Planet TV

D1105900

Planet TV
A Global Television Reader

EDITED BY

Lisa Parks and Shanti Kumar

New York University Press

NEW YORK AND LONDON

NEW YORK UNIVERSITY PRESS
New York and London

© 2003 by New York University
All rights reserved

Library of Congress Cataloging-in-Publication Data
Planet TV: a global television reader / edited by Lisa Parks and Shanti
Kumar.
p. cm.
Includes bibliographical references and index.
ISBN 0-8147-6691-9 (cloth : alk. paper)—ISBN 0-8147-6692-7 (pbk. :
alk. paper)
1. Television broadcasting—Social aspects. I. Parks, Lisa. II.
Kumar, Shanti.
PN1992.6 .P57 2002
302.23'45—dc21   2002008947

New York University Press books are printed on acid-free paper,
and their binding materials are chosen for strength and durability.

Manufactured in the United States of America

10 9 8 7 6 5 4 3 2 1

Contents

Acknowledgments   ix

Introduction   1
Lisa Parks and Shanti Kumar

PART I: Pulses
Historicizing "Global Television"   19

1   The Rise of the Global Media   21
    Edward S. Herman and Robert McChesney

2   Disjuncture and Difference in the Global Cultural Economy   40
    Arjun Appadurai

3   Who We Are, Who We Are Not: Battle of the Global
    Paradigms   53
    Michele Hilmes

4   *Our World*, Satellite Televisuality, and the Fantasy of Global
    Presence   74
    Lisa Parks

5   Flows and Other Close Encounters with Television   94
    Mimi White

PART II: Over the Air
Revisiting Western Imperialism   111

6   Media Imperialism   113
    John Tomlinson

7   Is There Anything Called Global Television Studies?   135
    Shanti Kumar

8   Reviving "Cultural Imperialism": International Audiences,
    Global Capitalism, and the Transnational Elite   155
    Ramaswami Harindranath

9   Going Global: International Coproductions and the
     Disappearing Domestic Audience in Canada   169
     Serra Tinic

PART III: Monitoring
           Television and National Identity   187

10   *Francophonie* and the National Airwaves: A History of
     Television in Senegal   189
     Jo Ellen Fair

11   On the Margins of the Constitutional State: Terrorism on
     German Television and the Rewriting of National Narratives   211
     Olaf Hoerschelmann

12   Television, Chechnya, and National Identity after the Cold War:
     Whose Imagined Community?   226
     James Schwoch

13   Television and Trustworthiness in Hong Kong   243
     Michael Curtin

14   Soothsayers, Politicians, Lesbian Scribes: The Philippine
     Movie Talk Show   262
     Jose B. Capino

PART IV: Uplink/Downlink
          Negotiating the Global and the Local   275

15   Act Globally, Think Locally   277
     John Fiske

16   Where the Global Meets the Local: Notes from the Sitting
     Room   286
     David Morley

17   Embedded Aesthetics: Creating a Discursive Space for
     Indigenous Media   303
     Faye Ginsburg

18   Local, Global, or National? Popular Music on Indonesian
     Television   320
     R. Anderson Sutton

19   Marriages Are Made on Television: Globalization and
     National Identity in India   341
     Divya C. McMillin

PART V: Channelsurfing
Imagining Transnationalism 361

20 Culture and Communication: Toward an Ethnographic
Critique of Media Consumption in the Transnational
Media System 363
Ien Ang

21 Narrowcasting in Diaspora: Iranian Television in
Los Angeles 376
Hamid Naficy

22 Postnational Television? *Goodness Gracious Me* and the
Britasian Diaspora 402
Moya Luckett

23 African American Television in an Age of Globalization 423
Timothy Havens

24 *Teletubbies*: Infant Cyborg Desire and the Fear of Global
Visual Culture 439
Nicholas Mirzoeff

Contributors 455

Index 459

Acknowledgments

The idea for this reader grew out of a discussion we had on a chilly winter evening some years ago at a coffee shop in Madison, Wisconsin. Since then, many colleagues and friends have contributed to making that idea a reality, and they all deserve our most sincere thanks. We are grateful to all the authors, who not only contributed their work, but also generously gave their time and energies to writing and rewriting the chapters in this book.

We also wish to thank our colleagues at the University of California–Santa Barbara and the University of Wisconsin–Madison, particularly Julie D'Acci, Michael Curtin, John Fiske, Michele Hilmes, Nietzchka Keene, Ed Branigan, Anna Everett, Dick Hebdige, Constance Penley, Bhaskar Sarkar, Janet Walker, and Chuck Wolfe. Finally we would like to thank our students at UW-Madison and UC–Santa Barbara for helping us discuss and think through television and globalization.

We thank Eric Zinner for supporting the book through its various stages as well as New York University Press. Cecilia Feilla served as editorial assistant in the earlier stages of the project's development, and we are deeply grateful to Emily Park and Despina Gimbel for their invaluable assistance, warm enthusiasm, and guidance.

We are indebted to Doug Battema, who came to our rescue many times during the preparation of the manuscript. We know that we would not have been able to complete this book without his generous help. Finally, we thank Melissa Stevenson and Mika Vipotnik, who provided assistance and support at the last stage of the book's completion.

Introduction

Lisa Parks and Shanti Kumar

Both of us are television and cultural studies scholars working in the United States. Shanti Kumar was born and raised in India and educated in the United States, he has traveled regularly to India and throughout parts of Southeast Asia. Lisa Parks was born and raised in the United States and has only recently traveled to Europe, Australia, and New Zealand. By no means does either of us claim to have a comprehensive understanding of television around the world. We begin this book with personal passages as a way of situating ourselves within the field of global television, to ground ourselves somewhere within it.

Shanti

My first recollections of watching television as a child growing up in India are from my primary school days in the city of Bombay. During lunch breaks we would quietly sneak into the school library and join some of our teachers and fellow students to watch the much-anticipated cricket test match between India and England that was being broadcast live on the Indian television network Doordarshan. In the early 1970s, television was still a very rare commodity in India. Many of us who lived in major cities like Bombay grew up watching television in public places such as the school library, or with friends and families who were among the lucky few to own a black and white television set at home. In the seventies there wasn't much to watch on television, but by the mid-eighties, there was more on TV than we could—or were allowed to—watch on weekdays and weekends. Our Sunday mornings began with a mix of Indian, Hungarian, Japanese, and Disney cartoons. Following breakfast, we would lounge on the family couch all morning watching great Indian epics like *Ramáyana*, folk mythologies like *Vikram aur Betal*, popular American shows like *I Love Lucy*, *Different Strokes*, *Star Trek*, and *National Geographic*, and German comedies and dramas like *The Didi Comedy Show* and *The Old Fox*. Our Sunday afternoons would consist of the occasional English film and regional language films. Our Sunday evenings started with sporting events from around the world and ended with a blockbuster Hindi film. If that wasn't enough, there were always the song-and-dance sequences from Hindi films on weekdays. We were India's first television generation. Television helped us mediate our imagined and real worlds, which were somewhere between the Indian and the Western, the modern and the traditional, the past, the present, and the future. Television and its images were part of a cultural repertoire that was a source of identity and alienation. It gave us a sense of community and fragmentation, of nationalist pride and internationalist ambitions. The arrival of satellite television in the 1990s opened other windows to the world. First there were MTV, BBC, Star TV, and other transnational media networks bringing with them images of Madonna, Michael Jackson, *Baywatch*, and *The Bold and the Beautiful*. They were soon followed by Zee TV, Channel V, and Sun TV, which gave us our "Indian" response to Madonna in Alisha Chinai, and our own curry-Western version of Clint Eastwood in "Shotgun Murugan." If television did not shape our world, it certainly changed our worldview.

Lisa

My first television memory is of a man walking on the moon. More than the image, I remember my parents' excitement as they encouraged me to touch the glowing screen of our TV set, shouting, "Lisa! There's a man on the moon!" Oddly enough, I could have been one of the babies born into a world of live-via-satellite television in June 1967, as my delivery had occurred in a hospital just two weeks before *Our World*'s. Despite the outward moves of the late 1960s, toward the new frontier of outer space and the fantasy of a global village, I led a pretty insular life, raised by a hardworking single mother and a steady diet of American television. As a kid I watched shows like *Mork and Mindy, Charlie's Angels, Solid Gold, Three's Company, Little House on the Prairie, Bonanza, The Love Boat, The Brady Bunch*, and *Grape Ape*. It was not until recently that I was able to travel outside the United States and begin to understand and experience the strangeness and dominance of my own television culture.

If we were to invert and extend the concept of television flow, it might generate something like this: a series of unscheduled fragments of global television caught by chance. In Alice Springs, Australia, I saw shows ranging from *A Country Practice* to *Beverly Hills 90210* to *Nganampa* on Imparja TV, an Aboriginal-owned and -operated direct satellite broadcasting service, which were interrupted again and again with special news bulletins about the tragic death of John F. Kennedy, Jr. In New Zealand a news report about Maori civil rights was followed by an episode of *Ally McBeal*. From a tiny hotel room in Denmark I watched *Big Brother*, a program that originated in Holland and was copied in the United States, and here I was watching a salacious German episode. In Holland I watched BBC World coverage of the mass slaughter of livestock with foot-and-mouth disease and turned the channel to find an Arabic song contest. In Bosnia local news coverage of Milosevic's arrest was followed by a Sade music video: her moody crooning synchronized with Banja Luka's postwar melancholia. In Slovenia I didn't have a chance to watch television, but I met fans of *Buffy the Vampire Slayer*. At home in Santa Barbara, I watch Japanese master chefs cook suckling pigs, lobsters, and chanterelles on *Iron Chef*, and I occasionally meet international tourists who are visiting only because they have seen the soap opera *Santa Barbara*.

Studying Global Television

One way to begin a discussion of a topic as broad as global television is to try to put into language the range and complexity of what we encounter on the screen. We introduce this book with our descriptions of the flickers and flows that make up global television, and we offer these personalized accounts as a way of encouraging the reader to begin reflecting critically upon his/her own knowledge and experience of global television. As Mimi White reminds us in her chapter in this book, one of the key theoretical concepts in television studies—that of "flow"—was generated as a kind of "traveling theory" when Raymond Williams sat in his Miami hotel room and tried to describe what he saw on the screen. One of the greatest challenges in studying global television is that of description. How do we begin to describe television as a global phenomenon? Where do we begin and where do we end? How do we write in a way that captures the movement of television programs across national borders and cultures? How do we describe the unequal technological access and television production around the world—what could be called global television's *ebbs and flows*? How can we describe television in places where we do not speak local languages? How do we study transnational audiences, viewers scattered across continents? How did certain television institutions and industries emerge in different parts of the world? The essays in this reader try to develop answers to some of these questions, but as we hope you will discover, there are no complete pictures of global TV. Instead, within this frame we will find a set of dynamic practices and industries, a medley of mixed signals and shifting screens.

Although this book is subtitled a "global television reader," it is not an attempt to geographically represent and intellectually tackle the entire globe; rather it is one possible "read" of what we hope will become a more international and intercultural field of television studies. To study global television, we need a sense of its intellectual history and some working definitions. So what is global TV? Global television should not be conceptualized as something "out there" to be explored and studied, something Other that is separate from us. Rather, it is part of the very social fabric that gives shape to us as individual subjects and imagined communities. We have in fact named this book *Planet TV* in order to call attention to television's relationship to lived social environments and material conditions. As we study global television we must recognize that no matter where we live in the world we are implicated within it. We are all shaped in one way or another by the social, economic, and cultural relations that the medium of television has historically worked to structure and reproduce. If we see ourselves as *part* of global television rather than *distinct from it*, perhaps we will become more active in struggling over the uses of the medium and its global futures. We hope that this book will help you not only to explore what it means to study and critique global television, but also to determine how to best help shape it.

Mapping the Emergence of Global Television Studies

The Global Village

For several decades now, communication and media scholars have been studying global television. The most widely publicized discourse on the topic came from Marshall McLuhan in his highly acclaimed book *Understanding Media*.[1] Published in 1964, in the midst of the Cold War and a growing nonaligned movement, McLuhan's book boldly prophesied that communication technologies would shatter political divides like the Iron Curtain and the ideological spheres of the First, Second, and Third Worlds, and make the world a smaller and more intimate place. McLuhan's vision of uniting the world into a global village emerged from his utopian faith in the power of new media technologies such as satellites, transoceanic cables, and television networks to cross boundaries and increase international and intercultural communication.

McLuhan's utopian vision of the global village managed to captivate the popular imaginary and thus became an important means of stimulating public discussion of television's globalization. However, the global village metaphor was also widely criticized for its underlying ideology of utopianism and its explicit emphasis on technological determinism. For instance, Raymond Williams in *Television: Technology and Cultural Form* critiques McLuhan's idealized version of the world as a global village of electronically linked tribes as being "wholly ahistorical and asocial."[2] While in McLuhan's early formulation, "the medium is the message," Williams finds an explicit celebration of the technological form, in the subsequent formulation, "the medium is the massage," Williams finds not only an ideological ratification of the medium as such, but also an attempt to marginalize all other questions about its effect and uses in society.[3] In McLuhan's work, Williams writes,

> The physical fact of instant transmission as a technical possibility has been uncritically raised to a social fact, without any pause to notice that virtually all such transmission is at once selected and controlled by existing social authorities. . . . But the technical abstractions, in their unnoticed projections into social models, have the effect of cancelling all attention to existing and developing (and already challenged) communication institutions.[4]

Therefore, Williams finds it "hardly surprising" that McLuhan's ideas have been most celebrated by those who support the existing interests and practices of media institutions. Moreover, McLuhan's critics are also concerned that the global village metaphor allows media practitioners to sidestep questions about unequal media flows and inequities of technological access in the world, especially since media flows occur so disproportionately from West to East and North to South. Further, they worry, the metaphor of global village has had the effect of suppressing the notion that these unidirectional flows might further elaborate Western cultural imperialism around the world.

World Systems/Cultural Imperialism

One of the most trenchant critiques of global television comes from international communication scholars influenced by the world systems theory of Immanuel Wallerstein[5] and Marxist theories of cultural imperialism.[6] There are several variants of the world systems theory and the cultural imperialism thesis, which emerged in the 1960s not only from scholars based in universities across the United States and Europe, but also from academics and activists in the newly independent nations of Asia, Africa, and Latin America.[7] These international communication scholars were primarily concerned with questions of freedom and fairness in media flows between developed and developing countries, and were central to the debates over, and demands for, a New World Information and Communication Order (NWICO) in the 1960s and the 1970s. Decades of debates and demands for free and fair media flows in the New World Information and Communication Order culminated in the publication of the UNESCO-sponsored MacBride Report.[8] However, the impasse reached after the publication of the MacBride Report pointed to a fundamental problem in international communication research: that is, it elided discussion of television as a sociocultural phenomenon and spent time counting and quantifying unequal media flows.[9] Although an important corrective to McLuhan's overly optimistic picture of an idyllic global village, international communications research on media flows in a sense reinforced what we already knew—that the United States and Western Europe powerfully dominated the global television economy.

Moreover, as John Tomlinson points out, international communication research that looks at media flows solely in terms of world systems theory or the cultural imperialism thesis fails to account for the creative power of audiences to resist domination in even the most exploitative contexts of global television.[10] By subordinating the creative autonomy of audiences, this research equates the economic power of the global television industry with its effects on political ideologies and cultural values around the world. When it does acknowledge the power of audiences to resist global media flows, it falls prey to empirically unsubstantiated myths of "authenticity" and politically regressive theories of "nativism" by characterizing non-Western societies as being "traditional" and previously unspoiled by contact with modern (Western) cultures.

Political Economy

Another body of work that has been influential in exploring the implications, extent, and history of domination in global television is the political economy approach.[11] The political economy approach has been a key intervention in that it brought into focus what is at stake when a small percentage of the world controls the rest of the world's communication technologies and content. More recent works in the political economy approach have focused on the importance of democratic values of free speech, public access to new communication technologies, personal control over information, and protections against privacy infringements by transnational corporations.[12] Although academically rigorous and activist in tone, this work has tended to focus more and more on structures of big business and corporate institutions to the exclusion of the role that television and other media play in people's everyday lives.

For instance, Edward Herman and Robert McChesney in their book *The Global Media: The New Missionaries of Corporate Capitalism*, argue that the globalization of media industries in recent decades has led to greater homogenization of global culture.[13] They point to the concentration of corporate ownership and the drive toward commercialization in the global media as threats to artistic freedom and cultural diversity around the world.

Both the political economy approach and the media flows research in international communication have pointed out the need to consider and analyze global television as an unequal set of economic relations that have serious political effects. These research traditions have been extremely important in mapping out some of the grave inequalities and injustices with respect to the distribution of television resources around the world. However, by focusing on the political and economic workings of the media industries, such analyses fail to recognize the multiplicity of meanings that are always at play in the processes of globalization. Recent trends in the globalization of television, for example, reveal a vast array of political, economic, cultural, and technological transformations around the world. Some of the most significant changes in global television are taking place not only in the media capitals of the United States, Western Europe, or Japan, but also in small towns and villages across Brazil, China, India, Indonesia, and South Africa. Therefore, even as we recognize that the dominant political-economic players in the global television industry are based in the United States, Western Europe, and Japan, it is important to look at the globalization of television from other perspectives in the world. These global transformations of television, however, cannot be analyzed in terms of an overarching theory that is applied from afar. Instead they can only be understood through close examination of the television industries, programs, technologies, and audiences in specific cultural contexts.

Global Television Studies

Planet TV thus makes a departure from these approaches in that it tries to explore global television as a set of overlapping industrial, textual, and audience practices. The chapters in this book are influenced by approaches from television and cultural studies, which has until recently focused largely on the study of television within the national cultures of industrialized Western nations. Books such as *Television: The Critical View; Channels of Discourse; Television Culture; Remote Control; Televisuality; Television, Audiences and Cultural Studies; Feminist Television Criticism;* and *The Uses of Television* (to name a few) have helped to establish television studies as a viable discipline that draws upon and combines approaches from film and literary studies, cultural studies, sociology, anthropology, and communication.[14] Instead of detailing the emergence of television studies here, we would like to briefly highlight work in the field that has helped to catalyze what might best be described as a global turn in television studies. We do not mean to suggest that television scholars have only now begun studying television in different parts of the world, or that scholars in other fields have not addressed issues of media globalization. Rather, we are interested in exploring how already existing work in television studies can be recast in relation to issues of globalization.

There are several examples of research in television studies that can be considered in this context. Early studies of the television series *Dallas* by Ien Ang and Elihu Katz and Tamor Liebes provided studies of the narrative structure and reception of this American series as it migrated through and between different national and local cultures.[15] Although these studies focused on meaning-making processes and the politics of pleasure, they also complicated the cultural imperialist assumption that the globalization of U.S. television resulted inevitably in the "Americanization" of world cultures. Readings of *Dallas* proved much more complicated than that, and suggested the need to develop transnational and intercultural analytical models that account for the migrancy of television cultures.[16]

Another important work that signaled a global turn early in television studies was Eric Michaels's book *The Aboriginal Invention of Television*.[17] As television studies began to emerge in Western Europe and North America in the 1980s, Eric Michaels traveled from Texas to central Australia to conduct research on Aboriginal television and video. His work, some of which was published posthumously in *Bad Aboriginal Art*, encouraged scholars to consider not only how indigenous societies were negotiating the globalization of television, but how they "reinvented" the medium in the process.[18] Michaels's work has been supplemented by research on indigenous media in South and North America, Canada, and Australia by scholars in television studies, communication, and visual anthropology.[19] Some of this work has been coproduced by scholars and indigenous peoples and it has appeared in video formats rather than in scholarly journals or books.[20] It is crucial that we imagine global studies of television as possibly taking different cultural forms since, obviously, we do not all speak the same languages, adopt the same critical theories, or have access to the same technologies.

Television studies researchers in the United Kingdom have long been concerned with issues of national identity and globalization. In London in 1984 and 1986, major international television studies conferences brought together hundreds of scholars from at least thirty-three countries.[21] Even before this, David Morley's book *The "Nationwide" Audience* analyzed class and national identity among British television viewers in the early 1980s, and his more recent books *Spaces of Identity* (cowritten with Kevin Robins) and *Home Territories* explore television more explicitly in relation to issues of globalization.[22] Even earlier, however, Raymond Williams—one of the gurus of British cultural studies and television studies—conceived television as a site of not only national but global culture as well. In 1974, a decade after the first international satellite television experiments, Williams recognized that "A world-wide television service, with genuinely open skies, would be an enormous gain to the peoples of the world. . . . But the probable users of the technology are not internationalists, in the sense of any significant mutuality."[23]

This global consciousness among British television and cultural studies scholars can be read as symptomatic of a combination of factors ranging from England's liberal and leftist intellectual climate, to its legacy of public service broadcasting, to its history of colonial empire. More concretely, however, the development of cable and direct broadcast satellite (DBS) systems throughout Western Europe, Asia, and South America during the 1980s and 1990s pushed these issues to the fore, as satellite spillovers and the "Americanization" of television industries were seen as compromising sovereign national boundaries.[24]

Even though particular approaches to television studies may have emerged in the industrial West, scholars around the world have been studying television for decades. They too have had to contend with the globalization of American media, often to the detriment of their own national media industries, as made evident in works ranging from Edward Said's *Orientalism* to Ariel Dorfman and Armand Mattelart's *How to Read Donald Duck* to Tony Dowmunt's *Channels of Resistance.*[25] To help global television studies emerge, however, Western scholars will need to engage and interact further with television programs and researchers from different parts of the world.

Since television studies is a relatively new field in the United States, it has been more inwardly directed and historically focused, working to legitimate itself within the academy. The global impulse in television studies in the United States has come primarily from feminist television critics who have been analyzing gender, class, race/ethnic, and national differences for nearly two decades, and who have been the only group of television studies scholars to hold a yearly international conference: "Consoling Passions." This conference has led to the formation of a transnational community of feminist television scholars. While much of this research has been concentrated on television in the industrial West, it has offered analytical models that might be appropriate for adaptation and use to study television in different national or international contexts, or to study television itself as a site of difference. Moreover, feminists' ongoing concerns with issues such as multicultural representation, the social construction of television and new media technologies, and various forms of media activism are pressing and relevant in a global context.

Many of the new chapters in this collection have been influenced in one way or another by an approach that Julie D'Acci has called the "integrated model" of television studies. This model conceives of television as a set of discursive negotiations involving television institutions, texts, audiences or reception, and sociohistorical contexts. The model thus accounts for power relations in and between these four sites. The integrated approach, D'Acci explains,

> illuminates the power of socially dominant "ideological" representations and definitions, as well as the simultaneous presence and power of socially subordinated, oppositional, and simply *different* ones. It traces how these many definitions interact, overlap and clash within the individual sites as well as between and among them.[26]

In one sense *Planet TV* explores how the integrated model plays in the context of television's globalization. Several questions emerge when we consider the integrated model as a traveling theory. In terms of industrial analysis, we might ask, How did early television executives imagine television's global future, and what strategies did they develop to pursue it? How do we study transnational media conglomerates that have no national homeland? For textual analysis, we could ask, How does the critic or historian from one culture analyze television structure and meaning making in another? Can television studies be conceived as a site of translation studies? With respect to audience and reception studies, we might ask, How does the critic analyze audiences that are scattered across national territories? How do transnational audiences make sense of the same text? Does the Internet offer new possibilities for conducting reception analyses of audiences? Finally, when considering sociohistorical contexts, how does one draw the lines and limits of contextualization, particularly when examining television across different national cultures? Does the process of contextualization ever end in a global context?

One of the areas we add to the integrated model is that of "technology." It, too, is a site of ongoing power struggles and negotiations that determine television's content and form. Television technologies shape and are shaped by industrial, audience, and textual negotiations as well as changing sociohistorical conditions. And the meanings of television technology are contingent and take on different properties and practices in different parts of the world. When does color TV emerge in Greenland? How is the remote control used in Senegal? Who manufactures satellite dishes in China and India? Where are TV sets repaired in Beruit? When discussing the globalization of television, then, we might keep in mind that television technology is never a constant or given. The history of the insides of the television set (which we are not meant to see) is in fact as dynamic and lively as the surface of the screen. At the current moment the meanings of "television" are undergoing major shifts as the medium converges with digital technologies. While these changes are significant, they did not happen overnight. It is important that TV scholars and cultural analysts not leapfrog discussion of television in a race to become part of the cyber-euphoria of the present. The histories of television, computers, and satellites not only parallel one another, but they intersect dramatically. And the technologies of global television are not only mechanisms of popular entertainment, they emerged as technologies of military and scientific power as well.[27] Histories and analyses of television as a technology of military intelligence or scientific knowledge are often suppressed, however, in favor of discussion of its more pleasurable forms. Global television thus involves layers of technological negotiations that must be explored as well.

Scope of the Book

Throughout the book we have reprinted influential essays that have been useful to the process of rethinking television studies as a field of global study. While most of the new chapters use approaches from television studies (especially aspects of the integrated model), the reprinted chapters come from various disciplines, including communication, philosophy, anthropology and cultural studies. Global television studies must engage with interdisciplinary work on globalization while simultaneously establishing itself by further developing (and in some cases, recontextualizing) its own analytical models and approaches.[28] *Planet TV* thus presents new work in television studies along side influential work on globalization to foster this process.

The title *Planet TV* is meant to suggest that television not only floats through the ether and orbit and onto viewers' screens, but also permeates lived social environments and earthly matters. In other words, the globalization of television is not an amorphous and de-territorialized process that takes place only within the boardrooms of multimedia conglomerates. It is planetary in a most material way. *Planet TV* is organized according to metaphorical properties of television, which are also part of an ongoing process of making sense of the unique potentialities of the medium. TV as a technology is not defined by these technical properties alone, however. We have linked television's properties to critical theories on globalization that have emerged during the past three decades. Our critical approach to global television imagines the apparatus in relation to changing sociohistorical conditions determined in different ways by forces of imperialism, nationalism, postcolonialism, and transnationalism. Again, while we include essays about television from different parts of the world, we resist totalizing or comprehensive claims to represent the entire globe: the book is one possible read of global television, a partial account of an irreducible field. It is not a survey of television around the world. Instead, it is an attempt to encourage intercultural and interdisciplinary dialogues and approaches that will give future shape and meaning to a field of global television studies.

Pulses: Historicizing "Global Television"

The globalization of television is often associated with the rise of satellite communication during the 1960s, but it emerges in the earliest moments of broadcasting's history when scientists and technicians in different parts of the world were competing to invent an electronic medium of "remote seeing." The book's first part offers historical and critical perspectives on the economic and cultural structures of global media with reprinted essays from Edward S. Herman and Robert McChesney and Arjun Appadurai, followed by three new chapters. The new chapters historicize and concretize global television, demonstrating that one cannot explain this phenomenon from the perspective of political economy or cultural theory alone. Michele Hilmes' essay, "Who We Are, Who We Are Not: Battle of the Global Paradigms," examines the formation of the dominant broadcasting paradigms of Britain and the United States that emerged in radio during the 1930s. Focusing on the rhetoric and international exchanges of broadcasters in the United States and Britain, Hilmes moves beyond a nationalist framework and explores how the public and commercial broadcasting models took shape *in relation* to one another.

Where Hilmes develops a model for exploring how national broadcasting paradigms emerge, Lisa Parks explores global television through a site of satellite and television convergence. Her chapter reveals that the 1967 live satellite program *Our World* constructs a fantasy of "global presence" based on Western discourses of modernization, cultural unity, and planetary control. Parks complicates McLuhan's "global village" metaphor by demonstrating how, despite its unifying title and liberal humanist aims, this satellite broadcast divided the world and reinforced Western hegemony in the context of decolonization, outer space exploration, and Cold War geopolitics.

In yet another effort to historicize the meanings of global television, Mimi White turns to the discourse of television criticism. Her chapter, "Flows and Other Close Encounters with Television," reveals that the concept of television flow emerges as a "traveling theory." Reading the writings of TV critics Raymond Williams and John Ellis as ethnographies, White reveals that "flow" (arguably one of the most important concepts in television studies) was generated as English scholars' "first contact" with the strangeness of American commercial television. Her chapter reminds us that global television studies will involve rereading and reflecting on the very processes by which our theories take shape. Combined, then, these chapters examine global television through the rhetoric of early broadcasters, the content of television programs, and the discourse of television critics.

Over the Air: Revisiting Western Imperialism

One of the ways that television scholars have approached the debates over globalization is through cultural imperialism, which forcefully foregrounds the inequities of media resources and flows in international communication. However, in recent years, cultural imperialism has come under heavy criticism for its inability to adequately theorize the power of audiences to creatively subvert the power of global television. As a result, it has become a less fashionable academic position in the 1990s than it was during the 1970s and 1980s. The new essays in part 2 critically engage with the notion of cultural imperialism, and seek to interrogate its relevance for global television in the twenty-first century. They follow a reprinted essay by John Tomlinson, which establishes an intellectual history of the concept.

Shanti Kumar examines the historic inequities of communication between the East and West in relation to the emerging field of global television studies. He anticipates some of the directions that global television studies could take and the problems it may face. Advocating caution, he argues that the practitioners of global television studies must be as critical of the theories and methodologies underlying their practice as they are of the television images they view on the screen. Otherwise, Kumar concludes, global television studies may end up perpetuating the categorical imperialism of Western academic discourse that has historically dominated East-West exchanges in major and minor disciplines alike.

In his essay, "Reviving 'Cultural Imperialism': International Audiences, Global Capitalism, and the Transnational Elite," Ramaswami Harindranath argues for a reinstatement of the cultural imperialism thesis in a new theoretical garb to account for recent developments in the global television industries. Responding to critiques of its demise, he argues that cultural imperialism remains a useful theory to examine the relationship between television and its audiences in terms of an emerging group of transnational, cosmopolitan elites who are impervious to national boundaries or nationalist sentiments.

Serra Tinic interrogates the cultural imperialism debate in terms of the regulatory and economic pressures that have made international coproductions and joint productions increasingly common in Canada. Tinic finds that as television programs are increasingly being produced for a global market, the demand to make programming palatable to international audiences is rapidly obliterating a particular sense of place that domestic television had previously sought to create in Canada. However, she argues, the universalizing and homogenizing tendencies of international coproductions and joint productions may ironically induce Canadian television audiences to seek out programs that establish a shared sense of place and community.

Monitoring: Television and National Identity

Television has always been central to debates about nationalism. Countless scholars have cited Benedict Anderson's famous formulation "imagined communities" to describe how, since the 1960s, television has been absolutely crucial to creating and sustaining a national identity.[29] At the same time, as television becomes an indispensable part of nationalist imaginations, there emerges a certain anxiety in the state about having to regulate both the technological apparatus and content/cultural meanings of television. The tension between the nationalist desire to sustain its imagined community through the airwaves and the statist anxiety to regulate the form and content of television remains a central concern for nation-states. All the essays in part 3 deal with the unresolved—and, some argue, unresolvable—tension that television produces in the imagined communities of nationalism in different parts of the world.

In the case of Senegal, Jo Ellen Fair argues that television was not a strong force for cultural nationalism. However, she suggests, it was an important medium for imaginations of a new Francophone culture among urban Senegalese. Fair describes how the personalities of powerful figures, political calculations of nationalist leaders, state regulations of media, and the programming tastes of diverse audiences have shaped the growth of television and national identity in Senegal. Recounting the history of French television in Senegal, she suggests that Senegalese culture—both urban and rural—will always stand apart from the global *francophonie* that France seeks to create through the global flows of French cultural products.

Olaf Hoerschelmann deconstructs the imagined community of nationalism in relation to representations of terrorism on television in Germany. He explores how the narrative and settings of a made-for-television docudrama, *Todesspiel* (Death Game), broadcast on German television in 1997, were appropriated by the nation-state to reimagine a unified Germany. He critiques the nationalist recasting of the televisual narrative of *Todesspiel* for its portrayal of terrorism as a useful Other against which to construct a post-fascist national imaginary. Television coverage of terrorism in Germany, Hoerschelmann concludes, is a telling representation of the uneasy relationship between the media, terrorism, and the state in many Western nations.

James Schwoch argues that traditional definitions of imagined communities in television—signified by national audiences, national networks, and national programming—may no longer be adequate for understanding newer imaginations of community and identity in the post–Cold War world. As a case study, he looks at Western imaginations of Chechnya in a made-for-television production on the Family Channel, *Candles in the Dark*. Such Western imaginings of Chechen identity, he argues, are consistent with an emerging strategy of resistance known in the Baltics as the "CNN defense concept," which has been used by Chechnya in an effort to deliver televisual representations of its national identity to audiences in the West. Schwoch's essay maps the shifting topographies of television in the post–Cold War era.

In his chapter, Michael Curtin describes the recent history of Hong Kong society and developments in local television. Outlining how television grew in Hong Kong during the early 1970s, Curtin examines the conceptual relationship between publicity, public trust, and the rule of law in society. He shows how television dramas during the 1970s and 1980s contributed to the constitution of a local identity by constructing characters who were distinguished by their social origins rather than their Chinese ethnicity.

Jose B. Capino describes the historical role that television has played in blurring the boundaries between showbiz and politics in the national culture of the Philippines. Through a critical appraisal of the television genre known as the movie talk show, he describes how action superstars, soft-core porn actors, and aging starlets have used the media visibility of the show to launch their political careers. Although at first glance it may seem like a televised catfight between thespians and scribes, the movie talk show, Capino concludes, also functions as a venue for the conduct of public affairs in the Philippines.

Uplink/Downlink: Negotiating the Global and the Local

As we have suggested, people often think of the interconnected world as a global village. More recently globalization theorists have used the terms "global/local" and "glocalization" to invoke the many ways globalization is negotiated in specific local conditions. It is important to remember, however, that local conditions themselves are always in flux and necessitate new understandings and critical approaches to globalization. As the essays in part 4 demonstrate, the local negotiations of global television industries, texts, and audiences can significantly rearticulate the very definition of globalization. We include reprinted essays by John Fishe, David Marley, and Faye Ginsburg, which provide frameworks for and case studies of global/local relations.

The first new essay in part 4, by R. Anderson Sutton, considers how television contributes to the negotiation of local cultures and global flows in Indonesia. Focusing on popular music on Indonesian television, he examines three hybrid genres: MTV music videos (both Indonesian and foreign), *dangdut* (a national genre with roots in Indian film music and regional music from Sumatra), and *Dua Warna* (a postmodern pastiche of mainstream pop and assorted regional idioms). Through close readings of the local appropriations of Western formats in these genres, Sutton shows that music television in Indonesia is both subject to and resistant to the homogenizing tendencies of globalization.

Divya C. McMillin describes how the marriage of the global and the local is taking place in Indian television through hybrid programming in which Western genres have been appropriated to fit different audience tastes and preferences. Through critical examination of a game show *Adarsha Dampathigalu* (The Ideal Couple) on a regional-language cable channel Udaya TV, she argues that audience anxiety over and enjoyment of the show are symptomatic of the uneasy articulation of the nation through the global and the local. Combined, the essays in this part use the categories of the global and the local to complicate any easy or essentialist distinction between them.

Channelsurfing: Imagining Transnationalism

The final part uses the navigation of multichannel environments as a metaphor for global television as a field of cultural and economic hybridity, flux, and migration. While the reprinted chapters by Ien Ang and Hamid Naficy represent established frameworks for transnational television analysis, the new chapters examine TV series that migrate across national borders in one way or another, taking on hybrid forms or spurring the formation of new social identities. Moya Luckett's "Postnational Television? *Goodness Gracious Me* and the Britasian Diaspora" suggests that the series *GGM*, one of the only British series written by and starring Asian actors, is symptomatic of the BBC's reorganization in the context of globalization. As Luckett argues, the show points to a significant change in the organization of terrestrial broadcast British television, and represents a move away from predominantly racially conceived programming for 'minorities.' Luckett considers how the production and reception of television comedy has been recast in relation to postcolonial diasporas.

Timothy Havens continues the focus on comedy, but explores the global syndication of African American sitcoms. In his chapter, Havens argues that business practices in international markets influence the way domestic U.S. producers craft TV representations of blackness. For years media buyers' beliefs, U.S. production firms' distribution priorities, and various social factors have limited the range of African American representation, but Havens contends that globalization may offer opportunities for a greater diversity of representation. The growth of niche channels and television's rising popularity in developing countries may trigger innovations in American producers' representation of nonwhite peoples and cultures.

The final chapter, "*Teletubbies*: Infant Cyborg Desire and the Fear of Global Visual Culture," by Nicholas Mirzoeff, focuses on *Teletubbies,* a television series that addresses the world's newest generation of viewers and consumers, infants and toddlers under three. His chapter discusses the global migrations of this BBC children's series from England to South America to Eastern Asia and North America. In its transnational contexts *Teletubbies* has become a site of media synergy, taking on guises ranging from dolls to Web sites to lunchboxes. As the Teletubbies travel and proliferate in their cyborg incarnations, Mirzoeff suggests, they provoke moral panics and crises over childhood as well. If the discourse surrounding *Teletubbies* is any indication, global television continues to be a lively site of intergenerational politics, technological convergence, and cultural posturing and appropriation. Part 5 thus brings *Planet TV* back where we began, examining how one of the most powerful TV institutions on earth, the BBC, has reinvented itself in the age of media globalization, markedly contradicting 1930s public service broadcasting rhetoric described by Michele Hilmes in her chapter.

NOTES

1. Marshall McLuhan, *Understanding Media: The Extensions of Man* (New York: Routledge, 1964).

2. Raymond Williams, *Television: Technology and Cultural Form* (New York: Schocken Books, 1975), 128.

3. Marshall McLuhan and Quentin Fiore, *The Medium Is the Massage* (New York: Bantam, 1967).

4. Williams, *Television*, 128.

5. Immanuel Wallerstein, *The Modern World System* (New York: Academic Press, 1974); Immanuel Wallerstein, *The Capitalist World-Economy* (Cambridge: Cambridge University Press, 1979).

6. See Oliver Boyd-Barret, *The International News Agencies* (Beverly Hills: Sage, 1980); Cees Hamelink, *Cultural Autonomy in Global Communications* (New York: Longman, 1983); Kaarle Nordenstreng and Tapio Varis, *Television Traffic: One-Way Street?* (Paris: UNESCO, 1964); Armand Mattelart, *Multinational Corporations and the Control of Culture: The Ideological Apparatuses of Imperialism* (Atlantic Highlands, NJ: Humanities Press, 1979); Herbert I. Schiller, *Mass Communications and American Empire* (New York: Augustus M. Kelly, 1969).

7. See, for instance, Ahmed Abdel-Fattah, *Communication for Population and Development Programmes: An Egyptian Experience* (Paris: UNESCO, 1983); Binod Agarwal, *Satellite Instructional Television Experiment—Television Comes to the Village: An Evaluation of SITE* (Bangalore: Indian Space Research Organization, 1978); Goodwin C. Chu, *Radical Change through Communication in Mao's China* (Honolulu: East-West Center, 1977); Frank Okwu Ugboajah, ed, *Mass Communication, Culture and Society in West Africa* (Munich: Hans Zell Publishers, 1985); Niko Vink, *The Telenovela and Emancipation: A Study on TV and Social Change in Latin America* (Amsterdam: Royal Tropical Institute, 1988).

8. UNESCO, *Many Voices, One World* (New York: UNESCO, 1980).

9. See Peter Golding and Phil Harris, eds., *Beyond Cultural Imperialism: Globalization, Communication and the New International Order* (Thousand Oaks, CA: Sage, 1997); Ali Mohamadi, ed., *International Communication and Globalization* (Thousand Oaks, CA: Sage, 1997); Kaarle Nordenstreng and Herbert Schiller, eds., *Beyond National Sovereignty: International Communication in the 1990s* (Norwood, NJ: Ablex, 1993).

10. John Tomlinson, *Globalization and Culture* (Chicago: University of Chicago Press, 1999); John Tomlinson, *Cultural Imperialism: A Critical Introduction* (London: Pinter, 1991).

11. See, for instance, Edward Herman and Noam Chomsky, *Manufacturing Consent: The Political Economy of Mass Media* (New York: Pantheon, 1988); Nicholas Garnham, *Capitalism and Communication: Global Culture and Economics of Information* (London: Sage, 1990); Dallas W. Smythe, *Dependency Road: Communications, Capitalism, Consciousness and Canada* (Norwood, NJ: Ablex, 1981).

12. Sandra Braman and Annabelle Sreberny-Mohammadi, eds., *Globalization, Communication and Transnational Civil Society* (Cresskill, NJ: Hampton, 1997); Mashood Bailie and Dwayne Winseck, eds., *Democratizing Communication? Comparative Perspectives on Information and Power* (Cresskill, NJ: Hampton, 1997); Peter Dahlgren, *Television and the Public Sphere* (Newbury Park, CA: Sage, 1995); Oscar H. Gandy, Jr., *A Political Economy of Personal Information* (Boulder; Westview, 1993).

13. Edward S. Herman and Robert W. McChesney, *The Global Media: The New Missionaries of Corporate Capitalism* (London: Cassell, 1997).

14. Horace Newcomb, ed., *Television: The Critical View*, 4th ed. (New York: Oxford University Press, 1987); Robert Allen, ed., *Channels of Discourse Reassembled* (Chapel Hill: University of North Carolina Press, 1992); John Fiske, *Television Culture* (London: Routledge, 1987); Ellen Seiter et al., eds., *Remote Control: Television, Audiences and Cultural Power* (London: Routledge, 1989); John Caldwell, *Televisuality: Style, Crisis, and Authority in American Television* (New Brunswick: Rutgers University Press, 1995); David Morley, *Television, Audiences and Cultural Studies* (London: Routledge, 1992); Charlotte Brunsdon, et al. eds., *Feminist Television Criticism* (Oxford: Oxford University Press, 1997); and John Hartley, *The Uses of Television* (London: Routledge, 1999).

15. Ien Ang, *Watching Dallas: Soap Opera and the Melodramatic Imagination* (London: Routledge, 1991); Tamor Liebes and Elihu Katz, "On the Critical Abilities of Television Viewers," in Seiter et al., *Remote Control*.

16. For cultural studies work that addresses issues of migrancy and mobility, see David Morley, *Home Territories: Media, Mobility and Identity* (London: Routledge, 2000); Iain Chambers, *Migrancy, Culture, Identity* (London: Routledge, 1994); and John Urry, *Sociology beyond Societies* (London: Routledge, 2000).

17. Eric Michaels, *The Aboriginal Invention of Television, 1982–1986* (Canberra: Australian Institute of Aboriginal Studies, 1986). For a discussion of this work, see Tom O'Regan, "TV as Cultural Technology: The Work of Eric Michaels," *Continuum: The Australian Journal of Media and Culture* 3, no. 2 (1990).

18. Eric Michaels, *Bad Aboriginal Art: Tradition, Media, and Technological Horizons* (Minneapolis: University of Minnesota Press, 1994).

19. See, for instance, Philip Baty, "Singing the Electric: Aboriginal Television in Australia," in *Channels of Resistance: Global Television and Local Empowerment*, ed. by Tony Dowmunt (London: British Film Institute, 1993); Donald R. Browne, "Aboriginal Radio in Australia: From Dream Time to Prime Time?" *Journal of Communication* 40, no.1 (winter 1990): 111–20; Faye Ginsburg, "Embedded Aesthetics: Creating a Discursive Space for Indigenous Media," *Cultural Anthropology* 9, no. 3 (1994): 366; Steven Leuthold, *Indigenous Aesthetics: Native Art, Media and Identity* (Austin: University of Texas Press, 1998); K. Madden, "Video and Cultural Identity: The Inuit Broadcasting Corporation Experience," in *Mass Media Effects across Cultures*, ed. F. Korzenny and S. Ting Toomey (Newbury Park, CA: Sage, 1992).

20. In Brazil, Australia, and Canada, for instance, indigenous people have produced videos that can be considered part of the discourse of global television studies. See, for instance, videos such as *The Spirit of Television and Video Cannibalism*, coproduced by media sociologists and Kayapo Indian communities in Brazil. In Australia media activists have worked with CAAMA (Central Australian Aboriginal Media Association) to produce videos such as *Satellite Dreaming, Stories of the Dreamtime*, and *Benny and the Dreamers*, as well as CD-ROMs and Web sites. In Canada Inuit peoples have recently produced soap operas. For further discussion of indigenous media see Faye Ginsburg et al., eds., *Media Worlds: Anthropology on New Terrain* (Berkeley: University of California Press, 2002).

21. Some of the conference papers were published in *Television in Transition*, ed. Phillip Drummond and Richard Paterson (London: British Film Institute, 1985), and *Television and Its Audience: International Research Perspectives*, ed. Phillip Drummond and Richard Paterson. (London: British Film Institute, 1988).

22. David Morley, *The "Nationwide" Audience* (London: British Film Institute, 1980); David Morley and Kevin Robins, *Spaces of Identity: Global Media, Electronic Landscapes and Cultural Boundaries* (London: Routledge, 1995); Morley, *Home Territories*.

23. Williams, *Television*, 144.

24. See Drummond and Paterson, *Television and Its Audience*; and Phillip Drummond et al., *National Identity and Europe: The Television Revolution* (London: British Film Institute, 1990).

25. Edward Said, *Orientalism* (New York: Pantheon, 1978); Ariel Dorfman and Armand Mattelart, *How to Read Donald Duck: Imperialist Ideology in the Disney Comic* (New York: International General, 1975); and Dowmunt, *Channels of Resistance*.

26. See Julie D'Acci, *Defining Women: The Case of Cagney and Lacey* (Chapel Hill: University of North Carolina Press, 1994), 2.

27. For work that emphasizes such intersections, see Armand Mattelart, *Mapping World Communication: War, Progress, Culture* (Minneapolis: University of Minnesota Press, 1995); and Armand Mattelart, *Networking the World, 1794–2000* (Minneapolis: University of Minnesota Press, 2000).

28. For an example of this work, see Frederic Jameson and Masao Miyoshi, eds., *The Cultures of Globalization* (Durham: Duke University Press, 1998). For examples of media studies research that has incorporated such theories, see Ella Shohat and Robert Stam, *Unthinking Eurocentrism: Multiculturalism and the Media* (London: Routledge, 1994); and, James Curran and Myung-Jin Park, eds., *De-Westernizing Media Studies* (London: Routledge, 2000).

29. Benedict Anderson, *Imagined Communities* (London: Verso, 1983).

Pulses
Historicizing "Global Television"

Chapter One

The Rise of the Global Media

Edward S. Herman and Robert McChesney

The emergence of a truly global media system is a very recent development, reflecting to no small degree the globalization of the market economy. Although global media are only one part of the overall expansion and spread of an increasingly integrated global corporate system, they complement and support the needs of nonmedia enterprises. On one hand, the global media play a central economic role, providing part of the global infrastructure for nonmedia firms, and facilitating their business just as the growth of domestic commercial media supports corporate growth within countries. The global media provide the main vehicle for advertising corporate wares for sale, thereby facilitating corporate expansion into new nations, regions, and markets. On the other hand, the global media's news and entertainment provide an informational and ideological environment that helps sustain the political, economic, and moral basis for marketing goods and for having a profit-driven social order. In short, the global media are a necessary component of global capitalism and one of its defining features.

Although the establishment of an integrated global media market only began in earnest in the late 1980s and did not reach its full potential until the 1990s, the roots of a global media system can be traced back decades, even centuries. In this chapter we outline the evolution of the global media from their modern origins to the present day. In our view, media, global or otherwise, can only be understood in a political economic context, so we will emphasize the relationship of media to capitalism. We devote most of our attention to the second half of the twentieth century and, within that, to the rise of neoliberal "free market" policies in the 1980s and 1990s. This will explain why the global media system is so thoroughly dominated by western, and especially U.S., media firms. Moreover, as we are primarily concerned with the media's ability to provide a public sphere for democracy, our analysis of capitalism includes discussion of its relationship to political institutions. Only by understanding global corporate capitalism's social and political implications can we possibly make sense of the global media's important social and political role.

The Origins of Global Media

. . . Global media developed haltingly in the nineteenth century. Newspapers and periodicals were written almost exclusively for domestic audiences, which combined with language problems to limit their potential for export. In fact, to this day newspapers remain the media industry that is least integrated into the global media system. When much of the planet was formally colonized by Europe and the United States in the late nineteenth century, the colonial powers generally permitted their home-based press interests a role in shaping the colonial media systems, which were understood to be of major importance in maintaining imperial rule. (This would also be the case later, with the development of colonial radio systems.) The growth and expansion of capitalism encouraged the growth of new transportation and communication technologies to expedite commercial interaction. The coming of the telegraph and underwater cables in the mid-nineteenth century marked the dawning of the telecommunication age: for the first time, information could reliably travel faster than people. Increasingly, as global trade grew in importance, there was great commercial value in the rapid communication of world news via the wires.

Hence the wire-based international news agencies were the first significant form of global media. The French Havas, German Wolff, and British Reuters were com- mercial news agencies established in the nineteenth century as domestic enterprises, but with particular interest in foreign news. They produced the news and then sold it to newspaper publishers. Reuters, Havas, and Wolff established the "Ring Combi- nation" in the 1850s, a cartel which divided the entire world market for news production and distribution among themselves. When the U.S. Associated Press (AP)—a cooperative service formed by U.S. newspaper publishers—came along later in the nineteenth century, it gradually worked its way into the cartel. So did the commercial United Press, established by rival U.S. newspaper interests which felt discriminated against by the AP.[1]

From the beginning, global news services have been oriented to the needs and interests of the wealthy nations which provide their revenues. These news agencies were, in effect, *the* global media until well into the twentieth century, and even after the dawn of broadcasting their importance for global journalism was unsurpassed. Indeed, it was their near monopoly control over international news that stimulated much of the resistance to the existing global media regime by Third World nations in the 1970s, as is discussed below. Yet these news agencies were not so much media as wholesalers of content to other commercial media in their home nations primarily, but also to the media in many nations which could not support their own global news services. Only with the emergence of genuinely global media, in the late twentieth century, has the influence of the news agencies waned.

The crucial change for global capitalism, which laid the groundwork for the rise of global media, was the emergence and ascension of the transnational corporation (TNC). A TNC is one that maintains facilities in more than one country and plans its operations and investments in a multi-country perspective. The modern TNC emerged out of the steady growth of corporate enterprise in the wake of the Indus- trial Revolution in the nineteenth century. Increasing numbers of U.S. firms began to think of foreign markets in the 1870s and 1880s as they became national companies, found themselves with manufacturing surpluses, and sought to exploit their technical prowess and product differentiation advantages or to attain further economies of scale. British and continental European foreign direct investment (FDI) abroad also reached substantial levels before 1914; that of Britain was heavily concentrated in the Empire and the United States, whereas FDI of the continental powers was most often in other parts of Europe.

Money and capital markets among the Atlantic powers were already well integrated by the 1890s, and financial industries were already spreading aggressively abroad. The first real general surge in U.S. FDI and TNC growth came during and after the huge wave of mergers at the turn of the century. The TNC became increasingly significant during the twentieth century, and contributed most importantly to "globalization" when its reach became wide, extending to many countries, when its facilities were more integrated and not independent ("stand alone"), and when there developed many firms of this character, thus making for a more profound integration of economic activity across borders.

Film and Radio Broadcasting

Two new media technologies—motion pictures and radio broadcasting—contributed to the development of global media in the first half of the twentieth century. In the case of motion pictures, unlike the earlier history of newspapers and magazines, there was no long drawn-out period of small-scale industrial competition followed by concentration. Instead, in keeping with the then ascendant corporate (and TNC) forth of industrial organization, the film industry developed quickly into an oligopoly dominated by a handful of very large studios. Moreover, the film industry was the first media industry to serve a truly global market.

The members of this new oligopoly were almost all American, based in Hollywood, and with close ties to major financial interests on Wall Street.[2] As early as 1914, 85 percent of the world film audience was watching American films.[3] In 1925 American-made films accounted for over 90 percent of film revenues in the United Kingdom, Canada, Australia, New Zealand, and Argentina and over 70 percent of film revenues in France, Brazil, and Scandinavia.[4] Although the percentages declined with the rise of "talkies," the dominance of Hollywood was never challenged. The only barrier to complete U.S. control came from explicit state intervention in nations such as Britain and France to protect the domestic industries from obliteration. Throughout the first half of the century, motion picture production was preponderantly a European and North American phenomenon.

Radio broadcasting emerged around 1920 with the establishment of stations on the medium wavelengths.[5] Broadcasting was international by nature, because the airwaves respect no political boundaries, but its international utilization as signal transmission over long distances was expensive. Furthermore, broadcasting could only be conducted on a limited number of frequencies and only by a small number of broadcasters at any given time to avoid damaging interference. This was a particular problem in Western Europe with its large population, numerous nations, and relatively small land mass. A series of conferences in the 1920s and 1930s allocated the medium-wave frequencies among the various nations, leaving most with only a handful of channels to exploit. The question, then, of how best to develop the limited number of radio channels became a political battle in nearly every independent country in the world. In most nations, there was a general consensus that broadcasting served too important a function—akin to, say, education—to be left to commercial exploitation, thus leading to various forms of state-directed broadcasting systems. The most famous and successful of these systems was the British Broadcasting Corporation (BBC), which banned advertising and was supported by an annual license fee paid by listeners. As a rule of thumb, the more democratic a given society, the more publicly accountable would be its broadcasting system. At the other extreme from the "public service" systems of Britain, Canada and The Netherlands were the centralized, tightly controlled and highly propagandistic state-run systems of Third Reich Germany and the Soviet Union.

In the United States, on the other hand, corporate interests were quick to grasp the commercial potential of radio as an advertising-supported medium, and they used their immense political leverage to seize control of the industry before a public service system could be established. The two dominant national networks—the National Broadcasting Company (NBC)[6] and the Columbia Broadcasting System (CBS)—had successfully fought off and eliminated the opposition to commercial broadcasting by 1934.[7] NBC and CBS immediately sought to expand their commercial broadcasting empires globally, but they met severe resistance from the public service systems in the desirable wealthy nations. By affiliating with Latin American broadcasters, however, NBC and CBS were able to establish rudimentary Spanish-language "Pan-American" networks for commercial broadcasting by the late 1930s. Yet the real profits in radio were to be made in the advanced nations. For example, in 1945, fully two-thirds of radio receivers were in the United States and Great Britain, and most of the remainder were in Western Europe.[8] As the enormous profitability of commercial broadcasting became evident, corporate and advertising interests throughout the world clamored for the creation of commercial broadcasting to replace the existing public service systems. By the 1930s, business interests had established several commercial English-language stations in France and Luxemburg aimed directly at Britain. The tension between commercial and noncommercial broadcasting remained throughout Europe and wherever else public service systems existed for the balance of the century.

Broadcasting became truly global with the development of the shortwave band (3,000 to 30,000 kilohertz) in the late 1920s. Shortwave broadcasting was less reliable than medium-wave broadcasting and was poorly suited to local or even national coverage. Due to the nature of the radio spectrum in the shortwave band, however, it provided an inexpensive means to broadcast globally from within the borders of a single nation. The initial shortwave broadcasters tended to be the national majors, like the BBC, NBC, and CBS, who merely rebroadcast much of their domestic programming on the shortwave frequencies for international consumption. Shortwave reception became quite popular, and by the late 1930s almost all radio receivers included shortwave bands. NBC and CBS quickly conceived of shortwave as a means to broadcast in numerous languages, permitting them to bypass all of the local national broadcasters and to broadcast U.S. commercial advertising directly into the world's homes. The experiment was carried the furthest in Latin America. Nonetheless, this was an idea well ahead of its time and neither NBC nor CBS found sufficient interest among U.S. advertisers to make the project viable. Indeed, shortwave broadcasting has never proved to be serviceable for commercial purposes; the global vision of CBS and NBC would have to wait for better times and more reliable technologies.

If shortwave broadcasting was inhospitable to commerce, it was a tool of extraordinary power for international politics, and no period has had more intense international politics than the 1930s and 1940s. The Soviet Union began foreign-language shortwave broadcasts in the 1920s and fascist Italy followed suit soon after. The Nazis commenced foreign-language shortwave broadcasting upon taking power in Germany and the BBC added foreign-language broadcasting to its English language service in 1938. By 1939, twenty-six nations were broadcasting in shortwave in languages other than their native tongues, and many of those nations were doing so in several languages. At its peak, the BBC was broadcasting in forty-six languages. Shortwave broadcasting became a major component of ideological warfare across the political spectrum. When the United States entered the war in 1941 it effectively took control of shortwave broadcasting from NBC and CBS and established the Voice of America as a shortwave broadcasting service funded and directed by the federal government. By the end of World War II, fifty-five nations had formal foreign-language shortwave broadcasting services.[9]

The experience with film, radio broadcasting, and propaganda in general elevated the importance of communication in the minds of policy-makers during the interwar years. There was little debate regarding the geopolitical and economic importance of control of media and, even more important, telephony and telecommunication systems. If, prior to World War I, U.S. media firms had rarely ventured abroad, U.S. firms were soon establishing themselves as global enterprises with the active support and encouragement of the U.S. government. These ventures met with resistance in Europe, but were more successful in Latin America, where the U.S. government policy was one of applying "the principle of the Monroe Doctrine into the field of Communications."[10] Accordingly, the U.S. government established the Office of the Coordinator of Inter-American Affairs in the early 1940s under Nelson Rockefeller with the express mission of expanding U.S. commercial and political influence over Latin American media and culture. By 1943, U.S. planners understood that after the war the United States would have a dominance of the world not seen since the heyday of the British Empire, as even its victorious allies were being reduced to rubble in the war effort. A major priority was for the United States to usurp the European role in international communication and thereby consolidate U.S. hegemony.

The Postwar Era: U.S. Hegemony and TNC Dominance

The ending of World War II in 1945 marked the beginning of a new era of rapid growth. The United States emerged from the war stronger than ever, while its capitalist world rivals were either defeated and devastated (former enemies, Germany and Japan) or allies who had suffered severe wartime damage and losses (Great

Britain, France). With its unique power, the United States was able to organize a new world order serviceable to its political and economic interests. Just as Great Britain, at the peak period of its competitive power and hegemonic status, wanted open markets, so did the United States after 1945. It therefore pressed steadily for an ending of wartime capital controls and in favor of convertibility of currencies, a gradual reduction of tariff barriers through international agreements and bilateral arrangements, and open-door policies everywhere. It used the leverage from its control over the International Monetary Fund (IMF) and International Bank for Reconstruction and Development (World Bank), its direct loans and gifts under the Marshall Plan and other programs, and the Cold War, Soviet Threat, and North Atlantic Treaty Organization (NATO) to force open doors that might otherwise have been closed to its businessmen and bankers. The United States dominated foreign lending and FDI for almost two decades after 1945, and its great TNCs in the auto, chemicals, pharmaceutical, computer, petroleum, electrical machinery, and financial industries made enormous global advances. In 1960, the U.S. share of world FDI was a staggering 49.2 percent of the total. Although the U.S. portion of the global economy would decline thereafter with the rise of Germany and Japan as major economic powers and rapid growth elsewhere, the United States remained far and away the largest international investor, as well as dominant military power, in the late 1990s.

In the postwar period the United States championed the notion of the "free flow of information" as a universal principle. With its new-found power, the United States was able to get the "free flow" principle enshrined as official policy in the newly formed United Nations Educational, Scientific, and Cultural Organization (UNESCO). Free flow was at once an eloquent democratic principle and an aggressive trade position on behalf of U.S. media interests. The core operational idea behind the principle was that transnational media firms and advertisers should be permitted to operate globally, with minimal governmental intervention. In the view of U.S. policy-makers, this was the only notion of a free press suitable for a democratic world order.

The U.S. attempt to establish a global media system in its own image was aided by its influence over the postwar reconstruction of German, Italian, and Japanese media systems. U.S. officials pushed them as much as possible on the path to U.S.-style commercial systems.[11] But the United States met with only partial success in this effort as strong public broadcasters emerged in all three of these occupied countries. Beyond the U.S. sphere of influence, the Soviet Union led a group of self-described communist nations, including China after 1949, which opted out of the global capitalist system and refused to play by the rules of the market. Western leaders were gravely concerned by the spread of anti-market politics, and very quickly the Soviet Union and "communism" replaced fascism as the primary threat to the status quo. By 1950 the global shortwaves had returned to ideological (Cold War) combat, helped along by the fact that they had limited reach in the lucrative western markets and were unattractive commercially. In the United States, for example, shortwave was no longer included on standard radio receivers in the postwar era. The U.S. Voice of America was soon the largest broadcasting organization in the world, and it complemented the covertly funded Radio Liberty and Radio Free Europe as well as the BBC World Service in ideological battle with the massive Soviet shortwave operations. Otherwise, the communist role in global communication was minuscule relative to the size of the communist nations. Although the Soviet Tass news agency ranked in size with the "Big Four," it had little influence outside of the communist world. As state-subsidized enterprises, communist media did not have the same commercial imperative to expand as did their capitalist counterparts, nor is there any reason to think a more aggressive posture would have met with success in global media markets. Indeed, whereas the communist economic and social model may have had some appeal to many people in the world as an alternative to capitalism—especially in the underdeveloped areas—the communist media system generated little enthusiasm anywhere.

It was in the postwar years that the contours of the contemporary global media system became apparent. An important factor helping to shape this system was the combination of the global power of the United States and the imperial legacy of Britain, which effectively made English the global "second" language, if not the language of choice. This was of considerable value in assisting U.S. media activities abroad. At the same time, the dominant U.S. TNCs began to invest heavily overseas, and U.S. advertising agencies followed in their wake. The commercial media also moved abroad and began to consolidate and establish empires across formerly distinct media industries, with leading media firms acquiring significant holdings in film, music, publishing, and broadcasting. These were, and are, all long-term processes that did not realize their potential until the last decades of the century. The full effect of these developments became clear when they were linked with the extraordinary technological advances in communications of the latter part of the twentieth century, advances that permitted a degree of media conglomeration and global integration unthinkable in 1945 or even 1970.

Prior to 1945, aside from shortwave broadcasting, the dominant activities in global media had been those of the "Big Four" news agencies and the global film industry centered in Hollywood. In the postwar period the German Wolff news agency, failing to recover from its affiliation with the Third Reich, collapsed, and the French Havas was recreated as the Agence France-Presse (AFP). In keeping with the U.S. role in the world, both the AP and the UP (to become UPI in 1958) gained ground globally on Reuters and AFP; aside from the Soviet Tass, this western grip on the global print news agency reporting was unchallenged. The new "Big Four" expanded their services to include radio. Television presented a greater challenge, and for that medium a handful of specific "newsfilm agencies" emerged to provide television companies and networks with international newsfilm and videotape footage. Reuters allied with the BBC and several other broadcasting companies to establish Visnews, while UPI linked up with British commercial media broadcasting interests to form UPITN. The other two significant international newsfilm agencies were connected to the U.S. television networks CBS and ABC. As with the news agencies, international newsfilm was conducted by a select group of western firms, based in Britain and the United States.

The global film industry, too, remained primarily in the hands of a few U.S. firms—Columbia, Twentieth Century-Fox, United Artists, MGA (Universal), Warner Brothers, Metro-Goldwyn-Mayer, and Paramount—in the postwar years. Large domestic film industries emerged elsewhere, for example, in India and Japan. But the global export industry was synonymous with Hollywood. Film exports grew so rapidly that by the mid-1960s some U.S. studios were generating more income from foreign sources than from the U.S. market, though that would not become the general rule until the 1990s. By the 1960s, one-half of the non-communist world's motion picture theaters were offering dominantly Hollywood fare.[12]

In many respects the film industry remained at the forefront of advances in the global media system. Hollywood studios, for example, began to purchase foreign movie theaters to guarantee control of markets.[13] With a significant proportion of revenues generated outside of the United States, the Hollywood firms began to extend production overseas. The postwar surge of U.S. media included Hollywood's effective takeover of the British film industry, the remaining competitor for global audiences. As one British producer told the trade publication *Variety* in the 1960s: "We have a thriving film production industry in this country which is virtually owned, lock, stock and barrel, by Hollywood."[14] . . .

The most dramatic and important media technology to emerge in the postwar period was television. As with other media, television usage was initially heavily weighted toward the advanced capitalist nations. As late as 1961 there were more television sets in the United States than in the rest of the world combined.[15] In the most lucrative European markets and in many of the newly independent Third World nations, television was established as a nonprofit and sometimes noncommercial national service, thus limiting the possibilities for global media expansion. What could be exploited commercially, however, was the pressing need for television programming. In this regard, the U.S. program producers had years of experience and economies of scale to make them virtually unbeatable in the world market. U.S. television programming sales abroad increased from $15 million in 1958 to $130 million in 1973.[16] Many nations imported a majority of their television programs and the United States was the main beneficiary. It exported twice as many hours of programming as all other nations combined in the early 1970s.[17] Due to U.S. broadcasting regulations (subsequently eliminated), the U.S. networks NBC, CBS, and ABC were restricted in what they could produce for domestic broadcast. Thus the major U.S. program producers, and therefore the major global TV production studios, were the film studios of Hollywood.

Despite these regulatory constraints, NBC, CBS, and ABC were hardly inactive as global TV players. They sought to export in the two program areas that they were permitted to control, news and sports, although these were minor in comparison to entertainment programming. Along these permissible lines CBS and ABC established global newsfilm services. As the broadcasting services of all the other industrial powers were nonprofit, the U.S. networks faced little direct competition as they attempted to establish commercial networks abroad. Wherever possible, the U.S. networks invested in local broadcasting companies. ABC was by far the most aggressive of the U.S. networks, and by 1965 it had financial stakes in fifty-four stations in twenty-four countries in Latin America, Africa, and Asia.[18] ABC also established WorldVision, a global commercial broadcasting network. This initial wave of U.S.

television network expansion was only marginally viable. Dealing with a series of national bureaucracies and regulations was expensive and time-consuming, and global advertisers were primarily interested in the affluent Western European markets, where broadcast advertising was restricted or heavily regulated.[19] . . .

The U.S. advertising industry, working for its own and its large corporate clients' interests, contributed significantly to the struggle to commercialize global broadcasting. Its members used, and helped make prosperous and politically powerful, commercial media abroad, and they regularly threw their weight behind efforts to commercialize publicly owned media. The J. Walter Thompson agency—based in the United States—was notorious for its behind-the-scenes role in the decision to introduce advertising to British broadcasting in the 1950s.[20] As early as 1960, advertising industry observers predicted that all but the communist world would experience commercial broadcasting within a generation. Indeed, by 1970 only Belgium and the Scandinavian countries still forbade television advertising altogether.[21] Most of the Third World nations which had hoped to establish public service systems also found the appeal of turning to advertising support difficult to resist. In the late 1960s, even All India Radio, which in the BBC tradition had a thirty-year record of opposition to commercial broadcasting, began to accept paid advertising. The nonprofit broadcasting systems of Europe and Asia remained intact, and often quite influential, but their missions were beginning to change in response to commercial and political imperatives.

The NWICO Debate

By the 1970s the trajectory and nature of the emerging global media system were increasingly apparent; it was a largely profit-driven system dominated by TNCs based in the advanced capitalist nations, primarily the United States. At the same time, the world had changed considerably in the preceding quarter-century. During this period almost all of the European colonies in Asia and Africa gained political independence. And while the 1960s had seen growth in media usage in what came to be called the Third World, there was little reason to expect the disparity between the media haves and have-nots to diminish for generations, if at all. The revolutionary development of geosynchronous communication satellites in the 1960s and 1970s fanned the flames of concern about global media. Satellites did for television—indeed for all sorts of communication—what shortwave had done for radio broadcasting; it made possible instantaneous, inexpensive global interactive communication and broadcasting, and of a much higher quality than shortwave could ever achieve. Satellites held out the promise of making it possible for Third World nations to leapfrog out of their quagmire into a radically more advanced media system, but at the same time satellites posed the threat of transnational commercial broadcasters eventually controlling global communication, bypassing any domestic authority with broadcasts directly to Third World homes.

Historically, communication policy debates had been almost exclusively local or national in scope. In many Western European capitalist nations—as in the Third

World—commercial media interests were powerful but not omnipotent. There were strong traditions of nonprofit media and communication services. The commercial interests battled with other segments of society over communication policy. In the United States, however, corporate media and communication firms ruled with little opposition and the only communication policy battles of consequence were among business rivals. International communication politics, on the other hand, historically refereed relations between nation states, accepting the existing balance of power as given. It tended to favor technocratic responses to the international regulation of communication, and eschew controversy. Now, for the first time, global politics dealt with the social implications of the emerging global media system. Moreover, the major global institutions that dealt with communication issues—the United Nations, UNESCO, and the International Telecommunication Union (ITU)—now had majorities comprised of Third World nations and sympathetic communist governments. The impetus for the global media debate came from the Movement of the Non-Aligned Nations (NAM), which comprised over ninety member nations by the 1970s.

The NAM criticized the global media system at several different levels. Global communication was attacked for the "flagrant quantitative imbalance between North and South" and the corresponding "inequality in information resources."[22] A central criticism revolved around the western monopoly of global news services, with their almost exclusive service to the needs of the developed nations. There was almost no journalism by people in the nonaligned nations for the developed nations or for each other. Likewise, the domination of entertainment programming across the Third World was criticized as a cultural imperialism that implanted alien western values on audiences. The role of transnational media in undermining national sovereignty was another major concern. At its strongest, the NAM critique of global media was linked to a critique of global capitalism and economic imperialism; the global media were seen as working primarily to serve TNGs and advertisers, thus reinforcing the inequalities of the global economy. As one NAM resolution noted, "a new international order in the fields of information and mass communications is as vital as a new international economic order." The nonaligned position included a socialist critique of capitalist media[23] and a nationalist critique of imperialist media.

Although there was rough consensus on the critique, given the diversity of the NAM membership—which ranged from democratic socialist governments to corrupt dictatorships to stridently pro-capitalist nations—moving beyond the critique to meaningful reform proposals was more problematic. Indeed, the 1970s and 1980s campaign for a New World Information and Communication Order (NWICO) was more a rhetorical challenge than an organized political threat to the global status quo. For many of the nations, the actual commitment to the NWICO was limited; most Third World nations could have done far more than they were doing to promote indigenous media and alternative news services. Much of the campaign was a "begging" operation, asking western media firms to curtail profitable operations (while getting nothing in return) and western governments to donate capital for Third World communication investment, for no apparent reason except the spirit of Christian charity. As such, this campaign was doomed to failure from the outset. The same problems plagued the campaign on behalf of a new international economic order.

Representatives of the developed nations naturally disputed the NWICO critique, and they argued strenuously against any changes that would seriously disturb the global media system. To the NAM, the state was the only body that could effectively represent the will of the people against the interests of powerful global corporations and institutions. In U.S. thinking the state was the sole enemy of a free press, and therefore only a market-based, profit-driven system could legitimately claim democratic credentials. Instead of increased state involvement with media and communication, the developed nations suggested that groups like UNESCO, ITU, and the World Bank should work to improve the communication infrastructure of Third World nations. To proponents of the NWICO, this was simply a continuation of postwar policies that had barely made a dent in the global media crisis.

The primary arena for the NWICO debate was UNESCO, which in 1976 established what became known as the MacBride Commission to study global communication and suggest solutions. In 1978, UNESCO passed a Mass Media Declaration, which referred to the "moral, social, and professional responsibilities of the mass media." Then, in 1980, the MacBride Commission issued its report, vaguely endorsing the NWICO. Upon receiving the MacBride Commission report, UNESCO passed a resolution in support of the call for eliminating global media imbalances and having communication serve national developmental purposes. UNESCO's resolution, and the MacBride Commission report itself, reflected compromise with western concerns; it rejected state media monopolies and supported "freedom of journalists" and "freedom of the press." It accepted UNESCO's traditional support for a "free flow" of information, adding a call for "wider and better balance" and a "plurality of channels and information."[24]

These fuzzy generalities and contradictory appeals had little intellectual force and hardly moved U.S., British, or other great power leaders. These, and the TNCs and western media, never had the slightest sympathy for the NWICO, the media regarding it as a direct attack on their *modus operandi*. To the western establishment, the NWICO was anathema because it gave governments, and not markets, ultimate authority over the nature of a society's media. The western media mounted an aggressive, no-holds-barred attack in the 1980s against both the NWICO and UNESCO itself, as the agency that sanctioned the NWICO. Proponents of the NWICO were characterized as tinhorn dictators who wanted to censor the press to keep the truth from their peoples and the world. (For some of the NWICO's supporters, such a charge had credence.)[25]

The heavily biased news coverage, however, gave U.S. readers no context for evaluating the nearly hysterical charges against the NWICO proposal and UNESCO, the bulk of whose activities had nothing to do with the NWICO.[26] The campaign was effective. Both the United States and Great Britain withdrew from UNESCO in 1985, and the chastened new leadership of UNESCO quickly retreated from NWICO controversies and rhetoric, confining media concerns to building infrastructure and training journalists. The UNESCO retreat reflected the weakening power of the Third

World, with many Third World nations too concerned with survival and too dependent on western governments and the IMF and World Bank to take positions hostile
to the dominant global interests. By the end of the decade, as Herbert Schiller
contends, UNESCO was "cowed and enfeebled," and had become "fully compliant
with Western media interests."[27] The withdrawal from UNESCO also reflected a
broader change in U.S. and western politics in the 1980s, a move toward aggressive
global pro-market policies, personified by Thatcher and Reagan and often referred
to as neoliberalism. . . .

In short, globalization has gone far and is proceeding apace: increasing numbers
of firms—financial and nonfinancial—plan investment and operations on a regional
or global basis and run operations that are integrated across borders; these are
supplemented by a dense set of cross-border relationships via alliances and outsourc-
ing arrangements. As the UN Conference on Trade and Development (UNCTAD)
puts it, integrated international production

> reaches deeper into the fabric of international relations. As a result, it places economic
> activities that were previously subject solely to national control also under the common
> governance of TNCs. As this form of governance becomes more widespread and encom-
> passes a larger share of world output, the nature of the world economy changes: national
> economies—still subject to domestic governance structures—are no longer linked
> through markets alone, but rather are increasingly integrated at the level of production,
> with this production (and attendant transactions) under the governance of TNGs. In
> addition, the linkages established through the governance are further strengthened by
> the flow across borders of norms, values and routines (business culture) that are
> becoming of central importance to international competition in a more integrated world
> economy.[28] . . .

Ideology of Global Corporate Capital

The world is in a paradoxical condition: technologies exist and are on the horizon
that will radically improve labor productivity and could lead to higher living standards as well as the ability to address environmental damage and social inequality.
Yet in the reigning "free market" context productivity advances slowly, environmental threats grow, and inequality increases. The problem facing the victims and critics
of the global corporate order is not that alternative courses are *technically*
impossible—they are in fact more possible than ever before—as much as they are
seemingly unthinkable. The triumph of TNG power has for the time being removed
any feasible alternative, and the system's capacity to keep in check even mild social
democratic reforms suggests that the "problem of transition" to social democracy
itself has become a formidable challenge.

This power is not only economic and political, but extends to basic assumptions
and modes of thought; that is, to ideology. To no small extent the stability of the
system rests upon the widespread acceptance of a global corporate ideology. Ideology
has played the role of rationalizing and sanctifying inegalitarian relations in most
societies historically—in premodern times it generally took the form of religion—

and it is certainly necessary in the present order with its extreme and growing disparities in wealth, income, and power. As is natural, this ideology is embraced enthusiastically by those at the top of the socioeconomic pyramid, as they are prime beneficiaries of the status quo. But a strong ideology extends to non-beneficiaries and genuine victims, many of whom accept it in the face of contradictory experience. Those who question its postulate of benevolence may still not escape its assumptions of naturalness and inevitability, which induce quiescence and passivity. This is what makes ideology such an important mechanism of social control—far better than the risky option of employment of force.

So what are the main components of the new global corporate ideology? Its core element and centerpiece is the idea that the market allocates resources efficiently and provides *the* means of organizing economic (and perhaps all human) life. There is a strong tendency in corporate ideology to identify "freedom" with the mere absence of constraints on business (i.e., economic, or market, freedom), thus pushing political freedom into a subordinate category. In defense of this priority system it is argued that economic freedom is basic and deserves top billing because in the long run it will allow or even cause political freedom to emerge. This is unproven and somewhat cynical in that it helps rationalize support of regimes that serve business well, but crush political freedom as part of the process of creating a "favorable climate of investment"[29] as with Pinochet in Chile, Marcos in the Philippines, and Suharto in Indonesia.

A second and closely related element of global corporate ideology is that government intervention and regulation tend to impose unreasonable burdens on business that impede economic growth. In this view, governments enlarge in a process of self-aggrandizement and in response to pressures of special interests. They should ideally confine themselves to the maintenance of law and order and the protection of private property; the market will do the rest. Government is best which governs least, except where business needs its support in the interest of "competitiveness." In the ideology of the market there is a closely related tendency to ignore or downplay "externalities," the existence of "public goods," and other forms of "market failure," which have been discussed at length by economists over the years and which would seem more relevant in today's interdependent and ecologically threatened world of rapid growth, proliferating chemicals, radioactive materials, and biological innovations. Market failure, however, implies a greater role for government, which conflicts with the ideological core, so it is not only mainly disregarded, but academic ideologues have developed theoretical models to show that the market does not fail,[30] or that failures are so small that their costs are less than are likely to follow from their attempted correction by inefficient governments.[31]

A third element of global corporate ideology is the belief that the proper objective of the economy and economic policy should be "sustainable economic growth."[32] Sustainable means non-inflationary, as inflation allegedly always tends to accelerate and eventually must be halted by draconian means. It is in fact very debatable whether low and moderate levels of inflation do accelerate,[33] but whatever the truth of the matter this criterion is extremely important to the professional investment community (bankers, brokers, mutual fund managers), as is evident in press reports of their near-hysterical reactions to reports of unexpected employment gains or "unfavorable" wage settlements (wages go up too much). Their great and overriding fear is of inflation, and they much prefer slow growth, substantial unemployment and zero inflation to more rapid growth at the cost of even mild inflation. What is more, the financial markets have the power to enforce their preferences by their reactions to economic events.

Given the necessary control over inflation, the aim of macro-policy and criterion of progress, in corporate ideology, is economic growth, measured by real (inflation-adjusted) increases in gross domestic product (GDP) or per capita income. What is excluded from this schema of objectives is progress in the distribution of income or improvement in the condition of the poor. Globalization and other recent trends in technology and economic and political power have greatly increased income inequality and in many countries reduced the real incomes of those at the bottom of the income ladder[34]—and the corporate attacks on the welfare state have tended to reinforce these regressive tendencies of today's free market. It is understandable, therefore, that corporate ideology should focus on total and per capita growth: these figures not only show the progress benefiting those who underwrite the dominant ideology; they conveniently exclude measurement of the condition of the non-beneficiaries and victims of the contemporary growth process.

A final important element of corporate global ideology is the belief in the desirability of privatization. This derives in part from the core belief that the market can do it all, and the derivative belief that the government is self-aggrandizing and inefficient. Getting the government to sell off its assets to private entrepreneurs will, in this view, improve efficiency. There are other motives underlying the recent enthusiastic support of privatization, however: one is the desire to weaken government. A government that owns and manages assets is likely to be more powerful and better informed than one that is outside markets; and it therefore poses the threat that, being potentially subject to democratic political control, it might effectively serve non-corporate interests. Making it small and dependent reduces this threat. A further motive is making money—either by fees in selling government properties or profits from buying government properties at favorable (below true market) prices, a phenomenon that is characteristic of a sizable fraction of privatized assets (they tend to be sold off by governments elected with the support of many of those interested in buying such assets, so that non-competitive selling and privileged buying is commonplace).[35]

The widespread acceptance and internalization of global corporate ideology rests on the enormous economic and political power of its sponsors. Its ideological domination is not complete, however, and in every country there are resistant classes, groups, cultural bodies, and individuals who expound alternative analyses, visions, and programs. But these are poorly funded, not effectively linked together, frequently work at cross purposes, and have little leverage in mainstream institutions and the mass media. Lavishly funded pro-corporate thinktanks, academics and public relations agencies, on the other hand, are significant propagators of the corporate ideology.[36] Their influence is large and growing in the—media system. Corporate interests also dominate electoral campaigns with their ability to fund candidates, thereby minimizing the possibility of dissident voices entering the political debate.[37]

But it is the commercial media that play the central role in this process. The development of a global commercial media system that tends to regard corporate domination as natural and benevolent was and is the logical outgrowth of the "free market" communication policies that have come to dominate globally in the 1980s and 1990s. The global media are the missionaries of our age, promoting the virtues of commercialism and the market loudly and incessantly through their profit-driven and advertising-supported enterprises and programming. This missionary work is not the result of any sort of conspiracy; for the global media TNGs it developed organically from their institutional basis and commercial imperatives. Nor are the global media completely monolithic, of course, and dissident ideas make their occasional appearance in virtually all of them. But their overall trajectory of service to the global corporate system at many levels is undeniable.

The Global Media System in the 1980s

Every bit as striking as the global media's emergence as exponents of the ideology of global corporate capitalism has been the overall increase in importance of media and communication as an economic component of the global economy. In 1980 communication, broadly construed, accounted for $350 billion or 18 percent of world trade. By 1986, the annual worldwide output of the communication and information industries was valued at $1,600 billion and it was growing rapidly.[38] Along with financial markets, communication and information have become the most dynamic features of the globalizing market economy, and the development of global commercial media has been crucial to the development of the global marketplace.

Neoliberal policies have been applied aggressively to global media and telecommunication, and have stimulated their commercial development. The twin hallmarks of neoliberalism were (and are) deregulation and privatization. In communication, this has meant the simple denial of the formerly important issues of whether the media had social, moral, and political obligations beyond the pursuit of profit. In the 1980s these policies were applied increasingly to national broadcasting and telecommunication systems that were traditionally regulated and often publicly owned and operated. As these public services were often large and politically influential, the pace of deregulation, attendant commercialization, and privatization ebbed and flowed, and it varied from nation to nation. Even in the United States, where corporate power in the media field has been exceptional, the attempt to thoroughly deregulate U.S. domestic broadcasting was partially derailed by public and congressional opposition. Nonetheless, the commercial media lobbies have few rivals for political influence and the general trajectory of the deregulation and privatization process was unmistakable across the planet.

The other critical development in the 1980s was the advance of communication technologies, spurred on by global business's demand for the most rapid and reliable global communication networks possible. In the 1980s videocassette recorders and the expansion of satellite and cable communication made the global distribution of media far more feasible. Satellite services such as the Cable News Network (CNN), Music Television (MTV), and the Entertainment and Sports Network (ESPN) were launched in the United States and eventually grew into global enterprises. Combined with privatization and deregulation, these new technologies also provided the basis for an extraordinary increase in the number of television channels, which sought commercial advertising and programming.

Consequently, the 1980s was a period of unprecedented expansion for global media, making the preceding thirty-five years appear almost like mounds of dirt against the backdrop of a mountain range. Hollywood's European exports (including films, television programming, and videotapes) increased by 225 percent between 1984 and 1988, to some $561 million annually.[39] Hollywood's worldwide exports doubled in value between 1987 and 1991 from $1.1 billion to $2.2 billion. (At the same time, film and television imports to the U.S. totaled $81 *million* in 1991.) Exports of recorded music also doubled from 1987 to 1991, to a total of $419 million by 1991. Moreover, the global market was increasing in importance relative to the domestic industry. In the second half of the 1980s, foreign sales increased from 30 percent to 40 percent of U.S. film and television industry revenues.[40] Using a broader definition of media products, Anthony Smith calculates that Hollywood's exports to Europe nearly doubled in the 1980s to reach a total of more than $5 billion by 1989.[41]

The number of hours of television watched globally nearly tripled between 1979 and 1991.[42] In the new deregulatory environment, global advertisers were eager to serve this translational client base and provide commercial support to the burgeoning global television industry. Advertising in Europe more than doubled between 1980 and 1987, and it continued at that pace well into the 1990s. As one European advertiser put it in the late 1980s, the European Union considers advertising to be a "vital component in the creation of a Single European Market."[43]

Deregulation and new technologies not only stimulated global media expansion, they also provided the basis for a striking new wave of corporate consolidation in the media industry. In the United States, for example, where most of the major media firms had their headquarters, in the early 1980s fewer than fifty firms dominated the vast majority of output in the film, television, magazine, newspaper, billboard, radio, cable, and book publishing industries. Almost all of these firms operated in several media sectors. By the end of the decade that total was cut in half, due to mergers and acquisitions.[44] The very same process transpired in Western Europe. Perhaps the most intense process of concentration took place in the global advertising industry. After a wave of mergers and buyouts, by 1990 the leading seven advertising agencies accounted for $73 billion in billings. Five of these agencies were either U.S., or U.S. and British, while the other two were Japanese and French.[45]

Most important, the late 1980s gave birth to the development of a truly global media market, where the dominant firms were increasingly transnational firms. As the 1980s drew to a close, the leading translational media firms, having activities located across the world, included, among others, Bertelsmann, Capital Cities/ABC, CBS Inc., Matsushita (owner of then MCA), General Electric (owner of NBC),

Rupert Murdoch's News Corporation, Disney, Time Warner, Turner Broadcasting, and the Sony Corporation (owner of CBS Records and Columbia Pictures). By the early 1990s some of these firms—like News Corporation—rejected national identities and regarded themselves as global concerns. Although dominated by firms based in the United States, a critical development in the 1980s was the diffusion of ownership of the transnational media firms among investors and firms in the advanced capitalist world. Hence the Japanese hardware manufacturers Sony and Matsushita became members of the club through their purchases of U.S.-based media firms. Indeed, by 1990 over 10 percent of the U.S. workforce that worked for foreign-based firms worked in the film and television industries, a 2,000 percent increase over the same figure for 1980.[46] Tunstall and Palmer note, "Hollywood seems to have become steadily more powerful in the world, while becoming less American-owned."[47] Herbert Schiller concluded that it was no longer appropriate to speak of American cultural imperialism, as much as one should speak of transnational corporate cultural imperialism with a heavy American accent.[48]

Yet even the stunning growth of the late 1980s was just the tip of the iceberg. All the major postwar global media trends were gaining momentum. Deregulation and privatization still had considerable ground to cover, and there remained enormous untapped potential for commercial expansion. In 1990, for example, European television advertising spending per household was only one-quarter of the U.S. rate.[49] Large sections of Asia had barely been incorporated into the global commercial media market. New technologies were on the horizon that could further revolutionize global media. A true global media market with its own logic and dynamics was emerging. The decade ended with the nascent global media industry in a state of flux. When Time merged with Warner Communications in 1989, Time's president stated that by the year 2000, worldwide media would be dominated by "6, 7, 8 vertically integrated media and entertainment megacompanies."[50] One industry observer captured the spirit of the moment: "By all accounts the 1990s promise a rate and speed of change that will make previous decades uneventful by comparison."[51]

NOTES

From Edward S. Herman and Robert McChesney, "The Rise of the Global Media," in *The Global Media: The New Missionaries of Corporate Capitalism* (London: Cassell, 1997). Reprinted by permission of the Continuum International Publishing Group, Inc.

1. See Oliver Boyd-Barrett, *The International News Agencies* (Beverly Hills: Sage, 1980).

2. Ian Jarvie, *Hollywood's Overseas Campaign: The North American Movie Trade, 1920–1950* (Cambridge and New York: Cambridge University Press, 1992), p. 330.

3. Tapio Varis, *The Impact of Transnational Corporations on Communications* (Tampere Peace Research Institute Reports, No. 10, 1975), p. 2.

4. Jarvie, p. 315.

5. These are the frequencies from around 550 to 1500 kilohertz, or what is regarded as the AM band today.

6. NBC was split in half in the early 1940s and the third U.S. network, the American Broadcasting Company (ABC) was formed.

7. Robert McChesney, *Telecommunications, Mass Media, and Democracy: The Battle for the Control of U.S. Broadcasting, 1925–1935* (New York: Oxford University Press, 1993).

8. Barnard Bumpus, *International Broadcasting* (UNESCO: International Commission for the Study of Communications Problems, Document 60, 1980), p. 1.

9. *Ibid.*, pp. 3–5.

10. Statement of Owen D. Young, Chairman of General Electric and founder of the Radio Corporation of America. Quoted in Emily S. Rosenberg, *Spreading the American Dream: American Economic and Cultural Expansion, 1890–1945* (New York: Hill & Wang, 1981), p. 95.

11. Jeremy Tunstall, *The Media Are American* (New York: Columbia University Press, 1977).

12. Varis, p. 33.

13. Thomas Guback and Tapio Varis, *Transnational Communication and Cultural Industries* (Paris: UNESCO, 1982), p. 28.

14. Quoted in Thomas H. Guback, "Film as international business," *Journal of Communication*, 24 (1) (Winter 1974), 100.

15. Robert S. Fortner, *International Communication: History, Conflict, and Control of the Global Metropolis* (Belmont, CA: Wadsworth, 1983), p. 180.

16. Cited in Guback and Varis, p. 9.

17. Fornter, p. 180.

18. Varis, p. 18.

19. See Chin-Chuan Lee, *Media Imperialism Reconsidered: The Homogenizing of Television Culture* (Beverly Hills, CA: Sage, 1979).

20. H. H. Wilson, *Pressure Group: The Campaign for Commercial Television* (London: Secker & Warburg, 1961).

21. Noreene Z. Janus, "Advertising and the mass media in the era of the global corporation," in Emile G. McAnany, Jorge Schnitman and Noreene Janus (eds), *Communication and Social Structure: Critical Studies in Mass Media Research* (New York: Praeger, 1981), p. 310; Karl Sauvant, "Multinational enterprises and the transmission of culture: the international supply of advertising services and business education," *Journal of Peace Research*, 13 (1) (1976), 51.

22. Mustapha Masmoudi, "The new world information order," *Journal of Communication*, 29 (2) (Spring 1979), 172–3.

23. Quoted in Howard Frederick *Global Communications and International Relations* (International Thompson Publishing, 1997), p. 165.

24. UNESCO, *Many Voices, One World* (New York: UNESCO, 1980).

25. See Armand Mattelart, *Mapping World Communications: War, Progress, Culture* (Minneapolis: University of Minnesota Press, 1994), pp. 182–3.

26. William Preston, Edward Herman, and Herbert Schiller, *Hope and Folly: The United States and Unesco 1945–1985* (Minneapolis: University of Minnesota Press, 1989).

27. Herbert I. Schiller, *Mass Communications and American Empire* (2nd edn), (Boulder, CO: Westview Press, 1992), p. 24.

28. UNCTAD, *World Investment Report 1994* (New York: UN, 1995), p. 141.

29. The classic statement was that of Argentine Finance Minister Martinez de la Hoz during the rule of the generals: "We enjoy the stability that the Armed Forces has guaranteed us. This plan can be fulfilled despite its lack of popular support. It has sufficient political support . . . that provided by the Armed Forces." *Bulletin of the Argentine Information Service Center, Argentina Outreach*, March–April 1978, p. 3.

30. This is the most famous insight of Chicago School economist and Nobel Prize Laureate Ronald Coase's work, spelled out in his article "The problem of social cost," *Journal of Law and Economics*, October 1960.

31. See "Over-regulating America: tomorrow's economic argument," *The Economist*, July 27, 1996, pp. 19–21.

32. This was the economic policy objective put forward in June 1995 at a G-7 gathering; see in particular the remarks of Wim Duisenberg, president of the Bank for International Settlements, in the *Financial Times*, June 13, 1995, p. 1.

33. See Robert Eisner, *The Misunderstood Economy* (Boston: Harvard Business School, 1994), chapter 8; Edward Herman, "The natural rate of unemployment," *Z Magazine*, November 1994, pp. 62–5.

34. Edward Herman, "Immiserating growth (2): The Third World," *Z Magazine*, March 1995, pp. 22–7.

35. See Chapter 3, "Privatization," in Edward Herman, *Triumph of the Market* (Boston: South End Press, 1995), and citations given there.

36. See Alex Carey, *Taking the Risk Out of Democracy: Propaganda in the US and Australia* (Sydney, NSW: University of New South Wales Press, 1995); Edward Herman and Gerry O'Sullivan, *The "Terrorism" Industry* (New York: Pantheon, 1990); John Saloma, *Ominous Politics: The New Conservative Labyrinth* (New York: Hill & Wang, 1984).

37. See Thomas Ferguson, *Golden Rule: The Investment Theory of Political Parties in a Money-Driven System* (Chicago: University of Chicago Press, 1995).

38. Cees J. Hamelink, *The Politics of World Communication: A Human Rights Perspective* (London: Sage, 1994), p. 33.

39. Jeremy Tunstall and Michael Palmer, *Media Moguls* (London: Routledge, 1991), p. 26.

40. National Technical Information Service, *Globalization of the Mass Media* (Washington, DC: Department of Commerce, 1993), pp. 20–1, 1–2.

41. Anthony Smith, *The Age of Behemoths: The Globalization of Mass Media Firms* (New York: Priority Press Publications, 1991), p. 23.

42. Fortner, p. 261.

43. Statistics and quotation in Tunstall and Palmer, p. 94.

44. Ben Bagdikian, *The Media Monopoly* (4th edn) (Boston: Beacon Press, 1992).

45. See Tunstall and Palmer, p. 221.

46. National Technical Information Service, p. 14.

47. Tunstall and Palmer, p. 209.

48. Schiller, pp. 14–15.

49. Schiller, p. 14.

50. Statement of Nick Nicolas. Quoted in U.S. House of Representatives, Committee of Energy and Commerce, 101st Congress, 1st Session, *Globalization of the Mass Media* (Washington, DC: U.S. Government Printing Office, 1990), p. 1.

51. Marc Doyle, *The Future of Television: A Global Overview of Programming, Advertising, Technology and Growth* (Lincolnwood, IL: NTC Business Books, 1993), p. 1.

Chapter Two

Disjuncture and Difference in the Global Cultural Economy

Arjun Appadurai

Homogenization and Heterogenization

The central problem of today's global interactions is the tension between cultural homogenization and cultural heterogenization. A vast array of empirical facts could be brought to bear on the side of the homogenization argument, and much of it has come from the left end of the spectrum of media studies (Hamelink 1983; Mattelart 1983; Schiller 1976), and some from other perspectives (Gans 1985; Iyer 1988). Most often, the homogenization argument subspeciates into either an argument about Americanization or an argument about commoditization, and very often the two arguments are closely linked. What these arguments fail to consider is that at least as rapidly as forces from various metropolises are brought into new societies they tend to become indigenized in one or another way: this is true of music and housing styles as much as it is true of science and terrorism, spectacles and constitutions. The dynamics of such indigenization have just begun to be explored systemically (Barber 1987; Feld 1988; Hannerz 1987, 1989; Ivy 1988; Nicoll 1989; Yoshimoto 1989), and much more needs to be done. But it is worth noticing that for the people of Irian Jaya, Indonesianization may be more worrisome than Americanization, as Japanization may be for Koreans, Indianization for Sri Lankans, Vietnamization for the Cambodians, and Russianization for the people of Soviet Armenia and the Baltic republics. Such a list of alternative fears to Americanization could be greatly expanded, but it is not a shapeless inventory: for polities of smaller scale, there is always a fear of cultural absorption by polities of larger scale, especially those that are nearby. One man's imagined community is another man's political prison. . . .

The new global cultural economy has to be seen as a complex, overlapping, disjunctive order that cannot any longer be understood in terms of existing center-periphery models (even those that might account for multiple centers and peripheries). Nor is it susceptible to simple models of push and pull (in terms of migration theory), or of surpluses and deficits (as in traditional models of balance of trade), or of consumers and producers (as in most neo-Marxist theories of development). Even the most complex and flexible theories of global development that have come out of the Marxist tradition (Amin 1980; Mandel 1978; Wallerstein 1974; Wolf 1982) are inadequately quirky and have failed to come to terms with what Scott Lash and John Urry have called disorganized capitalism (1987). The complexity of the current global economy has to do with certain fundamental disjunctures between economy, culture, and politics that we have only begun to theorize.[1]

I propose that an elementary framework for exploring such disjunctures is to look at the relationship among five dimensions of global cultural flows that can be termed (a) *ethnoscapes*, (b) *mediascapes*, (c) *technoscapes*, (d) *financescapes*, and (e) *ideoscapes*.[2] The suffix *-scape* allows us to point to the fluid, irregular shapes of these landscapes, shapes that characterize international capital as deeply as they do international clothing styles. These terms with the common suffix *-scape* also indicate that these are not objectively given relations that look the same from every angle of vision but, rather, that they are deeply perspectival constructs, inflected by the historical, linguistic, and political situatedness of different sorts of actors: nation-states, multinationals, diasporic communities, as well as subnational groupings and movements (whether religious, political, or economic), and even intimate face-to-face groups, such as villages, neighborhoods, and families. Indeed, the individual actor is the last locus of this perspectival set of landscapes, for these landscapes are eventually navigated by agents who both experience and constitute larger formations, in part from their own sense of what these landscapes offer.

These landscapes thus are the building blocks of what (extending Benedict Anderson) I would like to call *imagined worlds*, that is, the multiple worlds that are constituted by the historically situated imaginations of persons and groups spread around the globe. An important fact of the world we live in today is that many persons on the globe live in such imagined worlds (and not just in imagined communities) and thus are able to contest and sometimes even subvert the imagined worlds of the official mind and of the entrepreneurial mentality that surround them.

By *ethnoscape*, I mean the landscape of persons who constitute the shifting world in which we live: tourists, immigrants, refugees, exiles, guest workers, and other moving groups and individuals constitute an essential feature of the world and appear to affect the politics of (and between) nations to a hitherto unprecedented degree. This is not to say that there are no relatively stable communities and networks of kinship, friendship, work, and leisure, as well as of birth, residence, and other filial forms. But it is to say that the warp of these stabilities is everywhere shot through with the woof of human motion, as more persons and groups deal with the realities of having to move or the fantasies of wanting to move. What is more, both these realities and fantasies now function on larger scales, as men and women from villages in India think not just of moving to Poona or Madras but of moving to Dubai and Houston, and refugees from Sri Lanka find themselves in South India as well as in Switzerland, just as the Hmong are driven to London as well as to Philadelphia. And as international capital shifts its needs, as production and technology generate different needs, as nation-states shift their policies on refugee populations, these moving groups can never afford to let their imaginations rest too long, even if they wish to.

By *technoscape*, I mean the global configuration, also ever fluid, of technology and the fact that technology, both high and low, both mechanical and informational, now moves at high speeds across various kinds of previously impervious boundaries.

Many countries now are the roots of multinational enterprise: a huge steel complex in Libya may involve interests from India, China, Russia, and Japan, providing different components of new technological configurations. The odd distribution of technologies, and thus the peculiarities of these technoscapes, are increasingly driven not by any obvious economies of scale, of political control, or of market rationality but by increasingly complex relationships among money flows, political possibilities, and the availability of both un- and highly skilled labor. So, while India exports waiters and chauffeurs to Dubai and Sharjah, it also exports software engineers to the United States—indentured briefly to Tata-Burroughs or the World Bank, then laundered through the State Department to become wealthy resident aliens, who are in turn objects of seductive messages to invest their money and know-how in federal and state projects in India.

The global economy can still be described in terms of traditional indicators (as the World Bank continues to do) and studied in terms of traditional comparisons (as in Project Link at the University of Pennsylvania), but the complicated technoscapes (and the shifting ethnoscapes) that underlie these indicators and comparisons are further out of the reach of the queen of social sciences than ever before. How is one to make a meaningful comparison of wages in Japan and the United States or of real-estate costs in New York and Tokyo, without taking sophisticated account of the very complex fiscal and investment flows that link the two economies through a global grid of currency speculation and capital transfer?

Thus it is useful to speak as well of *financescapes*, as the disposition of global capital is now a more mysterious, rapid, and difficult landscape to follow than ever before, as currency markets, national stock exchanges, and commodity speculations move megamonies through national turnstiles at blinding speed, with vast, absolute implications for small differences in percentage points and time units. But the critical point is that the global relationship among ethnoscapes, technoscapes, and financescapes is deeply disjunctive and profoundly unpredictable because each of these landscapes is subject to its own constraints and incentives (some political, some informational, and some technoenvironmental), at the same time as each acts as a constraint and a parameter for movements in the others. Thus, even an elementary model of global political economy must take into account the deeply disjunctive relationships among human movement, technological flow, and financial transfers.

Further refracting these disjunctures (which hardly form a simple, mechanical global infrastructure in any case) are what I call *mediascapes* and *ideoscapes*, which are closely related landscapes of images. *Mediascapes* refer both to the distribution of the electronic capabilities to produce and disseminate information (newspapers, magazines, television stations, and film-production studios), which are now available to a growing number of private and public interests throughout the world, and to the images of the world created by these media. These images involve many complicated inflections, depending on their mode (documentary or entertainment), their hardware (electronic or preelectronic), their audiences (local, national, or transnational), and the interests of those who own and control them. What is most important about these mediascapes is that they provide (especially in their television, film, and cassette forms) large and complex repertoires of images, narratives, and ethnoscapes to viewers throughout the world, in which the world of commodities and the world of news and politics are profoundly mixed. What this means is that many audiences around the world experience the media themselves as a complicated and interconnected repertoire of print, celluloid, electronic screens, and billboards. The lines between the realistic and the fictional landscapes they see are blurred, so that the farther away these audiences are from the direct experiences of metropolitan life, the more likely they are to construct imagined worlds that are chimerical, aesthetic, even fantastic objects, particularly if assessed by the criteria of some other perspective, some other imagined world.

Mediascapes, whether produced by private or state interests, tend to be image-centered, narrative-based accounts of strips of reality, and what they offer to those who experience and transform them is a series of elements (such as characters, plots, and textual forms) out of which scripts can be formed of imagined lives, their own as well as those of others living in other places. These scripts can and do get disaggregated into complex sets of metaphors by which people live (Lakoff and Johnson 1980) as they help to constitute narratives of the Other and protonarratives of possible lives, fantasies that could become prolegomena to the desire for acquisition and movement.

Ideoscapes are also concatenations of images, but they are often directly political and frequently have to do with the ideologies of states and the counterideologies of movements explicitly oriented to capturing state power or a piece of it. These ideoscapes are composed of elements of the Enlightenment worldview, which consists of a chain of ideas, terms, and images, including *freedom, welfare, rights, sovereignty, representation*, and the master term *democracy*. The master narrative of the Enlightenment (and its many variants in Britain, France, and the United States) was constructed with a certain internal logic and presupposed a certain relationship between reading, representation, and the public sphere. (For the dynamics of this process in the early history of the United States, see Warner 1990.) But the diaspora of these terms and images across the world, especially since the nineteenth century, has loosened the internal coherence that held them together in a Euro-American master narrative and provided instead a loosely structured synopticon of politics, in which different nation-states as part of their evolution, have organized their political cultures around different keywords (e.g., Williams 1976).

As a result of the differential diaspora of these keywords, the political narratives that govern communication between elites and followers in different parts of the world involve problems of both a semantic and pragmatic nature: semantic to the extent that words (and their lexical equivalents) require careful translation from context to context in their global movements, and pragmatic to the extent that the use of these words by political actors and their audiences may be subject to very different sets of contextual conventions that mediate their translation into public politics . . .

These conventions also involve the far more subtle question of what sets of communicative genres are valued in what way (newspapers versus cinema, for example) and what sorts of pragmatic genre conventions govern the collective readings of different kinds of text. So, while an Indian audience may be attentive to the resonances of a political speech in terms of some keywords and phrases reminiscent of Hindi cinema, a Korean audience may respond to the subtle codings of Buddhist or neo-Confucian rhetoric encoded in a political document. The very relationship of reading to hearing and seeing may vary in important ways that determine the morphology of these different ideoscapes as they shape themselves in different national and transnational contexts. This globally variable synaesthesia has hardly even been noted, but it demands urgent analysis. Thus *democracy* has clearly become a master term, with powerful echoes from Haiti and Poland to the former Soviet Union and China, but it sits at the center of a variety of ideoscapes, composed of distinctive pragmatic configurations of rough translations of other central terms from the vocabulary of the Enlightenment. This creates ever new terminological kaleidoscopes, as states (and the groups that seek to capture them) seek to pacify populations whose own ethnoscapes are in motion and whose mediascapes may create severe problems for the ideoscapes with which they are presented. The fluidity of ideoscapes is complicated in particular by the growing diasporas (both voluntary and involuntary) of intellectuals who continuously inject new meaning-streams into the discourse of democracy in different parts of the world.

This extended terminological discussion of the five terms I have coined sets the basis for a tentative formulation about the conditions under which current global flows occur: they occur in and through the growing disjunctures among ethnoscapes, technoscapes, financescapes, mediascapes, and ideoscapes. This formulation, the core of my model of global cultural flow, needs some explanation. First, people, machinery, money, images, and ideas now follow increasingly nonisomorphic paths; of course, at all periods in human history, there have been some disjunctures in the flows of these things, but the sheer speed, scale, and volume of each of these flows are now so great that the disjunctures have become central to the politics of global culture. The Japanese are notoriously hospitable to ideas and are stereotyped as inclined to export (all) and import (some) goods, but they are also notoriously closed to immigration, like the Swiss, the Swedes, and the Saudis. Yet the Swiss and the Saudis accept populations of guest workers, thus creating labor diasporas of Turks, Italians, and other circum-Mediterranean groups. Some such guest-worker groups maintain continuous contact with their home nations, like the Turks, but others, like high-level South Asian migrants, tend to desire lives in their new homes, raising anew the problem of reproduction in a deterritorialized context.

Deterritorialization, in general, is one of the central forces of the modern world because it brings laboring populations into the lower-class sectors and spaces of relatively wealthy societies, while sometimes creating exaggerated and intensified senses of criticism or attachment to politics in the home state. Deterritorialization, whether of Hindus, Sikhs, Palestinians, or Ukrainians, is now at the core of a variety of global fundamentalisms, including Islamic and Hindu fundamentalism. In the Hindu case, for example, it is clear that the overseas movement of Indians has been exploited by a variety of interests both within and outside India to create a complicated network of finances and religious identifications, by which the problem of cultural reproduction for Hindus abroad has become tied to the politics of Hindu fundamentalism at home.

At the same time, deterritorialization creates new markets for film companies, art impresarios, and travel agencies, which thrive on the need of the deterritorialized population for contact with its homeland. Naturally, these invented homelands, which constitute the mediascapes of deterritorialized groups, can often become sufficiently fantastic and one-sided that they provide the material for new ideoscapes in which ethnic conflicts can begin to erupt. The creation of Khalistan, an invented homeland of the deterritorialized Sikh population of England, Canada, and the United States, is one example of the bloody potential in such mediascapes as they interact with the internal colonialisms of the nation-state (e.g., Hechter 1975). The West Bank, Namibia, and Eritrea are other theaters for the enactment of the bloody negotiation between existing nation-states and various deterritorialized groupings.

It is in the fertile ground of deterritorialization, in which money, commodities, and persons are involved in ceaselessly chasing each other around the world, that the mediascapes and ideoscapes of the modern world find their fractured and fragmented counterpart. For the ideas and images produced by mass media often are only partial guides to the goods and experiences that deterritorialized populations transfer to one another. In Mira Nair's brilliant film *India Cabaret*, we see the multiple loops of this fractured deterritorialization as young women, barely competent in Bombay's metropolitan glitz, come to seek their fortunes as cabaret dancers and prostitutes in Bombay, entertaining men in clubs with dance formats derived wholly from the prurient dance sequences of Hindi films. These scenes in turn cater to ideas about Western and foreign women and their looseness, while they provide tawdry career alibis for these women. Some of these women come from Kerala, where cabaret clubs and the pornographic film industry have blossomed, partly in response to the purses and tastes of Keralites returned from the Middle East, where their diasporic lives away from women distort their very sense of what the relations between men and women might be. These tragedies of displacement could certainly be replayed in a more detailed analysis of the relations between the Japanese and German sex tours to Thailand and the tragedies of the sex trade in Bangkok, and in other similar loops that tie together fantasies about the Other, the conveniences and seductions of travel, the economics of global trade, and the brutal mobility fantasies that dominate gender politics in many parts of Asia and the world at large.

While far more could be said about the cultural politics of deterritorialization and the larger sociology of displacement that it expresses, it is appropriate at this juncture to bring in the role of the nation-state in the disjunctive global economy of culture today. The relationship between states and nations is everywhere an embattled one. It is possible to say that in many societies the nation and the state have become one another's projects. That is, while nations (or more properly groups with ideas about nationhood) seek to capture or co-opt states and state power, states simultaneously seek to capture and monopolize ideas about nationhood (Baruah 1986; Chatterjee 1986; Nandy 1989). In general, separatist transnational movements, including those that have included terror in their methods, exemplify nations in search of states. Sikhs, Tamil Sri Lankans, Basques, Moros, Quebecois—each of these represents imagined communities that seek to create states of their own or carve pieces out of existing states. States, on the other hand, are everywhere seeking to monopolize the moral resources of community, either by flatly claiming perfect coevality between nation and state, or by systematically museumizing and representing all the groups within them in a variety of heritage politics that seems remarkably uniform throughout the world (Handler 1988; Herzfeld 1982; McQueen 1988).

Here, national and international mediascapes are exploited by nationstates to pacify separatists or even the potential fissiparousness of all ideas of difference. Typically, contemporary nation-states do this by exercising taxonomic control over difference, by creating various kinds of international spectacle to domesticate difference, and by seducing small groups with the fantasy of self-display on some sort of global or cosmopolitan stage. One important new feature of global cultural politics, tied to the disjunctive relationships among the various landscapes discussed earlier, is that state and nation are at each other's throats, and the hyphen that links them is now less an icon of conjuncture than an index of disjuncture. This disjunctive relationship between nation and state has two levels: at the level of any given nation-state, it means that there is a battle of the imagination, with state and nation-seeking to cannibalize one another. Here is the seedbed of brutal separatisms—majoritarianisms that seem to have appeared from nowhere and microidentities that have become political projects within the nation-state. At another level, this disjunctive relationship is deeply entangled with . . . global disjunctures . . . ideas of nationhood appear to be steadily increasing in scale and regularly crossing existing state boundaries, sometimes, as with the Kurds, because previous identities stretched across vast national spaces or, as with the Tamils in Sri Lanka, the dormant threads of a transnational diaspora have been activated to ignite the micropolitics of a nation-state.

In discussing the cultural politics that have subverted the hyphen that links the nation to the state, it is especially important not to forget the mooring of such politics in the irregularities that now characterize disorganized capital (Kothari 1989; Lash and Urry 1987). Because labor, finance, and technology are now so widely separated, the volatilities that underlie movements for nationhood (as large as transnational Islam on the one hand, or as small as the movement of the Curkhas for a separate state in Northeast India) grind against the vulnerabilities that characterize the relationships between states. States find themselves pressed to stay open by the forces of media, technology, and travel that have fueled consumerism throughout the world and have increased the craving, even in the non-Western world, for new commodities and spectacles. On the other hand, these very cravings can become caught up in new ethnoscapes, mediascapes, and, eventually, ideoscapes, such as democracy in China, that the state cannot tolerate as threats to its own control over ideas of nationhood and peoplehood. States throughout the world are under siege, especially where contests over the ideoscapes of democracy are fierce and fundamental, and where there are radical disjunctures between ideoscapes and technoscapes (as in the case of very small countries that lack contemporary technologies of production and information); or between ideoscapes and financescapes (as in countries such as Mexico or Brazil, where international lending influences national politics to a very large degree); or between ideoscapes and ethnoscapes (as in Beirut, where diasporic, local, and translocal filiations are suicidally at battle); or between ideoscapes and mediascapes (as in many countries in the Middle East and Asia) where the lifestyles represented on both national and international TV and cinema completely overwhelm and undermine the rhetoric of national politics. In the Indian case, the myth of the law-breaking hero has emerged to mediate this naked struggle between the pieties and realities of Indian politics, which has grown increasingly brutalized and corrupt (Vachani 1989).

The transnational movement of the martial arts, particularly through Asia, as mediated by the Hollywood and Hong Kong film industries (Zarilli 1995) is a rich illustration of the ways in which long-standing martial arts traditions, reformulated to meet the fantasies of contemporary (sometimes lumpen) youth populations, create new cultures of masculinity and violence, which are in turn the fuel for increased violence in national and international politics. Such violence is in turn the spur to an increasingly rapid and amoral arms trade that penetrates the entire world. The worldwide spread of the AK-47 and the Uzi, in films, in corporate and state security, in terror, and in police and military activity, is a reminder that apparently simple technical uniformities often conceal an increasingly complex set of loops, linking images of violence to aspirations for community in some imagined world.

Returning then to the ethnoscapes with which I began, the central paradox of ethnic politics in today's world is that primordia (whether of language or skin color or neighborhood or kinship) have become globalized. That is, sentiments, whose greatest force is in their ability to ignite intimacy into a political state and turn locality into a staging ground for identity, have become spread over vast and irregular spaces as groups move yet stay linked to one another through sophisticated media capabilities. This is not to deny that such primordia are often the product of invented traditions (Hobsbawm and Ranger 1983) or retrospective affiliations, but to emphasize that because of the disjunctive and unstable interplay of commerce, media, national policies, and consumer fantasies, ethnicity, once a genie contained in the bottle of some sort of locality (however large), has now become a global force, forever slipping in and through the cracks between states and borders.

But the relationship between the cultural and economic levels of this new set of global disjunctures is not a simple one-way street in which the terms of global cultural politics are set wholly by, or confined wholly within, the vicissitudes of international flows of technology, labor, and finance, demanding only a modest modification of existing neo-Marxist models of uneven development and state formation. There is a deeper change, itself driven by the disjunctures among all the landscapes I have discussed and constituted by their continuously fluid and uncertain interplay, that concerns the relationship between production and consumption in today's global economy. Here, I begin with Marx's famous (and often mined) view of the fetishism of the commodity and suggest that this fetishism has been replaced in the world at large (now seeing the world as one large, interactive system, composed of many complex subsystems) by two mutually supportive descendants, the first of which I call production fetishism and the second, the fetishism of the consumer.

By *production fetishism* I mean an illusion created by contemporary transnational production loci that masks translocal capital, transnational earning flows, global management, and often faraway workers (engaged in various kinds of high-tech putting-out operations) in the idiom and spectacle of local (sometimes even worker) control, national productivity, and territorial sovereignty. To the extent that various kinds of free-trade zones have become the models for production at large, especially of high-tech commodities, production has itself become a fetish, obscuring not social relations as such but the relations of production, which are increasingly transnational. The locality (both in the sense of the local factory or site of production and in the extended sense of the nation-state) becomes a fetish that disguises the globally dispersed forces that actually drive the production process. This generates alienation (in Marx's sense) twice intensified, for its social sense is now compounded by a complicated spatial dynamic that is increasingly global.

As for the *fetishism of the consumer*, I mean to indicate here that the consumer has been transformed through commodity flows (and the mediascapes, especially of advertising, that accompany them) into a sign, both in Baudrillard's sense of a simulacrum that only asymptotically approaches the form of a real social agent, and in the sense of a mask for the real seat of agency, which is not the consumer but the producer and the many forces that constitute production. Global advertising is the key technology for the worldwide dissemination of a plethora of creative and culturally well-chosen ideas of consumer agency. These images of agency are increasingly distortions of a world of merchandising so subtle that the consumer is consistently helped to believe that he or she is an actor, where in fact he or she is at best a chooser.

The globalization of culture is not the same as its homogenization, but globalization involves the use of a variety of instruments of homogenization (armaments, advertising techniques, language hegemonies, and clothing styles) that are absorbed into local political and cultural economies, only to be repatriated as heterogeneous dialogues of national sovereignty, free enterprise, and fundamentalism in which the state plays an increasingly delicate role: too much openness to global flows, and the nation-state is threatened by revolt, as in the China syndrome, too little, and the state exits the international stage, as Burma, Albania, and North Korea in various ways have done. In general, the state has become the arbitrageur of this *repatriation of difference* (in the form of goods, signs, slogans, and styles). But this repatriation or export of the designs and commodities of difference continuously exacerbates the internal politics of majoritarianism and homogenization, which is most frequently played out in debates over heritage.

Thus the central feature of global culture today is the politics of the mutual effort of sameness and difference to cannibalize one another and thereby proclaim their successful hijacking of the twin Enlightenment ideas of the triumphantly universal and the resiliently particular. This mutual cannibalization shows its ugly face in riots, refugee flows, state-sponsored torture, and ethnocide (with or without state support). Its brighter side is in the expansion of many individual horizons of hope and fantasy, in the global spread of oral rehydration therapy and other low-tech instruments of well-being, in the susceptibility even of South Africa to the force of global opinion, in the inability of the Polish state to repress its own working classes, and in the growth of a wide range of progressive, transnational alliances. Examples of both sorts could be multiplied. The critical point is that both sides of the coin of global cultural process today are products of the infinitely varied mutual contest of sameness and difference on a stage characterized by radical disjunctures between different sorts of global flows and the uncertain landscapes created in and through these disjunctures.

The Work of Reproduction in an Age of Mechanical Art

I have inverted the key terms of the title of Walter Benjamin's famous essay (1969) to return this rather high-flying discussion to a more manageable level. There is a classic human problem that will not disappear however much global cultural processes might change their dynamics, and this is the problem today typically discussed under the rubric of reproduction (and traditionally referred to in terms of the transmission of culture). In either case, the question is, how do small groups, especially families, the classical loci of socialization, deal with these new global realities as they seek to reproduce themselves and, in so doing, by accident reproduce cultural forms themselves? In traditional anthropological terms, this could be phrased as the problem of enculturation in a period of rapid culture change. So the problem is hardly novel. But it does take on some novel dimensions under the global conditions discussed so far in this chapter.

First, the sort of transgenerational stability of knowledge that was presupposed in most theories of enculturation (or, in slightly broader terms, of socialization) can no longer be assumed. As families move to new locations, or as children move before older generations, or as grown sons and daughters return from time spent in strange parts of the world, family relationships can become volatile; new commodity patterns are negotiated, debts and obligations are recalibrated, and rumors and fantasies about the new setting are maneuvered into existing repertoires of knowledge and practice. Often, global labor diasporas involve immense strains on marriages in general and on women in particular, as marriages become the meeting points of historical patterns of socialization and new ideas of proper behavior. Generations easily divide, as ideas about property, propriety, and collective obligation wither under the siege of distance and time. Most important, the work of cultural reproduction in new settings is profoundly complicated by the politics of representing a family as normal (particularly for the young) to neighbors and peers in the new locale. All this is, of course, not new to the cultural study of immigration.

What is new is that this is a world in which both points of departure and points of arrival are in cultural flux, and thus the search for steady points of reference, as critical life choices are made, can be very difficult. It is in this atmosphere that the invention of tradition (and of ethnicity, kinship, and other identity markers) can become slippery, as the search for certainties is regularly frustrated by the fluidities of transnational communication. As group pasts become increasingly parts of museums, exhibits, and collections, both in national and transnational spectacles, culture becomes less what Pierre Bourdieu would have called a habitus (a tacit realm of reproducible practices and dispositions) and more an arena for conscious choice, justification, and representation, the latter often to multiple and spatially dislocated audiences.

The task of cultural reproduction, even in its most intimate arenas, such as husband-wife and parent-child relations, becomes both politicized and exposed to the traumas of deterritorialization as family members pool and negotiate their mutual understandings and aspirations in sometimes fractured spatial arrangements. At larger levels, such as community, neighborhood, and territory, this politicization is often the emotional fuel for more explicitly violent politics of identity, just as these larger politics sometimes penetrate and ignite domestic politics. When, for example, two offspring in a household split with their father on a key matter of political identification in a transnational setting, preexisting localized norms carry little force. Thus a son who has joined the Hezbollah group in Lebanon may no longer get along with parents or siblings who are affiliated with Amal or some other branch of Shi'i ethnic political identity in Lebanon. Women in particular bear the brunt of this sort of friction, for they become pawns in the heritage politics of the household and are often subject to the abuse and violence of men who are themselves torn about the relation between heritage and opportunity in shifting spatial and political formations.

The pains of cultural reproduction in a disjunctive global world are, of course, not eased by the effects of mechanical art (or mass media), for these media afford powerful resources for counternodes of identity that youth can project against parental wishes or desires. At larger levels of organization, there can be many forms of cultural politics within displaced populations (whether of refugees or of voluntary immigrants), all of which are inflected in important ways by media (and the mediascapes and ideoscapes they offer). A central link between the fragilities of cultural reproduction and the role of the mass media in today's world is the politics of gender and violence. As fantasies of gendered violence dominate the B-grade film industries that blanket the world, they both reflect and refine gendered violence at home and in the streets, as young men (in particular) are swayed by the macho politics of self-assertion in contexts where they are frequently denied real agency, and women are forced to enter the labor force in new ways on the one hand, and continue the maintenance of familial heritage on the other. Thus the honor of women becomes not just an armature of stable (if inhuman) systems of cultural reproduction but a new arena for the formation of sexual identity and family politics, as men and women face new pressures at work and new fantasies of leisure.

Because both work and leisure have lost none of their gendered qualities in this new global order but have acquired ever subtler fetishized representations, the honor of women becomes increasingly a surrogate for the identity of embattled communities of males, while their women in reality have to negotiate increasingly harsh conditions of work at home and in the nondomestic workplace. In short, deterritorialized communities and displaced populations, however much they may enjoy the fruits of new kinds of earning and new dispositions of capital and technology, have to play out the desires and fantasies of these new ethnoscapes, while striving to reproduce the family-as-microcosm of culture. As the shapes of cultures grow less bounded and tacit, more fluid and politicized, the work of cultural reproduction becomes a daily hazard. Far more could, and should, be said about the work of reproduction in an age of mechanical art: the preceding discussion is meant to indicate the contours of the problems that a new, globally informed theory of cultural reproduction will have to face.

NOTES

From Arjun Appadurai, "Disjuncture and Difference in the Global Cultural Economy," originally published in *Public Culture* 2, no. 2 (spring 1990). Reprinted by permission of the author.

1. One major exception is Fredric Jameson, whose work on the relationship between postmodernism and late capitalism has in many ways inspired this essay. The debate between Jameson and Aijaz Ahmad in *Social Text*, however, shows that the creation of a globalizing Marxist narrative in cultural matters is difficult territory indeed (Jameson 1986; Ahmad 1987). My own effort in this context is to begin a restructuring of the Marxist narrative (by stressing lags and disjunctures) that many Marxists might find abhorrent. Such a restructuring has to avoid the dangers of obliterating difference within the Third World, eliding the social referent (as some French postmodernists seem inclined to do), and retaining the narrative authority of the Marxist tradition, in favor of greater attention to global fragmentation, uncertainty, and difference.

2. The idea of *ethnoscape* is more fully engaged in Arjun Appadurai, "Global Ethnoscapes," in *Modernity at Large: Cultural Dimensions of Globalization* (Minnesota: University of Minnesota Press, 1996), 48–65.

BIBLIOGRAPHY

Ahmad, A. (1987) Jameson's Rhetoric of Otherness and the "National Allegory," *Social Text* 17:3–25.

Amin, S. (1980) *Class and Nation: Historically and in the Current Crisis*. New York and London: Monthly Review Press.

Barber, K. (1987) Popular Arts in Africa, *African Studies Review* 30 (3, September): 1–78.

Baruah, S. (1986) Immigration, Ethnic Conflict and Political Turmoil, Assam 1979–1985, *Asian Survey* 26 (11, November): 1184–1206.

Benjamin, W. ([1936] 1969). The Work of Art in the Age of Mechanical Reproduction. In H. Arendt (Ed.) *Illuminations.* H. Zohn (Trans.) New York: Schocken Books.

Chatterjee, P. (1986) *Nationalist Throught the Colonial World:A Derivative Discourse?* London: Zed Books.

Feld, S. (1988) Notes on World Beat, *Public Culture* 1 (1): 31–37.

Gans, E. (1985) *The End of a Culture: Toward a Generative Anthropology*. Berkeley: University of California Press.

Hamelink, C. (1983) *Cultural Autonomy in Global Communications*. New York: Longman.

Handler, R. (1988) *Nationalism and the Politics of Culture in Quebec*. Madison: University of Wisconsin Press.

Hannerz, U. (1987) The World in Creolization, *Africa* 57 (4): 546–59.

———. (1989 Notes on the Global Ecumene, *Public Culture* 1 (2, Spring): 66–75.

Hechter, M. (1975) *Internal Colonialism: The Celtic Fringe in British National Development, 1536–1966*. Berkeley: University of California Press.

Herzfeld, M. (1982) *Ours Once More: Folklore, Ideology and the Making of Modern Greece.* Austin: University of Texas Press.

Hobsbawm, E., and T. Ranger (Eds.) (1983) *The Invention of Tradition.* New York: Columbia University Press.

Ivy, M. (1988) Tradition and Difference in the Japanese Mass Media, *Public Culture* 1 (1): 21–29.

Iyer, P. (1988) *Video Night in Kathmandu.* New York: Knopf.

Jameson, F. (1986) Third World Literature in the Era of Multi-National Capitalism, *Social Text* 15 (Fall): 65–88.

Kothari, R. (1989) *State against Democracy: In Search of Humane Governance.* New York: New Horizons.

Lakoff, G., and M. Johnson (1980) *Metaphors We Live By.* Chicago and London: University of Chicago Press.

Lash, S., and J. Urry (1987) *The End of Organized Capitalism.* Madison: University of Wisconsin Press.

Mandel, E. (1978) *Late Capitalism.* London: Verso.

Mattelart, A. (1983) *Transnationals and the Third World: The Struggle for Culture.* South Hadley, Mass.: Bergin and Garvey.

McQueen, H. (1988) The Australian Stamp: Image, Design and Ideology, *Arena* 84 (Spring): 78–96.

Nandy, A. (1989) The Political Culture of the Indian State, *Daedalus* 118 (4): 1–26.

Nicoll, F. (1989) My Trip to Alice, *Criticism, Heresy and Interpretation.* 3: 21–32.

Schiller, H. (1976) *Communication and Cultural Domination.* White Plains, N.Y.: International Arts and Sciences.

Vachani, L. (1989) Narrative, Pleasure and Ideology in the Hindi Film: An Analysis of the Outsider Formula. M. A. Thesis, Annenberg School of Communication, University of Pennsylvania.

Wallerstein, I. (1974) *The Modern World System.* (2 Vols.) New York and London: Academic Press.

Warner, M. (1990) *The Letters of the Republic: Publication and the Public Sphere in Eighteenth-Century America.* Cambridge, Mass.: Harvard University Press.

Williams, R. (1976) *Keywords.* New York: Oxford University Press.

Wolf, E. (1982) *Europe and the People without History.* Berkeley: University of California Press.

Yoshimoto, M. (1989) The Postmodern and Mass Images in Japan, *Public Culture* 1 (2): 8–25.

Zarilli, P. (1995) Repositioning the Body: An Indian Martial Art and its Pan-Asian Publics. In C. A. Breckenridge (Ed.) *Consuming Modernity: Public Culture in a South Asian World.* Minneapolis: University of Minnesota Press.

Chapter Three

Who We Are, Who We Are Not
Battle of the Global Paradigms

Michele Hilmes

Across the globe the medium of broadcasting, in its early decades and indeed throughout its history, is associated strongly with the project of national identity formation. There are many reasons for this. Primarily, and not of course coincidentally, broadcasting's development corresponded with the crucial period of nationalism that followed the transgressions and disruptions of World War I, not only in Europe and the United States but in former colonial nations as they began to define and fight for an identity separate from their occupying powers. Just as radio had played a large part in the war effort itself, and with the bias toward military control of the medium that had to be supported or resisted once the conflict ended, so radio would be deployed in the ongoing process of redefining and reinforcing national boundaries.

Yet it is, paradoxically, the ability of radio to *transcend* the normal geographical borders of nations that mandated its nationalized structures of control. As Valeria Camporesi points out, "the international vocation of radio could only be restrained by means of political and economic agreements enforced by national governments."[1] Thus, here is one fundamental irony of radio, and later television: that a medium uniquely suited for crossing borders, transcending national boundaries, and permeating all strata of international culture should be so essentially linked to the tightest form of institutional control known to twentieth-century media.

This sort of irony has its flip side: finally, here was a medium that the state *could* control. Unlike books, newspapers, magazines, and films, which despite occasional attempts at licensing or censorship remained stubbornly resistant to the constraining ministrations of the state, broadcasting seemed to present the perfect excuse for the state to step in. Its necessary use of the electromagnetic spectrum, requiring allocation decisions; its expensive and tightly patented technology; the requirement that users go out and buy newly available specialized equipment, which could then be monitored and controlled, even licensed—all of these factors gave, in most countries, an opening for a level of state intervention only made acceptable by the mystification and ignorance about radio's eventual uses still prevalent in the early 1920s. During a time in which *internal* disruptions of unified national identity (renegotiations of social power around gender, class, and race/ethnicity) became as important as *exter-*

nal threats, it did not take long for most countries to see the advantage in a nationally owned, nationally run, or at least nationally chartered system of radio broadcasting that could unite the country in a simultaneous, controlled address simply impossible before, as well as protect its culture from airborne invasions from without. Far more effectively than any one newspaper, magazine, publishing house, or film studio, broadcasting became "the nation's voice" in countries across the globe. The project of defining "who we are, who we are not"—always a task that involves internal as well as external negotiations of identity—thus became a worldwide endeavor through the timely introduction of broadcasting technology in the second decade of the twentieth century.[2]

In this global nationalizing project, one dominant duality comes into play: a "battle of the paradigms" between two of the earliest and most prominent systems to establish themselves. One nation after another observed the privately owned, competitive commercial system of the United States and the state-chartered, public service monopoly of Great Britain and used their examples to craft local solutions. As this dualistic modeling extended across the globe in the 1920s and 1930s, more often than not it was the United States that came out the loser both rhetorically and practically. The vast majority of European countries installed some form of the noncommercial public service system modeled after the BBC, as did colonial nations, where such systems were often imposed by occupying powers. Often such systems were seen as the only defense against not only direct American influence but also the uncontrolled outbreak of popular culture—and oppositional national ideologies and identities—that a commercial system might provoke or encourage, as local elites moved to keep this new medium firmly under centralized control.

In Finland, for example—along with the other Scandinavian countries—an initial period of experimentation with privately owned stations ceded quickly to a conscious emulation of the British model, since "public service broadcasting would have an important role in fostering patriotism in the newly independent state."[3] In Germany private investment was allowed alongside the Lander, or regional, stations, until Hitler's government took control in 1932. After the war, a national state-run network worked in tandem with regionally owned stations, supported by a combination of advertising revenues and license fees. Italy's system was similar. France allowed a certain number of commercial radio stations to operate alongside the dominant state channel before World War II, but shut all but the state system down during the war and maintained the state system alone until the 1970s. Colonial nations such as India, South Africa, Rhodesia, and Egypt relied on the state-owned networks installed by their colonial governments, sometimes in addition to commercial stations, until well after movements for independence.[4] Throughout, as a Finnish broadcasting historian puts it, "the BBC held a pre-eminent position among the major national broadcasting companies."[5]

The introduction of television worked to challenge the dominance of state monopolies in many cases, including Great Britain itself. (Conversely, in the United States, the new possibilities represented by television reawoke the moribund reform movement, leading to increased pressure for educational and public service broadcasting.) By this time, both the United States and Britain had become active in recruiting other nations to their respective visions of media organization. In Israel, whose formative years relied on government-controlled radio vital to its precarious self-definition and defense, television threatened to introduce unwelcome instability. The Israeli government fought off American attempts to institute a commercial television system by relying on British help in establishing a state-controlled organization.[6] In South America, within the U.S. sphere of influence, U.S. networks actively invested in private broadcasting companies from the 1940s on, weakening state systems.[7] During the Cold War era, U.S. government agencies explicitly recruited the broadcasting industry into its expansionist plans, linking commercial television with democratic ideology and actively promoting its spread and growth (and not coincidentally opening up new American markets in the process). Susan Smulyan recounts the interesting example of occupied Japan, where after the war the United States confronted the contradictions in its easy equation of marketplace economics with democratic systems. While promoting a commercial, audience-research–based, pluralistic approach to broadcasting content, the occupying administration could not afford to permit truly alternative viewpoints to filter in to its hegemonic retelling of the "truth" of Japan's role in the war. A state-controlled, public service system worked better to accomplish American ideological goals.[8]

No other countries made more frequent and productive use of this contrast than the United States and Great Britain themselves. Historians of British broadcasting, from Briggs to Scannell and Cardiff, agree that comparison with the United States runs as a continuous constitutive undercurrent throughout the period in which the British Broadcasting Company and later the British Broadcasting Corporation were founded.[9] In the report of the Crawford Committee, which in 1926 formed the British Broadcasting Corporation divested of its traces of private ownership and made a state-authorized and funded entity, the negative example of the United States became a key support for the BBC's emerging public monopoly structure: "It is agreed that the United States system of free and uncontrolled transmission and reception is unsuited to this country, and that Broadcasting must accordingly remain a monopoly—in other words that the whole organisation must be controlled by a single authority."[10] Correspondingly, the figure of Great Britain appears frequently in the background of American radio history, emerging into prominence at certain crucial moments. In the heat of the debates of the early 1930s leading up to the ratification of the Communications Act of 1934, for example, the Federal Radio Commission itself echoed the familiar duality:

> This system is one which is based entirely upon the use of radio broadcasting stations for advertising purposes. It is a highly competitive system and is carried on by private enterprise. There is but one other system—the European system. That system is governmental. Under that system, broadcasting is conducted by the government or by some company chartered by the government. There is no practical medium between the two systems. It is either the American system or the European system.[11]

As we will see, it was no secret that it was the British system that provided the basic model for "the European system." I argue that this pattern of mutual projection and comparison was not simply strategic but determinant: if either system had not existed, the other would have had to invent it. From the earliest moments—1920 onward—the United States and the United Kingdom regarded each other across the Atlantic with an intense and selective scrutiny that provided ammunition for supporters of both systems. On both sides, publications and debates comparing the British system with that of the United States appeared frequently during radio's first decade, and would at various times subsequently shape public policy and engage nationwide deliberations.[12]

This history of mutual interdependence deserves a more lengthy study than I can give it here. The ways Great Britain and the United States defined, defended, and discursively constructed their competing systems had repercussions across the globe. It is worth taking a look at some of the foundational moments of this opposition in order to pick apart some of the basic assumptions, shortcomings, idiosyncrasies, and methods of deployment that underlie both commercial and public service broadcasting, as defined by their two dominant supporters during highly formative years. Comparative histories of this sort, though rarely undertaken, can provide a useful tool for deconstructing features of national institutions regarded as simply "natural" and to question "commonsense" knowledge about their structure and effects.[13] For the purposes of this chapter I will lightly skim over three significant episodes that demonstrate the practical effects of this mutual project of discursive construction of "who we are, who we are not" at a national level. I will focus primarily on the threat of "Americanization" to the public service system, as this is the dominant trend worldwide. The first episode involves the use of the concept of "American chaos" by British policy makers in the early 1920s, leading to the formation of the British Broadcasting Corporation in 1926 and the development of its influential public service model. I argue that projection of fear of the popular onto the specter of "American chaos" allowed the BBC in its early years to avoid some hard questions about the limited "public" nature of the British system. This created key elisions that would become fundamental to the elitist Reithian philosophy of "uplift" and service, not only in Great Britain but in many other nations as well. The second traces the flap created in 1933 when the U.S. National Association of Broadcasters (NAB), attempting to fight off broadcast reform at home, did so by publishing a highly one-sided rebuttal of the British system in the most prejudicial rhetoric available. Here we can see the philosophy of "marketplace democracy" emerging, in a historically specific form that would be used, over and over, to justify the weakness of public broadcasting in the United States and the aggressive recruitment of other nations into the commercial system. Finally, having briefly focused on U.S. networks' attempts in the 1930s to adopt BBC-derived programming strategies in order to defuse calls for reform, I will look at the ways the BBC at first distanced itself from, then adapted to, the "American" influence toward popular programming, consistent scheduling, and audience measurement. I will close with some reflections on the nature of the "public sphere" created under public service and commercial systems, with gender as the focus.

American Chaos

In Britain as in the United States, some of radio's earliest and most eager proponents were radio equipment manufacturers, who pressed in both countries for permission to set up stations and begin to market radio sets. In 1922 the British Post Office, under whose jurisdiction radio fell, entered into complex negotiations with the dominant radio interests in the United Kingdom. Records of these meetings reveal a slowly emerging compromise between the dominant company, Marconi, and its competitors to devise a means by which Marconi patents could be used but an effective Marconi monopoly could be avoided. It was not a nascent notion of public service to the nation, but rather Marconi head Godfrey Isaac's insistence that his company's cooperation depended on a noncommercial system (backed by the powerful Newspaper Proprietors' Association, which feared competition for advertising dollars) that finally broke the deadlock. The British Broadcasting Company was established in October 1922 as a consortium of manufacturers, pooling their patents to further radio development in the United Kingdom, jointly setting up noncommercial stations that would not compete with each other.

In the winter of 1921 the Post Office had dispatched its assistant secretary, F. J. Brown, to the United States to observe how the Americans were handling the radio situation. He embarked on a tour of the country over several months, and attended the first of the U.S. Radio Conferences convened by Herbert Hoover in January 1922. Brown, characterized by Briggs as "one of the leading figures in the history of broadcasting," exerted considerable influence on the eventual establishment of the BBC.[14] In the spring of 1923 his testimony before the Sykes Committee—convened to reauthorize the British Broadcasting Company—proved crucial in its deliberations. It is in Brown's reports and testimony that the strategic use of the concept of "American chaos" first appears. The goal of avoiding American chaos becomes the primary rationale for discouraging private ownership of radio in Britain and a way of avoiding discussion of the self-interested agendas of the radio companies and newspaper publishers in the process. Interestingly, in the light of what came later, Brown stresses that "The Post Office held that it was essential that there should be no monopoly" in British broadcasting, referring at this point to the danger of Marconi's dominant position.[15] He is questioned on this point by a member of Parliament, Mr. Trevelyan, who states, "There is no monopoly there [in America], and there are a large number of Broadcasting companies. That is how I come to question . . . why the Post Office here has set itself, apparently, to adopt an entirely different system from the American, whether it was because of the failure, in their view, of the American?" Brown answers, "Yes, it was. The American system was leading to chaos, it was doing so already while I was there, and because of that chaos Mr. Hoover called a Committee of Officials and Manufacturers . . . with the view of arriving at some agreed scheme for preventing that chaos."[16] Here he has managed to use the term "chaos" linked to the United States three times in a single sentence; obviously this is a crucial point. In the absence of any overtly expressed public service function for radio, the concept of "American chaos" stands in for a host of considerations and agendas that the BPO at this point felt it more expedient to conceal.[17]

This construction becomes a central one; it is echoed in the statement by Lord Gainford later in the proceedings: "Within six months we have achieved more than America did in two years, and have avoided the chaos which exists in the USA."[18] Or, as a BBC official statement summarized at the beginning of the Sykes Committee deliberations: "The initiative which led to the formation of the Company came from the Post Office. They knew that, if the American chaos were to be avoided, one broadcasting authority was essential."[19] And this broadcasting authority must be the state, not a commercial company or consortium.

What was this "chaos"? Though it is true that little regulation affected the growing numbers of experimental broadcasting stations springing up across the United States during this period, by 1922 large corporations such as Westinghouse and AT&T had begun to establish stations in the larger cities. With a well-tuned set it was possible to receive a variety of distinct signals in most locations, and various groups such as the American Radio Relay League had organized to produce codes, standards, and even "silent nights" so that distant signals could be received. In January 1922 the Interstate Commerce Commission had installed a system of licensing that divided broadcasters into A and B stations, with the B license and its more favorable and less crowded wavelength reserved for more established stations that followed certain restrictions.[20] This brought a considerable diminishment of voices to the spectrum. Even F. J. Brown was forced to concede that the chaos was not really observable in most places on a level of daily listening:

> Q: (Mr. Eccles) Did you listen in at all?
> A: (Brown) Yes, what I head was fairly good and was not interrupted.
> Q: (Mr. Eccles) What I heard was fairly good; I was wondering whether the chaos might not have been exaggerated?
> A: (Brown) It may have been exaggerated.[21]

But it is not on the literal technical level that the notion of "chaos" functioned in the British debates. Rather, it was the sheer *uncontrolled* potential of radio in and of itself, along with the dominance in the United States of commercial sales pitches and their attendant appeal to the unmitigated popular, that created a perception of unruliness and disorder. The BPO shifts its stance from wishing to *avoid* a monopoly to establishing a state-owned monopoly within a span of three short years, motivated by a need for control over this developing medium that the notion of "American chaos" came to symbolize, however inaccurately. Later, in a famous phrase, John Reith would attribute all the social good his public service system had managed to accomplish to precisely "the brute force of monopoly."

The crucial missing term here, of course, is "commercial." A state monopoly became the only way of avoiding a commercial broadcasting system, which, whether dominated by culturally suspect Marconi interests or permitting uncontrolled competition, threatened all parties involved. Not only would it compete for advertising revenues with the powerful newspaper industry, it would open the doors to the kind of populist access so readily observable in the United States. Advertising meant catering to popular—meaning middle- to lower-class, hence unauthorized—tastes and interests, as the press and film industry already did. Further, there is a sense that emerges from the debates at this time that Marconi, while a British company, was not truly one of "us" and that leaving such a vital national project as broadcasting in these slightly disreputable hands simply would not do.[22] That racial and class concerns underlay the decision making, in Britain as in most countries, can be seen in a speech given in 1926 by Prime Minister Baldwin in celebration of the BBC's first years of service.

> In the same way, it is too early yet to say what the influence on civilisation of the moving picture may be, but I confess that there is one aspect of it upon which I look with the gravest apprehension, and that is the effect of the commoner type of film, as representing the white races, when represented to the coloured races of this world. (Hear, hear). I need say no more on that subject except this, that in my view the whole progress of civilisation in this world is bound up with the capacity that the white races have, and will have, to help the rest of the world to advance, and if their power to do that be impeded by false ideas of what the white races stand for, it may well be that their efforts will not only fail, but that the conception of the white races generated in the hearts of the coloured races throughout the world may be an initial step in the downfall of those white races themselves. *I have ventured to say these things to you because we all felt here how different have been these past four wonderful years in the development of this great gift of science to mankind; how different from what they might have been had those in charge of them been actuated merely by mercenary and "get rich quick" motives.* (Cheers).[23] (emphasis added)

Here Baldwin explicitly links commercial culture and its "get rich quick" ethos to the destabilization of existing social hierarchies, and congratulates the BBC for adopting a system designed to keep threatening influences under control. Implicit is the argument that a commercial broadcasting system would have thrown open the airwaves to the disruption of the dominant cultural order.

The close connection of this discourse with the threat posed by an "Americanized" system is clearly articulated in another speech by Reith:

> In the beginning we were to some extent guided by the example of America. I do not mean that America indicated the path, but rather that America showed us what pitfalls to avoid; we learnt from her experience. Broadcasting in America was well under way, with a two years' start, when the service was first inaugurated in Great Britain, and it was soon common knowledge that the lack of control in America was resulting in a chaotic confusion. . . . Britain, as I say, benefitted by America's example, and a centrally controlled system of broadcasting stations was the result.[24]

In the context of the overall debate it is very clear that "American chaos" has come to stand in for "commercial competition" and its attendant "social unruliness" as a rationale for a unified system under centralized state-appointed control. Broadcasting in Britain would not be thrown open to individual or commercial entrepreneurship, as in the United States, but would be carefully controlled to limit the intrusion of "chaotic" voices from social groups and classes whose interests might clash with the maintenance of the existing social order and stability. This first and crucial displacement onto American practices of an unresolved tension at home—a "public" service open only to a very small and highly elite segment of the population—would be written into the very charter of the British Broadcasting Corporation by the Crawford Committee in 1926. This would help to justify the transformation of the commercially based Company into the government-chartered Corporation, and the rest, as they say, is history.

However, during the late 1920s and early 1930s the meaning of "American chaos" shifted in a significant way: emerging from behind its implied screen of technical or administrative disorder, it could now nominate more overtly the cultural disarray posed by American radio. It is possible that it was discourse on the American side of the equation, employed to help commercial broadcasters win their war over educational radio claims in the early 1930s, that pushed British commentators into a more inclusive condemnation of American practices. Certainly the National Association of Broadcasters was the first to throw down the gauntlet.

British Quality

As Robert McChesney has convincingly described, the early 1930s, before the passage of the Communications Act of 1934, represent one of the few times in U.S. history that the commercial basis of U.S. broadcasting was called into serious and effective question.[25] The efforts of educational broadcasters to secure public funding and reserve frequencies for a type of public service broadcasting that was evolving in Great Britain (and other countries) brought the topic of the structure and financing of the American system into question in a way never previously undertaken. U.S. broadcasters recognized this threat, and McChesney details the many tactics employed to defeat the scattered and underfunded league of education stations.

One tactic was to emphasize the public service that the major networks claimed to perform, modeled after the BBC. A sudden outpouring of symphonies, public affairs, and serious dramatic programs wafted over the American airwaves from 1933 to 1938, as broadcasters first promised to pull up their socks and then had to follow through, however briefly. Most of these efforts drew on a particular definition of "quality" programming taken from observation of BBC practices, and were (at first, at least) offered on a sustaining (nonsponsored) basis. NBC hired Arturo Toscanini to direct the NBC Symphony Orchestra, patterned after the BBC orchestra. Adaptations of literary and stage works, an area that the BBC had developed strongly, were emphasized in programs like the *Mercury Theatre of the Air*, the *Columbia Workshop*, and *Everyman's Theater*. Certain well-respected "radio auteurs" were given a freer hand than ordinarily, such as Orson Welles, Arch Oboler, and Norman Corwin, adopting the more authorial approach to drama that the BBC emphasized. Continuity acceptance departments were established at both major networks to provide some form of centralized control over the unruliness of programs created by sponsors and their agencies. The separation of women's programs into the separate but unequal daytime schedule helped to distance the "quality" pretensions of nighttime programming from the more overtly commercial, feminized daytime.

A particular aspect of network public image polishing involved renewing and reinvigorating links with the BBC itself. In 1933 NBC appointed an official representative to the BBC, Fred Bate; in the same year CBS employed Cesar Saerchinger, an American journalist already based in London, in a similar capacity. The BBC responded in 1935 by hiring Felix Greene as their man in New York—where he would play a much more vital role in advising the Canadian system than he did in the United States. These young men were meant to serve primarily as goodwill ambassadors, though they also worked at arranging various kinds of trans-Atlantic broadcasts and in facilitating guest performances on each other's outlets.[26]

Meantime, the head of the NBC, Merlyn Aylesworth, and John Reith of the BBC had developed a cordial and even personal friendship based on frequent, polite correspondence and a cross-Atlantic visit or two. Their letters, housed in the Wisconsin NBC papers, show an increasingly if somewhat affectedly intimate tone, especially on Aylesworth's part. They address each other as "My dear Merlyn" and "Dear Sir John" and Aylesworth signs off, "Affectionately yours." Reith visits Aylesworth at his home in the autumn of 1933, following up a 1931 visit made by Aylesworth to Britain. Aylesworth informs Reith in a letter written in December 1933 that "we all consider you as a part of our family" (which he copied to General Sarnoff).[27] Just a few weeks later the family was looking a bit dysfunctional.

The crisis in relations between the BBC and NBC arose as a part of the larger battle over commercial versus public service broadcasting. As one of their more effective volleys in the public opinion war, educational radio supporters persuaded the High School Debating League of the United States to take on as the subject of 1933's national debate competition the topic "Resolved: That the United States Should Adopt the Essential Features of the British System of Radio Control and Operation." This resulted in a flood of articles and publications on both sides of the issue, culminating in a 191-page pamphlet assembled by the National Association of Broadcasters entitled *Broadcasting in the United States*. It consisted of a thirty-two-page, highly complimentary description of "American Radio," with charts and graphs enumerating the many hours of high-quality sustaining and commercial broadcasting purportedly put out by American networks and stations, followed by a twenty-six-page denunciation of the British system called "The American vs. the British System of Radio Control." Similar to the British use of "American chaos," these two NAB-authored pieces made heavy use of the tactic of praising the U.S. system by denigrating the British:

> American radio is the most competitive in the whole world. Hundreds of local stations are forever looking for local entertainment talent. The two competing "chains" are forever trying to develop new competitive entertainment stars. Additionally the advertisers, in multitudes, are forever competitively flinging new entertainment stars into the radio firmament. You have to take the volcanic dust of their advertising convulsions along with the stars; but you get the stars. You get them because each of these competitors has to stay awake. . . . The British Broadcasting Corporation does not have to stay awake. It doesn't even begin broadcasting—for instance—till after ten o'clock in the morning, on week days; and on Sundays, till recently, it didn't begin broadcasting till three o'clock in the afternoon. And then, on Sundays, it always laid off and did no

broadcasting from six-thirty to eight in the evening. It can afford to rest. It knows that no rival will broadcast while it's sleeping. And it takes a sort of social revolution to wake it up.[28]

Here American initiative and "wide awakeness," all based on commercial competition, are contrasted with British complacency and sleepiness, with an underlying attribution of elitism that only a "social revolution" could shake free. This native American vitality was then linked to innate characteristics of the United States as a nation in contrast to England:

> It must be remembered that not only is Great Britain a small country, but that on the whole, its population possesses similar traits of mind and character—similar viewpoints and interests. There is not the marked diversity in racial, cultural, social and economic backgrounds which one finds in the United States. Each part of the country has priceless cultural heritages of its own, which color its viewpoint, and affect many of the radio programs it desires. Likewise the many races which have gone to make up our nation have a right to programs ministering to their racial consciousness, for each of them have brought something of great value to the evolution of the American character.[29]

Or, to put it another way,

> The nervously-active American is never in a mood to take educational punishment. You *must* interest him—or he quickly tunes you out. This characteristic is in only slightly lesser degree fundamental to any discussion of listener reaction in any country. It is the rule and the law and the testament upon which every successful broadcast structure is based. It is the risk, for instance, that Sir John Reith runs in Britain when he avowedly gives his public what he believes it is good for it to have.[30]

Here a liberal-pluralist concept of America's racial background is contrasted to Britain's homogeneity—this in a country that effectively barred African Americans from the airwaves and had made *Amos 'n' Andy* its most popular show. Education is termed "punishment" and commercial competition becomes practically a biblical mandate. After this diatribe, the pamphlet offers a compilation of various articles and talks about the competing paradigms by U.S. broadcasting spokesmen. This section included a collection of mostly critical responses to the BBC from the British press compiled by Major Joseph Travis of London, in the preface to which it is asserted, "the great mass of radio listeners, realizing that the BBC is a monopoly and can do as it pleases (which impression is given in most of the addresses and articles by BBC officials), have decided that it is a waste of time and money to send their criticisms to either the BBC or the press."[31] It concluded its most vehemently argued section, the reprint of a speech by news commentator William Hard, with the rhetorical flourish:

> I hold up to you the superior scholarship, the superior good taste, the superior urbanity of the British broadcasting system. It is all that can be said for it in comparison with ours. I hold it up to you and I ask you: Will you for that bribe surrender what America has given to you in your inherent passion for all feasible liberty of utterance? Will you for that bribe surrender all your chances of free expression on the whole American air to the autocratic determination of one selected citizen? If so, vote British. If not, vote American.[32]

Here John Reith himself has become the devil incarnate, with a suspect and auto-cratic "superiority" his only defense. The American Revolution is being fought again, this time in the air. The pamphlet appeared in early January 1934 and hit London like a bomb. On January 10 an urgent telegram from NBC's Fred Bate in London to Merlyn Aylesworth breathlessly wailed,

> DEEPEST RESENTMENT HERE NAB PUBLICATION EVEN REACHING CONSID-ERATION SEVERING RELATIONS STOP FEEL ADVISABLE YOU CBS DEFINE AT-TITUDE TOWARD STATEMENT SURE TO BE CHALLENGED STOP FAILURE ADVISE ME PUBLICATION IN TIME OR PROVIDE COPY RESULTED MOST EM-BARASSING SITUATION TODAY STOP. . . . SUGGEST LINE OF ACTION STOP SITUATION TENSE.[33]

A frantic, and rather humorous in retrospect, exchange of telegrams and letters ensues. Aylesworth attempts to reassure Bate and Reith, by downplaying the NAB as a fractious bunch of small-time station owners, as opposed to the big network guardians of more enlightened culture. Reith expresses his dismay, pointing out that many members of the reform opposition had lobbied for a BBC endorsement of their views, which the BBC had honorably rebuffed, only to be insulted in this way. Aylesworth again reassures Reith, at great length and with considerable disingenu-ousness, considering the strength of the reform movement in the United States: "We consider the whole matter of little importance in this country and just a lot of fun between school children who have a good time debating the subjects."[34]

NBC was obviously trying to have it both ways during this period, at once rigorously defending commercial broadcasting against any thought of a public service system in the United States, while simultaneously attempting to get credit for sup-porting and exemplifying the "high culture" goals of just such a system. It also displaced onto "Britishness" the whole concept of broadcast reform, projecting un-desirable "foreign" attributes onto those who objected to commercial radio's narrow limits. It limited the reformist agenda to a definition of "public service" that was eminently criticizable in American terms: elitist, focusing on high culture and formal education, and above all British. This effectively obscured well-founded and more radical criticisms of the commercial system made by the reform movement at home, such as the lack of political debate on the airwaves, the concentration of station ownership in mainstream commercial hands, corporate America's ability to keep anticorporate views off the air, and censorious network practices.

The "American" Popular

Though this episode blew over without marked incident—including any change to the American system of broadcasting, as the commercial broadcasters received just about every concession they wanted from Congress—it does mark a transition to the next stage of U.S./BBC relations. Beginning in the late 1920s, the threat of American "chaos" would be detached from the regulatory situation and rearticulated to a different, though related, set of concerns. Or, more accurately, the underlying fear of allowing private industry (i.e., Marconi) to dominate radio was allowed to emerge from behind its mask of Americanization into prominence once the danger of Marconi was safely defused. By the late 1920s, commercialism itself, and the cultural chaos it engendered, could be openly denounced as a threat to all that was good in British broadcasting, and once again the American model stood the BBC in good stead. In contrast to the United States, where as early as 1922 the commercial broadcaster was regarded by the powers that be as uniquely capable of serving the public, in Great Britain "national" interests become constructed as specifically opposed to economic interests. Sir William Mitchell-Thompson, Post Master General, justified continued funding of the BBC before Parliament in these terms:

> There were . . . at the head of the British Broadcasting Company men not merely of great organising and technical ability but men with vision, men with high purpose, men with wide outlook, *men who looked at the problem not from the trade angle but from the national angle.* . . . They set broadcasting upon a plane of high ideals, and they based it on a broad conception of their duty to the public and to public morality.[35] (emphasis added)

The man that Sir Mitchell-Thompson most had in mind was doubtless the imposing head of the BBC since 1922, John Reith. Reith's best-known statement of his views comes from his 1924 account of the BBC's early years, *Broadcast over Britain.*

> As we conceive it, our responsibility is to carry into the greatest possible number of homes everything that is best in every department of human knowledge, endeavour, and achievement, and to avoid the things which are, or may be, hurtful. It is occasionally indicated to us that we are apparently setting out to give the public what we think they need—and not what they want, but few know what they want, and very few what they need. . . . In any case it is better to over-estimate the mentality of the public, than to under-estimate it.[36]

Reith's task of uplift was made immensely easier by frequent and unfavorable contrast with U.S. radio programming, usually emphasizing the influence of the system of commercial broadcasting and the cultural chaos it brought in its wake. This is a tradition that begins very early, even by those who fundamentally admired American radio culture. Describing the United States in 1924, A. R. Burrows writes, "It mattered not whether one station overlapped another in wave-length or in hours of transmission, or whether the performance of a classical masterpiece was followed by an appeal on behalf of somebody's soap or pickles. It was all part of a new game."[37] Yet another British visitor to the United States in 1927, Peter Eckersley, observed of NBC's programs,

> Some of the concerts were good, but the majority suffered through commercialism, and to our ears would sound extremely crude. For example, I heard an announcement that a particular hour was to be the "Brightness Hour," brightness means smiles, smiles means white teeth, teeth will be whiter if you use X tooth paste, the manufacturers of which are responsible for the program. In other cases the advertisement is less crude.[38]

A 1929 editorial in *Radio Times*, the BBC-published (and advertising-supported) program magazine, put it even more strongly:

In America, the ether is racked and torn with competing broadcasting stations filling the air with advertising matter. . . . In America, even the wireless reception of a Beethoven Symphony cannot be free from association with someone's chewing gum or pills. In England, the tired worker who has been all day shouted at and advertised to in his newspaper, on the hoardings, in train or omnibus, may settle down to his evening's wireless entertainment with the feeling that at last he is free from the necessity to listen to someone who has something to sell.[39]

"Chaos" becomes articulated to the rampant spread of commercial mass culture, with its "crude" and "vulgar" and above all "American" manifestations. Another *Radio Times* opinion piece concludes,

The thoughtful listener will come away with the double impression that, while American radio has startling vitality in its method of presentation, its material, which largely consist of songs of the jazz order sung by artists of the genus "crooner," is, to British ears at least, confined within a rut of lowering and monotonous sentimentality . . . much that this vitality contributes to radio on that side of the Atlantic would be termed "vulgar" on this.[40]

That there are class and gender biases to these characterizations is not hard to discern. The undisciplined, feminized "mass" audience, indulging its own low, vulgar, sentimental, or crude tastes, became decisively associated with Americanness. And the devils goading them on were commercial culture and its handmaiden, advertising. The BBC increasingly came to see itself as the last best hope in Britain for the preservation of cultural standards somehow free from the taint of trade and populism. Yet with a system that collected license fees from the entire public, in a regressive structure that taxed the working classes as much as the upper classes, it could not entirely dismiss the claims that popular tastes and preferences made on broadcasting service. Better to convince oneself that the less welcome aspects of popular taste were not truly "British," but stemmed from American influence, and as such were permissible to resist.

Programmers began to resist the increasing intrusion of "American" elements into BBC programs, even as irresistible pressure to adopt more popular practices built up in the early to mid-1930s. In 1936 Cecil Graves, director of programming at the BBC, expressed his displeasure toward a new variety program called *Follow the Sun*:

What depressed me much more than all of this was the fact that it was another example of trying to introduce American methods and American phraseology into our broadcasting. . . . I notice it creeping in in various directions. . . . Such expressions as "we bring to you," "We offer you," etc. are examples, but it goes deeper than this and is noticeable in the form used as well as in the actual words. There is no demand for this kind of thing and we certainly don't want to create one. We are perfectly capable of producing first-class shows with first-class presentation without apeing American models.[41]

A responding memo from Peter Eckersley, generally an advocate of the popular expansion of BBC programming, shows the range of opinion on the subject.

I ventilated the matter of Americanisation, as you wished, at Programme Board this morning. . . . Coatman, as was to be expected, was violently opposed to any form of

Americanisation in our programmes. . . . He speaks of America as a country completely composed of barbarians, and it would do him a lot of good to go over there and see that there are plenty of things that they do just as well as we do here and that they have their own cultural ideals.[42]

Despite such attitudes, in the late 1930s certain "American style" programs were introduced to popular acclaim and became a cherished part of the BBC schedule. One of the first was the comedy/variety show *Band Wagon*, followed by the long-running *It's That Man Again*, described by its own producer as "An English version of the Burns and Allen show."[43] The British comedian Mabel Constanduros, having heard the radio serial *One Man's Family* while on a visit to the United States, adapted it into the first British comedy serial, *The English Family Robinson*, in 1937, which led to the long-running *Mrs. Dale's Diary*.[44] Of course, though these popular British programs might have drawn some inspiration from American models, as Valeria Camporesi points out, their deeper roots lay squarely in British traditions of popular culture, adapted to the new radio medium. Had the early management of the BBC not set its face so resolutely against more popular forms of expression, no doubt a British popular radio tradition would have emerged much earlier.

One of the most influential practices adopted by the BBC after the example of the United States, however, may well be the simple concept of regularly scheduled programming, which we now take almost wholly for granted as simply inherent to radio: that a program appear weekly, or daily, on a regular day at a regular time. This practice, called "fixed point" scheduling, was deplored as American and actively opposed by the early BBC since it worked against the British conception of the proper mode of broadcast listening. Program lengths were less standardized than in the United States. What U.S. broadcasters referred to negatively as "dead air" was considered entirely appropriate on BBC schedules; and the listener was expected to seek out desired programs and make a point of being available to listen to them, in contrast to the deplored "tap listener." By the mid-to late 1930s, however, fixed point scheduling had become more prevalent, based largely on what the BBC had begun to learn about the needs and wants of the public it served.

Which Public, Whose Service?

Here I turn to a consideration of the BBC's conception of its audience, the listening public that the BBC had been created to serve, a conception increasingly under fire as the 1930s progressed.[45] As has been noted, the early BBC viewed its audience from the top down, defining the "universal access" so key to public service concepts as the ability to *receive programs*, not to *participate* in decisions about what types of programming might be desirable or appropriate.[46] The BBC, as seen in the Reith quote above, had always held that audience research on any organized scale was not only impractical but actually undesirable. The point of broadcasting was to offer the public something above their own taste, "to lead, not to follow." It might seem contradictory that a broadcasting service created expressly to serve the public, funded by contributions paid directly by the public, would be so unconcerned about the opinions and characteristics of that public as to resist even regular surveys or opinion polls. And as early as 1930 the contradiction between planning broadcasting as a public service and the only very vague and tenuous connection most broadcasters had with the public had begun to seriously concern at least a few British broadcasters. Yet once again, audience survey methods were linked to commercial, American practices, making it easier to reject the entire notion. A move to initiate an audience measurement service, as was done extensively in the United States by this time, was launched not surprisingly by those in charge of the more popular forms of programming: Val Gielgud, head of Drama, in particular, urged that some kind of analysis be done. In a memo to the top BBC directors in 1930, he spoke frankly:

> I cannot help feeling more and more strongly that we are fundamentally ignorant as to how our various programmes are received, and what is their relative popularity. It must be a source of considerable disquiet to many people besides myself to think that it is quite possible that a very great deal of money and time and effort may be expended on broadcasting into a void. . . . I do not suggest that popular opinion is or should be the last word as to whether our programmes are or are not good and should or should not be continued in any particular form.[47]

Charles Siepmann, director of Talks (later to move to the United States, where he would contribute heavily to the FCC's stringent "Blue Book"), replied,

> Gielgud's memorandum interests me very much. I know exactly what he feels, and share his view that some alteration in our present system of measuring the reaction of the public is required. I do not share his view on the democratic issues. However complete and effective any survey we launch might be, I should still be convinced that our policy and programme building should be based first and last upon our own conviction as to what should and should not be broadcast.[48]

This distrust of public opinion and the ways it might be used underlay even the eventual establishment of a Listener's Bureau in 1936. Once again, study of the American system produced mixed reviews: American measurement methods might be emulated for their sophisticated techniques, but should never substitute for the judgment of the professional broadcasters of the BBC. This unwillingness to cater to the interests of the listening public and the insistence on the goal of uplifting and improving it seem to have produced one feature of British broadcasting that stands in great contrast to the American experience: the virtual exclusion of women from the masculinized public sphere created by the early BBC, as well as from significant participation in production and authorship. This would not change until the advent of war suddenly provoked a more urgent need to reach the wider public, if need be on their own terms.

It cannot be said that the BBC refused to recognize any differences in taste and program preference in its audience. Class and region were assumed to be important categories affecting radio listening habits, but gender almost never so, particularly when it came to entertainment. Survey after survey, during the early years of measurement, concentrate on class and region, and occasionally on age, but leave gender out as a category of analysis. In contrast, by the mid 1930s American daytime radio hours were filled with programs designed specifically for the frequently surveyed female audience, largely because of their much-vaunted consumer power. By no coincidence were those the parts of the day seen as most heavily, and deplorably, commercial. Such programming as the daily serials or "soap operas," talk shows, instructional programs, and musical formats, all directed primarily toward a female audience and mindful of women's interests, tastes, and concerns, arguably developed a new kind of feminized public sphere within radio's dominantly masculine address.[49] Female producers, writers, and actors found ample outlet for their talents, and introduced some of the most innovative and lasting forms that shaped American broadcasting. Though confined, until the war years, to the "women's ghetto" of the daytime, radio's feminized "subaltern counterpublic" sphere allowed for considerable expression and debate of controversial (and often "vulgar") topics, such as feminine sexuality, home versus career, family relationships, and forms of women's knowledge.[50] These expressions were certainly trammeled by the limitations of commercial sponsors' narrow interests, but a surprising diversity of voices based on program ownership and control developed in daytime. Entrepreneurs like Mary Margaret McBride developed their own programs, sought out their own advertisers, and determined the content of their shows, buying time on local stations and national networks. This limited the extent to which a dominantly masculine superstructure of decision makers could exercise control over feminine discourse.

In the United Kingdom such a feminine sphere was very slow to develop. In 1935 the BBC decided to turn its attention to a complete revision of program policy, with special emphasis on the daytime, an area that had been largely neglected. At no time in the study is the daytime audience of women even identified, much less deemed worthy of special programming consideration.[51] While some of the "talks" programming during the day addressed issues thought to be of special interest to women, such as cooking and child rearing, the notion of entertainment specially geared to the female audience remained undeveloped. The same applies to histories of British broadcasting: neither Briggs nor any other historian to date has made women's programs or the female audience during these early decades a subject of study. In the summaries of programming done by the BBC yearbook each year from 1929 until the late 1940s, women's programming is not even a recognized category.

Not until audience research had been under way for several years did the revelation that women's interests in programs differed from men's have much effect on BBC practices. The necessity of recruiting women into the war effort led to the first real attempts to create shows of varied content that appealed to women—and to treat them with the same respect as other programs and schedule them at times convenient for women to listen. By then, producers could use audience listening figures to bolster their arguments that the programs were popular and effective. Here it seems clear that the articulation of audience research to American-style commercialism had a distinctly negative impact on the ability of the British public service system to serve all members of its public equally well. The same could be said for class-based tastes and interests: the working and lower middle classes paid the vast bulk of the license fees that supported broadcasting, but their own tastes, concerns, and habits-like those of women-were considered by the BBC's early directors as matters only for discouragement, correction, and uplift-if they were considered at all. In the United States the "chaos" of the commercial system allowed market power (that possessed by white, middle-class women, in particular) to disrupt the social control that powerful broadcasters and regulators could exercise over the scope and content of programming. In the more homogenized and centralized system of Great Britain, social power combined with state power to present a formidable barrier to participation by members of subordinate classes, without the potential for disruption presented by "chaotic" competition and commercialism. This would begin to change rapidly during the war years and after the introduction of commercial television in the mid-1950s. On the other hand, American television would soon enter its most tightly controlled and restrictive decades, under the influence of restrictive regulation and the new system of network, rather than sponsor, production of programming.

Conclusion

We can see in these debates that both countries used the example of the other as a containment device: to limit the options available to a duality of extremes, in which differences were emphasized, similarities usually played down, and specific aspects enlarged to suit the strategic interests of each. In the United States, denigration of the BBC as a "government monopoly" producing "dull and sleepy" programming for a "superior elite" masked the dominance of the U.S. system by large corporations in fact serving some very similar functions. The major networks' two-faced role helped to narrow and defuse the reform movement, pushing it in an elite direction based on highbrow notions of "quality" programming, and away from more meaningful, radical changes. In the United Kingdom, very real threats of American industrial domination were reified into an effective and long-lasting system of projection of American "chaos," catering to the "vulgar (feminized) masses" and producing "sentimental, sensational" programming that "would never work in England." Under this cover could be swept the domestic threats of class, gender, and racial disorder and the imposition of control by cultural and economic elites. This distinction runs throughout the experience of both countries. Yet it should not be forgotten that strong currents ran against the dominant in each case: a sizable minority in each country actively lobbied for adoption of resistant elements of the other's broadcasting structure and habits, with the backing of not inconsiderable economic and institutional power.

In fact, much mutual influence marked the development of both systems, in the United States culminating in the public broadcasting system finally installed in the late 1960s; in Britain culminating in the introduction of commercial television in the 1950s and of local radio in the 1970s. The vital dualism developed in broadcasting's earliest decades shows no signs of abating, and indeed has spread across the globe, where "Americanness" is often employed to denote those elements of the popular that dominant local powers would like to repress (particularly in the area of gender), and defenses of "quality" programs draw on BBC-derived notions of artistic integrity, anticommercialism, and cultural uplift.[52] As new technologies break through the artificial barriers of broadcast nationalism, they often come attached to commercial economics that do not fall under the control of local elites and powers. An infusion of "chaos," often articulated with Western, and specifically American, programs and organizations, prompts the development of competing commercial broadcasting stations and networks, and disrupts state broadcasting monopolies. Some evidence indicates that, in many countries, women in particular have used this disruption of prevalent social norms to break with repressive local hierarchies and envision new roles and new aspirations.[53] On the other hand, such commercialized media often primarily empower the affluent, educated classes that can afford them, leaving the rest of the population with an impoverished alternative. The Western values that they bring may be useful to local populations in some ways, but may import problems as well. The debate over the value of preserving some aspects of a public service system, now on the defensive in many countries, takes on new urgency—not least in the United States.

However, this essay shows that the terms of the traditional public service/commercial opposition should not be taken at face value. If we are to defend public service broadcasting effectively in this era of challenge and breakdown, it might be well to ask Stuart Hall's question "which public, whose service?" We may have to acknowledge that highly elitist and repressive agendas can be concealed in a too-quick condemnation of those admittedly mixed offerings that a commercial system brings. On the other hand, commercial broadcasting often conceals as restrictive a system of representation and information behind a cover of inclusion, in which members of the "public" are defined primarily as consumers—which has both positive and negative aspects—and have even less chance of intervention by public debate.[54] Neither the Lord Reiths nor the Rupert Murdochs of this world deserve the final say on the shape of this increasingly vital medium, and it is my hope that this reconsideration of the uses of national identity might help to clarify the terms of the debate.

NOTES

Abbreviations:

BBC WAC: British Broadcasting Corporation Written Archives Center, Caversham Park, UK

NBC: National Broadcasting Company collection, Wisconsin State Historical Society, Madison, WI, USA

1. Valeria Camporesi, "Mass Culture and the Defense of National Traditions: The BBC and American Broadcasting, 1922–1954" (Ph.D. diss, European University Institute, Florence (1993), 3. I am grateful for the existence of this groundbreaking work, and have used it frequently to point the way to relevant documents and publications.

2. For further discussion of the aspects of internal national identity formation that took place in the United States during the 1920s through the 1940s, see Michele Hilmes, *Radio Voices* (Minneapolis: University of Minnesota Press, 1997).

3. Eino Lyytinen, "The Foundation of Yleisradio, the Finnish Broadcasting Company, and

the Early Years of Radio in Prewar Finland," in Rauno Enden, ed. *Yleisradio, 1926–1996: A History of Broadcasting in Finland* (Helsinki: Yleisradio 1996), 16.

4. The public service/commercial duality did not always work in total opposition. In Russia, China, Japan, and other countries where authoritarian governments held sway, centralized state systems sometimes combined commercialism with state control—operating for-profit stations supported by advertising, with profits going to the government. And Australia and Canada provide examples of productive—and highly contentious—combinations of public service and commercial broadcasting stations operating side by side.

5. Lyytinen, "Foundation of Yleisdradio," 19.

6. Tasha Oren, "A Clenched Fist and an Open Palm: Israeli National Culture, Media Policy, and the Struggle over Television" (Ph.D. diss, University of Wisconsin–Madison, 1999).

7. James Schwoch, *The American Radio Industry and Its Latin American Activities, 1900–1939* (Urbana: University of Illinois Press, 1990).

8. Susan Smulyan, "Now It Can Be Told: American Influence on Japanese Radio during the Occupation," in Michele Hilmes and Jason Loviglio, eds., *Radio Reader: Essays in the Cultural History of American Radio* (London: Routledge, 2001).

9. See Asa Briggs, *The Birth of Broadcasting*, vol. 1 (London: Oxford University Press, 1961), 58–68; Paddy Scannell and David Cardiff, *A Social History of British Broadcasting*, vol I 1922–1939 (London: Basil Blackwell, 1991); also R. H. Coase, *British Broadcasting: A Study in Monopoly* (London: Longman's Green, 1950), 8–23.

10. "Report of the Broadcasting Committee 1925 (Crawford Committee)," Cmd. 2599, R4/31/1, BBC WAC.

11. Federal Radio Commission, "Broadcasters Urged to Study Problems of Radio Advertising," *United States Daily*, 22 December 1931, VI, 2391–92.

12. For recent examples, see Michael Tracey, *The Decline and Fall of Public Service Broadcasting* (New York: Oxford University Press, 1998), Krishan Kumar, "Public Service Broadcasting and the Public Interest," in Colin McCabe and Olivia Stewart, eds., *The BBC and Public Service Broadcasting* (Manchester: Manchester University Press, 1986), 46–61; Wilf Stevenson, "Introduction," in Wilf Stevenson, ed., *All Our Futures: The Changing Role and Purpose of the BBC* (London: BFI Publishing, 1993), 1–22.

13. See Kate Lacey, "Radio and Political Transition: Public Service, Propaganda and Promotional Culture," in Hilmes and Loviglio, *Radio Reader*.

14. Briggs, *Birth of Broadcasting*, 94.

15. "Testimony of Mr. F. J. Brown, C.B., C.B.E., Assistant Secretary, General Post Office," R4/64/1, Sykes Committee—Minutes of 2nd Meeting—2 May 1923, 38–39, BBC WAC.

16. Ibid., 36–37.

17. Though the most common overt articulation of "chaos" was with the technical situation of radio (the necessity to control frequency use to avoid interference), this argument was never made very effectively. Coase demonstrates not only that it was spurious (which would have been readily revealed if anyone had cared to make a more than cursory examination of the U.S. situation), but also that it was frequently elided with *administrative* chaos. He notes that if it had been true, it would have been a preemptive argument in favor of monopoly; the fact that so many others were needed indicates its use as a smokescreen.

18. "Lord Gainford's Statement," 31 July 1923, R4/67/1, Sykes Committee—Precis of Evidence—1923, BBC WAC.

19. "Broadcasting Question: Official Statement by BBC," 14 April 1923, CO38/2, British Broadcasting Company—License and Agreement (1923) File 2—Feb, 1923-July 1926, BBC WAC. The "historical fact" of "American chaos" lives on in many more recent works: see the

BBC's historical Web page for a definition of early U.S. radio as "unregulated" (http://www.bbc.co.uk/thenandnow/history/1920s-1.shtml).

20. Hilmes, *Radio Voices*, 22.

21. "Testimony of Mr. F. J. Brown," 46–47.

22. The fact that the two second-largest companies had significant American investment could not have made the situation any simpler.

23. "Speech Given by Reith 16 December 1926, Dinner in honor of Prime Minister and retiring directors of the Company and Governors-designate of the British Broadcasting Company," p. 8, R44/540/2, Publicity—Speeches and Articles by Managing Director—Reith, Sir John—1925–26, BBC WAC.

24. John Reith, speech, n.t., n.d., 4–5, R44/540/2, Publicity—Speeches and Articles by Managing Director—Reith, Sir John—1925–26, BBC WAC.

25. Robert W. McChesney, *Telecommunications, Mass Media, and Democracy* (New York: Oxford University Press, 1993).

26. See, on the NBC end, box 34, folder 52, BBC—1935, and similar files in subsequent years. By 1937 Greene had made himself unpopular around the halls of NBC and CBS due to his general disdain for U.S., broadcasting culture (box 52, folder 27, BBC—Felix Greene—1937). At the BBC WAC, see the E1/113 group, "Countries—America—American Representative of the BBC." Cesar Saerchinger wrote a book about his experiences, called *Hello America! Radio Adventures in Europe* (Boston: Houghton Mifflin, 1938). In February 1934 NBC assigned two employees to prepare a detailed comparison of the BBC and NBC organizational structures. Box 24, folder 25, Correspondence—BBC—Jan–Aug, 1934, NBC.

27. See box 16, folder 26, Correspondence—BBC (1926–27), NBC.

28. NAB, "William Hard Has a Few Words to Say," in *Broadcasting in the United States* (Washington, DC: NAB Press, 1933), 95.

29. NAB, "American Radio," in *Broadcasting in the United States*, 48.

30. Ibid., 18.

31. Ibid., 114.

32. Ibid., 113.

33. Telegram from Fred Bate to Merlyn Aylesworth, 140 Jan, 1934, box 24, folder 25, NBC.

34. See box 24, folder 25, Correspondence BBC-Jan–Aug 1934, NBC.

35. Testimony before Parliament by Sir William Mitchell-Thompson, V199, Hansard Commons Deb 5s, c1573–1650, 15 November. 1926, BBC WAC.

36. John Reith, *Broadcast over Britain* (London: Hoddard and Stoughton, 1924), 34.

37. Arthur R. Burrows, *The Story of Broadcasting* (London: Cassell, 1924), 55

38. P. P. Eckersley, "American Radio Broadcasting," 1927, p. 1, E15/57, BBC WAC.

39. "Financial Broadcasting: 'Realism' and Reality," *Radio Times*, 21 June 1929, 610–11.

40. "The Big Broadcast,"*Radio Times*, 17 February 1933, 383.

41. Memo from CGG (Cecil Graves) to Peter Eckersley and Erik Maschwitz, "Follow the Sun: Broadcast of First Night," 5 February 1936, R34/918/1, Policy—Vaudeville and Variety—File 1—1926-August 1929, BBC WAC.

42. Memo from Peter Eckersley to Cecil Graves, 7 February 1936, R34/918/1, Policy—Vaudeville and Variety—File 1—1926–August 1929, BBC WAC.

43. Asa Briggs, *The Golden Age of Wireless* (London: Oxford University Press, 1965), 118.

44. These programs met with quite a bit of in-house opposition due to their popular emphasis, particularly the serial drama directed toward women. See R19/779/1, Entertainment—"Mrs. Dale's Diary" 1947-1951, especially memos from Val Gielgud, BBC WAC.

45. The title of this section comes from Stuart Hall, "Which Public, Whose Service?" in Stevenson, *All Our Futures*.

46. See Richard Collins, *From Satellite to Single Market* (New York: Routledge, 1998), esp. 51–74, for a thoroughgoing critique of this definition of Habermassian "access."

47. Memo from Mr. Gielgud to DP through ADP, "Listeners' Reactions to Programmes," 12 May 1930, R44/23/1 Publicity—Audience Research—File 1—1930–33 BBC WAC.

48. Memo from Mr. C. A. Siepmann to Director of Programmes, 26 May 1930, R44/23/1, Publicity—Audience Research—File 1—1930–33, BBC WAC.

49. See Hilmes, *Radio Voices*, chaps. 4 and 5.

50. Here I invoke Habermassian notions of the public sphere, as critiqued by Fraser, Negt and Kluge, Landes, McLaughlin, and others. It is surprising that, in the hundreds of articles that have appeared using public sphere theory to support and defend public service broadcasting systems, so few apply gender as a category of analysis to the BBC, though Kate Lacey makes the case compellingly in *Feminine Frequencies: Gender, German Radio, and the Public Sphere* (Ann Arbor: University of Michigan Press, 1996). See Nancy Fraser, "Rethinking the Public Sphere: A Critique of Actually Existing Democracy," in Craig Calhoun, ed., *Habermas and the Public Sphere* (Cambridge: MIT Press 1992), 108–42; Oskar Negt and Alexander Kluge, *The Public Sphere and Experience* (Minneapolis: University of Minnesota Press, 1993) Joan, Landes, "The Public and the Private Sphere: A Feminist Reconsideration," in J. Mcchan, ed., *Feminists Read Habermas* (New York: Routledge, 1995), 91–116; Lisa McLaughlin, "Feminism, the Public Sphere, Media and Democracy," *Media, Culture and Society* 15, no. 3 (1993): 599–620.

51. See Memo from E. R. Appleton, "Revision of Programmes," 17 December 1935, R34/874/2, BBC WAC.

52. For an extended grappling with this question, see Sakae Ishikawa, ed., *Quality Assessment of Television* (Luton: University of Luton Press, 1996).

53. See, for instance, Michael Curtin, "Feminine Desire in the Age of Satellite TV," *Journal of Communication* 49, no. 2 (spring 1999): 55–70; Bodil Folke Frederiksen, "Popular Culture, Gender Relations and the Democratization of Everyday Life in Kenya," *Journal of Southern African Studies* 26, no. 2 (June 2000): 209–25; and Szu-Ping Lin, "Prime Time Television Drama and Taiwanese Women" (Ph.D. diss. University of Wisconsin–Madison, 2000).

54. Irene Costera Meijer, "Advertising Citizenship: An Essay on the Performative Power of Consumer Culture," *Media, Culture and Society* 20, no. 2 (1998): 235–49.

Chapter Four

Our World, Satellite Televisuality, and the Fantasy of Global Presence

Lisa Parks

Designed by BBC artist German Fecetti, the logo for *Our World*—one of the first live international satellite television programs—incorporates a Da Vinci–inspired figure mapped over the Earth's grids of longitude and latitude with its arms encircling the globe.[1] In an evocative statement that collapsed global travel and world history within Da Vinci's iconic image of Western rational intellect, one of the show's producers declared, "It took three years of his life for Magellan to go around the world. The *Graf Zeppelin* took three weeks. A Russian cosmonaut made it in 90 minutes. . . . We are in a sense, electronic Magellans." The "electronic Magellan" not only became a powerful metaphor for the way that satellite technology promised to ricochet *Our World*'s viewers around the globe from the comfort of the living room, it also revealed how broadcasters in the industrial West imagined new technologies of space communication.

From 1962 to 1967 broadcasters in Western industrialized nations participated in a series of live international television exchanges using the Telstar, Early Bird, and Syncom satellites. These "live-via-satellite" television programs began just after the launch of the first United States commercial satellite, Telstar, in July 1962, and continued throughout the decade. While Telstar forged satellite connections across the Atlantic in a series of exchanges between the United States and Western Europe, Syncom established a satellite link across the Pacific, integrating East Asia within an expanding global satellite system. In 1964 Japan relayed the opening ceremony of the Olympics live to viewers across the Pacific. In 1965 a program called *The Town Meeting of the World* was relayed live via Early Bird across the Atlantic. But the most ambitious satellite spectacular of the decade was the 1967 broadcast of *Our World*.

What distinguished *Our World* from earlier satellite broadcasts was its deliberately global reach: it was intended to link nations across the Pacific and the Atlantic, the communist East and the democratic West, the industrialized North and the under-developed South. In addition, *Our World*'s producers fully exploited what they understood to be the unique properties of live satellite television: its capacity to craft a "global now." Described by critics as a "fabulous planetary swing," a "spectacular display of electronic wizardry," "a vast global happening," and "an old fashioned geography class gone electric," *Our World* was relayed live via satellite on June 25,

1967, to an estimated 500 million viewers in twenty-four countries.[2] The two-hour show, coordinated by the European Broadcasting Union and edited from master control at the BBC in London, required more than two years of planning, ten thousand technicians, four satellites, thousands of miles of land lines, and $5 million to produce. The show predicated itself upon the cultural legitimacy of public broadcasting, the benevolent paternalism of Western liberals, and the space age utopianism of satellite communication. Its visual design established precedents for subsequent global television coverage, combining live views of the television studio with global maps and remote locations, interpellating the viewer not only as "globally present" but as "culturally worldly" and "geographically mobile." Seen by millions of viewers throughout North America and Europe, this early live satellite experiment helped to determine (that is, shape and set the limits of) the cultural form of satellite television.

This chapter critically examines the content of and discourses surrounding *Our World* to explore the particular form of televisuality it generated. John Caldwell uses the term "televisuality" to refer to the aesthetic excesses that characterized U.S. television during the 1980s and 1990s—to "describe an important historical moment in television's presentational manner, one defined by excessive stylization and visual exhibitionism."[3] Such stylistic excesses and visual exhibitionism can be recognized in earlier moments of television's history as well, particularly in moments of its convergence with other technologies. In the 1960s, *Our World* and other satellite spectaculars constantly called attention to their immediacy and liveness, aggressively using mise-en-scène, graphics, narration, and publicity to construct a form of television that was imagined as fundamentally different from earlier forms.

During the 1960s a particular practice of *satellite televisuality* emerged. Generated at the peak of the Cold War, in the midst of the space race, and during the decolonization of the developing world, satellite televisuality first took shape as a series of live international broadcasts emanating from the United States, Western Europe, and Japan. These broadcasts exploited "liveness" as their defining stylistic feature, articulating it with Western discourses of modernization, global unity, and planetary control. These experimental broadcasts provide a way of complicating the technologically determinist assumption that satellites simply extended television's reach, and generated a harmonious global village. Not simply an "aesthetic," satellite televisuality also was the result of particular industrial practices, namely, a decentralized mode of international coproduction that involved live switching, translation, and transmission. *Our World*'s status as a "live" broadcast was somewhat ironic, however, since it required two years of international collaboration, preproduction planning, and technical preparation.

One of the most important structures established in the early satellite broadcasts is an imaginary construct or Western fantasy I shall call "global presence." As Jeff Sconce demonstrates, the concept of electronic presence dates back at least to the nineteenth century and has been variously described over the years as " 'simultaneity,' 'instantaneity,' 'immediacy,' 'now-ness,' 'present-ness,' 'intimacy,' 'the time of the now.' " As Sconce suggests, "this animating, at times occult, sense of 'liveness' is clearly an important component in understanding electronic media's technological, textual, and critical histories."[4] In this chapter I develop the term "global presence" to historicize the meanings of "liveness" or "presence" in the context of satellite and television convergence in the 1960s. During this time the meanings of "liveness" and "presence" were indistinguishable from Western discourses of modernization, which classified societies as traditional or modern, called for urbanization and literacy in the developing world, and envisioned mass media as agents of social and economic change.[5] Emanating from Western nation-states, the live satellite spectaculars were imagined as the cutting edge of the modern, the most current or present form of cultural expression. The end point of modernization, then, was the capacity to be technologically and culturally integrated within a new system of global satellite exchange. Less developed nations could construct their identities as "modern" only if they were in reach of U.S., Western European, or Japanese earth stations or television networks.

Setting the Global Stage

Telstar and Early Bird linked the United States and Europe, and Syncom connected the United States and Japan, but as industry executives foresaw the "swelling global audience" of "space-age TV," they sought to develop programming that was more fully global in reach.[6] Given their technical successes in the early 1960s, broadcasters were ready to take on a bigger challenge. As ABC's James C. Hagerty predicted, live satellite transmission from abroad would be limited almost entirely to "great human events—a coronation, a summit meeting, a sports event." He continued, "As for entertainment, the consensus is that after the novelty of Bob Hope live from London's Palladium wears off, such shows will be no factor. Furthermore, the time zone differences eliminate mass audiences most of the time."[7] Yet as broadcasters schemed to develop cultural events appropriate for live global satellite transmission, members of the United Nations debated the future of satellite communication, calling for uses of space technology that would benefit all the world's people.

Our World was conceived in 1965 by a handful of producers from the BBC's TV Features and Science Departments. The next year Aubrey Singer, the BBC producer responsible for *The Town Meeting of the World*, spearheaded what was initially called the "Round the World" project, gaining the support of the European Broadcasting Union and traveling to different countries to assess the availability of technical facilities and broadcasters' interest. The U.S. commercial networks shied away from the project and left it in the hands of NET, which later became PBS. In September 1966, representatives from eighteen nations met in Geneva to discuss the program's development.[8] At this meeting, participants agreed that the program would have no political content; that no item would be included without full knowledge of all participants; and that the entire program would be live.[9] This meant that *Our World* would differ from the Telstar Relays and *The Town Meeting of the World*, which focused heavily on the activities of political officials and featured postcard flashes of national monuments on both sides of the Atlantic.

Our World emerged amidst international discussions about the regulation of satellite communication. By 1967 a live international television program that not only linked the East and West but also North and South was both feasible and desirable, since many of the participants were also U.N. members who encouraged uses of space technologies that would "benefit all of mankind." In 1963 the U.N. General Assembly unanimously adopted the first of several Outer Space Treaties, which provided that "outer space and celestial bodies are free for exploration and use by all states in conformity with international law and are not subject to national appropriation."[10] To encourage further international cooperation in this area, UNESCO convened a special meeting of experts from around the world in December 1965. Scholars, engineers, political officials, and broadcasters were asked to advise on a long-term program "to promote the use of space communication as a medium for the free flow of information, the spread of education and wider international cultural exchanges."[11]

While the producers of *Our World* did not participate directly in the meeting, the discussions shed light on the various ways world leaders imagined life in the age of the satellite. Taking satellite access almost for granted, Western leaders were primarily concerned with shifts in lifestyle. Stanford professor Wilbur Schramm predicted that "the pace of living in the satellite age may require man to learn how to get along with less sleep, or at least to organize his working and sleeping hours so that they coincide better with time schedules in other parts of the world that most concern him."[12] The English broadcaster Lord Francis Williams suggested that with satellites "the opportunity . . . will exist for ordinary men and women to participate directly as observers in every event of public importance in the world as it actually takes place and with the same immediacy as if they were physically present."[13] And Arthur C. Clarke described satellites as the "nodal points" in the "nervous system of mankind," predicting an age in which they would "enable the consciousness of our grandchildren to flicker like lightning back and forth across the face of this planet. They will be able to go anywhere and meet anyone, at any time, without stirring from their homes."[14] Each of these comments posits a global era that privileges the West, whether by keeping track of the "areas that most concern him," observing "events of public importance in the world," or having the capacity to "go anywhere . . . without stirring from their homes." Their comments reinforce a fantasy of global presence organized not as a sphere of cultural exchange but rather as a return to the Western self.

Leaders from the Soviet Union had a different perspective. University of Moscow professor N. I. Tchistiakov emphasized the "equal right of participation of all parts of the world and all countries . . . to balance the powerful flow of broadcasting and information from developed countries by an equal flow from developing countries."[15] Third World nations such as Pakistan, Nigeria, and India insisted on subsidized access to satellites for underdeveloped nations and proposed that satellites be used in education initiatives throughout the developing world. Nigeria's I. O. A. Lasode proposed that a ground station be built in Nigeria so the African continent could become part of the global satellite system.[16] The Pakistani engineer M. M. Khatib felt that engineers and scientists from Asia, Africa, and Latin America should be included in the stages of satellite experimentation, trial, and observation so they could acquire technical knowledge and a sense of belonging to the world's satellite development group, making the global satellite system more genuinely a "world community project."[17]

In 1967, the same year *Our World* was produced, U.N. members signed the Outer Space Treaty, which provided for free use of outer space in accordance with international law, prohibited national appropriation of outer space, and made states the sole responsible entities for observing and enforcing its provisions.[18] Even before this treaty was signed, however, the United States and the USSR had been appropriating outer space for national security purposes, deploying top-secret satellite espionage systems in orbit. In addition, the United States had been actively working to commercialize the global satellite system since the early 1960s, when it formed two public corporations: COMSAT (the Communications Satellite Corporation) in 1962 and INTELSAT (the International Telecommunications Satellite Consortium) in 1964. Although both were public corporations, mandated to operate in the public interest (COMSAT) and to promote "world peace and understanding" (INTELSAT), they clearly were designed to benefit the U.S. economy first and foremost.[19]

Gestures toward international cooperation in the development, regulation, and use of satellites were always influenced by Cold War politics. On June 21, 1967, four days before *Our World* was scheduled for relay, the Soviet Union announced its withdrawal from the broadcast based on its belief that the United States, England, and West Germany were supporting Israeli aggression in the Middle East, compromising the program's original humanitarian aim.[20] Following the Soviets' lead, the other Eastern bloc participants—Poland, Hungary, East Germany, and Czechoslovakia—withdrew. Producers quickly added Denmark to *Our World*'s roster and ended up with fourteen rather than eighteen contributing countries, and beamed the show's signal to viewers in twenty-four rather than thirty nations. The communist bloc's withdrawal from *Our World* demonstrated the use of liveness for an overt political purpose: to call attention to what the Soviets felt was inappropriate Western intervention in the Six-Day War in the Middle East. As one Soviet leader declared, "The radio and television organizations of USA, England and the Federal Republic of Germany . . . are engaged in a slanderous campaign against the Arab countries and the peaceful policy of . . . socialist states."[21] The conspicuous absence of the communist nations on the day of the broadcast (especially since for months promoters had highlighted their participation) complicated the "globalist" claims of the show. But despite the last-minute cancellation of the USSR and its allies, *Our World* aired as scheduled.

Since many of *Our World*'s organizers either emerged from or supported the BBC tradition of public service broadcasting and were aware of U.N. discussions about the use of satellites in the interests of all humankind, they agreed that the program should have a humanitarian theme. At a meeting in January 1967, representatives of the participating nations agreed to develop the show's theme around the "population explosion" because it was deemed "equally valid and important to people all over the world."[22] During the 1960s population control was declared a potential global crisis by Western sociologists, economists, biologists, anthropologists, and geographers. Books such as *The Population Explosion* (1962), *The Population Dilemma* (1963 and 1969), *The Silent Explosion* (1965), and *The Population Bomb* (1968), to name a few, likened population growth in the developing world to a ticking time bomb that threatened to wreak havoc worldwide.[23] As Paul Ehrlich explained in his widely read book *The Population Bomb*, "each year food production in undeveloped countries falls a bit further behind the burgeoning population growth."[24] If population control measures were not instituted immediately, he argued, people in developing countries faced mass starvation.[25] The book's cover depicted a bomb with a short fuse above a panicky catch line: "While you are reading these words four people have died from starvation. Most of them children."

Our World's producers perceived the live satellite broadcast as a unique way of publicizing and visualizing what they believed was an urgent global crisis. They chose population control as a liberal humanitarian gesture, the theme divided the world once again. Where the Soviet withdrawal highlighted political tensions between the communist East and the democratic West, the population explosion reinforced divisions between the industrialized North and the underdeveloped South. As Ehrlich insisted, the world's countries "can be divided rather neatly into two groups: those with rapid growth rates and those with relatively slow growth rates."[26] And as the *Our World* script bluntly put it, the "growth rate is not equal all over the world; because in a sense our world is two worlds. If you are in reach of this programme, you almost certainly belong to the industrialised world." If developing countries did not have the science and technology for birth control or efficient forms of agriculture, so the logic went, how could they participate in a live satellite television program?

Since *Our World*'s remote cameras did not even venture into the Third World, the population problem was visualized as a series of statistics, graphics, and prerecorded images of "hungry people." Its population control theme said as much about the Western imaginary as it did about Third World living conditions. While producers may have had good intentions, the absence of both the Eastern bloc and developing countries within the show revealed its self-promotion as a "globe-encircling now" to be somewhat of a myth, if not a farce. The "global" scope of *Our World* was particularly problematic given that Nigeria, Pakistan, and India had expressed a desire to participate in such "world community projects" during the UNESCO meeting of 1965.[27] Popular intellectuals such as Arthur C. Clarke and Marshall McLuhan insisted that satellites would flatten social hierarchies and unite people across the planet in a "room-sized world" or a "global village." But such metaphors concealed the ways live satellite broadcasts were being used to reassert Western hegemony during a period of spatial flux, a period of decolonization, outer space exploration, and Cold War geopolitics. McLuhan and Fiore wrote in 1967, "Ours is a brand new world of allatonceness. 'Time' has ceased, 'space' has vanished. We now live in a global village . . . a simultaneous happening."[28] Rather than reiterate Western liberal ideals of world unity, however, I offer the term "global presence" to challenge and destabilize the "global village" metaphor by exposing neocolonial strategies at work in the "liveness" of early satellite television texts such as *Our World*.

Satellite Televisuality

Our World combined the conventions of the film newsreel, the travelogue, and the television variety show. It was divided into five major segments that emphasized problems faced by, and excellence within, the global community.[29] In the opening sequence, the words "Our World" appear in the frame and the show's title is announced and shown in several different languages. The BBC host enters a set furnished in minimalist, otherwordly space decor, and as satellite images of a cloud-covered Earth are projected on a seventy-meter-wide screen behind him he proclaims, "Twenty thousand miles up in the sky, satellites are beaming these pictures into millions upon millions of homes, and viewers in 24 countries all around the world are at this moment watching them together."[30]

Viewers then witness four live childbirths from maternity wards in Sapporo, Japan; Mexico City, Mexico; Edmonton, Canada; and Arhus, Denmark—representing both hopes for an egalitarian future and Western anxieties of an impending "population explosion." Remarkably, producers planned months in advance to represent "Mundo," the Mexican baby, as premature, describing him as "fresh, red and still unseparated from the umbilical." And the baby from Edmonton was a Cree Indian. Since two of the four babies were of color, their births were used to dramatize the population problem. As the babies are "delivered" live via satellite into the studio, the narrator explains, "We can represent the crowded, expanding world by charts and maps and symbols, but none of us can ever see it, at least not as a whole, not as one great family circle as we are at this moment." In short, the world's "great family circle" included only nations that could uplink and downlink with the industrial West. Still, the babies are offered as an expression of universal diversity and oneness, framed in a mosaic, as the narrator proclaims, "[Four] babies. Only [four] out of some eighteen hundred born in the few minutes since this programme began. [Four] whose lives are likely to be worlds apart: born at the moment in history when it is first possible to see round the planet in a moment of time."[31]

The program's narrative was structured around the lives of these babies literally born into a world of live satellite television. The announcer asks, "What sort of world have they come in to? What are people up to around the globe on this June evening in the late 1960s?"[32] These questions motivate the transition to "This Moment's World," a segment designed to immerse viewers in a "panoramic look at people and their activities at a precise moment in various parts of the globe."[33] It begins with a wide shot of the Earth—a "full disk" view impossible before ATS-1. Emphasizing the unique vantage point of the remote sensing satellite, the announcer explains, "This is our world as no one *on* the world can see it. Somewhere on this indistinct circle, over three thousand million people are working, playing or sleeping—or watching this picture."[34] Viewers then move from the orbital perspective of the satellite to a whirlwind tour around the globe, stopping at a traffic jam in Paris, a steel mill in Linz, and a weather station on Mount Fuji. Although it violated their apolitical intentions, producers added a last-minute visit to Glassboro, New Jersey, where President Johnson and Soviet Premier Kosygin were meeting to discuss world peace. Cameras revealed a horde of international television crews and crowds of protestors outside the meeting holding large signs reminding the leaders, "Peace Depends on You Two."[35] This political pit stop reminds us that live satellite television not only captures but also defines events of global significance by virtue of where its remote cameras land.

"The Hungry World" segment exploits the population explosion theme, opening with a prerecorded photomontage of masses of "hungry people" gazing into the camera as the announcer assures viewers, "We are doing something to help them. Around our world scientists are searching urgently for new means of feeding the ever-growing numbers of mouths." Rather than directly addressing the problem of world hunger (for instance, by critiquing the unequal distribution of resources), the segment focuses on "scientific and technological advances" designed to intensify food production. Viewers witness Ron Caldwell's "convoy of high tech [farm] machinery" in Wisconsin, a hyperproductive shrimp farm in Japan, and an algae lab in Canada. Ironically, the segment spotlights efforts to get species like shrimp and algae to overproduce unnaturally so that the proliferating human population can sustain itself.

"The Crowded World" segment reinforces the theme of overpopulation by proclaiming, "The sheer crowding together of people is an even greater threat to the quality of our children's lives. . . . if we go on growing at the same rate . . . the human race has only 450 years left . . . before extinction by proliferation. Our cameras could not reach the hungry world, but the crowded world is all around them." Viewers see helicopter perspectives of New York City skylines and crowds of Muslim worshippers and shoppers in Tunis. The segment also features housing plans designed to alleviate the pressures of overpopulation, such as Montreal's Habitat (a prefab apartment complex with the "most modern rooms in the world") and Scotland's Cumbernauld (a "visionary [suburban] town" where, the announcer explains, "you are free of the monster"—a reference to the slums of Glasgow only fourteen miles away, one of the unspoken side effects of industrialization).

The next segment, "Aspiration to Excellence," celebrates the physical and artistic talents of the industrialized world. This athletic segment sets out to reveal that "even in those parts of the world where men have conquered the basic problems of food and housing, striving does not stop. They are always trying to do something better and better."[36] Viewers watch the fifteen-year-old Canadian swimmer Elaine Tanner try to beat her own 100-meter butterfly world record, Swedes plunge through treacherous whitewater in tipping canoes, and the Italian D'Inzeo brothers jump over intimidating fences on champion horses. Another segment, "Artistic Excellence," profiles artists "whose work," we are told, "is our own pleasure," including Franco Zeffirelli directing a scene of *Romeo and Juliet* in Italy, Miro and Calder at work in the south of France, the opera *Lohengrin* in rehearsal at Bayreuth, pianists Van Cliburn and Bernstein rehearsing at Lincoln Center, Mexico City folk dancers, and the Beatles recording "All You Need Is Love" in a London studio. While the program positions people of the developing world as struggling for basic biological sustenance, Westerners are portrayed with the leisure to engage in abstract intellectual and aesthetic pursuits and to enjoy the body as an expression of individual excellence. In this way, the program masks class differences within industrialized nations by contrasting a culturally and economically *productive* West with an essentially *reproductive* Third World.

The program closes with "The World Beyond," pushing the narrative of Western scientific and technological progress into outer space, where, viewers are told, "man pushes forward the outer limits of his knowledge of our world and those beyond."[37] For the first time, cameras bring viewers to Cape Kennedy's Moonport and to an Australian astronomical observatory. Through a radio telescope in Parkes, Australia, viewers take "a voyage to the limits of the universe—a trip to the edge of time." As the camera pans across their faces, a group of scientists huddle around their instruments and interpret for the world their data about the Earth's interstellar origins. This final segment of *Our World* brings its claims to global presence full circle, for the power to see and experience the Earth as a unified totality brings with it the power to know and contextualize the relations of those dwelling upon it.

Global Presence

Producers promoted *Our World* as a unique televisual experience, as "the first time in history that man [could] ... see his planet as a single place in both time and space."[38] Not only did satellite vantage points and cartographic perspectives represent the "whole Earth" as a unified object via the Earth shot, a range of stylistic strategies were deployed and combined to construct the show's discourse of global presence. Indeed, the show initiates practices that have become the hallmarks of live global coverage. If, as Caldwell suggests, televisuality refers to the stylistic excesses and self-exhibitionism of the medium, then *Our World* is a key moment in this history. It reveals television pushing its own limits—extending itself, technologically, ideologically, culturally, and economically as a global system of seeing and knowing. To reinforce this point I will delineate four practices that emerged in *Our World* and that can be seen as part of an ongoing mode of global television production: spotlighting the apparatus; spatial relations of global presence; scheduled/canned liveness; and time zoning.

Spotlighting the Apparatus

Our World constructs its global presence by *spotlighting the apparatus*—that is, by constantly calling attention to its very mode of production as a spectacle. The live global mode of television production is made possible by a technical infrastructure that includes satellites, ground stations, signal converters, control rooms, studios, remote cameras, microwave links, cables, phone lines, and receivers. To prepare broadcasters for the program, producers distributed flow charts, which diagrammed the technical infrastructure supporting the show, and stylized versions of this preproduction document made their way to the screen. *Our World*'s liveness is organized in part as the visualization of the signal's real-time generation and movement through this infrastructure. The show, in other words, maps and displays the trajectory of the signal as it takes shape and moves from place to place. During the show cameras and control rooms are featured as part of mise-en-scène and narration is used to celebrate the wondrous mode of live global television production. In the show's first few minutes, the narrator invites viewers on a "journey round the globe through a network of landlines and microwave links and ground stations and satellites." He continues, "in 53 control rooms all round the world, production teams are monitoring and selecting the hundreds of pictures and sounds from five continents which will combine to make this historic programme." The experimental nature of the broadcast was exploited to create a sense of suspense. During the transition from Tokyo to Melbourne the narrator highlights the extensive yet delicate infrastructure, warning viewers, "this is the most difficult technical switch!" Here "liveness" is constructed through the spectacle of the working technical apparatus (which is always accompanied by the equally exciting possibility of technical failure). *Our World* would have been impossible without satellite technology, yet despite the show's continual celebration of other parts of the technical apparatus, the satellite itself remained invisible.[39] In this sense, satellite technology becomes a structuring absence: since the orbiting satellite itself could not be represented "live" (at least not in 1967), it is recoded in the broadcast as other space age stuff. It emerges, for instance, in the otherworldliness of the set design and in the unmotivated electronic noise seemingly emanating from "nowhere."

This spotlighting of the apparatus is connected to what Thomas Elsaesser identifies as television's "standby mode," which

> breaks through this staging of national self-identity and social role play towards the universally human(itarian). But it is always also a self-staging of television technology and power, as the whole hardware infrastructure of satellite hookups, equipment-laden camera crews, frontline reporters in Land Rovers, and telephone links via laptops becomes visible and audible, making time palpable and distance opaque.[40]

While Elsaesser alludes specifically to contemporary practices of global television networks such as CNN, we can trace such practices back to the first live satellite programs of the 1960s as well, as broadcasts like *Old World* dramatized television's standby mode.

Spatial Relations of Global Presence

Our World's global presence was also constructed through patterned alternations between studio, geographic, and remote spaces, a pattern I refer to as the *spatial relations of global presence*. In *Our World*, views of studio space are intercut with those of geographic and remote spaces. Whenever there is a transition between distant places (say, between Melbourne and Paris), a world map appears and the signal's trajectory is plotted from one point to another. "This Moment's World," for instance, intercut feeds of a Tunis camel driver listening to *Our World* on his transistor radio, aerial images of boats at Huelva, a roundup in Ghost Lake, Alberta, bikini-clad girls on the beach in Santa Monica, and road construction in Tokyo. The segment could only construct the show's "full circle round the world" by using maps to signify the transition from one part of the planet to another. This visual strategy was designed to concretize the concept of the "global village." As producers stated in a press release, "For two hours this afternoon the world will take a step closer to Marshall McLuhan's concept of a 'global village' as an estimated 500 million persons in 30 nations witness the first globe-girdling telecast in history."[41]

Global presence is thus encoded through a series of alternations among global (or geographic), studio (or technological), and remote (or performative) views. In this mode of television production, the studio space plays a central function as the repository for and regulator of live remote feeds coming in via satellite and landlines from around the world. Rather than being a static space of talking head narration, *Our World*'s studio set is a spectacular space of multiple screens, dynamic lighting, and technical activity/performance. Space age sounds, spotted patterns of floor light, and minimalist design construct the studio as an unearthly or otherworldly space, alluding to the show's own status as "deterritorialized"—as a set of fast-moving signals ricocheting to and from various parts of the planet via satellite.

At the same time, since the studio is filled with views and models of the earth, it works to harness or interiorize the global (and the orbital) within the rubric of the televisual. In the studio, the global is produced as a series of simulations: as a fourteen-foot 3-D model of Earth; as screen projections arranged to convey the infinite variety of the planet; and as television signals being instantly generated and transmitted. One sequence dramatizes this last form of simulation explicitly when a cameraman emerges from stage right, dolleys across the set (as if Fred Astaire), and points his camera at the enormous model of Earth dangling from the ceiling. The cameraman's Earth shot is instantaneously projected on a wide screen behind him and quickly transforms into several smaller frames, which feature the "achievements of man" arriving to the studio from remote locations. This sequence spotlights the technical apparatus while encouraging the viewer to see and understand the correspondence between the camera (boldly marked with the show's logo) and the "live global images" it delivers to the screen. In this sense, the television studio is constructed as a portal or gateway to the world "out there," filtering feeds that pour in and packaging them for the screen. Global presence is based on the positioning of the studio as simultaneously connected to and detached from the world: it assumes an orbital position distant enough to visualize and construct the world as a "whole sphere" while remaining instantly within reach of its most remote parts. This is one of the defining features of satellite televisuality-the visual celebration of simultaneous distance and connection perhaps best epitomized in the term "remote sensing."

Geographic maps are used as transitions between the studio and remote views to orient the viewer spatially and to symbolically "ground" the ethereal (or more appropriately the orbital) signal within an earthly field of representation.[42] After the map is displayed and the trajectory plotted, a "live" remote feed fills the frame and a local narrator introduces a particular activity or performance in his/her native tongue. These remote views are not static panoramas or tableaus; the cameras are extremely mobile, showing multiple perspectives of the same event and reinforcing the show's claim to global presence. On the set of Zeffirelli's film *Romeo and Juliet* in Tuscany, Italy, the camera lurks through the rehearsal as if a spy, following the cast and crew as they move through blocking points in an Umbrian church and zooming in to Zeffirelli's face as he directs. To feature a traffic jam in Paris, producers intercut mobile helicopter perspectives with those of several cameras stationed on intersecting freeways. Producers encouraged moving rather than static perspectives, insisting that the show be concerned with people, "for humanity is of the moment, whilst buildings and natural scenery are relatively timeless, static, and tend to make uninteresting television."[43] Thus the spatial relations of global presence were not only organized around the alternation of studio, geographic, and remote views, but were constructed through the camera's excessive mobility as well. Combined, these stylistic strategies worked to naturalize television's presence as part of earthly space itself.

Just as a "hierarchy of discourse" exists in the production of television news, a hierarchy exists in the spatial relations of global presence.[44] The live remote feed is the most volatile view, the most unpredictable site of televisual representation. As a result, it is never able to emerge raw, untended, unanchored. Put another way, the live remote signal is never seen; it is always screened, emerging through the map or the studio, or being "anchored" by narration. Any potential for the live-via-satellite view to reveal something unplanned or unstaged has historically been carefully regulated and contained by stylistic strategies. In the remote "live via satellite" view, then, we do not see the world simply unfolding, so much as we see the process by which everyday matter and motion have been packaged to support the Western fantasy of global presence.

Scheduled/Canned Liveness

Although *Our World* constantly called attention to itself as "live," specifically as the "miracle of a globe-encircling now," like other forms of television it was carefully scripted, meticulously planned, and ardently rehearsed. What distinguishes it from other television formats, which are often characterized by their repetitious structure, is its status as a unique occasion—a "spectacular." As such it anticipates the age of the global media event-an age in which the world's "liveness" is not only packaged but *scheduled* for maximum visibility. While there were many live shows "scheduled" during the 1950s, *Our World* was one of the first to expose the scrupulous scheduling of liveness. In this case, the *scheduling of liveness* involved buying or negotiating for time on several satellites, preempting national and local television schedules, arranging and timing each of the contributed sequences, programming the broadcast at a time when it could be seen simultaneously by the maximum number of viewers in different parts of the world, synchronizing the image with multilingual soundtracks, and ensuring that the program aired on time. In other words, *Our World*'s liveness was more a negotiation of preexisting temporal structures than a magically unfolding actuality, a "globe-encircling now."

Another way to think about this is to imagine *Our World*'s liveness as "canned," much like the laughter of a sitcom soundtrack. Just as the guttural dimension of the laugh has become harnessed by the televisual apparatus and transformed into the generic signature of the sitcom, the unpredictable volatility of remote occurrences becomes part of television's scheduled annihilation of time/space. While the sitcom promotes itself with a laughter that comes from nowhere, *Our World* celebrates itself as offering a liveness that comes from elsewhere. Still, a lurking tension related to the fantasy of authentic liveness remains in the live satellite broadcast, ultimately related to the possibility of technical failure. The more that *Our World* exposed its infrastructure, the more pronounced became the question of whether or not it would work. Indeed, the moment of transmission (especially of elaborate experimental broadcasts) is always underpinned by this question. But in *Our World* even the "breakdowns" were planned: the script included detailed instructions about what to do in the case of technical failures. It is the moment of technical breakdown that in fact takes us closest to gratifying the fantasy of liveness—a fantasy affirmed when we see the apparatus itself resisting its own timing, failing to conform to its own schedule. This is when the medium's presence is made most manifest. In *Our World* there were a few noticeable delays in the transmission when translation or local narration did not start on cue, or the image went black or fuzzy. Such gaps most indulge the fantasy of television's immediacy, for in these moments we become most aware of how televisual timing orders "our world."

Our World's most pronounced instance of "canned liveness" occurs in the Mexican cultural segment. Producers' concerns about Mexico's ability to deliver its remote feed on time meant the segment had to be prerecorded. It was presented as "live" but was actually the only prerecorded remote feed in the two-hour broadcast. The sequence featured Mexican folk dancers and singers performing in the city and countryside. The flashy performances, which included spectacular skirt-twirling, flying doves, cavorting cowboys, and singing señoritas, were repeatedly intercut with an image of two Mexican technicians watching what was presumably the videotaped version of the segment as it moved through a reel-to-reel player and out into the world. The performances were also juxtaposed with a corresponding image of several female performers huddled around a television monitor on a city park lawn watching themselves as part of *Our World*. The repeated representation of the moments of transmission and reception are important because they construct Mexico, one of only two developing nation participants, as part of the "global present"—even though its contribution had been recorded and edited days in advance so it could be transmitted on cue.

In the Mexican segment, liveness is articulated with Western discourses of modernization and development. The apparatus is displayed not only to celebrate the mode of production, as I have already suggested, but also literally to *generate* an electronic image of the "developing" nation. Producers sent instructions to local directors encouraging them to exploit the "developing element" of events whenever possible.[45] Since Mexico's performances had been prerecorded, the "developing element" was expressed through Mexico's capacity to transmit and receive a global television signal, which became a symptom of its own modernity. Indeed, in this first era of live global television, modern nationhood increasingly hinged on the capacity to achieve global presence—that is, to have the technical facilities and knowledge to uplink and downlink with the flows of a global media economy. Mexico's inclusion in *Our World* was particularly significant since it would host and relay live television coverage of the Olympic Games to the world via satellite a year later in 1968.

Time Zoning

As implied by the notion of "scheduled liveness," global presence is also constructed through temporal relations. I invoke the phrase "time zone" here not only to refer to the boundaries of Greenwich time, but also as a metaphor for the ways multiple temporalities (or time-based imaginaries) intersect in live satellite broadcasts. One of the most frequent and direct ways the show constructs its global presence is by referring to itself as a "globe-encircling now." Arjun Appadurai critiques this notion of a "global now" as reducing scattered and diverse lived world experiences into a Western expression of global modernity. As he suggests, Western intellectuals have "steadily reinforced the sense of some single moment—call it the modern moment— that by its appearance creates a dramatic and unprecedented break between past and present."[46] But as much as *Our World* tries to establish a singular simultaneity or a "global now," it does so only by interweaving various time-based imaginaries, which I refer to as a practice of *time zoning*. *Our World*'s narrative conflated such trajectories as the life spans of newborn babies, the modernization of the developing world, the history of Western civilization, the evolution of the Earth as an astronomical body, and the rate of population growth. In the age of satellite exchange, the "global now" should be reconceived as a zone of multiple temporalities, a zone in which various time-based imaginaries are assimilated, combined, layered, reordered, and rearticulated, a zone that the West struggles to control as *one* "time of the now." As Appadurai notes, "We cannot simplify matters by imagining that the global is to space what modern is to time. For many societies, modernity is an elsewhere, just as the global is a temporal wave that must be encountered in *their* present."[47]

At the most literal level *Our World* constructs itself as a "globe-encircling now" by virtue of its crossing of the boundaries of Greenwich time. One promotion pitched the show as an experience in televisual time travel, boasting, "Time differences around the world, and the ability to switch rapidly through the magic of space-age electronics, will allow cameras to take viewers from 'now,' back to 'yesterday,' and ahead to 'tomorrow.' "[48] Just as the viewer is oriented in global space with the geographic map, he/she is oriented in global time with the Greenwich clock, which was keyed over maps to indicate shifts in time with changes in place. *Our World* featured shifts in local time, however, only to highlight that they could be smoothly replaced with the "now" of live global television. To celebrate the speed of satellite transmission, an animated sequence stages the movement of dawn around the globe with special lighting effects and contrasts it with television signals beamed into different time zones via satellite. The announcer explains,

> The sun lights up only half the globe. But television can beat the sun. Our cameras can be where it is noon and midnight, dawn and sunset, summer and winter, today and tomorrow, and all at the press of a button. The dawn creeps around the equator at a mere thousand miles an hour, but our pictures flash around at a hundred and eighty six thousand miles a second.[49]

Satellite television is imagined as traversing world time zones and seasons, as having the capacity to outrun the earth's orbit around the sun. Symbolically, the sequence implies that the satellite has augured the dawn of a global age and new generation of television technology. Live satellite television becomes tantamount to solar power itself, and the speed of its transmissions is naturalized as a defining feature of global time/space.

We see in this historic moment of television's convergence with the satellite, decades before the widespread development and institutionalization of direct satellite broadcasting, the early imaginings of a satellite footprint. *Our World* is one of the first moments in history when an international boundary was drawn across the globe for the purpose of the simultaneous distribution of a television signal. Although direct satellite broadcasting services today operate with very different technical schemes, their footprints also function as time zones. Technically, the satellite footprint refers to the boundary in which a given satellite's signal can be received, but it involves the reconfiguration of temporal relations within that boundary as well. Viewers are constantly encouraged to negotiate local time and satellite television schedules with other time-based imaginaries such as the modern and the traditional, the fast and the slow, the developing and the underdeveloped. If we imagined *Our World* as a footprint, it would include Western Europe, North America, and East Asia—which is not surprisingly where the first direct satellite broadcasting services emerged in the 1980s and 1990s. Like *Our World*, contemporary direct satellite broadcasting services such as Star TV, Direct TV, and Imparja TV rely on temporal motifs to construct themselves as globally present, even if they are primarily regionally, nationally, or subnationally based.

Conclusion

Although *Our World* was promoted as a "global" program, it divided the world into two hemispheres, taking care to distinguish the "free" industrialized world from the impoverished and "hungry" developing world (not to mention the excised communist bloc). An astute *Denver Post* critic spotlighted the show's exclusionary globalism, noting, "There was a huge dark area stretching all the way from Japan to mid-Europe. As much as anything, the darkness dramatized the deep rift that divides the world."[50] This "dark area" contained Second and Third World nations, many of which lacked access to television and/or satellite technologies and thus remained disconnected from *Our World*'s historic "globe-encircling now"—a period of time that would eventually become known as the age of globalization. The dark area of *Our World*'s global map was also a stark reminder that "development" and "modernity" relied increasingly on access to new television and satellite technologies that enabled nations to participate in a sphere of global exchange. The modern and developed nation was necessarily one that could readily downlink and transmit the live *Our World* image. The fact that project leaders rushed memos to local producers encouraging them to continue promoting the show as "global" after the withdrawal of the Eastern bloc suggests some anxiety about characterizing the show in this manner.[51] Thus, the global was defined not simply through inclusion in a worldwide community, but as the ability to establish "presence" within Western satellite media.

Nevertheless, Western broadcasters took steps to ensure that *Our World* would be perceived as a "global" event. The "Our World Fact Book" emphasized the liberal humanism undergirding the "electronic miracle" of bringing the world together. It declared, "[The show] will . . . inspire men everywhere with the realization that time and distance are no longer effective separators of mankind in this twentieth century, that all men are neighbors in the same world and that mutual understanding and co-operation are in the best interests of all."[52] But while "global village"–inspired rhetoric touted the utopian promise of new satellite technology, it was complicit with Western discourses of development that worked to subjugate non-Western and postcolonial cultures and peoples. McLuhan's global village is predicated on the assumption that Western communication technology is the key to Third World progress. And although *Our World*'s promotional materials explicitly proclaimed that "time and distance are no longer effective separators of mankind," they *im*plicitly suggested that in the global future of satellite communications, the developing world will always have one foot in the past.

Perhaps the most quirky yet strategic element of *Our World* was how it united the primal site of childbirth and space age technology, connecting the satellite's global temporality to the life span of a newborn baby. This convergence brought infancy together with a satellite-regulated globalism, implying that the satellite itself had given birth to a new era. Nowhere is this more explicit than in a montage of extreme close-ups of the babies' eyes projected onto the studio screen. The last set of eyes dissolves to a shot of a huge metronome as the announcer says, "They are coming into our world at the rate of three every second. Every click of the Metronome is a new baby . . . 90 a minute, 84,000 a day. The population is increasing at the rate of over half a million every week."[53] The metronomes multiply on the screen and are replaced first by statistics of population growth, then by images of "hungry people" gazing into the camera.

The segment forcefully brings together the show's most troubling discourses of liberal humanism and anxieties about the "population explosion," echoing the racist and eugenicist undertones of the population control movements of the 1960s and 1970s.[54] Like the Rockefeller Foundation and the Nixon administration's Commission on Population Control and the American Future, *Our World* implies that the Third World population growth directly threatens Western economic and cultural suprem-acy.[55] The segment literally infantilizes the Third World as an object of paternal pity. But the innocent baby, the program asserts, is also a ticking time bomb that threatens to overrun the industrial world. The satellite, with its power to reconfigure time and space, is the key to maintaining the West's hegemony over "our world." Even while *Our World* imagines an ideal global future, it inscribes rigid spatial, temporal, and cultural boundaries between the industrialized and developing worlds. This technology, which in so many ways makes the "global" possible and knowable, has been used to perpetuate neocolonial structures of inequality. Satellite technology not only enabled the West to circulate knowledges about a "dangerous" and "reproducing" Third World in the 1960s, but in the same breath it sets the terms by which the Third World can enter the present.

As the nearly four decades since the launch of Sputnik have shown, the satellite's uses have fundamentally transformed the ways we come to know the contours of our world and the cultures that act on it. Beginning with such endeavors as *Our World*—and continuing in the now-commonplace news flashes of CNN, BBC World, and Star TV—satellite television has divided the world not only into First and Third, industrialized and developing, but also fast and slow. As Caldwell rightly points out, "Satellite broadcasts today seldom emphasize either immediacy or liveness."[56] As satellite use grew more common throughout the 1970s and 1980s, the technology was internalized as part of the televisual apparatus, naturalized as an extension of the medium, and imagined as a technology of signal distribution rather than as one of television production, textuality, and flow. In this chapter, I have explored how the West's global epistemologies—that is, ways of seeing and knowing the world, and particular worldviews—took shape in one of the first live satellite television programs. What I ultimately suggest, however, is that broadcasters' early uses of satellites were far from "global"; they dramatically reasserted the primacy of the West, transforming its cultural and economic systems into a stream of live, rapidly moving, and seemingly omnipresent electronic signals. The same structures of global presence continue today in the coverage of networks such as CNN and BBC, and in the footprints of direct satellite broadcasting services throughout Western Europe, Asia, and the Americas. But now the satellite is even more invisible, and thus, I would argue, in need of even more cultural analysis as it secretly structures our worldviews.

NOTES

1. "Photo Cutlines," *Our World* Press Packet, May 1967, NET Collection, National Public Broadcasting Archives, Hornbake Library, University of Maryland, College Park, MD.

2. See John Beaufort, "Girdling the Globe Electronically," *Christian Science Monitor*, June 26, 1967; Barbara Delatiner, "Global Show Displays Electronic Magic," *New York Newsday*, June 26, 1967; and Mary Ann Lee, " 'Our World' Sees Advent of New Eras in Television," *Memphis Press Scimitar*, June 26, 1967, all from NET Collection, series 6, box 7, folder 9, Wisconsin State Historical Society. The original title of the show was *Round the World in 80 Minutes*, evoking Jules Verne's prophecy, and then it became *Spaceship Earth—a View of Man on the Planet*. Other suggestions included *The World Is Ours* and *Without Horizons*.

3. John Thornton Caldwell, *Televisuality: Style, Crisis, and Authority in American Television* (New Brunswick: Rutgers University Press, 1995), 252.

4. Jeff Sconce, *Haunted Media: Electronic Presence from Telegraphy to Television* (Durham: Duke University Press, 2001), 6.

5. For further discussion of modernization theory in the 1950s and 1960s, see David

Harrison, *The Sociology of Modernization and Development* (London: Unwin Hyman, 1988), 29–31.

6. Donald Coyle, "TV's Global Future Awaits Those Who Take the Opportunity Today," *Variety*, January 4, 1967, 93.

7. "Telstar's TV Future Is Foggy," *Business Week*, July 7, 1962, 33.

8. Countries that participated in the planning of the show included Tunisia, Japan, Austria, France, Italy, Sweden, Spain, England, West Germany, East Germany, the Soviet Union, Czechoslovakia, Hungary, Poland, Canada, Mexico, the United States, and Australia. Lou Potter, "Memo to All Stations," May 12, 1967, NET Files, series 6, box 7, folder 9, NET Collection, Wisconsin State Historical Society.

9. " 'Our World'—Round the World Project Fact Book," May 1, 1967, NET Collection, National Public Broadcasting Archives, Hornbake Library, University of Maryland, College Park, MD.

10. For further discussion of the treaty, see Sara Fletcher Luther, *The United States and the Direct Broadcast Satellite: The Politics of International Broadcasting Space* (New York: Oxford University Press, 1988), 68–69.

11. UNESCO, *Communication in the Space Age: The Use of Satellites by the Mass Media* (Hague: UNESCO, 1968), i. For further discussion and critique of Western discourses on global television during the 1960s, see Michael Curtin, *Redeeming the Wasteland: Television Documentary and Cold War Politics* (New Brunswick: Rutgers University Press, 1995).

12. UNESCO, *Communication in the Space Age*, 20.

13. Ibid., 43.

14. Ibid., 38.

15. Ibid., 145.

16. Ibid., 120–21.

17. Ibid., 117–18.

18. Cited in Luther, *The United States and the Direct Broadcast Satellite*, 82–3.

19. The preamble to the INTELSAT agreement expressed the members' desire to establish a "single global commercial communications satellite system . . . which will contribute to world peace and understanding." Cited in Luther, *The United States and the Direct Broadcast Satellite*, 82.

20. Stan Levy, "Memo to All Stations," June 21, 1967, NET Files, series 6, box 7, folder 9, NET Collection, Wisconsin State Historical Society.

21. "Conflict Splits World Telecast," *Broadcasting*, June 26, 1967. The Six-Day War broke out on June 5, 1967, when Egypt concentrated forces in the Sinai Peninsula and conspired with Jordan, Syria, Algeria, Kuwait, and other Arabic states to threaten Israel's borders.

22. "Round the World Project," Report of Meeting Held in Geneva at the Hotel de la Paix, February 13, 1967, NET Collection, National Public Broadcasting Archives, Hornbake Library, University of Maryland, College Park, MD.

23. Jan Lenica and Alfred Sauvy, *The Population Explosion* (New York: Dell, 1962); Philip Hauser, ed., *The Population Dilemma*, 2d ed. (Englewood Cliffs, NJ: Prentice-Hall, 1969); Philip Appleman, *The Silent Explosion* (Boston: Beacon Press, 1965); and Paul R. Ehrlich, *The Population Bomb* (New York: Ballantine Books, 1968).

24. Ehrlich, *Population Bomb*, 17.

25. Western scientists and intellectuals imagined various ways of resolving the population problem, ranging from family planning to sending people to the moon and other planets in the solar system. Other alternatives included mass use of antifertility agents in the water or staple foods, temporary sterilization of all girls at puberty, compulsory abortions of illegitimate

pregnancies, and cash bonuses for men who get vasectomies. "Interstellar Migration and the Population Problem," *Heredity* 50 (1959) 68–70, and Frank W. Notestein, Dudley Kirk, and Sheldon Segal, "The Problem of Population Control," in Hauser, *The Population Dilemma*, 2d ed., 164.

26. Ehrlich, *Population Bomb*, 22.

27. In this sense, *Our World*'s globalist discourse resonated with earlier cultural forms such as Edward Steichen's 1955 traveling photographic exhibition *The Family of Man*, which, as Steichen explains, was "conceived as a mirror of the universal elements and emotions in the everydayness of life—as a mirror of the essential oneness of mankind throughout the world." Edward Steichen, introduction to *The Family of Man*, 30th anniversary edition (4th printing) (New York: Simon and Schuster, 1993), 3.

28. Marshall McLuhan and Quentin Fiore, *The Medium Is the Massage: An Inventory of Effects* (New York: Bantam Books, 1967), 63.

29. In this way *Our World* also resembled the NBC television series *Wide Wide World* (1954–57), which was a biweekly, ninety-minute "super-spectacular" featuring live transmissions from locations across North and Central America. Like *Our World*, the show addressed viewers as "armchair travelers" and emphasized themes of global mobility and "worldliness." For further discussion, see Lisa Parks, "As the Earth Spins: NBC's *Wide Wide World* and Early Live Global Television," *Screen* 42, no. 4 (winter 2001).

30. *Our World* script, June 1967, NET Collection, National Public Broadcasting Archives, Hornbake Library, University of Maryland, College Park, MD.

31. Ibid.

32. " 'Our World'—Round the World Project Fact Book."

33. Jack Wilson, press release regarding *Our World*, May 18, 1967, NET Files, series 6, box 7, folder 9, NET Collection, Wisconsin State Historical Society.

34. *Our World* script.

35. Lee, " 'Our World' Sees Advent of New Eras in Television."

36. Wilson, press release regarding *Our World*.

37. Ibid.

38. " 'Our World'—Round the World Project Fact Book."

39. This is in contrast to the late 1950s and early 1960s, when satellites emerged as spectacles in popular media and culture. See Lisa Parks, "Technology in the Twilight: A Cultural History of the First Earth Satellites," *Humanities and Technology Review*, fall 1997.

40. Thomas Elsaesser, "Digital Cinema: Delivery, Event, Time," in *Cinema Futures: Cain, Abel or Cable? The Screen Arts in the Digital Age*, ed. Thomas Elsaesser and Kay Hoffman (Amsterdam: Amsterdam University Press, 1998), 210.

41. *Our World* press release, June 25, 1967, NET Files, series 6, box 7, folder 9, NET Collection, Wisconsin State Historical Society.

42. One review described the broadcast as "an old fashioned geography class gone electric." See Lee, " 'Our World' Sees Advent of New Eras in Television."

43. *Our World*'s "Production Philosophy," p. 6. NET Collection, National Public Broadcasting Archives, Hornbake Library, University of Maryland, College Park, MD.

44. Colin McCabe first develops the concept of a hierarchy of discourse in his essay "Realism and the Cinema: Notes on Some Brechtain Theses-*Screen* 15, no. 2 (1974): 7–27."

45. Producers suggested, "Whenever possible individual remote contributions should be constructed so as to develop through time rather than across space; the metaphor in the producers' mind should be that of lighting a fuse rather than of going around a garden gathering flowers. We should pick a single operation and watch it develop rather than

looking at several which do not develop at all." " 'Our World'—Round the World Project Fact Book."

46. Arjun Appadurai, *Modernity at Large: Cultural Dimensions of Globalization* (Minneapolis: University of Minnesota Press, 1996), 3.

47. Ibid., 9.

48. "Photo Cutlines."

49. *Our World* script.

50. Bob Tweedell, " 'Our World' Impressive," *Denver Post*, June 26, 1967, series 6, box 7, folder 9, NET Collection, Wisconsin State Historical Society.

51. See, for instance, Potter, "Memo to All Stations."

52. *Our World* press release, "Babies Are Focal Point," May 1967, NET Collection, National Public Broadcasting Archives, Hornbake Library, University of Maryland, College Park, MD.

53. Ibid., 28.

54. For a discussion of the politics of reproduction in Third World countries, see Soheir Morsy, "Biotechnology and the Taming of Women's Bodies," in *Processed Lives: Gender and Technology in Everyday Life*, ed. Jennifer Terry and Melodie Calvert. (London: Routledge, 1997), 165–73.

55. Ironically, decades later, global satellite providers would aggressively target audiences and exploit markets in precisely those countries that were allegedly the primary culprits of the population explosion, including India, China, Brazil, and South Africa.

56. Caldwell, *Televisuality*, 31.

Chapter Five

Flows and Other Close Encounters with Television

Mimi White

In his essay on "The Work of Art in the Age of Mechanical Reproduction," Walter Benjamin quotes Paul Valery about the prospects for audio—visual systems in the impending future. "Just as water, gas, and electricity are brought into our houses from far off to satisfy our needs in response to a minimal effort, so we shall be supplied with visual or auditory images, which will appear and disappear at a simple movement of the hand, hardly more than a sign" (219). While Benjamin goes on to explore the implications of the arts of reproduction, Valery more explicitly describes something on the order of an audiovisual system of transmission. Indeed, Valery anticipates what has become one of the guiding terms for understanding broadcasting and other electromagnetic means of communication with the analogy to water, gas, and electricity, which *flow* into homes with a simple movement of the hand.

The specific term "flow" emerged in the 1970s as a keyword in television studies. It has been used as a core concept in the context of cultural studies and as a guiding concern for political economy approaches to global television. In this essay, I consider some of the prominent uses of the term "flow" and the implications for the ways the term positions television as an object of study. I start with a brief review of perspectives on flow that develop in the context of cultural television theory after Raymond Williams. I then return to Williams's 1974 account of how the idea of flow crystallized in a particular context, when he was watching American television while visiting the United States, and explore the implications of this "discovery." I also turn to political economic studies of the global circulation of media programming and information, focused on the study of media flows. Comparing the idea of flow in these formative but discrepant contexts of television studies—television cultural studies and global political economic media studies—exposes distinctive methodological emphases. But they also have something in common: they both implicate television as an object of study in various forms of global mobility—tourism, international trade, ethnography, and diasporic communities. And both introduce the same word, "flow," at very nearly the same time, to capture this aspect of the medium.

Flow and the Television Text

In *Television: Technology and Cultural Form*, Raymond Williams proposes the term "flow" to describe the distinctive nature of television. "In all developed broadcasting systems the characteristic organisation, and therefore the characteristic experience, is one of sequence or flow. This phenomenon of planned flow, is then perhaps the defining characteristic of broadcasting, simultaneously as a technology and as a cultural form" (Williams, 80). With this perhaps overly terse formulation, Williams suggests that flow has something to do with the organization of television as a textual system ("the characteristic organisation") as well as with viewing and reception ("the characteristic experience"), both in turn linked to—but not narrowly determined by—institutional prerogatives ("this phenomenon of planned flow"). In other words, as a conceptual term, flow represents the mediations between television technology (the flow of the broadcast signal), institutional terms of programming, and, ultimately of most significance, television textuality and viewer experience thereof. In elaborating on the concept of flow, Williams explains that the term is intended to express television's fundamental reconfiguration of the nature and experience of cultural texts. Specifically,

> the notion of "interruption," while it has still some residual force from an older model, has become inadequate. What is being offered is not, in older terms, a programme of discrete units with particular insertions, but a planned flow, in which the true series is not the published sequence of programme items but this sequence transformed by the inclusion of another kind of sequence, so that these sequences together compose the real flow, the real "broadcasting."(84)

The term "flow" has subsequently become a keyword of television theory and criticism, albeit with substantial elaboration, revision, and criticism.[1] As Lynn Spigel notes, "Perhaps because it has been so influential, the concept of flow has also been criticized for its attempt to explain too much about television by devising a covering law for the very diverse kinds of experiences we have when we watch TV" (Spigel, xxv). Scholars have applied a variety of refinements to the notion of flow in an effort to more precisely describe the nature of the cultural experiences it constitutes for viewers, in which television watching in general supersedes the individual bounded program (Ellis, Feuer, Newcomb and Hirsch, Fiske). Thus flow is reconstrued as segmentation (Ellis), as segmentation without closure (Feuer), as the viewing strip (Newcomb and Hirsch), and as the associative textual strategies generative of television's intertextuality (Fiske).

John Ellis offers an initial refinement of Williams's sense of flow, proposing that the textual system of television is best described as "segmentation," here borrowing from semiotic film theory (Metz). He introduces the term to characterize television's unique cultural/textual form, especially in contrast to cinema:

> Broadcast TV has developed a distinctive aesthetic form. Instead of the single, coherent text that is characteristic of entertainment cinema, broadcast TV offers relatively discrete segments: small sequential unities of images and sounds whose maximum duration seems to be about five minutes. These segments are organized into groups which are

either simply cumulative, like news broadcast items and advertisements, or have some kind of repetitive or sequential connection, like the groups of segments that make up the serial or series. Broadcast TV narration takes place across these segments. (Ellis, 112)

Jane Feuer offers further refinements on flow and on Ellis' idea of television as segmentation. She describes Williams's idea of flow as something of an illusion, because distinctive units of story and information are legible in television's textual system. "It would be more accurate to say that television is constituted by a dialectic of segmentation and flow. Television is based upon program segments, advertising segments, trailer segments, etc." (15). Indeed, she notes that unlike cinema, television segmentation is not a result of an analytic process, but is a manifest property of the text. "Williams should more accurately say that television possesses segmentation without closure, for this is what he really means by flow" (15–16). Feuer adds two additional qualifications to her discussion. First, she emphasizes that flow is an integral part of television as a commercial form, something planned by networks, stations, and programmers to maximize viewers, and therefore central to the commodity logic of the medium. "Flow as such is neither natural nor technologically determined. It is an historically specific result of network practice: 'flow charts' are constructed by network executives prior to being reconstituted by structuralists" (16). Second, she extends the idea of flow to the viewing situation. "The set is in the home, as part of the furniture of one's daily life; it is always available; one may intercept the flow at any point" (15).[2]

Horace Newcomb and Paul M. Hirsch draw on the idea of flow to ground a method for analyzing television appropriate to the medium's textual system. They propose the viewing "strip"—a sequence of programs—as the appropriate unit of analysis. (Nick Browne proposes something similar with the idea of the television "super-text.") This emerges in the context of developing an approach to understanding television as a "cultural forum," a site where prevalent social and cultural issues are debated and explored from diverse perspectives. "The emphasis is on process rather than product, on discussion rather than indoctrination, on contradiction and confusion rather than coherence." As a cultural forum, television programs address issues of social and cultural significance, and provide dramatic and narrative means for exploring issues from a variety of points of view. With this emphasis, and following Williams, they conclude that the best way to analyze the full range of television's cultural meanings is to study the viewing strip rather than individual programs or episodes. The idea of the viewing strip combines Williams' idea of flow, television's commercial programming system, and the awareness that particular viewers tend to watch more than one program at a time.

> Within these flow strips we may find opposing ideas abutting one another. We may find opposing treatment of the same ideas. . . . The forum model, then, has led us into a new exploration of the definition of the television text. We are now examining the "viewing strip" as a potential text and are discovering that in the range of options offered by any given evening's television, the forum is indeed a more accurate model of what goes on *within* television than any other that we know of. By taping entire weeks of television content, and tracing various potential strips in the body of that week, we

can construct a huge range of potential "texts" that may have been seen by individual viewers. (509–10)

Finally, the idea of flow influences John Fiske's formulation of television intertextuality. Initially, his approach to flow closely follows the ideas discussed above, as characteristic of the medium's foundational textual system.

> The television text, then, is composed of a rapid succession of compressed, vivid segments where the principle of logic and cause and effect is subordinated to that of association and consequence to sequence. Flow, with its connotations of a languid river, is perhaps an unfortunate metaphor: the movement of the television text is discontinuous, interrupted, and segmented. Its attempts at closure, at a unitary meaning, or a unified viewing subject, are constantly subjected to fracturing forces. (105)

Fiske notes that this textual system encourages meaning to be found across texts, creating a system that promotes interpretation among the continuities and discontinuities of the segments that comprise flow, rather than in terms of a specific, isolated segment or an individual program episode.[3]

All these accounts of flow build on Williams's initial articulation of the concept. Even when they revise his initial formulation, they aim at explaining the unique quality of television textuality, often in contrast to common understandings of film as a related, but distinct, cultural form. (This emphasis on film versus television is explicitly raised by Ellis and Feuer, and influences Fiske's discussion.) They also have implications for what constitutes a television "text" as a unit of analysis, and for developing the best possible interpretive approaches to television. This is the case even as flow is criticized for metaphoric implications of non-differentiation and smooth transition within programs and between programming segments (Ellis; Fiske).

John Caldwell offers a different approach in his criticism of "flow" as a key concept for television theory. In particular he addresses the way flow and related concepts in television theory are based on efforts to differentiate television from the cinematic apparatus, and the profound limits of this for making sense of television as an aesthetic and cultural set of practices. As a result, he offers a more wholesale critique of the idea of flow, suggesting that it does not begin to encompass a wide range of common textual practices and viewing habits that are clearly at stake in television. Caldwell challenges the emphasis on "flow" as a distinctive characteristic of television on several grounds. While I do not have time to review all of his perspectives, his basic framework is important, recasting television theory in productive ways. For instance, he proposes that flow highlights the continual, redundant, and monotonous aspects of television programming, to the detriment of understanding distinctions within the medium and its programs. "A great deal of television in the last fifteen years is significant precisely because it self-consciously rejects the monotonous implications of the flow" (19).

He also argues that the common acceptance of flow provides the basis for another faulty theoretical proposition, "glance theory": the idea that television does not engage viewers with any intensity of attention, especially in visual terms. First introduced by Ellis in direct contrast to the cinematic gaze, the idea that television invites the glance rather than the concentration of the gaze has wide currency in some approaches to television theory. While glance theory is partially premised on the quality of the broadcast television image before big-screen television sets, digital signals, and HDTV, Caldwell specifically draws attention to the conceptual relation between the distractedness allegedly encouraged by textual segmentation or flow and the pervasive distractedness attributed to the television viewing experience by glance theory. He also stresses that both flow and glance theory, as core concepts in television theory, developed in the context of efforts to discern essential differences between television and film, distinctions that may have little to do with the ways television programming is produced or engaged by viewers. "The morasslike flow of television may be more difficult for the TV viewer to wade through than film, but television rewards discrimination, style consciousness, and viewer loyalty in ways that counteract the clutter" (26). Rather than linking segmentation, with or without closure, to distraction, Caldwell proposes thinking about television in terms of its semiotic density, its complex visual/aural strategies and narrative paradigms that are just as likely to promote absorbed, intensive viewing attention as to only engage a distracted glance.

Beyond Caldwell's concerns about the limits of building television theory in distinction to cinema apparatus theory, the emphasis on flow as a unique quality of television, differentiating it from cinema, neglects important historical conditions of commercial programming. After all, the nature of flow first identified and named by Williams was not necessarily exclusive to, or invented by, American commercial television. Rather, it was arguably already in place in American commercial radio broadcasting, the model adopted and extended by television broadcasters. This is hardly surprising, given that the major American national radio networks worked hard to secure their position as the dominating force in the emerging national television networks in the post–World War II era (Boddy; Schwoch, 1990). Television theories that focus on differentiating television from cinema by and large pay inadequate attention to the significant relationship between radio and television broadcasting and its theoretical and historical implications for understanding television. In the process such theories risk mistaking a characteristic of commercial broadcasting (as a technology and a cultural form) for a specific trait of television.

Finally, Williams's and others' use of the term "flow" is criticized from institutional perspectives (Feuer; Budd). In particular these concerns focus on the fact that flow seems to describe television in its most advanced commodity form, undermining its value as a critical term for conceptualizing the medium apart from its consumerist imperatives. In this vein, for example, "flow" is a term used in the industry, involving the explicit determination of program schedules and marketing strategies. This includes the careful planning that informs the placement of commercials, efforts to maximize audience continuity on a particular channel, programming against other channels to draw a large audience share, and the intertextual proliferation of product tie-ins.

Traveling Theorists: Ethnography and Tourism

As a keyword and central concept in cultural and theoretical television studies, flow has thus achieved an ambiguous status. While it informs a substantial amount of television theory and criticism, it also seems at once too extensive and/or too confining for specific purposes of theoretical clarification or critical understanding. Yet there are other aspects of "flow" that remain unexplored. Notably, the idea of "flow" emerges in a number of contexts that approach television in terms of travel, tourism, and global mobility. Ultimately I want to suggest that the emphasis on "flow," whatever its limits, situates television according to a kind of "traveling theory," as scholars variously posit logics of tourism, global trade, and diaspora to explain the medium's institutions, texts, and modes of reception. This understanding initially emerges in Williams's own account of his "discovery" of flow—an account whose arguably apocryphal status is nonetheless made credible by its repetition in other contexts:

> One night in Miami, still dazed from a week on an Atlantic liner, I began watching a film and at first had some difficulty adjusting to a much greater frequency of commercial "breaks" [than is typical in British commercial programming]. Yet this was a minor problem compared to what eventually happened. Two other films, which were due to be shown on the same channel on other nights, began to be inserted as trailers. A crime in San Francisco (the subject of the original film) began to operate in an extraordinary counterpoint not only with the deodorant and cereal commercials but with a romance in Paris and the eruption of a prehistoric monster who laid waste New York. Moreover, this was sequence in a new sense. Even in commercial British television there is a visual signal—the residual sign of an interval—before and after the commercial sequences and "programme" trailers only occur between "programmes." Here there was something quite different, since the transitions from film to commercial and from film A to films B and C were in effect unmarked. . . . I can still not be sure what I took from that whole flow. I believe I registered some incidents as happening in the wrong film, and some characters in the commercials as involved in the film episodes, in what came to seem—for all the occasional bizarre disparities—a single irresponsible flow of images and feelings. (85–86)

Significantly, Williams does not dismiss this whole experience as aberrant, even though he characterizes himself as disoriented foreign traveler who is watching American commercial television.[4] After all, U.S. broadcasting is only one model for television, and is typically contrasted unfavorably—especially at the time he is writing—with the public service tradition of most European broadcasting systems, including British television, with which Williams was far more familiar.[5] Instead, Williams uses this avowedly untypical viewing experience to discern the *typical* nature of television. Indeed, it becomes a defining moment, crystallizing the full implications of flow, replete with its commercialism, textual overloading, and distinctive consequences for reception. On this basis he proposes as a *general rule* that flow is "the central television experience" (89).

Williams presents this experience of U.S. television, a narrative of "first encounter," as the foundation for a far more general theory of television. He proceeds to offer a comparative analysis of British and U.S. programs and programming as case studies of flow (72–112). Here, he theoretically assesses television as a cultural-technological "other," as opposed to assimilating it into a European cultural tradition through aesthetic analysis and canon construction. It is Europeanized nonetheless by virtue of being situated in terms of a Western anthropological perspective. The full meaning of this "other" cultural form reveals its basic nature—flow—to the European traveler, who considers it from the vantage of ethnography. It is thus in the formative stages of television theory that the medium is posited as an ethnographic discovery.[6]

Moreover, Williams's original experience of flow is repeatable, even decades later, for those who encounter American-style commercial broadcasting for the first time through direct exposure to American commercial television programming flow. The fact that these narratives of first encounter bear repeating seems to confirm their value as tales for the tourist-ethnographer scholar. For example, sixteen years after Williams, John Caughie published his own account of a "first encounter" with U.S. television, rediscovering the full impact of commercial flow:

> For all the preparation that one receives from conventional wisdom about the annoyance of the commercial interruptions on American television, their effect still catches me a little unprepared. It is much less the regularity of the interruption, or the wonderful blatancy of their placement, more the specific way they interrupt, the effect on (or, more exactly, in) the text. . . . On American television, Cagney looks out of the frame, and the answering reverse-field is a commercial for Mack trucks. The space of the commercial is continuous from the space of the fiction. . . . they can be read symptomatically as little contests between commercial logic—the need to deliver audiences to advertisers—and narrative logic—the need to hold audiences in identification. What is so striking to someone raised in the protective shelter of public service is the visibility of the context. I *experience* the effect which I had always known in theory: a quite radical destabilizing of the text as an autonomous and logical fictional space complete within its own boundaries. For a still "foreign" viewer, the experience of watching American television is never simply the experience of watching programs as texts in any classical sense, but is always also the experience of reading the specific forms of instability of an interrupted and interruptible space. (50)

Caughie's account bears considerable resemblance to Williams's description of "flow" both as an experience and as a theoretical concept. One signal difference is that Caughie remains more firmly committed to the idea of primary "texts," the narrative programs, *interrupted* by commercial and other interstitial sequences. This is precisely a distinction Williams had attempted to displace with the introduction of the word "flow" in the first place. That is, Williams's encounter with the American commercial model led to a different assessment of what the object-text was: television was not best understood or interpreted as a medium where primary texts (programs, news reports) were interrupted by advertisements, station identifications, and so on. Rather, the medium transformed the nature and notion of textual hierarchies, which were superseded by *flow*, sequences transformed by their ongoing juxtaposition with other sequences. As a result of this difference, the sense of being a tourist is much stronger in the Caughie account as he deploys his situated European gaze, holding up the British public service tradition, with its clearly delineated primary texts, as the standard against which U.S. broadcasting, with its disruptions, poses a potential crisis of meaning and stable subjectivity. He is not, in other words, willing to let American television flow constitute a general rule about the nature of television as a technology or a cultural form. Caughie's status as a foreign traveler watching television is also foregrounded as he details unexpected televisual encounters in other global locales. The story of his confrontation with commercial American TV programming flow is followed by anecdotes of stopping to drink in a Catalonian village only to see a dubbed version of *Dynasty* and the wedding of Prince Andrew and Fergie on the local television.

His status as a tourist is essential, signaling the extent to which his theoretical knowledge is intimately tied to *his* particular experiences around the world—whether in Spain, the United States, or Scotland. From the start he makes it clear that academic knowledge of flow is incommensurate with the experience of the first encounter. "I *experience* the effect which I had always known in theory," he says, with the clear implication that his experience (and not his academic knowledge) finally makes the theory salient: he had to watch American television *for himself* before he could truly grasp flow and, consequently, comprehend its relation to poststructural and postmodern theory. The theoretical and critical work of others—not only Williams, but also, especially, of native American informants (i.e., other television scholars)—was not only insufficient evidence but also inadequate as a way of knowing. Instead, ethnographic knowledge is advanced for the traveler as his own, selfsame subject of experience, knowledge, and study.

As a result, John Caughie (re)discovers flow through an originary and personal experience, which occurs while he is traveling, just like Raymond Williams. And even then, Caughie is much more guarded about the generalizability of this experience. This is the case despite the fact that the encounter with commercial television flow has comprised the daily experience of millions of "native" American television viewers for decades. "There is a real risk in the theorizing and, particularly, in the teaching of television of opening up a gap between the television which is taught and theorized and the television which is experienced," he asserts (50). Yet it is equally possible to understand "flow" precisely as a concept designed to articulate theory and experience, the structures of television and its modes of reception. This at least seems to be at the heart of Williams's initial exposition of the term and its theoretical import.

Despite these differences, both accounts express what might best be termed "the shock of the flow" as a signal experience for foreigners in America. Given the rhetorical nature of these accounts, it is not at all clear that the same experience— firmly inscribed in the strategies and practices of U.S. commercial television—is granted to the natives in theoretically or phenomenologically meaningful terms. The implication is that native viewers are too prone to absorption in the overwrought media environment that has been naturalized through routine exposure; they are all too likely to go with the flow. Because (we) Americans are always already natives within the culture of flow, innovations such as VCR, cable, and DBS, which seem to exacerbate and intensify flow, are a priori rationalized as the fulfilled promise of the system that has always existed. And because the native viewers are always already inside the system, they are implicitly cast as unable to recognize, or theorize, the implications of their own media experiences. Instead, the stories of first encounter claim this ability for traveling theorists.

As a result, the experience of flow-as-shock—the signal experience whereby flow achieves its full impact and can then be recognized in its full theoretical import—is reserved for tourists who watch American television from a Eurocentric ethnographic perspective. And if Williams and Caughie are any indication, there is a compulsion to recount the experience as a narrative of "first encounter" with a "native" system that is also posited as the most elaborated commercial version of the medium. In this context television exemplifies a nonprimitive ethnographic object of scrutiny and fascination, requiring a "thick description" so that it can be properly assimilated into the Eurocentric worldview. With "flow" as a keyword of television theory, the Euro-centric ethnographic perspective is inscribed as a founding epistemology of television cultural studies whose full force subsequently emerges in the elaboration of audience ethnographies. At the same time, this approach posits television as a cultural "other"—not an integral part of a European cultural or aesthetic tradition—no matter the context of its production and reception.

I even have my own anecdote to substantiate and extend the repeatability of this experience for foreigners who watch U.S. television. In 1994 I showed a taped episode of *The Simpsons* in a seminar I was teaching in Finland on American television culture.[7] I had carefully described the nature of American television, emphasizing flow and intertextuality as two key issues, as well as describing the multichannel world of cable and DBS systems. I was subsequently assured that this was elementary theory, basic knowledge with which the students, having read Williams and Fiske among others, were already thoroughly conversant. Yet shortly after I started the tape, as the program moved directly from opening titles to commercials, the students visibly blanched; and during the commercials they gingerly asked if I had recorded the program properly in sequence as it had been broadcast. Given the typical abrupt transition, in the American style, from titles to ads to program, they were certain I had mistakenly started and stopped recording over a previously recorded tape. In other words, despite my lecture and their previous reading, their immediate experi-ence of American commercial television flow—even a three-minute segment of one channel—had an impact that registered as startling, with the capacity to disorient: the shock of the flow.

Global Media Flows

As it happens, the Finnish students were already quite familiar with the program *The Simpsons* because it regularly aired on Finnish television; it was only the encounter with American television programming flow that was new to them. But this distinc-tive *experience* of programming flow was particularly salient precisely because of another dimension of flow explored by media scholars starting in the 1970s. This introduces a second register of issues regarding television, travel, and flow: the global distribution and circulation of programs. For even as Raymond Williams was introducing the term "flow" to account for the nature and experience of television as a system of programmed texts, the idea of "media flows" was being used by social scientists—particularly political economists—to study the ways news, information, and entertainment media were distributed around the globe (Mowlana; Varis, 1974, 1985).

The initial media flow studies were funded by UNESCO in the interests of understanding the uneven circulation of information and media programming at a global level. They were part of a larger intellectual project, motivated by concern with the relationship between mass communication technologies, media information flow, and development in Third World countries (MacBride; Mowlana and Wilson; Nordenstreng; Nordenstreng and Hannikainen; Nordenstreng and Schiller; Sreberny-Mohammadi). These projects were also in part a response to a Cold War conflict, mainly in Europe, over competition for TV viewership around the border of the Iron Curtain, a competition cast along the philosophical values of the free flow of information (Schwoch, 2001).

The classic flow studies along these lines are quite different from Williams in their basic impulse and understanding of the power of media. The number and range of programs imported/exported around the world were counted by nation-state, in an effort to quantitatively map the ways global power and influence are unevenly distributed. These studies propose that television programming—understood in terms of geographical origin relative to geographical points of reception—expresses something about spheres of influence and domination in international relations. These may be broken down into specific categories—aesthetic, political, cultural, ideological, and so on. But there is always a sense of structural causality and intentionality that hinges on an initial nation-state identity.

The methodological emphasis of the media flow studies involved extensive sample bases and aimed to generate both representative and predictive results. The analysis of data in this way proposed to yield meaningful strategies of intervention to change the distribution of nation-state interests. Influence was quantified in terms of the number of programs and kinds of information that were produced in one place and ended up in others, and in the proportion of total programming hours that were considered to come from "elsewhere." Because the data suggest that texts and information flow unevenly—predominantly from North to South and West to East—programs are seen as having the capacity for a neocolonial imposition of outside values (Euro-American commercial culture) on a host of nation-states around the world. In this approach television programs are effectively conceived as travelers, akin to an unwanted immigrant population that moves around the globe with the privilege of cultural empire, inevitably introducing their values at the places they alight. These findings became an important part of the political theory of cultural imperialism.

The problems and limits of such studies are sufficiently well-known (White, 1995; Hjarvard). Even the purveyors of flow studies acknowledge that the enumeration of where programs start and where they end up does not have much to say about the nature of their reception or interpretation (Mowlana; Varis, 1985). And, as Caughie (among others) notes, it also says little about the particular, local strategies of flow in which the programs are inserted (45–46). Nonetheless the persistence of the influence of this work is still apparent, especially in contemporary debates on globalization (Curtin).

Flow in Historical Perspective

More central to my purposes is the striking use of the same keyword—"flow"—to anchor two distinctive but simultaneous theoretical conceptions of television and television studies. Work in the area of media flows engages social science research methods, involving quantification, extensive sampling, and measurement, rather than the participant observation and "thick description" of texts and their reception that develop in the context of British cultural studies and television studies under the influence of Raymond Williams. Media flow studies see a disproportionate number of television programs representing, and imposing, the ideas and ideals of the Western developed, (post)industrial nations, especially including the United States, on the rest of the world. In the cultural studies paradigm, the Eurocentric ethnographic gaze experiences and diagnoses U.S. television culture as its "other." Yet despite these differences, both approaches not only share a keyword—"flow"—but also implicate a more general sense of television as mobile, involving travel on a global scale. Neither approach emphasizes television as an aesthetic or semiotic practice wherein the programs themselves constitute the central object of study and analysis. Instead, both approaches suggest that television is always, somehow, an "other" to its viewers, because of who is watching, where they are watching, or what they are watching.

These concerns also emerge in some of the earliest writing on television as a cultural/technological apparatus. Notably, in "A Forecast of Television," Rudolf Arnheim offers an account of the medium that stresses its capacity for global mobility, and explicitly dissociates it from the realm of aesthetics:[8]

> Television is a relative of the motor-car and aeroplane: it is a means of cultural transportation. To be sure, it is a mere instrument of transmission, which does not offer new means for the artistic interpretation of reality—as radio and film did. But like the transportation machines, which were a gift of the last century, television changes our attitude to reality: it makes us know the world better and in particular gives us a feeling for the multiplicity of what happens simultaneously in different places. (160–61)

For Arnheim, television at its best, by virtue of its ability to move us around the world, can offer a better sense of our relative place within it. "We come to recognize the place where we are located as one among many: we become more modest, less egocentric" (161). Yet this emergent global perspective is not guaranteed in advance, since he does not allow that most viewers have the sensibility or sensitivity of the ethnographer, and are unable to be instructed and transformed in their self-perception by the encounter with the world that television can afford. On the contrary, Arnheim offers a significantly gendered (and nationalized) image of the typical viewer-traveler. In this context, he hints at something like flow, in the "variety of visible things" that television brings:

People who know how to observe and to draw conclusions from what they see will profit greatly. Others will be taken in by the picture on the screen and confused by the variety of visible things. After a while they may even cease to feel confused: proud of their right to see everything and weaned from the desire to understand and to digest, they may feel great satisfaction—like those hardy British spinsters who after a trip around the world contentedly arrive in the train station of their home town in the same state of mind in which they left. (162)

Arnheim's association of television, female spectators, and travel as the embodiment of the worst television has to offer is not atypical. On the contrary, many early critics figured television's debased cultural status in similar terms, significantly including implications of "flow" even if that particular term is not used. For example, Lynne Joyrich has described Dwight MacDonald's writing on television and mass culture in precisely these terms:

Within his framework (as well as that of several other critics), this absence of form, the "nothing to see" of mass culture, is intimately tied to the notion of a female public and a feminized media: MacDonald defines mass culture as "a tepid, flaccid Middlebrow Culture that threatens to engulf everything in its spreading ooze." The aesthetic disorder he discerns in mass culture is therefore related to a particular spectator position. Remarking on the masses' lack of "cultural equipment," MacDonald associates mass culture with a childish, weak, and impotent viewer, condemning the media for encouraging overstimulation yet passivity, infantile regression, sentimentalism, and what he calls "Momism." (25)

As Joyrich elaborates in a footnote, MacDonald's use of the term "ooze" closely resonates with the idea of flow. Moreover, this sense of fluidity and lack of boundaries is commonly deployed by mass culture critics to figure the medium in terms of femininity and passivity (183–84). Historically, women and children are proposed as the avatars of this position, the most likely viewers to be engulfed by the ooze, absorbed in the flow. But as Joyrich and others have noted, American mass culture in general and all of its audiences are considered overly susceptible to these effects. This echoes the sense that American television viewers in general are believed to be unable to establish sufficient critical distance to make theoretical sense of the medium, even though European cultural critics and the occasional male middlebrow critic are able to gain appropriate critical perspective.

As a result, "flow" can be reconceptualized as a "master" term that is implicated in a gendered division of labor. In the linkages of mass culture—femininity, ooze, and "British spinsters" who travel around the world—television emerges as a debased mode of cultural expression, "not us" in the eyes of self-appointed guardians of a properly aesthetic national culture. In the context of (male) ethnographic and political economic work, the ability to diagnose "flow" conveys a more robust sensibility, exemplified by traveling scholar-viewers replete with the analytic skills necessary to assess, and as necessary redress, the terms of the medium's mobility, including the ability to differentiate and stanch the flow. Thus, as a keyword, "flow" encompasses various formations and permutations of television's status as a cultural other.

With flow as a core conceptual term, television gets defined and theorized in terms of global cultures and travel almost from the outset, even as the power and knowledge of the medium relative to its viewers are variously assessed. The medium's value as an ethnographic discovery and as an instrument of social domination, along with its devaluations as a feminized debased form of cultural expression, forestalls among other things substantial consideration of the medium in aesthetic and cultural terms. At the same time, the conditions for understanding this mobile, global apparatus can only be specified and understood through particular conjunctions—of viewers, texts, programs, and programming flows. This is even true in Arnheim's case, writing well before the institution of any widespread television broadcasting systems.

In this vein, Caughie argues for the importance of *locality* to any consideration of television. But ideas about "locality," standpoint knowledge, and national identities make sense only in the larger context of more generalized ideas about television tourism, with programs and viewers conceptualized as mobile entities. Caughie proposes that "The continued return to locality, whether it be of nation, race, class, gender, or generation, resists the easy rationality of a general category or a universal theory" (56). Even if this is the case, the local finds its meaning most acutely in encounters between viewers and programs that do not originate in the same place. When it comes to encounters with television, the local is always plural—a relation between at least two places or identities, and often more (e.g., a heterogeneous Chinese diasporic community watching a particular Chinese-language program on television in Chicago; or an American watching RAI-4 on cable in Helsinki, Finland, perhaps viewing an American or British television sitcom dubbed into Italian).

In both the ethnographic and social scientific paradigms of television studies, locality is defined in the context of a global condition. This immediately interposes a tacit subject-object distinction. The object-text, television, is never "us" to the scholars who study it or even to the viewers who watch it. In ethnographic approaches, the ethnographer is the subject distinct from the object of study—the diverse users and viewers of television with their particular identities and sites who are themselves, in turn, distinct from the programs they watch. In media flow studies, the national subjectivity of viewers is seen to be challenged by the foreign traveling object-text. Travel distanciates and dislocates subjects of reception from the texts they encounter. In this vein, John Fiske can argue that television reception can almost always be conceptualized as a form of resistance of viewing subjects to the object-texts they encounter, because the sources of programs—in terms of class, gender, sexuality, nationality, and so on—are usually discrepant from the multiple points of reception, with their particular local determinations and identities. Only in this vein can the ethnographer play at "going native," as Caughie does; the title of his essay is "Playing at Being American." At the same time, the European analyzers of media flow worry that diverse "natives" around the globe will mistake the values and ideas of the alien traveling object-texts as their own.

Caughie captures this subject-object distinction, and at the same time neatly indicates the differences between aesthetic methodologies on the one hand and ethnographic views on the other when he proposes that "we" television scholars are not implicated in the texts we study in the same way that film scholars were in the recent past of media studies (54). This is a performative declaration, assuring that no one mistakes his interest in television for actually enjoying or being captivated by the medium, and claiming his position as a general perspective for all worthwhile television studies. His intellectual gaze should not be confused with the distracted glance of typical television viewers. The split he notes, between film-text studies and television audience studies, is more profoundly premised on a distinction between aesthetics and ethnography, between "us" and "others," between European culture and global cultures. In the ethnographic tradition, U.S. television is part of native global cultures, whereas in the world of political economy and quantitative social science, the United States is more fully assimilated into a hegemonic Euro-American culture. But in both cases, travel and global mobility are founding conditions of television's perpetual otherness.

These issues are taken up from a different perspective by Hamid Naficy in *The Making of Exile Cultures,* a study of Iranian television in Los Angeles. He introduces the idea of ethnic flow and exilic flow to understand the place of Iranian television programs in the context of a particular local U.S. television market. In the process, he offers a reminder that even local and particular programming strategies are characterized by an excess yielding heterogeneous and contradictory meanings, based on the flow of programs and populations, both of which travel. In the process he also complicates the larger conclusions of the early media flow studies, with a case study that focuses on programs from the East and the South that have made their way to one of the centers of Western media production—Los Angeles. As Naficy explains,

> The ethnic flow at multiethnic stations is characterized not so much by seamlessness as by segmentation. It is also intensely hermeneutic, as varied politics, nationalities, ethnicities, religions, cultures, languages, classes, news values, narrative strategies, modes of address, physical locations, tastes, gestures, faces, sights, and sounds clash with one another. This segmentation penetrates to even below the level of nationality as many emigre and exile communities are themselves not homogeneous. (93–94)

This takes place in relation to communities of viewers who are by and large not "native" to the city (or the country) where these programs are shown. Ethnic television flow can be considered to interpellate all viewers as diasporic "tourists," as it encompasses situations where viewers, programs, and reception contexts are quite explicitly dislocated in relation to one another—at least one of them has traveled. This includes those who watch their "own" television when they are away from home, as well as those who watch television made by and for others from a place they identify as home. Exile television is at once global and local, traveling around the world, participating in global media, technology, and population flows, to address particularly situated audiences—situated in specific places and with specific national, ethnic, and/or linguistic identities.

Through the examination of various uses of the term "flow" as a keyword of television studies, I have tried to suggest that television has always functioned this way, as an apparatus of global mobility and dislocation. Of equal importance, at some level television has persistently been understood by theorists in these terms.

This has most prominently been expressed in the use of the term "flow," which has simultaneously served to naturalize television's global, gendered trajectories. In practice, this has often had the effect of making television scholarship a difficult and slippery enterprise. For as television is tacitly implicated as an agency of flow, its stability as an object of analysis is all too easily undermined. The practices and meanings of television are set up in advance as a moving target, so that scholarly engagement with particular programs, audiences, or formations of television are prone to challenge for being focused in the wrong place. The impact and meaning are always liable to lie elsewhere: not in this text, but another; not in the programs, but the audience; not in the aggregate audience, but with individual viewers; not with viewers, but in the economics of global distribution, and so on. In other words, the enterprise of television studies as a whole has been stymied because the implications of flow for understanding the medium have been taken for granted rather than interrogated.

Instead, understanding the limits and possibilities of flow as a concept requires acknowledging its epistemological implication in networks of global mobility—of people, programs, and models for programming. In the process of reopening consideration of the term, I am hoping to denaturalize, or at least highlight, these foundational assumptions. This includes foregrounding television's implications in discourses of globality and mobility; questioning easy assumptions about what is "us" and "other" when it comes to television; and calling for new ways of thinking about our implication in and estrangement from television in historical, social, cultural, and aesthetic terms. At the same time, these crucial issues in the constitution of television theory and television studies have to be placed in historical context. With rapid changes in global television—multitudes of stations, cable and satellite systems of distribution, commercialization, globalization, Americanization, and so forth—to say nothing of the rise of the Internet and its emerging audiovisual and information capabilities, the tale of the traveler/ethnographer is itself becoming something of a historical narrative, a story that can only be set in the past, at least in the terms that it has thus far been recounted. Yet perhaps it is precisely this historical distance that makes it possible to reassess "flow" in these terms.

NOTES

1. For another account of flow as a cultural and critical term in television studies, see Corner.

2. While a substantial body of television theory and history has emphasized the home as the central locus for television, in institutional, historical, and theoretical terms, Anna McCarthy's *Ambient Television* (Durham: Duke University Press, 2001) offers an alternative historical and theoretical perspective, with its examination of television in public spaces.

3. I have also analyzed specific forms of television intertextuality that promote a sense of continuity across programming flow. The emphasis is on specific textual practices that encourage viewers to recognize continuities across television's ongoing "segmentation without closure," rewarding discerning and regular viewers for their recognition of these connections by virtue of their regular viewing habits (White, 1986).

4. It is also interesting that Williams had been traveling by boat rather than plane, a mode of transportation that allows for gradual transition rather than abrupt shift. In this context, the impact of the "irresponsible flow of images and feelings" may have been exacerbated. It is unclear in the passage whether his week on the liner was a transatlantic crossing, ending up in Miami, or a vacation cruise; or whether this recounts his actual first encounter with American television broadcasting, or simply the moment when it had its distinctive revelatory impact.

5. Typically, even commercial channels that emerged alongside public service systems have had relatively strict guidelines about intervals, station breaks, and so on.

6. In these terms the cultural studies connection between Raymond Williams and more recent emphasis in television studies on audience ethnographies (Fiske, Jenkins, Morley, Seiter et al.) is quite direct.

7. My thanks, and apologies, to the seminar students in the Department of Film and Television at the University of Turku, whose experience I recount here.

8. By contrast, Arnheim did assess radio, with its restriction to the domain of the acoustic, in terms of a distinctive aesthetic capacity.

REFERENCES

Arnheim, Rudolf. "A Forecast of Television." In *Film as Art*, 156–63. 1958. Reprint, London: Faber and Faber, 1969.

———. *Radio*. London: Faber and Faber, 1936.

Benjamin, Walter. "The Work of Art in the Age of Mechanical Reproduction." In *Illuminations*. Ed. Hannah Arendt, trans. Harry Zohn. New York: Schocken, 1969.

Boddy, William. *Fifties Television: The Industry and Its Critics*. Urbana: University of Illinois Press, 1990.

Browne, Nick. "The Political Economy of the Television (Super) Text." *Quarterly Review of Film Studies* 9, no. 3 (summer 1984): 174–82.

Budd, Michael. "Television Flow and Commodity Form." Paper presented at Society for Cinema Studies annual conference, 1986.

Caldwell, John. *Televisuality: Style, Crisis and Authority in American Television*. New Brunswick: Rutgers University Press, 1995.

Caughie, John. "Playing at Being American: Games and Tactics." In *Logics of Television*, ed. Patricia Mellencamp, 44–58. Bloomington: Indiana University Press, 1990.

Corner, John. *Critical Ideas in Television Studies*. New York: Oxford University Press, 2000.

Curtin, Michael. "Dynasty in Drag: Imagining Global TV." In *The Revolution Wasn't Televised*, ed. Lynn Spigel and Michael Curtin, 245–62. New York: Routledge, 1997.

Ellis, John. *Visible Fictions*. London: Routledge and Kegan Paul, 1982.

Feuer, Jane. "The Concept of Live Television: Ontology as Ideology." In *Regarding Television*, ed. E. Ann Kaplan, 12–22. Los Angeles: American Film Institute, 1983.

Fiske, John. *Television Culture*. London: Methuen, 1987.

Hjarvard, Stig. "TV News Flow Studies Revisited." *Electronic Journal of Communication/La Revue Electronique de Communication* 5, nos. 2–3 (July 1995).

Jenkins, Henry, III. *Textual Poachers: Television Fans and Participatory Culture*. New York: Routledge, 1992.

Joyrich, Lynne. *Re-viewing Reception*. Bloomington: Indiana University Press, 1996.

MacBride, Sean. *Shaping a New World Information Order: Address to the "Forum 1979" Organized by the International Telecommunication Union*. Paris: UNESCO 1979.

Metz, Christian. *Film Language: A Semiotic of the Cinema.* Trans. Michael Taylor. New York: Oxford University Press, 1974.

Morley, David. *Television, Audiences, and Cultural Studies.* New York: Routledge, 1992.

Mowlana, Hamid. *International Flow of Information: A Global Report.* Reports and Papers on Mass Communication, no. 99. Paris: UNESCO, 1985.

Mowlana, Hamid, and Laurie J. Wilson. *Communication Technology and Development.* Reports and Papers on Mass Communication, no. 101. Paris: UNESCO, 1988.

Naficy, Hamid. *The Making of Exile Cultures: Iranian Television in Los Angeles.* Mineapolis: University of Minnesota Press, 1993.

Newcomb, Horace, and Paul M. Hirsch. "Television as a Cultural Forum." In *Television: The Critical View*, 5th ed., ed. Horace Newcomb, 503–15. New York: Oxford University Press, 1994.

Nordenstreng, Kaarle. *NAM and NIICO: Documents of the Non-Aligned Movement on the New International Information and Communication Order (1986–1987).* Prague: International Organization of Journalists, 1988.

Nordenstreng, Kaarle, with Lauri Hannikainen. *The Mass Media Declaration of UNESCO.* Norwood, NJ: Ablex, 1984.

Nordenstreng, Kaarle, and Herbert Schiller, eds. *National Sovereignty and International Communication.* Norwood, NJ: Ablex, 1979.

Schwoch, James. "Cold War Telecommunications Strategy and the Question of German Television." *Historical Journal of Film, Radio and Television*, 21, no. 2 (June 2001): 109–21.

———. "Selling the Sight/Site of Sound: Broadcast Advertising and the Transition from Radio to Television." *Cinema Journal* 30, no. 1 (fall 1990): 55–66.

Seiter, Ellen, et al., eds. *Remote Control: Television, Audiences, and Cultural Power.* New York: Routledge, 1989.

Spigel, Lynn. Introduction to *Television: Technology and Cultural Form*, by Raymond Williams. Hanover, NH: Wesleyan University Press, 1992.

Sreberny-Mohammadi, Annabelle, et al. *Foreign News in the Media: International Reporting in 29 Countries: Final Report of the "Foreign Images Study."* Reports and Papers on Mass Communication, no. 39. Paris: UNESCO, 1985.

Varis, Tapio. *International Flow of Television Programmes.* Reports and Papers on Mass Communication, no. 100. Paris: UNESCO, 1985.

———. *Television Traffic—A One-Way Street?* Reports and Papers on Mass Communication, no. 70. Paris: UNESCO, 1974.

White, Mimi. "Crossing Wavelengths: The Diegetic and Referential Imaginary of American Commercial Television." *Cinema Journal* 25, no. 2 (winter 1986): 51–67.

———. "Reconsidering Television Program Flows, or Whose Flow Is It Anyway?" *Electronic Journal of Communication/La Revue Electronique de Communication* 5, nos. 2–3 (July 1995).

Williams, Raymond. *Television: Technology and Cultural Form*, 1974. Reprint, Hanover, NH: Wesleyan University Press, 1992.

Part II

Over the Air
Revisiting Western Imperialism

Chapter Six

Media Imperialism

John Tomlinson

Media theorists have their own axes to grind, but in grinding them they produce a substantial element of the discourse of cultural imperialism. Though their discussions of media imperialism often remain tied to the particularities of media institutions and forms they are always, if sometimes unwittingly, in the thick of the conceptual and normative problems of cultural imperialism. Our aim is to explore these problems *through* the discourse of media imperialism and this should, and will, severely limit our scope.

We shall be concerned with three main issues. The first is the problem of specifying "the cultural" within a wider context of political/economic domination. The discourse of media imperialism often tugs back to one of economic domination, in which the specific moment of the cultural seems forever to recede. Looking at claims about media imperialism, then, will help us form a first view of what should and should not count as cultural domination.

The second issue is related to the first. Because of the constant tendency to revert to an economic account, where cultural "effects" of media imperialism *are* posited, they are invariably problematic. Either they are simply assumed and allowed to function in the discourse as a self-evident concomitant of the sheer presence of alien cultural goods, or else they are inferred using fairly crude interpretative assumptions. The second issue is the *hermeneutic naivety* of much of the discourse of cultural imperialism. Not only do the claims of some media analysts provide nice examples of this, there is an existing debate within media theory generally about the problems of inferring "media effects" to which we can conveniently refer.

The third issue has to do with the way in which the media figure in contemporary Western culture, thus in cultural imperialism seen as the "imposition" of this. The media are generally located at the centre of the culture of the capitalist West and there are several reasons for this, ranging from the pragmatic to the more theoretically principled. To understand the notion of cultural imperialism, we therefore need to think about the "mediated" nature of contemporary Western culture and to ask what it is that is "imposed" on other cultures. Is it simply a set of "media images" or a more complex "mediation" of cultural experience?

In pursuing these three issues we shall be parasitic on the discourse of media imperialism. This chapter will be neither a survey of the "media imperialism debate", nor will it involve itself directly in many of the specific and detailed arguments of media analysts. . . .

There is a strategic reason for us to avoid the fine grain of the media analysts' discourse, apart from the obvious question of space. This is the need to maintain the critical distance of our discourse from the various ways in which cultural imperialism has been discussed. Each particular discourse will tend to draw us in to its particularities. We can think of them . . . as "settled areas" in the terrain of cultural imperialism. What we must do is to resist becoming settlers as we visit each area. We must keep our distance. Ours must be a *nomadic* discourse.

Media Imperialism Theory and the Retreat of Culture

In 1981 Fred Fejes wrote an assessment of the state of play of research into media imperialism. His main conclusion was that the area was heavy on "empirical description of concrete examples of media imperialism", but light on unifying theory. What was mostly going on, Fejes argued, was a mass of detailed descriptions of the global operations of the media industries, focusing on the control exercised by the Western transnational corporations over the flow of information and the dissemination of media products worldwide. If there was to be any progress, he argued, this empirical description needed a coherent theoretical framework. Fejes spent much of his time arguing that the documentation of ownership and control of the global media be integrated into a broader political-economic analysis of relations between developing and developed societies.

Towards the end of his discussion—and the priority afforded the issue is significant—Fejes turned to media imperialism as cultural imperialism:

> A third concern that the media imperialism approach must address if it is to progress is the issue of culture. While a great deal of the concern over media imperialism is motivated by the fear of the cultural consequences of the transnational media—of the threat that such media poses to the integrity and the development of viable national cultures in Third World societies—it is the one area where, aside from anecdotal accounts, little progress has been achieved in understanding *specifically the cultural impact of transnational media on Third World societies*. All too often the institutional aspects of transnational media receive the major attention while the cultural impact, *which one assumes to occur*, goes unaddressed in any detailed manner.[1]

The key phrase here is "specifically the cultural impact of transnational media on Third World societies". This implies that there is a form of domination involved in the practices studied as media imperialism which can be recognised as "specifically cultural" as distinct from—what? Well, presumably a media domination which is, in some sense, describable as *other* than cultural. Immediately we are confronted with the problem of specifying "the cultural". If we use too broad an approach it will be difficult to exclude *any* human practices and certainly no activity associated with the media. So, what understanding of "the cultural" is implied here by Fejes? We can see that he means to distinguish between "the institutional aspects of transnational media" and the effects of media products on their consumers.

On the one hand there is that cluster of issues which has to do with the ownership and control of the media worldwide: with the manner in which media products—TV programmes, advertisements, news—are produced and distributed, and particularly with the market dominance of the powerful multinational corporations. On the other hand, there is the question of the *implications* of this market dominance for the people on the receiving end of these cultural goods. How does the consumption of foreign TV programmes and so forth affect the patterns of culture within a society? Does it significantly alter cultural values, for example spreading Western "consumerism"? Does it destroy, swamp or crowd out authentic, local, traditional culture?

The first cluster of issues would normally be considered as one of political economy, or of the "macro-sociology" of institutions. The domination involved here could be described largely in economic terms: it is part of the neo-imperialism which structures the overall relations between the First and the Third World. This is the domination which the "dependency theory" of developing societies advocated by Fejes describes. The second cluster of issues is "specifically cultural" in Fejes's formulation, as distinct from this economic imperialism. The idea implicit here is that there is a distinct level of analysis involved, having to do with the content of media texts, the reception of this content, and the impact of the reception, "on the lives and human relationships of Third World populations". This is "the cultural dimension of the media" which, according to Fejes and others,[2] theorists of media imperialism have generally failed to confront. This failure, Fejes suggests, derives from the inherent difficulties of "the cultural dimension": "There is very little consensus on the basic formulation of the questions to be asked, much less agreement on methods and criteria."[3]

We can agree with Fejes in a lot of this. Certainly much of the output of the media analysts *does* have to do with matters of political economy or media institutions. Equally, at the time that Fejes was writing, there was very little attempt to confront the issue of media effects in relation to media imperialism. Since then some attempts have been made and we will consider these in the next section. But we need to hold as *provisional* the view of "the cultural" that Fejes presents. If it were simply and indisputably the case that the cultural is the domain of texts and their reception, matters would be much more straightforward. The inherent ambiguity of the concept of culture with which we are saddled makes things rather more complicated.

In order to understand this complexity, let us look now at a representative discussion of media imperialism of the kind that Fejes criticises for stopping short, in his terms, of the specific moment of "the cultural".

The text we shall consider is a short paper by Herbert Schiller, "Transnational Media and National Development", which appeared in a much-cited collection edited by Nordenstreng and Schiller, *National Sovereignty and International Communication*, in 1979. . . .

Schiller begins by presenting a picture of how the world works economically. Following Wallerstein,[4] he describes a "modern world system" consisting of a global capitalist market economy in which the "core" countries of the developed industrial West. . . . dominate the allocation of human and natural resources. The nations of the Third World are located, according to this model on the "periphery", at a distance in terms of economic, technological, strategic and political power, from the centres of control. Thus, Schiller argues, Third World countries do not have the control of their economic (and even, arguably, of their political) development in the way that the term "national development" implies. Forces outside of nominally "independent" sovereign nations actually determine how development proceeds.

The ideas of a "world system" and a "core-periphery" model of global political-economic power are typical of the broadly neo-Marxist paradigm in development studies known as "dependency theory".[5] Dependency theory obviously stresses the way in which formerly colonial countries remain dependent on the West, but perhaps the key to the thinking here . . . is the integrated and *systematic* nature of modern global capitalism. The multinational corporation (MNC)—sometimes transnational corporation (TNC)—is of central importance in this approach, since it is generally held to represent the most significant unit in the "system" of global capitalism. The enormous economic power of the MNCs . . . and their interests in exploiting markets, natural resources and labour forces worldwide has, for many critics, come to represent the high point of capitalist development and the major determinant of the economies of the Third World. Dependency theory has much to recommend it, especially considering the paradigm in development studies—"modernisation theory"[6]—which it displaced. However, it must be said that Schiller tends to present a fairly simple version which glosses over some of the tricky conceptual problems involved and in which the notion of "the system" becomes reified and operates in a rather crude and rigid "functionalist" manner.

Schiller is out to show how the media fit into the world system of capitalism and his focus is on their provision of "the ideologically supportive informational infrastructure of the modern world system's core—the multinational corporations".[7] Multinational media corporations thus act as agents for "the promotion, protection and extension of the modern world system and its leading component, the MNC in particular."[8]

At the centre of Schiller's argument is the notion that media imperialism is an extension of the sort of commercial role the media have in developed societies—particularly in the United States—in relation to the "developing" societies, the media are seen primarily as vehicles for corporate marketing, manipulating audiences to deliver them as "good consumers" of capitalist production:

> The apparent saturation through every medium of the advertising message has been to create audiences whose loyalties are tied to brand named products and whose understanding of social reality is mediated through a scale of commodity satisfaction.[9]

The point to note is that there is simply an *assertion* of the manipulative and ideological power of the media here. Critical media theory has long grappled with the problems of assessing "media effects" and there are, as we shall later see, major difficulties involved. Schiller is not interested in these problems; what he wants to do is to chart the way in which "the system" spreads its tentacles. So, dwelling only long enough to register the manipulative role of the media within his analysis, he moves quickly on to the needs of the system to gain more and more markets and areas of exploitation, and to the strategies employed towards this end. The picture he draws is of the incorporation of successive media practices (print and broadcast media production, advertising, market research, public relations) and successive technologies (computing and data analysis, information technology, satellite broadcasting) into the integrated and integrative world system of capitalist domination. This description, with an accompanying suggestion of the clandestine role of US agencies like the CIA in "stabilising" the system's spread throughout the world,[10] occupies the rest of the paper.

Schiller's conclusion is most revealing. His summary describes the transnational media as, "inseparable elements in a worldwide system of resource allocation generally regarded as capitalistic," which "create and reinforce their audiences' attachment to the way things are in the system overall".[11] But he goes on from this specifically to *deny* the point of attempts to measure media effects at a detailed empirical level. Individual media texts are mutually reinforcing in their demonstration of the attractions of consumerism and the "American way". Their effects, though not directly quantifiable, are cumulative and "totalising" and "are observable as typifying a way of life". Thus the "effect" of the transnational media in Third World countries is, for Schiller, the institution of a developmental path:

> It is what has come to be recognised, with apologies to the Chinese, as the capitalist road to development. In this process, the media, now many times more powerful and penetrative than in an earlier time, are the means that entice and instruct their audiences along this path, while at the same time concealing the deeper reality and the long term consequences that the course produces.[12]

Schiller employs a broad notion of culture as a "way of life"—the culture of capitalism—and what is really significant about this way of life is the centrality of "the system" within it. He has a strong view, recalling some of the themes of the "critical theory" of the Frankfurt School,[13] of the incorporative power of the capitalist system. This is seen as shaping the way things are at all levels of Western societies, from the military-industrial complex to the personal-existential experience of citizen-consumers. Because this "totalising" view is so strong, Schiller sees neither point nor possibility in attempting to isolate and investigate, for example, the consumerist attitudes or the political values that exposure to particular media texts are said to promote. The evidence, as he sees it, is in the inexorable and undeniable spread of capitalism. . . .

Schiller is not idiosyncratic in this. Much of the output of an equally prolific writer on media imperialism, Armand Mattelart (some of whose work we will examine in the following section) has a similar focus on media institutions and multinational corporate strategies.[14] Nor is this general approach without its intellectual-strategic justification. Golding and Murdock, for instance, state that: "Cultural dependency is itself, however, an aspect of a more fundamental system of economic domination, and only *comprehensible* as such."[15] There is a strong sense in many of the media critics of the *priority* of a political-economic analysis in both analytical and political terms. A good example of this strategic sense is found in an a article by Rohan Samarajiwa documenting the control exercised by the Western transnational news agencies over the global news market. Samarajiwa's paper is not theoretically "totalising" in the manner of Schiller. It is a careful and informative discussion, which demonstrates how the sheer economics of the global news market acts as a barrier against the entry of agencies from the Third World. This sort of analysis is clearly most important in understanding the structural underpinnings of the silencing of Third World voices. But what is significant for us is the justification Samarajiwa offers for his analysis:

> This approach does not imply that news is nothing more than a commodity or that it should always be treated as a commodity. *The Third World interest in news derives precisely from its political and cultural significance. . . .* However the political and cultural objectives can be achieved, and the present order challenged, only by the adoption of realistic strategies that take into account the strengths and weaknesses of the present structure. A politico-economic analysis of the world market in news is an indispensable step in the formulation of such strategies.[16]

There are clear differences between a careful empirical analysis like Samarajiwa's and the more polemical heaping up of instances of domination in Schiller's work. But they share a sense of the priority of what they are doing. Reading the mass of research generated by the media analysts, there is a definite sense of the conceptual problems of the "moment of the cultural" being forever deferred. As Michael Tracey has put it:

> Those who favour the idea of cultural dominance through television have tended to study company reports, rather than the realities of individual lives; to describe the flow of communication in the abstract, rather than the cultural meaning of those flows.[17]

There are good reasons—particularly for Marxists—to try to clarify the material context of domination. But the question remains whether this sort of analysis will ever grasp the specificity of cultural domination.

Fejes clearly thinks it won't. For him there are questions of "cultural impact" to be addressed at the level of individual consumers. Part of his criticism of theorists like Schiller is that their broad sweep involves the unexamined *assumption* of the manipulative effects of media products:

> Generally, a perception of the cultural consequences of the control of various media products is based on a view of the mass media as primarily manipulative agents capable of having direct, unmediated effects on the audience's behaviour and world view.[18]

Schiller's totalising approach tends to assume that capitalism *is* culture; that the "effects" of the spread of the system are evident in the immersion of individuals within it. For Fejes, there is another stage in the analysis to be undertaken. This concerns the difficult question of *how* people experience the culture of capitalism. Perhaps it is not so powerfully manipulative—or its effects are experienced differently by different individuals? Perhaps the export of consumerist values and the ethics of the market-place are mediated by other factors as they cross cultural boundaries? Religion might be an obvious example of such a mediating influence. Such considerations suggest that Schiller's approach is too broad, too shallow, and perhaps too pessimistic.

The question remains, then, of how to get closer to the cultural implications of the political-economic analysis of media imperialism. Fejes suggests that we pursue media products into the realm of their reception by audiences. We need to examine the way in which media texts are *interpreted* and how these interpretations may be mediated in different cultural contexts. Is this a fruitful area of investigation and will it give us an adequate sense of "the cultural"?

Reading Donald Duck: The Ideology-Critique of the "Imperialist Text"

Contrasting with the broad sweep of Schiller's work are analyses that focus on particular media texts and aim to disclose their imperialist nature. These analyses are not nearly so numerous as the institutional analyses but they have a celebrated exemplar in a study by Ariel Dorfman and Armand Mattelart: *How To Read Donald Duck: Imperialist Ideology in the Disney Comic*.[19]

As the title suggests, Dorfman and Mattelart aim to demonstrate the imperialist nature of the values "concealed" behind the innocent, wholesome facade of the world of Walt Disney. The Disney comic is taken to be a powerful ideological tool of American imperialism, precisely because it presents itself as harmless fun for consumption by children. What Dorfman and Mattelart offer is an "oppositional reading" of Disney, which penetrates this veneer of innocence to reveal the ideological assumptions that inform the stories and that can, arguably, naturalise and normalise the social relations of Western capitalism. As Martin Barker summarises Dorfman and Mattelart's argument: "American capitalism has to persuade the people it dominates that the 'American way of life' is what they want. American superiority is natural and in everyone's best interest."[20]

How To Read Donald Duck was written in Chile in 1971 during the brief flowering of revolutionary socialism of Salvadore Allende's Popular Unity government and is closely identified with the revolutionary politics of this period. After the military coup of 1973 which, with the connivance of the United States, brought the junta led by General Pinochet to power, the book was publicly burned and its authors forced into exile. It was subsequently widely translated—the English translation being, for a time, banned in the United States—and has become somewhat of a classic of recent anti-imperialist cultural critique. John Berger, reviewing the English translation for *New Society* wrote: "It has become a handbook of de-colonization. It examines the meaning of Walt Disney comics: in doing this one thing precisely and profoundly, it illuminates a global situation."[21]

The Disney comics, which have been widely distributed in the Third World since the 1940s, could certainly be seen as potential "carriers" of American capitalist cultural values. In this sense, Berger is right to say that Dorfman and Mattelart's analysis "illuminates a global situation" in which media texts of Western origin are massively present in other cultures. But the key question is, does this presence represent cultural imperialism? Clearly the sheer presence *alone* does not. A text does not become culturally significant until it is read. Until it is read it has the same status as imported blank paper: a material and economic significance, but not a directly *cultural* significance. At this level of analysis, then, reading the imperialist text becomes the crucial issue in judging cultural imperialism. Thus, following Fejes's call for attention to the "cultural impact" of media texts, we need to ask how textual analyses—readings—like Dorfman and Mattelart's stand as evidence of cultural imperialism.

How to Read Donald Duck is a rather difficult book to assess. It is not a careful academic study, but an openly polemical work with a self-consciously political aim. Its analysis is not crude, but it is, as David Kunzle has said, "enraged, satirical and politically impassioned."[22] It is as much a *refusal* of American consumer-capitalist values as it is an analysis of them and their ideological effects on Chilean society. It also tends to conflate "America" with capitalism itself as "the class enemy." Because of these features, which arise from the particular historical context of the book's production, it is rather unfair to treat it as a coherent argument about the workings of cultural imperialism. But what it does contain is an implicit model of these workings which relies on the central notion of the *power of ideology* in the "imperialist text." There are two basic theoretical moves in the book: the identification of imperialist ideology, and the theorisation of its effect.

The first move receives by far the most attention. Dorfman and Mattelart reveal a catalogue of ideological themes in the comics: an obsession with money and a "compulsive consumerism;" the constant reference to "exotic" (that is, Third World) lands as the source of wealth "there for the taking" by adventurers from the West; the depiction of Third World nations in terms of racial and cultural stereotypes (and in particular the "infantilisation" of the peoples of these countries); the presentation of capitalist class relations as natural, unchangeable and morally justified; direct anti-communist and anti-revolutionary propaganda; the representation of women in stereotypically subordinate terms, and so on.

In many cases their interpretations are plausible and, to the "politicised" reader, often compelling. But in the very nature of interpretation there is always room for disagreement. The book is, of course, conceived as a disagreement with the self-representation of the Disney comics. But Dorfman and Mattelart's readings would also, no doubt, diverge from the "naive" readings of most children and, probably, a majority of adult readers. There is certainly evidence that other critics of the Disney comics see things differently . . .

What is finally at stake is not the literary-critical merits of Dorfman and Mattelart's interpretations, nor indeed the correctness of their socioeconomic analysis, but the crucial question of how ordinary readers read the comics: that is, the questions of if and how the text has its ideological effects.

Unless they can establish a convincing account of the influence the ideology they detect has on ordinary readers in Chile, Dorfman and Mattelart's work remains at the level of a politicised reading of the "imperialist text", not an argument about cultural imperialism. They do offer a sort of argument about influence, but it is scarcely a developed one. The most concentrated discussion comes in their final chapter, "Power to Donald Duck?":

> But how can the cultural superstructure of the dominant classes, which represents the interests of the metropolis and is so much the product of contradictions in the devel-

opment of its productive forces, exert such influence and acquire such popularity in the underdeveloped countries? Just why is Disney such a threat?[23]

How, in fact, does the American Dream travel? The first response Dorfman and Mattelart give to their own question is to stress the location of cultural imports like Disney within the wider economic context of dependency: "Our countries are exporters of raw materials and importers of superstructural and cultural goods."[24]

This explains the presence of alien cultural texts, but not yet their effects. They go on:

> To service our "monoproduct" economics and provide urban paraphernalia, we send copper, and they send the machines to extract copper and, of course, Coca Cola. Behind the Coca Cola stands a whole superstructure of expectations and models of behaviour, and with it, a particular kind of present and future society and an interpretation of the past.[25]

So, imported cultural goods—Coke, Disney—somehow "contain" the values of American consumer capitalism and offer an implicit interpretation of the good life. Still, we have yet to see how these cultural goods are supposed to transmit the values they contain and the social vision they "offer". When the explanation comes, it is frankly disappointing:

> The housewife in the slums is incited to buy the latest refrigerator or washing machine; the impoverished industrial worker lives bombarded with the images of the Fiat 125. [in the same way]. . . . Underdeveloped peoples take the comics at second hand, as instruction in the way they are supposed to live and relate to the foreign power centre.[26]

When it comes to the crucial question of ideological effects, Dorfman and Mattelart can only offer an unproblematised notion of the manipulative power of the media text. They simply *assume* that reading American comics, seeing adverts, watching pictures of the affluent *yanqui* lifestyle has a direct pedagogic effect. Their model of effects is thus precisely the one that, as we saw in the previous section, Schiller employs and Fejes criticises. For all that they focus on texts rather than institutions, Dorfman and Mattelart do not significantly advance the argument about cultural imperialism beyond Schiller. Any advance in this approach to cultural imperialism is dependent on an analysis of *the relationship between text and audience*. This is something that, as Boyd-Barrett points out, few critiques of cultural imperialism have addressed:

> The orthodox view of audiences in the West is now one that stresses the social context in which communications are received, and which stresses the individual's capacity for active selection and selective retention. This view does not seem to have carried over sufficiently to Third World contexts. . . . Individual capacity for psychological compartmentalization and rationalization is underestimated to an extraordinary degree. Much more attention needs to be given to the processes by which individuals and groups interpret, translate and transform their experiences of foreign culture to relate to more familiar experiences.[27]

Since Boyd-Barrett wrote this, some work has been done on these problems. In turning to this we shift our focus from Disney to another, more recent, *bête noire* of the critics of cultural imperialism, *Dallas*.

"*Watching* Dallas": *The Imperialist Text and Audience Research*

For many critics, the American TV series *Dallas* had become the byword for cultural imperialism in the 1980s. Ien Ang's study, *Watching Dallas* takes as its central question the tension between the massive international popularity of the Texan soap opera . . . and the reaction of cultural commentators to this "success". . . . Ang detects amongst European cultural critics an "ideology of mass culture" by which she means a generalised hostility towards the imported products of the American mass culture industry, which has fixed on *Dallas* as the focus of its contempt. She quotes Michelle Mattelart:

> It is not for nothing that *Dallas* casts its ubiquitous shadow wherever the future of culture is discussed: it has become the perfect hate symbol, the cultural poverty . . . against which one struggles.[28]

The evident popularity of *Dallas* juxtaposed with its hostile critical reception amongst "professional intellectuals" and the linked charges of cultural imperialism poses for us nicely the problem of the audience in the discourse of media imperialism. For the cultural critics tend to condemn *Dallas*, like Donald, with scant regard to the way in which the audience may read the text. Cultural imperialism is once more seen as an ideological property of the text itself. It is seen as inhering in the images of dazzling skyscrapers, expensive clothes and automobiles, lavish settings, the celebration in the narrative of power and wealth and so on. All this is seen to have an obvious ideological manipulative effect on the viewer. As Lealand has put it:

> There is an assumption that American T.V. imports do have an impact whenever and wherever they are shown, but actual investigation of this seldom occurs. Much of the evidence that is offered is merely anecdotal or circumstantial. Observations of . . . Algerian nomads watching *Dallas* in the heat of the desert are offered as *sufficient* proof.[29]

However, encouraged by developments in British critical media theory,[30] some writers have attempted to probe the audience reception of "imperialist texts" like *Dallas*. Ien Ang's study, although it is not primarily concerned with the issue of media imperialism, is one such.

Ang approaches the *Dallas* audience with the intention of investigating an hypothesis generated from her own experience of watching *Dallas*. She found that her own enjoyment of the show chafed against the awareness she had of its ideological content. Her critical penetration as "an intellectual and a feminist" of this ideology suggested to her that the pleasure she derived from the programme had little connection with, and certainly did not entail, an ideological effect. In reacting to the ideology in the text, she argues, the cultural critics overlook the crucial question in relation to the audience: "For we must accept one thing: *Dallas* is popular because a lot of people somehow *enjoy* watching it."[31]

Ang saw the popularity of the show, which might be read as a sign of its imperialist ideological power, as a complex phenomenon without a single cause, but owing a good deal to the intrinsic pleasure to be derived from its melodramatic narrative structure. The show's ability to connect with "the melodramatic imagination" and the pleasure this provides were, Ang thought, the key to its success, and these had no necessary connection with the power of American culture or the values of consumer capitalism. What the cultural critics overlooked was the capacity of the audience to negotiate the possible contradictions between alien cultural values and the "pleasure of the text".

Ang's study was based on a fairly informal empirical procedure. She placed an advertisement in a Dutch women's magazine asking people to write to her describing what they liked or disliked about *Dallas*. Her correspondents revealed a complex set of reactions, including evidence that some did indeed, like Ang herself, manage to resolve a conflict between their distaste for the ideology of the show and a pleasure in watching it. For example:

> *Dallas.* . . . God, don't talk to me about it. I'm hooked on it! But you wouldn't believe the number of people who say to me, "Oh, I thought you were against Capitalism?" I am, but *Dallas* is just so tremendously exaggerated, it has nothing to do with capitalists any more, it's just sheer artistry to make up such nonsense.[32]

Ang found such a high level of disapproval for the cultural values of *Dallas* in some of her correspondents that she speaks of their views being informed by the "ideology of mass culture" of the cultural critics. These viewers, she argues, have internalised what they perceive as the "correct" attitude towards mass-cultural imports—that of the disapproving professional intellectuals. They thus feel the need to justify their enjoyment of the show by, for example, adopting an ironic stance towards it. Alternatively, she suggests, an opposing "anti-intellectual" ideological discourse of "populism" may allow the *Dallas* fan to refuse the ideology of mass culture as elitist and paternalist, and to insist (in such popular maxims as "there's no accounting for taste") on their right to their pleasure without cultural "guilt".[33]

Ang's analysis of the ideological positioning and struggle around the text of *Dallas* is not without its problems.[34] But her empirical work does at the very least suggest how naive and improbable is the simple notion of an immediate ideological effect arising from exposure to the imperialist text. The complex, reflective and self-conscious reactions of her correspondents suggest that cultural critics who assume this sort of effect massively underestimate the audience's active engagement with the text and the critical sophistication of the ordinary viewer/reader.

The same message comes from most recent studies of audience response. Katz and Liebes, for instance, also looked at reactions to *Dallas*, but in a rather more formal empirical study than Ang's. Their work involved a large-scale cross-cultural study of the impact of *Dallas*, comparing different ethnic groups in Israel with a group of American viewers. Katz and Liebes situate themselves within the growing perspective in media research which sees the audience as active and the process of meaning construction as one of "negotiation" with the text in a particular cultural context. They argue that this perspective:

> raises a question about the apparent ease with which American television programmes cross cultural and linguistic frontiers. Indeed, the phenomenon is so taken for granted that hardly any systematic research has been done to explain the reasons why these programmes are so successful. One wonders how such quintessentially American products are understood at all. The often-heard assertion that this phenomenon is part of the process of cultural imperialism presumes, first, that there is an American message in the content and form; second, that this message is somehow perceived by viewers; and, third, that it is perceived in the same way by viewers in different cultures.[35]

Katz and Liebes, like Ang, are generally dubious about the way in which the media imperialism argument has been presented by its adherents. . . . Their study of *Dallas* thus represents perhaps the most ambitious attempt so far to examine the media imperialism argument empirically from the perspective of audience response. In order to do this, they organised fifty "focus groups" consisting of three couples each to watch an episode of *Dallas*. The idea of watching the programme in groups was essential to one of their guiding premises, that the meanings of TV texts are arrived at via a *social* process of viewing and discursive interpretation. They believe, in common with other recent views,[36] that TV viewing is not essentially an isolated individual practice, but one in which social interaction—"conversation with significant others"—is a vital part of the interpretative and evaluative process. This may be even more significant when the programme in question is the product of an alien culture and, thus, potentially more difficult to "decode".

The groups that Katz and Liebes arranged were all from similar class backgrounds—"lower middle class with high school education or less"—and each group was "ethnically homogenous":

> There were ten groups each of Israeli Arabs, new immigrants to Israel from Russia, first- and second-generation immigrants from Morocco and Kibbutz members. Taking these groups as a microcosm of the worldwide audience of *Dallas*, we are comparing their "readings" of the programme with ten groups of matched Americans in Los Angeles.[37]

The groups followed their viewing of *Dallas* with an hour-long "open structured" discussion and a short individual questionnaire. The discussions were recorded and formed the basic data of the study, what Katz and Liebes refer to as "ethno-semiological data".

The groups were invited to discuss, first, simply what happened in the episode—"the narrative sequence, and the topics, issues and themes with which the programme deals".[38] Even at this basic level Katz and Liebes found examples of divergent readings influenced, they argue, by the cultural background of the groups and reinforced by their interaction. . . .

More importantly, perhaps, Katz and Liebes found that different ethnic groups brought their own values to a judgement of the programme's values. They quote a Moroccan Jew's assessment:

Machluf: You see, I'm a Jew who wears a skullcap and I learned from this series to say, "Happy is our lot, goodly is our fate" that we're Jewish. Everything about JR and his baby, who has maybe four or five fathers, who knows? The mother is Sue Ellen, of course, and the brother of Pam left. Maybe he's the father. . . . I see that they're almost all bastards.[39]

This sort of response, which seems to be not just a rejection of Western decadence, but an actual reinforcement of the audience's own cultural values, extended from issues of interpersonal and sexual morality to the programme's celebration of wealth: "With all that they have money, my life style is higher than theirs." However, here, at the "real foundations", Katz and Liebes found a more typical response to be an agreement on the importance of money:

Miriam: Money will get you anything. That's why people view it. People sit at home and want to see how it looks.
[. . .]
Yosef: Everybody wants to be rich. Whatever he has, he wants more.
Zari: Who doesn't want to be rich? The whole world does.[40]

It scarcely needs saying that responses like these demonstrate no more than agreement with aspects of the perceived message of *Dallas* and cannot be taken as evidence of the programme's ideological effect. All cultures, we must surely assume, will generate their own set of basic attitudes on issues like the relationship between wealth and happiness. *Dallas* represents, perhaps, one very forceful statement of such an attitude, informed by a dominant global culture of capitalism. But it would be absurd to assume that people in any present-day culture do not have developed attitudes to such a central aspect of their lives quite independent of any televisual representations. We clearly cannot assume that simply watching *Dallas* makes people want to be rich! The most we can assume is that agreement here, as with disagreement elsewhere with the programme's message, represents the outcome of people's "negotiations" with the text.

Katz and Liebes are careful not to draw any premature conclusions from this complex data. But they do at least suggest that it supports their belief in the active social process of viewing and demonstrates a high level of sophistication in the discursive interpretations of ordinary people. They also make the interesting suggestion that the social and economic distance between the affluent denizens of the Southfork Range and their spectators around the globe is of less consequence than might be thought: "Unhappiness is the greatest leveller."[41] This thought chimes with Ang's argument that it is the melodramatic nature of the narrative and its appeal to the "tragic structure of feeling", rather than its glimpses of consumer capitalism at its shiny leading edge that scores *Dallas*'s global ratings.

The general message of empirical studies—informal ones like Ang's and more large-scale formal projects like Katz and Liebes's—is that audiences are more active and critical, their responses more complex and reflective, and their cultural values more resistant to manipulation and "invasion" than many critical media theorists have assumed. If we take this empirical work as an adequate response to Fejes's call for investigation of the impact of the "imperialist text" on "the lives and human relations" of audiences, we might conclude that this impact has been seriously overstated in the polemics of writers like Schiller, Dorfman and the Mattelarts. . . .

Media and Culture

It's worth pausing to take stock of the debate over research into media imperialism. Most of the discussion so far has cast doubt on the simple notion that "imperialist media" have a direct manipulative effect on the cultures they gain access to. No one really disputes the dominant presence of Western multinational, and particularly American media in the world:[42] what is doubted is the cultural implications of this presence.

We saw first how much of the research labelled "media imperialism" is conducted at the level of political-economic or institutional analysis and how the specific moment of cultural domination constantly recedes. Cultural domination, though conceived . . . as the object of analysis, constantly tugs back to economic domination.

We then noted how critics of this sort of "macro" approach like Fejes, Tracey and Boyd-Barrett, have called for a demonstration of the cultural effects claimed in terms of the actual impact of media texts on an audience. Analysis of texts themselves, even relatively sophisticated ideological readings like Dorfman and Mattelart's, cannot demonstrate this impact. What is at stake is the more difficult task of judging how audiences *respond* to an "imperialist text". What little work has been done on this tends to suggest that audiences are more active, complex and critically aware in their readings than the theorists of media imperialism have allowed. This belief in the "active audience" is supported by audience research within Western societies on the general issue of the supposed "ideological effect" of media texts: people generally, it seems, are less deceived than critical media theorists have supposed. . . .

The stress that studies like that of Katz and Liebes place on the social context of viewing directs our attention away from the text-audience nexus and towards much broader questions of the location of media forms within a culture. Seen in this way, the media imperialism argument might be shown by (or rather, via) empirical studies to be not so much *wrong* as *wrongly formulated*. Thus the cultural "impact" of the political-economic and institutional dominance that Schiller catalogues may be impossible to grasp in the interrogation of texts and audiences: it may involve a more complex form of cultural "mediation" than the research programmes of media specialists have so far offered. The cultural imperialism of media imperialism may even lie beyond the conceptual range of media studies. . . .

The major implication is that the relationship between media and culture needs careful thought. There is an assumption shared both by proponents and critics of the media imperialism case that the media are somehow at the centre of cultural processes and that issues of cultural domination therefore turn on issues of media domination. . . . There is a sense in which the media are the most obvious target, since the most public. But the danger of pursuing this obviousness is that we may take media issues as the substance of cultural imperialism, when they may be no more than indications of a more deeply structured cultural process. Lodziak warns against what he calls the "media-centredness" of media theory, by which he means the tendency of people working in this area to assume the cultural and ideological processes they study are at the centre of social reality. This narrow perspective he argues, distorts the overall social significance of something like television:

> Television's power is so strongly assumed that, rather than being the object of analysis, it tends to prescribe research practices and theoretical reasoning. . . . Media-centred reasoning is unable either to explain why television has become the dominant leisure activity in a majority of Western societies or to grasp the social significance of this.[43]

Lodziak is in effect challenging media theorists to gain a sense of orientation by performing a sort of "Copernican twist": by removing themselves from the centre of their cosmology. This is also sound advice for us. It is now worth interrogating the centrality generally assigned to the media in culture.

Let us begin with some of the strongest claims advanced by contemporary cultural theorists. These are found in the currently fashionable, though in many ways problematic, theories of "postmodernity" associated with thinkers like Jean Baudrillard, Jean-François Lyotard and Fredric Jameson . . . I want to register . . . the tendency within this sort of cultural theory to claim a virtual identity between "media" and "culture" in contemporary societies. As an example of this we can consider a claim about television made by . . . Arthur Kroker and David Cook:

> TV is, in a very literal sense, the real world, not of modern but of *postmodern* culture, society and economy—of society typified by the dynamic momentum of the spirit of technicisme triumphant and of real popular culture driven onwards by the ecstasy and decay of the obscene spectacle and that [*sic*] everything which escapes the real world of TV, everything which is not indicated as its identity-principle, everything which is not processed through TV as the technical apparatus of relational power *par excellence*, is peripheral to the main tendencies of the contemporary century. In postmodernist culture, it's not TV, as a mirror of society, but just the reverse, *it's society as a mirror of television*.[44]

Behind the hyperbole of this lies a not uncommon perception that contemporary culture is so thoroughly saturated by the mass media that it is impossible to separate out an immediate "real" cultural experience from those we experience through the flat surface of the television screen. Baudrillard, whom Kroker and Cook closely follow here, has been the most extravagant proponent of this idea, claiming that reality itself has given way to a media-produced "hyperreality" in which "the medium and the real are now in a single nebulous state whose truth is undecipherable".[45] In fact in Baudrillard's discourse the very power attributed to them transforms the concept of "the media". They can no longer be seen as the *means*—the forms and institutions—through which communication occurs! they become a sort of *principle* of (post)modern cultural experience which dissolves the notion of meaningful communication. This view connects both with a general mistrust of the possibility of immediate "lived reality" that is pervasive of the discourse of postmodernity, and with a very patronising stance towards the media audience—or as Baudrillard usually has it, "the masses".

Such claims are, of course, very easy to criticise from the perspective of orthodox media research, for writers like Baudrillard and Kroker and Cook simply fail to engage with any sort of empirical evidence or with the hermeneutic issues we have discussed in this chapter.[46] However it is possible to sympathise at least with what such theories are attempting to articulate: a shift in cultural practices that significantly alters the terms in which we can speak about cultural experience. For example, when Baudrillard speaks of the "obscenity" of television images he is trying to grasp a situation in which "the most intimate processes of our life become the virtual feeding ground of the media" (think of the lingering shots of private grief that seem obligatory in the coverage of any disaster), while at the same time "the entire universe comes to unfold arbitrarily on your domestic screen" (think of the vast range of disconnected images it is possible to conjure up by "zapping" across the channels). All this, Baudrillard claims, "explodes the scene formerly preserved by the minimal separation of public and private".[47] "Obscenity" is the state of extreme "visibility" of all phenomena. There is thus a sense in which television may radically alter our sense of cultural "boundaries", like the public and the private, making all experience equally visible but also equally "flat"—robbing us of the differentiations that give events particular significances.

The hyperbolic rhetoric of postmodernist media theory can be seen as an attempt to grasp the *feel* of a culture in which, as Harvey reminds us, "the average American is now reputed to watch television for more than seven hours a day".[48] But the big question remains: *whose* "feel of the culture" is being described? Does the average American actually experience the decomposition of cultural meanings that people like Baudrillard suggest are the concomitant of media practices? Or are we dealing with another example of the sort of gap between the world of the cultural critic and that of the media audience that Ang and others detect?[49]

We can pursue this by turning to a far less extreme, though still strong, argument about media centrality; that offered by Stuart Hall. Hall's analysis of the development of the mass media within Western societies leads him to suggest that:

> Quantitatively and qualitatively, in twentieth-century advanced capitalism, the media have established a decisive and fundamental leadership in the cultural sphere. Simply in terms of economic, technical, social and cultural resources, the mass media command a qualitatively greater slice than all the older, more traditional cultural channels which survive.[50]

This is to argue that the sheer enormous material presence of the mass media has marginalised other, older, means of social communication in modern societies in which people live "increasingly fragmented and sectionally differentiated lives". The mass media thus become the primary way in which people in massified, "anomic", socially fragmented capitalist societies gain a sense of the social "totality" and of their relation to it:

> This is the first of the great cultural functions of the modern media: the provision and the selective construction of *social knowledge*, of social imagery, through which we perceive the "worlds", the "lived realities" of others, and imaginarily reconstruct their lives and ours into some intelligible "world-of-the-whole."[51]

In Hall's view, then, the mass media are central to modern capitalist culture since they are the primary resource for the meaningful organisation and "patterning" of people's experience. In this they are intimately related to the technico-economic and social processes of modern capitalism, since these latter produce both the "bewildering complexity" of social modernity and the technical means for "mediation" of this complexity of experience. The cultural centrality of the media is thus a function of the type of society which engenders it: modern capitalist societies generate social experience in all sorts of modes and at all sorts of levels: "in regions, classes and sub-classes, in cultures and sub-cultures, neighbourhoods and communities, interest groups and associative minorities"[52] and, we may add, in familial, interpersonal and "existential" modes. The media do not supplant this experience (as Kroker and Cook suggest), they provide a way of organising it into a coherent and intelligible "whole"—it is in this sense of "managing" experience that the media has "leadership" in the sphere of culture.

Hall's argument is a strong one because it is cautious in its formulation—it doesn't suggest that the modern media have entirely swamped all forms of communication and cultural practice, merely that they have a unique managerial function. It is also plausible in terms of the routine social practices of people in advanced capitalist societies—for obvious instance, the way in which television viewing has tended to "colonize" most people's leisure time.[53] Yet for all this, there is a danger that the importance of the media may be overstated even here. For all its evidential problems, audience research does suggest that the media cannot have the undisputed managerial function that Hall implies, since media messages are themselves mediated by other modes of cultural experience: this is what is implied by the notion of the "active audience".

The undeniably high profile of the mass media in contemporary cultural practices, set against the evidence that people bring other cultural resources to their dealings with it, suggests that we can view the relationship between media and culture as a subtle *interplay of mediations*. Thus, we may think of the media as the dominant *representational* aspect of modern culture. But the "lived experience" of culture may also include the discursive interaction of families and friends and the material-existential experience of routine life: eating, working, being well or unwell, sexuality, the sense of the passage of time and so on. So the following relationship might suggest itself:

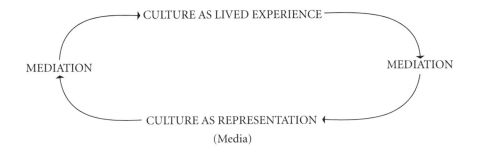

The relationship implied in this is the constant mediation of one aspect of cultural experience by another: what we make of a television programme or a novel or a newspaper article is constantly influenced and shaped by whatever else is going on in our lives. But, equally, our lives are lived as *representations to ourselves* in terms of the representations present in our culture: our biographies are, partly, "intertextual". We can make matters less abstract by giving an illustration of each "moment" in this interplay.

According to Hall's notion of the "managerial" role of the media, the average inhabitant of the Midlands city where I write this organises her or his "worldview" primarily in relation to the social knowledge furnished by television, newspapers, magazines and so on. On this account (which has the *prima facie* support of all the newsagents, video-hire stores, TV rental companies etc. in the city doing a healthy trade) what it is to be living in the late twentieth century in the capitalist West is made coherent by a perpetual flow of media images. Yet it is clear to me that the people I see around the city have a "real" cultural experience in their everyday lives which has a certain priority over any experience provided by the media. This lived experience is very probably closer to people's sense of what their lives are about: it is, indeed, what people think of as "real life" as distinct from the represented life of the media. So this mundane but existentially close level of experience—worrying about families, organising the routines of the day, having a headache, gossiping, daydreaming, sharing a joke—must itself "manage" people's use and perception of media images.

Let us take the example of romantic love. During an average week, television offers a range of versions of what love is all about: from the "realism" of soap operas to the "romance" of old black-and-white movies. These images will be mediated by the "real" experiences of viewers during that week: by their ongoing relations with their families or their lovers, by their knowledge of the problems or triumphs of friends and so on. What people come to judge as the cultural reality of "love" will thus be, in some sort, the public representation which accords best with the personal evidence of lived reality. This is what is behind the common criterion applied to fictional representations: whether they are "true to life" or not. This, then, is the moment of the dominance of lived reality over representation.

We can take the same example of romantic love to illustrate the other moment of dominance: that of representation over lived experience. The experience of "being in love" may seem to be deeply personal and "immediate": something we feel is unique to the person involved. In this sense we may think that *representations* of this experience are always derivative of the "real thing". attempts to grasp and convey something that is essentially "subjective". So when Gustave Flaubert says that Emma Bovary "was in love with" Leon Dupuis he is faced with the problem of representing this deeply personal feeling. This is how he describes the rather obsessive-neurotic nature of Emma's feelings of love:

> she sought solitude that she might revel in his image undisturbed. It marred the pleasure of her daydream to see him in the flesh. The sound of his step set her trembling. But in his presence, her agitation subsided, leaving nothing but an immense astonishment that worked itself out in sadness.[54]

If you respond to this, as I did, with enthusiasm for the psychological insight and the powers of emotional evocation—if this seems to strike some precise chord—you should ask, why? Is it that Flaubert manages to conjure up in language some particular aspects of "the real thing"? Well, Flaubert rather debunks this idea when he tells us that Emma's feelings for Leon owe a lot to the romantic novels she has read:

> They were all about love and lovers, damsels in distress swooning in lonely lodges, postillions slaughtered all along the road, horses ridden to death on every page, gloomy forests, troubles of the heart, vows, sobs, tears, kisses, rowing boats in the moonlight, nightingales in the grove, gentlemen brave as lions and gentle as lambs, too virtuous to be true, invariably well dressed and weeping like fountains.[55]

So this fictional experience of love is actually a product of other (fictional) fictions. And when *we* read Flaubert, doesn't this add to *our* sense of the "reality" of love? We don't need to go into all the complexities of discussing texts within texts to realise that the experience of love may be at least partly a product of representations. The implications are that every romantic novel we read, every soap opera we watch, may add to, shape or mediate our "real" experiences. This is not to say that these experiences are, as a consequence, any less "real" the point is that present "reality" must always be partly a function of our past experiences which generally, in modern cultures, include experiences of media texts.

What this suggests is that the dialectical relationship between "lived experience" and cultural (media) representations is one that cannot easily be analysed into its constitutive parts: of course people rightly discriminate between their own "real life" and the things they see on the television or read about in books. But if we think about it, there must be a constant interchange between, and mediation of, these levels of experience. It is just as implausible to think of real life as absolutely immediate experience entirely separate from cultural representations, as it is to think of television as "the real world" (Kroker and Cook).

Where does this view of the constant mediation of one level of experience by another leave us in situating the role of the media in modern culture? The key to this is, I think, in keeping a firm grasp on the idea of *mediation* itself. Extravagant claims for media power seem to arise where theorists come to see the media as *determining* rather than as mediating cultural experience—that is, as at the centre of things rather than as related to other practices and experiences. First we must bear in mind that all cultures involve interactions between representations and "lived reality"—even those "traditional" cultures which we may think of in distinction from modern mass-mediated ones. Modern societies clearly involve much more routine interaction with media texts than "traditional" societies, and, as Hall suggests, there are likely to be real historical differences between cultures subject to mass media(tion) and those less so. But this does not imply that the media are at the "centre" of modern cultures in the sense that people live their cultural reality entirely through the media. People in modern societies are involved in all sorts of relationships and practices other than watching television, and to do justice to these it is necessary to "decentre" the media from the position that they have gained in some cultural theories.

All this suggests that the most useful way to think about the effects of "imperialist" media on another culture may not be in the narrow terms of media imperialism, where this concentrates exclusively on media institutions and media texts. It will probably be better to think of cultural imperialism as a much broader process of cultural change which involves the media among other factors. If we think of the significance of the spread of Western media into the cultural life of "developing societies" it may be possible to think of this impact as a shift in the balance of forces in the "dialectic" of culture-as-lived-experience and culture-as-representation: of people coming to draw more on media imagery in their constructions of reality. This process, however, proceeds as part of a whole range of other changes in the way in which people experience their lives: living in cities, being dependent on large-scale capitalist industry both for income and for the satisfaction of needs, experiencing their lives as divided into a number of discrete "spheres"—work, consumption, "private life" and so on. These changes in routine lived reality (which, in all sorts of ways, also involve the mediations of media representations) may be described as the impact of capitalist modernity. . . . It is in terms of the spread of capitalist modernity that the idea of cultural imperialism is best understood.

NOTES

From John Tomlinson, "Media Imperialism," in *Cultural Imperialism* (Baltimore: Johns Hopkins University Press, 1991). Reprinted by permission of the Continuum International Publishing Group, Inc.

1. F. Fejes (1981) "Media Imperialism: an Assessment", *Media, Culture and Society*, Vol. 3(3), pp. 281–9 (p. 287).

2. Ibid. See also M. Tracey (1985) "The Poisoned Chalice? International Television and the Idea of Dominance", *Daedalus*, Vol 114(4), pp. 17–56.

3. Ibid.

4. See I. Wallerstein (1974) *The Modern World System*, New York, Academic Press.

5. See John Tomlinson (1991) "The Culture of Capitalism," in *Cultural Imperialism*, Baltimore, Johns Hopkins, pp. 105–8. For discussions of "dependency theory" see A. Webster (1984) *Introduction to the Sociology of Development*, London, Macmillan, and I. Roxborough (1979) *Theories of Underdevelopment*, London, Macmillan.

6. See the discussion of "modernization theory" in Tomlinson (1991) "Modernity, Development and Cultural Fate," in *Cultural Imperialism*, pp. 143–44.

7. H.I. Schiller (1979) "Transnational Media and National Development", in K. Nordenstreng and H.I. Schiller (eds) *National Sovereignty and International Communication*, New Jersey, Ablex, p. 21.

8. Ibid., p. 23.

9. Ibid.

10. One of the idiosyncratic features of Schiller's work is his tendency to suggest something *approaching* a "conspiracy theory" linking multinational industries with US strategic planning. See, for example, H.I. Schiller (1976) *Communication and Cultural Domination*, New York, M.E. Sharpe, pp. 19–23.

11. Schiller (1979), op. cit., p. 30.

12. Ibid., p. 31.

13. See the discussions in Tomlinson, "Culture of Capitalism," pp. 126–31 and "Modernity, Development, and Cultural Fate," pp. 144–46.

14. See, for example, A. Mattelart (1979) *Multinational Corporations and the Control of Culture*, Brighton, Harvester Press. The book by Dorlman and Mattelart that we will discuss in the following section is an exception to this general approach.

15. P. Golding and G. Murdock (1979) "Ideology and the Mass Media: the Question of Determination", in M. Barrett et al. (eds) *Ideology and Cultural Production*, London, Croom Helm, p. 222 (emphasis added). See also P. Golding (1977) "Media Professionalism in the Third World: the Transfer of an Ideology", in J. Curran et al. (eds) *Mass Communication and Society*, London, Arnold.

16. R. Samarajiwa (1984), "Third-World Entry to the World Market in News: Problems and Possible Solutions", *Media, Culture and Society*, Vol. 6(2), pp. 119–36, (pp. 120–1; emphasis added).

17. Tracey, op. cit., p. 45.

18. Fejes, op. cit., p. 287.

19. A. Dorfman and A. Mattelart (1975) *How to Read Donald Duck. Imperialist Ideology in the Disney Comic*, New York, International General Editions. See also A. Dorfman (1985) *The Empire's Old Clothes*, London, Pluto Press, and Mattelart's discussion of the American educational television programme, *Sesame Street*, in Mattelart (1979), op. cit.

20. M. Barker (1989) *Comics: Ideology, Power and the Critics*, Manchester, Manchester University Press, p. 279.

21. J. Berger, quoted in introductory pages to Dorfman and Mattelart, op. cit., p. 3.

22. D. Kunzle (1975) "Introduction to the English Edition", Dorfman and Mattelart, op. cit., p. 11–21 (p. 14).

23. Dorfman and Mattelart, op. cit., p. 97.

24. Ibid.

25. Ibid.

26. Ibid., p. 98.

27. J. O. Boyd-Barrett (1982) "Cultural Dependency and the Mass Media", in M. Gurevitch et al. (eds) *Culture, Society and the Media*, London, Methuen, p. 193.

28. M. Mattelart, quoted in J. Ang (1985) *Watching Dallas: Soap Opera and the Melodramatic Imagination*, London, Methuen, p. 2.

29. G. Lealand quoted in Tracey, op. cit., p. 36.

30. See particularly, D. Morley (1980) *The "Nationwide" Audience: Structure and Decoding*, London, British Film Institute.

31. Ang. op. cit., p. 4.

32. Ibid., p. 96.

33. Ibid., p. 113.

34. See the critique in D. Webster (1988) *Looka Yonder: the Imaginary American of Populist Culture*, London, Routledge/Comedia, p. 202. The main fault Webster Finds is that Ang overstates the "spontaneous" nature of the populism she describes, failing to acknowledge, for instance, the way in which the tabloid press may *organise* a populist discourse around television.

35. E. Katz and T. Liebes (1985) "Mutual Aid in the Decoding of *Dallas*: Preliminary Notes from a Cross-Cultural Study", in P. Drummond and R. Paterson (eds) *Television in Transition: Papers from the First International Television Studies Conference*, London, British Film Institute, p. 187.

36. See, for example, D. Morley (1986) *Family Television: Cultural Power and Domestic Leisure*, London, Comedia, and D. Morley and R. Silverstone (1990) "Domestic Communication—Technologies and Meanings", *Media, Culture and Society*, Vol. 12(1), pp. 31–55.

37. Katz and Liebes, op. cit., p. 188.

38. Ibid., p. 190.

39. Ibid., pp. 193–4.

40. Ibid., p. 194.

41. Ibid., p. 197.

42. But see Tracey's discussion of the complexity of TV distribution around the world, and his point that these flows do not fit neatly into the model of "total domination of international television by the United States"—Tracey, op. cit., p. 23.

43. C. Lodziak (1986) *The Power of Television: A Critical Appraisal*, London, Frances Pinter, pp. 2–3.

44. A. Kroker and D. Cook (1988) *The Postmodern Scene: Excremental Culture and Hyper-Aesthetics*, London, Macmillan Education, p. 268.

45. J. Baudrillard, quoted in D. Kellner (1989) *Jean Baudrillard: From Marxism to Postmodernism and Beyond*, Cambridge, Polity Press, p. 69.

46. See the critique in Kellner, ibid., pp. 73–6.

47. J. Baudrillard (1985) "The Ecstasy of Communication", in H. Foster (ed.) *Postmodern Culture*, London, Pluto Press, p. 130.

48. D. Harvey (1989) *The Condition of Postmodernity: An Enquiry into the Origins of Cultural Change*, Oxford, Basil Blackwell, p. 61.

49. Cf. Kellner's critique of Baudrillard's "theoreticism", Kellner, op. cit., pp. 74–5. See also Lodziak, op. cit., Chapter 4, "The Maligned Audience."

50. S. Hall (1977) "Culture, the Media and the 'Ideological effect,' " in Curran et al., op. cit., p. 341.

51. Ibid., pp. 340–1.

52. Ibid.

53. See H. Sahin and J.P. Robinson (1981) "Beyond the Realm of Necessity! Television and the Colonization of Leisure", *Media, Culture and Society*, Vol. 3(1), pp. 85–95.

54. G. Flaubert (1950) *Madame Bovary*, Harmondsworth, Penguin, p. 120.

55. Ibid., p. 50.

Chapter Seven

Is There Anything Called Global Television Studies?

Shanti Kumar

In recent years, there has been an unprecedented international boom in television studies. The emergence of an international televison culture and the internationalization of television studies have contributed to what John Hartley identifies as the global convergence of TV producers, TV studies, and TV audiences.[1] For Hartley, the tendencies of global convergence in television are more interesting and sustainable than the rhetoric of "internationalization" and "globalization" in everyday journalistic and corporate usage, where such terms are restricted to discussions about capital investment, commercial expansion, and technological integration. Hartley suggests that the "sustainable convergence" impacted by television "is among those global developments that suggest we are on the path towards the re-integration of our species."[2] Hartley optimistically writes,

> Mobility, migration, medical conditions—media—are all causing human consciousness to converge. Travel and television have actually fulfilled their most cliched function—they have literally "broadened the mind" of our dispersed, combative and boundary-loving species. This is a transmodern tendency; it began before modernity and will continue after it. Studying television is a "useful" way of checking out what is happening. Instead of speciating, and instead of pursuing policies of Mutually Assured Destruction to their logical conclusion, humanity has hearkened to a Mandelan, Gorbachevian, Dianan, televisual tune; it looks to *gather* populations not to defeat them. . . . cordialization of the species has reached epidemic proportions. We are all converging on one another like there's no tomorrow.[3]

There is a certain mythology about globalization that we embrace. In a world driven by media, medications, migrations, and mobility, globalization means different things to different people. From television sound bites to learned academic texts, the mythology of globalization reverberates throughout the world and is frequently invoked to signify sweeping changes in every aspect of our lives. Analyzing the many meanings of the term "globalization" in "politics, commerce, industry, scholarship, communication, environmentalism, and popular culture," Marjorie Ferguson identifies seven common myths: "Big Is Better," "More Is Better," "Time and Space Have Disappeared," "Global Cultural Homogeneity," "Saving the Planet Earth," "Democracy for Export via American TV," and the "New World Order."[4] These myths, Ferguson argues, interact with one another individually and collectively. Sometimes they refer to the journey of becoming global. At other times, they focus on globalization as a state of destination. Often these myths represent both the process of becoming and the state of being global. One encounters these mythologies of globalization in many recent bestsellers, ranging from academic works such as Francis Fukuyama's *End of History* and Samuel Huntington's *Clash of Civilizations* to journalistic writings such as Thomas Friedman's *Lexus and the Olive Tree* and Benjamin Barber's *Jihad vs. McWorld.*[5]

To these influential writers and their growing number of admirers who summarily dismiss critiques of globalization, one scarcely need remind that encounters of Western culture with other civilizations have been historically cast in a paradigm that espouses subordination of the non-West by the West and the nonwhite by the white. Mythologies of globalization more often than not focus more on the emergence of a common culture of consumption and style that pretentiously nurtures cultural diversity as a global commodity. As a mythology, globalization "sounds like a relatively value-neutral descriptor of a supranational universe of media interconnectivity" and cultural flows. On closer examination, "it reveals extensive causal assumptions, normative intentions, and value judgments." What are important are "the overtones of historical inevitability embedded in inferences of globalization as an irreversible process or a fait accompli." Worse, globalization is sometimes promoted as a scientific or a social-scientific doctrine that explains, predicts, and justifies an interlocking system of world trade and commodity traffic. It overlooks the empirical realities of irreducible differences in globalization discourse, thus neglecting the creative potential that lies in the dialogue of civilizations.

In the dialogue of civilizations, as Ashis Nandy asks, will an encounter between "a culture with a developed, assertive language of dialogue" and another with a "low-key, muted, softer language of dialogue" be potentially ethnocidal for the latter?[6] In such a situation, practitioners of global television studies must recognize the limitations of its assertive language as a discipline and be willing to engage with other languages of dialogue they encounter around the world—however "low-key, muted, and soft" they may be. The goal for practitioners of global television studies should not be the promotion of their version of discipline in the "others" they encounter. Instead the goal should be to creatively use the civilizational dialogues to move global television studies beyond its disciplinary straitjacket.

In this essay I address the problem of cultural representation in globalization; more specifically, the problematic double bind of global television that at once illuminates and blinds. The emergence of global television studies as a field of inquiry (if not yet a discipline) raises crucial questions about the nature, methodology, and direction of discourse—and maybe even about the wisdom of such an endeavor. These questions and many others urgently need to be addressed before a discipline called "global television studies" takes firm root. Any hurried, overambitious attempts in this direction may cause global television studies to end up in the hegemony of those very forces of globalization it seeks to interrogate. This essay is a tentative attempt to anticipate some of the directions the discipline of global television studies could take, and the problems it may face. Advocating caution, I argue for a radical transformation both in how its practitioners view the flow of images in the ever-changing global media universe, and in their own roles in an increasingly internationalist university system. I posit that media practitioners must be as critical of the theories and methodologies underlying their trade as they are of the television images they view on the screen. Using the example of teaching an introductory course on "global television studies," I conclude by outlining the challenges for media practitioners who recognize how their discipline may simultaneously free and fetter the cultural texts and audiences being represented in the classroom and in the living room. This essay is therefore centrally concerned with questions of incommensurability in the civilizational dialogues that must occur if the discipline of global television studies is to be truly global. Incommensurability, here, refers to the irreducible differences of language one encounters in the discourse of globalization—be it in the realms of politics, economics, technology, culture, and/or everyday life.

The Uses and Abuses of Global Television Studies

Historically, as Mikhail Bakhtin's brilliant work reminds us, languages of the incommensurable have always been marginalized as the voices of the unreasonable, the uncivilized, the uncouth, the unintelligent, or the unintelligible.[7] The historical legacy of perpetual suppression of incommensurablity as the voice of dissent in colonial and postcolonial discourse led Gayatri Spivak to wonder, "Can the subaltern speak?"[8] To which someone once added, "With the permission to narrate."

Large parts of the world may seek comfort in neat images and convenient myths, and large parts of academe may thrive in them, but practitioners of global television studies cannot afford to do so. As practitioners of global television studies, we are (or ought to be) the critics of the critics and the watchdogs of the watchdogs. We must look at the orchestrated power of images and myths in the world as challenges of our own intellectual discipline as well as those of our institutional disciplinarity. Unfortunately, even the best among practitioners of global television studies are not immune to the images and myths surrounding them. Our views are invariably influenced by personal biases, cultural imaginations, linguistic abilities, institutional constraints, nationalist interests, trade ties, historical alliances, and military relations. The conventional norms of teaching, learning, and publishing in academic discourse force us to confine our vocabulary to a laundry list of disciplinary catchphrases that compress complex global issues into convenient categories.

The crucial question is whether we as practitioners of global television studies can successfully address the incommensurability in our own discipline. Answers lie in some apparently more basic questions: How do we define the discipline of global television studies? What—if any—are its theoretical legacies? What—if any—are its methodological implications? In the last decade or so, there have been several introductory books on global television studies, most prominently *Television, Globalization and Cultural Identities*; *Global Television: An Introduction*; *Channels of Resistance: Global Television and Local Empowerment*; *New Patterns in Global Television*; and *Television: An International History*.[9] While introductory texts about global television emerge from a common concern with television in diverse and often international contexts, no two books share even a rudimentary definition of global television studies as a discipline. This returns us to the central problem of defining television studies as a global discipline, where no such definition exists. In most textbooks on global television, the reader is often left only with an overall impression of the discipline created through a sustained engagement with the various sections and chapters. Even in the more self-reflexive introductions to global television studies, such as Chris Barker's culturalist approach and Anthony Smith's internationalist attempts, the underlying—and at times explicit—emphasis is on certain historical precedents, geographic locations, academic traditions, and theoretical legacies that reveals the privileged position they occupy in international communications.

As John Hartley points out, television is "far too big as a textual system, far too complex in all its facets of production, programming and reception, far too varied across time and place." Since television is "too chaotic an object of study to be described detail by detail," Hartley suggests, "many books that introduce the general study of television tend to abandon any attempt to describe a coherent entity or phenomenon." Instead, Hartley finds, the general study of television is offered in one of three ways: (1) as an object of interdisciplinary analysis (where "contributing disciplines have been located in the humanities ... and social sciences"); (2) as intellectually distinct problems (where television is "studied in relation to such issues as power, social change, aesthetics, meaning, economics, marketing, identity, and technology); and (3) incommensurate phenomena (where "there is no 'essential' aspect of television that all studies must attend to").[10] In an attempt to "adopt an analytical framework that recognizes the complexity, diversity and even incoherence" of television as an object of study, Hartley substitutes the murky conceptual question of "what is television studies?" with a more analytically pragmatic question of "What are the uses of television studies?" He writes,

> While it is not possible to imagine "television" as a singular object of study, and not wise to reduce it to a single characteristic, it is possible to take a simple analytical approach by changing the question to one that is fundamentally historical. Not WHAT IS TELEVISION? But: WHAT IS TELEVISION FOR? WHAT ARE THE USES OF TELEVISION? (capitals in the original)[11]

The seemingly facile substitution of questions, Hartley concedes, is not innocent. It is, he contends, "already an allusion or homage to—or plagiarism of—Richard Hoggart's most celebrated publications." Following the lead of *The Uses of Literacy* and "yielding place" to questions about the uses of television, Hartley argues that Hoggart—or as he puts it, Hoggart(ism)—offers a new approach to television studies: "cross-demographic communication."[12] Hartley describes cross-demographic communication as "teaching people from 'they' communities how to operate successfully in institutions from school to 'life,' not of their own making."[13] Cross-demographic communication, he posits, cannot be understood simply in terms of ideological critiques of communication as an imperialist attempt to "take power over some actually or virtually colonized people."[14] Nor can cross-demographic communication be dismissed as populist celebration of the power of people without taking into account the real-life conditions of "both the communicator and the demographic group being addressed."[15] Instead, Hartley argues, cross-demographic communication is *teaching* "done by the likes of Rupert Murdoch as well as Richard Hoggart."[16] Proposing that "the best teacher of cross-demographic communication currently to hand is television," Hartley argues that television "is not just a teacher, but a good one." It is, he argues, not just a teacher of ideology, false consciousness, and bad habits, but a "teacher in the best sense."[17] In short, he concludes, *teaching* about the uses of television is more important than coming up with the "correct theory" of television, though he concedes that "the effort to theorize correctly is teaching."[18] Therefore, for Hartley, critical cross-demographic communication about the uses of television provides "the way to move on," once complicated questions of the theoretical definition of television have been set out.[19]

But is it time to move on? Given the historical inequities in cross-demographic communication—such as the colonizer-colonized relationship in the colonial world, or the East-West relationship in the postcolonial world—I submit that it may not be time to move on yet. Given recent trends in the global convergence of television and television studies—in which Western academics like Richard Hoggart and transnational media barons like Rupert Murdoch are more influential as teachers than those who teach in classrooms around the world—I contend that the problems of theoretical definition remain important, particularly in the non-Western parts of the world where new television cultures are emerging from the residual fissures and scattered hegemonies of imperialist and nationalist media systems. As television increasingly becomes an integral and indispensable part of globalization discourse—in both the classroom and the living room—Western definitions of television and Western theories of television studies are traveling into parts of Asia, Africa, Eastern Europe, and Latin America. At the same time, the rapid globalization of the media and of academia in recent years has induced television producers, audiences, and scholars in Western Europe and North America to become more aware of television industries, audiences, and texts from non-Western cultures. In this context, the three theoretical problems—of disciplinarity, intellectual diversity, and incommensurability—that Hartley identifies in television and television studies have become even more important for critical cross-demographic communication among media audiences, producers, and scholars.

Therefore, even as we focus for the sake of analytical simplicity on pragmatic questions of the use value of television, we must remember to ask a more polemical (and political) question about the exchange value of cross-demographic communication alluded to in the title of a lesser-known two-volume collection by Richard Hoggart, *Speaking to Each Other*.[20] As television producers, audiences, and academics increasingly speak to each other—through teaching, training, and traveling around the world—how will television studies be articulated as a global discipline? In the current geopolitics of international communication—or to use Hartley's preferred term for global convergence, cross-demographic communication—is there any direction that global television studies *ought* to take? These are questions to which it is tempting to prescribe a normative answer. Keeping in mind the folly of prescriptive scholarship, I will limit myself to articulating a position, with a caveat that it is a position arrived at by observation of the travels and travails of television studies in other disciplinary formations that have grappled with the theoretical problems of disciplinarity, diversity, and incommensurability that Hartley identifies in television studies. The disciplinary formation I take as an illustrative example is cultural studies, in which both Hoggart and Hartley have played key roles in the debates about the role of television and television studies in society.

Since the early writings of Richard Hoggart, much work has been done on questions of disciplinarity, intellectual diversity, and incommensurability in cultural studies; John Hartley's *Uses of Television* is one of the more recent texts in that exemplary tradition. In focusing on the disciplinary formation of cultural studies, I seek to acknowledge its central role in the articulation of international and interdisciplinary approaches to television and television studies across a variety of subjects and locations. In doing so, I also emphasize the need for global television studies to engage in a critique of the increasingly internationalist and interdisciplinary ambitions of cultural studies. In the disciplinary travails and interdisciplinary travels of television studies *through* cultural studies—its early blunders, later corrections, current advances, and future potential—lie some profound lessons for anyone who cares to learn from them.

Global Television and Cultural Studies

Some of the most prominent scholars in the field of cultural studies have recently directed their attention toward the hitherto unexplored area of the internationalization of the discipline. In a much-cited essay, "Cultural Studies in/and New Worlds," Lawrence Grossberg refers to the emergence of cultural studies as "something of a global intellectual commodity" and "something of a global fantasy."[21] Though the global fantasy of promoting cultural studies as a valuable commodity may be dangerous and undesirable—"at least in principle"—Grossberg argues that it does not necessarily negate its "use value." In asking how cultural studies should travel, Grossberg moves the debate from questions about the "use value" of cultural studies to the problem of its exchange value in globalization discourse in terms of "the relations between its local speaking positions and the increasingly dense and intense lines connecting these positions."[22] Refusing to impose what Tony Bennett has called "charismatic closure," Grossberg cautions against the dangers of identifying with a particular speaking position—such as the biographical identity of a speaker or his/her geographic location—in the global exchanges of cultural studies. Grossberg writes,

> Too much of the contemporary discussion of cultural studies is trapped in the fruitless opposition between the global and the local. The former tends to see cultural studies as "traveling theory" and consequently often fetishizes and reifies theory. The latter tends to emphasize local exigencies and political demands and often ends up substituting "political necessity" for theoretical work. . . . If the relation between the global and the local is itself an articulated one, with each existing in and constituting the other, cultural studies needs to map the lines connecting them. Only then can it begin to challenge some of these relations and offer new possibilities.[23]

In what is probably the first organized effort in this direction, a conference entitled "Trajectories: Toward an Internationalist Cultural Studies" was held in Taipei, Taiwan, in July 1992. Several anthologies, conference proceedings, international journals, and introductory readers in cultural studies have also attempted to bring together the leading scholars in cultural studies and ask the question, "What is cultural studies?"[24] "Nobody knew," says Stuart Hall, recollecting his early days at the Centre for Contemporary Cultural Studies at Birmingham.[25] Nobody does even today: "It is probably impossible to agree on any essential definition or unique narrative of cultural studies."[26] At its narrowest, it is a classical Marxist analysis of forces of production in a predominantly economic domain; at its broadest, it is a utopia "where the new politics of difference—racial, sexual, cultural, transnational—can combine and be articulated in all their dazzling plurality."[27]

James Carey offers a "jump-start" definition through a simplistic division of the field into two broad camps: "One that draws primarily upon continental sources and regularly invokes names like Derrida, Foucault, and Althusser; and one that draws primarily upon American sources and regularly invokes names like Dewey, James, and Rorty."[28] The first, commonly referred to as "British cultural studies" and popularized through the work of Richard Hoggart, Raymond Williams, and Stuart Hall, is essentially "Marxist" in orientation;[29] the second, popularized through the work of James Carey, has been called "American cultural studies": "idealistically American," placing faith in a liberal democracy in which "neighbors help one another out . . . lend out the lawnmower, come to the funeral, take part in the town meeting—but do not ask one another too many questions about their private lives."[30] To complete the list of "schools" of cultural studies in the international context, add to these two schools the emerging "Australian" school, which Graeme Turner says has been profoundly influenced by British cultural studies:

> In Australia, the cultural studies project has had to find space for itself within existing disciplinary boundaries—working within a strong tradition of left-conservative history, for instance, or within the critical and nationalist movements within literary studies, or the new interest in film and media studies . . . or look for a home within the eclectic and cautiously multidisciplinary field of Australian studies. . . . Australian cultural studies has so far concentrated very closely on local texts, and constitutive discourse while drawing its major theoretical categories and protocols from Europe, particularly from Britain.[31]

The Australian school, whose subject of analysis is a once-colonial culture seeking self-definition in a postcolonial environment, has woven the theoretical insights of what is popularly called postcolonial studies into the scholarship of television and cultural studies. Given the increasing interest in postcolonial scholarship around the world, no discussion about cultural studies (especially in the global context) will be complete without a mention of the subaltern studies collective. The subaltern studies collective, dispersed across North America, Latin America, Africa, Asia, Australia, and Europe, has come up with what Edward Said has described as "massively detailed, and frankly revisionist . . . fiercely theoretical and intellectually insurrectionary" accounts of marginalized subjects in the colonial and postcolonial worlds.[32]

Ranajit Guha writes that the word "subaltern" is used by the subaltern studies group "as a name for the general attribute of subordination in South Asian society whether this is expressed in terms of class, caste, age gender and office or in any other way."[33]

With expanding horizons, diminishing boundaries, and overlapping subject matters, distinctions among the various schools and positions are getting increasingly blurred. Even James Carey, one of the few self-professed followers of the "American" school, owes allegiance to names like Richard Hoggart and Raymond Williams. "American" scholars in cultural studies such as John Fiske have worked in Australia. Australian television studies scholars such as Tony Bennett and Graeme Turner have regularly invoked the writings of European social theorists such as Michel Foucault. Scholars in the "British" cultural studies tradition such as Lawrence Grossberg and Stuart Hall have recently addressed the issue of postcolonial discourse and subaltern identity. Postcolonial scholars such as Ranajit Guha, Homi Bhabha, and Gayatri Spivak have been at the forefront of theoretical debates in Western Marxism, Foucauldian discourse analysis, Lacanian psychoanalysis, Derridean deconstruction, feminism, and postfeminism. As Edward Said pointed out in his pathbreaking work *Orientalism*, historically European scholars in the colonial and the precolonial times were heavily influenced by Asian and African scholarship.[34] Subsequently, as Ashis Nandy demonstrates in *The Intimate Enemy*, many postcolonial scholars in Asia and Africa have an ambivalent love-hate relationship with Europe.[35] Moreover, as Dipesh Chakrabarty in *Provincializing Europe* regretfully concedes, many postcolonial scholars are now more familiar with the intricacies of Euro-American debates in Marxist, neo-Marxist, poststructuralist, feminist, and psychoanalytic theories than with even the most basic tenets of non-Western scholarship available in writings from Asia, Africa, or Latin America.[36] With blurring boundaries, traveling theories, and transnational theorists, it is no longer a fruitful endeavor—if it ever was—to define cultural studies in terms of "nationalist" origins.

Moving on to methodologies, introductory texts in television studies, such as *Channels of Discourse* and *Channels of Discourse Reassembled*, edited by Robert C. Allen, or the various editions of *Television: A Critical View*, edited by Horace Newcomb, provide a laundry list of methodologies commonly used in cultural studies: semiotics, structuralism, narrative theory, ethnography, genre study, ideological analysis, psychoanalysis, feminist criticism, and postmodern criticism. The list is endless, and it is impossible to define global television studies in terms of its methodologies. Using the leeway provided by the "unstable" disciplinary base of cultural studies, most practitioners of television studies have implicitly or explicitly—and sometimes unproblematically—relied on the leading luminaries in the Euro-American canon. In *Rethinking Popular Culture*, Chandra Mukerji and Michael Schudson suggest that the blurring of boundaries among various "schools," "theories," and "methodologies" is a success of the growing interest in cultural studies.[37]

It may be too early to decide whether the blurring of boundaries in cultural studies is a success of the discipline. What must be noted with extreme caution, however, is that the spatial dispersion of Euro-American cultural theory into Australia, Asia, Africa, and Latin America and the blurring of boundaries among the metropolitan centers of international academic discourse cannot be considered a "success" of any particular global significance. At the same time, any "disciplining" of cultural studies to make sense of the incommensurability in its diversity can only be detrimental to its endeavors. What do leading practitioners of cultural studies have to say about that? Stuart Hall, while recognizing the dangers of "disciplining" cultural studies, says, "Although cultural studies as a project is open-ended, it can't be simply pluralist."[38] Similarly, Grossberg, while admitting that "policing the frontiers of cultural studies is a dangerous endeavor," wonders what will be lost if cultural studies "becomes increasingly content-free" as a global discipline.[39]

To interrogate the incommensurability between the ideals of disciplinarity and diversity in cultural studies, Arjun Appadurai invokes two meanings of the term "discipline" that emerge from the dual responsibilities of teaching and research in the modern university. In terms of teaching, the idea of discipline emerges from a liberal arts perspective of diversity, which "aims to cultivate a certain sort of cosmopolitan liberal self among students."[40] In the practice of research, on the other hand, the idea of discipline as the cultivation of a liberal self does not coincide with the ideals of departmental disciplinarity. When doing research, Appadurai argues, discipline refers to "the means and techniques for scrutinizing the world and producing knowledge that is both new and valid."[41] The inherent tension between the goals of teaching and research, Appadurai finds, points to the incommensurability of the two meanings of discipline, namely, disciplinarity and diversity:

> Departmental disciplinarity frequently advances its interests by invoking its special status in the fostering and protection of research. At the same time, when departments argue their interests (in matters of curriculum, certification, hiring, and budgets) against other departments or organized fields, they not only invoke the aura of research, but also imply that discipline in the prime sense of "care, cultivation, and habit" (the hallmark of the liberal arts and the building of cosmopolitan selves) is somehow the extension of the ideal of research. In fact, both conceptually and historically, the reverse is true. The first step towards articulating a more fruitful relationship between disciplinarity and diversity is to recognize the suture that the ideal of research permits between the discourse of departmental disciplinarity and the more general liberal ideal of scholarly discipline.[42]

One way to articulate the link between disciplinarity and diversity, Appadurai suggests, is to "consider the problems and potential of area studies," which, due to their status as "minor disciplines," are representative of diversity "in the current dispensation of the American academy." In using the term "minor disciplines" to describe area studies, Appadurai draws on Felix Guattari's notion of "minor literatures," which he suggests "can be used to explore the historicities that constitute the relationship between majority and minority in disciplines."[43] In historicizing the location of "area studies" thus, Appadurai refers to "the particular organization of funds, centers, pedagogical methods developed in the United States after 1945 to study those areas of the world—Africa, Asia, Latin America, and the Middle East—considered both strategic for United States global interests and civilization."[44] For Appadurai, the tension between minoritarian and majoritarian views of the future of area studies provides crucial insights into the efforts of "scholars, policy makers, and funders to find a new way for American universities to internationalize themselves and participate in the making of a new world order." In this framework, Appadurai argues that cultural studies of "other parts of the world" (i.e., area studies) "contains the potential for a new and critical internationalism" that may help "restore the primacy of the liberal-cosmopolitan ideal of discipline over the later, research-driven ideal of disciplinarity."[45]

Although university administrators, policy makers, and academics in "major" disciplines have been eager to pay attention to area studies in recent efforts to grapple with globalization, most scholars in area studies have always been forced to deal with the global dimensions of their disciplinary formations, which emerged during the heyday of the Cold War. An overview of the various trajectories of globalization in the exchanges between "major disciplines" like comparative philosophy and literature and "minor" disciplines like area studies can be gained by turning toward the East West Center in Hawaii, which has been both a geographical and an intellectual nexus for East-West discourse throughout the twentieth century.

Global Television Studies and East-West Discourse

The East-West Center—or more accurately, the Center for Cultural and Technical Interchange between East and West—was established by the U.S. Congress in 1960 to "promote better relations and understanding between the United States and the nations of Asia and the Pacific through cooperative study, training and research."[46] As part of its mandate, the East-West Center has been involved in the conduct of research and training projects, conferences, and seminars as well as the publication of reports, conference proceedings, books, and journals in diverse disciplines in the humanities and the social sciences.[47]

The earliest East-West conferences held in Hawaii, however, predate the formation of the East-West Center. The first East-West conference was held at the University of Hawaii in 1939.[48] It was an ambitious attempt by Western (and Western-educated Eastern) scholars in comparative philosophy, religion, and area studies to examine the feasibility of constructing a grand unified system of philosophy by neatly compartmentalizing the "East" as the "other half" of the West. Wing-Tsit Chan, who was present at the conference, recalls,

> It was a very small beginning. There were only five of us: Charles A. Moore, the organizer, and Filmore S. C. Northrop from Yale representing the West, George P. Conger of Minnesota representing India, Takakusu Juniro, the eminent Buddhist scholar representing Japan, and I, representing China. We dealt with generalities. We dealt with generalities and superficialities and lumped Brahman, Tao, and Buddhist Thusness together. We hardly went beyond Spinoza in western philosophy and confined Chinese thought largely to the pre-Christian era. We saw the world as two halves, East and West. In his book, which resulted from the conference, Northrop neatly but sharply contrasted the entire East, as using doctrines out of concepts by intuition, to the West, as constructing its doctrines out of concepts by postulation.[49]

In hindsight, with a fifty-year legacy of scholarship and the luxury of rereading history, it may be easy for Chan and his fellow participants at the East-West Center conferences to laugh off their early "utter, albeit well-meant naivete."[50] But in those early decades of East-West conferences, a grand unified theory was an alluring possibility. The second East-West conference in comparative philosophy in 1949 was a more definite and confident effort toward establishing the grand unified system of philosophy.[51] Although the papers presented at the conference revealed a rich diversity of viewpoints, the underlying current of the conference was to seek and promote the commonalities among the various viewpoints. The proceedings of the third, fourth, fifth, sixth, and seventh East-West conferences in comparative philosophy reveal greater critical assessments and self-reflexivity in scholarship, as well as a willingness to accept a diversity of viewpoints within and across disciplinary formations.[52]

However, a disconcerting point in East-West discourse—including the most recent comparative philosophy conference on cross-cultural perspectives in justice and democracy, held at the East-West Center in 1996—have been unable to escape the lure of "comparison," which is necessarily an unequal discourse. Gerald James Larson, analyzing back issues of the journal *Philosophy East-West* and the proceedings of the various East-West conferences, finds five biases that consistently show up in comparative scholarship in East-West discourse:

1. A tendency to favor disciplinary boundaries that separate philosophy from religion, art, literature, law, science, and other cognitive pursuits.
2. A tendency to favor philosophical boundaries of European thought since Descartes for identifying conceptual problems in general.
3. A tendency to favor large holistic boundaries of language, culture, and history.
4. A tendency to treat conceptual boundaries as "entities" or "things" that can be externally compared.
5. A tendency to favor similarities in comparative work while ignoring or glossing over differences.[53]

In East-West discourse, when comparison is the preferred mode of analysis, there is always a danger that the East meets the West in a game that is played by "Western" rules, is framed in "Western" theories, and uses "Western" jargon. This is not to suggest that this is part of an overt hegemonic effort by Western scholars to colonize Eastern scholarship. After all, one must acknowledge that the conferences held by the East-West Center have brought together some of the most insightful scholars, both Western and non-Western, from across a range of disciplines in the humanities and the social sciences.

I focus on the follies of comparison in East-West discourse through the lenses of "major" disciplines like philosophy and minor disciplines like "area studies" only to highlight the dangers and challenges of the comparative approach that confront the emerging discipline of global television studies. Clearly, any attempt to create a grand unified theory of global television studies—as the early experiments at the East-West conferences suggest—is doomed to failure. Moreover, as the experiences of disciplines like comparative philosophy, literature, religion, and area studies demonstrate, even the best-intentioned attempts at comparative studies of globalization from the theoretical and methodological frameworks of four or five dominant perspectives would be detrimental to the enterprise of global television studies, which seeks to understand television industries, programming, and audiences from all parts of the world.

As Raimundo Panikkar would say, the main difficulty in comparative studies of East-West discourse is that one always starts—consciously or unconsciously—from an initial philosophical position, or a stance, influenced by the images and the myths of one's own culture and location.[54] Thus, even in the most careful of hands, a comparative approach to global television and television studies will be flawed, for the nature of discourse in this arena would be dialectical: the subjective "thesis" of the scholar (or media producer or audience member) meets the antithesis of the television culture under observation, resulting in the synthesis of what Hartley describes as cross-demographic communication among television audiences, producers and scholars. But as long as one enters cross-demographic communication with a guiding "thesis" (influenced by one's own cultural location), the emerging "synthesis" will necessarily be dependent. Moreover, as comparative studies in East-West discourse have demonstrated, the "antithesis" will always be described, inscribed, and/or judged in terms of the theories and practices of the guiding "thesis" and through the cultural location of the interpreting scholar, producer, or viewer.

Using Panikkar's argument in a slightly different context, we could argue that the "thesis" and the "antithesis" are theoretical options in global television and television studies, for a cultural synthesis has already occurred in most television cultures.[55] For instance, the publicity blurb on the back cover of Albert Moran's recent book on global television, *Copycat Television*, summarizes the cross-demographic communication taking place through television programming as follows:

> The radio game show *What's My Line?* moves from the NBC Radio Network in the US to BBC Radio and later becomes a popular television program; the British sitcom *Men Behaving Badly* is adapted as a US television series *It's A Man's World* while the Australian soap *The Restless Years* gives rise to *Goede Tijden, Slechte Tijden* in the Netherlands and *Gute Zeiten, Slechte Zeiten* in Germany. It is indeed a copycat world in the international broadcasting industries.[56]

Granted, the synergy-driven industries of global television create a synthetic world of hybrid programming where there are no longer cultural "theses" and "antitheses" guiding the overdetermined contexts of media networks, programming, and audience preferences. Nevertheless, it can be argued that the theoretical question raised about the merits of understanding global convergence of television audiences, producers, and scholars through a comparative approach remains important. The degree of diversity/disciplinarity in the dialectical "syntheses" that a comparative approach to global television and television studies will effect depends largely upon how willing or able practitioners of the discipline are to allow for expression of incommensurability. The more porous the disciplinary framework of global television studies, the greater will be the possibility for diverse expressions of incommensurability.

And that is one of the most daunting of challenges to an emerging discipline like global television studies. Despite an increasing sophistication in scholarship, comparative study remains alluring to the academic enterprise because its dialectical trajectory fuels what Panikkar describes as the "universalization characteristic of western culture."[57] Therefore, Panikkar finds a need to move the academic dialogue away from the dialectical approaches of comparison toward what he calls the dialogical approach of imparison. An imparative approach, as Panikkar defines it, engages in the East-West dialogue with "an open philosophical attitude ready to learn from whatever philosophical corner of the world" without making a value judgment about one or the other from an "objective, neutral, or transcendent vantage point."[58] The significance of the shift from comparison to imparison—that is to say the move from a dialectical to a dialogical discourse—is evident for television studies as a global discipline: all television practitioners—be they television audiences, producers, or academics—engaged in East-West discourse open themselves up to a dialogue with others, and in the process undergo changes. Thus the goal of dialogical studies of television is not to *teach* but to *learn*, not to rescue the "other" but to understand the "self" through the incommensurability of irreducible differences one encounters in the dialogue. Incommensurability, then, is not merely in the theoretical domain of one's discipline, but in the everyday encounters of civilizational dialogues: religious, political, economic, philosophical, cultural, and academic.

In terms of a dialogical approach, the questions of disciplinarity, diversity, and incommensurability can be stated as follows: how can a discipline such as global television studies, whose disciplinary power/knowledge enforces certain truth-claims over the nature of reality and media representations, not only recognize the existence of other disciplines and their disciplinary versions of "truth" but also legitimize their claims in its own discourse? As Panikkar puts it, "If truth is one, how can there be a plurality of philosophies, each of them claiming ultimate truths?"[59]

The solution to the problematic of incommensurability is dialogical in that it does not assume any hermeneutical circle of discourse (such as "thesis" and "antithesis"). It does not prescribe a dialectical encounter wherein the rules of discourse are established even before the dialogue occurs. The hermeneutical circle of discourse is created and constantly modified in dialogical encounter. The dialogical encounter brings "one culture, language, philosophy into another culture, language, or religion, making it understandable." The dialogical encounter is thus a rigorously self-critical process that demands an ability to "plunge into a participatory process," the outcome of which is impossible to predict. As Panikkar says, only those who have "existentially crossed the borders of at least two cultures and are at home in either" can hope to succeed in a dialogical encounter.[60]

Although necessary, the existential border crossing that Panikkar advocates may not be a sufficient condition for success in a dialogical encounter. What the brief history of East-West discourse in area studies and comparative studies reveals is that international ventures of border crossing, such as the ones held at the East-West Center, have not always circumvented the dialectical logic of comparison. Rather, as the interdisciplinary border crossings in a variety of disciplines—ranging from comparative philosophy to literature to cultural studies—have shown us, the use of "interdisciplinarity" from within a particular "discipline" may paradoxically aid its undisciplined growth in the classroom and in the world around us.

The incommensurability of disciplinarity and diversity demonstrates that no easy answers exist to most questions raised about the philosophical, theoretical, method-ological, and cultural contexts of the discipline of global television studies. The caution with which leading practitioners of television studies practice their discipline—in terms of its two meanings—becomes more of an exception than a rule in less careful hands. Thus what has been the strength of the discipline of television studies in the American or the British context may become its major weakness in the global context. While any form of theoretical or methodological closure applied to preserve the disciplinarity of the discipline could be detrimental, an undisciplined global consumption of diversity in television studies will only lead to a categorical imperialism of what Jacques Derrida refers to as "Hegelian didactism"—the dialectical master-student relationship in the modern university and in modernity at large.

Therefore, the question one needs to address when dealing with the theoretical challenges of disciplinarity, diversity, and incommensurability in global television studies can be stated as follows: how can the discipline be used to provide others a voice in one's own discourse in a world that *appears* to accommodate diversity, yet is unable and/or unwilling to accommodate its own incommensurability? The chal-lenge is enormous, the demands of the discipline punishing. My critique of the problematic of global convergence in television and television studies—which Hart-ley identifies as teaching in cross-demographic communication—emerges from my understanding of how a particular kind of discipline essentially shapes one's self and informs representations of others in one's own discourse.

Teaching/Learning Global Television Studies

The journal *College Literature* once devoted an entire issue to the question of teaching in the classroom.[61] In the introductory essay, Cary Nelson argued that the traditional boundaries of disciplines, theories, and methodologies rigidly policed until the early 1970s are threatened today by discourses such as feminism, Marxism, structuralism, poststructuralism, postcolonialism, and so on. The increasing alliance between so-cially engaged projects of cultural recovery and academics has opened possibilities to recover the political edge of academic discourse.[62] According to Nelson, the primary question facing academics is whether to acknowledge the historicity and politics of academic discourse and work openly with them in the classroom, or to suppress them in favor of "a more neutral, decontextualized liberal notion" of academics as providing a series of intellectual options.[63] Favoring a more open approach, Nelson points out that if we agree that "apparently essentialist tendencies can have multiple and different consequences in different contexts," then it is "particularly misguided to continue the tradition of seeking a single, essential identity for critical practices."[64]

For Nelson, among the contexts where multiple consequences are possible is the classroom, and among the audiences for whom critical texts can have varied mean-ings are undergraduate students, who constitute "audiences representing different subcultures, different majority and minority groups, different academic disciplines."[65] Nelson argues that to teach by focusing on the kinds of cultural work texts can do to and for different student audiences is, of necessity, to foreground the politics of cultural texts. "But I would argue," writes Nelson, "that the only powerful reasons for teaching theory now are political reasons."[66]

Although Nelson's arguments are mainly in the context of literary and cultural studies, the problematic he outlines is relevant for most other disciplines, including television studies. However, as Nelson observes, the general historical conjuncture outlined above "is not replicated in the same way in every local department" even within literary and cultural studies:

> [G]raduate students interested in theory are likely to take theory courses in several different departments and likely as well to encounter a good deal of disciplinary critique in jointly taught courses and multidisciplinary colloquia. The undergraduate experience . . . [on the other hand] is quite different, since a large percentage of undergraduate courses is taught by faculty members antagonistic to theory. Many undergraduates thus never have any contact with recent theory, and those who do encounter the politics of the discipline rather directly. Undergraduates who become interested in feminism, for example, are guaranteed punishment for that interest if they try to pursue it in a variety of other courses. Undergraduates will even sometimes be prohibited from writing about women and minority writers because instructors consider these insufficiently important subjects for term papers.[67]

Needless to say, this complicates matters further for teachers who rarely have the luxury of embarking on multidisciplinary graduate seminars, and must make a living by teaching freshmen introductory classes twice or thrice a week, each semester. As David Kaufer and Gary Waller put it,

> It's easy enough for department heads or full professors bought out of their teaching by prestigious grants, to speculate on self-indulgent play, dehierarchizing hierarchies, finding the tracks along which meanings may (or may not) be possible; but what of those of us who must teach the 8:30 A.M. freshman . . . class?[68]

Disagreeing with Kaufer and Waller, Kevin LaGrandeur favors interrogations of the master-student didactic in the freshman classroom. For LaGrandeur, deconstruction offers teachers dialogical strategies of teaching/learning that, "instead of appearing as seamless deliveries of knowledge to our students, may show the seamy underside of the pursuit of truth, the difficulty of its construction."[69] For LaGrandeur, the openness or undecidability of teaching/learning deconstruction provides a way of subverting what Roland Barthes called the potential tyranny of pedagogical speech.[70] According to LaGrandeur, at the heart of a deconstructive classroom is the dialogical experience of incommensurability by both the teacher and the learner:

> a moment or a series of moments in a text or con-text which for both teacher and student leads to an impasse, or "aporia." As Miller describes this phenomenon, it is the point at which a text (which for our purpose we have defined as the result of any play of language—including classroom dialogue—that tends toward the inscription of meaning) no longer quite makes rational sense. . . . Sooner or later there is an encounter with an "aporia" or impasse. The bottom drops out, or there is an "abyssing," an insight one can almost grasp or recognize as part of the familiar landscape of the mind, but not quite, as though the mental eye could not quite bring the material into lucid focus.[71]

Such dialogical encounters with uncanniness and disciplinary incommensurability in the classroom enable teachers/students "to see not only the end results of *our* investigations into knowledge—that is, the 'facts' and 'readings' we present to them—but to see and participate in the struggle for knowledge."[72] How might such a classroom operate, in practical terms? It may be instructive to consider what Derrida has to say on the question of deconstruction as teaching/learning. In a "lecture" delivered at St. Louis College, Brussels, in 1979, titled "le titleer" (Title [to be specified]), Derrida began by spelling out the letters "t-i-t-l-e-e-r" instead of pronouncing it, and continued: "Were I to venture stopping here, to pronounce this, the t-i-t-l-e-e-r, had I audacity enough to be satisfied with it, or be convinced to leave you with what I have just uttered, no doubt you still could not tell how to take it." Yet he did not stop here; he would not stop, he told his audience, with spelling out the title because he had entered a contract with the university system to appear on a specified date and to deliver a lecture. Derrida found it his binding duty to "respect the fundamental contract." Yet, by threatening to leave the audience after merely uttering the title, Derrida also attempted to defy and breach the contract. Derrida succeeded in simultaneously honoring and defying the master-student contract by never beginning his lecture, instead remaining on its border by confining his discussion to a theory of titles. He was thus able to show how a lecture could violate the law of the lecture and to provide a rationale for doing so, while remaining firmly obedient to the law (that is, the master-student didactic).[73]

I argue that it is possible to pursue a similar dialogical strategy of teaching/learning deconstruction in an undergraduate course titled "Global Television Studies 101." In the first class meeting, the teacher would begin—à la Derrida—by merely writing out the title of the course and initiating the dialogue by asking the students what, in their view, the title "Global Television Studies" signifies or represents. Possible answers could include CNN, MTV, BBC, Rupert Murdoch, satellite TV, transnational corporations, American programs like *Baywatch* or *The Bold and the Beautiful*, media imperialism, global culture, and so on. Of course there will be some other less expected views (given that it is an introductory undergraduate freshman class, or there may be no views at all—an aporia of a different kind to begin with)!

Without committing to any definite answer, the teacher and the students engage in a dialogue to reach some kind of understanding (if possible) of the signifier "Global Television Studies." The rationale of this strategy is that in each class meeting, the teacher and the students will be forced to confront what the title of the course signifies in terms of the reading material for that class, but at the end of each discussion, recognize the inadequacy of any text to represent the signifier "Global Television Studies." For instance, if students were assigned to read Chris Barker's excellent *Global Television*, the class would bring into discussion points in the text where Barker painstakingly describes the different ways of thinking about global television that caution against universalization—but is forced to resort to several universalizing descriptors in order to illuminate the different meanings of globalization.[74]

Through the semester, as the students recognize the inadequacy of any concept, phenomenon, or theory to comprehensively "represent" "Global Television Studies," they will also recognize that the signifier "Global Television Studies" itself is an inadequate title to represent the complex set of cultural discourses/texts they encounter during each class session. The initial aporia of the first class meeting, after a diversity of dialogical encounters with the discipline of global television studies, thus propels the class into another aporia (of the awareness of its own incommensurability) from which it is both impossible and necessary to escape: impossible because there can be no universal signifier, and necessary because anything that must be represented needs some kind of signifier to generate a dialogue in the global context.

Therefore, I caution against hasty acceptance of slogans that announce the end of disciplinarity. I argue that questions like "What is a discipline?"—or "What is global television studies"—are nonquestions. This is not because I find the issues of "discipline" unworthy of serious attention, but because I recognize their worth in the modern university and find it necessary to remain a faithful disciple of the "discipline" that sustains my own discourse. But then, is the most faithful disciple to be blamed when the "discipline" breaks down only on him who has chosen to remain with it to the limit? As Derrida's subtle insight into disciplinary formations suggests, the paradoxical logic of "discipline" that governs academic disciplines breaks down only on those who actively promote the search for knowledge creation at the limits of disciplinarity in the modern university and in modernity at large. After all, radical "interdisciplinarity" runs against the grain of discipline formation in the modern university and in society. Over the centuries, careful accumulation of knowledge has been achieved in the modern university (and modernity) through assiduous cultivation of disciplinarity. Without the shared knowledge of a particular discipline, it would be impossible for the kind of dialogue essential for any community of coworkers to occur.

My concern, therefore, is not that emerging disciplines like global television studies—or for that matter, more established disciplines like comparative philosophy, literature, or cultural studies—lack "discipline." Rather, my concern is that scholars in global television studies (and other more conventional disciplines alike) may not always be disciplined enough. If we remain truly faithful to our "discipline" to the limits of its own incommensurability, wouldn't "disciplinarity" and "interdisciplinarity" necessarily mean the same thing?

The point is that the discipline of global television studies is at once necessary and impossible: necessary because only global studies of television will reveal the multiplicity of television cultures that is critical for fighting the universalizing tendencies in Western discourse; impossible because any global study of television in the current geopolitics of international communication necessarily means an unequal discourse. Therefore, within the university system practitioners of television studies may need to shed all pretensions of being "interdisciplinary," and engage with its disciplinarity by extending the discipline to its dialogical limits where, paradoxically, it breaks down.

NOTES

1. John Hartley, *Uses of Television* (New York: Routledge, 1999).

2. Ibid., 8.

3. Ibid., 10.

4. Marjorie Ferguson, "The Mythology about Globalization," *European Journal of Communication* 7 (1992): 74.

5. Francis Fukuyama, *The End of History and the Last Man* (New York: Free Press, 1992); Samuel P. Huntington, *The Clash of Civilizations and the Remaking of World Order* (New York: Simon and Schuster, 1996); Thomas L. Friedman, *The Lexus and the Olive Tree* (New York: Farrar, Straus, Giroux, 1999); Benjamin R. Barber, *Jihad vs. McWorld* (New York: Times Books, 1995).

6. Ashis Nandy, *Traditions, Tyranny and Utopias: Essays in the Politics of Awareness* (New Delhi: Oxford University Press, 1987).

7. Mikhail Bakhtin, *Rabelais and his World* (Cambridge: MIT Press, 1968); Mikhail Bakhtin, *The Dialogic Imagination: Four Essays* (Austin: University of Texas Press, 1981).

8. Gayatri Chakravorty Spivak, "Can the Subaltern Speak?" in Cary Nelson and Lawrence Grossberg, eds., *Marxism and the Interpretation of Culture* (Urbana: University of Illinois Press, 1988), 271–313.

9. Chris Barker, *Television, Globalization and Cultural Identities* (Buckingham Open University Press, 1999); Chris Barker, *Global Television: An Introduction* (Oxford: Blackwell, 1997); Tony Dowmunt, ed., *Channels of Resistance: Global Television and Local Empowerment* (London: British Film Institute, 1993); John Sinclair, Elizabeth Jacka, and Stuart Cunningham, eds., *New Patterns in Global Television* (New York: Oxford University Press, 1996); Anthony D. Smith, *Television: An International History* (1995; Oxford: Oxford University Press, 1998).

10. Hartley, *Uses of Television*, 17.

11. Ibid., 25.

12. Richard Hoggart, *The Uses of Literacy: Aspects of Working-Class Life with Special Reference to Publications and Entertainment* (Harmondsworth: Penguin, 1958).

13. Hartley, *Uses of Television*, 31.

14. Ibid.

15. Ibid.

16. Ibid., 32

17. Ibid.

18. Ibid.

19. Ibid., 25.

20. Richard Hoggart, *Speaking to Each Other: Essays*, vol. 1, *About Society*; vol. 2, *About Literature* (London: Chatto and Windus, 1970).

21. Lawrence Grossberg, "Cultural Studies in/and New Worlds," in *Bringing It All Back Home: Essays on Cultural Studies* (Durham: Duke University Press, 1997), 344.

22. Ibid., 343–44.

23. Ibid., 346.

24. See, for instance, Lawrence Grossberg, Cary Nelson and Paula Treichler, eds., *Cultural Studies* (New York: Routledge, 1992); Cary Nelson, and Dilip Gaonkar, eds., *Disciplinarity and Dissent in Cultural Studies* (New York: Routledge, 1996).

25. As quoted in Grossberg, Nelson, and Treichler, *Cultural Studies*, 2.

26. Grossberg, Nelson, and Treichler, introduction to *Cultural Studies*, 3.

27. Lata Mani, "Cultural Theory, Colonial Texts: Reading Eyewitness Accounts of Widow Burning," in Grossberg, Nelson, and Treichler, *Cultural Studies*, 392.

28. James Carey, "Cultural Studies and the Political Correctness Debate," *Journal of Communication Research* 42, no. 2 (1992): 56.

29. "Marxist" as defined by Lawrence Grossberg, "Strategies of Marxist Cultural Interpretation," *Critical Studies in Mass Communication* 1 (1984): 392–421. Grossberg outlines three approaches: Classical, Hermeneutic, and Discursive approaches; and ten positions under these three approaches, which range from classical Marxist "false consciousness" to theories of mediation to postmodernist views; invoking names from Marx and Engels to Althusser, Derrida, and Foucault.

30. Carey, "Cultural Studies and the Political Correctness Debate," 56.

31. Graeme Turner, " 'It Works for Me': British Cultural Studies, Australian Cultural Studies, Australian Film," in Grossberg, Nelson, and Treichler, *Cultural Studies*, 643.

32. Edward Said, foreword to Ranajit Guha and Gayatri Chakravorty Spivak, eds., *Selected Subaltern Studies* (New Delhi: Oxford University Press, 1988), v.

33. Ranajit Guha, preface to Guha and Spivak, *Selected Subaltern Studies*, 35.

34. Edward Said, *Orientalism* (New York: Pantheon, 1978).

35. Ashis Nandy, *The Intimate Enemy: Loss and Recovery of Self under Colonialism* (New Delhi: Oxford University Press, 1983).

36. Dipesh Chakrabarty, *Provincializing Europe: Postcolonial Thought and Historical Difference* (Princeton: Princeton University Press, 2000).

37. Chandra Mukerji and Michael Schudson, eds., *Rethinking Popular Culture: Contemporary Perspectives in Cultural Studies* (Berkeley: University of California Press, 1991).

38. Stuart Hall, "Cultural Studies and Its Theoretical Legacies," in Grossberg, Nelson, and Treichler, *Cultural Studies*, 279.

39. Grossberg, "Cultural Studies in/and New Worlds," 344.

40. Arjun Appadurai, "Diversity and Disciplinarity as Cultural Artifacts," in Nelson and Gaonkar, *Disciplinarity and Dissent in Cultural Studies*, 32.

41. Ibid.

42. Ibid.

43. Ibid.

44. Ibid.

45. Ibid., 33.

46. The center's Web site is www.ewc.hawaii.edu.

47. See, for instance, publications in the East West Conference Series, *Literary Studies East and West* (vol. 1, 1989–vol. 16, 2000) and the proceedings of conferences in comparative philosophy—East and West.

48. See Charles A. Moore, *Philosophy East and West* (Princeton: Princeton University Press, 1944).

49. Wing-Tsit Chan, "Chu Hsi and World Philosophy," in Gerald James Larson and Eliot Deutsch, eds., *Interpreting across Boundaries: New Essays in Comparative Philosophy* (Princeton: Princeton University Press, 1988), 5, 230.

50. Gerald James Larson, "The Age-Old Distinction between the Same and the Other," in Larson and Deutsch, *Interpreting across Boundaries*, 9.

51. See Charles Moore, *Essays in East-West Philosophy* (Honolulu: University of Hawaii Press, 1949).

52. See Charles A. Moore, ed., *Philosophy and Culture East and West: East-West Philosophy in Practical Perspective* (Honolulu: University of Hawaii Press, 1959); Charles A. Moore, ed.,

The Status of the Individual in East and West (Honolulu: University of Hawaii Press, 1968); Eliot Deutsch, ed., *Culture and Modernity: East-West Philosophical Perspectives* (Honolulu: University of Hawaii Press, 1991); and Ron Bontekoe and Marietta Stepaniants, eds., *Justice and Democracy: Cross-Cultural Perspectives* (Honolulu: University of Hawaii Press, 1997).

53. Larson, "Age-Old Distinction between the Same and the Other," 9–16.

54. Raimundo Panikkar, "What Is Comparative Philosophy Comparing?" in Larson and Deutsch, *Interpreting across Boundaries*.

55. Ibid., 131.

56. Albert Moran, *Copycat Television: Globalisation, Program Formats, and Cultural Identity* (Luton, U.K.: University of Luton Press, 1998).

57. Panikkar, "What Is Comparative Philosophy Comparing?" 116.

58. Ibid., 127.

59. Ibid., 129.

60. Ibid., 130.

61. Literary Theory in the Classroom, *College Literature* 18, no. 2 (June 1991), Special Issue.

62. Cary Nelson, "Teaching Theory Today," *College Literature* 18, no. 2 (June 1991): 2.

63. Ibid.

64. Ibid.

65. Ibid., 4.

66. Ibid.

67. Ibid., 3.

68. David Kaufer and Gary Waller, "To Write Is to Read Is to Write, Right?" in G. Douglas Atkins and Michael L. Johnson, eds., *Writing and Reading Differently* (Lawrence: University Press of Kansas, 1985), 66.

69. Kevin LaGrandeur, "Aporia and the Emptied Teacher: Deconstruction and the Unraveling of (Con) 'Texts,' " *College Literature* 18, no. 2 (June 1991): 72–73.

70. Ibid.

71. Ibid., 73.

72. Ibid.

73. This incident is narrated by Gregory L. Ulmer in "Textshop for Post(e)pedagogy," in Atkins and Johnson, *Writing and Reading Differently*, 39–40.

74. Barker, *Global Television*.

Chapter Eight

Reviving "Cultural Imperialism"
International Audiences, Global Capitalism, and the Transnational Elite

Ramaswami Harindranath

"The biggest weapon wielded and actually daily unleashed by imperialism against collective defiance [of the oppressed]," the Kenyan writer Ngugi Wa Thiong'o writes in *Decolonising the Mind*, "is the cultural bomb. . . . Amidst this wasteland that it has created, imperialism presents itself as the cure and demands that the dependant sing hymns of praise with the constant refrain: 'Theft is holy'. Indeed, this refrain sums up the new creed of the neo-colonial bourgeoisie in many 'independent' African countries" (1986: 3). This sentiment accurately captures the stance of critical thinkers in most developing countries who perceive increasing levels of globalization as the spread of capitalist values and forms of production. However, voices from the non-West are rarely recognized within the current fashions of academic writing and publication, a form of willful blindness that contributes to an intellectual form of imperialism and restricts debates to the finer points of theoretical analysis and conceptual accuracy. There is a growing need not only to familiarize oneself with the contributions of theorists and researchers from outside Western academia, but also to acknowledge the lived reality of a majority of the world's population; in other words, to reinstill a political and social consciousness to a debate that appears to have its edge blunted by an array of criticisms—a few productive, others merely adopting the latest academic fad.

The concept of cultural imperialism, which formed the basis of a considerable body of critical work in international communications, has especially since the early 1990s come under sufficiently strong critiques for it to be consigned to a former period in the intellectual history of mass communication studies/cultural studies. What had been a hotly debated issue is currently seen as a once-useful concept devoid of much political value: as Tomlinson declares, "the idea of cultural imperialism has been heavily criticized and, as a result, is far less fashionable a critical position in academic circles in the 1990s than it was during the 1970s and 1980s" (1999: 79–80). This essay is a plea for its reinstatement, perhaps in a novel theoretical garb, which, while acknowledging some of the more insightful critiques leveled against it, nevertheless sees it as a necessary critical tool with which to account for recent developments in global communications, advances in information and communication technology, the internationalization of neoliberal economics, and international audiences. To lose sight of the relationship between, for instance, satellite television—the technology, the reach, the ideologies—and the global spread of particular forms of capitalist production and consumption in the academic hair-splitting ventures of a lot of recent writing about audiences who are seen to inhabit apparently disparate cultural spaces (on the basis, at times, of belonging to different ethnic groups—in itself a difficult conceptual jump), or about the apparent conceptual weaknesses underlying arguments regarding cultural imperialism (Tomlinson 1991) is to be blind to both the political aims and aspirations of cultural studies and critical communication research as well as to the socioeconomic conditions in which the majority of the world's populations live. As Golding and Harris observe, media scholars have been blinkered about the debates and critical interventions being presented in other disciplines such as sociology and politics: "the myopia and insularity to which we allude is not that of parochialism, but of intellectual provincialism" (1996: 4).

This essay attempts to rectify this lack by addressing three "sites" of the debate, beginning with an assessment of one of the main critiques of the cultural imperialism thesis, which comes from audience studies in the form of an "active" audience theory that challenged the easy assumption of a program's ideology being uncritically accepted by an ingenuous audience, a concept supported by empirical research (most famously by Liebes and Katz 1993). The concept of "hybridity" developed in postcolonial theory and cultural studies is particularly relevant to this debate, by both revealing the flaws in the argument about the ideological content of the media and providing a platform from which to begin reconceptualizing the relationships assumed in the debates for and against cultural imperialism. Second, attention will be drawn to the broad socioeconomic context in which globalization currently operates, namely, neoliberalism. The removal of import restrictions, the liberalization of the economy, and the increasing privatization of industry in countries such as India and China have to be considered alongside questions of satellite broadcasting and its ownership and control. The final part of the essay begins the process of reconfiguring the critical emphasis of cultural imperialism by arguing the case for conceiving the relationship between the economic, political, and cultural elite and the nonelite not in terms of geographical space conceived either by way of nation-states or of regions, but in terms of the emergence of a transnational, cosmopolitan elite impervious to national boundaries or nationalist sentiments (as Rupert Murdoch's switching of nationalities demonstrates). This transnational bourgeoisie benefits from the deregulation of national communication policies and economies and from the resulting unarrested flow of global finance and products. It is no longer accurate to think solely in terms of the West suppressing the Rest, but who gets co-opted into this exclusive "club" of the international elite, and how, and who doesn't and what the consequences are.

To begin, we must reconceptualize the cultural imperialism thesis by acknowledging the validity of some of its critics—for instance, Garofalo (1993) and Tomlinson (1991, 1999)—who point out flaws in the assumptions underlying the argument while accepting, to differing degrees, the need for an intellectual intervention into the relationship between international media and the continuing patterns of global inequality. Both point to the assumed connection between economy and culture at the heart of the thesis, the acceptance (among some cultural imperialism theorists) of "authentic" cultures previously uncontaminated by external influences, and the presumption of an uncritical audience. These are relevant issues, highlighting the inadequacies of the conceptualization of cultural imperialism that have limited the value of this concept, as Golding and Harris suggest (1996: 5). Tomlinson devotes the majority of his book to discussions of "four ways to talk about cultural imperialism" (1991: 19), which include conceiving of it as media imperialism, as a discourse of nationality, as the critique of global capitalism, and as the critique of modernity. He concludes by recommending that we regard the growing interrelationship between various parts of the world as globalization, since "it is a far less coherent or culturally directed process" than imperialism:

> The idea of "globalization" suggests interconnection and interdependency of all global areas, which happens in a far less purposeful way.... More importantly, the effects of globalization are to weaken the cultural coherence of *all* individual nation-states, including the economically powerful ones. (1991: 175; emphasis in the original)

Tomlinson's suggestion betrays a fundamental flaw: if imperialism implies a deliberate and "culturally directed" attempt at exploitation of natural resources, labor, and so on, his definition of globalization goes to the other extreme, removing any sense of unequal relations between developing countries and the West. "Interconnection" and "interdependency" suggest a process of equal exchange, an equal partnership, which belies the fundamental inequality in the flow of the media, the flow of capital, and the international division of labor. This inequality is also evident in the other aspect of globalization that Tomlinson mentions: the weakening of the cultural coherence of various countries. While it is relatively simple to admit to the truism of changes occurring as a result of closer "interconnections"—any cultural encounter contributes to changes to both sides—it overlooks the economic dimension that guarantees that these changes occur mostly in one direction. For instance, the effects of the increased flow of immigrants to the West ought to be recognized: "the Other has installed itself within the very heart of the western metropolis.... Through a kind of reverse invasion, the periphery has now infiltrated the colonial core" (Robins 1991: 32). However, to treat this as an instance of merely a cultural *mestizaje*, as Tomlinson does in his celebration of hybridity (1999), means ignoring the conditions of migration, the politics of global ethnic conflict, and the patterns of immigration control—a perfect instance of the exercise of power. Massey makes this point in her idea of the "power geometry" of globalization, whereby "some people are more in charge of it than others; some initiate flows and movement, others don't; some are more on the receiving end of it than others; some are effectively imprisoned by it" (1994: 149).

In other words, one cannot equate the (often literally) cosmetic changes in Western culture brought about by encounters with other cultures (in the form of the presence of diasporic communities and the appropriation, through "ethical trade,"

An Indian family watches a broadcast by British Prime Minister Tony Blair on the BBC. Photograph by Dr. Shobha Das.

of "authentic" products from Asia and Africa) on the one hand and, on the other, the fundamental modifications to the material conditions and even the existence of non-Western cultures as a consequence of direct and indirect forms of imperialism. To equate the two is to be blind to the social "lived" realities in the developing world. What this implies in terms of the theorization of the cultural imperialism thesis is that it must encompass both the requirements of theoretical niceties demanded by its critics *and* the empirical investigations whose conclusions have challenged the more simplistic dimensions of the project.

Cross-Cultural Audiences and "Hybridity"

As Roach (1997) notes, the major challenge to the argument about cultural imperialism was posed by the concept of the active audience, who—rather than being seen as passively accepting the ideological content of media representations—were conceived as being able to interact "actively" with the program and even resist its ideological advances. This "populist" conception of the audience (Seaman 1992), along with Fiske's (1987) concept of polysemy, posed a more or less direct threat to the political economy approach with its emphasis on the relationship between the economy of media ownership and the ideological power of the media. Fiske (1987) even goes to the extent of arguing that the diversity of audience interpretations of programs such as *Dallas* was itself a contribution to the maintenance of healthy cultural diversity.

To remind ourselves of how the power of the media was theorized by international communication researchers, we recall Schiller's attempt to link multinational media organizations with capitalist domination. For him, the ideological content of the media consisted of presentations of a capitalistic way of life: "It is what has come to be recognized, with apologies to the Chinese, as the capitalist road to development. In this process, the media . . . are the means that entice and instruct their audiences along this path while at the same time concealing the deeper reality and the long term consequences that the course produces" (1979: 31). Schiller's emphasis was thus on patterns of media ownership and on the media as carriers of capitalist ideology— in this framework of research, audiences were "read into" the media content. Given this context, it is not difficult to see the effect of the transfer of "power" from the text to the audience facilitated by the active audience theory and the qualitative reception research it engendered. The widespread acceptance of the inherent "resistance" of audiences to media ideology, supported by empirical evidence allegedly demonstrating the diversity of culturally differentiated audience groups, has contributed to the creation of an intellectual camp opposing the apparent excesses of political economy, so much so that the debate has reached a stalemate. Before we examine one of these empirical studies, it is worth noting Fiske's position vis-à-vis the economy-culture nexus that is at the core of the cultural imperialism thesis:

> Hollywood, and to a lesser extent, Europe, may dominate international flow of both news and entertainment programming, yet there is little evidence of a global surge of popularity for the Western nations and their values. The domination in the economic domain may not necessarily produce the equivalent domination in the cultural field. (1987: 320)

The similarities between Fiske's comment and Tomlinson's flawed conceptualizations discussed earlier are striking. In his uncritical celebration of the variety of audience interpretations as indicative of a semiotic democracy devoid of hegemonic intent or content, Fiske is able to make a sweeping generalization of the lack of evidence of "a global surge of popularity for Western values." Apart from the rhetorical excesses of that statement and its ill-defined call for "evidence," its deliberate separation of the cultural and economic spheres is undergirded by a sentiment similar to that of Tomlinson's view that the cultural imperialism argument "makes a leap of inference from the simple presence of cultural goods to the attribution of deep cultural or ideological effects. . . . Culture simply does not transfer in a unilinear way" (1999: 83–84). This argument about the localized appropriation or "indigenization" of cultural goods is predicated on the conclusions of empirical studies of international audiences.

As mentioned earlier, one of the studies often cited as demonstrating the differences in interpretation among culturally diverse audiences is Liebes and Katz's (1993) comparison of the interpretations of episodes of *Dallas* by audiences from different ethnic groups in Israel and the United States This study involved families from different ethnic groups (Israeli kibbutzim, Arabs, Moroccan Jews, Russian Jews, and

Americans) watching an episode of *Dallas* and being interviewed extensively about their interpretations of that episode. In the study's conclusion the researchers linked these interpretations and their underlying ethical stands directly to ethnic belonging. For instance, the discussions of the Arab and the Moroccan groups were considered to be inspired by their "traditional" culture, as opposed to those of the "modern" Israeli and American groups. I have presented the politically problematic aspects of their conclusions elsewhere, but in attempting to distinguish the differences between the interpretations of "traditional" communities such as the Israeli Arabs and the Moroccans from those of the more "modern" groups such as the Russians, the Israelis, and the Americans, Liebes and Katz sought to demonstrate the apparent weaknesses inherent in the argument about the ideological influences of Western, particularly American, television programs on international audiences. Their conclusions supported the notion of socially situated audiences actively interpreting such media content in different ways—in this case not so much influenced as determined by a reductionist conceptualization of ethno-culture.

Apart from the easy correlation between ethnicity and interpretive (and by implication other kinds of) behavior, the other problem with Liebes and Katz's study is their inadequate theorization of the links between culture and interpretation: how do sociocultural contexts affect interpretation of texts? This is not the place to provide a theoretical bridge to fill this gap; what is pertinent in the present context, however, are the findings of my study comparing the interpretations of documentaries by audiences in India and Britain (Harindranath 1996). This project involved audience groups from different educational and economic backgrounds watching documentaries made by Indian and European filmmakers. Their discussions of these documentaries were subsequently analyzed in terms of their acceptance or rejection of the documentary genre's claim that it depicts "truth" and their use of critical frames for interpreting the films. The implicit assumption at the start of this project was that national cultures would perform a normative function similar to Liebes and Katz's categories of ethnicity. However, the "Indians" (as an ethnic group) did not conform to one type of interpretation. The unexpected results pointed in another direction that required a different cartography, a level of theoretical commitment that allowed for the presence of different interpretive frameworks among respondents who apparently shared other social beliefs. The surprising finding—given the initial assumptions mentioned earlier—was that the interpretations of the documentaries by some of the Indian respondents were closer to those of the British respondents than to their Indian counterparts. Without providing too much detail, I will note that these differences had to do with the employment of "transparent" or "critical" frameworks of interpretation riding on the acceptance or rejection of the documentary's claims of veridicality as a genre. Also significant was that the most important variable was the level of education among the Indian respondents. Those with university education interpreted the documentaries the way the British respondents did, while those with no higher education read the films employing a more or less completely "transparent" framework that accepted the genre's claims.

This raises two relevant issues. First, we must reappraise the category of culture, in terms of both nationality and ethnicity, each of which betrays a conception of cultural worlds as timeless, unchanging, and homogeneous. If Liebes and Katz can be criticized for reifying ethnicity as a static essentialized category, a similar accusation can be leveled against the reification of national belonging as a marker for cultural distinction. Yet some of the arguments for and against cultural imperialism take such a conceptualization for granted. Tomlinson, for instance, rightly raises questions about the conceptual validity of "this very general way of speaking about cultural imperialism: as the domination of one national culture by another" (1991: 68), and identifies four problematic categories: "the specification of a national culture," "the complex ideological-psychological processes though which a sense of national identity may arise," the tendency to think of cultural imperialism in "predominantly spatial terms," and "the question of how domination is conceived in this discourse" (1991: 69–70). These are relevant points that must be considered in any reconceptualization of cultural imperialism. However, it is surprising that Tomlinson fails to critique similarly Liebes and Katz's use of the category of ethnicity in essentially normative terms. If, as Tomlinson points out, the idea of national culture can be co-opted by the Right and is therefore problematic, the same can surely be attributed to the correlation of ethnicity with culture and the "ideological-psychological processes" of ethnic identity, as well as the direct connection between ethnic and national identities.

Second, my data suggest the presence of differential access to cultural capital, manifest in different interpretive "repertoires" that do not coincide with distinctions based on a conception of "national" cultures. Normative categories premised on notions of cultural purity, in other words, are problematic. Interpretations of televisual texts, be they documentaries or fiction, and by extension other forms of cultural influence, are much more untidy and engendered by diverse resources—cultural, economic, and social. The data generated by my study indicate the importance of university education, which in India is largely Western-oriented, in most cases uses English as the medium of instruction, and contributes to the creation of a cultural and political elite. In my study, the interpretations of university-educated Indians were closer to those of the British audiences and used markedly different interpretive frameworks than those of Indians without university education. I have discussed various aspects of this observation elsewhere (Harindranath 1998), but it is useful to remind ourselves that this is symptomatic of a majority of former colonies in the developing South. What Anderson (1991) refers to as "mental miscegenation" was very much a characteristic of colonial relations as a means of creating an elite among the colonized populations for administrative purposes, as go-betweens. This is recalled in Macaulay's infamous description of the native elite: ethnically inferior, but closer to the colonizer in intellect and cultural taste—in other words, a hybrid who would perform the function of "translating" between the colonizer and the colonized. It is unproductive to conceive cultural imperialism in terms of geographical regions or even nation-states, since, as suggested by my study, cultural capital is not uniform among all Indians, nor (by extension) among all citizens of other developing societies. That there are differences in the interpretive frameworks of different groups has been amply demonstrated by various audience studies in the West, but our concern is with its significance to the notion of cultural imperialism. We must take into account the role of the in-betweens, the hybrid or *comprador* community, who are ethnically non-Western but culturally Western.

The concept of hybridity has played an important critical and theoretical role in postcolonial studies, but tends to be less familiar to communication scholars. Yet this notion, modified to reflect the inegalitarian nature of the cultural, economic, and political aspects of the current global order, is invaluable for the task of beginning to reconceptualize the cultural imperialism thesis. One of the most influential theorists of hybridity, Homi Bhabha (1985, 1994), builds on Fanon's seminal *Black Skin, White Masks* to reconfigure the colonizer-colonized dichotomy in terms of a Lacan-inflected, psychologically complex in-betweenness that transcends the "corporeal malediction" of the colonized, and affects both sides. For Bhabha, colonial discourse —contrary to Said's distinction between the West and the Orient—is marked by ambivalence since its object is both derided and desired in the case of both the colonizer and the colonized. Colonial identity thus lies between them: it is an ambivalent identification containing fear and desire, aggression and narcissism. Bhabha treats the resulting ambivalence with an optimistic twist, suggesting that on the one hand this state of affairs undermined the authority of the colonizer, while on the other hand it contributed to the possibility of anticolonial resistance. For him, resistance is neither a political act of straightforward opposition nor a simple rejection of another culture, but "the effect of an ambivalence produced within the rules of recognition of dominating discourses as they articulate the signs of cultural difference" (1985: 153).

Thus hybridity, seen as a cross-fertilization of cultures, reconceptualizes the relationship between the colonizer and the colonized and stresses the mutuality of the process of cultural interaction. This reconceptualization, evading the notion of external imposition, emphasizes the new formations arising from the inevitable clash of cultures in an imperialist encounter. Postcolonial theory "emphasizes how hybridity and the power it releases may well be seen to be the characteristic feature and contribution of the post-colonial, allowing a means of evading the replication of binary categories of the past and developing new anti-monolithic models of cultural exchange and growth" (Ashcroft et al. 1995: 183).

It is this possibility of overcoming binary oppositions afforded by the concept of hybridity that I want to stress here.

> If the effect of colonial power is seen to be the production of hybridization rather than the noisy command of colonialist authority or the silent repression of native traditions, then an important change of perspective occurs . . . enabl[ing] a form of subversion, founded on the undecidability that turns the discursive conditions of dominance into the grounds of intervention. (Bhabha 1994: 112)

However, I want to add an important caveat. As the first part of this quote suggests, hybridity as a critical notion enables a transcendence of the unproductive and conceptually suspect opposition between the colonizer and the colonized, or for our purposes, between the West and the developing countries. If, on the other hand, following the second part of the quote on the "undecidability" of discursive conditions, we were to utilize Bhabha's notion of resistance to negotiate the differences in audiences' readings of, say, an episode of *Dallas* or a documentary on the environment, interpretative ventures of both Liebes and Katz's "traditional" communities and the Indian respondents without university education in my study can be theorized as inhabiting this ambivalent space. These audiences would therefore be in the cusp of a resistant reading since they are at least partially aware of the rules of the dominant discourses. This position will be quite close to that of Fiske (1987) in that it facilitates the celebration of a plurality of interpretations as itself indicative of a semiotic democracy, yet cannot be understood as revealing the presence of unequal cultural resources.

By changing the emphasis of the constituents of this hybrid relationship, we can construct a more productive framework. Instead of assuming, as Bhabha does, that the ambivalent relationship between the colonized and the colonizer contributes to a lack of closure to colonial representation and thereby to possible resistance, I contend that the various forms of socialization—including education, religion, the bureaucracy, and so on—that created the hybrid also facilitated the co-option of the colonized elite into a position of relative power. The colonized elite were the "mimic men," hybridized in different ways. In terms of identity, of power and status, and of economic and cultural capital, they were superior to the "native," but still inferior to the Westerner: "not white not quite." These elite who benefit from their role as "cultural translators" are those who are, willingly or otherwise, appropriated hegemonically by the colonial power, thus changing the colonial relationship from simple subjugation to a much more complex and insidious form of exploitation.

Global Capitalism and the Transnational Elite

To return to the main theme of our discussion, what this *comprador* class implies is, first, that it is not entirely accurate to think of cultural imperialism as an imposition of Western ideology on an unadulterated non-Western culture. Apart from reifying unproductive forms of essentialism, such a notion also ignores the long history of cross-cultural contact and exchange, of conquest and exploitation. The more recent part of this history is taken up by colonialism, which was predicated on various forms of exploitation and of which, as Said (1993) has shown, cultural imperialism was an important feature. Therefore a more constructive way of conceptualizing contemporary forms of cultural imperialism is to think of it as a continuation of the colonial relationship, in which television and other media have taken over the role of the nineteenth-century novel in the discourse of power. As in the colonial relationship, the contemporary world order is not one of a simple subjugation of the rest by the West, but a more insidious and consequently more effective hegemonic appropriation of certain sections of the developing world. Such a conceptualization reorders the relationship between what Giddens (1991) refers to as " 'out there' and 'in here,' " between the global and the local, in terms of a dialectic instead of merely the global erasing the traces of the local. Cultural imperialism is thus not simply an "out there" phenomenon, occurring only at the level of international communication. It is neither only the ideological content nor the hegemonic potential inherent in global media. It is instead a phenomenon evident in these places *and* in forms of consumption and production: in the relations of contemporary capitalist production in which increasingly mobile capital is able to move from one region to another in search of cheap labor.

Second, the *comprador* class impels a fundamental change in the cultural imperialism thesis by demonstrating the role of the local, indigenous elite spreading capitalist production and consumption. While it is still the case that the international system is split into the center and the periphery, "the center-periphery contrast is in the process of transformation, the former contrast of industrialized nations versus non-industrialized areas giving way to new polarization mechanisms which are based upon financial, technological, cultural and military domination" (Amin 1997: 19). In this changed system, the role of what Appiah refers to as the "comprador intelligentsia" is crucial: "a relatively small, Western-style, Western-trained group of writers and thinkers, who mediate the trade in cultural commodities or world capitalism at the periphery" (1996: 62).

In this context, the apparently "unexpected" data from my study referred to earlier assume a certain significance beyond demonstrating the unreliability of normative categories such as ethnicity or national culture. They indicate as well the unequal distribution of cultural resources, with consequences for the analysis of the media, the public sphere, and citizenship. Moreover, in the university-educated Indian they reveal the presence of Appiah's "comprador intelligentsia," for whom Westernized (particularly English) education is a necessary step toward assuming political, economic, and social power. It is important to emphasize that not all university-educated Indians are in thrall to Western, capitalist values. A critical intelligentsia has always existed, as have other forms of active resistance; as Roach argues, for writers such as Said and Ngugi Wa Thiong'o imperialism as a historical fact and the existence of various forms of resistance to it are two sides of the same coin. In my research on cross-cultural audiences, it is both the adoption of critical frameworks of interpretation by the university-educated Indians and the content of their criticism of the documentaries that set them apart from the other Indian respondents. While the former shows them as possessing certain cultural capital, the latter demonstrates to a certain extent a critical attitude to the rhetorical devices adopted by the films, as well as to their main arguments. This finding suggests the inadequacy of conceiving audiences along purely ethnic lines, as Liebes and Katz (1993) have done.

This apparent paradox replicates Guha's critique of the "universalist assumptions of liberal ideology." He conceptualizes the institutional, modal, and discursive aspects of the exercise of colonial power in India as the interaction of Dominance (D) and Subordination (S):

> While these two terms, in their interaction, give power its substance and form, each of them, it its own turn, is determined and indeed constituted by a pair of interacting elements—D by Coercion and Persuasion, and S by Collaboration and Resistance. . . . But while D and S imply each other logically and the implication applies to all cases where an authority structure can be legitimately defined in those terms, the same is not true of the other dyads. There the terms imply each other contingently. (1997: 21)

In our example, the employment of a particular form of cultural capital acquired from Westernized university education for the critique of documentary texts as discourses of Western ideology is one of the contemporary versions of the paradoxes that Guha characterizes as a "tissue of paradoxes" (1997: 62) comprising the political culture of the colonial era.

On a broader scale, Guha's revisionist historiography provides the initial framework for a radical overhaul of the cultural imperialism thesis. The universalism of Dominance and Subordination and the more contingent aspect of the other constituents of the matrix of power are useful in formulating a thesis that, while recognizing the global spread of capitalist forms of production through neoliberal ideology, acknowledges the contingent nature of the coercion and persuasion toward, collaboration with, and resistance to the implementation of neoliberal policies in various parts of the developing world. It is in this context that cultural imperialism ought to be examined and theorized. Such an analysis, I suggest, will overcome the apparent gap between economy and culture noted by Tomlinson (1991, 1999).

Toward a Reconstituted Thesis of "Cultural Imperialism"

In the context of recent developments in India, for instance, an analysis of the political and cultural implications of cable and satellite broadcasting is inadequate without due consideration of the liberalization of the economy. The "complexity of cultural appropriation" to which Tomlinson (1999: 84) refers must be considered, in other words, not only in terms of possible "indigenization," but also, and more significantly, within the material context of the indigenous collaboration with and resistance to global capitalism. Cultural appropriation is not uniform, as demonstrated in my study comparing reception of documentaries in India. The differences in interpretation indicate that cross-cultural reception ought to be considered in the context of what it could imply regarding the sociocultural and economic conditions of this historical contingency covering developments in India, as well as the nature of the global political and economic order—in other words, globalization. As Salinas and Paldan argued two decades ago, "culture, as both a specific sphere of ideal reflections and a system of meanings attributed to the existing reality, cannot be separated from the basic socioeconomic structure of a given society" (1979: 83).

Let us continue on the specificities of contemporary India and consider two aspects of neoliberal ideology. In emphasizing competition between individuals as the motivating force of the economy, neoliberal theory favors capital, especially the unbridled flow of transnational capital; ignores the conditions of production; and emphasizes the culture of individualism and consumption (Gill and Law 1988: 50-51). For instance, the lowering of import restrictions in India in the early 1990s, which contributed to the free flow of capital and goods into the country, was particularly welcomed by both indigenous and global bourgeoisie. While the latter are interested in the growing middle-class market for goods, the local economic elite celebrates the weakening of state control on the domestic economy. As Ahmad has argued,

> Most national bourgeoisie have achieved a far greater level of capital accumulation [as a result of economic liberalization] and have therefore developed a contradictory attitude towards their nation-state: they wish to more or less bypass the regulatory aspects of this state (through liberalization, marketization, etc.), and yet utilize it both for securing the domestic conditions of production favorable to capital . . . and for facilitating the articulation of domestic and foreign capitals. In other words, the new national bourgeoisie, like imperialist capital itself, wants a weak nation-state in relation to capital and a strong one in relation to labor. (1995: 11)

Given this context of the local elite's contradictory attitude to the nation-state, which implies both national culture and state politics, it is imperative to modify the basic parameters of the cultural imperialism thesis to remove from it the simple supposition of the West's imposition of a particular form of culture on the "pure" peripheral regions, and to accommodate the presence of an economic, political, and cultural elite "hybrid" class who are transnational collaborators with the global capitalist culture. Such transnational capitalist classes "identify with the global capitalist system, reconceptualize their several national interests in terms of the global system, and take on the political project of reconceptualizing the national interests of their co-nationals in terms of the global capitalist system" (Sklair 1991: 134).

The second aspect of neoliberal ideology of interest here is that of the creation of an individualist culture of consumption. Schiller's (1976, 1979) thesis regarding international media as contributing to the dissemination of (if not coercion of the developing world into) a capitalist "way of life"—what Tomlinson dismisses as Schiller's "totalising approach" (1991: 40)—begins to make sense in this context. The challenge for researchers of international communication is to analyze systematically the connections between populations in developing countries as consumers and audiences, taking into account both the economic and media policies of the individual countries and the material and social conditions of consumption and reception. To dismiss contributions from scholars of political economy such as Schiller is to ignore an important aspect of global media and the spread of neoliberalism.

In sum, the cultural imperialism thesis is still valid, but must be revitalized. In order to sharpen its critical edge, scholars must reassess and reconfigure it to the current global environment. Contemporary forms of imperialism retain some of the characteristics of the colonial relationship, chief among them being the presence of the *comprador* class; only now the collusion of the indigenous elite with the global powers is much more pronounced, since their economic and political interests are best served by overt cooperation with the forces of neoliberalism. It is, therefore, inaccurate to conceive of this relationship as simply between the imperial West and the subjugated developing world, either in terms of cultural imperialism or economic exploitation. For while many of the current manifestations of global inequality support such an assertion, it is theoretically unsophisticated and overly simplistic. We must recognize that although the relationship between the West and the rest continues to be fundamentally unequal, characterized by the exploitation of labor, the rise in consumerism, the spread of neoliberal values, and so on, the role played by the hybrid, Westernized "local" elite is crucial to this relationship.

I have attempted to demonstrate the importance of rethinking the idea of cultural imperialism within the context of the economic and political aspects of neoliberalism. As in older forms, contemporary imperialism is not confined to the cultural sphere alone. In order to grasp this scenario in its entirety, researchers ought to consider manifestations of cultural imperialism alongside developments in local forms of economic production, the adoption of neoliberal policies removing restrictions to the movement of global capital, the rise of right-wing politics, and so on—in other words, the economic and political spheres. I support Wallerstein in his denial of "the presumed autonomy of the three spheres of economics, politics, and culture" (1990: 64).

Such a project will not only redress the pronounced lack of scholarly interventions from the developing world in the debate, but also overcome the dissatisfaction Tomlinson displays toward those expressing "the cultural viewpoint of the concerned Westerner confronting a perplexing set of global phenomena" (1991: 107). A reconceptualized cultural imperialism thesis that takes on board the essentially unequal relations that underpin the global capitalist system is vital for a proper investigation of the production and consumption of international communication.

REFERENCES

Ahmad, Aijaz. "The politics of literary postcoloniality." *Race and Class* 36, no. 3, (1995).

Amin, Samir. "Reflections on the international system." In *Beyond Cultural Imperialism*, ed. Peter Golding and Phil Harris. London: Sage, 1997.

Anderson, Benedict. *Imagined Communities: Reflections on the Origin and Spread of Nationalism*. London: Verso, 1991.

Appiah, K. A. "Is the post in postmodernism the post in postcolonialism?" In *Contemporary Postcolonial Theory: A Reader*, ed. P. Mongia. London: Arnold, 1996.

Ashcroft, Bill, et al., eds. Introduction to the section on "Hybridity," *The Post-Colonial Studies Reader*. London: Routledge, 1995.

Bhabha, Homi. *The Location of Culture*. London: Routledge, 1994.

———. "Signs taken for wonders: Questions of ambivalence and authority under a tree outside Delhi, May 1817." *Critical Inquiry* 12, no. 1 (autumn 1985).

Dorfman, Ariel, and Armand Mattelart. *How to Read Donald Duck: Imperialist Ideology in the Disney Comic*. New York: International General Editions, 1975.

Fiske, John. *Television Culture*. New York: Methuen, 1987.

Garofalo, G. "Whose world, what beat: The transnational music industry, identity, and cultural imperialism." *World of Music* 35, no. 2 (1993).

Giddens Anthony. *Modernity and Self-Identity: Self and Society in the Late Modern Age*. Cambridge: Polity Press, 1991.

Gill, Stephen, and David Law. *The Global Political Economy: Perspectives, Problems and Policies*. New York: Harvester/Wheatshelf, 1988.

Golding, Peter, and Phil Harris, eds. *Beyond Cultural Imperialism: Globalization, Communication and the New International Order*. London: Sage, 1996.

Guha, R. *Dominance without Hegemony: History and Power in Colonial India*. Cambridge: Harvard University Press, 1997.

Harindranath, R. "Cross-cultural interpretation of television: A phenomenological hermeneutic inquiry." Ph.D. diss., University of Leicester, 1996.

————. "Documentary meanings and interpretive contexts: Observations on Indian 'repertoires.' " In *Approaches to Audiences*, ed. Roger Dickinson et al. London: Arnold, 1998.

————. "Ethnicity, national culture(s), and the interpretation of television." In *Ethnic Minorities and the Media: Challenging Boundaries*, ed. Simon Cottle. Milton Keynes: Open
University Press, 2000.

Liebes, Tamar, and Elihu Katz. *The Export of Meaning: Cross-Cultural Readings of* Dallas.
Cambridge: Polity, 1993.

Massey, Doreen. *Space, Place and Gender*. Cambridge: Polity, 1994.

Ngugi, Wa Thiong'o. *Decolonising the Mind: The Politics of Language in African Literature*.
London: James Currey, 1986.

Roach, Colleen. "Cultural imperialism and resistance in media theory and literary theory."
Media, Culture and Society 19 (1997).

Robins, Kevin. "Tradition and translation: National culture in its global context." In *Enterprise
and Heritage*, ed. J. Corner and S. Harvey. London: Routledge, 1991.

Said, Edward. *Culture and Imperialism*. New York: Knopf, 1993.

Salinas, R., and L. Paldan. "Culture in the process of dependent development: Theoretical
perspectives." In *National Sovereignty and International Communication*, ed. Kaarle Nordenstreng and Herbert Schiller. Norwood, NJ: Ablex, 1979.

Schiller, Herbert. *Communication and Cultural Domination*. Armonk, NY: M.E. Sharpe, 1976.

————. "Transnational media and national development." In *National Sovereignty and International Communication*, ed. Kaarle Nordenstreng and Herbert Schiller. Norwood, NJ:
Ablex, 1979.

Seaman, W. "Active audience theory: Pointless populism." *Media, Culture and Society* 14
(1992).

Sklair, Leslie. *Sociology of the Global System*. London: Prentice Hall, 1991.

Tomlinson, John. *Cultural Imperialism*. London: Pinter, 1991.

————. *Globalization and Culture*. Cambridge: Polity, 1999.

Wallerstein, Immanuel. "Culture is the world-system: A reply to Boyne," *Theory, Culture and
Society* 7 (1990).

Chapter Nine

Going Global

International Coproductions and the Disappearing Domestic Audience in Canada

Serra Tinic

> The new reality of international media is driven more
> by market opportunity than by national identity.
> —Steven Ross, former head of Time-Warner

In the new global media landscape, economic contingencies are winning out in the ongoing struggle between market forces and national cultural development goals. As financial and political support for national public broadcasting institutions around the world dwindles, producers in countries with relatively small domestic markets— such as Canada—have turned their attention to international audiences and coproduction partners to piece together the requisite funding to tell their stories. In the growing body of scholarship on media globalization, debates over the rapid increase in international television flows have emphasized the potential for either cultural homogenization or fragmentation at both the national and global levels. For some (e.g., Robertson 1990), the extension and consolidation of a global media system as part of the larger process of economic globalization have led to a singular perception of a cultural system wherein people cannot help but think in global terms. For others (e.g., Smith 1990), the globalization of the electronic media does not inevitably translate into the dissolution of national communities and identifications, but contributes to increasingly complex formations of supranational and subnational community affiliations as cultural forms and symbols are no longer territorially fixed. Though not always explicit, concerns over potential cultural homogenization in a global media arena often imply that homogenization equals *Americanization*. Given Hollywood's disproportionate presence internationally, this is not surprising. However, thus far, little attention has been given to the ways emergent television production practices outside the United States have contributed to the global circulation of American-inflected television programs.

This essay examines the growing trend toward international television coproductions and joint ventures and addresses the cultural ramifications of producing for the global market. The analysis draws on current discourse in industry trade publications as well as my own fieldwork in the television and film production community in Vancouver, British Columbia. Beginning in 1978, the B.C. government consciously strived to develop and promote Vancouver as a locations site for the U.S. television and film industry as part of the province's larger global diversification strategy. Today, Vancouver is the third-largest production center for Hollywood television series and movies, behind only New York and Los Angeles. Frustration with federal definitions of national culture, combined with decreasing financial support for regional domestic television production, has led Vancouver producers to move away from the initial nation-building goals of Canadian media policies and take advantage of the Hollywood presence to pursue co-venture agreements with American producers and coproduction projects with other international partners to develop programs for global audiences. In this respect, Vancouver provides a strategic location from which to examine the cultural implications of the globalization of television production strategies.

The role of cultural producers is often elided in the literature of media globalization, which, by either emphasizing the rapid flow of media content in abstract terms or privileging textual analysis for intrinsic cultural meanings, rarely examines the negotiations behind the images displayed on television and movie screens around the world. This essay redresses this gap by exploring the dual nature of television production as both a symbolic and an economic activity. The study integrates cultural studies and political economy perspectives as a means to analyze artisanal and industrial visions of television and "conceptualizes the relations between these two sides of the communications process—the material and the discursive, economic and cultural—without collapsing one into the other" (Murdock 1989, 436).

I first consider the rationale underlying the various forms of international media co-ventures, then examine the cultural negotiations producers must engage in when developing a project with a foreign partner or selling an existing idea or program to an international broadcaster. I give specific attention to the debate over the potential for cultural homogeneity as producers attempt to "universalize" the culturally specific narratives and styles of their local and national communities to increase their global resale value. As the Vancouver case study shows, the global audience is not a vague or nebulous construction in the imaginations of international producers and media corporations. In fact, the preferred *global* audience for most international producers, given its sheer size as a single, English-language target market with a high percentage of domestic television ownership, is the *American* audience (Alvarado 1996, 68). This fact, plus their cultural and geographical proximity to Hollywood, makes Canadian producers particularly attractive coproduction partners for media companies around the world. The final section examines how tensions between cultural homogeneity and cultural fragmentation operate in terms of domestic audience expectations. Canadian audiences, despite their engagement with and enjoyment of American television, continue to support programs that reflect their own sociocultural circumstances and sense of *place* at the local and national levels. The implication is that global media production is detrimental to a sense of national and local community only to the extent that it supplants, rather than supplements, domestic media offerings.

Turning Toward the Global: The Rationale behind International Coproductions

Canadian television producers and broadcasters have long been reconciled to the fact that international sales of domestic media programming are vital to the ability to generate revenue for future productions. Over the past decade, however, the international media market has become increasingly important to the production and distribution of domestic television programs. International joint ventures (IJVs) with foreign production partners have become the preferred mode of production for countries with potentially small domestic audiences. With forty-four international coproduction treaties, Canada is one of the leading nations in formalizing production agreements with television producers around the world. While the majority of these agreements are with European nations, Canada has recently signed treaties with various countries in South America, Africa, and Southeast Asia.

The economic benefits of IJVs are significant, since they allow producers to share the financial risks of project development while providing both parties with access to one another's government cultural subsidies and tax incentives. Perhaps most important, a formal coproduction allows a television program to qualify as domestic content in both countries, assuring access to markets where cultural protection barriers exist. IJVs vary in structure, content, and the extent to which a production will be accepted as a domestic property. Of the numerous contractual forms that fall under the umbrella term of "international joint venture," official coproductions, co-ventures, and twinning packages are the predominant types of international television production agreements.

Official coproduction agreements are the preferred format for producers wishing to gain unimpeded access to another country's market while reaping the benefits of national subsidies both at home and abroad. To qualify as an official coproduction, both countries must make a roughly equal financial and creative investment in the project. While exact contributions vary with every agreement, both countries are generally expected to supply a lead actor to the project and (in the case of the Canadian contribution) invest at least 30 percent in the total production budget. Co-ventures differ by being less restrictive in terms of relative contributions to the project and, under new, stricter government guidelines, are more difficult to qualify for domestic subsidies and tax incentives in Canada. Co-ventures are developed between producers in countries that do not have a formalized coproduction treaty; the primary goal is to share the costs and financial risks of the production process. A twinning package, finally, is an agreement in which the producers in both countries develop and produce comparable yet distinct domestic projects and then partner them so that each will receive airtime in the other's broadcast market (Hoskins and McFadyen 1993).

International coproductions evolved in the early 1950s as European nations attempted to revitalize the postwar film industry by sharing costs and resources, as
well as increasing access to larger audiences (Taylor 1995). In the early stages of
proliferating international joint ventures across Europe and later in North and South
America, media researchers often presupposed that foreign television partnerships
would develop along the lines of geolinguistic compatibility, resulting in new cultural
blocs or regions of media development. However, as Attallah (1996, 181) points out,
the IJVs and coproduction agreements in the current global television landscape
depend less on cultural and linguistic similarities than on congruent regulatory
environments in the participant countries. This is evident in the recurring patterns
of Canadian coproductions. While Britain might seem to be a natural coproduction
partner for Canadian television projects, few such partnerships exist. Because Britain
does not have a domestic content quota system, most agreements between the two
countries tend to be twinning packages (Attallah 1996, 180). Instead, the French are
the most important and frequent coproduction partners for Anglo-Canadian
producers—particularly since 1992, when France designated all Franco-Canadian
television productions, even those developed in English, as European works. Consequently, these coproductions qualify as domestic content throughout the European
Union (Collins 1994, 395). As for co-ventures, Canadian partnerships in these areas
tend to be with U.S. producers as there is no formal coproduction treaty between
the two countries. The benefits of co-ventures for Canadian producers stem from
sharing the production costs. For U.S. producers, the goal is to cede a minimum of
creative control while ensuring sufficient Canadian content (CanCon) points to
access the Canadian market as domestic content. As a result, the majority of these
co-venture projects are derivative of American formulas, stories, and settings, and
many are merely service locations for U.S. productions.

The proximity to and understanding of the U.S. production system often make
Canada such an attractive coproduction partner for other countries. These factors,
combined with the market importance of English-language productions, afford the
possibility that a coproduction project with a Canadian producer may provide access
to the American market. (For American producers, a co-venture with a Canadian
producer may similarly offer an avenue into the more restrictive markets of the
European Union.) What makes Canadian projects particularly appealing to European
media buyers and distributors, however, is that they portray popular conceptions of
North America while remaining subtly distinct from American television. According
to a Dutch media consultant, "Canadian features with universal themes translate well
in Europe because 'Canadian sensibilities are more European than American'" (interviewed in Armstrong 1996, 3). This reference to a different Canadian "sensibility"
was also often invoked by the producers with whom I spoke in Vancouver. As an
elusive cultural identification it was frequently described as a sense of marginality
both within the nation and internationally—a way of seeing the world from the
periphery as a former colony of Britain and as a perceived cultural satellite of the
United States. While the ways this negative sense of identity (describing oneself by
what one is not—not British and not American) translates into television programs
will be explored later, the above commentary provides insight into the success of

Canadian television productions in the international market. In fact, after the United States, Canada is the largest exporter of television programming worldwide. In 1995 Canadian-produced television programs and movies generated $1.4 billion in international sales, an increase of 175 percent from 1993—a volume that producers believe will increase as the number of international coproduction treaties continues to grow (Winsor 1997, A7).

While the success of Canadian television exports in the international marketplace bodes well for the continued participation of Canadian producers in the industry, the suggestion that Canadian stories have "universal themes" raises the question of how—and whether—distinctly "Canadian" stories will be produced in the global cultural economy. As Sinclair, Jacka, and Cunningham observe, participation in coproductions and international media trade markets changes the target audience for domestic producers. The "primary audience which regulates the flow of peripheral programming internationally" becomes the foreign media buyers and distributors who enter into agreements where "rough-and-ready genre expectations are in play" (1996, 19–20). Moreover, the world's audiences have already been divided into psychographic genre zones for the purpose of television sales. For example, police series are popular in Germany while "environmentally conscious Scandinavians" tend to be interested in ecological documentaries (Rice-Barker 1996, 24). Implicit is the notion that if Canadian producers concentrate their attention on the export market, then the interests of foreign audiences, as defined by media buyers, will drive the types of programs produced more than will the interests of domestic audiences.

This dilemma highlights the central tension in the growing trend toward international coproductions and the emphasis on the global audience market. While IJVs and international sales are crucial to small-market producers seeking development funding in an environment of diminishing government support for domestic production, the concomitant loss of cultural specificity can be the first sacrifice in negotiating control over the development of programming. While examples of generic "Euro-pudding"–type programs abound, a recent miniseries about one of the most Canadian of all institutions, the Hudson's Bay Company, provides an illuminating case.[1] When producer Michael Levine decided to produce a television miniseries about the Hudson's Bay Company, he realized that the project's success would depend on international financing. As a result of investment by British and U.S. production companies, the story of Canada's penultimate trading post emphasized its roots in imperial Britain:

> Now, we could take it and we could plant the entire story in Montreal and on Hudson's Bay and in Winnipeg, and we could tell it from a Canadian viewpoint in a way that I could guarantee that absolutely nobody would have bought it.... The way to do it is to focus on the Orkneys and the Scots and the money men in London and the British Royal Family, so you see an international story.... That's the dilemma of export, because the minute you export, by definition you are speaking to universals. (Michael Levine interviewed in Saunders 1997, C1, C3)

This perceived need to universalize the culturally particular became a recurrent theme in my conversations with Vancouver television producers, as the push to internationalize has reconciled most producers to accept a level of homogeneity in their future development plans. In this context, questions about representing the specificities of *place* and community become particularly problematic.

Negotiating Culture in the Global Economy: Looking for the "Universal" in the "Particular"

According to Waters, under the processes of globalization material and economic exchanges tend to bind social relations to the local while symbolic exchanges, in the form of information, culture, and entertainment, "liberate relationships from spatial referents" as they "appeal to human fundamentals that can often claim universal significance" (1995, 9). The differentiation of *place* and *space* takes on new dimensions in debates over postmodernity and the "dilemmas" of cultural fragmentation or homogenization. As Harvey (1990, 301–4) explains, *place* (local culture and community) becomes crucial to marginalized groups, both intra- and internationally, as they have a better command over cultural definition at this site than over *space*, which is the terrain of national institutions and global capital. The translation of the sociocultural specificities of quotidian experiences and social struggles and contestations within the immediate community (*place*) into television narratives has been a fundamental goal of nation-building broadcasting policies in Canada. In Vancouver's production context, this "de-spatialization" of cultural production assumes two forms. First, stories that represent the particularities of *place* are able to achieve universal resonance because of the global restructuring of the community, and, second, stories are developed to de-emphasize *place* in order to appeal to universal "human fundamentals" that may obscure the specificities of *place*.

An example of the first kind of de-spatialization arose during a conversation with an independent filmmaker who had produced a movie about the intergenerational cultural conflicts facing a Chinese-Canadian family in Vancouver. Although the film, which later aired on Canadian television, explicitly referenced Vancouver as the site of the story about a young Chinese woman's struggle to navigate between two cultural worlds, the production resonated with audiences in urban centers across North America:

> When we screened [the movie] in New York people came up to me and they thought we had shot it in San Francisco. It was distinctive; it was about the Asian immigrant experience in Vancouver but as I said people in New York thought it could be San Francisco. The story had universal themes that were carried through. Of course people in Vancouver look at it and know right away. The landmarks are so distinctive, that comes through. . . . All of the actors were Canadian, the writer-director was Canadian, the producer was Canadian. Everyone who saw it in Vancouver knew it was a Vancouver-made film and everyone who saw it in Toronto knew it was a made-in-Vancouver film. (interview by author, July 22, 1997)

As this example suggests, the symbolic exchanges transforming globalizing cities contribute to new forms of community and cultural interaction that are simultaneously *place*-specific and universally recognizable to people in other global urban centers. In this respect, media content can "liberate relationships from spatial referents" without denying the sociocultural dimensions of the *place* of origin. In the example above, the producer wanted an international audience for a story set in Vancouver and was unwilling to sacrifice the story line to placate distributors. Concessions that would erase the specificity of the city did not need to be made since the culturally particular elements of the film reflected universal themes of the immigrant experience.

However, such productions are the exception rather than the rule in the global cultural economy. In the case of television and film productions intended for the global market, and especially in the case of IJVs, the second form of de-spatialization—whereby the particularities of place are de-emphasized in favor of universal themes and representations—is usually most evident. Hoskins, McFadyen, and Finn explain this form of de-spatialization as a consequence of the "cultural discount" given media content that is too culturally specific: "[a] particular program rooted in one culture and thus attractive in that environment, will have diminished appeal elsewhere as viewers find it difficult to identify with the styles, values, beliefs, institutions and behavioural patterns of the material in question" (1994, 367). International media buyers are unwilling to pay top dollar for programs that carry a cultural discount, if they are willing to buy them at all. In an effort to avoid the cultural discount, most international coproductions aim at a form of universalism that homogenizes television content so that stories take place in, as the producer Martyn Burke put it, a "no-where land" (interviewed in Saunders 1997, C3). Even members of large private Canadian production companies, such as Michael MacMillan of Atlantis, contend that culturally specific domestic programming will be scarce if IJVs become the only available means of television production: "In the world of international deals, the homogenization of program content is inevitable. We're not supposed to talk about that but it's happening, and only government support will ensure that our own stories keep getting told" (quoted in Zemans 1995, 154–55).

For some producers, however, the major concern is not that domestic stories will be "watered down" to meet international buyers' criteria, but that they will not even be proposed or developed. As the CBC producer Mark Starowicz said, "the decision-making point is at the buy-in. We don't change our stories, we murder them in the crib" (interviewed in Saunders 1997, C3). Thus the question that begs to be asked is, If Canadians are not telling their own stories, then whose stories are they telling? The trend in international coproductions is to tell formulaic stories that emulate those currently popular among the preferred audience market: the United States. In fact, the concept of a "nowhere land" in television production is a misnomer: most stories have to exist in a time and place and, in the case of IJVs, that context is often a (re)presentation of an American city.

Highlander and *Poltergeist: The Legacy* are two international television coproductions that illuminate the generic processes of global production strategies. Based on a 1986 feature film, *Highlander: The Series* is a Canadian (Filmline International) and French (Gaumont Television) coproduction about the travails of immortals battling for supremacy, while *Poltergeist*, also a Canadian (Trilogy Entertainment Group) and

French coproduction, follows a group of supernatural sleuths who attempt to eradicate evil, otherworldly forces from the "natural" realm. Both series fulfill the requirements for domestic government support through equal investment, use of lead actors from each country, and production location (Vancouver and, sometimes, Paris). However, neither program references national narratives or social processes. Moreover, despite their physical production location, both series are set in the United States: Vancouver stands in for Seattle in *Highlander* and for San Francisco in *Poltergeist*. The narrative structures also follow the recognizable American formula wherein good prevails over evil within the hour, facilitating international distribution and syndication sales within the United States.

In this respect, American television and movies are able to maintain a hegemonic presence in the global cultural economy. The United States has "written the 'grammar' of international television" (Morley and Robins 1995, 223) to the extent that audiences around the world recognize and accept the American mode of television production; moreover, foreign producers seek to reproduce that style to serve as an international common denominator. The result is not that audiences naturally prefer U.S. television or that these programs inculcate an American value system, but that American (or American-style) television programs begin to dominate international markets. As Sinclair et al. explain, "The cultural imperialism theory failed to see that, more fundamental than its supposed ideological influence, the legacy of the USA in world television development was in the implantation of its systemic model for television as a medium" (1996, 9). With an increase in global competition in television productions aimed at the American market, many Canadian writers and producers are bypassing the middle ground offered by IJVs and attempting entry directly into U.S. network or cable television.

"Nowhere Land" or "Somewhere, U.S.A."?

The goal of accessing the American market, whether through an IJV or a direct sale to a U.S. network, fundamentally changes the content and style of a Canadian program. The extent to which cultural specificity is lost in an IJV is largely dependent on the countries involved in the production partnership. As stated earlier, Canada is a preferred partner because it brings a North American style and sensibility to the project without producing a completely American story. Foreign producers see their Canadian partners as willing to negotiate on cultural points to the extent that both countries are able to reference their specific national contexts even when following a generically American format. As the French producer/director Michael Mitrani explains, this is not the case when dealing directly with American producers and broadcasters: "Co-productions with Americans invariably suffer from identity problems. . . . The American determines the script. There are no compromises" (quoted in Hoskins and McFadyen 1993, 231). In any international joint venture involving the United States, the American production team enters the agreement from a position of power, since it is in the unique position among Western countries of usually recouping or absorbing production costs wholly within their domestic market. Thus the desirability of gaining access to the American audience tends to make an IJV with a U.S. partner more beneficial to foreign producers than to their American counterparts. As a consequence, "locals go as supplicants" (Morley and Robins 1995, 117) when pitching story ideas or co-venture proposals to U.S. production companies and broadcasters.

My conversation with one independent producer in Vancouver illustrates the differences between coproductions with European partners and co-ventures with U.S. producers and broadcasters. This producer was one of the first producers to sell a Canadian story as a movie of the week (MOW) directly to an American network (CBS) and one of the first to enter into an official coproduction agreement with a British partner. In the case of the British coproduction, a children's story, the cultural negotiations were minor; the primary point of contention was whether or not the lead character should be an aspiring Little League baseball player when the sport is not overly popular in England. The agreement with CBS, however, demanded a complete script overhaul. The original script was a reality-based story of a woman murdered in Vancouver. Along with the rights to the story, the producer had secured releases for interviews with all parties involved in the case and had approval to use their real names and details from the legal proceedings. This attention to detail proved unnecessary as CBS insisted that the names, nationalities, and personality traits of the main characters be changed to suit the network's formula for "true-crime" MOWs. Consequently, the story was placed in "small-town America" (though filmed in Vancouver) and the psychological complexities of the main characters were eliminated so that the generic "good guys" could be distinguished from the "bad guys." According to this producer, CBS was steadfast in following formulas that appealed to their perception of the U.S. audience:

> The audience is rural Ohio or Indiana—the Midwest—especially the CBS audience. And they homogenize things for that audience. They don't care. American network television doesn't even really do authentic or historical stuff about their own culture. If you want to get into stuff like that you'll go to the cable companies—Turner, Showtime, HBO, A&E. (interview by author, August 7, 1997)

American cable stations may have a greater appetite for unique or specialized programming but, as my interviews with other Vancouver producers also indicated, they are not far removed from the broadcast networks in their expectations of formula, style, and U.S. audience composition. One producer, who had recently completed a historical documentary for A&E, described the U.S. television industry as a risk-averse environment in which the commodity form of production and audience marketing dictated adherence to genre and style expectations:

> There's a real formula to television. Especially American television. Different [U.S.] networks have different formulas. . . . They want people to turn to their channel and recognize a look, a kind of show, a voice, an approach. . . . We had to show what the stereotypical pictures in people's heads would be. . . . It's a type of mentality that they're in the market, really competitive, and people sit with their remotes in their hands and you can't afford to have any chances, any time where you're increasing the odds that they'll look at something else. They're a business and that's first. So whether we might

have done it differently because it would be nicer that way, or have a better pace or feel when the explanations came later—to them it was a business concern. (interview by author, July 10, 1997)

Similarly, another Canadian producer shared her experiences in trying to negotiate around the restrictive codes of U.S. television that dictated the detailed conventions of the medium down to the level of timing and cueing the audience's attention:

> you have to have a music cue every twenty seconds, whether there is drama or not. And if there is drama, then you have to accentuate it. . . . In post-production on my first [production]—it was a courtroom drama and we were on a tight close-up of one person. And it was a very dramatic part of the script. It was riveting. And we had to put music cues in it. Now, really! We fought with the distribution people over that. They said, "Well, you have to have that. It's been silent for forty-five seconds." (interview by author, August 19, 1997)

Although these comments indicate stylistic differences between Canadian and U.S. television programming, they also speak to the divergent sensibilities of the two countries and to the negotiation of these sensibilities in television programs. The combination of a culture defined by a consistent questioning of Canadian identity and a broadcasting tradition rooted in realism and documentary has resulted in a television style that encourages open-ended ambiguity and risk taking in both narrative content and form. A brief examination of some Canadian programs that were unable to gain access to the U.S. television market illuminates these distinctions and foregrounds the rationale of producers who call for increased support of public broadcasting by the Canadian Broadcasting Corporation (CBC).

Canadian television programs and MOWs are marked by a sensibility for presenting controversial and often disturbing depictions of social issues and problems in a nonglamorous albeit fictional form. Even humor and satire tend to explore the darker side of the Canadian condition through the perspectives of realistic characters and without the benefit of a laugh track, such that much of the decoding work is left to the audiences. In Canada many television programs that have attracted the largest audiences have dealt with uncomfortable issues, including youth crime (*Little Criminals*), incest (*Liar, Liar*), mistreatment of Native peoples (*Where the Spirit Lives*), and abuse in Catholic orphanages (*The Boys of St. Vincent's*).

Given the restrictive framework of U.S. television, particularly its fear of alienating advertisers, it is not surprising that Canadian producers have had a difficult time selling the above programs to U.S. networks. What is considered prime-time viewing in Canada is seen as a risky encounter with taboo subjects in the United States. In the case of *Where the Spirit Lives*, a CBC MOW about the physical abuse of Native children placed by the government in parochial schools, the producer, Keith Ross Leckie, found that he could not even sell it to the more highbrow PBS:

> They liked the script but said their audience wasn't interested in Native issues so they wanted to make it a regular orphanage; they said they couldn't show any abuse or even imply abuse of children, so that would have to come out; and they said it couldn't be negative toward a religious organization. (interviewed in Leger 1996, 16)

Little Criminals and *Liar, Liar* met with similar reactions from the U.S. commercial networks and PBS despite being sold to, and well received in, several other countries, including England, Brazil, Italy, Malaysia, South Africa, and several Scandinavian countries.[2] *Little Criminals*, with its realistic portrayal of Vancouver youth crime, was not of interest to any U.S. network or broadcaster. In fact, the show's producer doubted that the show would ever have been developed through a coproduction, a co-venture, or a private Canadian broadcaster: "CBC is the only broadcaster in the world who would have done this film and financed it" (interviewed in Leger 1997, 28).

The ability to produce programs like *Little Criminals* and *Liar, Liar*, and their consequent popularity with Canadian audiences, underlines the role that television plays in exploring the sociocultural specificities of *places* and the capacity of the medium to negotiate and "construct collective memories and identities" (Morley and Robins 1995, 91). It is this capacity that many local producers worried could be lost in the trend toward audience market expansion in the global cultural economy.

It is also important to understand the rationale underlying U.S. broadcasters' disinclination to buy and air these types of programs. While much of this reluctance signifies the cultural disjunctures between the two countries, it also illustrates the divergent motivations of market-oriented and public service broadcasting institutions. In the United States the commercial imperative of private broadcasting results in a risk-averse environment in which the fear of offending advertisers leads network executives to construct an image of the audience that falls toward the more conservative side. The CBC, conversely, has been able to take greater risks in programming as it has traditionally relied on advertising for only 30 percent of its revenue. Moreover, Canadians have learned the grammar of CBC television and are more accustomed to television that breaks the rules of the U.S. model. It is also not implausible that the U.S. networks lack an understanding about their own audiences' tastes and competencies.[3] When *Liar, Liar* was eventually sold to CBS, after profitable international sales and high domestic audience ratings, the MOW received CBS's highest weeknight ratings in eighteen months. It was the top-rated show of the night and the fourth-highest of that week. According to Ivan Fecan, former CBC vice president of English television,

> They [CBS] scratched their heads about it and said, "Well, you've broken all the rules. You tell a story that's a lot blunter than we'd ever tell it, you don't have anybody who is known to an American audience in it, in the court scenes your lawyers wear "costumes"; this violates every single development rule we have and yet you've done better than we have for four months. What's going on here? (interviewed in Miller 1996, 473)[4]

Such successes aside, specifically Canadian stories remain difficult to sell to U.S. broadcasters. Despite positive audience response to such fare, there has not been a subsequent flurry of production activity to develop programs that forthrightly address the intricacies of American social and political issues. Perhaps U.S. network executives perceive these successes as "flukes" or are only willing to gamble on them once they have seen evidence of their success in other markets. Whatever the reasoning behind the American reluctance to purchase programming about foreign cultures rather than "universal" programming, Canadian producers rarely develop such projects with a U.S. sale at the forefront of their budgeting decisions. Rather, for these types of programs, a future sale to an American network is fortuitous while support from Canadian broadcasters, specifically the CBC, is essential.

It is not surprising that only those producers most committed to developing domestic stories do not dilute the specificity of cultural narratives to appease a coproduction partner or to enter the U.S. market. With decreased federal support for the CBC and virtually no funding for independent regional producers available, such television content is becoming a relative rarity in Canada. In the face of mounting frustrations with Canadian funding, most of the producers with whom I spoke expressed a greater openness to dealing directly with U.S. networks or cable stations, even if it meant a loss of control over the style and content of a story idea.

Past success with American sales and co-ventures encourages independent producers to continue seeking direct access to the U.S. market by universalizing their projects. The comparative ease with which agreements and funding arrangements are finalized with U.S. broadcasters, as opposed to the circuitous process of acquiring funding in Canada, has encouraged some producers to opt out of the domestic television sphere altogether.

In the midst of this increasing move of production away from the regional and the national, it is often assumed that Canadians are not interested in or do not enjoy domestic television because they watch a disproportionate amount of U.S. programming. However, as ratings for quality domestic programs indicate, Canadians appreciate seeing their stories and everyday lives represented in dramatic form. It is not that an insufficient number of Canadians are watching domestic programming that resonates with their feeling of *place* and community, but that there are not enough potential Canadians watching to make it profitable for many producers to neglect the international market. Consequently, Canadians become a marginal market within the global media economy. However, Canadian audiences are vocal supporters of domestic television that provides them with a sense of collectivity and shared experience in both a universal and a particular context.

Bringing It Home: The Canadian Audience for Domestic Television

To speak of a "Canadian" audience is problematic, given the salience of regionalism and other intersecting forms of cultural identification in the Canadian national context. However, to the extent that Canadian broadcasters rationalize their programming decisions in the discourse of national audience share, reach, and ratings, it is difficult to ignore the ways the audience's voice is constructed within the Canadian television industry's production strategies. This section explores Canadians' attitudes and responses to Canadian and U.S. programming as reflected in industry research reports and public participation in broadcasting debates and lobby efforts. The conclusions drawn from these forms of audience representation correspond with the work of media scholars (e.g., Silj 1988) who argue that, when given a choice, audiences will select Canadian television content over American content when both are available and of equal production quality.

Unlike commercial television broadcasters, national public service broadcasting institutions are compelled to develop programming that appeals to audiences as publics/citizens rather than as markets/consumers (Ang 1991). Consequently, programming is supposed to address significant sociocultural issues rather than cater to popular acceptance of the formulaic productions that characterize private television networks. In this respect, these institutions are intended to create a sort of electronic public sphere that enables ritual participation in the continual construction and reconstruction of the national community. The attainment of this goal has been challenging for the CBC, given its private-public structure. For Canada's national public broadcaster the audience, of necessity, has been constructed simultaneously as a public and a market.[5]

Despite, or perhaps because of, this contradictory view of the audience, the CBC conducts extensive quantitative and qualitative audience research. In addition to commissioning AC Nielsen ratings, the corporation relies on focus groups and a regular audience survey panel that provides detailed comments on CBC programs every week. The CBC also mails viewing questionnaires to approximately a thousand Anglo-Canadians throughout the year. In 1991 the CBC completed its most comprehensive audience study of the decade. In its subsequent internal report, *How People Use Television*, the CBC research department examined Canadians' engagement with and enjoyment of domestic public and private television programs and of U.S. programming. The study found that Canadians watch a disproportionately greater number of U.S. entertainment programs than Canadian dramas. However, 62 percent of respondents also reported that "U.S.-made programs had too great an influence" on Canadian life. This number had increased by 4 percent from a similar study conducted five years earlier (CBC Research 1991, 11).

Although the CBC found it had an audience reach—the number of viewers who watch at least one minute of programming a week—of 80 percent, 70 percent of audience members interviewed described the CBC as less entertaining, more formal, and less regionally attuned than Canadian private broadcasters. However, when the questions turned to entertainment programming, viewers indicated that many of the Canadian drama and comedy programs they watched were CBC productions. This is not an unexpected finding considering that Canadian private broadcasters produce few domestic dramas. More intriguing, however, were the findings that when quality Canadian alternatives to U.S. programs were available they received a higher rating on the CBC's "Enjoyment Index." For instance, the CBC dramatic series *Street Legal*, about a group of lawyers in a small storefront office in Toronto, was rated "more enjoyable" by Canadian audiences than the U.S. hit program *Dallas* (CBC Research 1991, 84).[6] The audience portrait painted by *How People Use Television* suggests that Canadians want quality dramatic programs that both entertain and reflect the sociocultural specificity of their community at the national and regional levels. In the meantime, U.S. television programs fill the void left by the dearth of Canadian alternatives. In this respect, the conclusions of the CBC study underline Straubhaar's description of "cultural proximity," which contends that audiences "first seek the pleasure of recognition of their own culture in their programme choices, and that programmes will be produced to satisfy this demand, relative to the wealth of the market" (in Sinclair et al. 1996, 14). In the case of Canadian television, there is audience demand for "culturally proximate" programs, but the potential number of viewers does not constitute a "wealthy market" for producers.

Canadians are aware of their lack of market appeal to most independent and private producers, and while their support for domestic television may not be reflected adequately in the ratings, it is evident in public participation and protests in debates concerning cutbacks to the CBC. While CBC television may not dominate the viewing schedules of most Canadians, the CBC is still seen as the primary source of domestic social and cultural expression in popular programming. This recognition is evidenced in public support for the CBC during recent funding cutbacks and implied threats of privatization. Most notable were the "Keep the Promise" campaign and the CBC "unity train" organized by the lobby group Friends of Canadian Broadcasting. In the spring of 1997, during yet another round of cutbacks that would amount to over $400 million in lost revenue for the CBC, the Friends of Canadian Broadcasting held public meetings across the country to protest further decimation of the CBC's production capabilities. Timed to coincide with the upcoming federal election, signs and stickers reading "CBC: Keep the Promise" covered lawns, apartment windows, and car bumpers throughout Canada. In late April of that year, the same group organized a cross-country railroad journey that picked up Canadians from East to West to congregate in support of the CBC on Parliament Hill in Ottawa one month before the election. Although these efforts did not prevent the final round of cutbacks to the CBC, the symbolism of thousands of Canadians riding the "unity train" was not lost on federal politicians. Using the railroad was not only a salient symbol of Confederation but also served as a reminder that the Canadian Pacific Railway was the first producer and disseminator of radio programming that later fell under the auspices of the CBC—a resonant signifier of Canadian unity and cultural sovereignty.

This is not to say that Canadians show their support for domestic cultural production only through grand acts in times of crisis. There are, in fact, several television programs that receive extraordinarily high ratings (in Canadian terms) and vociferous support through the public hearings process mandated by the Canadian Radio-Telecommunications Commission (CRTC). This has been particularly apparent in the case of comedy programming and in the fight for a second window for two of the most popular domestic programs, *The Royal Canadian Air Farce* and *This Hour Has 22 Minutes*. Both programs are sketch comedies providing political and social satire of power structures in the form of the federal and provincial governments, the United States, and the legacy of British colonial rule. These comedies reaffirm a collective sense of Canadian identity vis-à-vis Britain and the United States to the extent that a viewer must be an insider to understand the references inscribed within the cultural codes to "get the joke."

In October 1997, shortly after the voyage of the "unity train," the privately owned Baton Broadcasting Corporation and the Canadian Association of Broadcasters

(CAB) brought a grievance before the CRTC protesting the CBC's use of its specialty channel, CBC Newsworld, as a second outlet for the two comedies. At the time, *Air Farce* and *22 Minutes* generated audiences of over 1,000,000 and 1,310,000 respectively each week during their first airings on the CBC main network. The same episodes captured equally large audiences in their second airing later that week on Newsworld. Their scheduling, which coincided with the rerun hour of syndicated U.S. programming on private stations, drew audiences away from the commercial broadcasters. However, this was not the rationale that Baton and CAB used to bring the CRTC into a content and licensing debate over CBC Newsworld. Rather, the private broadcasters argued that airing comedies on a specialty news channel violated the mandate and licensing requirements of specialty programming as defined in CRTC regulations. The CBC countered by stating that since both programs were satires of news and current events they did not violate the "news-only" licensing requirement of Newsworld.

The *Air Farce/22 Minutes* dispute is salient for two reasons. First, the CRTC found itself in the ironic position of siding with private broadcasters airing American programs, despite its role as the national guardian of Canadian content, due to the technicalities of broadcast licensing regulations. Second, as all hearings before the CRTC must be publicized so that all Canadians may respond with their opinions, the *Air Farce/22 Minutes* case received close to record responses from the public; 1,274 interventions were filed in support of the CBC. While acknowledging the programs' popularity, the CRTC denied CBC's claim:

> A majority of the Commission . . . is not convinced that such programs are a suitable component of a news specialty service such as CBC Newsworld, and is concerned that their inclusion in the service could have unwelcome implications and consequences for the Canadian specialty services industry. (CRTC Decision 97–575, 2–3)

Although the CBC lost that round with the CRTC, the public's response underlined both the popularity of Canadian programs and the importance of the public forum on cultural issues to the Canadian psyche. This level of public participation resurfaced in January 1999, when CBC Newsworld held a call-in "town forum" in which CBC executives responded to questions and comments from Canadians across the country concerning their views and requests of the CBC. The response was so overwhelming that Newsworld added an hour to the program to accommodate callers—in addition to a two-hour forum that had occurred earlier that day on CBC radio. The vast majority of people phoning in expressed their belief that the CBC was essential to the continued depiction of Canadian stories and experiences on television.

The extent to which Canadians participate in the cultural realm illustrates the importance afforded the continued support for domestic storytelling on Canadian television. Moreover, the success of certain shows underlines the capacity to produce popular programs that contribute to a shared sense of community. The ability to produce stories connected to the sociocultural specificities of *place*, however, will depend on the future of public service broadcasting and cultural development policies in a global media arena. If the domestic audience continues to be constructed as a marginal market and funding for national broadcasting continues to decrease, television producers will be more motivated to pursue international coproduction agreements that provide access to global audiences.

As this essay indicates, IJVs provide contradictory implications in the debate over cultural homogenization within the context of media globalization. As the global continues to infuse the local, some of the cultural particularities of local *places* become universally resonant in their translation into television programming. The central question now facing global television scholars is whether or not stories that are *too* particular to the sociocultural experiences of small nations will be diluted in the cultural and economic negotiations between international coproduction partners —if they are produced and aired at all.

NOTES

This chapter is an excerpt from a larger work generated by a yearlong fieldwork investigation of the globalization of the Vancouver television industry. In-depth interviews and informal conversations with fifty-two members of the television production community formed a central component of the study.

1. As the members of the European Union negotiated cultural policy goals in "Television without Frontiers," they sought to avoid programs that hid or erased national cultural differences by appealing to a formulaic genre that could be defined as uniformly European. The term "Euro-pudding" defines this hodgepodge type of production that would attempt to characterize cultural elements of all the nations and thereby reflect none.

2. *Degrassi High*, an internationally acclaimed Canadian youth series, faced similar problems with PBS. Although PBS bought the series, several of the more "realistic" or controversial themes were edited or removed from selected episodes. A notable example was an episode concerning a lead character having an abortion. At the end of the episode a right-to-life protestor pushes a "fetus doll" into the young girl's face. This was edited out of the PBS broadcast despite the fact that the image became a recurring theme in future episodes. As Miller (1996, 336) notes, there is a perception among Canadian producers that "As a country we are a lot more open or we can talk more honestly to our audience."

3. The creators of the British adult-animation series *Bob and Margaret* met with similar responses from U.S. broadcasters, who wanted to make the program more accessible to Americans by changing several key creative aspects of the series (see Doherty 1998). Ultimately, the British creators formed a coproduction agreement with the Canadian animation company Nelvana, which was willing to leave the initial concept intact.

4. The "costumes" referred to are the black barristers' and solicitors' robes that Canadian lawyers must wear when appearing before the Court of Queen's Bench. It is a part of British judiciary protocol and remains a part of the Canadian system.

5. The CBC relies on advertising for 30 percent of its revenue; the remainder is provided through federal appropriations. The corporation must continually negotiate advertisers' constructions of the "desired" audience in its production decisions as it is uncertain how much funding will be provided by the government from year to year.

6. In *East of "Dallas,"* Silj (1988) similarly found that *Dallas* lost Peruvian audiences to a popular locally produced comedy program.

REFERENCES

Alvarado, Manuel. 1996. Selling Television. In *Film Policy: International, National and Regional Perspectives*, ed. Albert Moran, 62–71. London: Routledge.

Ang, Ien. 1991. *Desperately Seeking the Audience*. London: Routledge.

Armstrong, Mary Ellen. 1996. TIFF Buyers Focus on Ancillary Markets. *Playback*, 9 September, 3.

Attallah, Paul. 1996. Canadian Television Exports: Into the Mainstream. In *New Patterns in Global Television: Peripheral Vision*, eds. John Sinclair, Elizabeth Jacka, and Stuart Cunningham, 161–91. New York: Oxford University Press.

Beginnings. 1996. *Reel West*, March–April, 31.

CBC Research. 1991. *How People Use Television: A Review of TV Viewing Habits*. Ottawa.

Collins, Richard. 1994. Trading in Culture: The Role of Language. *Canadian Journal of Communication* 19:377–99.

Doherty, Mike. 1998. No Nudity or Violence, Unless It's Essential. *National Post*, 2 December, B4.

Harvey, David. 1990. *The Condition of Postmodernity*. Cambridge, MA: Blackwell.

Hoskins, Colin, and Stuart McFadyen. 1993. Canadian Participation in Co-Productions and Co-Ventures. *Canadian Journal of Communication* 18: 219–36.

Hoskins, Colin, Stuart McFadyen, and Adam Finn. 1994. The Environment in Which Cultural Industries Operate and Some Implications. *Canadian Journal of Communication* 19:353–375.

Leger, Louise. 1996. Writers: The Real Story. *Playback*, 17 June, 14+.

———. 1997. "Criminals" Emotional Truth Pays Off. *Playback*, 27 January 28+.

Miller, Mary Jane. 1996. *Rewind and Search: Conversations with the Makers and Decision-Makers of CBC Television Drama*. Montreal and Kingston: McGill-Queen's University Press.

Morley, David, and Kevin Robins. 1995. *Spaces of Identity: Global Media, Electronic Landscapes and Cultural Boundaries*. London: Routledge.

Murdock, Graham. 1989. Cultural Studies: Missing Links. *Critical Studies in Mass Communication*, December, 436–40.

Rice-Barker, Leo. 1996. Canadians Cash In at MIPCOM. *Playback* 21 October, 1+.

Robertson, Roland. 1990. Mapping the Global Condition: Globalization as the Central Concept. In *Global Culture: Nationalism, Globalization, and Modernity*, ed. Mike Featherstone. London: Sage.

Saunders, Doug. 1997. Exporting Canadian Culture. *Toronto Globe and Mail*, 25 January, C1, C3.

Silj, Alessandro. 1988. *East of "Dallas": The European Challenge to American Television*. London: British Film Institute.

Sinclair, John, Elizabeth Jacka, and Stuart Cunningham. 1996. Peripheral Vision. In *New Patterns in Global Television: Peripheral Vision*, eds. John Sinclair, Elizabeth Jacka, and Stuart Cunningham, 1–32. New York: Oxford University Press.

Smith, Anthony. 1990. Towards a Global Culture? In *Global Culture: Nationalism, Globalization, and Modernity*, ed. Mike Featherstone. London: Sage.

Taylor, Paul W. 1995. Co-productions—Content and Change: International Television in the Americas. *Canadian Journal of Communication* 20 (3): 15–20.

Waters, Malcolm. 1995. *Globalization*. London: Routledge.

Winsor, Hugh. 1997. New Content Rules in the Wind, Copps Says. *Toronto Globe and Mail*, 15 February, A1+.

Zemans, Joyce. 1995. The Essential Role of National Institutions. In *Beyond Quebec: Taking Stock of Canada*, ed. Kenneth McRoberts, 138–62. Montreal and Kingston: McGill-Queen's University Press.

Part III

Monitoring
Television and National Identity

Francophonie and the National Airwaves
A History of Television in Senegal

Jo Ellen Fair

The growth and content of television programming in Africa since the 1960s could be read as a story of media imperialism. The flood of Western programming into Africa alone makes this reading credible. Television's rapid transmission of distant words and pictures has challenged cultural practices that once emerged from particular geographic spaces. Indeed, as audiences view television, they now claim membership in several communities at once: the group of family and friends seated in the room; the entire community of nationals filtering televised images in ways unique to that national culture; and the international community of media cognoscenti, people around the world bound together in their knowledge of the language, rhetoric, and quirks of this or that program or program genre. Globalized media create this cognoscenti in Africa as they do everywhere, encouraging cosmopolitanism as they introduce and even impose attitudes that are, by all evidence, at least at the outset, foreign.

Media imperialism is too simple a concept, however. We know that local conditions check and modulate the flow of cultural products into Africa from the West. Neither state nor public waits impassively for the arrival of imported culture. The range of media products that become available in a country and the preferences that develop over time depend on an interplay of politics and taste on the national scene and the world at large.

This chapter explores the political and cultural history of television in Senegal. Its purpose is to show how the personalities of powerful figures, political calculations at a range of scales, the state's structure and regulation of media, and the preferences and tastes of diverse national populations have shaped the growth of television and the content of programming there. Television was introduced to Senegal in the mid-1960s, soon after independence from France, but it has never been a strong force for cultural nationalism. In fact, television has been important in creating a new urban culture in Senegal, and a sense in that culture of belonging to a larger francophone community, which France purports to lead ("Francophonie par satellite," *Jeune Afrique* 5–11 December 1990; Tudesq 1992, 197–213; Silla 1994; Ager 1996, 44–62). Despite the constant flow of French cultural products through the airwaves into Senegal and their partial absorption into daily life, especially in the cities, Senegalese cultures, urban and rural, will always stand apart from the French and the global *francophonie* France seeks to create. An additional purpose of this chapter, therefore, is to recount the history of French television in Senegal and to show how it has shaped urban Senegalese discourse around regional, national, and international cultural identities.

Senegal's Colonial Past

Senegal long has had a unique relationship with France. For example, during the colonial period, which extended from 1885 to 1960, Senegal was the only colony in sub-Saharan Africa where France fully applied its ideas of colonial assimilation, whereby Senegal was granted its own governmental assemblies and municipal councils, and whereby a small class of assimilated elites (*evolués*) could qualify for French citizenship (Gellar 1995, 5–19). For some, the connection between Senegal's colonial history and its contemporary environment, especially in relation to the emergence and development of television, may seem remote and even tenuous. But as many observers of Senegal have noted, the country's colonial experiences have influenced its present-day political, economic, and social organization, as well as its cultural life profoundly (Gellar 1995, 8; Martin 1995; Schraeder 1997; see also Coulon 1988; Diop and Diouf 1990, 251–81; Boone 1992, 344–49; McNamara 1989, 95–141).

Through the colonial policy of *la mission civilsatrice*, France sought to consolidate its power by spreading French language and culture. When Senegal became independent, France abandoned its formal civilizing mission. Instead, government officials and diplomats embarked on policies for a new period of decolonization, which centered discursively on notions of cooperation among French-speaking countries (Martin 1995; Ager 1996; Schraeder 1997). Replacing the colonial mission of "French-ifying" the Senegalese was *francophonie*, which in its most literal sense means the community of those having the ability to speak French. But in a more political sense it invokes a global French-speaking partnership led by France and concerted efforts (particularly by states) to keep this cultural-political alliance intact (Miller 1990, 182–201; Hargreaves and McKinney 1997, 3–6; Léger 1987; Schraeder 1997; Tétu 1987).

The first two presidents of Senegal, Léopold Sédar Senghor (1960–1980) and Abdou Diouf (1981–2000), have been keen to maintain the country's participation in the francophone community and reinforce Senegal's special relationship with France (Chipman 1989, 227–55; Diop and Diouf 1990, 251–81; Gellar 1995, 83–107; Schraeder 1997). However, it is difficult to understand fully *francophonie*'s cultural and political force without exploring its modes of operation (Hargreaves and McKinney 1997, 3–6; Miller 1990, 182). In many ways, the French presence and its ties to *francophonie* in Senegal have been developed and maintained first through the development of a national television service in the 1960s and then through the introduction of primarily French television in the early 1990s (McNamara 1989, 133; Silla 1994). Yet the French cultural intrusion never has been complete and always has been complicated by national (Senegalese) cultural groups who have appropriated, reformed, and come

Images of television permeate popular Senegalese culture. In this cartoon, a frustrated youth takes his set to a serviceman whose tools and shop location tell us that that he was a blacksmith (*forgeron*) before getting into the TV/VCR repair business. The sign on his shop says that he repairs "all brand" (none of the French used in the cartoon would pass muster with the Académie Française). One onlooker observes, "Hey, this guy didn't turn off his TV." Another says, "Mine smokes a lot less than that."

up with new or hybridized uses, meanings, and understandings of television and its programming.

The remainder of this chapter addresses television in Senegal in relationship to its development by the French and more recent trends in terms of the introduction of French and other international television channels. The discussion is organized around the institutional history of television in Senegal and the country's contemporary broadcast landscape. Throughout, the discussion explores the interplay among stakeholders—state, capital, market, and the public—that combine to shape Senegalese television.

The Sénégalisation *of Television*

By nearly any measure, Africa remains the least connected, the least wired, and the least developed of all the world's media environments. As access to television has expanded rapidly and widely in other regions, Africans generally still see little of the medium. According to U.N. statistics, in 1965 there were 192 million TV receivers in the world, of which 600,000 receivers were in Africa (compared with 84 million in North America). By the mid-1990s, there were 1.3 billion receivers, of which 37 million were in Africa (compared with 338 million in North America). As of 1996, there are some 320,000 receivers in Senegal, a country of nearly 10 million people.

Senegalese television first began its operations in Dakar, the capital city, in 1964.

At the outset, the government declared the mission of telecasting to be purely educational and developmental. In an address to officials of his party, the Union Progressiste Sénégalaise, President Senghor noted that television's mission was to serve as a base of "knowledge and training for the masses," which ultimately would facilitate "our march toward progress" (Congrès de l'Union 1969).[1] Funded by UNESCO, the U.N. Development Program, and the French and Canadian governments, the television service provided viewers in Dakar with information and training to improve farming, nutrition, health, and entrepreneurial skills.[2] The six-year experiment was modest in scale. Some offices at Radio Sénégal were converted for television production, producers and technicians were sent to France for training, a dozen or so television receivers were imported, and programs were aired for an hour or two in the evenings. In the early part of the experiment, from 1964 to 1966, programming on housekeeping, nutrition, and hygiene was targeted to five hundred women. These women were organized into groups or télé-clubs so that they could watch and discuss programs together. Later, from 1966, the experiment focused on general adult literacy training (Fougeyrollas 1967; Head 1974, 302; Katz and Wedell 1977, 84–89; Carlos 1985).

The emphasis of Senegalese television on education is not at all surprising, given the era in which the experiment was launched. Broadcast media—both radio and television—were hypothesized to be capable not only of transforming "traditional" societies into "modern" ones but also of fending off communism (Lerner 1958; Schramm 1964; Simpson 1994). These objectives made U.N. agencies, as well as Western governments such as the French, keen to fund them. Moreover, the French, ever influential in Senegal, transferred their state-dominated, noncommercial, public service model of broadcasting to former colonies through the training of broadcasters, in the assistance of program production, and through technology imports. For its part, the Senegalese government recognized the poor state of general education, a legacy left by the French in many of its former colonies, and sought a remedy through broadcasting (Head 1974, 302; Cruise O'Brien 1985; Tudesq 1992, 47–59).

For Senghor, both radio and television broadcasting contributed to Senegalese society by providing information, knowledge, and culture that would elevate average Senegalese citizens, transform them qualitatively, and stave off "subversive attempts" (Congrès de l'Union 1969). What is somewhat unusual about the experiment's development-oriented programming was that it was exclusively in Wolof, the largest national (but not official) language. Most television services of newly decolonized countries in the early 1960s used former colonial languages with the intent of building them as lingua francas. The president himself widely promoted French language use as a means by which Senegalese society could remain a part of a global francophone community. He saw French as central to the "convergence of [French-speaking] civilizations," as well as to the "consciousness of a society marching toward modernity" (Allocution de M. le Président 1968). In particular, he pushed for the use of French in print media (Allocution de M. le Président 1968). Yet he supported Wolof, rather than French, as the language of television. Interestingly, Senghor's nuanced position on media language allowed him to achieve various political aims. Television in Wolof allowed the government to appear to reach out to the masses in an attempt to transform society and to resist continued French cultural influence by promoting a national language. At the same time, promoting French as the language of print media allowed Senghor and his government to stay "engaged in the project of *francophonie. . . .* our cultural reality," a long and important obsession of Senghor's (Allocution de M. le Président 1968).

When funding for the television experiment was exhausted in 1969, television in Senegal simply ended. At the time, there was no intention of developing a general service, though wealthy expatriate French, Lebanese, Moroccan, and Portuguese communities could and perhaps would have given substantial support to telecasting that emphasized entertainment programming over development (Head 1974; Carlos 1985). Nonetheless, Senghor opposed the continuation of television broadcasting as too expensive for the country, which was faced with mounting debt and declining living standards (Congrès de l'Union 1969; see also Gellar 1995).

Soon after the end of the experiment, rich expatriates and Senegalese elites began to exert pressure on the Senghor government to relaunch television as a conventional entertainment medium. By 1972, television in Senegal was reintroduced, despite the opposition of many government ministers, including the president. In fact, one minister called television "a jewel for the tired and spent bourgeoisie" (Katz and Wedell 1977, 87). In considering whether to have any television at all, the government began by revisiting its experimental model from the 1960s. One government report suggested that using existing equipment and facilities from the earlier experiment would keep down the cost of reintroduction. The report also raised the question of how the government might "facilitate individual reception through the acquisition of television sets" when in the earlier experimental phase all viewing occurred communally (Compte rendu du Conseil interministériel 1971). In the end, the government's decision to relaunch television was made easier by an offer from Thomson-CSF, a French manufacturer, to donate the necessary equipment. In an arrangement negotiated through the French Ministry of Cooperation, Thomson-CFS gave a number of television sets to be used for communal viewing around Dakar, which was the only viewing area. But more important, the French company became the sole supplier of television sets bought by elites and imported into Senegal.

After a ground station was installed in Gandiol (just south of Saint-Louis), Senegal's second try with television began just in time for the 1972 Olympics. Innumerable newspaper ads for Thomson-CSF television sets promoted sales so that Senegalese could join the rest of the world watching the Olympics live and in color. But as letters and columns to various local newspapers suggest, many potential Senegalese television viewers were frustrated by the sets' prohibitive cost. Television remained a medium for elites. As one man asked rhetorically in a letter to the government newspaper, *Le Soleil,*

> "For us, a developing country, with still limited means, having just recently obtained television, the provider of information, education, and entertainment, . . . what kind of television should we have? And also, for whom? The elite or the masses?" ("Télé—des émissions pour qui?" 13 August 1972).

This frustration also was recorded in a person-on-the-street poll conducted by *Le Soleil*. One man queried in the poll worried that television sets would become mandatory in dowries given when daughters married. Another man said he wondered why the government made receivers so expensive when they were supposed to be used by all for development purposes. A woman ventured that the government should make businesses sell sets on credit. Still another man interviewed thought that buying a television was ridiculous if the government did not have plans to continue broadcasting entertainment programs after the end of the Olympics ("L'enquête," *Le Soleil* 29 August 1972). Indeed, letters and columns indicate widespread concern about who would have access to television. In an article published in a small opposition newspaper, the writer complained that telecasting was intended not for the people but for elites:

> We have learned that the government has "ordered" the installation of some 100 television sets. "In the homes of all the ministers; all members of the cabinet; the secretaries general; and some of the members of the National Assembly, the Supreme Court, the Economic and Social Counsel, and the governor of Cap-Vert." This information sounds a little overstated.... Nonetheless, only about 50 televisions were installed for the entire UNESCO project [of the 1960s]. ("Télé-Munich 'Ministériel'?" *La Lettre Fermée* 11–24 August 1972)

Though the government initially planned to have broadcasts only for the three weeks of the Olympic Games, demand for television's continuation, especially among buyers of sets, was strong enough that the Senghor government decided not to pull the plug. In a report recommending the formation of a broadcast policy committee, the secretary general's office noted that television would continue because it had become an "irreversible part of modern life" (Projet de décret portant création 1972). In fact, the government went so far as to encourage further sales of receivers when it decided against adopting license fees and dropped the 105 percent import tax ("Baisse effectivement des prix," *Le Soleil* 15 March 1973).

In December 1973 with the passage of Law 73–51, the government formed a new broadcast structure, the Office de Radiodiffusion-Télévision Sénégalaise (ORTS). Administratively, ORTS was modeled on the French broadcasting authority (ORTF). Established as a public corporation with oversight from the Ministry of Communication, ORTS expanded its mandate from purely educational objectives to include entertainment ("La télé continue," *Le Soleil* 14 September 1972; Projet de loi abrogeant 1977). Newly conceived, the medium was no longer "only educational, but a television of the masses at the same time informative, cultural, and entertaining" ("Décisions hier au Conseil," *Le Soleil* 5 October 1971). Senghor recognized, though apparently with reluctance, the powerful draw of television. In a speech given at a ribbon-cutting ceremony of a transmitter in Thiès (seventy kilometers northeast of Dakar), the president said,

> why all this passion for television? Why, every day, under the stars, do men, women, young and old, poor and rich, commune, immobile and silent, as with a ritual, in the front of the little screen? It's because television fulfills mankind's dream permitting him

to witness the world: to live in the universe and share the feeling of being a citizen of the planet. (Allocution de M. le Président 1976)

Part of being this global citizen meant speaking French and participating in the francophone community. Unlike the UNESCO television experiment in which broadcasts were in Wolof, the new service used French almost exclusively ("L'ORTS est né," *Le Soleil* 23 November 1973). At the time, the French government, through ORTF, was responsible for most of the new service's technology, training of technicians and producers, and programs (Compte rendu du Conseil national 1976). In the mid-1970s, about 75 percent of programs aired on Senegalese television were imported (Katz and Wedell 1977, 157). Though ORTS broadcast some literacy and development-oriented shows in national languages, the program schedule had taken a decidedly entertainment turn, with most shows being action-adventure, family-situation dramas, soap operas, and films. Programs originated most often in France and the United States (which were then dubbed) (Katz and Wedell 1977, 156–66; Carlos 1985, 166–68; Ly Diop 1989, 23–24). French feature films and series such as *Animals of the World* and European soccer were popular among viewers. American shows such as *Mannix*, *Columbo*, and *Gunsmoke* also attracted audiences. Despite the movement of ORTS into entertainment, Senghor still thought of television as playing a grander role in Senegalese society than mere "distraction":

> Our television is not a commercial one whose chief objective would be the conditioning of viewers to make themselves into commodity consumers. We have deliberately opted for a different solution, because it is the best way to assure consideration of the general concerns and interests of all Senegalese, and especially to stay rooted in our place, while at the same time to be open to all civilizations of the world. (Allocution de M. le Président 1976)

As the president continued, television was "to serve 'Homosénégalensis,' to assist him in development, to enrich his personality, that is the task of 'Télésénégalaise'" (Allocution de M. le Président 1976). To fulfill that role, Senegalese television had to be both outward and inward looking: It had to connect Senegalese citizens outward to the francophone world and to provide programs that were thought to be culturally relevant by the government. In the same speech, Senghor begins to make use of the terms *sénégaliser* (infinitive) and *sénégalisation* (noun) to suggest that television, though primarily in French, must be made to feel Senegalese and imbue Senegalese values.

The challenge to the *sénégalisation* of television was that ORTS lacked the funds to create programs that were of the technical quality of the imports. While attention was being paid to the quality of the French language used in broadcasts ("L'ORTS est né," *Le Soleil* 23 November 1973), shows were being produced in the same poorly equipped television studio, once converted from a radio office, used for the UNESCO project ("Quand le petit écran," *Le Soleil* 28 May 1973). *Sénégalisation* came to mean, in government mandates to ORTS, expansion of television diffusion beyond Dakar, an increase in locally produced programs in national languages and French, diversification of programming, better-quality programs, collaborative work between film and television producers, and a decrease, between 25 to 30 percent, of imported programs (see, e.g., Conseil national de l'audio-visuel 1978; Allocution de M. Cherif Thiam, l'ORTS 1985).

Making Senegalese television more Senegalese was going to be expensive. While the president talked about ORTS's importance to *francophonie* and to nation building, the government—like many other newly decolonized countries—found it had to reconcile demands for the *sénégalisation* of television with the budgetary realities of a failing economy. Some critics, such as Abdou Rahman Cissé, acting commissioner of the Ministry of Information from 1962 to 1964, have suggested that television was intentionally underfunded so it could remain a toy for the amusement of elites rather than a tool of social change (personal interview 14 July 1996). Because the government's attentions were turned toward Senegal's high rates of unemployment and inflation, funding for television seriously stagnated and plans for *sénégalisation* stalled from the mid-1970s through the 1980s ("Conseil interministériel," *Le Soleil* 26 October 1983). Though some 80 percent of ORTS's operating budget came from the government during this period, ORTS still had to seek ways of keeping itself afloat. The governments of France and Germany were courted and gave financial and technical support ("Plan d'urgence," *Le Soleil* 2 November 1979; "300 millions," *Le Soleil* 28 April 1981). The government, now led by President Abdou Diouf, also tried tinkering with ORTS's mandate as a way to make the service revenue-generating. According to a revision of the law that created ORTS as purely a public corporation, ORTS was redefined as a "public corporation with industrial and commercial features," freeing the service to pursue advertising, corporate, and other nongovernmental revenue (Projet de loi 1977; Secrétariat du Conseil des Ministrès 1985).

RTS and Canal Horizons in the 1990s

Throughout the 1970s and 1980s, ORTS hobbled along on its tight budget. But political, economic, and social currents in Senegal were undergoing change. In the early 1990s, Diouf began to suggest the need to open Senegal's media landscape. Scrapping the language of *sénégalisation*, Diouf set out a new course:

> our country, engaged in a battle of image and sound on a global level, must find appropriate responses that affirm Senegal's spirit and preserve its cultural identity. Today, the proliferation of television signals that crisscross the world and the development of direct satellite television have brought about a competition, a conquest of audiences not only national but transnational. The African continent can no longer be sheltered from these upheavals of the global broadcast landscape. The risks of cultural erosion and the fragmentation of our national audiences are real. But this situation can and must be for us, a developing country, an opportunity to transform ourselves, to evolve qualitatively, and to renew our imagination. (Allocution de M. le Président 1990)

With this statement Diouf then announced two key changes in government broadcast policy: the restructuring of ORTS into a new entity, Radiodiffusion-Télévision Sénégalaise (RTS), and the approval of the French satellite subscription channel, Canal Horizons, to begin operation in 1991. The purpose of the reorganization of ORTS into RTS was to permit the service to pursue revenue generation further. Passed by Law 92-02 in January 1992, RTS remained a state-run entity but was defined as a "national company" rather than a public corporation. Though it retained its educational, development, and nation-building mandates, it also was newly charged with creating programs of sufficient quality that they could be exchanged internationally. To fulfill these objectives, the government intended for RTS to become more efficient and financially self-sustaining by handing over day-to-day management to a "dynamic cadre capable of improving [RTS's] production potential" (Projet de loi portant approbation 1992; see also "La RTS passe société nationale," *Le Soleil* 30 January 1992).

Despite the restructuring of ORTS into RTS, the Senegalese television authority faced intense public criticism. As one viewer commented, "RTS translated by the young people of Podor [a town just south of the Mauritanian border] means 'nothing on every night' " (a play on words: "Rien Tous les Soirs" [RTS]) ("Podor sans télé," *Sud Quotidien* 5 August 1993). Many letters to the editor in newspapers such as *Le Soleil*, *Sud Quotidien*, and *Wal Fadjri* described RTS programming as "dull," "poor quality," "silly," and as involving "too much talking." Wrote one columnist, "In brief, we have not a public service television but a state television, and with that, inertia, controls, and heavy handedness" ("Le télé unique, un mal unique," *Sud Quotidien* 31 December 1993).

The president's calls for RTS's programming "to contribute to civil society," "to reflect the political, cultural, religious diversity of the Senegalese people," and "to prompt a national democratic dialogue" ("Edifier un paysage," *Le Soleil* 2 November 1990) were met with skepticism by many. Opposition party members began to argue that there could be no democratic debate if RTS was the sole television outlet. As one guest columnist, showing his frustration, wrote to the government newspaper, *Le Soleil*, "Democratic dialogue can only take place when ideas compete. It's necessary at minimum to open the media of the state not only to the opposition, but also to civil society" ("Recentrer le débat," 2 November 1990).

By the late 1980s and early 1990s, Diouf's government had been dogged by a number of political crises—university strikes, conflict with Mauritania, rioting in the capital, and charges of corruption of elections. He was very much in need of regaining his political authority (Coulon 1988; Diop and Diouf 1990; Diouf 1996; Gellar 1995). When he first announced in his 1990 speech the creation of RTS and the launching of the French Canal Horizons, he suggested that both would "improve and diversify programming, and stimulate national production" (Allocution de M. le Président 1990). Certainly, improving and diversifying programming at the national level would help to satisfy domestic critics and perhaps to deflect some of the political heat focused on him. Seemingly responding to criticism that RTS could not foster and sustain democratic dialogue, pluralism, and civil society, the government created the Haut Conseil de la Radio Télévision (HCRT) in 1991 (Law 92-57). The task of the High Council was (and is) to provide opposition parties with some access to RTS. It was described as an independent structure that would guard pluralism and guarantee freedom of information by allowing Senegalese political parties to have broadcast time to present their platforms ("L'ère de responsabilité," *Le Soleil* 27–28 July 1991). Still, many found the government's opening of Senegalese airwaves to be little more than an empty gesture. As one Ministry of Communication official, who later became a High Council member, said,

> I would like to think the Council will work. But the problem of television in Senegal is that the opposition doesn't have access to RTS. Even with the electoral code [which set out airtime allocations], the opposition doesn't have the same access, what with the president and ministers shown day in and day out. (personal interview with Moussa Paye 5 July 1994)

In fact, several parties complained that their time on RTS was too limited or that they received broadcast time only when there would be few viewers (Ly 1993, 98; "L'opposition boycotte," *Le Soleil* 15 March 1992; "Dialogue sur l'utilisation des mediats d'état," *Le Soleil* 22 January 1993). The government argued that the High Council was necessary to ensure access to RTS at a time when the government saw itself as undergoing a "change of direction toward deregulation" ("L'ère de responsabilité," *Le Soleil* 27–28 July 1991; see also, "Respecter les principes du pluralism," *Le Soleil* 10 December 1992). Some media professionals fretted about the potential chilling effect that government broadcasting directives might have on actual political debate (Paye 1992; "Parlez, il en restera," *Wal Fadjri* 8–14 January 1993; personal interview with Mame Less Camara 12 July 1996). Yet others, such as journalist and playwright Boubacar Boris Diop, defended the HCRT, suggesting it was a show of "good will on the part of the state to encourage greater pluralism" ("L'HCRT vu par les professionels," *Le Soleil* 4 September 1991; see also "Les objections du RND," *Le Soleil* 19 September 1991). The reorganization of RTS, which brought about the subsequent creation of the HCRT, was an important element in the government's rehabilitation of its political image. By embracing discourses of democracy and pluralism, the Diouf government could point to RTS as the domestic forum that would "contribute to the enrichment of national political debate" (Haut Conseil de la Radio-Télévision 1994, 25).

But Diouf also had a second communications strategy for improving his political fortunes by opening the broadcast environment: the introduction of international broadcasting into Senegal. Given the long and sometimes vitriolic debate about the impact of Western media on "developing" societies seen in the discussions of the New World Information and Communication Order, it seems almost counterintuitive that the Senegalese government would invite a major French communications corporation to broadcast within its borders. Earlier in his presidency, Diouf expressed concerns about the impact of global informational and entertainment imbalances (Allocution de M. le Président 1986). But just months after his 1990 speech, Diouf announced the introduction of Canal Horizons. Serge Adda, Canal Horizons' director general, soon arrived in Dakar to help set up shop. Canal Horizons is a subsidiary of Canal Plus and a French public broadcast agency (Société Financière de Radiodiffusion, SOFIRAD) that manages international broadcast operations. Adda, touting the Canal venture and appealing to national pride, noted that the country would "play a pioneering role in Africa" with the opening of the service in Senegal, Tunisia, and Gabon ("CH montre ses grilles," *Le Soleil* 19 October 1990; see also "La France multiplie les médias," *Jeune Afrique* 11 December 1990). Furthermore, using some of the language of the president, he told Diouf that Canal programs would support "pluralism, dialogues of cultures, and equal relations between North-South." Adda also promised to help fund Senegalese programming on the station ("CH montre ses grilles," *Le Soleil* 19 October 1990).

Diouf liked what he heard. A month later, he said that Canal Horizons would be "an axis of cultural development, a lever for the creation and production of Senegalese television, and a melting pot of cultural dialogue, notably North-South, but otherwise too" ("CH en vue," *Le Soleil* 21 November 1990). What Diouf and his government had in mind by allowing Canal Horizons to broadcast in Senegal is not exactly clear. At home, he allowed a slight opening of RTS to the opposition. With Canal Horizons, he could engage in a ruse: He could tell opponents that they could voice their issues on Senegal-produced programs airing on Canal Horizons, though he probably suspected (correctly) that there would be none. Either way— with the reorganization of RTS and the introduction of Canal Horizons—Diouf could look like a proponent of free, pluralistic, democratic dialogue.

The Canal Horizons deal also afforded the Senegalese government another payoff. Via RTS and SONATEL, the then parastatal telephone service, the government received 15 percent of Canal Horizons earnings in Senegal. The private Senegalese investors, two former ministers (one of whom was restored to office in late 1991), a prominent Muslim cleric, and six businessmen, took a total of 70 percent (the other 15 percent presumably went to France; figures vary according to source; "Sénégal; Images très privées," *Jeune Afrique* 25 July–1 August 1990; "CH en vue," *Le Soleil* 21 November 1990; personal interview with Anne Marie Senghor Boissy 7 July 1994). Additionally, Fara N'Diaye, former deputy and closely affiliated with Abdoulaye Wade, who was Diouf's chief opposition in the 1988 and 2000 elections, was appointed president of the Senegalese franchise.

Certainly, media groups such as Canal Horizons did not enter African countries because they thought they would be hugely profitable. African media markets were and remain the smallest and poorest in the world. In many instances, the French government, through a host of agencies, urged French media corporations to enter Africa. Maintaining a French presence in Africa was as much a goal as turning a profit was ("Un paysage audiovisuel," *Jeune Afrique* 18 December 1991–8 January 1992; "Les chaînes d'Afrique," *Jeune Afrique* 3–9 February 1994). The introduction of Canal Horizons into Senegal permitted the notion of *francophonie*, and Senegal's connection to the rest of the French-speaking world, to continue shaping the country's broadcast landscape. The francophone connection was vital enough that three years later, in 1994, another service, this one explicitly devoted to preserving the French language and protecting francophone cultures, entered the Senegalese market at the request of the Diouf government. Negotiations began at the 1989 Francophonie Summit, held in Dakar, where Diouf pleaded with delegates to help create an African television channel. Such a channel was seen as too costly, so Diouf seized the idea of expanding TV5, a television consortium of French-speaking countries, into francophone Africa ("Une chaîne pour l'Afrique," *Jeune Afrique* 9–15 July 1992; Silla 1994; "Les chaînes d'Afrique," *Jeune Afrique* 3–9 February 1994). Planning of this expansion was facilitated through the French Ministry of Francophonie. Senegalese Mactar Silla, who became the president of the TV5 Afrique, described the service as "the channel for cross-cultural meeting and diversity, the channel of francophones and francophiles" ("L'apport de TV5," *Le Soleil* 1 October 1992). TV5 began in 1984 with five member groups: three French channels (TF1, Atenne 2, FR3), one Belgian (RTBF), and one Swiss (TSR). Later, a Québec channel (CTQR) joined TV5, with each participating channel contributing French-language programming.

By 1994, some thirty years after television in Senegal was first launched, broadcasting had evolved in ways that Senghor would not have anticipated. The introduction of French and francophone television into Senegal also came at a time when radio broadcasting was undergoing great change. As it did with television, by the early 1990s the government began to allow international radio broadcasters into Senegal. The first of these were Radio France Internationale (RFI) and Afrique No. 1. Then, on July 1, 1994, Sud FM became Senegal's first private commercial radio station. The station's owner, Babacar Touré of the newspaper *Sud Quotidien*, had negotiated with the government for seven years, and at various points his production equipment had been seized (personal interview with Touré, 27 June 1994). Sud FM was soon followed by other privately owned Senegalese radio stations, such as Duniya and Nostalgie. A Ministry of Communication official, Moussa Paye, suggested that the government had to privatize radio if its stated "commitment to opening all forms of communication was not to be a charade" (personal interview 5 July 1994; see also "L'antenne ne sera pas à tous," *Wal Fadjri* 23 November 1993). Indeed, the private radio stations carried many call-in and talk show programs that frequently turned political. Despite the fact that radio reaches far more Senegalese than television does, the government did not acquiesce to pressures from business and religious sectors to permit private Senegalese-owned and operated television. There was too much potential that such stations could become venues for domestic political challenge. Instead, the government preferred the appearance of openness that international television services afforded.

Though the government continued to discuss broadcasting for rural development purposes, that line of discourse all but disappeared in the context of major urban areas such as Dakar and Saint-Louis (see, e.g., "Quelles programmes pour l'Afrique" and "Les antennes diaboliques," both *Jeune Afrique* 17–23 November 1994). While TV5 itself was largely devoted to news, information, documentaries, talk shows, and some films, the service provided a "bouquet" of other channels, including Canal France Internationale (CFI), CNN (which the French opposed because it operates in English and is U.S.-based), MCM, a French music video channel, and Portuguese and Moroccan television. Canal Horizons continued to be devoted, as ever, to entertainment: movies, many of which were American and dubbed into French; sports, particularly soccer but also Worldwide Wrestling Federation events; cartoons, such as *Tintin*; and music, especially jazz. RTS, which rightly surmised that it could not compete on a technical level with TV5 or Canal Horizons, continued to show largely imported entertainment programs (around 75 percent, according to the RTS journalist Adrienne Diop, personal interview 7 July 1994) but also found a niche in game shows, religious programs, Senegalese wrestling (*bëre* or *làmb* in Wolof), regional news, theater, storytelling, and music in Wolof and other national languages ("Les programmes de la nouvelle grille," *Le Soleil* 2, November 1990; "TV: La grille du changement?" *Le Soleil* 8 October 1992).

Because of all the publicity surrounding Canal Horizons and TV5, demand for these services grew. But access to these channels was limited to major cities and to those who could afford the start-up costs and/or monthly fees for special equipment. For example, viewers of TV5 needed a special (MMDS) antenna, which, in 1994, cost 100,000 CFA or about $182. Likewise, to receive Canal Horizons, viewers needed a decoder box, which was bought (not rented) for 50,000 CFA or about $91, with an additional monthly subscriber fee of 17,000 CFA or about $31. A television set itself cost about 300,000 CFA or $545 in 1994. These prices were steep for many Senegalese, who had seen their French-backed currency, the CFA franc, devalued by 50 percent in January 1994. Responding to the economic situation while trying to build their audience base, Canal Horizons and TV5 offered subscribers special breaks in prices (personal interviews with Wahab Touré of TV5 5 July 1994; and Boissy of Canal Horizons 7 July 1994). Particularly around major holidays and special events—Ramadan, Christmas, the Africa Cup, the Olympics—ads in newspapers and on radio and television (including RTS) publicized price reductions for services. Even particular groups, such as civil servants and teachers who were just on the fringe of being able to afford Canal Horizons and TV5, were targeted in campaigns.

The relations among the three television services were largely noncompetitive. Each had its own market niche and saw itself as complementing or supplementing the others (personal interviews with W. Touré 5 July 1994; Diop and Boissy 7 July 1994). RTS saw itself as appealing to viewers who wanted Senegalese programs. Of course, the tight budget for programming was a constant issue as RTS tried to create new shows to generate new ad revenue (personal interview with Diop 7 July 1994). As Babacar Diagne, RTS's director for television, noted, "My ambition is not to compete with Canal Horizons in the international domain. We haven't the means. I will invest in another area: national life" ("Les programmes de la nouvelle grille," *Le Soleil* 2 November 1990). For its part, Canal Horizons saw itself as a provider of international entertainment. Its marketing research revealed that in Dakar and its environs (about two million people in and around a thirty five-Kilometer perimeter of Dakar, Rufisque, and Bargny), there were some 65,000 households with television sets. Of those 65,000, Canal Horizons sought to subscribe 25,000. By 1994 the service had reached into 11,000 homes. An additional 3,500 households subscribed periodically when they could scrape together enough to pay the monthly fee. Of Canal Horizons' subscribers, 70 percent were Senegalese (personal interview with Boissy 7 July 1994). Because its service had only recently been introduced, TV5 had the smallest audience share in 1994. According to a TV5 marketing survey of 525 Dakar residents, the service had somewhat less than half of Canal Horizons' subscribers. TV5's Wahab Touré put the figure at about 5,000.[3] He also suggested that because TV5 was more affordable than Canal Horizons and because of the channel's emphasis on informational programming, the service was reaching largely well-educated Sene-

Secular Santa sells the Canal Horizons television service in this 1993 ad, which appeared in several newspapers, including *Le Soleil* and *Sud Quotidien*. Just in time for the Christmas season—and in a country where some 95 percent of the population is Muslim—Canal Horizons reduces the price of decoder boxes from 100,000 CFA to 50,000 and offers one month of free service. As the ad suggests, December is the month of gifts for family, friends, and clients, with Canal Horizons being the gift that allows Senegalese "to always see more."

galese (personal interview 5 July 1994). To help build an audience base by stabilizing the cost of the services, Canal Horizons began to distribute the TV5 "bouquet" of channels in late 1994, offering various kinds of price packages for basic and premium services, which included TV5.

Though all three television services had worked out their appeals to various segments of Senegalese viewers, Canal Horizons and TV5 at their launchings had promised to facilitate North-South dialogues. In practice, for Canal Horizons that meant little more than increasing the number of films from the "South" to about 12 percent ("Les chaînes d'Afrique," *Jeune Afrique* 3–9 February 1994). By contrast, TV5 had vowed to help African producers create new programs for broadcast. At the 1993 Francophonie Summit, promises were made, in particular through the French government's Agence de Coopération Culturelle et Technique (ACCT), to coproduce five African programs that would air two hours a day. The funds for this level of coproduction never materialized. But there have been attempts at some coproduction. The first was a soap-style show set in Senegal called *Fann Océan* and described as "le 'Dallas' sénégalais." The program—six fifty-minute shows—was created through efforts of RTS, the Belgian TV5 partner, and the French ACCT, and it aired in 1992 on RTS. While some viewers wrote to newspapers to say that as Senegalese they were proud that *Fann Océan* had been produced, press reviews of the program were fairly harsh ("Le Fann," *Sud Quotidien* 7 January 1992; "Les bons and les méchants," *Sud Quotidien* 8 October 1993). One avid television viewer said of the show, "Just thinking about it gives me a headache."[4]

Whether *Fann Océan* was bad may matter little. One of the outcomes of the program was that it served as an opportunity to train Senegalese producers and helped them land positions on other coproductions. The letters, reviews, and reactions to *Fann Océan* also are all examples of a larger debate about the role Senegalese audiences think television should play in the national discourse. For many viewers, programs such as *Fann Océan* evoked a national pride. Others whom I interviewed or corresponded with said that television helped them to think about Senegal's relation to the rest of world, particularly outside francophone regions. For these respondents, Paris was no longer the single metropole to which they looked for knowledge and inspiration concerning economics, politics, education, immigration, and even fashion. The anglophone world was in, and many shifted their sights toward New York and Washington, D.C. For example, the arrest of O. J. Simpson, with all the accompanying discussions of *Miranda* rights and due process, allowed many Senegalese viewers both to question legal code inherited from the French and to consider in a new light the government's harassment of political opponents.

By no means are domestic and international television services accepted uncritically. The impact of television, particularly Western programs, on the values and attitudes of young people has been the source of much public discussion. Columnists in the press have argued that Western programs on any of the channels carry values that are not compatible with those of Senegal, influencing, for example, the manner in which children address parents, how young girls dress, sexuality, and life expectations ("Un mal nécessaire?" *Le Soleil* 4 February 1992; "Une autre télévision pour les riches," *Wal Fadjri* 7 July 1993; "A consommer avec modération," *Wal Fadjri* 29

September 1993; "Promiscuité familiale," *Sud Quotidien* 1 October 1993; "Des jeunes africains," *Le Soleil* 9 July 1996; see also "Doit-on interdire à nos enfants," *Sudonline* 16 February 1999). In both interviews and questionnaires, many Senegalese viewers suggested that television did not have any effect on their lives. As several Senegalese described television's impact: "I'm autonomous in my thinking"; "I'm independent in what I believe"; and "I think for myself, then talk with family and friends." Perhaps summarizing this view best, a student at the Université Gaston Berger said, "I know Westerners think Africans aren't very smart and so will think TV will have a big influence on us, but it's not true. We know what is real and what is not real on TV. I can judge." But while many regular viewers of television claimed that television did not affect them, they argued that it influenced others. Notably, male viewers often said that television shaped the attitudes and behaviors of young women too much, and women said that television swayed children too much. Many pointed toward changes in fashion—preference for Western clothes, length of dresses, emphasis put on slimness, wearing of dreadlocks, and the use of rap/hip hop language and posturing—as examples of how television influences young people for the worse.

Others argued that television has divided Senegal further into "haves" and "have nots," especially in terms of class but also region ("Une autre télévision pour les riches," *Wal Fadjri* 7 July 1993; "Ma télé? Il n'en a pas," *Sud Quotidien* 19 July 1993; "Télévision: Les paraboles des riches," *Sud Quotidien* 27 September 1993). Because of the cost associated with obtaining Canal Horizons and TV5, those services in particular have been criticized for their elitism. Both Moussa Paye of the Communication Ministry and Babacar Touré of *Sud* (personal interviews 5 July 1994 and 27 June 1994) have suggested that the Senegalese government allowed Canal Horizons and TV5 to enter the country to meet elites' demands for the trappings of "modern" society. Many of my respondents echoed this view and added that they felt the French and francophone channels helped the Senegalese government divert viewers' attention away from local reporting on domestic issues. Many Senegalese I talked with said they did not want to be swamped by imported television programming; they valued Senegalese shows, though they wished they were of higher technical quality. Some viewers suggested that they wanted the government to intervene to ensure greater educational or cultural content, but many more said that the government should have no interest in RTS or the other international channels because such involvement was undemocratic.

Conclusion

While there has been a good deal of research that has explored how older and/or traditional forms and functions of popular art in Africa have been transformed through interaction with foreign cultures (see, e.g., Arnoldi, Geary, and Hardin 1996; Barber 1997a, 1997b), there has not been a corresponding interest in media. In the past thirty years, television has become part of the Senegalese popular imagination, with images and ideas about television making their way into songs, *sous verre* (under glass) painting, cartoons, postcards, wood carvings, magazines, and radio talk shows.

The entry of television into Senegalese thought and national discourse and the form that television in Senegal has taken are closely tied to a uniquely Senegalese postcolonial history. Senegal has not been simply inundated since independence by a larger flood of images and programming coming from the West. Rather, the attenuated introduction of television to the country and the array of programming made incrementally available to different segments of Senegalese society suggest a nation and its leaders trying, largely unsuccessfully, to manage cultural life according to their own designs. Government decisions have set parameters for television growth and content, but the overall effect of policy has been to contribute to the eclecticism of Senegalese airwaves, rather than shape television content. Television, like the rest of Senegalese cultural life, is variously parochial and cosmopolitan, but distinctly Senegalese in its combination of values.

Central to the emergence of this eclecticism have been the idiosyncratic thought and careful political positioning of key leaders such as Senghor and Diouf, navigating through decades of political and cultural change in their country. As shown here, they have needed at various times to appeal to particular ethnic and class constituencies, and these appeals have led to ad hoc and therefore often inconsistent decisions about media, especially television. The increasing cosmopolitanism of the Senegalese population at large, partly a function of world travels of Senegalese citizens from a surprising variety of ethnic and class backgrounds, is a major cultural condition that leaders are navigating now (Perry 1997). Openings to world television during the 1990s have only partly satisfied the demand for variety and quality. The trend toward media openness and a free market of cultural ideas is likely to continue because large segments of the Senegalese population demand it. State oversight has a long tradition in Senegal, however, and the continued opening of media markets is likely to be a state-managed process until such time as available technology has overridden the capacity of the state to control it.

NOTES

The author would like to thank her family for enduring the long absences, especially during the flood of 1996. Also, many thanks go to Papa Demba Sarr for his assistance with the project. This project was supported by the University of Wisconsin Graduate School and the African Studies Program. The West Africa Research Association and colleagues at Université Gaston Berger de Saint-Louis were very helpful.

1. All translations from French to English are by the author. Texts of speeches, government documents, and news clippings were gathered at the Senegalese National Archives in Dakar. The newspaper *Le Soleil*, which is government-owned, is treated as part of official government discourse. *Le Soleil* calls itself the "Official newspaper of Senegal." Stories used from other private (often opposition) newspapers, such as *Sud Quotidien* and *Wal Fadjri*, were gathered at the newspapers' libraries in Dakar.

2. With a .05-kilowatt transmitter, broadcasts did not reach beyond thirty kilometers, roughly the city limits.

3. Finding just how many people watch television or have access to television is quite difficult. For instance, though a single household may subscribe to Canal Horizons, viewing

usually occurs in groups, with neighbors, friends, and family, and sometimes interested passersby who are invited to watch. People also watch television in bars, restaurants, and appliance shops, especially during soccer championships, when large groups assemble. According to both Boissy and W. Touré, women usually made the decision as to whether a household subscribed to the television services. Boissy also noted that women were more likely than men to complain about Canal Horizons programming, saying that the channel had too many sporting events.

4. During the summers of 1994 and 1996, I conducted a series of informal interviews with Senegalese television viewers in Dakar and Saint-Louis. Additionally, I asked other television viewers to complete a questionnaire about their television habits (when and how often they watched, what programs they liked best, what they thought of RTS, Canal Horizons, and TV5, who they watched with, where they watched, etc.), My research assistant, Papa Demba Sarr, and I collected some eighty-eight completed questionnaires in 1994 and another forty-six in 1996. Any quoted material is anonymous. Though the results have not been systematized and were part of a convenience sample, there were a variety (age, gender, ethnicity) of respondents. However, I do not try to generalize but only report some anecdotes and apparent patterns.

REFERENCES

Books and Journal Articles

Ager, D. 1996. *"Francophonie" in the 1990s: Problems and opportunities.* Clevedon, England: Multilingual Matters.

Appadurai, A. 1997. *Modernity at large: Cultural dimensions of globalization.* Minneapolis: University of Minnesota Press.

Arnoldi, M. J., C. M. Geary, and K. L. Hardin, eds. 1996. *African material culture.* Bloomington: Indiana University Press.

Barber, K., ed. 1997a. *Readings in African popular culture.* Oxford: James Currey Press.

———, guest ed. 1997b. Audiences in action. *Africa* 67 (3): 347–490.

Boone, C. 1992. *Merchant capital and the roots of state power in Senegal, 1930–1985.* Cambridge: Cambridge University Press.

Carlos, J. 1985. La radio et la télévision en faveur de la participation à la vie culturelle: Le cas du Sénégal. In *La fonction culturelle de l'information en Afrique,* ed. by J. G. Sorgho, 157–90. Dakar: Les Nouvelles Editions Africaines.

Chipman, J. 1989. *French power in Africa.* Oxford: Basil Davidson.

Coulon, C. 1988. Senegal: The development and fragility of semidemocracy. In *Democracy in developing countries: Africa,* ed. L. Diamond, J. Linz, and S. Lipset, vol. 2, 141–78. Boulder, CO: Lynne Rienner.

Cruise O'Brien, R. 1985. Broadcast professionalism in Senegal. In *Mass communication, culture and society in West Africa,* ed. by F. O. Ugboajah, 187–99. Munich: Hans Zell.

Diop, M., and M. Diouf. 1990. *Le Sénégal sous Abdou Diouf.* Paris: Editions Karthala.

Diouf, M. 1996. Urban youth and Senegalese politics: Dakar, 1988–1994. *Public Culture* 8:225–49.

Fougeyrollas, P. 1967. *L'education des adultes au Sénégal.* Paris: UNESCO.

Gellar, S. 1995. *Senegal: An African nation between Islam and the West.* 2d ed. Boulder: Westview.

Gueye N'Diaye, P. 1981. Cultural development in Africa: Evolution, experiences, and prospects. In *Cultural development: Some regional experiences,* 5–22. Paris: UNESCO.

Hannerz, U. 1996. *Transnational connections: Culture, people, places.* London: Routledge.

Hargreaves, A., and M. McKinney. 1997. *Post-colonial cultures in France.* London: Routledge.

Head, S. W. 1974. *Broadcasting in Africa: A continental survey of radio and TV.* Philadelphia: Temple University Press.

Katz, E., and G. Wedell. 1977. *Broadcasting in the Third World.* Cambridge: Harvard University Press.

Léger, J.-M. 1987. *La francophonie: Grand dessein, grande ambiguïté.* Québec: Hurtubise HMH.

Lerner, D. 1958. *The passing of traditional society.* Glencoe, IL.: Free Press.

Ly, S. 1993. Senegal: Pluralism in radio broadcasting. In *Radio pluralism in West Africa,* ed. and trans. Lena Senghor, vol. 3, 91–118. Paris: PANOS.

Ly Diop, F. 1989. *Communication, audio-visuel et education: Etude de l'impact des émissions de télévision sur les enfants.* Projet de recherche dans le cadre du diplôme d'études approfondies d'anthropologie. Dakar: Chiekh Anta Diop.

Martin, G. 1995. Continuity and change in Franco-African relations. *Journal of Modern African Studies* 33:1–20.

McNamara, F. T. 1989. *France in black Africa.* Washington, DC: National Defense University.

McPhail, T. 1987. *Electronic colonialism: The future of international broadcasting and communication.* 2d ed. Newbury Park, CA: Sage.

Miller, C. 1990. *Theories of Africans: Francophone literature and anthropology in Africa.* Chicago: University of Chicago Press.

Nederveen Pieterse, J. 1993. *Globalization as hybridization.* Hague: Institute of Social Studies.

Paye, M. 1992. La presse et le pouvoir. In *Sénégal: Trajectoires d'un état,* ed. M. C. Diop, 331–77. Dakar: CODESRIA.

Perry, Donna L. 1997. Rural ideologies and urban imaginings: Wolof immigrants in New York City. *Africa Today* 44 (2): 229–60.

Schraeder, P. 1997. Senegal's foreign policy: Challenges of democratization and marginalization. *African Affairs* 96: 485–508.

Schramm, W. 1964. *Mass media and national development: The role of information in the developing countries.* Stanford: Stanford University Press.

Silla, M. 1994. *Le paria du village planetaire our l'Afrique de la télévision mondiale.* Dakar: Les Nouvelles Editions Africaines du Sénégal.

Simpson, C. 1994. *The science of coercion: Communication research and psychological warfare, 1945–1960.* New York: Oxford University Press.

Swigart, L. 1994. Cultural creolisation and language use in post-colonial Africa: The case of Senegal. *Africa* 64: 175–89.

Têtu, M. 1987. *La francophonie: Histoire, problématique et perspectives.* Montréal: Guérin.

Tomlinson, J. 1991. *Cultural imperialism: A critical introduction.* Baltimore: Johns Hopkins University Press.

Tudesq, A.-J. 1992. *L'Afrique noire et ses télévisions.* Paris: Anthropos/INA.

Government Documents and Records

Allocution de M. le Président de la République [Senghor] à l'occasion de l'inauguration de l'exposition de la presse de langue française. 10 December 1968.

Allocution de M. le Président de la République [Senghor] à l'occasion de l'inauguration du centre émetteur de télévision de Thiès. 21 July 1976.

Allocution de M. le Président de la République [Diouf] au Conseil intergouvernemental des ministrès de l'information des pays non-alignés. 9 January 1986.

Allocution de M. le Président de la République [Diouf] au Conseil national. 28 May 1990. *La corrélation entre la communication et le développement est évidente.*

Allocution de M. Cherif Thiam, ORTS. 7 May 1985. *L'ORTS et la télévision en milieu rural. Première semaine nationale de l'audiovisuel et de l'ORTS.*

Compte rendu du Conseil interministériel. 25 October 1971. Secrétariat général du gouvernement, no. 5493.

Compte rendu du Conseil national de l'audio-visuel. 30 January 1976. Secrétariat général du gouvernement.

Congrès (VIIe) de l'Union Progressiste Sénégalaise (Maison de Parti). 27–30 December 1969. *Résolution sur la Presse.*

Conseil national de l'audio-visuel. 3 July 1978. Ministère de l'Information et des Télécommunications changé des rélations avec les Assemblées, Jean Pierre Bondi.

Haut Conseil de la Radio-Télévision. 1994 and 1995. *Rapport annuel au président de la république,* Dakar: Tandian and TECNOEDIT.

Projet de décret portant création du Comité National de l'action culturelle et des moyens audio-visuel. 13 September 1972. Secrétariat général du gouvernement, no. 04258.

Projet de loi abrogeant et remplaçant le 2 alinea de l'article premier de la loi, no. 73–51, du 4 déc. 1973, transformant la radiodiffusion nationale en Office de Radiodiffusion-télévision au Sénégal (ORTS). 13 January 1977. Secrétariat général du gouvernement.

Projet de loi portant approbation des statuts de la radiodiffusion télévision sénégalaise, 12 February 1992. République du Sénégal. Ministère de la Communication.

Secrétariat du Conseil des Ministrès, 14 January 1985. *Rapport de présentation du projet de decret fixant les règles d'organisation et de fonctionnement de l'Office de la Radiodiffusion-télévision.*

Newspaper Articles

Le Soleil

L'apport de TV5-Afrique. 1 October 1992, by Moudo M. Faye.

Baisse effectivement des prix, mais les vendeurs ne font pas de crédit sur les téléviseurs. 15 March 1973.

CH en vue. 21 November 1990, by Lassana Cissokho.

CH montre ses grilles. 19 October 1990.

Conseil interministériel sur les objectifs et les moyens de la communication audio-visuel: Réhabilitation des stations régionals. 26 October 1983, by Abdallah Faye.

Décisions hier au Conseil interministériel, augmentation de la subvention à la radio; mise à l'étude d'un projet de télé. 5 October 1971.

Dialogue sur l'utilisation des médiats d'état. 22 January 1993.

Edifier un paysage a-v national, credible, et compétitif. 2 November 1990, by Amadou Mbaye.

L'enquête. 29 August 1972, by M. Touré.

L'ère de responsabilité. 27–28 July 1991, by Seeyni Ndiaye.

L'HCRT vu par les professionels. 4 September 1991.

Des jeunes Africains face à la culture "mediatique" transnationale. 9 July 1996, by Moustapha Gueye.

Les objections du RND. 19 September 1991.

L'opposition boycotte. 15 March 1992.

L'ORTS est né. 23 November 1973, by Ibrahim Mansour M'Boup. Plan d'urgence pour ORTS. 2 November 1979.

Les programmes de la nouvelle grille. 2 November 1990, by Amadou Mbaye.

Quand le petit écran fait relanche. 28 May 1973.
Recentrer le débat. 2 November 1990, by Mouhamadou Dia.
Respecter les principes du pluralism. 10 December 1992, by Papa Boubacar Samb.
La RTS passe société nationale. 30 January 1992, by Abdoulaye Elimane Kane.
Télé—Des émissions pour qui? 13 August 1972.
La télé continue. 14 September 1972.
300 millions d'Allemagne fédérale pour ORTS. 28 April 1981.
TV: La grille au changement? 8 October 1992, by El Hadj Amadou Mbaye.
Un mal nécessaire? 4 February 1992, by A. F. Bodian.

Sud Quotidien

Les bons et les méchants. 8 October 1993, by Boucar Niang.
Le Fann. 7 January 1992.
Ma télé? Il n'en a pas. 19 July 1993, by Oumar Ndao.
Podor sans télé. 5 August 1993, by Ahmed Sy.
Promiscuité familiale. 1 October 1993.
La télé unique, un mal unique. 31 December 1993, by Boucar Niang.
Télévision: Les paraboles des riches. 27 September 1993, by M. T. Talla.

Wal Fadjri

A consommer avec modération. 29 September 1993, by Valérie Gas.
L'antenne ne sera pas à tous. 23 November 1993, by Jean Meïssa Diop.
Parlez, il en restera quelque chose. 8–14 January 1993, by Jean Meïssa Diop.
Une autre télévision pour les riches. 7 July 1993, by Jean Meïssa Diop.

Jeune Afrique

Les antennes diaboliques. 17–23 November 1994. 1767: 56–57, by Assou Massou.
Les chaînes d'Afrique se déchaînes. 3–9 February 1994. 1726: 60–63, by Jean-Luc Eyguesier.
La France multiplie les médias. 11 December 1990. 1562: 78–70, by Pierre Huster.
Francophonie par satellite. 5–11 December 1990. 1562: 85–87, by Yves Gallard.
Un paysage audiovisuel en pleine mutation. 18 December 1991–8 January 1992. 1616–1617: 59, 61–63, by Phillipe Tranchard.
Quelles programmes pour l'Afrique? 17–23 November 1994. 1767: 47–48, 51, by Bernard Duhamel.
Sénégal: Images très privées. 25 July–1 August 1990. 1543: 27–30, by Ariane Poissonnier.
Une chaîne pour l'Afrique. 9–15 July 1992. 1644: 34–35, by Frédéric Dorce.

Other

"Télé Munich 'Ministériel' "? *La Lettre Fermée.* 11–24 August 1972, by Abdou Rahman Cissé.

Personal Interviews

Boissy, Anne Marie Senghor, assistant director general, Canal Horizons. 7 July 1994, Dakar.
Camara, Mame Less, secretary general, SYNPICS (Syndicat des professionnels de l'information et de la communication du Sénégal). 12 July 1996, Dakar.
Cissé, Abdou Rahman, acting commissioner of the Ministry of Information from 1962 to 1964 and former publisher of *La Lettre Fermée.* 14 July 1996, Dakar.
Diop, Adrienne, journalist and programmer at RTS. 7 July 1994, Dakar.
Paye, Moussa, official at the Ministry of Communication. 5 July 1994, Dakar.

Touré, Babacar, publisher of *Sud Quotidien* and owner of *Sud FM*. 27 June 1994, Dakar.
Touré, Wahab, director general, TV5. 5 July 1994, Dakar.

Web Sites

Doit-on interdire à nos enfants de regarder la television? 16 February 1999, by Arame Gaye
    Diop. http://sudonline.com/Rubriques%20infos/opinion2.htm (20 February 1999).
RTS, http://www.primature.sn/rts.

Chapter Eleven

On the Margins of the Constitutional State
Terrorism on German Television and the Rewriting of National Narratives

Olaf Hoerschelmann

The so-called German Autumn of 1977 created a significant trauma in the Federal Republic of Germany. It involved the abduction and murder of Hanns-Martin Schleyer, the head of the German Employers' Union, by the terrorist group RAF (Red Army Faction) and the hijacking of a Lufthansa tourist airplane by a Palestinian terrorist group, both designed to force the German state to release a number of imprisoned RAF terrorists. The abductions, the refusal of the German government to release imprisoned terrorists in exchange for Schleyer or the abducted tourists, and the insufficiently explained deaths of the imprisoned terrorists established the German Autumn of 1977 as a highly controversial topic. Numerous media texts related to this subject have been centrally involved in negotiating the identity of the West German nation-state and the legitimacy of its institutions and representatives on a national and international scale.

The subject of this essay is the made-for-television docudrama *Todesspiel* (Death Game), broadcast on German national television in two parts in 1997—twenty years after the events outlined above.[1] It claimed to provide an authentic account of the events of 1977 by combining fictional segments, pieces of historical television footage, and interviews with a variety of witnesses involved in some of the events. This essay argues that the extensive attention and praise *Todesspiel* received point to its importance as a "new national narrative"[2] for the unified German nation-state.

The institutional organization of broadcasting and the prevailing social and political discourses on terrorism in Germany lead to the creation of programming that does not address the social and historical complexity of terrorist movements. The media coverage of terrorism in Germany serves as a particularly telling example of the uneasy relationship between the media, terrorism, and the state that exists in many Western nations.

The Terrors of Nationalism in Postwar Germany

In *Nation and Narration,* Homi Bhabha emphasizes the textual character of national identity, arguing that "to encounter the nation *as it is written* . . . [is a] partial,

overdetermined process by which textual meaning is produced through the articulation of difference in language."[3] Postwar West Germany specifically pointed to the
overdetermined character of traditional national symbols such as monuments, rituals,
military uniforms, and the reason of the state. Invalidated by Germany's recent
history of fascism, these elements became sources of embarrassment and guilt rather
than sources of a reifiable national identity. As Ian Buruma points out, postwar
Germany was characterized by the deliberate erasure of national symbols. Reminders
of the past—not just Hitler's past—were destroyed, blown up, removed. Sites of
concentration camps were used for some time to house German prisoners, but as
soon as possible they were either razed or abandoned.[4] Thus, there were few national
symbols readily available in West Germany. The oak tree, for example, seems to have
an ongoing appeal as a symbol of the persistence and steadfastness of the German
nation. It first appears in Germanic mythology and is then used as the Emperor's
Oak (Kaisereiche) in the second German empire, as the Hitler Oak (Hitlereiche)
during Nazi rule, and as the German Oak (Deutsche Eiche) in postwar Germany.[5]
Similarly, the "Deutsche Michel" is another symbol that expresses national character:
"The point about the 'Deutsche Michel' is that his image stressed both the innocence
and simple-mindedness so readily exploited by cunning foreigners, and the physical
strength he could mobilize to frustrate their knavish tricks and conquests when
finally roused."[6] However, none of these symbols is powerful or appealing enough to
be utilized as a center for a strong national identity. The erasure of old metaphors
for the nation and the lack of new strategies to symbolize it left Germany with a
vacuum of national narratives and a highly fragmented national identity. Thomas
Elsaesser thus argues that narratives of guilt and defeat seem to fill Germany's
historical imagination:

> Since 1945 solutions to the German question, official attitudes to German history and
> many of the moral and political judgments on the war and fascism had been, as it were,
> imposed *from outside*. The defeat of Hitler, the creation of West and East Germany,
> rearmament and the division of the German nation were seen as external interventions,
> rather than expressions of national resolve.[7]

West Germany then was characterized by the defeat of grand national narratives
and the dominance of an unusable past that left Germany's national identity fragmented and tortured.[8] The strongest sense of national identity came from the reconstruction of Germany and the early prosperity of West Germany's economy. Germany's fascist past not only led to a lack of coherent national narratives, but also left
postwar Germany vulnerable to internal criticism. In the 1950s and 1960s, a new
generation of Germans born during and after World War II (the German equivalent
of American baby boomers) voiced substantial criticism of postwar West Germany.
The persistence of Nazi elites in politics and business and the restoration of restrictive
social structures in family, church, and education led to a further delegitimation
of dominant structures in the eyes of the emergent German youth culture. The
criticism found its expression in a series of riots as well as in the growing student
movement of the 1960s. A critique of the restrictive character of postwar Germany
can also be found in many films of the New German Cinema, which, along with

other leftist media, was heavily involved in the discursive struggles over German national identities.[9]

The television documentary *The Police State Visit* (Der Polizeistaatsbesuch) by Roman Brodmann, covering the visit of the Persian shah to Germany in 1967, exemplifies the position of the German New Left and the student movement in particular toward the West German nation-state.[10] The postwar generation of German filmmakers frequently cooperated with West Germany's public broadcasting channels, receiving funding from these institutions and presenting their works on German TV. However, *The Police State Visit* stands out for its outspoken political stance and its observations about crucial events in Germany's postwar history. The shah's visit generated intense debate in German culture and triggered numerous student protests. The shah was seen as a representative of a repressive, fascist system with strong connections to international militarism. The demonstrations against the shah's visit quickly turned violent, mainly due to extremely aggressive police activity, which first led to the death of one student and ultimately to the escalation of violence in Germany. As a final step, the shah's visit also contributed to the development of the Red Army Faction (RAF) terrorist group, since many student leaders and other activists became convinced that nonviolent protest would not lead to significant change in German society and culture.

Even though *The Police State Visit* was produced with the help of one of West Germany's state-supported public television channels, it still addressed a number of the troubling continuities and blind spots in German postwar culture. It articulated many of the critical positions of the German Left. The film frequently pointed to the continuities between Nazi Germany and the present, for example in scenes that emphasized archaic military ritual or the use of conservative folk costumes and music, and especially in a scene that connected the shah's visit to a small town directly to the visit of Adolf Hitler some thirty years earlier. In using these representational strategies, *The Police State Visit* adopted strategies similar to those of the New German Cinema, which was itself heavily involved in debates over Germany's past and its historical memory of fascism.

In the following decade, these strategies of delegitimation served as an important justification for the political violence exerted by the RAF. Both the student movement and the terrorist movement of the 1970s attacked Germany's problematic national identity in the Cold War era and pointed toward its repressiveness and its residual fascist character. From 1966 until 1972, the two largest political parties in West Germany, the Social Democrats (SPD) and the conservative Christian Democrats (CDU/CSU) formed a coalition to consolidate German politics into one large consensus. This "great coalition" meant that any sort of significant political dissent was removed from the main forum of German politics and effectively silenced. Left wing politicians and the leftist student movement in particular felt betrayed by the Social Democrats and did not perceive themselves as having any political influence. Following unsuccessful demonstrations against the shah's visit and the Vietnam War, and in response to increasing state violence, the student movement became increasingly fragmented, and parts of it turned toward violence. Parts of the student movement formed the RAF, which initially committed bank robberies, vandalism, and arson—

for example, setting fire to the Berlin headquarters of the Springer Press, an ultraconservative publishing house that publishes the *Bild-Zeitung*, Germany's biggest daily tabloid. The *Bild-Zeitung* was seen by the RAF as a particularly appropriate target, due to its archconservative politics and its role in creating public sentiment against the student movement. It was widely assumed in the student movement that the *Bild-Zeitung* played a significant role in the escalation of violence during the shah's visit. Rudi Dutschke, the most prominent student leader, summed up the sentiment that led to the ultimate escalation of violence into terrorism thus: "Violence against objects, such as fences, might be acceptable. Because of the role of the Springer Press in the publishing business and the great coalition in the Federal Republic [of Germany], dissenting minorities are not even noticed anymore without provocations."[11]

As the RAF increasingly turned toward terrorism as a radical form of political dissent, the student movement as a whole was moved into an even more marginal position. While the destabilization of West Germany's dominant social order was an important project of the German Left, the wave of terrorism of the 1970s and particularly the German Autumn of 1977 led to an increase in restrictive state policies against radical political dissent, such as the formation of special police forces and the use of special antiterrorist legislation. The RAF presented an even greater threat to the German state when it became obvious that it had developed connections to international terrorism. The RAF cooperated with a network of antifascist groups worldwide, such as the French Action Directe, the Italian Red Brigades, and the PLO. For example, several members of the RAF were trained on weapons and in guerrilla warfare in various Palestinian camps in the Middle East. Especially during the Vietnam War, the imperialist politics of the United States and its allies (such as West Germany, France, and Israel) were seen as one of the main targets of the RAF and its international collaborators, who selected a variety of representatives of the military, politics, and finance as their main targets. In 1977 the RAF unleashed three particularly violent acts that represented the height of the terrorist movement: first, the RAF assassinated the German attorney general (Generalbundesanwalt), Siegfried Buback, on April 7, then assassinated the well-known banker Jürgen Ponto on July 30, and on September 5 abducted Hanns-Martin Schleyer. Along with the hijacking of a Lufthansa airplane by Palestinian allies of the RAF, these acts created panic and hysteria in Germany and attracted heavy international attention.

In response, the mainstream German press increasingly demonized terrorists and their sympathizers as an internal Other against which German national identity could be defined. The press coverage of the events in the fall of 1977 shows that dominant media outlets had a strong interest in exerting their definitional power over terrorism, clearly marking the RAF as deviant, and possibly anti-German.

> From the viewpoint of the attorney general we are dealing with a "gang" that commits "terrorist acts"; from Croissant's [attorney of the RAF] point of view they are "fighters" in a "resistance movement" against a "fascist state" that he sees represented in a Social Democratic/Liberal government.[12]

This passage from *Der Spiegel*, a left-leaning weekly magazine, summarized the central discursive struggle in German culture: the attempt to negate the political

Editorial cartoon from *Die Zeit*, no. 33 (1977): 1. Reprinted by permission.

dimension of terrorism and instead characterize terrorists as common criminals. In editorial cartoons of German newspapers and magazines, terrorists were portrayed as rats (see fig. 11.1) or even characterized as "Hitler's children" (see fig. 11.2). Figure 11.1 portrays the assassination of Jürgen Ponto (where terrorists delivered roses with a gun hidden in the bouquet) and uses a rat to represent the terrorists. In the caption, the phrase "with insidiousness" makes a clear moral judgment without having to engage in an actual discussion of the underlying issues at stake from a larger political perspective.

These strategies ultimately help to diminish the threat that terrorism poses to the nation-state's monopoly on violence: "Control of the means of violence is an essential feature of the modern state—though not by any means the only one—and holds the key to the exercise of power within the political order."[13]

Editorial cartoon from *Der Spiegel*, no. 38 (1977): 33. Reprinted by permission.

While the wave of terrorism in 1977 posed a significant threat to West German politics, it also provided the *opportunity* to redefine German national identity in opposition to a terrorist Other. As a highly illegitimate movement, terrorism is not able to fundamentally question the legitimacy of the nation-state. Only when a liberal democracy such as West Germany cannot balance its exertion of force against terrorism does it face what Philip Schlesinger calls the "liberal state's dilemma":

> Either the state can play it by its own rules and bring the terrorists to trial thereby giving them a platform for their views and an opportunity to mobilise public opinion. Or it can violate its principles, dispense with due process and eradicate the terrorists without a trial, thereby undermining the popular consent on which its legitimacy rests.[14]

Schlesinger's point seems to apply to the end of the wave of German terrorism in the autumn of 1977. A special paramilitary unit from Germany was able to free the passengers of the abducted Lufthansa airplane in Mogadishu. Shortly after the end of the hijacking, however, the government announced the death of three terrorists— Andreas Baader, Gudrun Ensslin, and Jan-Carl Raspe—imprisoned in the high-security prison of Stuttgart-Stammheim. These deaths have respectively been characterized as suicides (by prison officials and the German government) or as murders (by members of the radical Left). Many questions regarding the deaths have not been sufficiently explained: How did the prisoners know of the events in Mogadishu, when they were supposed to be completely cut off from the outside? How were inmates of a high-security prison able to obtain two guns to shoot themselves? While these questions ultimately overshadow the larger, underlying social issues that terrorism raises, they nevertheless provide a moment of fracture in the West German national imaginary. Instead of becoming a moment of closure and legitimacy for postwar Germany, the German Autumn thus becomes an overdetermined moment of disclosure that displays the Janus-faced nature of German nationalism.[15]

The Institutional Context

The broadcast of *Todesspiel* was promoted heavily in the German media and received a tremendous amount of critical attention in the months following its original broadcast in June 1997. For example, a week before the original broadcast of *Todesspiel*, the popular weekly magazine *Stern* (Star) featured a ten-page story on the German Autumn, promoting the program and essentially reproducing the main lines of argument in *Todesspiel*.[16] Among the awards that *Todesspiel* and its director, Heinrich Breloer, received were several of the top honors for television productions in Germany: Telestar, Bambi, Goldene Kamera, and Special Honors, Baden-Baden Television Drama Festival. The presentation speech for the Bambi award stands out in particular, since it was delivered by Hans-Jürgen Wischnewski, one of the government representatives centrally involved in the hostage negotiations in 1977:

> The film succeeds at reproducing, in three hours, 45 days of the most difficult situation for the Federal Republic of Germany, full of drama, full of danger. For me, this film is a *historical document*. . . . You, dear Dr. Breloer, your actors and actresses, and your collaborators have gained merit in the representation of German history through the film *Todesspiel* (emphasis mine).[17]

What is striking about these remarks is their insistence on characterizing *Todesspiel* as reality or *true* history. Not only do Wischnewski's remarks deny the contingent character of history, but he manages to elevate the conjectural claims of the program about terrorism and German history into absolute truths. The reception of *Todesspiel* in a variety of media festivals thus reinforced the discursive strategies used in the program to streamline German history. The close concurrence among media texts, institutions, and dominant cultural forces in Germany can similarly be observed in the organizational structures of the main institutions that produced the program. *Todesspiel* was coproduced by the WDR (Westdeutscher Rundfunk) and the NDR (Norddeutscher Rundfunk)—both regional affiliates of the state-owned ARD television channel—and supported by the Deutsche Welle and the Filmstiftung Nordrhein-Westfalen, two other state-supported media institutions. While these institutions claim to be free from direct state influence in their programming policies, their institutional structures do not support that claim. For example, the Rundfunkrat, one of the main governing bodies of the Westdeutscher Rundfunk (WDR), consists exclusively of members appointed by established political, social, and cultural institutions such as Protestant, Catholic, and Jewish organizations, employers' and employees' organizations and unions, and the state parliament (Landtag). The Landtag-appointed members of the Rundfunkrat are all members of the Landtag, the Bundes-tag (state parliament), or the European Parliament. Thus, each member is affiliated with one of the dominant parties in Germany's political system. In other words, virtually all the members of the Rundfunkrat are closely connected to dominant forces in German culture, making a reliance on dominant viewpoints in program-ming decisions very likely.

The close relationship between the media and the state becomes visible in the cooperation of public broadcasters with state agencies in instituting a month-long news freeze in the fall of 1977, during the Schleyer abduction. Print and television journalists quickly gave in to a request by West Germany's government to have a blackout of all news related to the Schleyer abduction. Further, the media agreed to use caution when contacted by the terrorists or their helpers:

> The media were asked to co-operate with the Federal Government in reporting the news in the newspapers or on radio and television, and they were also asked not to endanger the investigation by the police. This was supported by the National Press Council in Germany, a professional organization, which agreed that the press should abide by these rules.[18]

As Schlesinger points out, there often is a "persistent effort to control the media's use of language, sounds, images and frameworks of interpretation" on the part of various political forces.[19] However, the willing self-censorship of the German press in 1977 illustrates that frequently this relationship is cooperative rather than coercive. Generally, we can assume that a direct intervention of the state and its officials is not necessary to produce programming that conforms to commonly held beliefs. Instead, the German media system demonstrates that the consent and cooperation of media institutions and practitioners already exist, because of the peculiar position of media organizations in German national culture. In other words, the theoretical separation of the media and the state has almost completely been erased in the case of terrorism on German television.

Playing with Death: Twenty Years After

Todesspiel bears witness to the fact that the controversies about the deaths of Baader, Ensslin, and Raspe have not stopped to this day, and in their moral ambiguity still provide fuel for debate. Jean Baudrillard refers to the ongoing discussions regarding the Stammheim deaths as a "hysterical search for truth," which ultimately only obscures the systemic violence of a political system in which the German Autumn of 1977 became possible.[20] *Todesspiel* picked up crucial questions about the German nation-state, its history and legitimacy, that have never been successfully resolved. Nevertheless, *Todesspiel* entered the debates about German terrorism trying to give fixity to the events of the German Autumn. Intended as a reworking (*Aufarbeitung*) of recent history, the program was involved in remaking the events of 1977 into a usable past. As Brennan points out, modern fictional forms such as the novel often attempt to create a people with a direct, political purpose.[21] Similarly, *Todesspiel* had clear political overtones, providing a unified narrative about terrorism in Germany. The creation of a unified, usable past seems to be one of the general ideological functions that German public broadcasting serves in this context, and possibly of public service broadcasting in general. Since it is the explicit purpose of these broadcasting systems to address a unified national audience, the narratives they produce also tend to create and naturalize a common ground for imagined national audiences.

As a docudrama, *Todesspiel* was presented in a form that exists at the intersections of fictional and documentary modes—a form that has also sparked a significant degree of scholarly debate. While some authors such as Alan Rosenthal argue that docudrama has a quasi-journalistic relationship toward the events it deals with and thus has a negligible ideological effect, others have pointed out the tendency of docudrama to affirm basic belief systems.[22] Todd Gitlin argues that "the 'docudrama' was aptly named for it exists not to comprehend but to document, to authenticate the validity of surface detail, to establish that this really happened."[23] Derek Paget provides a more comprehensive definition of this hybrid genre:

> In the dramadoc/docudrama, documentary's promise of privileged access to information is added to drama's promise of understanding through "second-order" experience. The camera accesses two different kinds of reality—a record of external events (which still constitutes the basis of the documentary's appeal) and a simulated reality of acted event.[24]

I argue that docudrama has the ability to claim privileged access not only to information, but ultimately to truth. John Corner outlines a set of crucial issues in regard to this genre: (1) "What tightness of relationship does the program claim with real events?" (2) "Is there an attempt to imitate the codes of documentary and thereby generate reportage values?" (3) Are viewers "encouraged to give truth status to unsubstantiated or purely imaginary events?" (4) "In what way does the point of view given prominence in the program relate to 'official' positions and attitudes?"[25]

Todesspiel used three different types of footage. It relied primarily on fictional footage, reenacting key scenes from the Schleyer abduction, the airplane hijacking, internal political debates at West Germany's political headquarters in Bonn, and events in the Stammheim high-security prison. A second source of material was archival documentary footage and newscasts from Germany's three public service channels, and a third source consisted of interviews with people involved in the events of 1977 conducted specifically for this program. Director Breloer has a reputation for his documentary work in Germany's public service television, giving him easy access to archival material and a wide variety of interview subjects. Otherwise, *Todesspiel* did not feature famous actors, leaving its topic and its interview subjects as the main attraction.

The major claims to truth in *Todesspiel* were accomplished through the combination of interviews and fictional scenes. In this respect, the construction of a suicide motive for the Stammheim prisoners seems to be of prime importance for the program. As mentioned above, the deaths of three imprisoned terrorists were a source of significant controversy. *Todesspiel* deliberately seemed to present these deaths as unambiguous, indisputable suicides. Both parts of the program pointed toward the suicidal tendencies of Baader, Ensslin, and Raspe. In several interviews, prison guards and government representatives who were in contact with the imprisoned terrorists mentioned that the terrorists seemed to have given up, "didn't seem of this world anymore," or were extremely sedate. What is striking about these responses is not only their unanimity, but the fact that in each case the interview question to which the subjects responded was edited out. It is very likely that interviewees were specifically asked whether the inmates had suicidal tendencies, so that a coherent case for the suicide thesis could be built. The seamless construction of a suicide argument for the imprisoned terrorists was carried through the entire three-hour program. It demonstrated that part of the strategy of *Todesspiel* was to create the impression that the docudrama presented unmediated reality rather than a particular viewpoint on a controversial historical event.

Todesspiel also suppressed other questions related to these deaths, especially questions regarding the origin of the weapons found in Andreas Baader's and Jan-Carl Raspe's prison cells. In the concluding sections of part 2 of *Todesspiel*, Baader and Raspe were shown removing guns from hiding places in their high-security prison cells and shooting themselves. Additionally, Baader was shown deliberately planting signs of a fight in order to make his death appear as a murder. Similarly, Gudrun Ensslin was clearly shown hanging herself with some string in her prison cell.

Todesspiel thus followed the official interpretation of the terrorists' deaths very closely, leaving little space for any ambiguity. The program illustrated the suicides in its fictional scenes and provided additional support for this interpretation of events through its interview footage. Since any controversies regarding the deaths in Stammheim were not even mentioned in the program, *Todesspiel* obviously aimed to remove any doubts regarding the terrorists' suicides. As a result, the program managed to *demonstrate* that the Federal Republic of Germany abided by its own rules. By combining fictional footage and edited interviews, the program resolved the "liberal state's dilemma" and reaffirmed Germany's claims to legitimacy.[26]

A second important feature of *Todesspiel* was the way it dealt with the political dimension of terrorism and the history of the RAF. Hints of the political agenda of the RAF were almost completely absent. In discussions with their hostage, Hanns-Martin Schleyer, the terrorists were hardly able to make any reasonable arguments, so that neither Schleyer's involvement in the SS nor his leading role in West Germany's military-industrial complex came under any close scrutiny. Any mention of Schleyer's Nazi background by his captors was thus treated as rude behavior rather than political debate. In a key scene in which Schleyer's Nazi past was under debate, Schleyer ultimately told the terrorists, "you think you're the good sons and I'm the evil Nazi father." Criticism of postwar German culture and its Nazi heritage was thus reduced to an act of deviant, youthful rebellion with psychoanalytic overtones. Interestingly, Schleyer's remarks also referred to the connection between terrorism and Hitler constructed in the press coverage of the RAF mentioned above (see fig. 11.2).

The historical background of the terrorist movement and its roots in the student movement of the 1960s are also minimized in the docudrama. A short sequence of about ten seconds showed scenes from the student demonstrations against the shah's visit, accompanied by a voice-over by Ulrike Meinhoff, one of the leading intellectual figures in the RAF. The voice-over was, however, almost unintelligible, and, along with the demonstration footage served as an alibi by making minimal mention of the historical background of terrorism. However, it did so without giving any serious consideration to the background of political violence in Germany.

Robbed of their crucial political agenda, the terrorists in *Todesspiel* were primarily portrayed as psychologically unstable and at times childish. Schlesinger et al. identify this process of infantilization as a popular convention for televised terrorism: "Terrorists are further separated from 'us' by being presented as fanatics and psychopaths who lack the normal human qualities."[27] The behavior of both the German terrorists and the Palestinian hijackers is shown as excessive in movement and speech, a strategy that is underlined by the program's visual strategies as well: interview footage with former terrorists and individual shots of (fictional) terrorists usually rely heavily on extreme close ups, a shot size that puts heavy emphasis on facial expressions.

In addition, harsh, high-contrast (almost chiaroscuro) lighting was used in shots of both fictional and real-life terrorists, further emphasizing their threatening and unstable qualities. In combination, these techniques created an aesthetic reminiscent of mug shots, further implying the RAF's illegitimacy and the threatening character of the terrorists. The strategies used to represent terrorists contrasted sharply with the visual style of interviews conducted with former politicians and victims of the hijacking. In these instances, the director was more likely to use medium close-ups or medium shots. Similarly, these subjects were lit fairly evenly using standard three-point lighting. *Todesspiel* thus managed to portray politicians and hijacking victims as stable and nonthreatening, underscoring their presumably reasonable and balanced remarks during interviews. I argue that these techniques result in an affective delegitimation of the terrorists, a strategy that undermines the intellectual and political dimensions of terrorism on a nondiscursive level. The audience was not given details on the political or intellectual background of German terrorism. *Todesspiel* followed a common political strategy of the nation-state vis-à-vis terrorism: it silenced the terrorists' political agenda and ultimately denied that terrorism has a political agenda at all.

These strategies came to a climax in scenes that prominently featured the Palestinian terrorists involved in the Lufthansa airplane hijacking. They were shown wearing (supposedly authentic) bright red Che Guevara T-shirts, making them almost into comic book villains. The incompetence of these terrorists was emphasized throughout part 2 of *Todesspiel*. Their frequent mistakes, their paranoid reaction to anything resembling the Star of David, their broken English, and their sudden violent outbursts all added to their psychotic appearance. The Palestinian terrorists were represented as stereotypical, bumbling Orientals—dirty, irrational, and violent. This representational strategy is commonplace in Western media. As Schlesinger points out, the use of images of alien Others is a standard device in Western media:

The simplest device is to make the terrorists into physical aliens, foreigners who have arrived from elsewhere and don't share our political ideals or ways of doing things. Images of "foreignness" and the residual racism and xenophobia on which they trade are still central to a good deal of popular fiction about terrorism.[28]

What is particularly striking about the portrayal of Palestinian terrorists on *Todesspiel* is the resemblance of these images to fictional films such as *Delta Force* and *True Lies*.[29] In each case the violent nature, irrationality, and incompetence of the terrorists were emphasized, so that they remained flat characters without personality or political agendas. The use of these characterizations in fictional films, docudramas, and even news programming forms a continuum that naturalizes negative images of the terrorist as Oriental Other for primarily Western audiences. Furthermore, flat characters without a distinguishable personality also do not invoke audience identification or sympathy, so that violence against these characters or even their death becomes easily legitimated. This is again illustrated in *Delta Force* and *True Lies*, where the deaths of Arab or Palestinian terrorists are accepted and even celebrated within their narratives. These representational strategies also made it particularly easy to dispose of the fictional terrorists in *Todesspiel*.[30]

Todesspiel framed much of its narrative in terms of the effect of terrorism on a variety of families. It considered the effect of the abduction of Schleyer on his wife and children and set up the narrative of the airplane hijacking as a story about rescuing families and reuniting a separated couple. The program ended with the official funeral services for Hanns-Martin Schleyer and the liberation of the abducted airplane's passengers. As it moved toward this climax, *Todesspiel* increasingly attempted to create narrative closure, providing two sets of protagonists representing one tragic and one happy ending respectively. The main narrative progression of the program was provided through the efforts of politicians and police units to free the terrorists' hostages. Because of this specific focus, "there is little scope to explore the critiques offered by the alternative and oppositional perspectives."[31] Thus, official perspectives were almost automatically dominant as this docudrama utilized narrative conventions borrowed from the action-adventure and detective genres.

The focus on the family worked primarily on an affective level to create a persuasive conclusion to the program. The ritual of Schleyer's funeral in particular served an important ideological function. All rituals are intended to incorporate a larger community and to extend the meaning embedded in the ritual across this community. The Schleyer funeral served to address the entire nation as a substitute family that partakes in the ritual and its ideological affect. By implying a national consensus in response to terrorism and encouraging the audience to identify with the families at the center of its narrative, *Todesspiel* invoked the ideological trope of the nation as family united in its opposition to illegitimate violence. Consequently, the narrative closure of *Todesspiel* was closely connected to its ideological closure. At the same time that *Todesspiel* provided a happy ending to the airplane hijacking, it also reemphasized the fundamental threat of terrorism to the extended family of the German nation.

The Return of the Repressed

The above sections point to the high degree of coherence in the production of a stable interpretation of the German Autumn of 1977. I have discussed the institutional production of a closed narrative, a usable past without contradictions or opposition. However, Homi Bhabha emphasizes the fact that the "nation as it is written displays the temporality of culture and social consciousness more in tune with the partial, overdetermined process by which textual meaning is produced."[32] To paraphrase Bhabha, it is impossible to ultimately contain the meaning of a nationalist narrative such as *Todesspiel*. While dominant conventions of reading and institutions of textual exegesis aim to give fixity to textual interpretation, they cannot provide a permanently stable meaning for a narrative. Consequently, we must also look for ruptures in the textual operation of *Todesspiel* through which the "traditional authority . . . of national objects of knowledge" can be contested.[33]

There are a number of sites of tension within the program that point to the text's internal contradictions as well as to contradictions in the official German discourse on terrorism. Shortly after a special paramilitary unit (GSG 9) freed the hostages on the Lufthansa plane, the German chancellor Helmut Schmidt was shown receiving a phone call from Mogadishu, indicating that the operation had been successful. While only one hostage had been killed, *Todesspiel* showed the bloody shooting of three of the terrorists in some detail. However, Schmidt announced to his fellow politicians that "there have been no deaths." In an act of symbolic annihilation, we were informed that the deaths of the Palestinian terrorists had been no deaths at all. It would seem that their status as irrational, Oriental Others significantly diminished the importance of their execution.

This episode complemented other scenes emphasizing military operations and the military experience of several leading German politicians. In the early stages of the airplane hijacking, the commander of the GSG 9 paramilitary force, Ulrich Wegener, explained in an interview that ending such a hijacking was "a mission we had been waiting for for years." Wegener thus offered a glimpse of the fact that an armed confrontation with terrorism might be violent, but not necessarily undesirable for state forces. It offered the opportunity to showcase the exertion of legitimate state violence and thus served as a reminder of the state's monopoly on violence.

In an extended sequence of interviews with the leading politicians of the late 1970s, several of the interviewees boasted of their military experience. The chairman of the conservative Christian-Social Union (CSU), Friedrich Zimmermann, said, "we had to accept the declaration of war [by the terrorists]. . . . Second Lieutenant Zimmermann, First Lieutenant Schmidt, and First Lieutenant Strauss [another conservative politician] knew what war was." What was left unsaid here is that these politicians accumulated all their military experience as officers in the Third Reich. While emphasizing their competence and military experience, Zimmermann and other politicians also pointed to one of the major repressed elements of postwar Germany, that is, their Nazi past.

Finally, in a fictional segment, the German chancellor Helmut Schmidt summed up this feeling of eagerness to combat terrorism when he announced to his fellow

politicians, "we will pursue these murderers with all our determination and tough-
ness, with all means available, even if we have to go to the margins of the constitutional state in the process." The viewer, however, was left to ponder how far *beyond*
these margins they were willing to go. At these small but important points of fracture,
Todesspiel starts to showcase the contested character of Germany's history and opens
up the text for a variety of unintended interpretations. While *Todesspiel* demonstrates
the close connection between broadcasting and the state in the creation of a new
national identity, it cannot perform its task without allowing ideological contradictions to surface.

Todesspiel demonstrated the heavy investment that public broadcasting systems
have in addressing commonly held beliefs of their nationwide audiences. The process
of producing these narratives of national consensus operates through the reiteration
of widely held beliefs and widely circulated assumptions about terrorism and political
insurgency. The production of an imagined national consensus in *Todesspiel* was
accomplished through the erasure of the social and historical dimensions of terrorism. Despite its efforts at glossing over the ideological tensions between terrorism,
the state, and the media, *Todesspiel* inadvertently revealed the dual character of the
nation as it is written. It aimed at stabilizing Germany's post-reunification identity
at the same time as it failed to contain the excess of meaning that it produced.

NOTES

1. *Todesspiel* [Death Game] (Heinrich Breloer, Cinecentrum Köln, Westdeutscher Rundfunk, Norddeutscher Rundfunk, Deutsche Welle, 1997).

2. Homi Bhabha, "Narrating the Nation," in *Nationalism*, ed. John Hutchinson and Anthony D. Smith (Oxford: Oxford University Press, 1990), 306–12.

3. Homi Bhabha, "Dissemination: Time, Narrative, and the Margins of the Modern Nation," in *Nation and Narration*, ed. Homi Bhabha (London: Routledge, 1994), 307.

4. Ian Buruma, *The Wages of Guilt: Memories of War in Germany and Japan* (New York:
Farrar, Straus and Giroux, 1994), 203.

5. Eric Hobsbawm, "The Nation as Invented Tradition," in Hutchinson and Smith, *Nationalism*, 76–82; Michaela Pohl, "Ideologies of Identity: *Volk* and *Narod* in Nazi and Stalinist
Folkloristics," *Indiana Center on Global Change and World Peace Occasional Paper*, 28 (1995),
27.

6. Hobsbawm, "The Nation as Invented Tradition," 81.

7. Thomas Elsaesser, *New German Cinema* (New Brunswick: Rutgers University Press,
1989), 248.

8. Eric Hobsbawm, *The Invention of Tradition* (Cambridge: Cambridge University Press,
1983), 5.

9. See, for example, the work of Rainer-Werner Fassbinder and Margarethe von Trotta.

10. *Der Polizeistaatsbesuch* [The Police State Visit] (Roman Brodmann, Südwestfunk, Germany, 1969).

11. *Der Spiegel*, no. 41 (1977): 34.

12. *Der Spiegel*, no. 42 (1977): 44.

13. Philip Schlesinger, *Media, State and Nation: Political Violence and Collective Identities*
(London: Sage, 1991), 8–9.

14. Philip Schlesinger, Graham Murdock, and Philip Elliott, *Televising "Terrorism": Political Violence in Popular Culture* (London: Comedia, 1983), 99.

15. Bhabha, "Narrating the Nation," 308.

16. "Der Deutsche Herbst" [The German Autumn], *Stern*, June 19, 1997, no. 26, 42–52.

17. Hans-Jürgen Wischnewski, "Keine Widersprüche" [No contradictions] (database online), Cologne, Germany: Westdeutscher Rundfunk Print Archive, 1997; available from http://www.wdr.de/wdrprint/archiv/1997/12/profile2.html.

18. Hans Josef Horchem, "Terrorism in West Germany," *Conflict Studies* 186 (1986): 17.

19. Schlesinger, *Media, State and Nation*, 3.

20. Jean Baudrillard, *In the Shadow of Silent Majorities, or The End of the Social and Other Essays* (New York: Semiotext(e), 1983), 118.

21. Timothy Brennan, "The National Longing for Form," in Bhabha, *Nation and Narration*, 50.

22. Alan Rosenthal, "Taking the Stage: Developments and Challenges," in *Why Docudrama? Fact-Fiction on Film and TV*, ed. Alan Rosenthal (Carbondale: Southern Illinois University Press, 1999), 1–11.

23. Todd Gitlin, *Inside Prime Time* (New York: Pantheon, 1983), 162. See also Douglas Gomery, "*Brian's Song*: Television, Hollywood, and the Evolution of the Movie Made for TV," in Rosenthal, *Why Docudrama?* 78–100.

24. Derek Paget, *No Other Way to Tell It: Dramadoc/Docudrama on Television* (Manchester: Manchester University Press, 1998), 81.

25. John Corner, "British TV Dramadocumentary: Origins and Developments," in Rosenthal, *Why Docudrama?* 45.

26. Schlesinger et al., *Televising "Terrorism,"* 99.

27. Ibid., 84.

28. Ibid.

29. *The Delta Force* (Menahem Golan, Golan-Globus Productions 1986). *True Lies* (James Cameron, Twentieth Century Fox, Universal Pictures, Lightstone Entertainment, 1994).

30. Ironically, one of the actors playing a Palestinian terrorist is the Turkish actor Birol Uenel. The image of Turks as Oriental Others thus seems to transfer easily from postwar German reality to fiction.

31. Schlesinger et al., *Televising "Terrorism,"* 79.

32. Bhabha, "Narrating the Nation," 308.

33. Ibid., 307.

Chapter Twelve

Television, Chechnya, and National Identity after the Cold War

Whose Imagined Community?

James Schwoch

In the wee hours of 27 August 2000, fire broke out in the Ostankino Television tower in Moscow, destroying the top third of the world's second-tallest freestanding structure and claiming at least four lives. Coming on the heels of the disaster of the *Kursk* submarine and a decade-long decline of Russian physical, social, financial, technical, and political infrastructures, the month became known in Russia as "Black August." As with the *Kursk* disaster, a full understanding of the causes of the Ostankino fire remains murky. The rumor mill for the causes of both disasters turned to the range of usual suspects, most prominently centering on sabotage by Chechens (or an Islamist-militant variation thereof). Some observed that if there was a Chechen cosmonaut aboard the slowly de-orbiting *Mir*, then all the problems of the Russian Space Agency could be pinned on the Chechens as well.

Such comments are indicative of the deep irony prevalent in Russian humor. Nevertheless, the ongoing conflict with Chechnya, if not literally responsible for the Ostankino fire, has played a major role in torching the Russian mediascape since the end of the Cold War, as well as providing a foul bonfire, reeking with the stench of propaganda. Researchers poking through this televisual rubble must don the intellectual equivalent of fire suit, heavy gloves, gas mask, and goggles, thus significantly problematizing the search for accuracy, representation, and understanding. Yet through the fog and smoke of war one can discern events, patterns, and trajectories that tell a story of television and national identity in the wake of the Cold War.

This essay is built around the premise that the rapid globalization of television we are witnessing is linked in many ways to the end of the Cold War. Since the fall of the Berlin Wall in 1989, the number of television sets in the world has more than doubled, surpassing 1 billion sets in use in 1994. Most of this growth is taking place outside North America, Western Europe, and Japan. One implication of this unprecedented growth is that the traditional understanding of television as the exclusive province of the world's most advanced industrialized societies has become outmoded. Television now hovers close to the baseline of human existence, and is now more likely to be part of everyday experience than the automobile. Since the fall of the

Berlin Wall, over twenty nations have orbited their own satellite, and the number of commercial launch sites on Earth is expected to reach twenty-five to thirty within the next ten years. The traditional national networks of the industrialized world have seen significant erosion of market share and audiences. But does it still make sense to make comparisons of single stand-alone national audiences the way we did in the past? Do these comparisons still mean what they meant in the days of a stable Cold War TV world?

This essay posits another question aimed not at the object of study (television after the Cold War), but at those who study the object. Do the assumptions, methods, categories, frames, and units of analysis developed and nurtured during the Cold War TV era—an era in which the units of analysis consisted of a small number of stable, nationally demarcated networks and audiences—still carry the same currency, value, and explanatory powers as they did in the past? Do the changes in our object of analysis since 1989 imply that we also need changes—or at least careful rethinking—in the ways we examine that object? With so little of the bipolar television world remaining, one is hesitant to assume that traditional notions of national identity in television—signified by national audiences, national networks, and national programming—will continue on the same terms we believe we recognize. Too often analysis ends up either critiquing or confirming narrative explanations of something—a stable, nationally demarcated, Cold War TV world—that no longer exists.

Technological innovations such as videocassettes, portable production equipment, and satellites have expanded the parameters of what television could present to audiences and changed how audiences could perceive what they saw. Private enterprise has public systems on the run. Programming has expanded exponentially in number of hours and in the formulas or genres utilized. Politics and television, from the local through the global, have developed a complex and evolving set of relationships that cannot be explained through a simple reductionist boiling-down to the Cold War paradigms of capitalism and Marxism. What was once accepted as an accurate description of global television—each nation with its own small number of national networks operating in the long shadow of the United States or perhaps the shorter shadow of the USSR—has now become the historical and cultural origins for global television in the twenty-first century. Television still contains strong elements of those historical and cultural roots but also elements of fragmentation, rapid growth of stations and sets, new forms of program distribution, and a wide range of nations providing globally distributed programming.

We have witnessed in the last decade the globalization of representations and institutions of television, a process that is having profound impact on governments, cultures, and citizens around the world. The shift toward the global has raised the significance of television for the world at large, because television itself is now a major determinant in shaping how we know the world. This includes shaping the understanding of one's own place and identity in relation to "others" around the world. Television is a site where one comes to understand his or her own similarities with and differences from others, as well as forming political and cultural suppositions that will inform future understandings of others. The global trajectories of television over the past ten or so years have undone the trajectories of the previous fifty years. These trajectories with which we have become so comfortable no longer describe the present but have receded into the past.[1]

But there is another factor to add to globalization, and that is the concept of civilizations.[2] In a seeming paradox, a globalizing world unshackled from the Cold War shows distinct signs of civilizational heterogeneity at the same time that it shows distinct signs of material homogenization. One might think that the conditions exist for all the world to become intellectually the same, but seemingly older, semi-forgotten, and little-understood civilizational contours now appear more visible than at most times during the period from 1917 to 1989. To account for this paradox, I offer the metaphor of the hurricane and the sunken pirate ship. When hurricanes hit the western shores of the North Atlantic Ocean, their speed and flow are usually such that they destroy and bury things. Sometimes—on rare occasions—the increase in the speed and flow of wind and water can uncover and reveal something that was long buried and existed only as rumor, like a sunken ship or a treasure chest.[3]

The massive increase of speed and flow brought on by the storm does not always bury things. In the case of a post-1989 world, the massive increase in the speed and flow of—well, of everything—that is the *sine qua non* of globalization is taking on a trajectory like that of the rare hurricane, uncovering and revealing civilizational contours formerly buried and therefore difficult if not impossible to discern until now. Rather than destroying civilizational difference by burying difference, the hurricane called globalization is recovering some of the differences of civilizations. Which differences will be uncovered by this storm and which will be reburied have yet to be learned, for the storm still blows strong. In fact, the storm has already blown so strong that several of the grandest edifices of the twentieth century have collapsed in its path. It is also too early to tell what from this century will survive, what will be buried, and what will be destroyed. The only thing certain is the storm has taken us all to the twenty-first century, where we will eventually learn what from the past was changed: what the storm destroyed, what the storm buried, what the storm revealed, and what survived the storm. For the intellectual community of media researchers, it may well be that our mainstream twentieth-century model of global television briefly described above will not survive as anything other than a relic or, more charitably, a historical narrative.

Post-1989 and the End of a Bipolar Cold War TV World

While we remember Marshall McLuhan for conceptualizing the global village, I want to return to the question of media research in and about a post–Cold War TV world with another McLuhan concept. I wonder if we have a bit of a case of rearview mirrorism here-what we think we see in front of us is actually something we have just passed by. This is bound up in television and the question of universalism, particularly the tendency of many Americans to think that the rest of the world wants to be just like us or else totally reject us, which, for example, is the basic premise of Benjamin Barber's *Jihad vs. McWorld*.[4] This new reductionism—attempting to replace the old bipolar reductionism of capitalism and communism—is a case of massive rearview mirrorism by the American public. A contemporary examination of global developments in television produces scenarios suggesting that the global dominance of U.S. television is not at its zenith, but rather at the beginning of the end—the first moments of a long, glorious sunset.[5] From this perspective, the post-1989 globalization of television looks less like the enduring global triumph of U.S. television and more like the warm send-off of a historical institution whose time has now passed.

The Cold War period not-so-coincidentally coincided with a period of global stability and incremental growth in television, marked above all else by the slow emergence of a limited number of national networks, clearly and neatly demarcated along the lines of nation-state units. The post-1989 period of global television development has already witnessed a significant destabilization of the bipolar system of demarcated nation-states operating either in the long shadow of the United States or the shorter shadow of the USSR. This is the historical and political backdrop for the second half of this chapter which is a case study on the televisual identity of Chechnya.

Television, Chechnya, and the Western Imagination—Via Estonia

I begin with a made-for-television production, an obscure film never fully released on video and cablecast only for three weeks in December 1994 on the Family Channel, a U.S. cable network.[6] *Candles in the Dark* was shot on location in Estonia in 1993, the first feature-length film for international distribution to be shot in post-Soviet Estonia. Directed by Maximilian Schell, the film tells the story of Estonian resistance movements in the last days of the Soviet era, focusing on the budding romance between an American exchange student (Alyssa Milano) and a young Estonian student resister (Chad Lowe). The Estonian resisters long to celebrate Christmas again in the ways they did before communism, and in Tallinn (the capital city) dare to occupy a long-shuttered church and hold services. To do so they risk being shot down by Soviet troops, but the troops do not kill them—in fact, they do not open fire—and the resisting worshippers succeed. In many ways it is the type of movie one would expect from the Family Channel, linked to Pat Robertson and the religious Right, and the Family Channel helped finance the film.

In the confrontational scene at the church, the Estonians find the Tallinn streets blocked by Soviet troops, guns ready. There is disagreement among the troop commanders, however. On the one hand, a KGB man screams at the troops to shoot the protesters. The Soviet military commander (played by Schell), however, chooses to do nothing, and the troops remain frozen in their spot on the street while the protesters slowly move through the soldiers and then past them to occupy the church. As the KGB man screams in impotent fury, he and the Soviet general, now handcuffed, are in a car. When the car begins to pull away, a young soldier, one of several portrayed throughout as unenthusiastic about the Soviet regime and occasionally willing to help the resistance (or at least look away) during skirmishes with the resisters, says with genuine sincerity, "Good luck in Moscow, General." The film ends with a chorus of religious Christmas songs, concluding with an Americanized rendition of a classic German Christmas hymn, "Silent Night" (Stille Nacht).[7]

Candles in the Dark is a loose adaptation of the breakdown of Soviet rule and the rise of the Estonian national resistance movement in the late 1980s, although I know of no specific church occupation that clearly correlates to the depicted event—that old cliché, "artistic license," applies here.[8] There was, however, during the late 1980s a Soviet general based in Estonia who did nothing to stop the growing Estonian nationalist resistance movement in the last days of the Soviet Union. This real general is far removed in his personal and moral demeanor from the womanizer Schell gives us. But there are similarities at the political and nationalistic level. This general went so far as to offer assistance to Estonians in flying the then-banned Estonian flag and met on several occasions with the clandestine Estonian parliament to discuss the future of an independent Estonia. This general left Estonia in 1991 and reemerged elsewhere in global consciousness. He was Dzhokhar Dudayev, the president of the breakaway Republic of Chechnya until reportedly assassinated in April 1996 by a Russian missile programmed to find his cellular phone.[9] *Candles in the Dark* is a film, paid for and disseminated by the Christian-based American religious Right, telling the story of anticommunism and the role of religion, and featuring as one of its heroes the future president of a Muslim breakaway republic. The ambiguous convergences of religious identities and national identities in a post–Cold War context are striking, indicative of what Matti Klinge calls the "Grand Reversal" of 1989.[10] Of course, no one knew when production began what would ultimately happen to Dudayev and Chechnya, and the story of *Candles in the Dark* is fictional. I want to leap from the fictional, however, to the reality of contemporary global issues, and discuss the linkages between Estonia and Chechnya in the context of television and national identity.

In many ways, the Chechnya breakaway movement is tied to resistance strategies developed by Estonia and the other Baltic nations at the very end of the Cold War period (roughly 1988–1992). Some of the strongest evidence of this is in the realm of media texts and national identity, and Chechnya adapted both theory and practice from the Baltics: the theory that a media-delivered representation of national identity must be aimed at audiences in the West, and the practice of this theoretical application from several specific Baltic tactics, which will be discussed. Chechnya consciously represented for Chechen and Baltic political and military leaders a test case for a defense strategy often called the "CNN defense concept." The heart of this defense concept is in the successful textual representation of national identity in global television.

The "CNN defense concept" and the linkages between Baltic and Chechen defense strategies are described in the following passage from the 1 February 1995 issue of *Soviet Press Digest*:

> An analysis of hostilities in Chechnya has led Baltic military quarters and politicians to conclude that resistance to an aggression against a small country should involve its entire population. . . . the emphasis ought to be placed on local militias. . . . (according to Estonian Chief-of-Staff Ants Laaneots) the Chechen scenario might be used against

Estonia at any time. . . . He urged to use the Chechen tactic. . . . Until recently, while planning resistance to possible Russian comeback attempts, the Baltic strategists pinned all their hopes on so-called CNN defense concept, which implied that they would hold out against an invading force until CNN and other mass media alerted the world public to give help. Now, looking at Chechnya, the military are increasingly inclined to count on their own forces.[11]

This raises some key questions: Did Dudayev help conceptualize the CNN defense concept during his time in Estonia? Did he think it would come into play in Chechnya? The Baltics were among the first nations to call for the world to recognize the national sovereignty of Chechnya; did they think their call for sovereignty was an important component in deploying the CNN defense concept, and hope to lead other nations into recognizing the sovereignty of Chechnya?[12] One even wonders whether religious identity came into play, because early in the fighting (which began in December 1994) a Christmas tree inexplicably appeared in central Grozny, drawing television cameras as if it were a magnet. Curiously, the first resistance scene in *Candles in the Dark* shows resisters substituting a white Christmas star for a red Soviet star at the top of a tree on display in Tallinn's old town, transforming the tree from a signifier of a secular Soviet New Year holiday to a symbol of a religious civilizational Christian holiday.

It appears that if the CNN defense concept was part of the operative strategy for Dudayev and Chechnya—and given the connections between Dudayev and Estonia, there is reason to think it was—then the CNN defense concept, based on eliciting a rapid response and intervention from the West, failed. This suggests that the easy conclusions offered by many media analysts about CNN's global reach and influence are overstated. Attempts to find a new bifurcation, such as Barber's *Jihad/McWorld*, to replace capitalism and Marxism are shown to lack particularities and nuance. Perhaps a new counterintellectual condition is emerging that rejects or critiques Cold War foundational assumptions of the desirability of parsimonious methodologies, universal solutions, constant conditions, and the elimination of social contentiousness. These values appear overdetermined in a post–Cold War intellectual climate that places greater value on nuances, particularities, and an increasing tendency to reject the foundational assumptions of Enlightenment thought.[13] The CNN defense concept in its original incarnation is not only a military failure for resistance movements, it is also an intellectual failure on the part of Western media analysts who attempt to carry the bifurcated, nationally demarcated world of the Cold War into a post–Cold War age. Besides, when it comes to media strategies, the Chechens never put all their eggs in the CNN defense concept basket anyway.

Although there was insufficient evidence in late 1994 of a Western-imagined, televised Chechen national identity,[14] the Chechens, by deploying the CNN defense concept and other media strategies, unexpectedly opened the door for a new Russian televisual national identity to emerge—and this Russian identity became "imagined" as much if not more by the West than by the Russians themselves. Only the Russian television audience saw the full brutality of this war daily. As one report noted, "The war, deeply unpopular throughout Russia, dominates the evening news on television night after night with its ghastly images of charred bodies, smashed homes and weeping refugees."[15] This raises another set of questions that undermine conventional assumptions about the globalization of television as a process of Americanization and CNN dominance: Why did a war televised to almost 100 million homes on a daily basis attract so little sustained attention in the West? Why was a war televised on a daily basis to almost 100 million homes by an entity other than CNN? Have Western television agencies such as CNN covered this war in detail? The West—with partial exceptions in some areas of Europe, including Finland—had not, certainly not in the United States, up to the events of August 1996. The CNN defense concept of the Chechens did not rapidly deploy onto CNN, but rather onto the post-Soviet television networks, which were attempting to globalize and, in the case of the Chechnya war, began operating along a CNN-like trajectory (albeit with their own values and on their own terms). Simply put, the Chechen deployment of the CNN defense concept helped create the conditions for CNN-like practices and institutions to emerge outside the sphere of U.S. and Western media influences. This contradicts the assumptions and predictions of conventional media researchers who never saw the possibilities of a globalization of television that had vast amounts of space for other entities, but saw globalization and Americanization of television as bipolar, intertwined, and reductionist, continuing the liberal trajectory of the Enlightenment. Such coverage of Chechnya was unexpected in the mainstream world of media representations and international relations, and Chechnya became the first huge war story covered by non-Western television networks in a manner formerly seen exclusively in the West.

Further fuel for the argument that a new Russian rather than—or perhaps along with—a Chechen national identity descended onto television is found in the aftermath of the Budyonnovsk incident of June 1995, in which Chechen soldiers invaded the Russian city of Budyonnovsk, engaged Russian ground forces, and were driven into the local hospital. A tense four-day standoff ensued; live televised negotiations between Chechen commander Shamil Basaev and Russian prime minister Viktor Chernomyrdin prevented further bloodshed and became the impetus for peace negotiations that significantly (albeit temporarily) reduced the warfare in Chechnya. These live televised round-the-clock negotiations were viewed by many Russians, continuing a post-Soviet pattern of the live televised coverage of political crises. But for the first time, the crisis did not devolve into the coup-like scenarios of 1991 and 1993, but instead transformed into the first tentative steps toward a peace process.[16] Whose national image in the minds of the West was transformed? Certainly not Chechnya, which at that time continued to be represented as an inauthentic nation and an unruly population that needed to be reabsorbed into the Russian Federation. The televisual identity of Russia itself, however, changed over this four-day period such that the *Economist* would comment that "The bloodiest act of terrorism on Russian territory since the second world war may, paradoxically, offer a chance of peace and sound government" and that through his negotiating skills Chernomyrdin demonstrated "stability" heretofore lacking in the image of the post-Soviet Russian political corpus.[17] Despite a war of independence and a miraculously successful resolution of an invasion and hostage situation that appeared to portend the extermination of the Chechen fighters, the televised national identity of Chechnya remained largely unimagined by Western audiences at the end of the crisis, while some imagined they saw a new Russian televisual national identity descend from the nascent political career of Viktor Chernomyrdin and the unexpected absence of Boris Yeltsin. Russian television had indeed changed; there was now room for more than one effective national leader on the Russian television screen, and there was a new televisual narrative in response to irrepressible political crisis: negotiation and peace.

Thus the "goal" to originate within Western imaginations a Chechen national identity via television (first through the application of the CNN defense concept, then through the opportunity of a live, televised crisis) was not yet fully realized by the Chechens. What the Chechens created, however, was the opportunity for Western audiences to believe they saw evidence of a new post-Soviet Russian political identity of nascent democracy descend into the representational sphere of global television.[18] In time, of course, the Budyonnovsk process became subsumed to the trajectories and flows of Moscow politics, which is where it all began in August 1991 anyway. Few now remember that Boris Yeltsin hailed Dudayev in September 1991 for his stance against the pro-Soviet coup attempts of that year.[19] The imagination of the West, both encouraged and tailored by Western elites in such a manner as to perceive that what television events demonstrate is a new democratic Russia and not an independent Chechnya, held into the summer of 1996.

The initial conceptualization of the CNN defense concept by Chechnya and the Baltic nations was based on eliciting a rapid response from the West, which did not materialize. While the CNN defense concept was a central component of an overall Chechen media strategy, it was not the only component, and other strategies of media representation—carefully borrowed from the Baltics and tailored to the West —are also apparent. Some strategies are direct adaptations of the experiences of the 1988–1991 Estonian revolution. Despite a two hundred-year history of Chechen resistance to Russian rule, public events such as protest songs, linking hands, and social demonstrations—all important to the Estonian movement and the Baltic independence movements of the late 1980s—only began to appear on a regular basis in Chechnya in 1991–1992. In addition to this adaptation of Baltic-style public protest, television news crews and reporters got surprisingly generous access, given the intensity of this war, to Chechen leaders.[20] Chechen leaders adapted to the "electronic revolution" of the 1980s—decentralized, portable, and instant are the keywords here —more quickly than their Moscow counterparts. In essence, the Chechens seem to have understood the theories of scholars like Paul Virilio, particularly Virilio's notions of speed and flow through permeable borders, ostensibly without having read them.[21]

Finally, the Chechens at this time played what might be called the "religious card" with care and skill, both in the long term (links to Muslim identity but not to Islamic extremism) and in singular events, such as putting up a Christmas tree in Grozny in December 1994. This adds up to a strategy of media representation by the Chechens, deployed in conjunction with a war of independence and designed to allow the West to begin imagining Chechnya as a community. These strategies play not to the imaginations of Chechens themselves, who have always imagined themselves as a community, but rather to the imaginations of the West. This raises questions about the notion of the imagined community—whose community, and whose imagination are at play—in the process of national identity. Is it the community itself, or those outside, who do the imagining? Or both (and maybe more)?

As part of this interrogation of imagination, community, and national identity I consider two theorists, Benedict Anderson and Immanuel Wallerstein, not so much in opposition to each other but in conjunction with each other.[22] In *Imagined Communities*, Anderson persuasively argued for the concept of an "imagined community" that reaches its nationalist awareness through its self-recognition. Mass culture is a key factor in stimulating and maintaining this communal self-awareness and the ability to sustain and act upon a collective imagination of the realized community. Thus Anderson helps account for the importance of mass culture and the circulation of information in imagining communities and, ultimately, in the emergence of nation-states. While Anderson helps account for the individual case, Wallerstein offers a key comparative dimension regarding national identity. He argues that national identity is valuable to a given populace only in a comparative context: national identity derives its ideological power when that populace possessing national identity simultaneously possesses the awareness that, somewhere else, there is a population without a national identity. This notion helps us get to the other side of Anderson, namely, the equal importance of "unimagined" communities in the emergence of national identity. Anderson correctly points out that mass culture plays a crucial role in allowing individuals to imagine themselves as a community, but does mass culture, particularly the global dromology (or speed) and topography of media texts, also play a role in providing what Wallerstein identifies as another key aspect of nationalism, the ability to prove to a population possessing a national identity that somewhere else there is another population without a national identity? The question thus becomes, Does television represent both imagined and unimagined communities in comparative contexts and to global audiences?

It may be that television can confirm both the presence and absence of national identity. If so, the most important historical function of the television text in terms of national identity has been to confirm its absence in other populations to those populations who possess (and can see on television) a textual representation of their own national identity. This would be in keeping with the structure of a Cold War TV world based on a small number of nationally demarcated networks. Thus the text of television is perhaps the other side of Anderson's imagined communities: that which allows for the effective representation of an absence of the national identity of others to those who possess national identity. Simply put, television is capable of simultaneously representing and comparing both an imagined community and an unimagined community to viewers.

How, then, did Chechnya finally come to be imagined by the West? The interface between nascent Russian democracy and the Chechnya war was key, although the final result of the long series of two rounds of presidential elections, the rise of Alexander Lebed, and the seemingly unimaginable Chechen triumph in the battle for Grozny in August 1996 were results of what Bruno Latour calls the contingencies of history—many possibilities existed at the start of that period, but only a few remained at the end.[23] It may come to pass that Chechnya will become an independent nation, recognized as such by both Russia and the West, although this possibility is now dim compared with 1996. If this day should come, it will not come from the assistance of the great powers of the world, who have resolutely turned their backs on Chechnya, none more so than when President Bill Clinton put U.S. history to an unprecedented use in comparing the Chechnya war to the American Civil War by noting that Abraham Lincoln died to preserve the idea that individual states could not leave the federal union.[24] If Chechnya compares to anything in U.S. history, as Richard Clogg noted, it is the genocidal U.S.-Indian wars of the late nineteenth century.[25] Clogg is right, and indirectly suggests that for the United States to imagine Chechnya, it must face the worst of its own national history. An imagined, recognized, independent future nation-state called Chechnya—if it comes to pass—will not be welcomed but instead will be forced upon the collective imaginary of the West as the result of the aggressive diplomatic efforts of small states, of decentralized power, of nuances, particularities, and anti-rationalist philosophies rather than universal conditions and Enlightenment-style intellectual reasoning, of a mastery of the topographies, dromologies, and chronoscopes of global media culture. It will secure a spot within the collective Western imagination that emerges in someplace other than the West's utopian dreams of its own future. The lack of a Western imaginary by Western political leaders regarding Chechnya as a nation-state is hardly surprising—what rational, enlightened, liberal politician would want to imagine such a community? A post-liberal nation-state like that is truly frightening.[26]

Instead of the West's own utopian dreams, Chechnya is most likely to locate itself elsewhere in the Western imaginary, a place darker and more foreboding than the place of utopian dreams: the place of dystopian nightmares. Perhaps that has already begun to happen; mystery, intrigue, and rumor surround Dudayev's death, and some Russian military figures are convinced that Dudayev—known to use doubles in the past—faked his own death. Others have pointed to the lack of a corpse, the non-adherence to Muslim burial laws (scrupulously followed by Chechens throughout the conflict), and a paucity of witnesses to the events surrounding his death. One unnamed Russian official, commenting on the possible resurrection of Dudayev, offered de facto evidence that the identity of the Chechen nation was indelibly etched in the darkness of his own imaginary and in his understanding of global media culture: "Our biggest nightmare is Dudayev showing up on television in a month's time, just before the presidential elections. . . . Dzokhar sightings are going to be like the Elvis sightings in America, except they'll be real."[27]

A Fragile Peace, Tentative Elections, and a Return to War

A fragile peace broke out in Chechnya in the fall of 1996, strong enough at that time to sustain the election of Aslan Maskhadov as president. He too has Baltic political roots, having been present as a Soviet officer the night of 13 January 1991 in Vilnius when a protester threw herself to her death, crushed under a Soviet tank. Yeltsin, like Dudaev, also eventually disappeared, replaced by Vladimir Putin. In August 1999, with causes still unclear, this conflict again became one of blood, with hardened attitudes on both sides and, as was the case from 1994 to 1996, the bulk of casualties taken from the ranks of ordinary people rather than soldiers, mercenaries, and freedom fighters. The renewed conflict began in neighboring Dagestan, but Chechnya quickly became its main theater of engagement and conflict. The current battle shows no signs of abating.

Many in the United States rightfully lament our failed opportunity to realize a peace dividend and argue that we have too little to show from our victorious end of the Cold War. I agree. At the same time, I am equally concerned about and sympathetic with those ordinary people of the former Soviet Union who have the unending detritus of the Cold War everywhere in their daily existence. They have no choice but to live with the material surplus of the history of twentieth-century warfare, both hot and cold. Unlike Bataille's "accursed share"—accursed because it must be expended for the organism to survive—the material Cold War surplus weighing on the everyday lives of former Soviets is difficult, if not impossible, to expend.[28]

Bataille teaches us that the organism must expend something in order to survive, and the question for the ordinary people of the former Soviet Union becomes, What should be expended? The choice is intellectual and ideological rather than material, choosing to expend and reject selective portions of the history of the twentieth century. Is it any wonder that they reject the intellectual surplus of twentieth-century ideology in favor of the ideology of other eras, while simultaneously surrounding themselves with as much material from the twenty-first-century world of consumer culture as possible? Without the option of expending that accursed share of material surplus (in such forms as inadequate worker housing, military overindustrialization, and ecological disasters everywhere), in order to survive the only choice is to expend the intellectual surplus of twentieth-century modern society. From this perspective, it should come as no surprise that the peoples and nations of the former Soviet Union put their hearts and minds into topographies and dromologies that encourage the intellectual history of the twentieth century to disappear as they head into the future, for the scrap heap of the twentieth century will be with them for a long time. This is the tragic dynamic (and the brilliant response) of these people, which helps account for the reemergence of civilizational contours in the rare hurricane of globalization that battered the world in the aftermath of the Cold War. When the storm finally came to this part of the world, the people were understandably willing to batten down their specific civilizational identities and let the storm instead sweep away as much of the twentieth century as possible.

The civilizational contours of globalization are becoming apparent in the growing tendency for peoples around the world to reject, alter, or rewrite the intellectual history of the twentieth century: modernity, industrialization, stasis, conformity, Wilsonian or Leninist liberalism, and mass everything—most especially mass warfare, death, and destruction. People and their leaders are willing to consider going into the twenty-first century bridged not to the twentieth century but to an alternative past. The architectural revival of Tartu, which I witnessed for a few days in May 1996, is one benign example: beautiful, state-of-the-art, twenty-first-century shops are going into the ground floor of eighteenth- and nineteenth-century buildings that remain basically unchanged on the upper floors. Homes maintain a large woodpile while they install a new satellite dish. Witness also the revival of Tamerlane in Uzbekistan, the frankly bizarre politics of the Cossacks, and the often-horrific return of much of the Balkans to pre-1914 conditions. These are identities that exist less for the West to consume and are instead identities and imagined communities rewritten in ways specific and particular—and not always pleasantly—for old, even ancient, communities that drift in and out of mainstream Western consciousness. Is a new fragmentation of national identity occurring—one set of identities for the world community of the twenty-first century and another, only partially overlapping, set of identities from that past that remains for "domestic use only"? In other words, is national identity now built on at least two imagined communities and two audiences: the nation itself and the community of nations it seeks to join? Is success for a new nation in the emergent world contingent on keeping these identities distinct, one identity perhaps even hidden on occasion from the other? Does a new nation-state emerging out of the whirlwind of globalization and civilization need a double identity: one for the world, one for itself?

In response to the last of several sets of rhetorical questions within this essay, I offer these final thoughts. The West has seen many examples of (but not always paid attention to) the media sophistication of Chechnya, as the Chechens—working outside modern public relations practices and after many trials, disappointments, and irreplaceable losses—succeeded through a combination of war and television in forcing the West to grudgingly imagine a Chechen community that could someday be a nation. Yet evidence also exists of a televisual identity for Chechnya, by Chechens, that is aimed not at Western audiences but at Chechens themselves. Within Chechnya there are many vendors of Chechen videocassettes that tell, in epic fashion the story of the Chechnya war of liberation. These tapes are not for circulation in the West, nor are they intended for Western audiences. They are not "broadcast quality" in any sense of the word. When they are played, there is constant signal dropout and image/sound degradation typical of too many generations of dubbing. They violate copyright practices by culling material from a number of different broadcasters. They tell their story in a mind-boggling mélange of filmic techniques, from Soviet montage of the 1920s to standard Western broadcast journalism to music video formats to classical Hollywood cinema to rank amateur video.

Ironically, the Chechen use of home-brew videocassettes to articulate Chechen history increasingly appears to be a process whereby a historical narrative is told using a technological medium that is no longer central in the theater of war and instead is heading toward the dustbin of history. The propaganda war between Russia and Chechnya has, since the burning of the Ostankino tower, turned away from television and toward the Internet. All parties increasingly turn toward Web-based activities in both promulgating their own message and blocking the other's message.

The shifting battleground from televisual to cybervisual space is not without its casualties. In the most graphic example, Adam Deniyev, deputy head of the pro-Moscow Chechen civil administration, was killed in April 2001 by a bomb blast while reading from the Koran over a local Chechen TV channel. Deniyev had gained notoriety in 2000 as a mysterious go-between during the kidnap and release of the Radio Liberty reporter Andrei Babitsky, who believed Deniyev was working under

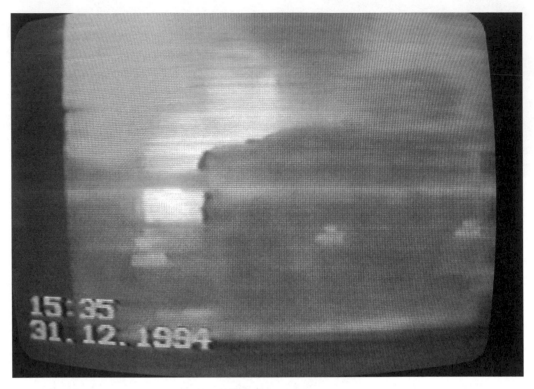

This blurry image is a screen capture from a Chechen resistance video, which was shot to document the destruction caused by Russian military attacks on 31 December 1994.

the supervision of the Federal Security Service or FSB (formerly KGB). In a whirl-wind of impossible-to-verify accusations, Deniyev had also been accused of being an FSB colonel; being involved in the kidnap and murder of Red Cross officials in 1996, blood feuds, and racketeering; and being an aspirant to the Chechen presidency.[29] This micro-incident coincided with a month of macro-actions by the Kremlin against press freedom in Russia—most notably the successful ouster of a management and ownership team at NTV, Russia's most independent TV news outlet, which led to mass resignations of the NTV news team.[30]

Now that the major independent broadcast voices have been suppressed, the war is going off-air and coming on-line.[31] An FSB spokesman, Aleksandr Zdanovich, has said that the FSB plans to begin revealing the identities of journalists involved in waging information warfare against Russia, including "those who hold a pen in their hands and those who sit at computers."[32] All this is occurring in a region where barely 1 percent of the population has Internet access. The same ordinary citizens who want no part of this never-ending conflict, and who pay the price with their lives, remain invisible and lack any identity in an escalating physical conflict and cyber-war with no end in sight.

Those same citizens, in conjunction with nongovernmental organizations (NGOs) and other nonstate actors in the local area, are turning toward consumer-level video equipment combined with noninstitutional distribution systems to build an audiovisual database that opposes state propaganda. This ad hoc volunteer coalition is undertaking the gruesome task of videotaping the discovery of mass graves, bombings, plunder, and corpses with clear signs of death by execution.[33] In one example, a video documenting the execution of civilians is circulating in refugee camps in neighboring Ingushetia. The description of this video says more than I could offer as my own conclusion:

> The bodies are laid out on rough blankets, the documents open on their bellies. All have their hands held up, palms out, as if trying to shield their faces. The boys, who look younger than their ages, are dressed in rubber boots, inexpensive sweatshirts and sweaters. One is emblazoned across the chest with the word "KIDS" in English. Ragged cuffs dangle from the elder Alsultanov's raised wrists. A surgeon from the regional hospital dons rubber gloves and examines the bodies. All have dents on the front or sides of their heads about the size of rifle butts. Each has two gunshot wounds to the head, one to the temple from point-blank range. One boy has an eye half-open, peering out quizzically from his misshapen skull as if trying to make sense of the situation. The blood on their faces is still red.[34]

Muskhadzhiyeva, the videographer, began to cry as she watched the film. "After such hell, such impunity, such horror—who now could want to remain a part of Russia?" she asked.

NOTES

An earlier version of James Schwoch's essay, "Television, Chechnya and National Identity after the Cold War," was published in *Writing Media Histories: Nordic Views*, ed. Raimo Salokangas, James Schwoch, and Kalle Virtapohja (Jyvaskyla: University of Jyvaskyla Press, 1997). Reprinted by permission.

My thanks to my coeditors and the University of Jyvaskyla, Peeter Vihalemm, Aune Unt, Epp Lauk, and Halliki Harno of the University of Tartu; Anatol Lieven of the International Institute of Strategic Studies; and many colleagues at Northwestern University, including Charles Ragin, John Bushnell, and Georgi Derluguian, for their advice. Thanks also to Norbert Strade, moderator of the chechnya-sl@yahoogroups.com e-newsletter, a priceless source of information.

1. For a similar argument on the new trajectories of telecommunications policy, see James Schwoch, "Global Dialogues, Paradigmatic Shifts, and Complexity: Emergent Contours of Theory and Praxis in Telecommunications Policy," *Emergences* 11, no. 1 (May 2001): 133–52.

2. Samuel Huntington, "The Clash of Civilizations?" *Foreign Affairs*, summer 1993, 22–49.

3. "Storms Uncover Medieval Settlement," AP Newswire, 9 February 2001, recounts such an incident in Wales.

4. New York: Times Books, 1994.

5. For a televisual metaphor, think about how *Dallas* has been replaced in the global imaginary with *Baywatch* and its endless Pacific sunsets.

6. The Family Channel graciously supplied me with a promotional copy of *Candles in the Dark*, for which I am grateful. Studies informing this discussion include John F. R. Wright et al., eds., *Transcaucasian Boundaries* (London: UCL Press, 1996); Michael Mandelbaum, ed., *The Rise of Nations in the Soviet Union* (New York: Council on Foreign Relations Press, 1991);

Matti Klinge, *The Baltic World* (Helsinki: Otava, 1994); Anatol Lieven, *The Baltic Revolution: Estonia, Latvia, Lithuania and the Path to Independence* (New Haven: Yale University Press, 1993); Rein Taagepera, *Estonia: Return to Independence* (Boulder: Westview, 1993); Suzanne Goldberg, *Pride of Small Nations: The Caucasus and Post-Soviet Disorder* (London: Zed, 1994); John Hiden and Patrick Salmon, *The Baltic Nations and Europe: Estonia, Latvia and Lithuania in the Twentieth Century* rev. ed. (New York: Longman, 1994); Svennik Hoyer, Epp Lauk, and Peeter Vihalemm, eds., *Towards a Civic Society: The Baltic Media's Long Road to Freedom* (Tartu: Nova Baltica, 1993); Kristian Gerner and Stefan Hedlund, *The Baltic States and the End of the Soviet Empire* (London: Routledge, 1993); Carlotta Gall and Thomas De Waal, *Chechnya: Calamity in the Caucasus* (New York: New York University Press, 1998); and Anatol Lieven, *Chechnya: Tombstone of Russian Power* (New Haven: Yale University Press, 1998). For two excellent studies on the general contours of Soviet and Russian television, see Ellen Mickiewicz, *Split Signals: Television and Politics in the Soviet Union* (New York: Oxford University Press, 1988), and Mickiewicz, *Changing Channels: Television and the Struggle for Power in Russia*, rev. and expanded ed. (Durham: Duke University Press, 1999).

7. Ostensibly sung in a gospel rendition, although to my ears, not very well done.

8. I have discussed this film with Estonian colleagues (all of whom knew of the film); in general they felt that the film corresponds to nothing specific, but it's really not made for Estonians anyway—the target audience is the West. This idea that you can have a film or any media text telling a story tied up in national identity aimed at audiences other than the citizens of that nation is extremely important, and one to which I shall return. This is only one of several absolutely vital ideas my colleagues at Tartu were generous enough to share with me. The church scene may be adapted from well-known events taking place in Leipzig during the 1989 collapse of the German Democratic Republic.

9. Alternative spellings include, at least in the American press, "Jokhar" and "Dudaev." In this essay I have decided to begin by retaining the spelling first used in the American press when the Chechnya war began in December 1994, although I am also aware that "Dudaev" now seems the spelling of choice. I use both of these spellings later in the paper. This eventual dropping of the letter *y* in the English spellings of the names of several Chechens can make keyword-based computer searches difficult, so researchers are forewarned. The Internet Web site "Chechnya Official Home Page" has this quote from Dudayev on Chechen names: "Chechenian tradition of naming was different. We were forced to the wrong standards. The right Chechenian way to call my name would be the following: at first, should be mentioned the name of my grandfather, then his son's, only after that comes my name—Dudi Musi Jokhar. Chechenian should be able to count minimum seven generations of his clan. Dudaevs have maintained 13—the whole our clan, however only by paternal line." Here at the Web site the spelling is Jokhar Dudaev: www.chechnya.org/, downloaded 21 March 1997.

10. Klinge, *The Baltic World*, 168–74.

11. Laaneots was second in command to Dudayev in Estonia during the late Soviet period. On the CNN defense concept, see also Steven Livingston and Todd Eachus, "Humanitarian Crises and U.S. Foreign Policy: Somalia and the CNN Effect Reconsidered," *Political Communication* 12 (1995); Jonathan Mermin, "Television News and American Intervention in Somalia: The Myth of a Media-Driven Foreign Policy," *Political Science Quarterly* 12, no. 3 (1997).

12. Along with this recognition of sovereignty Dudayev was awarded the 1995 Baltic Freedom Award by the Baltic American Freedom League at a ceremony in Los Angeles in March 1995. In his absence the award was accepted by Romualda Hofertiene, a Lithuanian parliament member and chair of the Baltic States Committee in Support of Chechen Independence. See *PR Newswire*, 6 March 1995.

13. For a critique of those who currently critique the Enlightenment, see "Crimes of Reason," *Economist*, 16 March 1996, 93–95. On Cold War intellectualism, see James Schwoch, "Origins, Paradigms, and Topographies: Methodological Considerations Regarding Area Studies and Broadcast Histories," *American Journalism* 9, nos. 3–4 (summer–fall 1992): 111–30.

14. There are always the exceptions, of course, such as the front cover of the *Economist* on 17 December 1994 with the headline "Chechnya Requests Independence" and a photo of an elder Chechen with binoculars, rocket launcher, pistol, and (I think) a sword. Of all major English-language news media I have surveyed, including extensive online research through the LEXIS/NEXIS database, I would have to say that the *Economist* was, surprisingly, the first— and for a long time, really the only—one of this group to report Chechen independence as a real possibility. Supposed stalwarts of American liberalism such as the *Nation* were very slow, in comparison, to "narrate" the Chechnya story. On mainstream U.S.-reporting of the Baltic and Chechnya crises, see Wanda Siu, "Media Framing and U.S. Foreign Policy: A Comparative Analysis of Baltic and Chechnya Crises" (conference paper, Midwest Graduate Conference on Mass Communication, University of Wisconsin, April 2001). Siu reaches similar conclusions on the relative lack of U.S. reporting.

15. *International Herald Tribune*, 1 April 1996.

16. "See Hostage-Takers Let Go! Live, on Every Russian TV!" *New York Times,* 20 June 1995; "Russia's Premier: Too Popular for His Own Good?" *New York Times*, 26 June 1995, both give analyses of the Budyonnovsk television coverage of June 1995.

17. "From the Party of War to the Party of Power," *Economist*, 8 July 1995, 43.

18. A typical response was found in the editorial pages of the 1 August 1995 *Chicago Tribune*, which noted that even though an emergent peace settlement ducked the issue of Chechen independence, the settlement and concomitant decisions by the Russian Constitutional Court both supporting and criticizing the Russian actions in Chechnya meant that "the community of nations can feel more confident today that, in its struggle to reach modernity, Russia is a healthier democracy than it was when troops moved into Chechnya last December." For a similar analysis written prior to the Budyonnovsk incident, see Doug Ford, "The Legitimacy of Separatism: Does Chechnya Have a Right to Independence?" *Foreign Service Journal*, April 1995, 42–47.

19. Suzanne Goldenberg, "Background Note: Reflections on Chechnya," in Wright et al., *Transcaucasian Boundaries*, 11–13.

20. The interviews by Finland's MTV 3 in March 1996 are but one example.

21. See Paul Virilio, *Open Sky*, trans. Julie Rose (London: Verso, 1997); Virilio, *The Information Bomb*, trans. Chris Turner (London: Verso, 2000); and James Der Derian, ed., *The Virilio Reader* (London: Blackwell, 1998).

22. Benedict Anderson, *Imagined Communities: Reflections on the Origin and Spread of Nationalism*, rev. ed. (London: Verso, 1991). Two recent publications that address Wallerstein's thinking about the importance of "absenting" nationalism are *Geopolitics and Geoculture: Essays on the Changing World-System* (Cambridge: Cambridge University Press, 1991) and *After Liberalism* (New York: New Press, 1995).

23. Bruno Latour, *We Have Never Been Modern*, trans. Catherine Porter (Cambridge: Harvard University Press, 1993).

24. This comment, which came at the end of the 1996 Moscow G7 summit, got huge media play in Europe. See *International Herald Tribune*, 22 April 1996.

25. Clogg is in the European Studies Center at St. Antony's College, Oxford; quoted from his letter to the editor, *Independent*, 1 May 1996.

26. One other route would be a revival/simulation of superpower ideology. The Bush

administration recently announced that it intends to pursue a diplomatic dialogue with the Chechen government of Aslan Maskhadov. *RFE/RL Newsline*, 21 March 2001.

27. *Times* (London), 28 April 1996. Even in 2001, occasional rumors that Dudayev lives still surface in contemporary Russian media. These rumors echo the legend of Imam Shamil, the nineteenth-century Chechen freedom fighter who resurfaced from the dead after a long period in hiding. See Lieven, *Chechnya*, 301–11.

28. Georges Bataille, *The Accursed Share*, vols. 1–3, trans. Robert Hurley (New York: Zone Books, 1988–91).

29. "Kadyrov's Man Murdered in Front of TV Camera," www.gazeta.ru, 14 April 2001; "Chechen Quisling Blown Up during Television Filming," *Independent*, 14 April 2001.

30. This story has been extensively covered in the Western media. For the reaction of the U.S. State Department, see "Closure of Independent Media in Russia Politically Motivated," Press Release, 18 April 2001, at www.state.gov/r/pa/prs/ps/2001/index.cfm?docid=2319.

31. See, for example, www.ichkeria.org/indexen.html for a leading Chechen Web site. A recent meeting of Russian occupiers in Chechnya concluded that television should now "be required to broadcast the ploughed fields and picturesque hills against the peaceful blue skies of Chechnya instead of disfigured, unidentified corpses in mass graves," "Calls for Correct Media Coverage on Chechnya," 20 March 2001, at www.gazeta.ru (via chechnya-sl@yahoogroups.com).

32. *RFE/RL Newsline* 5:78, part 1, 23 April 2001.

33. "Chechen Fighting Ebbs, but Information War Rages On," *Los Angeles Times*, 24 April 2001.

34. Ibid.

Chapter Thirteen

Television and Trustworthiness in Hong Kong

Michael Curtin

The paradoxical qualities of Hong Kong television are many. For instance, it emerged as one of the few truly local services in the history of the medium. That is, from its very beginning in 1967, broadcast TV in Hong Kong was primarily focused on the concerns of residents within the colony. It had no national agenda nor was it connected to a network of stations. Unlike other TV services around the world, Hong Kong broadcasters very quickly began to produce the vast majority of their shows at local studios and, as time wore on, this small territory of roughly six million people had two (sometimes three) stations almost exclusively devoted to local programming, ranging from variety shows to dramas to news. Perhaps most interestingly, the medium emerged at the precise moment when residents of the colony were beginning to think of themselves as a distinctive social grouping. Unlike other societies that developed their identities during the eras of print, film, or radio, Hong Kong's collective consciousness came to fruition through and on television. Consequently, the medium initially proved to be enormously popular and profitable until it reached a period of maturity in the 1980s, when profit growth began to taper off. Local stations then began to turn their attention to international markets, investing in video distribution networks and cable services in countries throughout East Asia, Europe, and North America. Hong Kong television therefore developed as a fundamentally *local* and *global* medium, almost completely evading the politics of nationalism. This is contrary to the experience of TV services in such places as the United Kingdom, India, and Egypt, where television developed first and foremost as a national medium.

Yet just as Hong Kong broadcasters began to expand their operations overseas, they encountered yet another unique challenge: the territory's "return to China." In the early 1980s the British government, which had ruled the colony since the mid-1800s, agreed to hand it back to the Chinese government in 1997. This enormously prosperous and modern city with a reputation for openness and independence—despite its colonial status—would thereafter become a part of mainland China, a developing country with an authoritarian central government. Never before had a television industry experienced such a phenomenon. Although guaranteed fifty years of autonomy as an interim period to smooth the transition to Chinese rule, institutions throughout the colony confront the daunting task of transforming relations that had been "glocally" constituted into ones that must conform to the interests of the Chinese nation-state. Now, as the territory continues to navigate the return to Chinese sovereignty, the economic viability and survival of Hong Kong media depend on their ability to respond simultaneously to local, national, and transnational market conditions. But just as importantly, it depends on their ability to sustain relationships of trust with their core audiences. That is, the value and the popularity of Hong Kong television have been crucially reliant on the ability of broadcasters to fashion programs that respond to the needs of local citizens and diasporic Chinese communities around the world. With the transition to Chinese sovereignty, those relationships will undergo profound changes. Only by examining the historical context of the medium's development can we begin to glimpse the complex social, cultural, and geographical forces that will influence the future development of East Asia's most influential media capital.

This chapter interweaves the recent history of Hong Kong society with developments in local television. The opening section shows how the medium emerged in Hong Kong during the early 1970s at a moment when residents of the colony were first developing a sense of local identity. At the time, TV portrayals of government investigations into widespread corruption helped to define the core values that citizens hold dear, including a faith in social mobility and the rule of law. Because television played a central role in local identity formation around these shared values, the essay then turns to an examination of the conceptual relationship between publicity, public trust, and the rule of law. Here an emphasis is placed on drawing distinctions between Western conceptions of the media and local conceptions, showing how the surveillance of corruption is perhaps one of the paramount missions of Hong Kong media. The third section shows how television dramas during the 1970s and 1980s further contributed to the constitution of a local identity by constructing characters who were distinguished by their social origins rather than their Chinese ethnicity. Local Chinese characters were portrayed as modern, diligent, and lawful, while mainlanders were often represented as a corrupting influence from the outside. Thus, Hong Kong identity rested to a large extent on the opposition between local residents and mainlanders. The fourth section focuses on the ways media institutions began to register a shift in their representations of mainland Chinese after the 1984 agreement to return the colony to China. Moreover, local media firms have shown strong interest in expanding their operations across the border. In order to win the support and cooperation of Chinese officials, Hong Kong television firms now face the difficult challenge of sustaining the trust of local audiences while also pursuing new audiences in mainland China. Consequently, the key challenge confronting Hong Kong TV between now and the middle of the century is the extent to which it can manage the demands and pressures that national interests will bring to bear on a historically distinctive glocal industry.

Dropping the I

On June 4, 1997, only one month before the official handover ceremonies, Hong Kong's incoming Chinese administration announced that the word "Independent" would be dropped from the title of the Independent Commission against Corruption (ICAC), a watchdog agency that monitors not only government and police bureaus but business organizations as well.[1] For example, the ICAC has successfully prosecuted high-profile cases in the fashion, travel, real estate, and publishing industries. Nevertheless, the new government reasoned that since the Basic Law of the new Special Administrative Region (SAR), drafted with Beijing's guidance, made no specific mention of an independent commission, the term would be eliminated. Some saw this as a deferential gesture to China's Communist Party leadership, which has a reputed aversion to words like "free" and "independent," especially in the titles of organizations. The announcement immediately caused an uproar in the Hong Kong news media and within the ranks of the civil service. The head of the ICAC, Lily Yam Kwan Pui-ying, was unabashed in her response, saying, "As far as we are concerned, it will stay." After several weeks of intense lobbying, the SAR leadership quietly withdrew the proposed name change and commission head Yam breathed a public sigh of relief. "Some people might say: 'What's in a word?' But this is not just a word, it is a crucial word."[2]

Indeed, the *I* in ICAC means a lot to inhabitants of Hong Kong. The impartiality and activism signified by this single letter grew out of a highly charged historical era when the local Chinese population made its first significant strides into the political arena. Prior to the establishment of the ICAC in 1974, Hong Kong government and business were awash in corruption. Huge fortunes were made and lost not on the basis merit or enterprise but through personal connections and intrigue. As one local media critic told me, the battle against corruption marked a defining moment for local inhabitants. "It was our Watergate," he said. "And the thing that made me the proudest was that the investigations went right to the top and they prosecuted people without regard to their social position, ethnic background, or political connections."

The formation of the ICAC was itself part of a broader period of social ferment and reform that stretches back to the late 1960s. Before that time political involvement was a rarity among Hong Kongers, since most residents had been born elsewhere and perceived their identity as connected to places they left behind, usually somewhere in mainland China.[3] Furthermore, the colonial administration treated most Chinese inhabitants as refugees, providing little in the way of public services, social welfare, or political standing. Yet by the late 1960s, this refugee generation had sunk its roots in Hong Kong: raising families, establishing businesses, and increasingly participating in the myth, if not the material rewards, of upward social mobility. Their children, born and raised in the territory, would in turn play a leading role in the contagion of political, social, and cultural activism that began with fierce protests against fare increases on the Star Ferry in 1966.[4]

Personal and public memories of the ICAC investigations that took place in the midst of this era of ferment might therefore be seen as more densely textured and meaningful for citizens of the territory than memories of Watergate are for many in the United States. Like Watergate, the ICAC investigations were connected to an era of political activism and reform that generated massive amounts of media attention. But unlike Watergate, this was one of Hong Kong's earliest experiences with an open political process. It was also the very first time that residents of the territory invested substantial amounts of time and energy deliberating about the distinctive qualities of public life in Hong Kong. What made the city different from the mainland and from other parts of Asia? What particular values, attitudes, and aspirations did Hong Kongers share? What specifically did it mean to identify oneself as a Hong Konger?

At the center of these political and cultural deliberations was local television, which was then in its very infancy but rapidly becoming a common household appliance. TV news organizations lavished tremendous attention on the corruption investigations, which were in turn followed by locally produced dramas that drew huge audiences, earned widespread praise, and sparked intense controversy regarding issues of censorship and creative freedom under the colonial regime. Moreover, the popularity of these TV shows inspired numerous film projects that played an important role in reviving the then moribund Cantonese movie industry.[5] In other words, the ICAC investigations were embedded in a matrix of political and cultural developments that most critics point to as central elements during Hong Kong's era of identity formation.

Even today popular representations of the struggle against corruption remain one of the defining characteristics of the city. Despite the fact that powerful business interests continue to conspire and collaborate and that triad gangs still exercise an unwelcome influence in many sectors of society, the fact remains that Hong Kong is one of the cleanest, best managed cities in Asia, if not the world. Citizens take great pride in this attribute, saying that theirs is a society governed by the "rule of law." Perhaps the intensity of their pride is connected to the fact that Hong Kong's success as a global financial center rests largely on its reputation as a "level playing field."[6] Conversely, this pride may also be a product of widespread public awareness of the city's reputation as an entrepot for transnational drug dealing, smuggling, and other forms of illicit behavior. Upon this uneasy dualism—civic probity and its repressed other—rests Hong Kong's identity, helping one to understand the delicate balance that seemed threatened by the very suggestion that the incoming SAR government would drop the *I* in ICAC.

Publicity and Public Trust

Yet the significance of Hong Kong's ongoing struggle against corruption extends further into the cultural matrix of the territory. As social theorists such as Anthony Giddens have remarked, one of the central features of modernity is the elaborate set of institutional roles and relationships that help to sustain trust among the members of a society who for the most part remain anonymous to one another.[7] According to Giddens, one trusts that certain actions will reliably generate a limited range of responses. When depositing money at a bank, one trusts that it will be available for withdrawal at some time in the future. Should a problem arise, one furthermore trusts that it would be resolved according to clearly stipulated guidelines and that one would ultimately have the right to seek redress in the courts as a guarantee that one is treated fairly. One trusts the bank teller, the bank manager, lawyers, judges, and a vigilant free press to insure that one is treated fairly by people and institutions that one hardly knows. In other words, the functioning of modern society is crucially dependent on a web of relationships based on trust.

One's repeated experiences with relatively trustworthy institutions and institutional actors may have more far-ranging implications as well. For example, Hong Kong's reputation for relatively impartial government and market operations not only marks the territory as a modern cosmopolis, it also helps to buttress public faith in the myth of upward social mobility, which is perhaps the paramount value binding the culture together. The city's early and continuing attraction to immigrants has been based on its reputation as a place where one could work hard to build a career, a business, or a lifestyle with a reasonable expectation that one's aspirations would not be dashed by a capricious exercise of power or privilege.[8] One could trust that anonymous others would be held accountable to more or less the same standards as oneself. This contrasts dramatically with characterizations of China as the second most corrupt nation among those studied by Transparency International.[9]

Not surprisingly, therefore, the single most pervasive fear that Hong Kongers expressed about the transfer of sovereignty to China is the threat it poses to the "rule of law." Public opinion polls in the year leading up to the handover show that corruption is the most commonly shared concern about the future, a finding corroborated in my personal conversations with acquaintances, friends, and colleagues. For example, a poll conducted by Professor Michael DeGolyer and his colleagues at the Hong Kong Transition Project found that 72 percent of respondents identified corruption among government officials as their biggest worry after the colony was returned to China. Corruption was seen as a greater concern than free speech, voting rights, or educational policy. Many respondents furthermore conveyed a fatalistic attitude, saying they felt they had little control over the future of the territory and simply hoped that they and their families would not be adversely affected.[10]

On the face of it, these polls might be interpreted as showing a callous fixation on material welfare, as opposed to more lofty spiritual and political concerns. Corruption seems more important than free expression or political representation and many said they were simply resigned to their fate under an authoritarian regime in Beijing. Yet I would suggest that these concerns regarding corruption in Hong Kong are emblematic of a widespread understanding of an important relationship between media and public life. This becomes most apparent when one compares global media coverage of the official handover with more regional and local media representations. At the global level, news reports focused on the issue of free speech and were full of dire predictions about the fate of "democracy" in Hong Kong. Martin Lee Chuming, a local legislator, attracted international acclaim for his heroically defiant pronouncements in the face of mounting pressure from leaders in Beijing who sought to attenuate the influence of democratically elected local representatives. Lee's public statements seemed to conform to Western perceptions of what citizens of the territory should be saying. Yet even though local opinion polls showed that many agreed with Lee, they nevertheless were stoical if not fatalistic about the transition. In part they were responding tactically to an inevitable transfer of power. But their sentiments also may have resulted from the fact that they conceive of political rights in ways that vary from Enlightenment concepts prevalent in the West. That is, local citizens seemed less concerned about the mechanics of political representation than they were about accountability and transparency in government and commerce. In his essay "Going Public," Benjamin Lee urges scholars to consider such variations around the globe when discussing concepts like democracy, publicity, and public life. In particular, he points to some of the distinctive ways that these concepts have been employed in post-Tiananmen China and in the larger transnational spheres of Chinese cultural and political discourse.[11]

Picking up on Lee's suggestion, we should note that Westerners tend to think of human rights in relation to abstract principles of democracy and personal expression. Some of the images we commonly associate with these abstractions are heroic moments of personal defiance: the Declaration of Independence, the Magna Carta, the storming of the Bastille. The fact that each of these confrontations stemmed in large measure from more mundane issues such as taxation tends to recede in our mythology, so that what remain are visions of heroic patriots battling an arrogant despot for universal rights of free expression and democratic representation.

At each of these mythical moments, the role of the printing press looms large because, as Jurgen Habermas suggests, the seeds of these revolutions in the West were cultivated by an emerging public dialogue that took place via the printed word. Publicity was the means by which the Enlightenment subject elevated his discourse above the level of private self-interest and inquired as to the greater good of society as a whole.[12] The resulting appeal to the rational, the universal, and the abstract no doubt invested the bourgeois subject with a sense of historical mission, a means by which the individual was both constituted and fulfilled through the discursive engagements of public life. To make one's issue public was to position personal experience as part of a national discourse of abstract political reflection. Moreover, this vision of publicity became connected to emerging literary and artistic movements that based their popular appeal on the construction of middle-class characters who would come to represent the fundamental unit of commercial and political power—the individual. Representative governance was premised on popular sovereignty ("one man, one vote"); in the marketplace, exchanges between individuals were construed as the fundamental basis for all economic activity. Consequently, Western societies tend to privilege free expression and personal fulfillment as fundamental rights that form the cornerstone of society. At the time of the Hong Kong handover, it therefore is little wonder that Western media reports would pay more attention to abstract rights of free speech than they would pay to the more practical benefits of publicity, such as surveillance of state abuses that arise from corruption, burdensome taxation, or capricious uses of administrative power.

Yet for many Hong Kongers, free expression seems not so much connected to abstract principles or individual rights, as it is to matters of accountability, transparency, and trust. Having been raised in a colonial school system that gave short shrift to academic subjects such as civics and contemporary history, most Hong Kongers tend not to speak freely and casually about human rights.[13] They had limited rights under the British regime and expect a similarly truncated form of citizenship under Bejing's rule. By comparison, United States citizens, partially as a result of their schooling, are as likely to quote from the Bill of Rights as any other official text.

Likewise, they are quick to reformulate many issues of public concern into a debate over rights. Whether the topic is taxes, pollution, or suggestive rock lyrics, Americans want to know first and foremost whether someone's rights have been jeopardized or violated. This is not to say by way of comparison that Hong Kongers do not care about rights, but that their concerns have a different inflection and a different history. For many citizens of the territory, free expression is a means to an end. It is a way to insure fair and impartial treatment in everyday life, a guarantee against abuses of power. It is less a matter of achieving personal fulfillment or defending an abstract, universal principle.

This does not diminish the importance that is attached to individual rights, but it does suggest a significantly different inflection to the concept. This difference helps to explain why many in the territory despaired over Hong Kong's inability to achieve postcolonial independence, while nevertheless believing that the city could still have a viable and prosperous future as part of China. In other words, the colonial history of the territory meant that until very recently citizens enjoyed limited rights under a British regime that was fixated on the expansion of commerce and the production of wealth. Hong Kongers now hope that the Beijing leadership is similarly disposed to promote free market principles above communist doctrine or nationalist politics. Although their ambitions for full political autonomy and democratic governance have been dashed by the Basic Law that set the terms of the handover, many citizens say they could tolerate the current situation if the existing commercial and social systems were left more or less intact, something that would be possible only if the media were allowed to continue to interrogate, criticize, and lampoon corruption and abuses of power.[14] Media surveillance of corruption is therefore seen as a fundamental necessity if Hong Kong is to remain a society based on the "rule of law."

TV Drama and the Rule of Law

This emphasis on the more practical aspects of publicity is linked to significant cultural concerns as well. As mentioned earlier, belief in the rule of law is one of the most prominent ways that Hong Kongers have distinguished themselves from mainland Chinese. This difference is perhaps all the more important because in fact citizens of the territory share racial, cultural, and historical legacies with their counterparts across the border. Almost all Hong Kongers are Han Chinese, which is by far the dominant ethnic group on the mainland.[15] Little ethnic difference exists between residents of the territory and their counterparts across the border. But as Eric Kit-wai Ma points out in his study of local drama shows since the 1970s, television producers have repeatedly constructed mainland characters who immigrate to Hong Kong and then have trouble adjusting to public life in the territory.[16] Symbolically, mainland characters represent a threat to social order, since they are often portrayed as troublemakers or even gangsters. By comparison, local characters are portrayed as industrious and law-abiding. The struggle against corruption is therefore more than an economic or civic issue, it helps to define the very identity of Hong Kong people.

For example, in 1979 TVB, the leading broadcaster in the city, began to televise what would become one of the most popular television programs in its history. *The Good, the Bad, and the Ugly* ran on a nightly basis for eighty episodes, consistently drawing audience ratings in the 70s and 80s. It is the story of a "typical" Hong Kong family who suddenly receive a letter from Ah Chian, a long-lost brother from the mainland who is finally able to sneak across the border to Hong Kong to rejoin his parents and adult siblings.[17] What should be an occasion for great rejoicing turns out to be something of a familial nightmare. Ah Chian, separated from his family for twenty years, has grown up in the lawless and tumultuous era of the Cultural Revolution. At the very time when Hong Kong was going through a period of economic growth and modernization, China had been plunged into a period of political turmoil and widespread poverty. Ah Chian therefore had grown up under very different circumstances and seemed alienated from his family in manners, tastes, and education. From the very outset, Ah Chian does not fit in. He wears a T-shirt and flip-flops on the street, spits in public, and speaks Cantonese with a heavy provincial accent. When he first arrives at his family's home, he eats greedily, uses foul language, and stays up all night watching television. "All through the story," writes Ma, "he seems to have an insatiable appetite, devouring any sort of food that he can get hold of."[18]

Ah Chian furthermore finds that life in the territory is not at all like his fantasies of luxury and easy money. Soon after his arrival he tells his brother Wai that he dreams of becoming rich and powerful. Wai responds that it takes patience and hard work to succeed in Hong Kong, but Ah Chian protests that he has no doubt that he will succeed; he *deserves* to get rich. His family sends him to night school, but Ah Chian fails to study hard and spends much of his time at discos. He aspires to wealth, but fails to grasp the social cues regarding appropriate behaviors leading to success. For example, he wants to become a wealthy Hong Kong businessman, so he shows up at an interview for an entry-level clerical job wearing a suit and tie, only to be told that he need not dress so formally, since he will be working initially as an errand boy. He aspires to the top, but fails to understand the many steps along the road to success. He is ridiculed for this failure and for similar forms of inappropriate behavior. Over time, Ah Chian, along with his buddies from the mainland, become convinced that the only way they will strike it rich in Hong Kong is by turning to crime.

By comparison, brother Wai graduates from university and gets a job at a company where he works his way up the ladder by helping to modernize its operations. He installs a computer network, helps to launch a successful promotional campaign, and convinces the boss to open more chain stores. Yet even then his success is not assured. Due to economic reversals, Wai falls from the top and his family experiences hard economic times. He nevertheless remains determined and industrious, even driving a cab by night to help support his parents. He asks for no favors or advantages from friends or family, relying instead on his meritorious labor. Wai is a character who plays by the rules and is rewarded for his hard work. He embodies the myth that Hong Kong is an open society and anyone can succeed if they work hard enough.

In the end, Ah Chian and his pals rob a bank and are caught by police and put

The family from *The Good, the Bad, and the Ugly.* The "good brother" in the middle is played by Chow Yun-Fat.

on trial. Although the family attends the trial, their support for Ah Chian is rendered ambiguous by their seeming relief when he is found guilty and sentenced to prison. As Eric Ma suggests, although Ah Chian is considered part of the Ching family, even that powerful bond is ultimately undermined by his status as a mainlander. In this case, local identity was represented as more significant than ethnic or familial solidarity.

Over 90 percent of Hong Kong households viewed at least part of this series and the narrative was such a compelling subject of popular discourse that Ah Chian entered the popular lexicon as a nickname that is commonly used to tease someone whose actions, language, or attire were considered offbeat or grotesque. Like English-language references to someone who is "fresh off the boat," the nickname conjures up the image of an awkward outsider, but it also suggests something more foreboding in that the term associates the mainlander with an inclination toward lawlessness that might manifest itself in street crime, corruption, or political terror. As Ma points out, the stereotypical characters in the series were neither fair nor accurate representations of mainlanders or of local residents. Yet the stereotypes marked some of the most important differences on which the Hong Kong identity was constructed during the 1970s. Television became the site where citizens of the territory saw themselves portrayed as diligent, educated, and law-abiding citizens—a sharp contrast from images of cronyism, chaos, and lawlessness across the border.

Consequently, residents of the colony were more than a bit disturbed when, during the early 1980s, deliberations over the renewal of the British lease of the territory turned into negotiations between the Beijing and London governments regarding the restoration of Chinese sovereignty. Commercial concerns were obviously at the forefront, but Hong Kongers also faced the daunting proposition that fundamental local values would be undermined by the transfer of power. Nevertheless, once the negotiations were completed and the Basic Law was adopted, television and film began to play an active role in the process of adaptation. By the late 1980s, representations of differences between Hong Kongers and mainlanders began to diminish in part because of the inevitable transfer of sovereignty and in part because of optimism over political reforms in China and increasingly vibrant transborder economic ties. Indeed, popular media began to register a growing fascination with social and cultural roots on the mainland. Historical dramas based on Chinese myths and legends proved especially popular, especially legends that focused on famous leaders of ancient dynasties. Not only did this somewhat mitigate the stigma attached to representations of the mainlander, it also sparked a reassessment of Hong Kong's relationship to mainland society.[19]

At the very same moment, China was going through its own process of change as the Beijing leadership promoted policies of social and economic liberalization. As a result, cultural flows into the mainland started to loosen up and Chinese citizens got their first taste of music, drama, and comedy from the outside world. Television, which was generally unavailable in China in 1980, became extremely popular. It was not only a new source of information and entertainment, it also became a mark of one's improved social status and prosperity. In many cases, people opened new businesses and worked extra hours because they were saving to buy a TV. By the end of the 1980s, the medium was widely available in cities throughout China. And in the southern part of the country, where modernization was proceeding most rapidly, TV shows and video copies of movies from Hong Kong were especially popular. In a way, television was mediating two related processes of transition: China's journey into the post-Mao era of modernization and Hong Kong's journey back into the fold of Chinese sovereignty.

Consequently, global fascination with television reporting of the heroic Tiananmen demonstrations of 1989 was nowhere more intense than it was in Hong Kong. What is often forgotten, however, is that the "pro-democracy" movement in China during this period began with demonstrations against corruption. Indeed, the Beijing protests were the culmination of several years of concerted political organizing by educated young people opposed to bribery, nepotism, and other forms of chicanery at all levels of Chinese society. Their ambitions for social mobility were interwoven with their yearning for public accountability and legal guarantees. And it is perhaps for this very reason that Hong Kongers empathized with the concerns of demonstrators in Beijing. Feverish fundraising efforts in the territory at the time of the Tiananmen protests yielded a dramatic outpouring of contributions of food, tents, sleeping bags, and cash that helped support the efforts of the demonstrators at the square. So much so that when Beijing government officials criticized the influence of "outside agitators," they made pointed reference to the efforts of Hong Kong organizers. Indeed, enthusiasm for the protest was running so high in the colony that when the Chinese government staged its late-night assault on the square, citizens of Hong

Kong responded in grief and outrage when they heard the news. More than one million people—one-sixth of the population—took to the streets, staging a massive memorial service for the slain demonstrators and venting their outrage at the actions taken by the Beijing government.

An annual commemoration of the Tiananmen protests continues in Hong Kong to this day. In 1997, on the very same day that the incoming SAR leadership announced it would remove the *I* from ICAC, an estimated fifty-five thousand people turned out in Hong Kong's Victoria Park to honor the martyrs of June 4. Although nowhere near the figure of one million people who took to the streets eight years earlier, the turnout was nevertheless impressive both because it has been an annual event ever since the bloody military crackdown and also because the turnout actually increased in 1997, only a month before the handover. Demonstrators gathered despite the entreaties of incoming chief executive Tung Chee-hwa, who went on TV several days before the event to plead that Hong Kongers "put aside the baggage of June 4."[20] In the face of mounting pressures from the government, such continuing demonstrations are a remarkable expression of public concern regarding corruption and the rule of law in China.

Yet the memorial observance, the largest of its kind anywhere in the world, also seems to represent the ambiguous status of Hong Kong society and institutions. As one reporter attending the tenth anniversary observed, "In some ways, this annual vigil has become a way for Hong Kong to reaffirm its differences from mainland China. In contrast to Beijing, where nervous officials sealed off Tiananmen Square for renovation [in June 1999], police presence in Hong Kong was light and officials treated the vigil as a routine event."[21] Hong Kongers continue to see themselves as significantly different from mainlanders, despite the fact that they increasingly perceive themselves as part of China. Unlike the 1970s, when it seemed an urgent necessity to define the distinctive qualities of one who was born and raised in Hong Kong as opposed to one who had recently migrated there, the last decade has witnessed a fluctuating but nevertheless pervasive need for popular media to explore ethnic and historical links between Hong Kong and China. This has become even more important now that the political and economic fortunes of the two are so inextricably connected. Shot through this rapprochement, however, is the average Hong Konger's unwavering distrust of the Beijing leadership. This in turn breeds an atmosphere in which media organizations maneuver cautiously. On the one hand audience tastes within the territory encourage popular media to nurture a distinctive Hong Kong identity, while on the other hand government leaders advocate that the mass media promote the official policy of reintegration. Similarly, media attempts to comment on corruption are now tempered by a concern that they not be seen by government leaders as a destabilizing influence.[22]

A Representational Shift

As a result, representational strategies have subtly but significantly shifted at almost every media enterprise in Hong Kong since the mid-1990s. Many news organizations have restrained their coverage of issues and events; dramatic television series seem to scrupulously avoid controversial contemporary topics; and the movie industry has conspicuously sought to promote its fare as pure entertainment.[23] Indeed, *Made in Hong Kong*, which won best picture at the 1998 Hong Kong Film Awards, stands out because the film is sharply critical of middle-class living conditions and the myth of social mobility. Set in government housing estates, where more than 40 percent of the local population resides, the film conveys the gritty reality of teenage alienation, dysfunctional families, and the economic tensions of daily life among the lower-middle-class. Unlike the character Wai from *The Good, the Bad, and the Ugly*, the lead character in this film is a local Hong Konger who dropped out of junior high school and spends his time playing basketball and engaging in petty crime. Autumn Moon, as he calls himself, is cynical about the myth of social mobility and expresses more faith in his chances to rise up the ladder of success in local gangs than in local business. Although something of a ne'er-do-well, his tender heart makes it difficult for him to succeed even as a gangster. When his boss orders him to collect an overdue loan from a single mother, he ends up falling in love with the woman's daughter, who he eventually discovers is ill with a terminal disease. Most of the characters in the film are lovable losers, who live outside the conventional values of middle-class achievement and respectability. Even though the film avoids any direct criticism of the Beijing regime or the SAR leadership, it is sharply critical of middle-class living conditions and the myth of social mobility.

As a result, theatrical exhibitors were reportedly reluctant to show the film when it was released shortly after the handover. Apparently, it was not the content of the story so much as the critical tone that made distributors wonder whether it might draw criticism from the authorities. Uncertainty and mistrust seemed to have been their main concerns rather than overt administrative restrictions. Distributors and exhibitors were probably less fearful of explicit retaliation or regulatory action than they were of the possibility that their future efforts to expand into mainland markets might at some point be undermined by Beijing officials who perceive them as a potentially disruptive influence.[24]

As with most every act of self-censorship in the territory, the film industry's restraint is animated by the powerful attraction of the mainland film markets. For the past sixty years, these markets have been largely inaccessible to Hong Kong producers, who, as a result, staked their success on the popularity of Hong Kong feature films among audiences in Southeast Asia, Taiwan, Korea, and Japan. These overseas audiences—particularly in the Cantonese-speaking diasporic communities of Southeast Asia and elsewhere—sustained the city's film industry throughout an era of censorship and economic chaos in China.[25] Yet recent reversals in these traditional markets have encouraged filmmakers to reassess their relationship to the mainland, and many now agree that the future growth of Hong Kong film depends on opportunities across the border.[26] Having experienced a serious slump in revenues since about 1993, the film industry is exceptionally anxious to establish itself in mainland markets, where its products are now widely circulated through cable TV and video rental, much of it on a pirated basis. This strategy of expansion into the mainland market therefore requires the cooperation of government officials to enforce anti-piracy laws so that the Hong Kong movie industry might reap the benefits of its popularity.

As for broadcast television, Chinese markets also figure prominently in the calculations of Hong Kong executives. The territory's diminutive market of six million viewers has been profitable only because the city is dominated by one major station (TVB) and its ill-fated competitor (ATV). As the prosperity of the average family spiraled ever higher over the last three decades, TVB came to dominate television advertising and ultimately captured well over half of total annual advertising expenditures in Hong Kong. Tightly regulated production budgets and almost complete control of exhibition meant that TVB was able to wring massive profits from a relatively small market. But as profit growth began to taper off in the late 1980s, the industry began to look to overseas markets, achieving notable successes in Taiwan and parts of Southeast Asia.[27] Yet many of these markets are now becoming crowded and intensely competitive. Early successes with overseas Chinese viewers have been solidified, but it is unclear how well Hong Kong programs will fare with non-Chinese audiences. Consequently, further expansion in these international markets is uncertain. Like their counterparts in film, TV executives seem to feel that mainland markets offer greater growth potential, ultimately playing an important role in the industry's future profitability.[28]

Under these circumstances, television executives have been remarkably cautious about program content over the past several years. During the season leading up to the handover, the entertainment division of TVB produced and heavily promoted a documentary series that rewrote the postwar history of Hong Kong in a manner that was sympathetic to the Chinese leadership. Sharp criticism from local journalists and commentators did not dissuade the station from this rather explicit attempt to curry the favor of the Beijing leadership.[29] Later that same season, when the TVB news division was asked to submit some of its programs for the annual Human Rights Awards competition, sponsored by Amnesty International, staff members responded to the invitation enthusiastically. Yet shortly thereafter, top executives pressured them to withdraw their submissions, which they did, quietly and without explanation.[30] As for the annual June 4 memorial, TVB's coverage of the event has been modest and unremarkable, especially compared to its extensive coverage of the official handover ceremonies, an occasion that generated little public enthusiasm.[31]

One could speculate that TVB is becoming a political instrument of the Beijing regime, but this would be too simplistic an explanation. TVB, like commercial media firms in most postindustrial societies, is generally agnostic about program content. At the very same time that it has been pursuing an ideologically cautious programming strategy in Hong Kong, it has developed an innovative, audacious, and extremely popular cable TV news service (TVBS) in Taiwan, where it has built a reputation for taking public officials to task on issues of widespread social concern. Because the island's mainstream broadcasters are all intimately connected to powerful political factions, most of their news coverage tends to be deferential and circumspect. By comparison TVBS quickly earned a reputation for independent and aggressive news gathering, as well as other innovations. It staged Taiwan's first televised political debates and created satirical political programs such as *Long Live the Election.*

Likewise, TVBS's lively Taiwanese talk shows, with their no-holds-barred approach, have sparked a programming craze throughout the island. As Taiwan goes through its current process of democratization, TVBS is tracking audience tastes and responding with programs that are innovative and populist but nevertheless unlikely to invite government restraints that might jeopardize its commercial standing.[32]

Meanwhile, in Hong Kong TVB is pursuing a very cautious programming strategy not because it fears censorship but because its perception of the market is shaped by anticipated developments on the mainland, where its broadcast signal is widely retransmitted via cable. In southern China alone, TVB has more viewers than it does in Hong Kong; most cable operators simply appropriate the extremely popular Hong Kong programs and replace TVB's commercials with local advertisements. Thus it would require extensive cooperation from government officials for TVB to recoup licensing or advertising revenues from programs viewed in southern China. Despite protracted negotiations on this very issue, prospects for change most importantly hinge on the cooperation of mainland officials.

Yet television and film companies in Hong Kong have repeatedly expressed frustration with the mixed signals they get from policy makers and bureaucrats who control access to Chinese media markets. To some extent the confusion is understandable given the tremendous changes that have taken place in China over the last few years. Only months before the territory's return to the mainland, the death of Deng Xiaoping engendered pervasive uncertainty among Chinese bureaucrats who were keeping a wary eye on the power transition within the Beijing leadership. Although Jiang Zemin appears to have solidified his support among "moderates" and "modernizers," some say his hold on power remains somewhat uncertain. The Mao nostalgia craze that China recently experienced is only one indication that periods of tremendous political and social transformation often foster strong criticisms of foreign cultural influences. Indeed, Jiang chose to mollify conservative factions within the Communist Party in 1996 by mounting a highly visible initiative to revive Mao's campaign for "spiritual civilization." In the year leading up to the handover, this involved repeated appeals to cultural workers in China to be wary of letting bourgeois sensationalism and moral decay influence their art. Given these pronouncements, it is unclear where Hong Kong media stand in relation to government policy. Sometimes they are reviled as a contaminating outside influence, while at other times they are seen as a bellwether of the changes sweeping the mainland. Yet even though pirated versions of Hong Kong film, television, and music are extremely popular throughout China, the industry's future ability to cash in on this success depends on cooperation and official approval from Beijing, something that China's leaders have so far been unwilling or unable to deliver. Indeed, many officials are not even sure at this point whether to count Hong Kong media products as imported or domestic.[33]

A Conflicted Future

In this atmosphere of uncertainty, Hong Kong media firms constantly weigh the strategic value of local audiences, overseas viewers, and the growing potential of mainland markets. The very same television and film industries that played an important role in the initial development of a Hong Kong identity during the 1970s now seem conflicted as to their future mission. The local market is not large enough to sustain their current level of productivity and previously established overseas markets offer limited or diminishing potential. Future growth will have to come from the mainland, which is why industry leaders anxiously monitor for signals from the Chinese bureaucracy, while media producers consciously attempt to fashion products that might prove marketable on a national basis.[34] In this respect, one could say that Beijing has already taken control of cultural production in the SAR without explicitly flexing its regulatory muscle. Hong Kong media now find themselves maneuvering between their various roles as local, regional, global, and most recently, national producers. The first role helped citizens of the territory achieve and sustain a distinctive identity; the second kept diasporic Chinese communities in touch with the cosmopolitan center of Cantonese culture; the third exploited the potential of international markets with action genres that translated well across cultures; now the fourth role demands that Hong Kong media participate in the national project of modernization initiated by the late Deng Xiaoping. The extent to which they can manage all four roles without serious conflict remains to be seen.

In early October 1997, only months after the handover, a state propaganda official in Beijing announced that a ninety-second documentary about the Chinese national anthem, "March of the Volunteers," had just been released for mandatory exhibition with all domestically produced films shown in China. The implication that this propaganda effort would extend to Hong Kong triggered two weeks of heated debate both in the SAR and in overseas Chinese communities. As with most other challenges to Hong Kong's autonomy during this transition period, Beijing has so far shown conspicuous restraint, ultimately issuing a clarification that the initiative would not be extended to Hong Kong.[35] Nevertheless one cannot help but wonder how cooperative these very same bureaucrats will be as Hong Kong media producers attempt to expand their operations into China. What will be the price of their cooperation? And how might that affect the popularity of Hong Kong products with local, regional, and global audiences?

At its most explicit level, this conundrum may involve issues such as the playing of the national anthem in cinemas, but at a more subtle and profound level it may affect the very nature of media texts themselves. As suggested above, one could argue that the popularity of Hong Kong film and television is dependent on their ability to respond to deep-seated longings among their various audiences for a society with impartial and transparent forms of legal, political, and economic process. In part this means producing texts that sustain the myth of social mobility, but it also requires the maintenance of media institutions that will criticize and parody corruption and privilege without reservation. Whether the industry can continue to do this is an extremely complicated question to which there are only partial and contingent answers. It is not so much that media practitioners need to take a heroic stand on abstract issues of free expression and human rights, but they will need to find a way to nurture the values and ideals that made Hong Kong television so popular during its heyday.

These challenges are made all the more complicated by the fact that both the film and television industries are currently in a serious slump. Many critics contend that shrinking markets and political uncertainties have fostered a "quick buck" mentality that has diminished the quality of the industry's output and made them ever more susceptible to pressures from Hollywood competitors. When and how they might come back is anyone's guess, but most media practitioners are nevertheless happy to have the transfer of sovereignty behind them in hopes that relations with the mainland will begin to stabilize.

Although on the face of it, political forces appear to be the greatest threat to Hong Kong's cultural autonomy, market influences may be just as significant. The very same media industries that played such a prominent role in the construction of a distinctive Hong Kong identity now are motivated by commercial incentives that seem to be driving them into the embrace of the national government. The grimmest potential outcome could be a media industry cowed by the national government and therefore unable to sustain the interest of audiences at home or abroad. The most optimistic scenario might portray this as a moment of opportunity that could mark the dawning of yet another revival in the artistic and commercial fortunes of Hong Kong film and television. If the latter scenario proves true, Hong Kong's impact on China may prove to be far more remarkable than the mainland's influence on the SAR.

NOTES

1. Niall Fraser, "Handover ICAC Title Sparks Clash," *South China Morning Post*, 4 June 1997, 1.

2. Niall Fraser, "Graft-Busters Gird for New Battle," *South China Morning Post*, 4 June 1997, N14. Interestingly, "independent" is not a component of the Chinese characters that are used to represent the commission, a fact that Hong Kong's incoming administration pointed to as partial justification for dropping the *I*. Popular understanding of the commission's function, however, emphasizes its independence and even Chinese-language press reports will often refer to it as the ICAC, rather than resorting to the Chinese characters.

3. Victor Hao Li, "From Qiao to Qiao," in Tu Wei-ming, ed., *The Living Tree: The Changing Meaning of Being Chinese Today* (Stanford: Stanford University Press, 1994); and Steve Fore, "Home, Migration, Identity: Hong Kong Film Workers Join the Chinese Diaspora," in Kar Law, ed., *Fifty Years of Electric Shadows: Hong Kong Cinema Retrospective* (Hong Kong: Hong Kong Urban Council, 1997), 126–35.

4. See, for example, Benjamin K. P. Leung, *Perspectives on Hong Kong Society* (Hong Kong: Oxford University Press, 1996); and Joseph Man Chan, "Mass Media and Socio-Political Formation in Hong Kong, 1949-1992," *Asian Journal of Communication* 2, no. 3 (1992): 106–29.

5. Cheuk Pak-Tong, "The Beginning of the Hong Kong New Wave: The Interactive Relationship between Television and the Film Industry," *Post Script* 19, no. 1 (fall 1999): 10-27. James Kung and Zhang Yueai, "Hong Kong Cinema and Television in the 1970s: A Perspective," in Li Cheuk-to, ed., *A Study of Hong Kong Cinema in the Seventies* (Hong Kong: Hong Kong Urban Council, 1984), 14–17; Choi Po-King, "From Dependence to Self-Sufficiency: Rise of the Indigenous Culture of Hong Kong, 1945–1989," *Asian Culture* 14 (April 1990): 161–76;

and Terence Lo and Chung-bong Ng, "The Evolution of Prime-Time Television Scheduling in Hong Kong," in David French and Michael Richards, eds., *Contemporary Television: Eastern Perspectives* (New Delhi: Sage, 1996), 200–220.

6. It is estimated that international business employs 49 percent of the territory's work-force. Fraser, "Graft-Busters Gird for New Battle," N14.

7. Anthony Giddens, *The Consequences of Modernity* (Stanford: Stanford University Press, 1990).

8. This has been the city's reputation among Chinese communities around the world, whether on the mainland, in Southeast Asia, or in the Chinatowns of Europe or North America.

9. Fraser, "Graft-Busters Gird for New Battle," N14.

10. Angela Li, "Corruption Heads List of Fears for Handover," *South China Morning Post*, 14 March 1997, 3; "ICAC Fights Corruption Creeping from the North," *Inside China Mainland*, 1 September 1997.

11. Benjamin Lee, "Going Public," *Public Culture* 5 (1993): 165–78.

12. My use of the masculine pronoun here is intentional. As scholars such as Nancy Fraser, Joan Landes, and Lauren Berlant have pointed out, this conception of the public sphere privileged the white male as the universal political subject. Michael Warner also shows how self-abstraction through the printed word became the means by which the bourgeois subject erased the traces of his particularity. See Jurgen Habermas, *The Structural Transformation of the Public Sphere*, trans Thomas Burger (1964; Cambridge: MIT Press, 1989); Joan Landes, "Jurgen Habermas, the Structural Transformation of the Public Sphere: A Feminist Inquiry," *Praxis International* 12, no. 1 (April 1992): 106–27; Nancy Fraser, "Rethinking the Public Sphere: A Contribution to the Critique of Actually Existing Democracy," Lauren Berlant, "National Brands/National Body: Imitation of Life," and Michael Warner, "The Mass Public and the Mass Subject," in Bruce Robbins, ed., *The Phantom Public Sphere* (Minneapolis: University of Minnesota Press, 1993).

13. In the early 1980s, when it became clear that the territory would be returned to Chinese sovereignty, the British colonial administration began to reconsider its policy of keeping politics, civics, and local history out of the school system. Especially during the final years of British rule under Governor Chris Patten, educators attempted to teach and encourage democratic citizenship. Nevertheless, those who graduated more than a decade ago mention with some bitterness how little they know about the history and politics of their homeland. Indeed, this was a key point made by numerous members of the media community when discussing the often apolitical nature of Hong Kong films. See panel on "Operations of the Hong Kong Film Industry," at the conference "Hong Kong Cinema: Fifty Years of Electric Shadows," Hong Kong, 1997. The slow process of politicization is analyzed by Anthony Fung, "Parties, Media and Public Opinion: A Study of Media's Legitimation of Party Politics in Hong Kong," *Asian Journal of Communication* 5, no. 2 (1995): 18–46.

14. See, for example, "How Our Views Have Changed," *South China Morning Post*, 26 June 1997, 21; and Wendy Kan, "Identity crisis," *South China Morning Post*, 5 July 1997, R1.

15. Han Chinese make up an estimated 93 percent of the mainland population. Although there are significant linguistic and cultural differences between Chinese populations in the north and south of the country, the fact is that Hong Kongers distinguish themselves from all groups on the mainland. Regarding the linguistic and cultural regions of China, see S. Robert Ramsey, *The Languages of China* (Princeton: Princeton University Press, 1987).

16. Eric Kit-wai Ma, *Culture, Politics, and Television in Hong Kong* (London: Routledge, 1999).

17. The romanized spelling of this character's name has been rendered in a number of ways, including A Can, Ah Tsarn, and Ah Chan.

18. Ma, *Culture, Politics, and Television*, 68.

19. Sek Kei, "Hong Kong Cinema from June 4 to 1997," in Law, *Fifty Years of Electric Shadows*, 120–25.

20. Chris Yeung, Linda Choy, and No Kwai-yan, "Mourners Struggle to the End," *South China Morning Post*, 5 June 1997, 1; Anthony Spaeth, "Solidarity," *Time* (Asian Edition), 16 June 1997, 16–19; Bruce Gilley, "Show and Tell," *Far Eastern Economic Review*, 19 June 1997, 20–21.

21. Mark Landler, "Tiananmen Protestors Gather in Hong Kong; Heavy Turnout in 'Little Island of China,'" *International Herald Tribune*, 5 June 1999, 2. Interestingly, Nexis-Lexis, which regularly archives all the news stories of the *Hong Kong Standard* and the *South China Morning Post*, has no record of stories about the memorial in 1997, although stories on the memorial had been archived in previous years.

22. Part of the concern is political, but much is economic as well. Business reporters have indicated that even before the handover, they started to restrain their criticism of businesses linked to the Chinese government. These so-called red chip companies were the object of heated stock market speculation in the first half of 1997, their value was based largely on access to particular Chinese leaders rather than on tangible assets. Some critics worry that without an independent and critical business press, the territory may ultimately be headed toward a market meltdown not unlike the reversals that have recently beset the economies of Thailand, Indonesia, and South Korea. Comments to this effect were made during sessions of "News Traditions and Transitions: Hong Kong Media in a New Era," a conference sponsored by the Freedom Forum, Hong Kong, June–July 1997.

23. The ideological shift in newspaper coverage has been tracked by Joseph Man Chan and Chin-Chuan Lee in their many articles and commentaries on the Hong Kong press, but it is most comprehensively examined in their volume *Mass Media and Political Transition: The Hong Kong Press in China's Orbit* (New York: Guilford, 1991). Changes in the representational strategies of the film industry are discussed in Kei, "Hong Kong Cinema from June 4 to 1997" and in recent volumes published by the Hong Kong International Film Festival. The institutional and representational shifts in the television industry are examined on an annual basis in *The Other Hong Kong Report* (Hong Kong: Chinese University of Hong Kong Press). It should of course be observed that Western-based media enterprises such as Disney, Fox, and CNN have similarly attempted to accommodate the Beijing government in various ways. An interesting counterexample to this tendency among both global and local firms is Hong Kong's *Apple Daily*, which after its start-up in 1995 quickly rose to be the second most popular newspaper in the territory based in part on its avowed independence. Although it succeeded at the newsstand, the *Apple Daily* experienced problems securing additional capital for its expansion plans in 1997—problems that numerous critics attribute to caution on the part of financiers who do not want to be associated with the paper's oppositional editorial stance. An analysis of the ideological trends and future prospects of Hong Kong media can be found in Paul S. N. Lee and Leonard L. Chu, "Hong Kong Media System in Transition: A Socio-Cultural Analysis," *Asian Journal of Communication* 5, no. 2 (1995): 90–107; and Leonard L. Chu and Paul S. N. Lee, "Political Communication in Hong Kong: Transition, Adaptation, and Survival," *Asian Journal of Communication* 5, no. 2 (1995): 1–17. Regarding trends in media ownership in Hong Kong, see Anthony Y. H. Fung and Chin-Chuan Lee, "Hong Kong's Changing Media Ownership: Uncertainty and Dilemma," *Gazette* 53 (1994): 127–33.

24. Edward A. Gargan, "For China to Ponder: The Dark Side of Easy Street," *New York Times*, 14 November 1997, 2.

25. Grace L. K. Leung and Joseph M. Chan, "The Hong Kong Cinema and Its Overseas Markets: A Historical Review, 1950–1995," in Law, *Fifty Years of Electric Shadows*, 136–51.

26. At the conference staged in conjunction with the twenty-first Hong Kong International Film Festival, film directors and distributors repeatedly emphasized the importance of the mainland market to the future of the film industry. A report on these deliberations can be found in Berenice Reynaud, "High Noon in Hong Kong," *Film Comment* 33, no. 4 (1997): 20–23.

27. Yiu-ming To and Tuen-yu Lau, "Global Export of Hong Kong Television: Television Broadcasts Limited," *Asian Journal of Communication* 5, no. 2 (1995): 108–21.

28. In background interviews conducted during the spring of 1997, marketing executives from ATV, TVB, Wharf Cable, and Star TV all offered similar assessments of the importance of the China market to their future operations.

29. Eric K. W. Ma, "Reconstructing Hong Kong: A Thick Description of 'Electronic Memory'" (paper read at the Fifth International Symposium on Film, Television, and Video, Taipei, 1997); and C. K. Lau, "The Politically Correct Past," *South China Morning Post*, 25 August 1997, 11.

30. This account was related to me by a member of the judges' panel and was later corroborated by two other sources.

31. In fact, before the handover many viewers contacted Hong Kong's Television Licensing Authority to express their fear that massive coverage of the handover would unnecessarily interfere with regular programming. Performers slated to participate in the TVB variety show were similarly unenthusiastic about the "celebration," complaining that they were not being financially compensated for their appearance. Said James Wong Jim, "If I get paid, I will do the job. If I don't get paid, I will not do it. This is the virtue of capitalism and the essence of 'one country, two systems.'" See Alex Lo, "TV Vows to Make Handover a Turn-On," *South China Morning Post*, 7 April 1997, 1; Glenn Schloss, "Protests at Saturation Coverage," *South China Morning Post*, 22 February 1997, 3; and Wanda Szeto, "No Money, No Talk, Say TV's Handover Hosts," *South China Morning Post*, 24 June 1997, 1.

32. It should be pointed out that TVBS is a joint venture with Taiwan's ERA Communications and that the station is almost entirely staffed by Taiwanese personnel. Nevertheless, TVB has played an active role in program development as well as other aspects of the station's operations, suggesting that the firm is willing to support controversial programming in a different social and political context. "Control Panels," *Cable and Satellite Asia*, July 1997, 22; *Television Broadcasts Limited Annual Report 1996*, 11.

33. In an attempt to control the rapid spread of satellite receiver dishes in China, the government started to promote inexpensive cable TV access in cities across the country. China now has tens of thousands of cable systems, each one with its own mix of program offerings. Unofficial quotas on imported programs have been developed by the Ministry of Radio and Television, but they are interpreted differently by each cable operator. Some, for example, apply the term "foreign" to any imported program, while others apply only it to Western programs, thereby categorizing Hong Kong and Taiwan programs and films as Chinese programming.

34. For example, *Comrades, Almost a Love Story*, a film that nearly swept the Hong Kong Film Awards in the spring of 1997, was consciously adjusted in hopes of making it marketable on the mainland, according to director Peter Chan Ho-san, interview with the author, 11 April 1997.

35. Andy Ho, "Sense of Identity Lacking," *South China Morning Post*, 7 October 1997, 19.

Chapter Fourteen

Soothsayers, Politicians, Lesbian Scribes
The Philippine Movie Talk Show

Jose B. Capino

On a typical episode of one of Philippine television's most popular genres, one could tune in to any of the following scenes: A gay alderman and optometrist, who also moonlights as a talent scout of porn actors, introduces his new roster of "discoveries," all of them named after rightist military leaders who led the most recent bloody putsch against Corazon Aquino's presidency. Most of them don sequined garb, indicating their recent career in go go bars and brothels. A tomboyish correspondent of a movie fan magazine, dressed in male drag, presses an overly accessorized starlet of teeny bopper movies for her opinion on the subject of virginity. A senatorial candidate from society's upper crust appears on a pretaped video interview just to say that she is flattered by comments from journalists who compare her to a famously unattractive singer-actress. A soothsayer named Madam Auring, dressed like a carnival fortune-teller, stops by to promote her new beauty products and to announce that she has finally found a boyfriend. Before the end of the show, a production assistant ushers in the day's lineup of lost-and-found children who may be picked up the next evening at the studio (the reunion scene would be accompanied by extremely sappy music).

In a country where show business and politics both speak the language of spectacle and melodrama, it is not surprising that a television genre such as the movie talk show would occupy such a prominent role in public discourse.[1] Although the genre comes in many formats, the basic formula is simple: think of the American political talk show *Firing Line* and replace its quorum of political correspondents and government officials with a wild bunch of ruthless gay and lesbian entertainment journalists and the actors who *lie* to them. And while it may seem at first glance that the genre is primarily devoted to the mission of televising catfights between thespians and scribes, the movie talk show also functions as a venue for the conduct of public affairs, as when it is invaded by politicians who appear on the program to boost their popularity and to sling mud at their opponents. Moreover, the same cast of action superstars, soft-core porn actors, and aging starlets who inhabit the show have found great success in launching their own political careers on the sole basis of their media visibility. By conducting their personal and public affairs as empty spectacles and maudlin social dramas, these show biz politicians have accelerated the disappearance of the boundary between show biz and political discourse in both the movie talk show and real life. It is this complex and promiscuous interplay between the cultures of show business and politics, mediated through the feminine and effeminate popular discourse of television talk, that this essay seeks to elucidate as it constructs a history and critical appraisal of this, the most interesting of Philippine television genres.

The genre's origins can be traced back to a similar format on AM radio, where Inday Badiday, the queen of movie talk shows, began her media career by interviewing celebrities, reading show biz news, and taking phone calls from quarrelsome fans who engaged in publicly defaming the rivals of their show biz idols. In the seventies, Badiday migrated to television, where she hosted programs with such appropriately gossipy titles as *Nothing but the Truth* and *Would You Believe?* But it was in her third show, *See True*, that Badiday and the movie talk show genre enjoyed an unprecedented national prominence, its popularity buoyed by the newfound success of the public affairs talk show (which also had its own long but lackluster history in Philippine television).[2] It was when TV talk became such an important conduit of political power during the mid-1980s that it began to attract serious public attention and acquired a distinctly new coloration. How this came about necessitates a brief explanation here: Shortly after the assassination of Senator Benigno Aquino, Jr., in 1983, a string of public affairs talk shows surfaced on Philippine television. The hitherto unpopular television genre became a venue where the country's leftist intellectuals could openly pose rhetorical questions to the Marcos government about its involvement in the Aquino assassination, about the role of cronyism in the nation's unprecedented economic crisis, and about the military's dismal human rights record. This newfound ability to critique the dictatorial power was refreshing in a media environment still haunted by the ruthless censorship practices during the recently ended martial law regime, during which media companies were permanently shut down and journalists silenced by the barrel of a gun. The public affairs talk show captured the imagination of an increasingly restless middle class, which found release and affirmation in the format's public ritual of interrogation and discussion, denial and confession. Through programs such as *Viewpoint* and *Tell the People*, anchored by prominent lawyers and journalists, the educated, English-speaking middle class claimed a crucial space in television to discuss the country's most pressing concerns.

Shortly thereafter, on the same network that aired *Viewpoint*, a peculiar sister of the public affairs talk show emerged and—in very little time—skyrocketed in popularity. It was called *See True*. Like any public affairs talk show, it featured a panel of hard-hitting journalists moderated by a seasoned interlocutor and provocateur, Inday Badiday. But quite unlike any public affairs show, *See True* was less interested in querying the state of the nation than in questioning the virginity of the country's newest teen starlets. *See True*'s guest journalists—mostly effeminate men and unfeminine women—mercilessly demanded that actors confess whether they preferred to sleep in the nude or in briefs, who they have been sleeping with, and whether or not they sustained an erection while shooting a love scene for a forthcoming action flick. The same proudly Christian nation that sought the Vatican's help in bringing down the Marcos dictatorship tuned in in record numbers to support these entertainment

Inday Badiday on the set of *Eye to Eye*, the hybrid public affairs and movie talk show she helped create to boost the genre's credibility. Advertisers boycotted her previous show, *See True*, amidst criticism of the genre's overall trashiness. Photograph courtesy of Dolly Anne Carvajal, LOCA Productions.

journalists in their noble quest for the elusive show biz truth. They rooted for Babette Villarruel, a chubby queen who playfully twirled his head in circles to the musical accompaniment of Lionel Richie's "Say," before posing killer questions. (He was, incidentally, famous for maintaining an unusual collection of celebrity pubic hair.) They cheered for Lolita Solis, a butch female scribe who always sported police-style Ray Ban glasses, as she goaded out admissions of pregnancy from pretty teenyboppers. They adored Badiday—whose deep hoarse voice and excessive makeup resembled those of a drag queen—when she subtly provoked the scribes into asking racy questions while feigning surprise when an actress suddenly broke into tears or when a burly action star erupted into an obscene diatribe directed at one of the malicious "faggot" journalists. As in the case of the public affairs talk show, the program's live broadcast served as a convenient excuse for uttering highly censorable material. "Sorry about that," the moderator typically sighed in embarrassment. "We broadcast live, so anything goes." The stakes of confession were further increased by "extremely candid" questions from the home viewers, whose inquiries were relayed by an unseen announcer with a booming masculine voice. A loud alarm would sound at otherwise dull moments in the show, allowing the announcer to interrupt the discussion and read the phoned-in questions of extremely knowing televiewers. "Petra from Malabon asks if it is true that you and [actor's name] are more than good friends?" In a literal rendition of *vox populi, vox dei*, the announcer's voice-of-god interrogation commanded nothing but the truth, for it came from an anonymous and thus unremittingly fearless voice.

For the most part, the content of the early movie talk shows was decidedly nonpolitical. Some examples: A bitchy gay journalist asked an aging character actress why—considering how many men she's been rumored to have slept with—her screen name should not be changed from Laila Dee to Laila "Do"? An effeminate male psychic, who claimed he was occasionally possessed by the spirit of the Infant Jesus, read his litany of predictions, including a number of celebrity deaths. In another episode, a scribe asked a teen starlet point-blank to respond to rumors that she's "preggy." The starlet admitted, broke into tears, and uttered one of the most famous lines in the history of Philippine television. To paraphrase: "I know people think I'm a disgrace, but deep in my heart I believe that God was with us when we did it." Dr. Rey dela Cruz (the gay optometrist–turned–talent scout I introduced earlier), who dressed flamboyantly like a seventies pimp, introduced his other bevy of porn starlets, all of them named after soft drinks: Coca Nicolas, Pepsi Paloma, Sarsi Emanuelle. (After Pepsi Paloma committed suicide, dela Cruz returned weeks later with her replacement, Pepsi Paloma II.) On other nights, dela Cruz introduced the "street beauties" (named after famous roads in the country) such as Ms. Aurora Boulevard and the "prominent families beauties" (from names that graced the pages of the society columns). Dela Cruz was also notorious for placing an absurd guarantee of virginity on his newest discoveries: "This is Maureen Mauricio, eighteen years old. Very fresh and a guaranteed virgin. You could even ask a gynecologist to examine her and he would say the same thing." One evening, dela Cruz staged a dramatic confrontation between one of his porn starlets, her mother, and a gaunt, foul-mouthed ex-prostitute who claimed to be her biological mother. When asked for proof, all that the latter could say was, "When you were a child, I asked you to wash my sanitary napkin." Weeks later, dela Cruz admitted that it was all a hoax, staged to boost the sagging popularity of his client.

One of the few exceptions to the "purely" show biz content was the live appearance on *See True* of Kris Aquino, the daughter of Benigno Aquino and president Corazon Aquino. The event caused the show's audience share to rise to a unprecedented 89 percent.[3] Prior to this appearance, the pretty young Aquino granted Badiday an interview during her mother's campaign in the snap presidential elections of 1986. When her mother was installed into power following the 1986 revolution, Kris Aquino joined show business as a comedic and dramatic actor. Her poor acting skills and turbulent personal life (she had an affair with an unruly action star and was later impregnated out of wedlock by yet another action star) later served as fodder for talk show dish, especially when her mother's poor leadership became a target of criticism by the media. (A libelous column accused her of hiding under her bed during a coup d'état.) It is important to note, however, that the movie talk show was not simply an escapist and intellectually vacuous mimicry of the public affairs talk show performed in chimp drag. Its relationship to social and political discourse can be explained by three related propositions, which I have begun and shall continue to elucidate in this essay. First, the movie talk show created a space for nontraditional political spectators (e.g., homemakers and wet market vendors) to participate in the solidarity of public discourse that was so crucial to Philippine society at that given time. The contemporaneous rise to prominence of the public affairs talk show and the movie talk show should be interpreted as having issued from a similar incitement to discourse that was pursued, content-wise, in different directions. Here gossip, as Patricia Meyer Spacks suggests, embodied "an alternative discourse to public life . . . a language for an alternative culture."[4]

Second, even if the subject of discourse shifted from the practice of democracy to the absence of chastity, the rhetorical mode of show biz gossip was decidedly produced by, and is a highly strategic response to, the same sociopolitical ferment in Philippine life. Gossip's rhetorical mode—its predilection for speculation, its accusatory tone, and its incitement to confession—was well in line with the way information about the Aquino assassination and the atrocities of the Marcos administration circulated hush-hush in Philippine society. Since newspapers and newscasts were censored for the entirety of martial law and beyond, gossip became an important means of communication. During martial law, for instance, highly coded ephemeral media emerged: reports of military atrocities were written on blackboards that could be instantly erased, television news anchors raised their "editorial eyebrows" when reading sanitized reports. In the aftermath of the Aquino assassination, a new form of medium was used: "white paper," a term for speculative news, anonymously written and quietly circulated in offices across the metropolis through photocopies.

Third—and this is getting ahead of the discussion—the convergence of political and show biz cultures (epitomized by the election of movie stars to major public offices) after the 1986 EDSA revolution has made the renarrativization of political events through show biz discourse into a valid (and potentially empowering) means of social and political dialogue. The movie talk show and Philippine show biz culture offered—and continue to offer—tools for discoursing about Philippine society itself through narratives that dramatically (if simplistically) represent social reality. History and current events are renarrativized into family scandal, fantasy, and melodrama: they are transformed into tales of the politician who steals government money to finance his flashy lifestyle and pamper his show biz paramours; the water peddler who rises to superstardom because of her extraordinary talent, only to fall back into poverty because of the excesses of fame; the suffering poor whose illnesses could not be nursed by an uncaring government but who are instantly cured by their faith in a miraculous statuette of the Infant Jesus.

A Televised Revolution

The intermingling of public affairs and media culture was intensified and complicated by the EDSA revolution of 1986, which was staged as much on television as it was on the streets. This grand social drama in which a freedom-loving nation reclaimed its liberty through the intercession of two female figures—Corazon Aquino and the Blessed Virgin Mary—was covered second-for-second on television by prominent broadcasters who seized the government-owned broadcast station to produce a televised revolution.

What was essentially an uneventful, four-day human barricade outside a military camp that housed dissidents against the Marcos government was dramatized into a major social upheaval through a combination of panicked and spontaneous live television and radio news coverage, panel discussions with impassioned politicians from the opposition, guest appearances by actors who encouraged the televiewers to go to EDSA (E. Delos Santos Avenue) and join the revolution, and stirring song numbers from prominent entertainers who recycled old ditties (such as "Tie a Yellow Ribbon" and "Onward Christian Soldiers") into a revolutionary battle cry. The participation of high-profile show biz celebrities was remarkable: they entertained the crowd that kept vigil outside the military camps, mobilized their resources to feed the protesters, and even provided protesters from the nearby provinces with money for bus fare.

In the first senatorial and local elections after the revolution, numerous show biz personalities were elected as senators, congressmen, mayors, and aldermen. The trend continues to this day: the current president, Joseph Estrada, is a former action star. Indeed, since so many of our elected public officials are show biz personalities, it would not be unreasonable to declare that the figure of the show biz–politician has truly succeeded the figures of the lawyer-politician and the cleric-politician who dominated Philippine politics during the American and Spanish colonial periods, respectively. This newfound prominence of the show biz–politician is, I believe, linked to what I described earlier as a renarrativization of Philippine politics itself, from one of efficient governance to that of *visible* governance. The charisma of celebrity has become a guarantee of approachability, affection for the masses, honesty, and the liberal exercise of media surveillance to get work done and to expose those who wish to take advantage of the voting public. One may also say that, pragmatically, for some, politics is renarrativized into an absolute spectacle. In an unchanging political system where nothing can be done anyway, the least voters could get out of their elected officials is entertainment: in the form of public appearances at funerals and town fiestas, business openings and local beauty pageants. It is rumored that in the next local elections Inday Badiday, the host of *See True*, will run for mayor of Pasig City.[5] Perhaps then, the connection between movie talk shows and Philippine politics will become perfectly apparent.

The Movie Talk Show after 1986

A series of scandals forced the cancellation of *See True*, its old rival, *Scoop*, and its new rival, *Rumors, Facts and Humor*. *Movie Magazine*, a sister program of *See True* produced by Badiday, conducted an interview in which the ill and impoverished father of a prominent chanteuse (Kuh Ledesma) accused his daughter of being an ingrate for not taking care of him.[6] The musicians' equity association, OPM, appealed to advertisers to boycott such shows because of their callous invasion of privacy. *See True*, being a bigger fish, suffered the brunt of the boycott. The show's new rival, *Rumors, Facts and Humor*, came to an abrupt end shortly after a former porn actress pounded a microphone on the head of Dr. Rey dela Cruz, who accused her of

The set of a typical 1980s talk show featured separate areas for celebrities, moderators and entertainment journalists. Photograph reprinted by permission of ABS-CBN Broadcasting Corporation.

hypocrisy for criticizing the acting ability and moral standards of his "soft drink beauties."

Badiday returned a few seasons later with a program called *Face to Face*, which claimed to be more worthwhile than its predecessor because it focused on discussing public affairs issues but with a more appealing panel of show biz personalities rather than politicians. Stupid actors and bitchy journalists discussing public affairs? Everyone yawned, and the show was immediately canceled. Badiday returned again the next season with *Eye to Eye*, a public affairs show with a few show biz interviews thrown in. To maintain its appeal, producers devoted a significant part of the program to featuring actors engaging in charitable work. Badiday and her staff also capitalized on the popularity of occultists who appeared on *See True*. One of them, Madam Elma, tried to bring on stage a cadaver that she would bring back to life. *Eye to Eye* ran features on animals borne of human beings (e.g., a woman who gave birth to a catfish) and humans who look like animals (e.g., a child whose legs resemble those of a crab). Reports were also filed about cultists who believed that some recently exhumed well-preserved corpses (one of an infant boy, the other of an old lady) worked miracles for those who either touched the corpses or drank the foul liquid that dripped from the carcasses. Compared to the popularity of the actors who appeared on *Eye to Eye*, the freaks, soothsayers, and corpses truly held their own, soon meriting a section in the show. The juxtaposition of show biz and the occult brings to mind another important intertext of the movie talk show: the supermarket tabloid, with its surreal mix of show biz, politics, and the supernatural.

Reflecting half a decade later on the rationale for such juxtapositions, Badiday wrote insightfully, in a column for the *Philippine Daily Inquirer*,

Also, like Oprah, I had my share of brickbats for the kind of television I dished out. The critics dubbed it trash TV. I called it a mirror of reality. For whenever I showed the life of prostitutes and pimps, the plight of battered wives and abused children and the adventures of cuckoos and other curiosities, I only meant to present what reality was as actually lived—or imagined—by people on the other side of the tracks.[7]

Badiday's perceptive take on how movie talk shows (and other popular forms such as the supermarket tabloid) constitute some sort of interpretive reality for its less-educated, less economically privileged audiences is further clarified in the following quote, also from the same column:

We live in a world of projection. It's all a matter of public perception. The Image becomes the real thing. For how else would you explain the fact that if I did a story on what went on inside a brothel, it was tacky; but if, let's say, Tina Monzon-Palma [a prominent, English-speaking newscaster] tackled the same material, it was a sociological study? Or if I chronicled what went on in the life of rugby boys [boys who sniff Rugby, a brand of rubber cement] and street children, it was exploitative; but if Tina did the same story, it was social commentary?[8]

Her crude articulation of postmodernist and Marxist theory notwithstanding, Badiday is cogent in defending why her kind of public affairs show must be hybridized with elements from the movie talk show and show biz itself. Not only is the sensibility of her viewers able to embrace these seemingly disparate juxtapositions of the political, the occult, and the filmic; all these elements have already insinuated themselves into Philippine social reality whether her critics chose to acknowledge it or not. An important indicator was the contemporaneous rise to popularity of a controversial newscast format that adopted the language and concerns of the tabloid newspaper. *TV Patrol*, anchored by the same announcer who used to read the phone-in questions in *See True*, privileged sensationalism and spectacle over objectivity, purveying images of bloodied corpses and brothel raids on prime-time TV.

In very little time, *TV Patrol* took first place in the ratings game, dislodging the long-standing tradition in Philippine broadcasting of conservative newscasts delivered in English.

When *Eye to Eye* was finally canceled in the mid-nineties due to a number of reasons (not all of them pertaining to ratings), the talk show returned with a vengeance. The rhetoric of decency and media responsibility that stigmatized the movie talk show disappeared. The efficient but ho-hum affairs of Fidel Ramos's administration did not deliver the high doses of show biz and political scandals that the media were accustomed to. The panel-style movie talk show was replaced by a new format: a cross between an entertainment magazine show and a celebrity talk show. The format resembles the American show biz magazine program *Entertainment Tonight*, including its use of flashy computer graphics and on-location interviews. The sensibility, however, was very Filipino—it was invigorated by the ruthless confessional discourse of earlier Philippine movie talk shows (it featured a lot of crying

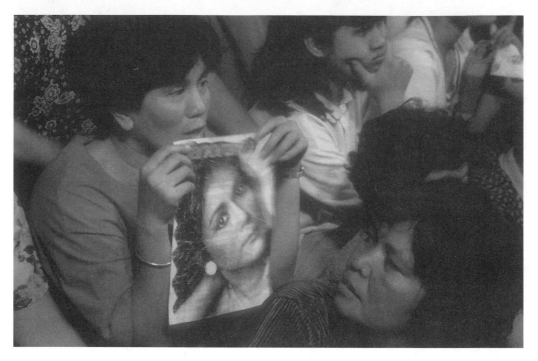

Women and gay men dominate the live studio audience of the movie talk show. In this photo, a movie fan flashes a photocopied magazine cover of superstar Nora Aunor when the latter appeared on *Star Talk*. Reprinted by permission of ABS-CBN Broadcasting Corporation.

from jilted lovers and confessed drug users).[9] The new format also accommodated the commercial interests of film studios (owned by the same television networks that aired movie talk shows) that wanted to promote their products through behind-the-scenes features and celebrity interviews. The most popular of these movie talk shows were *Showbiz Lingo* (produced by ABS-CBN Broadcasting Corporation, which owns Star Cinema Productions) and *Star Talk* (produced by GMA Network, which owns GMA Network Films). The interlocutors of these shows, typically composed of two to three actors and scribes, were generally kinder to stars of films produced by their network's affiliates; however, after the run of these films ended, they got the same foul treatment as everyone else.

Gay Slang

When *Showbiz Lingo* debuted in the early 1990s, it employed as an anchor a literally screaming faggot (played by actor Ogie Diaz) who announced the program's highlights from within a box office set. His loud and hysterical show barking brought attention to an important aspect of the movie talk show that has always been too obvious to notice: its language, sensibility, and constituency were primarily effeminate and feminine. In the heyday of *See True* during the mid-1980s, a substantial number of Filipino televiewers participated in these gay and female-inflected discourses of society (and politics), embracing their concerns and marveling at their often hysterical sense of social drama. Current affairs were filtered through the sensibility of gay and lesbian entertainment journalists, who in turn represented the concerns of lower-class gay hairdressers, fishmongers, housewives, and domestic helpers. *Showbiz Lingo* embodied an even bolder step: its influential use of gay slang on television extended beyond the boundaries of the movie talk show to other programs in the network.

The writers of *Showbiz Lingo* took their cue from movie gossip magazines, which, in the mid-1980s, began using in their especially bitchy articles the imaginative language of the gay subculture. Hardly understandable, "sward speak" or "gay lingo," as it is popularly called in the Philippines, became a status symbol of being "inside," being in the know. One can get the juiciest gossip only if one knew how to decode the strange language. For instance, the slang for ugly was "chaka," in reference to the American singer Chaka Khan, who is considered a paragon of unattractiveness. The gossip magazines included glossaries to educate their readers—mostly women and gays. When some of the gossip columnists from these magazines appeared on *See True* in the mid-1980s, they occasionally used a few words of gay lingo. The famous scribe and publicist Oskee Salazar, for instance, coined neologisms for porn movies that were so influential they are still used in Philippine film historiography. Salazar named three porn film movements based on their sexual content: the *penekulas* ("pene" plus "pelikula," or "films with penetration") of the mid-1980s, the ST (sex trip) films of the early 1990s, which were big on tease but not on nudity, and the TF (titillating film) of the late 1990s, which trafficked heavily in breasts and butts due to more relaxed censorship laws. Lolita Solis, a regular in *See True* who eventually ended up with her own movie talk show, also coined the pervasive term "datung," evoking the sound of crisp peso bills that she believes should be paid to journalists for writing favorable articles about actors and forthcoming releases. In general, however, the use of gay slang prior to the debut of *Showbiz Lingo* was quite sparing.

Showbiz Lingo did more than feature a gay anchor liberally speaking gay slang. Its "coming next" teasers, mostly rendered in crude Monty Python–style computer animation, featured more obscure gay slang delivered in an extremely bitchy, hysterical tone. At times, correspondents filed reports with gay lingo titles and played their very own theme songs with playful gay lingo lyrics. A delightful example is a report entitled "Brunei-yukla" ("Brunei" plus "yukla," a contraction of "dyukla," sward speak for "gay"), about a scandal involving a Filipina actor who allegedly attempted to prostitute herself to the sultan of Brunei but was immediately sent home because she was mistaken for a drag queen. The extremely mean ditty that bookended the report was playfully sung in gayspeak to the tune of the Hawaiian "Hukilau Song." A handful of movie talk shows followed *Showbiz Lingo*'s liberal use of sward speak. *Star Talk*, its rival program on the channel that formerly carried *See True*, continues to feature two correspondents, one of whom is a gay man and the other a woman whose voice is dubbed by a (literally) screaming faggot.

The irresistible pleasure of speaking and understanding gay slang became so popular that it began to be spoken not only in movie talk shows but also in teasers for other TV shows and in commercials written by gay copywriters. This explosion of gay slang in mainstream television prompted the *Philippine Daily Inquirer*, the nation's leading broadsheet, to run a feature article on "The Homosexualization of Television." The article examined the growing influence of gay language and gay sensibility in the boob tube. Its interviewees—prominent scholars and public figures, some of whom were openly gay—agreed on the unprecedented ubiquity of gay slang in television. A gay literary scholar offered a corrective, however, arguing that "The Homosexualization of Television" should be reconceptualized as "The Faggotization of Television." What could have potentially erupted into a media scare did not catch on, and the TV plugs and the ads gradually grew tired of the playful language. It is important to note, however, that the influence of gay slang extended to such high-profile advertising campaigns as the most recent one for Sprite. The big-attitude "Get real" slogan of the famous soft drink was translated by Filipino copywriters to the gay-inflected "Magpakatotoo ka, sister!" (Get real, sister!"). "Sister" is, of course, used in gay lingo to connote one's fellow homosexuals.

Predictably enough, the acceptance of gay lingo has also engendered a warmer reception toward the subculture that produced it. As gay slang became popular even among the upper crust (who delighted in the salacious gossip carried by the language), so did gayness acquire a modicum of "hipness." So much so that former First Lady Imelda Marcos, appearing in 1999 in the movie talk show *Star Talk*, did not take offense when her interviewer suggested that she had become the queen of Philippine faggots. The dynamics of this unexpected "faggotization" of Asia's iron butterfly is amusingly captured in the following exchange:

> *Rosanna Roces:* Why does it seem as if you've suddenly become the queen of faggots? So many gay hairdressers and fashion designers look up to you as their idol.
> *Imelda Marcos:* [Embarrassed, but still flashing a grin] Oh, maybe it's because, like me, they're also allergic to ugliness. Everyone knows of my longtime commitment to the true, the good and the beautiful . . . When we see ugliness, we [gays and myself] cringe.
> *Rosanna Roces:* You're awesome, madam. And so . . . gay!
> *Imelda Marcos:* [Her face registers shock but quickly feigns delight]
> *Rosanna Roces:* Your daughter, Imee is also that way. Both of you have a soft spot for faggots.
> *Imelda Marcos:* Well, as the saying goes, like mother, like daughter.[10]

Mrs. Marcos's initial shock and embarrassment were allayed by the fact that her unexpected coronation as queen of faggots was meant as a compliment. Whereas in the past, such a label would connote a grotesque hyperfemininity that easily served as the target of drag queen impersonations, Marcos's sort of faggotization was—in her own interesting, salvaging construct—supposed to connote a benevolently excessive amount of flair. That Marcos was honored to accept such a title means either of two things: that gayness has become chic or that she is desperate enough to welcome even such an unflattering distinction. But the question remains: should drag queens be flattered by the coronation of Marcos or is she way too vile to be an honorary member of that community?

Conclusion

At present, the popularity of the various movie talk shows continues. Badiday's new show, *The Truth and Nothing But*, debuted in August 2000. A range of formats, derived from the movie talk show's long history, is represented in current offerings, including the magazine format, the public affairs format, and the celebrity interview format. *The Truth and Nothing But* promises to be the "ur" movie talk show by combining all the formats in one package.[11]

The prevailing production values are higher than ever, the hosts are dressed more elegantly (some, like publicist-turned-TV host Boy Abunda, routinely speak English), and the audience composition has increased in diversity, including upper-middle-class women. Show biz culture itself, with its newfound alliance with political power, has acquired a new prestige. In the fifteen-year life of the movie talk show, Philippine society had witnessed a remarkable legitimation of woman's talk, gay slang, effeminate and feminized discourses, and the affirmation of their value (and appeal) not only to a rarefied fantasy culture inhabited by moviegoers but to Philippine society at large. In this second heyday of the movie talk show, the outcasts of the conservative, mostly Christian Philippine society—the hairdressers, the fishwives, the soothsayers, the lesbian transvestites, the immoral teen mothers, the porn actors—openly continue to party on television, and the public faithfully joins them. I am happy to note the unprecedented integration of these figures into the larger society and, as a maker and scholar of media, proud to find that one of my family's guilty pleasures has turned out to be quite socially productive. However, in the last presidential, senatorial, and local elections, my fondness for both show biz and politics came to bite me (and my country) in the behind. A stupid porn actor was elected alderman of my town. A pretty but unintelligent newscaster became the top senator-elect. And, worst of all, one of the most shamefully inarticulate superstars of Philippine action movies suddenly became president. You probably know the feeling.

NOTES

1. I am using the term "movie talk show" instead of the more recent "show biz talk show" out of tradition. I recognize, however, that the latter is more precise, since the genre's concerns extend well beyond the world of cinema.

2. The history of *See True* and Badiday's earlier efforts is briefly discussed in Ricky Lo, *Star Studded* (Makati, Metro Manila: Virtusio Press, 1995).

3. Inday Badiday, "Magical Moments," *Philippine Daily Inquirer*, 15 January 2000.

4. Patricia Meyer Spacks, *Gossip* (Chicago: University of Chicago Press, 1985), 46.

5. Ricky Lo, "Are They Really Running," *Philippine Star*, 15 January 2000.

6. Badiday briefly discusses this event in "Trashing Trash TV," *Philippine Daily Inquirer*, 22 May 1999.

7. Ibid.

8. Ibid.

9. I am evoking Michel Foucault's notion of the confessional discourse as provocatively

applied to television by Mimi White in *Tele-Advising: Therapeutic Discourse in American Television* (Durham: University of North Carolina Press, 1992).

10. This episode, which aired the day before Mother's Day in 1999, is distributed in the United States as "Star Talk/S-Files # 120" by RNJ Video. The company is located at 1330 E. 223rd St., Ste, 516, Carson, CA. 90745-4326, tel. 1-800-816-0400.

11. An article in the *Manila Bulletin* ("Inday Badiday Now on RPN 9," 26 June 2000) describes the show's format:

> Inday's show promises to deliver exciting segments such as: "inDAY News," . . . which features the hottest showbiz news that transpired during the week. "True To, O!" [Truly!] is a one-on-one interview segment. Showbiz and nonshowbiz personalities are the subjects. What makes this segment doubly-entertaining are the location shoots that give televiewers a glimpse into the celebrities' private lives. "inDAY Past" is the flashback portion. It features VTR clips of past events and controversies. "Sagot sa Gusot" [Ironing a Kink] is the "celebrity with a cause" portion of the show. It highlights a celebrity and the foundations that he [*sic*] supports, plus the causes and issues she [*sic*] favors. "Pa-is-staran" ['Outshining Each Other'] is the fashion section of the show. It aims to commend the best-dressed and most glamorous showbiz personalities and advises the rest on how to dress well and carry oneself with grace. "Showbiztuhan" [Showbiz Revelations] is the panel-discussion portion. Capping *The Truth and Nothing But* is a showbiz calendar of events for the upcoming week. It aims to inform viewers of their favorite stars' future concerts, movies, launching, birthdays, and weddings.

Part IV

Uplink/Downlink
Negotiating the Global and the Local

Chapter Fifteen

Act Globally, Think Locally

John Fiske

A culture of power is a culture of representation. The intellectual, ethical, religious discourses of power may well tend towards high art (great representations), and their more economic, pragmatic ones towards industrialized art (mass representations), but both rely on their ability to produce representations of the world and, more importantly if less explicitly, of themselves in the world. . . .

Cross-cultural communication which is initiated and directed by the more powerful of . . . two cultures (for power difference is always part of cultural difference) always runs the risk of reducing the weaker to the canvas upon which the stronger represents itself and its power. This risk increases in proportion to the power difference between the two cultures. To point this out is not to propose that cultures should isolate themselves from each other, for intercultural communication is becoming more, not less, necessary for a peaceful planet, but rather to warn that the weaker of the two cultures must always exert a satisfactory (to it) degree of control over the communicative relationship. It must be able to say what it wants to with reasonable confidence that it will be listened to: it must, in other words, be able to represent itself rather than be the object of representation. This entails a distinction, which is necessary but often difficult to draw, between one culture listening to another, and one exoticizing the other. In the first case, cultural difference can produce genuine diversity in the imagination of the listeners, but in the second it serves only to reinscribe existing power relations and to constrain and constrict imagination. Any attempt to hear and learn from what another culture wishes to say works towards equalizing power relations, particularly when what is said may not be what the listener wishes to hear. Listening is the opposite of representation, which is why the first act of the power-bloc on rising in the morning is to insert its ear plugs.

A culture of representation, therefore, is not limited to what is often thought of as representational art. Abstract art, for instance, can represent the ability to impose an external order upon even those parts of nature (subjective feelings) which appear to be most disordered, most entropic: it can give a public form to the most private of experiences. Its ability to extend control into those realms of experience which once seemed to be well beyond its reach may be one reason why it is the style of art most collected by multinational corporations to hang in their foyers and boardrooms:[1] multinational capitalism represents itself in the abstracted, insidious ordering of what is not non-representational art. But, despite the Navajo pot on the white bookshelves and the Jackson Pollock in the boardroom, the workings of representation can best be traced in what is most commonly meant by the term "realistic reproductions" and it is on these that this chapter focuses.

Representations are representative in three ways. In the first the sampled miniaturization of reality (which is what a text is) is taken as representative of the whole. The Navajo pot is representative of "Navajoness"—the ugliness of the word appropriately represents the process of giving a colonizer's meaning to the colonized. Similarly, the Victorian capitalist in his machine-made frame (no longer my grandfather) is representative of his era or he could not re-present it. In the second a representative is one who speaks for us, one who promotes our interests in the wider world and is thus instrumental in extending our power beyond our immediate conditions. The business representative on the road or the politician in the House of Representatives are power-extenders. In the third, a *re*presentation presents again selected features of an absent "reality" or referent. By presenting us with a particular experience or knowledge of the real a representation actually produces that reality, for our experience/knowledge of it becomes reality-for-us. Reality is always represented, we cannot access it raw: it never exists in its own terms, but is always "reality-for-someone."

One of the key representational strategies is "othering." The "other" is always a product of representation and, as such, whatever form it may be given, always applies the discursive and material power of the representing social order upon that part of the world it has made into its other. Edward Said and Frantz Fanon,[2] for example, show how European and US imperializations have worked consistently throughout history to other the Middle East, Africa, Asia and Latin America. This othering works in two ways. First it imposes upon the so-called (or othered) "third" world meanings that bear, as their unspoken obverse, the superiority of the "first" (representing the "third" world as "third" is a fine example of this process), and second it represents the "third" world as the terrain where the power of the "first" is quite properly exercised. Similarly, feminist scholars have shown how the power to other the feminine works both to settle meanings of inferiority upon it and to naturalize it as the object of patriarchal power. Representing the other is representing "our" power in it, and is not just a semantic sleight of hand but is a material exercise of power. Representation is *really*, not symbolically, powerful.

TV news *represents* the world, in all three uses of the word. A story, broadcast by CBS on 17 April 1991, is representative of the news's work of representation:

> *anchor:* On the Turkish side of the Iraqi border, US troops and Western volunteers are just starting to get a handle on the refugee crisis, Allen Pizzey is on the scene.
> *reporter:* Thousands of refugees are finally being taken off the mountainsides where they were starving and without clean water. Their new home is a camp on a flat plain where it should be easier to help them, but so far the Turkish government hasn't supplied enough food and the refugees complain there still isn't adequate medical help for sick children.
>
> Back in the mountains it's still a hell hole, but there's a new "can-do" spirit in the air and US special forces hit town today. They came up the road in a truck and

were greeted with smiles and waves. The first thing they did was make friends with the kids, the way soldiers always do, they handed out smiles and candy.

nat sound: (soldiers talking) All right men let's do it.

reporter: Then they linked up with the other "can-do" people of the camp, the Dutch branch of Doctors Without Borders set up the doctors' operation here without Turkish permission, because the refugees needed it. While Turkish soldiers were beating refugees away from food supplies, the Dutch doctors have had people lining up to the only medical care in the camp.

nat sound: (doctor holding a baby) She's had no food and she has diarrhea.

reporter: Ground is already being cleared for a field hospital. George Bellas, an American Fulbright scholar teaching in Turkey decided this was the place to spend his spring break.

george: I mean people die up here and they shouldn't die. There's no reason for people to die.

reporter: They still do die, but there is a palpable improvement in the camp's atmosphere. The military men say the camp is full of talented people who want to help themselves.

soldier: We've done a leaflet drop asking these people that when we come in to come up and identify themselves, and they're coming up to us in droves and offering assistance.

reporter: There are US army men all over the camp trying to figure out what to do where.

nat sound: (radio voice) All right Roger-wilco and out.

reporter: That meant persuading refugees to move their tents from the proposed landing zones so they wouldn't be blown away. The refugees still stuck here seem to know that it's not going to be as bad as they feared or even as bad as it was.

The problems of this camp were so massive that no one group could hope to solve them alone, but it looks like the right people are finally getting together to do the job many of them say the Turks should have at least started weeks ago.

The CBS images of refugees or of sick and starving children are like the Navajo pot in the white living room: they represent the "third" world to and for the "first". They represent US power in it, not just mimetically by showing US soldiers benevolently at work but more insidiously by presenting the "third" world as the proper field for US power, a field that is only knowable by this power, for without it, it is unformed and useless, The "third" world is not and cannot be represented in its own terms, for in "first" world imperializing knowledge there are no such things: its mode of representation is a "first" world product which reproduces the "first" world in all that it represents. Within such representation of the "first-in-the-third" world, US soldiers can move easily from bombing Iraq to setting up field hospitals for Iraqi Kurds, because bombing Iraq was "really" setting up a field hospital for Kuwait. The "new can-do spirit in the air" represents (the) US (of A) in them, for it is the spirit that put *us* into the driving seat of the "developed" world and which the "developing" world is now discovering in itself: for it is "full of talented people who want to help themselves" but who are represented as incapable of doing so without US aid:

> We've done a leaflet drop asking these people that when we come in to come up and identify themselves, and they're coming up to us in droves and offering assistance.

This is a miniature representation of US foreign policy in general: the economics and politics of its distribution of international aid are a product of its discursive representation of the relationships between the "first" and "third" worlds, and their realities circle back into the discourse to guarantee its representation and "prove" its accuracy. It is significant that the phrase "these people" is used here as a benignly disempowering representation. . . .

What is represented in the second paragraph of the reporter's introduction and the visuals that accompany it is representative of this imperializing discourse. The "third" world is a "hell hole" of inadequacy: The US provides both the spirit and the means to "develop" it.

This representation continues down to the smallest detail of the story. The phrase "to get a handle on" is accented by US vernacular speech; it sounds like the "authentic" America breaking through the official language of public events. But the word accented by this vernacular authenticity is "handle," an instrument of control. Similarly, the vernacular "trying to figure out" authenticates the Americanness of scientific rationalism which has turned the "can-do spirit" via technology into material achievement. The American national identity represents itself in its representations of "the refugee crisis." The power to represent the world in this way is the power to behave in the world in this way. The US military and US television represent US similarly, and the presence of the TV crew in the "third" world is, in the operation of power, identical to the presence of the soldiers. . . .

The "third" world also exists within US cities. And suddenly, early in 1991, a representation in which it spoke, or rather screamed, for itself was widely circulated by the media. On 3 March, LA cops stopped an African American driver, Rodney King, for a motoring offense, pulled him out of his car and beat him so severely that the fillings were knocked out of his teeth. He survived. This was not an unusual occurrence, but what was unusual about it was, first, that a nearby resident videotaped the event, and second that local and then national TV played and replayed the videotape so that it became one of the most widely heard Black statements of the year. This was one of the rare occasions when a text can be shown to have direct social and political consequences. It provoked a passionate nationwide debate over the ways in which the social relations between the police and minorities were embodied and enacted, as opposed to institutionally represented. What the video represented was not the "third" world as the proper field of power, but the "first" world as the improper exercise of that power.

The police officers involved were charged, a new hotline for civilian complaints was set up and averaged thirty calls a day over the next six months, and a civilian commission of inquiry reported virtually unchecked racism throughout the LAPD's 8,300 members. In the midst of all the other repercussions, Daryl Gates, the long-time, hard-nosed chief of police, agreed to take "early retirement." Most significantly of all, Amnesty International announced that it would investigate the LAPD to see if brutality, racism and a disregard for human rights were systematic in the department. Amnesty International's usual sphere of operations is the "second" and "third" worlds—a fact that was not lost on an LA Police Commissioner who complained on CBS News that "They're treating us like a third world country."[3] When the report was released, in July 1992, Police Chief Gates, on his last day in office, replied to its charges of brutality occasionally amounting to torture, by denouncing Amnesty International as "a bunch of knucklehead liberals" who "attack everything that is good in the country . . . and good in the world."[4]

Tom Bradley, the Mayor of Los Angeles, himself an African American and a former cop, admitted that he had long known of such racism and brutality within the LAPD but, without a way of representing that knowledge to the public and thus of making it powerful, he was hamstrung. When it was his own, personal knowledge it was localized and restricted: while he might have been able to use it in his own locale as an African American citizen he could not, apparently even as Mayor, translate that knowledge into an anti-imperializing one that was "strong" enough to challenge white imperialist power in its own sphere.[5] Only when that knowledge was made representational (in all senses of the word) could it gain the power to "imperialize"—that is, to extend its power far beyond the immediate conditions of those who know it experientially rather than representationally. African American and other racial minorities "knew" policing in this way from their localized experience of it, but while the European Americans may have known *about* it, such knowledge was distanced and marginalized in their consciousness. The power to represent reality makes its representations real; it is a real power and police racism became known as reality. . . .

Realism, as a mode of representation, is particularly characteristic of Western cultures and, therefore, in the modern world, of capitalism. It is as powerful and attractive as it is because it grounds our cultural identity in external reality: by making "us" seem real it turns who we think we are into who we "really" are. To achieve this, it must "know" reality in the way that science "knows" it, as an objective universal whose existence and truth are independent of culture.

Realism and scientific rationalism go hand in hand, and both grew in parallel to become the dominant ways of knowing of post-Renaissance Europe. The secular humanism which is common to both taught that man (sic) could, through reason, control his own destiny by using that reason to understand, represent and control the reality within which that destiny would evolve. Similarly, the new capitalism taught that man could control his own economic destiny. The historical conjuncture of humanism, scientific rationalism, representationalism and capitalism launched European societies on their voyage to dominate the world. These are the-isms of power which worked as effectively for the West in the modern world as they did for Greece and Rome in the classical.

The power to represent the world in the way that . . . CBS . . . did is a power to map the world in a particular way. Maps are crucial to imperial power, for we cannot control what we do not know, and we cannot know a territory until we can map it. In general, non-imperializing societies do not produce maps, but instead give their members directions for travel. Directions for travelling through a territory differ significantly from a map of it, and the differences are produced by different power/ knowledge relations between a society and its physical environment. Maps are powerful discourse, for they bring together science and representation to function as explicit instruments of control.

The TV news of the Gulf War constantly represented it to us in the form of maps. The maps gave us the objective, all-seeing, all-powerful truth of the world. Equally importantly, of course, they gave the US military the all-seeing eye that Iraq lacked. In maps representation and scientific technology become one. The scientific way of knowing, coupled with its will to know, produced the ability to build the satellite which reproduced its own way of knowing in the form of maps. These representations were as instrumental as the bombs and tanks. American power was the power of knowledge as well as of heavy armor and high explosive. The war was represented to us-US, in part at least, as being one between smart technology and blind faith. The Iraqi army was blind because they could not see Saddam Hussein any more clearly than they could see US troop movements. Being able to see or know is not just a prerequisite for control, it is part of that control. The mapping disparity was as great and as influential as the hardware disparity.

This is not news, for it has always been so. Europeans mapped the world as they explored, exploited and colonized it. The maps produced by Mercator's projection, his scientific way of representing a globe on a flat surface, have become part of Western common sense because they represent, not just the world, but Western power in and over it. To flatten the curvature of the earth, Mercator made the meridians parallel and so progressively widened the distance between them as they travelled northwards. To compensate for this, he enlarged the distances between the parallels proportionately. The result was a map that empowered Europe in two ways. Instrumentally it was an efficient navigational tool because it allowed a straight line on its surface to be sailed by a straight compass bearing on the surface of the earth: it distorted the distance but held the bearing. When time and distance were less crucial than direction, the map was a superb technology for capitalism for it allowed the merchants and the military of Europe to find their way to any part of the known world and bring back to Europe the resources and the glory of their power to see and to sail. Representationally, the projection enlarged Europe. Flattening the curve of the earth entailed enlarging the northern land masses which "happened" to be the ones occupied by Europeans. But this was not Mercator's only representational technique. Because most of his customers needed to know about and sail about the northern hemisphere, he dropped the equator to almost two thirds of the way *down* his map. He also standardized the idea that the north should be on top—in the position of discursive as well as political and economic power. Europe became the enlarged center of the world. . . .

This Eurocentric representation of the world was part of Eurocentric action in the world, for knowing and doing are continuous. European-derived societies have retained it as one of their commonest maps, if not the normal one, because we are still engaged in much the same global enterprise as the seventeenth-century helmsmen. . . .

The news of the world and the maps of the world both constitute the world as a sphere of knowledge and therefore action for those whose power enables them to know it as they do. The connections between news and maps as ways of knowing are close. The maps and atlases of the sixteenth and seventeenth century were consistently entitled "new" or "newly described," and Pieter van der Keere, a printer and engraver who worked with Mercator in the production of his atlas, also produced the first English-language newspaper: in 1620 he printed the single sheet *coranto* (the name means "current" or "new"), which has come to be regarded as London's first newspaper.

The other period of energetic European imperialization was in the nineteenth century: its representational arm of power this time worked less through maps than through news. At least three major factors motivated the nineteenth-century development of the news industry. Imperialization produced the need to know the world more efficiently: the spread of literacy produced a larger public for that knowledge and the rising standard of living made that public a source of profit. And finally technology made possible the mass production and distribution of newspapers: the telegraphic cable system enabled news to be collected, the stream and then rotary press accelerated printing from 150 copies per hour in 1814 to 12,000 by 1848, and the new railways enabled the overnight distribution of the papers themselves. International news agencies grew rapidly to provide the required knowledge. In 1869 the imperially named Agency Alliance Treaty did away with unprofitable competition between the three major agencies, and divided the world up so that each could have its own colony of knowledge. Reuters of London controlled the knowledge of the British Empire and the Far East, Wolff of Berlin that of Northern Europe and Russia, and Havas of Paris that of France, Spain, Portugal, Italy and their respective empires. Subsequent reorganization brought US players into the game (Associated Press and United Press International) so that now the news of the world is controlled by five agencies: AP, UPI, Reuters, AFP (Agence France-Presse, the successor to Havas), and Tass. These are all under the control of European-derived, imperialist powers. So, too, is the technology by which their power is applied: the satellites which distribute the information (and incidentally produce both our modern maps and that specialized news called military intelligence) are, inevitably, part of the same societies as the agencies.

As the development of cartography in early modern Europe had a strong commercial dimension, so did the development of news. Not only was news itself commodified, but newspapers distributed commercial knowledge (called "advertisements") inseparably from, and uncontradictorily with, their imperializing knowledge (called "news"). News and advertising travel on each other's backs. Imperializing knowledge always has multiple dimensions—political, military, economic, representational.

The power of imperializing knowledge works . . . by both oppression and repression. It oppresses first by "othering" or exoticizing its object of knowledge, and thus producing it as the terrain for imperialization. The imperializing agency may be abstracted from this terrain, as are the . . . US TV crew in Turkey, and the greedy European navigator in Mercator's world, or it may be embodied in visible representatives such as the benign GIs on the Turkish border. But whether we see the agency or not, it is always part of the process of representation.

Powerful knowledge exerts its control not only over what it chooses to represent as real, but also in its repression of what it chooses to exclude. But the power to repress is rarely total, so traces of the repressed remain obstinately present in the representation. The US "representatives" in the Middle East wear military uniform, and no representation of their benignity can obliterate the knowledge that soldiers kill and have killed. So, too, the pictures of Kurdish families and the information about their wide range of talents contain traces of social identities and a social order which is theirs and which can, and should, be known quite differently from their US representation. . . .

Mercator's map, the most scientific and hence instrumentally powerful of all the representations, represses other ways of knowing more efficiently than do the others. But they are possible and they do exist. Mercator's projection exists competitively with others, even if the knowledge of that competition is repressed. In 1974, Arno Peters, for example, produced a projection which represented the size of all countries in the world with proportionate accuracy.[6] It is still a "scientific" map, indeed, its supporters claim that it exemplifies better science than Mercator's. To the white world, in whom Mercator has been normalized, the effect was shocking. North America, Europe and the USSR appear to be squeezed and misshapen. Africa, South America and the south appear elongated. Not surprisingly Peters's projection has been enthusiastically promoted by members of the "third" world and by organizations such as the UN or international churches. Those who believe that the best way of knowing the world as we move towards the twenty-first century is one that respects its diversity and minimizes power difference between nations find that this map represents their knowledge more realistically (accurately) than does Mercator's. Equally unsurprisingly, the Peters projection has been rejected or ignored by most of the agencies of the power-bloc in the West—school boards, the major map and atlas publishers, the TV news networks and the federal government. CBS news could hardly backdrop its account of the US military in the Gulf or in the Kurdish refugee camp with Peters's way of representing the world.

People live in places. The power to control place is always the power to control people. Power is never exerted only through technological control, but always through discursive control as well: the power to do and the power to know are inseparable. George Bush's line drawn in the sands of Saudi Arabia and the US tanks that enforced it were part of Mercator's projection of the world, not Peters's. Science and rationalism produce knowledge about the physical and social worlds which enable those who possess it to dominate and exploit those worlds for their own ends. It is not surprising, then, that those nations whose power-blocs have promoted scientific and rationalistic ways of knowing have come to dominate and exploit the world, just as, within those nations, those same power-blocs have used those same ways of knowing to dominate and exploit other social formations within their own nation. Such an instrumentally powerful way of knowing disguises its political instrumentality with the rhetoric of objectivity. This displaces its truths and locates them in external nature or reality rather than in the power of those who produce and use them, and in so far as it is effective in this (and in general terms its effectiveness is almost total), it naturalizes this power by casting it not as the effect of a history of domination but as the effect of being able to know the truth. The physical and political instrumentalities of this knowledge are mutually endorsing and interdependent: they are two sides of the same coin.

Representation is control. The power to represent the world is the power to represent us in it or it in us, for the final stage of representing merges the representor and the represented into one. Imperializing cultures produce great works of art (great representations) which can be put to work discursively as armies and trading houses work militarily and economically. Shakespeare, Jane Austen and maps were as important to English Imperial power as was the East India Company, the British army and the churches of England. It is no coincidence that modern Europe, the Europe of colonization, was also the Europe of "great art," and no coincidence either that it was the Europe of great map makers, for unless we can control the world discursively by maps we cannot control it militarily or economically. Mercator, Molière, Columbus and Captain Cook imperialized in different ways, but they all imperialized, and ultimately the effectivity of one depended upon and supported the effectivity of all the others. Similarly the US form of contemporary colonization, which involves occupying economies and political parties rather than physical territories, is accompanied by the power of both Hollywood and the satellite to represent the world to and for the US.

NOTES

From John Fiske, "Act Globally, Think Locally," in *Power Plays, Power Works* (London: Verso, 1993). Reprinted by permission of the publisher.

1. Roseanne Mantovella, *Corporate Art* (New Brunswick, NJ: Rutgers University Press), 1990.

2. Edward Said, *Orientalism* (New York: Random House, 1978); and Frantz Fanon, *Black Skin, White Masks* (New York: Grove, 1967).

3. CBS News, 23 September 1991.

4. Jack Miles, "Blacks vs. Browns," *The Atlantic Monthly*, October 1992, p. 64.

5. The *Star Tribune*, 28 July 1991, p. 19A reports him as saying:

Without something of a dramatic fashion to hit the people squarely between the eyes, there was no way that you could convince the majority of the people in the city that these kinds of (abuses) happen. . . . I have seen evidence of it from time to time and knew that there was much more of this racism and excessive use of force present in that department. . . . Had that tape not been there, these officers no doubt would have denied that it took place and we would have had the same kind of situation: charges, allegations, denial, matter dismissed. That videotape, I think, has shaken not only law enforcement in this city, but across the nation.

6. Ward L. Kaiser, *A New View of the World, a Handbook to the World Map: Peters Projection* (New York: Friendship Press, 1987).

Chapter Sixteen

Where the Global Meets the Local
Notes From the Sitting Room

David Morley

For most people there are only two places in the world—
where they live and their TV set.

(DeLillo 1985: 66)

Foucault observes that "the great obsession of the 19th Century was, as we know, history ... [but] the present epoch will perhaps be above all the epoch of space" (Foucault 1986:22). Jameson (1984) argues for the spatial specificity of the cultural logic of (postmodern) "Late Capitalism". As Soja notes, some years ago, John Berger argued: "Prophesy now involves a geographical rather than historical projection; it is space, not time, that hides consequences from us" (quoted in Soja 1989: 22). It is in this context that we should heed Foucault's injunction "A whole history remains to be written of *spaces*—which would at the same time be the history of *powers* ... from the great strategies of geopolitics to the little tactics of the habitat" (Foucault 1980b: 149).

I have, with Kevin Robins, elsewhere (see Morley and Robins 1989, 1990 and 1992) begun an exploration of the issues at stake once we try to think of communications processes within the terms of a postmodern geography, and once we begin to consider the role of communications in the ongoing construction and reconstruction of social spaces and social relations. At a meta-level Robins (1989) has argued that, in the present period, we are involved in fundamental processes of political and economic restructuring and transformation which presage (if not already reflecting) a shift beyond the Fordist system of accumulation and social regulation. Robins's central point is that, at the heart of these historical developments, is a process of radical spatial restructuring and reconfiguration which is "at once a transformation of the spatial matrix of accumulation and of the subjective experience of, and orientation to, space and spatiality. Its analysis ... demands a social theory that is informed by the geographical imagination" (Robins 1989: 145).

The point, for my present purposes, concerns the fact that the image industries ... are implicated in these socio-spatial processes in significant and distinctive ways.

Thus, as Robins argues, "issues around the politics of communication converge with the politics of space and place: questions of communication are also about the nature and scope of community" (ibid., 146). The further point, for the argument of this chapter, is that such theoretical work as has begun to take on board these questions — for instance, in the context of debates around satellite television and cultural identity, has done so at a very abstracted level, principally in the context of international geopolitics. However, the force of Foucault's remarks quoted earlier is, of course, to remind us that the "geographical imagination", and its refocusing of the relation of communications and geography, needs to be applied, as he puts it, to the "little tactics of the habitat" every bit as much as to the "great strategies of geopolitics". If one of the central functions of communications systems is to articulate different spaces (the public and the private, the national and the international) and, necessarily, in so doing, to transgress boundaries (whether the boundary around the domestic household, or that around the nation), then our analytical framework must be capable of being applied at both the micro- and the macro-level.

It is in this context that this chapter addresses the question of the place of ethnographic studies of media consumption in the analysis of the simultaneous dynamic of globalization and localization in contemporary culture. The key issue is that of the status of small-scale studies of micro-process(es) in the analysis of these macro-issues. The argument of the chapter is that it is precisely through such detailed "domestic" or "local" studies, focused, in the first instance, on the "politics of the sitting-room", that we will most effectively grasp the significance of the processes of globalization and localization (or homogenization and fragmentation) which have been widely identified as central to contemporary (or even "postmodern") culture.[1]

Clearly, any analysis which ultimately offers us *only* an understanding of the micro-process of consumption in this or that domestic context, without reference to the broader cultural (political and ideological) questions at stake, is going to be, ultimately, of only limited value . . . Conversely, any analysis of these macro-processes which is not grounded in an adequate understanding of the complexities of the process of (principally domestic) consumption runs the equal and opposite risk of being so over-schematic as to hide all the differences that matter. Put another way, it is a question of steering between the dangers of an improper romanticism of "consumer freedoms", on the one hand, and a paranoiac fantasy of "global control" on the other. It is, as Murdock (1989) argues, a question of finding ways of combining interpretative studies of people's "lifeworlds" with attempts to map the contours of the wider formations that envelop and organize them.

I shall attempt to address these issues, in the first instance by reviewing some recent debates about the consumption of television and the "activity" of the television audience.

Romantic Readings?

If for much of the 1970s the audience was largely ignored by many media theorists in favour of the analysis of textual and economic structures which were presumed to impose their effects on the audience, the 1980s, conversely, saw a sudden flourishing of "audience" (or "reception") studies. However, the more recent period has also seen a small but significant flurry of articles and papers questioning whether all (or, indeed, any) of this "audience research" is getting us anywhere.[2]

On the one hand, there are the methodological difficulties pointed to by Feuer (1986), Hartley (1987) and Clifford and Marcus (1986), all of which raise doubts about the validity and viability of recent empirical audience research. A whole series of scholars has now argued that contemporary audience researchers, in their desire to avoid a "hypodermic" effects model, have ended up uncritically celebrating the supposed "creativity" of the audience and, in effect, endorsing the worst commercial products, on the grounds that if they are popular, then they are, *ipso facto*, good (cf. Ericson 1989; Schudson 1987; Gripsrud 1989; Brunsdon 1989). I shall not attempt to deal here with all of those critiques but will focus on those offered by . . . Morris (1988) and Willemen (1990).

Morris (1988) acidly sums up what she takes to be the cosy (old-fashioned) "cultural studies" orthodoxy in relation to the audience and the question of "reading". As she notes, many versions of this "theory" have now been offered—from Fiske's (1987) notion of a "reader's liberation movement", through Nava's (1987) analyses of the "contradictions of consumerism", to Chambers's (1986) accounts of counter-hegemonic forces in popular culture, all extolling the creative energies of the much-maligned consumers of popular culture. As far as Morris is concerned, the "Ur-thesis" of this kind of cultural studies runs perilously close to the banal observation that, as she puts it, "people in modern mechanised societies are complex and contradictory; mass cultural texts are complex and contradictory; therefore people using them produce complex and contradictory culture" (Morris 1988: 24–5).

I would agree with Morris that some of this work is indeed problematic, but for a rather different reason from that which she adduces. For me, it is the lack of a sufficiently sociological dimension to Fiske's or Chambers's work that is the problem. Certainly, if, as Morris notes, our analyses finally say only that "it's always complex and contradictory", then that is a banal observation. The point, however, is, in my view, an *empirical* one: the question is one of understanding (and here I continue to believe that Bourdieu has much to offer in this respect) just how "complex" or "contradictory" it is, for *which* types of consumers, in *which* social positions, in relation to *which* types of texts or objects. The "distinctions" are all, in this respect, and if Fiske and Chambers can be faulted for failing to help us see them, Morris seems not even to realize that they are what we need to look for. Everything might simply be "complex and contradictory" at one level of abstraction—but the banality of that observation is, to my mind, ultimately a function of the level of (over-) abstraction of Morris's argument, and of the lack in her own analysis, of an explicitly sociological perspective. . . .

Willemen has argued that many "left cultural commentators" have made the "tragic mistake" of "conniving" with the capitalist logic of "multinational commodification" of culture. Willemen's specific point is that my own *Family Television* book, for instance, is vitiated by the "lack of attention to the capitalist logic over-determining cultural production" (Willemen 1990: 109) in so far as, he claims, I "construe the site of plurivocality, the space for resistance, as a space only invested by the power relations that obtain *within* family or peer group situations" (my emphasis), ignoring the powerful pre-structuring agency of capitalist cultural production in setting all the significant boundaries to what people can do within these structures. Willemen argues that this work focuses wrongly on "the way the TV as a piece of sound-and-image emitting furniture is used in interpersonal relations, that is, the immediate commodity aspect of the use of TV" (ibid., 109) to the detriment of these broader questions. Thus, according to Willemen, the consequence is an analysis of "the uses of TV-as-furniture" which is improperly substituted for an analysis of "the things people can, and more importantly, cannot do with TV discourses", where the analysis of all the important issues of cultural power is consequently sidestepped (ibid.). . . .

Micro- and Macro-Issues

Willemen's critique . . . arises from a misperception on his part—it is clearly not the case that the only power relations relevant to the process of consumption are those that obtain "*within* family or peer group situations". In the case of the *Family Television* study (Morley 1986), for example, and its focus on gender relations, these are not simply an "internal" factor of family life. Rather, the argument is that the gender roles adopted within the family, which then function as the immediate determinants of viewing practices, are themselves structured by the dominant public discourses of gender within the particular culture being researched (cf. Althusser 1972, on "overdetermination").

Willemen's argument in fact operates within a structuralist (and indeed, over-determinist) perspective which entirely reduces the micro to an effect of the macro (and reduces people to the function of "tragers" of their structural positions), rather than seeing structures as only themselves reproducible through agency (cf. Giddens 1979, on "structuration"). As for the charge that *Family Television* . . . is *only* concerned with the "uses of TV-as-furniture" in interpersonal relations, Willemen would be quite right to be concerned if that were the exclusive focus of the research. However, the whole point of the research is that it is attempting to integrate this level of analysis (and its consequent focus on the complexities of the immediate processes of domestic consumption), with the analysis of the "broader questions" to which Willemen refers. The argument is rather that these "broader questions" have to be approached via this "necessary detour" into the detail of domestic consumption, if we are in fact to understand their pertinence.

To do so otherwise is finally to relegate the domestic context of television consumption, once more, to the status of mere backdrop—to be "recognized" and then immediately forgotten, as if this context had no effectivity of its own. As Slack puts it, "more often than not 'context' is invoked as a sort of magical term, as if by claiming to take context into consideration, one could banish the problems of its specificity" (Slack 1989: 329). The question is precisely one of addressing contextual specificity in relation to broader structural factors. . . .

The objective, from this point of view, is not to substitute the one (micro-)level of analysis for the other (macro-)level, but, rather, to integrate the analysis of the "broader questions" of ideology, power and politics what Hall (1988a) has described as the "vertical" dimension of communications) with the analysis of the consumption, uses and functions of television in everyday life (the "horizontal" dimension of communications, in Hall's terms). It is not a question, finally, of understanding simply television's ideological (or representational) role, or simply its ritual (or socially organizing) function, or the process of its domestic (and more broadly social) consumption. It is a question of how to understand all these issues (or dimensions) in relation to each other.

From this perspective, the challenge lies precisely in the attempt to construct a model of television consumption which is sensitive to both the "vertical" dimension of power and ideology and the "horizontal" dimension of television's insertion in, and articulation with, the context and practices of everyday life. Silverstone and I have argued elsewhere (Morley and Silverstone 1990) that we need to develop a "double focus" on television viewing, so that, for instance, we can understand viewing as, *simultaneously*, a ritual whose function is to structure domestic life and provide a symbolic mode of participation in the national community *and* an active mode of consumption and production, *and* as a process operating within the realm of ideology. To debate whether we should regard television viewing as either one or the other is to miss the point.... Our objective ... ought to be the production of analyses of the specific relationships of particular audiences to particular types of media content which are located within the broader framework of an analysis of media consumption and domestic ritual. These analyses, of course, must be sensitive to empirical variation.

Communications Technologies: Scenarios of the Future

In this section of the chapter, I want to try to make a number of arguments concerning (a) the question of the "effects" of communications technologies; (b) the ways in which these technologies have been claimed to be responsible for *both* the "fragmentation" and the "homogenization" of contemporary culture; and (c) how abstract (and technologically determinist) futuristic scenarios of this kind need to be informed by the analysis of the economic, social and cultural determinations of technology's impact, "take-up" and use.

Erni argues bluntly that "in the context of the enormous changes in television technology" (such as the increasing use of video technology and the development of "television—computer—telephone hybrids") audience research work focused on broadcast television "becomes somewhat obsolete" (Erni 1989: 39). In a not dissimilar vein, Lindlof and Meyer argue that the "interactive" capacities of recent technological developments fundamentally transform the position of the consumer:... "The received notion of the mass communications audience has simply little relevance for the reality of mediated communication," (Lindlof and Meyer 1987: 2). The technological advances are often seen to have transformative (if not utopian) consequences for the television audience. . . .

The problem, of course, is that many of these arguments run the danger of abstracting these technologies' intrinsic "capacities" from the social contexts of their actual use. In understanding such technological developments, we could usefully follow Bausinger in his concern with the question of how these technologies are integrated into the structure and routines of domestic life—into what he calls "the specific semantics of the everyday." His basic thesis is that technologies are increasingly "absorbed" into the everyday ("everyone owns a number of machines, and has directly to handle technical products"), so that everyday routines themselves are constructed around technologies which then become effectively "invisible" in their domestication. The end result, he argues, is the "inconspicuous omnipresence of the technical" (Bausinger 1984: 346). The key point is to understand the processes through which communications and information technologies are "domesticated" to the point where they become inconspicuous, if not "invisible" within the home. The further point is then to focus on the culturally constructed meanings of these technologies, as they are "produced" through located practices of consumption. I will return to these points later in the chapter. First, however, I want to point to the parallel between these arguments about the individualizing effects of these new communications technologies and those "postmodern" scenarios which simultaneously point to their homogenizing effects. . . .

In recent years, writers such as Carey (1989), drawing on, among other sources, the work of Innis (1951), have rightly drawn our attention to the historical role of communications systems, both physical and symbolic (cf. also de la Haye 1979) in transforming our senses of space and time. . . .

Carey is concerned with, among other things, the role of communications in the construction of empire and the administration of power. Thus, Carey notes, the economic influence not only of the coming of the railways but, more dramatically perhaps, of the coming of the telegraph, which "permitted for the first time, the effective separation of communication from transportation . . . allowing messages to be separated from the physical movement of objects" (ibid., 203), thus freeing communication from the constraints of geography, and to that extent "making geography irrelevant" (217) and "diminishing space as a differentiating criterion in human affairs" (222).

In order to make my task easier here, rather than attempting to deal with Carey's carefully nuanced historical work on the mutual influence of communications technologies and social development, I shall choose as an example of contemporary scenario-writing Meyerowitz's (1985) fascinating (if overblown) analysis of the impact of electronic media on social behaviour, in transforming the "situational geography of human life." Meyerowitz's concern is with the way in which electronic media have undermined the traditional relationship between physical setting and social situation, to the extent that we are "no longer 'in' places in quite the same way" (Meyerowitz 1989: 333), as these media "make us . . . audiences to performances that happen in other places and give us access to audiences who are not physically present" (Meyerowitz 1985: 7). Meyerowitz's central argument is that these new media re-define notions of social position and of "place", divorcing experience from physical location.

He argues that the electronic media have transformed the relative significance of live and mediated encounters, bringing "information and experience to everyplace from everyplace," as "state funerals, wars . . . and space flights are dramas that can be played on the stage of almost anyone's living room" (ibid., 118) and, in Horton and Wohl's (1956) terms, viewers develop forms of "para-social interaction" with media figures and "stars" they have never met. In this way, these media, according to Meyerowitz, create new "communities" across their spaces of transmission, bringing together otherwise disparate groups around the "common experience" of television, in a process of cultural "homogenisation of here and there." Thus, argues Meyerowitz, television acquires a similar status to that of the weather, as a basis of common experience and source of conversation, as a sort of "metaphysical arena" (ibid., 146), so that "to watch TV is to look into . . . the [common] experience: . . . to see what others are watching." Thus, Meyerowitz argues,

> the millions who watched the assassination of JFK . . . were in a "place" that is no place at all . . . the millions of Americans who watch TV every evening . . . are in a "location" that is not defined by walls, streets or neighbourhoods but by evanescent "experience" . . . more and more, people are living in a national (or international) information-system rather than [in] a local town or city. (Meyerowitz 1985: 145–7)

Postmodern Geography and the "Generalized Elsewhere"

It is in this sense, Meyerowitz argues, that the electronic media are destroying our sense of locality, so that "places are increasingly like one another and . . . the singularity . . . and importance of . . . locality is diminished" (Kirby 1989: 323). This may be to overstate the case, as Meyerowitz admits in his reply to Kirby, but, minimally, the function of these electronic media is certainly likely to "relativize" our sense of place —so that "locality is no longer necessarily seen as the centre stage of life's drama" (Meyerowitz 1989: 330). That centre stage is, then, according to Meyerowitz, taken by national television in the home, bringing us news of the "generalized elsewhere" of other places and "non-local" people and their simultaneous experiences—thus undermining any sense of the primacy of "locality", as the "unifying rhetorical space of daily TV extends into the living rooms of everyone" (Berland 1988: 47).

As Meyerowitz notes, part of the point is that, for instance, access to non-local people (for instance, via the telephone) is often faster and simpler than access to physical neighbours. The "community" is thus "liberated from spatial locality" and many intimate ties are supported by the telephone rather than by face-to-face interaction (cf. the telephone advertisement: "Long distance is the next best thing to being there"). Thus, it seems, we should no longer conceive of community so much in terms of a local clustering of relationships as in terms of types of social relationship, whether local or distant—a "psychological neighbourhood" or a "personal community" as a network of (often non-local) ties (Wellman 1979; quoted in Meyerowitz 1989). Thus, "community" is transformed: living physically near to others is no longer necessarily to be tied into mutually dependent communication systems: conversely, living far from others is no longer, necessarily, to be communicationally distant. Thus, it seems, locality is not simply subsumed in a national or global sphere; rather, it is increasingly bypassed in both directions—experience is both unified beyond localities and fragmented within them.

Such fragmentation, however, is rarely random; nor is it a matter of merely individual differences or "choices" (cf. Morley 1980). Rather, it is a question of the socially and culturally determined lines of division along which fragmentation occurs. Central among these lines is, of course, that of gender. . . . here is an increasing recognition of the "gendering" of technologies such as the telephone, which is an effect of the socially organized positioning of gendered categories of persons across the public/private division. As Garmarnikow and Purvis (1983) note, the public/private split can, of course, itself be seen as a fundamental metaphor for the patterning of gender. "Place" and "placelessness" can certainly be seen to be (among other determinations) highly gendered experiences.

The vision of an "emergent placelessness" (cf. Berland 1988: 147) offered (celebrated?) by a number of postmodern commentators can be criticized on a number of different counts. On the one hand, it offers little recognition of the particular operations of power, in so far as what emerges across this electronic ("placeless") network is what Mattelart *et al.* identify as the "time of the exceptional and the spectacular, the product of an international industrial entertainment culture" (Mattelart *et al.* 1987: 97)—a heavily standardized televisual language which will tend to disqualify and displace all others. On the other hand, as Ferguson (1989) argues, the "techno-orthodoxist" world view, which proclaims that satellite and other new ICTs have effectively reduced time/space differences to insignificance, is badly overabstracted. Principally, this is because the argument has little empirical grounding and operates at a level of abstraction which does not permit us to answer questions about *how* these media shift our everyday understandings of time and space, or about *which* media-forms influence *which* people in *which* ways in their conceptualization of duration and distance (cf. Bryce 1987). What is needed, in this respect, is "qualitative research into *how* electronic communications magnify . . . time-space imperatives and *which* forms produce *which* kind of intended and unintended consequences" (Ferguson 1989: 171).

If the homogenization of space and time in contemporary culture has not yet abolished all differences, still we must attend to the need to construct a properly postmodern geography of the relations between communications and power and the contemporary transformations of the public and private spheres. As Ferguson notes, despite the grand claims of the techno-orthodoxist "homogenizers", it remains true that "just as they have differential access to new and old communication media, so do different cultures, social groups and national sources of power perceive, categorise and prioritise temporal and spatial boundaries differently" (ibid., 153) . . .

Rather than presuming a uniform effect in which, from a crudely technologically determinist perspective, new ICTs impose new sensibilities on peoples across the globe, it may be more realistic to conceive of them as overlaying the new upon the old (cf. Rogge and Jensen, in Lull 1988). Thus, a new technology such as the home computer may often be principally "made sense of" via its integration into the very old "technology" of the peer-gossip network. Rather than the new media promoting a "boundless media-land of common understandings", a variety of senses of "temporal elasticity and local indeterminacy" may be the more likely result, where "formerly finite absolutes take on a notably relativist character . . . and old certainties . . . [are undermined, to some extent by] new ambiguities" (Ferguson 1989: 155). This seems both a more realistic (cf. Miller 1992) and a richer perspective from which to analyse the interaction of local definitions and larger communications systems. As Miller (ibid.) argues in his analysis of the consumption of American soap opera in Trinidad, the "local" is not to be considered as an indigenous source of cultural identity, which remains "authentic" only in so far as it is unsullied by contact with the global. Rather, the local is often itself produced by means of the "indigenization" (or "domestication") of global or "foreign" resources and imputs. . . .

If "geography matters", and if place is important, this is not only because the character of a particular place is a product of its position in relation to wider forces, but also because that character, in turn, stamps its own imprint on those wider processes. Moreover, places are not static or fixed, easily definable, or bounded entities into which external forces somehow (improperly or problematically) intrude, as those working in the Heideggerian tradition would often seem to imply. . . . As Massey (1991) argues, places are to be seen as themselves processes; they are frequently riven with internal conflicts and divisions (they are not internally homogeneous) and are perhaps best seen not as "bounded areas" but as "spaces of interaction" in which local identities are constructed out of resources (both material and symbolic) which may well not be at all local in their origin. But then perhaps, as Miller (op. cit.) observes, we should define "authenticity" *a posteriori*, rather than *a priori*, as a matter of local consequences, rather than of local origins. Similarly, to the extent that imported television programmes penetrate local meaning systems, rather than thereby "homogenizing" diverse cultures, their principal effect may be a rather variable one—in so far as they introduce a relativizing perspective, as an "uncertainty principle" which may work to undermine established and dominant frameworks of meaning in a variety of ways (cf. Hebdige 1988 and Worpole 1983, on the effects of "foreign" cultural artefacts in under-mining the hierarchies of national taste cultures; but cf. also Chen 1990, on the significance of the fact that the "foreign" is so often represented by the "American").

From the Sitting Room to the (Inter)nation(al)

In recent years, one line of criticism of researchers such as Lull, Silverstone and myself has been that, in our concern with the domestic context of television-viewing, we were busy conducting an ill-considered (if not hasty) "retreat" into the private realm of the "sitting-room" and away from the important "public" issues of power, politics and policy which constitute the proper subjects of the study of communication. I shall argue that this critique is misguided, on a number of counts. It is not only that the average sitting-room (in my experience) is the site of some very important political conflicts—it is, among other things, one of the principal sites of the politics of gender and age. It is also that, in my view, the sitting-room is exactly where we need to start from, if we finally want to understand the constitutive dynamics of abstractions such as "the community" or "the nation." This is especially so if we are concerned with the role of communications in the continuous formation, sustenance, recreation and transformation of these entities. The central point precisely concerns television's role in connecting, for example, the "familiar" or domestic, and the national and international spheres, and in sustaining both the image and the reality of the "national family" and of various trans-national "communities". . . .

Chaney (1983) analyses the role of broadcasting in enabling the public to participate in the collective life of the nation. As Chaney points out, a "nation" is a very abstract collectivity, in so far as it is too big to be experienced directly by the individual. To that extent, the "we-feeling" of community has to be continually engendered by opportunities for identification, as the sense of "nation" is manufactured. Chaney is particularly concerned with the role of mass media in relaying civic rituals (coronations, royal weddings, etc.). As he notes, if such rituals are "dramatizations" of the nation as symbolic community, then the infinite reproduceability of media performance makes the "audience" for them possible on a scale previously unimaginable (Chaney 1983: 121). Recalling Silverstone's definition of television's role in establishing "the space of intimate distance" (1988: 23), Chaney analyses the "quasi-democracy of intimate access" . . . created by the presence of the television camera, "representing" the public in the most intimate moments of symbolic ritual. At the heart of the process is an ambivalence, in which public figures are simultaneously humanized through vicarious observation (and the camera often gives the audience at home a closer view than those physically present—D.M.) but also distanced through the dramatic conventions of media presentation (Chaney 1986: 121).

Chaney is concerned with the spectacular character of ceremonial occasions, arguing finally (in a curious reversal of Ellis's (1992) comments on broadcast television as the "private life of the nation state") that "spectacular forms of mass communication are the public life of a mass culture" (Chaney 1986: 132). Contrary to the established view that "ritual" is less significant in secularized industrial societies than it was in earlier times, Chaney argues that, because of the scale and nature of these societies (where the entire citizenry simply cannot be personally acquainted and a sense of collective identity must be continually invented), ritual becomes more salient as a mode of dramatizing (indeed, constituting) "community". Thus, Chaney notes that "collective ceremonies have patently not disappeared from the calendar of institutional identity and reproduction; indeed they have been made more accessible and less arcane through their dramatisation as media performances" (132). . . .

It is this "interfacing" of the public and the private that concerns us here. On the one hand, the audience for such national events is usually atomized, either attending individually or in small groups such as the family or peer group. On the other hand, each such group sits in front of a television set emitting the same representations of this "central" event. The "public" is thus experienced in the private (domestic) realm:

it is "domesticated". But at the same time the "private" itself is thus transformed or "socialized". The space (and experience) created is neither "public" nor private in the traditional senses.

In unravelling these connections, the work of Dayan and Katz (1987) on the representation of the royal wedding of 1981 on British television may be of some help. Drawing on Austin's (1962) theory of "performative" speech acts, Dayan and Katz are concerned to analyse television's role in constructing (literally "performing") media events such as the royal wedding. In this connection, they argue, television should be seen not as "representing" the event but as constructing the experience of it for the majority of the population. Television, they argue, is not so much reporting on the event as actively involved in "performing" it. Television is not simply transmitting such an event (or commenting on it) but is bringing it into existence.

General de Gaulle's concept of television as the face of the government in the sitting-room can, of course, be argued to apply only to broadcasting under quite particular conditions, specifically where broadcasting is allowed very little autonomy from direct governmental control. However, if we take our lead from the work of Chaney and Dayan and Katz (see above), we can not only begin to see the crucial role of television in articulating "governmental" (cf. Foucault 1980a, 1980b) or "public" with domestic space; we can also pose the more fundamental question as to the extent to which it still makes sense to speak of broadcast media as "reporting" on political developments. The problem is that to pose the question this way is to presume that there exists some separate realm of "politics" on which television then, subsequently, reports. In an age when international sporting events are routinely arranged to suit the convenience of broacasting schedules and acts of war are timed with reference not so much to military requirements as to maximizing PR advantage, this may seem obvious. The fundamental issue is of some long standing. As early as 1974, Pateman argued a similar point in relation to electoral politics. His point was that television can only "cover" an election when the campaign has an existence independent of the presence of television, and that nowadays these campaigns no longer have any such existence, being principally designed and planned—in terms of "photo-opportunities", "sound-bites", etc.—with reference to their televisualization. Thus, Pateman argues, "we do not have television coverage of an election, we have a television election" (1974). Pateman's point can be extended well beyond the specific field of "elections" to cover "politics" in a much more general sense: for the majority of the population, "politics" is principally a "media event", and their participation in this realm is a heavily mediated one.

We are back, once again, with the politics of "being there". This is, increasingly, a complex issue. The *Guardian*'s South Africa correspondent, David Beresford, offered a telling account (*Guardian*, 17 April 1990) of his attempt to report Nelson Mandela's speech in Cape Town on his release from prison—where "being there" physically unfortunately entailed being unable to see or hear Mr. Mandela. This Beresford accounts as an experience of "being there and not being there" where being the "man on the spot" has the perverse effect of being unable to witness the images available to the rest of the global village. In a similar vein, Dayan and Katz refer to the seemingly puzzling (but increasingly common) behaviour of those physically present at public events who, if they can, also take with them a portable television, so they too can see "what is happening". Physical contiguity does not, then, necessarily equate with effective participation; and, of course, vice versa. . . .

The question that Dayan and Katz pose is what happens to public ceremonies when, instead of being attended in person, they are delivered to us at home. As they note, being physically distanced from the ceremonial forms and isolated from each other, television audience do not form "masses" or "crowds" except in an abstract, statistical sense (cf. Ang 1991). The question they pose is that of whether we can still speak of a public event when it is celebrated at home—and whether we can speak of a collective celebration when the collectivity is scattered (cf. Siskind 1992). . . .

The analogy which Dayan and Katz offer is that of the Jewish Passover "Seder" ritual—a collective ceremony without a central "cultic temple", which translates the public celebration into "a multiplicity of simultaneous, similarly programmed, home-bound, micro-events" (ibid., 195). Thus, Dayan and Katz imply, the television audience, as a dispersed community, can usefully be seen as being regularly united (both by its occasional viewing of special events and by its regular viewing of the "news" or favorite soap operas) through precisely this kind of "diasporic ceremony". While "media events" such as a televised royal wedding clearly constitute a special case, in which this issue is brought into particular prominence, this model can clearly be extended to the quotidian level—so that the regular viewing of the nightly television news or of a long-running soap opera can be seen in the same light—as a discourse which constitutes collectivities through a sense of "participation" and through the production of both a simultaneity of experience and a sense of a "past in common" (cf. the debates on "popular memory": Wright 1985).

The Production of Cultural Identities

In this connection, Schlesinger (1987) has rightly argued that the conventional question concerning the "effects" of new information and communication technologies (satellite television etc.) on cultural (or "national") identities is mal-posed. His argument is that we should, rather, invert the terms of the question: rather than starting with a set of supposedly "pre-given" objects ("national cultures") and investigating the "effects" which communications technologies have on them, we should begin by posing the question of identity itself and ask what importance "communications" of various sorts might have in its constitution.

In a similar vein, Donald (1988) argues that we should focus our analyses on the apparatuses of discourses, technologies and institutions which produce cultures. As he suggests, from this perspective, the "nation" is an effect of these cultural technologies, not their point of origin. A nation is not reflected in or expressed through its culture: rather, it is cultural apparatuses (among other things) that produce the nation. The point is increasingly well taken, as demonstrated by the essays collected in Rutherford 1990 and Bhabha 1990, the latter directly addressing the question of the relationship between "nation" and "narration" and focusing on the "performativity" of language and discourse in constructing the narratives of national and cultural identities. Clearly, the point applies at both micro- and macro-levels—just as we should, then, be concerned with the role of communications technologies in the constitution of national identity, so with the analysis of the role of these technologies in the construction of identities at the domestic level.

One of the critical issues, as argued earlier, concerns the relationship between community and geography, when, as Rath (1985) puts it, we increasingly live in a "television-geography", where the invisible electronic networks defined by spaces of transmission (and distribution) cut across established geographical boundaries. By way of indication of some of the issues involved in developing this work further, we can also usefully refer to the work of Gillespie (1989), who offers an insightful analysis of the role played by the video-recorder in the negotiation of ethnic identities among Asians in Britain (who utilize the video to arrange regular showings of Indian films and similar material unavailable on broadcast television in Britain—a process which can be found among other ethnic groups (Turks, Moroccans, etc.) in other European countries). In this way, new communications technologies are mobilized in the (re-)creation and maintenance of traditions and of cultural and ethnic identities which transcend any easy equation of geography, place and culture, creating symbolic networks throughout the various communities of the disapora. The point here is that such groups have, thus far, usually appeared in the research frame on the understanding that theirs is a particularly problematic position—as "immigrants." In this respect Hall (1988b) usefully reminds us of the increasing centrality of the "migrant" experience throughout contemporary culture, even if we might still want to distinguish between "voluntary" and "involuntary" cosmopolitans (cf. Hannerz 1990; Hebdige 1990).

If the traditional *equation* of community with geographical boundary and physical place is something which we simply have to ditch in order to understand contemporary culture and communications, this is *not* to say that these terms will have *no* effective relation—simply that it is increasingly misleading to reduce the former to either of the latter. As long ago as 1933, the art historian and psychologist Rolf Arnheim foresaw the social consequences of television as a means of distribution:

> it renders the object on display independent of its point of origin, makes it unnecessary for spectators to flock together in front of an "original" . . . it takes the place of other means of distribution . . . Thus TV turns out to be related to the motor car and the aeroplane—as a means of transport for the mind. (quoted in Rath 1985: 199)

As I said in the Introduction, I am finally interested in articulating the analyses of micro- and macro-processes in relation to the simultaneous processes of homogenization and fragmentation, globalization and localization in contemporary culture. Certainly, as we enter the era of narrow-casting and audience segmentation, it may well be (*pace* Scannell) that many of us will have less broadcast "experience" in common with anyone else—and anyway video allows us both to time-shift broadcast materials so as to consume them at times that fit our "private" schedules, and to consume non-broadcast materials—so the model of a "necessary simultaneity" of shared social experience, provided by broadcasting, becomes problematic. However, at the same time, new developments in broadcasting (whether the occasional Global

Totemic Festivals of the "Live Aid" variety or the regular construction of a Europe-wide youth audience for music programming) begin to combine us into not just national but international collectivities, especially as the supply of programmes to national broadcasting systems is increasingly dominated by a small number of trans-national corporations. But then, as Coca Cola put it, "we are not a multi-national, we are a multi-local" (cf. D. Webster 1989; Robins 1989).

Even more confusingly, we have yet to recognize the full implications of globalization for commercial strategies, not least the emergence of the "decentred" or "polycentric" corporation, operating increasingly with an "equidistance of perspective" (Kenichi Ohmae; quoted in Robins 1991: 26), and treating all strategic markets with the same attention as the "home" market. Ohmae sees Honda, operating in Japan, Europe and North America as a typical case, where, "the very word "overseas" has no place in Honda's operating vocabulary, because the Corporation see itself as equidistant from all its key customers" (ibid.). What is required, in this context, is an analysis which can deal both with the global/local dynamic of these cultural processes at a substantive level and with the need to articulate the micro- and macro-dimensions of our analyses, so as both to ground our theories, and to theorize our ground, in an attempt more effectively to connect our analyses of the domestic, the local, the national and the inter- or trans-national aspects of communications.

NOTES

From David Morley, "Where the Global Meets the Local: Notes from the Siting Room," in *Television, Audiences, and Cultural Studies* (New York: Routledge, 1993). Reprinted by permission of the publisher.

1. The theoretical backdrop to the approach taken in this chapter is derived in some part from the work of Fernand Braudel (see especially his *Civilisation and Capitalism: The Perspective of the World,* London: William Collins, 1988). Most particularly, my emphasis here is on attempting to transcend the sterile dichotomy, characterized by Immanuel Wallerstein, between, on the one hand, the limitations of the "idiographic", empirical, "concrete" perspective of both narrative history and classical anthropology and, on the other hand, the absurdities of the "nomothetic" approach which has traditionally dominated the social sciences in their search for the transcendental laws of social life (see Wallerstein's *Unthinking Social Science*, Cambridge: Polity Press, 1991, for an exposition of this argument). The attempt made here to reconceptualize the relation of the "micro-" and the "macro-" levels of analysis (to relate "event", "conjuncture" and "structure", in Braudel's terms) is in many ways parallel to that offered by the analyses collected together in K. Knorr-Cetina and A.V. Cicourel (eds), *Advances in Social Theory and Methodology: Toward an Integration of Micro- and Macro-Sociologies*, London: Routledge & Kegan Paul, 1981.

2. See Seaman (1992) for a recent critique of "active audience theory" which entirely fails to grasp the original point of the analysis of popular culture and media audiences. In the wake of the emerging critique of "populism" in cultural studies, the pendulum of intellectual fashion seems to be swinging fast. A number of voices, besides Seaman's, can now be heard issuing clarion calls for a return to the "old certainties" of political economy and conspiracy theory and to models of imposed "dominant ideologies" which seem to be quite innocent of any recognition of the complexities of the concept of hegemony.

BIBLIOGRAPHY

Althusser, L. (1972) *For Marx*, Harmondsworth: Penguin Books.

Ang, I. (1991) *Desperately Seeking the Audience*, London: Routledge.

Austin, J. (1962) *How to Do Things with Words*, Oxford: Oxford University Press.

Bausinger, H. (1984) "Media, technology and everyday life," *Media, Culture and Society* 6(4).

Berland, J. (1988) "Placing television", *New Formations* 4.

Bhabha, H. K. (ed.) (1990) *Nation and Narration*, London: Routledge.

Brunsdon, C. (1989) "Text and audience" in E. Seiter *et al.* (eds), *Remote Control*, London: Routledge.

Bryce, J. (1987) "Family time and television use", in T. Lindlof (ed.) *Natural Audiences*, Norwood, New Jersey: Ablex.

Carey. J. (1989) *Culture as Communication*, London: Unwin Hyman.

Chambers, I. (1986) *Popular Culture: The Metropolitan Experience*, London: Methuen.

Chaney, D. (1983) "A symbolic mirror of ourselves: civic ritual in mass society", *Media, Culture and Society* 5(2).

————. (1986) "The symbolic form of ritual in mass communication", in P. Golding *et al.* (eds.) *Communicating Politics*, Leicester: Leicester University Press.

Chen, K. H. (1990) "Postmarxism", Taiwan: Institute of Literature, National Tsing-Hua University.

Clifford, J. and Marcus, G. (1986) *Writing Culture*, Berkeley: University of California Press.

Dayan, D. and Katz, E. (1987) "Performing media events", in J. Curran *et al.* (eds) *Impacts and Influences*, London: Methuen.

de la Haye, Y. (1979) *Marx and Engels on the Means of Communication*, New York: International General.

DeLillo, D. (1985) *White Noise*, London: Picador.

Donald, J. (1988) "How English is It?", *New Formations* 6.

Ellis, J. (1992) *Visible Fictions*, London: Routledge.

Ericson, S. (1989) "Theorising popular fiction", in M. Skovmand (ed.) *Media Fictions*, Aarhus: Aarhus University Press.

Erni, J. (1989) "Where is the audience?", *Journal of Communication Enquiry* 13(2).

Ferguson, M. (1989) "Electronic media and the redefining of time and space", in M. Ferguson (ed.) *Public Communication*, London: Sage.

Feuer, J. (1986) "*Dynasty*", paper presented to International Television Studies Conference, London.

Fiske, J. (1987) *Television Culture*, London: Methuen.

Foucault, M. (1980a) "The eye of power", in C. Gordon (ed.) *M. Foucault: Power/Knowledge*, New York: Pantheon.

————. (1980b) "Questions on geography", in C. Gordon (ed.) *M. Foucault: Power/Knowledge*, New York: Pantheon.

————. (1986) "Of other spaces", *Diacritics* 16.

Garmarnikow, E. and Purvis, J. (1983) "Introduction" to E. Garmarnikow and J. Purvis (eds) *The Public and the Private*, London: Heinemann Educational Books.

Giddens, A. (1979) *Central Problems in Sociological Theory*, London: Hutchinson.

Gillespie, M. (1989) "Technology and tradition", *Cultural Studies* 3(2).

Gripsrud, J. (1989) "High culture revisited", *Cultural Studies* 3(2).

Hall, S. (1988a) [Introductory Address, International Television Studies Conference, Institute of Education, London, July 1988].

————. (1988b) "New ethinicities", in K. Mercer (ed.) *Black Film, British Cinema*, London: Institute of Contemporary Arts.

Hannerz, U. (1990) "Cosmopolitans and locals in world culture", in M. Featherstone (ed.), *Global Culture*, London: Sage.

Hartley, J. (1987) "Television audiences, paedocracy and pleasure", *Textual Practice* 1(2).

Hebdige, D. (1988) "Towards a cartography of taste", in D. Hebidge, *Hiding in the Light*, London: Comedia/Routledge.

————. (1990) "Fax to the future", *Marxism Today*, January 1990.

Horton, D. and Wohl, R. (1956) "Mass communications and para-social interaction", *Psychiatry* 19.

Innis, H. (1951) *The Bias of Communication*, Toronto: University of Toronto Press.

Jameson, F. (1984) "Postmodernism: the cultural logic of late capitalism", *New Left Review* 146.

Kirby, A. (1989) "A sense of place", *Critical Studies in Mass Communication* 6(3).

Lindlof, T. (ed.) (1987) *Natural Audiences*, Norwood, NJ. Ablex.

Lindlof, T. and Meyer, T. (1987) "Mediated communication: the foundations of qualitative research" in T. Lindlof (ed.) *Natural Audiences*, Norwood, NJ: Ablex.

Lull, J. (ed.) (1988) *World Families Watch Television*, Newbury Park and London: Sage.

Massey, D. (1991) "The political place of locality studies", *Environment and Planning (A)* 23(2).

Mattelart, A. *et al.* (1987) *International Image Markets*, London: Comedia.

Meyerowitz, J. (1985) *No Sense of Place*, New York: Oxford University Press.

————. (1989) "The generalised elsewhere", *Critical Studies in Mass Communication* 6(3).

Miller, D. (1992) "The young and the restless in Trinidad", in R. Silverstone and E. Hirsch (eds), *Consuming Technologies*, London: Routledge.

Morley, D. (1980) *The "Nationwide" Audience*, London: British Film Institute.

————. (1986) *Family Television*, London: Comedia/Routledge.

Morley, D. and Robins, K. (1989) "Spaces of identity", *Screen* 20(4).

————. (1990) "No place like Heimat", *New Formations* 12.

————. (1992) "Techno-orientalism", *New Formations* 16.

Morley, D. and Silverstone, R. (1990) "Domestic communications", *Media, Culture and Society* 12(1).

Morris, M. (1988) "Banality in cultural studies", *Block* 14; reprinted in P. Mellencamp (ed.) *Logics of Television*, Bloomington: Indiana University Press, 1990.

Murdock, G. (1989) "Critical Inquiry and audience activity", in B. Dervin *et al.* (eds) *Rethinking Communication*, Vol. 2, Newbury Park and London: Sage.

Nava, M. (1987) "Consumerism and its contradictions", *Cultural Studies* 1(2).

Pateman, T. (1974) *Television and the February 1974 General Election*, London: British Film Institute.

Rath, C.D. (1985) "The invisible network: television as an institution in everyday life," in P. Drummond and R. Paterson (eds) *Television in Transition*, London: British Film Institute.

————. (1988) "Live/life: television as a generator of events in everyday life," in P. Drummond and R. Paterson (eds) *Television and its Audience*, London: British Film Institute.

Robins, K. (1989) "Reimagined communities", *Cultural Studies* 3(2).

————. (1991) "Tradition and translation", in J. Corner and S. Harvey (eds) *Enterprise and Heritage*, London: Routledge.

Rogge, J. U. and Jensen, K. (1988) "Everyday life and television in West Germany", in J. Lull (ed.) *World Families Watch Television*, London: Sage.

Rutherford, J. (ed.) (1990) *Identity: Community, Culture, Difference*, London: Lawrence & Wishart.

Scannell, P. (1988) "Radio times: the temporal arrangements of broadcasting in the modern world", in P. Drummond and R. Paterson (eds) *Television and its Audience*, London: British Film Institute.

——. (1989) "Public service broadcasting and modern public life", *Media, Culture and Society*, 11.

Schlesinger, P. (1987) "On National Identity", *Social Science Information* 26(2).

Schroder, K. (1987) "Convergence of antagonistic traditions?", *European Journal of Communications* 2.

Schudson, M. (1987) "The new validation of popular culture: sense and sentimentality in Academia", *Critical Studies in Mass Communication* 4(1).

Seaman, W. R. (1992) "Active audience theory: pointless populism", *Media, Culture and Society* 14.

Silverstone, R. (1988) "Television, myth and culture", in J. Carey (ed.) *Media, Myths and Narratives*, London: Sage.

Siskind, J. (1992) "The invention of Thanksgiving: a ritual of American nationality", *Critique of Anthropology* 12(2).

Slack, J. D. (1989) "Contextualising technology", in B. Dervin *et al.* (eds), *Rethinking Communication*, Vol. 2, London: Sage.

Soja, E. (1989) *Postmodern Geographies*, London: Verso.

Webster, D. (1989) "Cocacolonisation and national cultures", *Overhere* 9(2).

Wellman, B. (1979) "The community question", *American Journal of Sociology* 84.

Willemen, P. (1990) [Review of J. Hill *Sex, Class and Realism: British Cinema* 1963–1965], in M. Alvarado and J. O. Thompson (eds) *The Media Reader*, London: British Film Institute.

Worpole, K. (1983) *Dockers and Detectives*, London: Verso.

Wright, P. (1985) *On Living in an Old Country*, London: Verso.

Chapter Seventeen

Embedded Aesthetics
Creating a Discursive Space for Indigenous Media

Faye Ginsburg

> The closing years of the twentieth century are witnessing
> a radical re-orientation of thought in the human sci-
> ences which defies conventional disciplinary boundaries
> and demands a new "turning": away from the rational-
> ising modes of modernity and towards a different grasp
> of the nature of knowing itself. . . . The power of visual
> media as a means of knowledge-creation is only hesi-
> tantly grasped by many in public life. . . . But, from the
> viewpoint of the emergent visual-aural culture of the
> twenty-first century, "what's on" creates the context for
> what is known and hence finally for what "is."
> —Annette Hamilton

Since the late 1970s, Aboriginal Australians (and other indigenous people) have been
engaged in developing new visual media forms by adapting the technologies of video,
film, and television to a range of expressive and political purposes. Their efforts to
develop new forms of indigenous media are motivated by a desire to envision and
strengthen a "cultural future" (Michaels 1987a) for themselves in their own communities and in the dominant society. Aboriginal cultures, of course, are extremely
diverse, as Aboriginal cultural critic and anthropologist Marcia Langton has pointed
out in her recent book on indigenous media production. "There is no one kind of
Aboriginal person or community," she writes:

> There are [two] regions which can be characterised, however, with reference to history,
> politics, culture and demography. . . .
> The first region is "settled" Australia . . . where most provincial towns and all the
> major cities and institutions are located, and where a myriad of small Aboriginal
> communities and populations reside with a range of histories and cultures. . . .
> The second region is "remote" Australia where most of the tradition-oriented Abo-
> riginal cultures are located. They likewise have responded to particular frontiers and
> now contend with various types of Australian settlement. [Langton 1993:12–13]

Aboriginal media productions are as various as Aboriginal life itself, ranging from low-budget videos made by community-based media associations for both traditional people in remote settlements and groups in urban centers; to regional television and radio programming for Aboriginal groups throughout Central Australia made by organizations such as the Central Australian Aboriginal Media Association (CAAMA); to legal or instructional videos (often quite creative) made by land councils as well as health and other service groups; to documentaries and current affairs for national broadcasting; to independent features directed by cosmopolitan Aboriginal artists such as Tracey Moffatt whose first feature film, *Bedevil*, premiered at Cannes in 1993. Such works are inherently complex cultural objects, as they cross multiple cultural boundaries in their production, distribution, and consumption. For example, Aboriginal producers often collaborate with non-Aboriginal media workers, be they media advisers to remote settlements or staff at Australia's national television stations. Works themselves are often hybrid, combining traditional ritual knowledge and/or performance with MTV-style special effects. In terms of circulation and reception, these productions are seen by multiple audiences, including other Aboriginal and non-Aboriginal viewers in Australia, via circulation of video letters as well as local, regional, or national broadcasts, or by diverse overseas audiences through film festivals and conferences.

With an interest in enlarging analyses of film texts to account for broader contexts of social relations,[1] I have found it helpful to think of Aboriginal media as part of a *mediascape*, a term created by Arjun Appadurai to account for the different kinds of global cultural flows created by new media technologies and the images created with them in the late 20th century. Appadurai argues for situated analyses that take account of the interdependence of media practices with the local, national, and transnational circumstances that surround them (Appadurai 1990:7). Using such a model for indigenous media helps to establish a more generative discursive space for this work which breaks what one might call the fetishizing of the local, without losing a sense of the specific situatedness of any production. The complex mediascape of Aboriginal media, for example, must account for a range of circumstances, beginning with the perspectives of Aboriginal producers, for whom new media forms are seen as a powerful means of (collective) self-expression that can have a culturally revitalizing effect. Their vision coexists uneasily, however, with the fact that their work is also a product of relations with governing bodies that are responsible for the dire political circumstances that often motivated the Aboriginal mastery of new communication forms as a means of cultural intervention.[2] Such contradictions are inherent to the ongoing social construction of *Aboriginality*. Cultural critic Fiona Nicoll offers a helpful explication of the term that has been the subject of considerable debate.[3] As she writes:

> "Aboriginality" . . . [is] a colonial field of power relations within which Aborigines struggle with the dominant settler culture over the representation of things such as "identity," "history," "land," and "culture." In contrast to the category "Aboriginal culture," which is always defined in opposition to a dominant "non-Aboriginal culture," the concept of "Aboriginality" must be thought in *relation* to "non-Aboriginality." For it was the while settlers who lumped the various indigenous peoples under the homog-

enizing name of "Aborigines," then brought into being the categories of "Aboriginal history," "Aboriginal culture," "Aboriginal experience" and "Aboriginal conditions." [1993:709]

Thus, not only are Aboriginal film and video important to Aboriginal Australians, but they cannot be understood apart from the contemporary construction of Aboriginality. As nation-states like Australia increasingly constitute their "imagined communities" (Anderson 1983) through the circulation of televisual and cinematic images of the people they govern, Aboriginal media have become part of the mediascape of the Australian *national imaginary*.[4] Put in concrete terms:

> "Aboriginality" arises from the subjective experience of both Aboriginal people and non-Aboriginal people who engage in any intercultural dialogue, whether in actual lived experience or through a mediated experience such as a white person watching a program about Aboriginal people on television or reading a book. [Langton 1993:31]

Discursive Spaces/Social Action

This essay is an extension of a larger effort initiated by Aboriginal cultural activists to develop a "discursive practice"—both for Aboriginal makers and for others who make and study media—that respects and understands this work in terms relevant to contemporary indigenous people living in a variety of settings (Langton 1993). Specifically, it examines how Aboriginal media makers understand their own work. How, one might ask, do people understand indigenous media works as they move through the complex circuits sketched above? What are the aesthetic standards—the discourses and practices of evaluation—that are applied to indigenous productions as they are positioned differently in various exhibition contexts? Are Aboriginal ideas about their "beauty/value" able to cross over cultural borders? I am concerned in particular with how notions of the value of indigenous media are being negotiated at different levels of Aboriginal media production.[5] While there are multiple arenas of Aboriginal production (local, regional, urban, etc.), in this essay I will focus on three sites of Aboriginal media work: remote communities; national television; and transnational networks of indigenous media producers that form around events such as film festivals or coproductions.

In these different arenas, Aboriginal producers from very different backgrounds use a language of evaluation that stresses the *activities* of the production and circulation of such work in specific communities as the basis for judging its value. In communities where traditional Aboriginal cultural practices are still relatively intact, such evaluation is culturally very specific, corresponding to notions of appropriate social and formal organization of performance in ceremonial or ritual domains. In her analysis of Aboriginal media production, Marcia Langton argues that such media from remote areas are "community-authored" (1993:13). Summarizing studies in the 1980s of the organization of video production at the remote Warlpiri settlement of Yuendumu (Michaels and Kelly 1984). Langton writes that "the camera and camera person are attributed with the ritual role of *kurdungurlu* (ritual managers) . . . because they are witnesses to events and affirm their truth," while those in front of the camera are *kirda* (ritual owners) with acknowledged rights and obligations to tell and perform certain stories and ceremonies (1993:65). Based on my own contact with Yuendumu in 1992, it is unclear whether these specific arrangements still endure in the 1990s. However, the general principle of kin-based rights to tell certain kinds of stories and ceremonial knowledge continue to shape production practices. More generally, then, "[t]here are rules, which are somewhat flexible, for the production, distribution and ownership of any image, just as there are under traditional law for sacred designs which ... refer to ancestors and ancestral mythology" (Langton 1993:65).

In ways that are both similar and different, urban Aboriginal mediamakers are also concerned with their media productions as a form of social action. While their works are more typically understood as authored by individuals (Langton 1993:13), many urban Aboriginal producers nonetheless see themselves as responsible to a community of origin (for example kin and friends in the urban neighborhood of Redfern in Sydney), although it is a sense of community less bound by specific cultural rules than that of people in remote settlements. This is especially true of those working for Australian state television who shoulder the specific burden of creating an "authentic" Aboriginal presence in the mass media and, more broadly, in Australia's national imaginary.[6] This tendency to evaluate work in terms of social action is striking to an observer schooled in Western aesthetics. With few exceptions, questions of narrative or visual form are not primary issues for discussion per se, despite the obvious concern for it in individual works. Rather, for many Aboriginal producers, the quality of work is judged by its capacity to embody, sustain, and even revive or create certain social relations, although the social bases for coming to this position may be very different for remote and urban people.[7] For the sake of discussion, I will call this orientation *embedded aesthetics*, to draw attention to a system of evaluation that refuses a separation of textual production and circulation from broader arenas of social relations.[8] For example, Eric Michaels, an American researcher who helped develop Aboriginal media production with Warlpiri people at Yuendumu in Central Australia, noted that for the people he worked with:

> [Aboriginal] art or video objects become difficult to isolate for analysis because the producer's intention is the opposite. Warlpiri artists demonstrate their own invisibility in order to assert the work's authority and continuity with tradition. They do not draw attention to themselves or to their creativity. [Michaels 1987a:34]

My argument, then, is that this new and complex object—Aboriginal media—is understood by its producers to be operating in multiple domains as an extension of their collective (vs. individual) self-production. However, it is important to recognize that Aboriginal producers from various locales and backgrounds—remote, urban, rural—come to their positions through quite different cultural and social processes. In the case of urban Aboriginal mediamakers, their embrace of *embedded aesthetics* may be an extremely self conscious choice, produced out of contact with a variety of discourses. In the cases below, I will sketch the multiple ways that this kind of positioning of indigenous media emerges from very different social bases for the understanding of Aboriginality and its representation, especially as it passes across cultural and national borders.

Remote Control: Media in Traditional Communities

My first examples are drawn from two successful community-based Aboriginal media associations developed at relatively traditional remote settlements in the Central Desert area of Australia. The first is Ernabella on Pitjantjatjara lands in South Australia, just south of Uluru (Ayers Rock). The second settlement is Yuendumu on Warlpiri lands in Central Australia, northwest of Alice Springs, home to the Warlpiri Media Association since 1982. Both are Aboriginal settlements with highly mobile populations that can vary from 500 to 1500 over the course of a year. Founded by missionaries in the 1940s, they became self-governing by the 1970s and retain infra-structures consisting of a community store, a town office, a police station, a primary school, a health clinic, a church, an art association, and local broadcast facilities (Langton 1993).

In 1983, people at Ernabella began producing video programs with the encourage-ment of white schoolteachers and advisers, in particular Nell Turner, who settled in the community, learned the language, and facilitated the development of Ernabella Video Television (EVTV) from its inception to the present. Established in 1985, EVTV operates from a small video production, editing, and playback facility and an inex-pensive satellite dish that provides local broadcasts of work produced by EVTV as well as items selected from national television feeds. Determined to be as independent as possible from government subsidies, EVTV has supported itself successfully through a self-imposed tax on cold drinks in the community store, the sales of EVTV videos, and occasional public and private grants (Batty 1993: Molnar 1989; N. Turner 1990).

Over the first decade of its existence, EVTV has produced over eighty edited pieces as well as thousands of hours of community television under the direction of a respected couple, Simon and Pantiji Tjiyangu, and a local media committee made up of male and female elders. Their concerns range from monitoring the content of work shown—so that images are not circulated that violate cultural rules regulating what can be seen (e.g. tapes of women's sacred ceremonies are not edited and are only accessible to appropriate senior women)—and the timing of viewing so that television transmission, whether locally produced or the national satellite feed, does not interfere with other cultural activities.

Perhaps because the supervision of EVTV is largely in the hands of elders, the video work of Ernabella is distinguished by its emphasis on ceremonies, in particular the stories, dances, and sand designs that are associated with the Kungkarangkalpa (Seven Sisters Dreaming) (which explains the origins of the Pleiades constellation). In adapting such forms to video, EVTV producers include in their tapes the produc-tion process itself, which can involve the whole community, including children, dancers, storytellers, and video crew. For example, in tapes such as *Seven Sisters Dreaming: Tjukurpa Kungkarangkalpa Tjara* (made in 1985) one sees not just a performance as we understand it in the West. Dances and enactments of the story of the Seven Sisters are preceded by extensive preparation and participation by those members of the Pitjantjatjara community who are responsible for ritual knowledge and ceremony. This aspect of Pitjantjatjara ritual performance has been reconfigured to accommodate video production: the tape includes not only ritual preparation but also other participants offering their comments on the ritual as they sit at night by the campfire to view the day's rushes (Leigh 1992:3). Such reflexivity is not a Brechtian innovation; rather, it authorizes the reconfiguring of traditional practices for video as "true" and properly done.

In addition to such framing of the production process, the value or beauty of such videos for the Pitjantjatjara videomakers is extratextual, created by the cultural and social processes they mediate, embody, create, and extend. The tapes underscore the cosmological power of ceremonies to invigorate sacred aspects of the landscape; they reinforce the social relations that are fundamental to ritual production; and they enhance the place of Pitjantjatjara among Aboriginal groups in the area, as well as for the dominant Australian regional culture. Over the last decade, people from Ernabella frequently have been invited to "perform" in nearby cultural centers such as Adelaide. Knowledge of these issues is important to understanding the value of EVTV tapes as texts that cross over cultural borders, reaching other Aboriginal and non-Aboriginal audiences. As media activist Philip Batty commented:

> The work of EVTV had the effect of engendering a kind of local renaissance in traditional dance, performance and singing. The various video programmes depicting the actual land where the dreaming lines were located gave renewed strength to traditional beliefs and values within the communities. [Batty 1993:113]

As another example of indigenous media work emerging from remote Aboriginal settlements, the Warlpiri Media Association (WMA) began producing tapes in 1982 and established their own unlicensed local television station similar to that of EVTV, in April 1985. Francis Jupurrurla Kelly, a young Warlpiri man, became a key videomaker and central figure in developing WMA. Much of what has been written about that group for outsiders came out of the work of Eric Michaels, for the (then) Australian Institute of Aboriginal Studies, which commissioned him to research the impact of Western media on traditional Aboriginal people in Central Australia. When he arrived at Yuendumu, he discovered that:

> [t]here was, in the early 1980s, a considerable creative interest among Aborigines in the new entertainment technology becoming available to remote communities. There was equally a motivated, articulate, and general concern about the possible unwanted consequences of television, especially among senior Aborigines and local indigenous educators. In particular, the absence of local Aboriginal languages from any proposed service was a major issue. [Michaels 1987a:11]

As a result, Michaels also brought an interventionist approach to his research, encouraging people to produce their own videos without imposing Western conventions of shooting and editing. The broader concern that Michaels shared with Yuendumu videomakers was that, if people could make videos based on Aboriginal concerns, they might escape the more deleterious effects of broadcast television by substituting their own work for mainstream satellite television signals. While they had not tried video production before, Yuendumu residents were familiar with mainstream cinema, as well as the active production of Aboriginal popular music, as well as radio programs in Central Australia.[9] Since 1982, Warlpiri videomakers have produced hundreds of hours of tapes, on a range of subjects including sports events, health issues, traditional rituals, and their own history, as in *Coniston Story*, a tape in which the Aboriginal descendants of a revenge massacre of Warlpiri people by whites go to the site of the tragedy and tell their version of this "killing time." In an analysis of *Coniston Story*, Michaels notes that "one is struck by the recurrent camera movement, [and] the subtle shifts in focus and attention during the otherwise even, long pans across the landscape," shifts that Western interpreters might see as "naive" camerawork (1987a:51). Rather, Francis Jupurrurla Kelly (the Warlpiri producer/ director and camera operator) explains that the camera is following

> the movement . . . of unseen characters—both Dreamtime [ancestral] and historical— which converge on this landscape. . . . Shifts in focus and interruptions in panning pick out important things in the landscape, like a tree where spirits live or a flower with symbolic value: [Cited in Michaels 1987a:52]

Jupurrurla's explanation suggests that in developing a new mode of telling Warlpiri history through video, his concerns were consistent with traditional Aboriginal cosmology in which the particular geographic features of the areas they inhabit (and the kin-based rights and responsibilities attached to them) are central to authorizing myths and ceremonies. Michaels argued that this emphasis on the meaning of landscape is apparent in many Warlpiri tapes and accounts for the value and beauty of such sequences for Warlpiri viewers (Michaels 1987b).

What is not immediately visible in the tapes themselves is that people organize themselves around media production in terms of the responsibilities of specific groups for knowledge and practices associated with certain geographic areas, similar to the case of Ernabella discussed above. In other words, the ways in which tapes are made and used reflect Warlpiri understandings of kin-based obligations for ceremonial production and control of traditional knowledge, as these index cosmological relationships to particular features in regional geography (Michaels and Kelly 1984). "The credibility of the resulting tape for the Warlpiri audience is dependent upon knowing that these people were all participating in the event, even though the taped record provides no direct evidence of their presence" (Michaels 1987a:46). Thus, for Warlpiri videomakers, cultural production—if it is of any value—is understood as part of a broader effort of collective self-production always associated with the *jukurrpa*, the ontological system of kin-and land-based ritual knowledge, translated into English originally as "the dreaming" (Stanner 1956) and now also as "the law." Notions of value embedded in jukurrpa run contrary to Western notions of the social relations of aesthetic production that emphasize the creative "self-expression" of individuals who are assigned responsibility as authors. Rather:

> stories are always true, and invention even when it requires an individual agent to "dream" or "receive" a text, remains social in a complex and important sense that

assures truth. Rights to receive, know, perform, or teach a story (through dance, song, narrative, and graphic design) are determined by any identified individual's structural position and social/ritual history within an elaborately reckoned system of kin. Novelty can only enter this system as a social, not an individual invention. Not only is one's right to invent ultimately constrained, it is particularly constrained with respect to the kinship role for it is the geneaology of an item—not its individual creation—which authorises it. [Michaels 1987b:65]

These principles through which some Aboriginal videos from remote settlements are mediated within and across cultural borders are consistent with the evaluative processes used for other "hybrid" Aboriginal media such as acrylic paining. As Fred Myers writes regarding the evaluations Pintupi painters from the Central Desert area make of their work, "the painters themselves have been unforthcoming about such aesthetic considerations." (Myers 1994:15). Indeed

The[ir] principal discourse . . . emphasizes their works as vehicles of self-production and collective empowerment . . . these are not necessarily interpretations that are outside the processes of representation themselves. [Myers 1994:35]

In addition to providing a means for enhancing forms such as ritual performance, Aboriginal film and video offer innovative possibilities for collective self-production. As novel forms, these media provide sites for the re-visioning of social relations with the encompassing society, an exploration that more traditional indigenous forms cannot so easily accommodate. In media production, Aboriginal skills at constituting both individual and group identities through narrative and ritual are engaged in innovative ways that are often simultaneously indigenous and intercultural, from production to reception. For example, Yuendumu residents have produced a series of children's programs designed to teach literacy in Warlpiri. The series was invented by elders and schoolteachers, both white and Aboriginal. With grants written with the help of a media adviser, they received funding from the Australian government and hired a local Anglo-Australian filmmaker, David Batty (with whom they had worked before), to create the series *Manyu Wana* ("Just for Fun"). The result has been an ongoing series of collaborative community-based productions where kids, teachers, and filmmaker work together to improvise and then enact humorous short sketches to illustrate both written and spoken Warlpiri words in ways that seem to engage multiple audiences. Immensely popular in Yuendumu and neighboring Aboriginal communities. *Manyu Wana*, despite its very local origin and monolingual use of local language, has also been seen and appreciated all over the world.

National Imaginaries

Since the early 1980s, the demand for more Aboriginal participation and visibility in the Australian mediascape has been increasing, not only for local access to video in remote areas, but also for more Aboriginal representation on mainstream national television. This concern is not simply about equal access but a recognition that distortion and/or invisibility of Aboriginal realities for the wider Australian public can have a direct effect on political culture. Continuing exclusion of work by Aboriginal people from Australia's media institutions has sharpened Aboriginal awareness of the connections between political enfranchisement and the need to control their own images in the public sphere.

Aboriginal people—in terms of content and staffing—are still virtually absent from Australia's three commercial television networks (Langton 1993:21).[10] However, two important efforts to increase an Aboriginal presence on public television were initiated in 1989. These were (1) the Aboriginal Programs Unit (APU) of the Australian Broadcasting Corporation (ABC) the state-owned national television station that reaches all of Australia; and (2) the Aboriginal Television Unit of the Special Broadcast Service (SBS),[11] Australia's state-funded station set up to provide culturally and linguistically appropriate programming, both imported as well as locally produced, for Australia's many ethnic communities.

In April 1989, the Special Broadcast Service initiated a 13-part television series devoted to Aboriginal issues, called *First in Line*, the first prime-time current affairs show in Australia to be hosted by two Aboriginal people. This was a border crossing of considerable significance to Aboriginal cultural activists.[12] The producers and crew were primarily Aboriginal, and they consulted with communities throughout Australia for items stressing the positive achievements of Aborigines (Molnar 1989:38–39). Eventually, *First in Line* was discontinued, and an Aboriginal unit was established with Rachel Perkins at the head, a young Aboriginal woman who had trained at the Central Australian Aboriginal Media Association (CAAMA). She has been creating programming through the use of work such as *Manyu Wana* from regional and local Aboriginal media associations. In 1992, she commissioned and produced a series, *Blood Brothers*, comprised of four documentaries on different aspects of Aboriginal history and culture (Rachel Perkins, interview, May 2, 1992). While these efforts are important, the SBS has a relatively small audience and budget.

By contrast, the state-controlled and-funded Australian Broadcasting Corporation (ABC) has a much greater resource base and reaches a national audience. In 1987, the ABC set up the Aboriginal Programs Unit (APU),[13] but it was not until 1989 that their first Aboriginally produced and presented program, *Blackout*, began broadcasting on a Friday evening time slot. This series, a weekly magazine show on Aboriginal issues, is still being produced. (In 1992, it was awarded the United Nations Human Rights Media Award.) Additionally, APU programs occasional series such as *The First Australians*, an eight-part series of independent documentaries on Aboriginal topics broadcast on Thursday nights in 1992.[14]

Unlike the producers from remote settlements, Aboriginal producers at APU grew up in urban or "settled" areas, are bicultural, often hold university degrees, and are sophisticated about the ins and outs of national television vis-à-vis their interests as indigenous makers. People like Frances Peters and Rachel Perkins are new kinds of cultural activists who are regular *border crossers*, a position they occupy as part of their own background (from Aboriginal families educated in the dominant culture's pedagogical system) and out of a recognition that they must speak effectively to (at least) two kinds of Australians. Like the more remote-living Aboriginal media makers discussed above, they are concerned with their work as part of a range of activities engaged in cultural revival, identity formation, and political assertion. Through their work in televisual media production, they have been able to assert the multiple realities of contemporary urban Aboriginal life, not just for their own communities but also in the national public culture where Aboriginal activism and political claims are generally effaced from the official histories.

For example, in 1991, Peters worked with fellow APU producer David Sandy to produce the first documentary special of APU for broadcast in 1992. The title, *Tent Embassy*, refers to the event that galvanized the beginning of what some have called the "Aboriginal civil rights movement." On Australia Day (January 26) 1972, four young Aboriginal men erected a small tent on the lawns of the Parliament House in Canberra and declared themselves a sovereign nation. The action succinctly dramatized the issue of Aboriginal land rights in the Australian imagination and helped catalyze a broader social movement. The return, in 1992, of some of the original activists, now in their forties, to the site of the original protest to reassert their claims and to occupy Parliament House as well becomes the occasion for the film to explore the last 20 years of Aboriginal politics. The history moves from the confrontational activism of the Aboriginal Black Power and the Black Panther movements in the 1970s, to the establishment in the 1980s of the Aboriginal and Torres Straits Islanders Commission (ATSIC), a five-billion-dollar bureaucracy that has been criticized by some activists as co-opting Aboriginal political power. *Tent Embassy* is built out of the stories of key activists—lawyer Paul Coe, scholar and activist Roberta Sykes, public figure Charles Perkins—as we see them in archival footage, in extended contemporary interviews. It opens with a wonderfully humorous dramatic recreation that suggests the spontaneous origins of the first protest and holds fast to the principle of making people primary over issues. Other events are tracked through archival footage, not only of the embassy protest, but also of crucial events leading up to it, such as the discovery of bauxite on Aboriginal lands in the 1960s, which helped put land claims on the national political agenda.

For productions like *Tent Embassy* to be effective in reaching large, mixed audiences, they require aesthetic considerations that negotiate multiple cultural perspectives. The challenge for producers is to create visions of Aboriginal culture and history that simultaneously address the realities of Aboriginal communities and intervene in representations of Australian national histories in ways that will attract both Aboriginal and non-Aboriginal audiences. Frances Peters (and a number of other Aboriginal producers) are exploring how to reposition cultural authority in their works by using satire, humor, and drama. These provide complex commentaries on their own identities and on their relationships with the dominant society, without simplifying or reducing the Aboriginal experience for what are still predominantly white audiences. In Peters's words:

> Aboriginal people in Australia are not one nation; the differences are there, but we're all Aboriginal. . . . I [am] trying to break a lot of image stereotypes. I think those stereotypes may have something to do with why many indigenous artists are moving away from documentary and into fiction or drama films. We are sick of the documentary format; we've seen so many of them about us . . . so unfortunately what we've done

is associate documentary with just another form of stereotyping. We've got the opportunity as aboriginal filmmakers to change that. [Peters 1993:102]

Producers at APU are engaged in more than the creation of media images of themselves that alter their place in the world of representations. In considering this kind of work in relation to questions of indigenous aesthetics, one must recognize the value they place on media production as a form of social action. Frances Peters articulated this position clearly to me in discussing her position as an Aboriginal producer:

> Unlike you, we can't remove ourselves from the programs we're making because they're about us as well. And because they are about us, we always have that responsibility to our Aboriginal culture and country . . . we can't walk away and just make a program on a different theme next time. . . . Ultimately you're not really answerable to a hell of a lot of people. . . . But with us, with every program that we make, we are ultimately responsible to a larger Aboriginal community. And we can't remove ourselves from that responsibility. [Frances Peters, interview, April 30, 1992]

Peters's comments speak to the complex and embedded sense that indigenous producers bring to their work, never seeing it as existing apart from the mediation of social relationships, especially with communities of origin, whether urban or remote. However, *community* is not, for her, some romantic notion of a unified social position. It is, rather, a complex and unstable social construct, implicated in the changing understandings of Aboriginality in Australia today, as bureaucratic structures for the administration of Aboriginal funding and policies have proliferated. As much as she feels accountable to a broader Aboriginal world, she queries the concept:

> Which community? Our communities have become bureaucratized and class-stratified. Accountability is riddled with fear of being made to feel guilty, or that you aren't Aboriginal enough. [Peters 1993:105]

Her positioning (along with that of other producers) intersects and is influenced by emerging Western theoretical discourses in the arts, built on frameworks of multiculturalism, which emphasize "cultural diversity as a basis for challenging, revising, and relativizing basic notions and principles common to dominant and minority cultures alike, so as to construct a more vital, open, and democratic common culture" (T. Turner 1993:413). In the world of Aboriginal media making, an approach built out of contemporary identity politics (which has influenced many urban-based Aboriginal producers) intersects with concerns that shape the work of more traditional Aboriginal producers from remote communities, thereby creating a sense (or even illusion) of coherence in the ways that a broad range of Aboriginal makers evaluate their work. Regardless of this outcome, it is important to recognize that urban Aboriginal producers working in bicultural settings have embraced an *embedded aesthetic* as a strategic *choice*. Their efforts to develop an alternative approach to their work, while emerging from their experiences as Aboriginal Australians, are nonetheless self-conscious; the Western aesthetic conventions of the dominant society are culturally available to them as well. This sense of self-conscious positioning is evident in Frances Peters's description of coming to consciousness in her days as a student and Aboriginal radio producer:

> So, I was going to university, getting a formal education, and then spending my Saturday afternoons having great fun at an Aboriginal radio station [Radio Redfern], breaking all the rules. We were creating our own sounds, basically, we were promoting our music, and we were telling our own news in ways and forms that we chose. All that raised a lot of questions for me about the media and how I was going to see myself working in it. It was hard; it was a battle, and I used to fight in every one of those classes at University. [Peters 1993:99]

Transnational Mediations

For most producers, their sense of community is very local. However, new and more expanded communities of identity are emerging through collaborative activities that transcend the boundaries of the nation-states that encompass them. Over the last five years, indigenous media productions have increasingly become part of *global cultural flows*. Connections are being built by indigenous producers who have been organizing a transnational indigenous network via film festivals and conferences, as well as joint productions such as the Pac Rim initiative, a documentary series being made jointly by indigenous filmmakers from Australia, New Zealand, the United States, and Canada. These events are becoming the basis for constituting an emergent organization of indigenous media producers. For example, the First Nations Film and Video Makers World Alliance (FNFVWA) was formed at the September 1992 Dreamspeakers Festival in Edmonton, Canada, itself the first indigenously organized international Aboriginal film and video festival. In such exhibition venues organized by and for indigenous people, media workers frame their work with a discourse of self-determination, clearly placing collective and political interests over those of individual expression. Such positioning is evident, for example, in the following statement of aims of the FNFVWA drawn up in 1992:

> a. to raise awareness of First Nations issues
> b. to establish a film and video communication network
> c. to ensure that tr2aditional lands, language, and culture are protected
> d. to implement work and training exchanges
> e. to establish a world conference
> f. to ensure environmental protection and management
> g. to promote our teachings of history and culture
> h. to distribute and market our own films.
>
> A major concern of all those indigenous filmmakers who attended Dreamspeakers was the need for our works to be distributed amongst other indigenous groups in other countries, that we are our own international market. The problem we felt was that our works are almost always received [more positively] by overseas audiences than by those in our own countries.

This statement of principles developed by a group of indigenous attendees (and the weeklong Dreamspeakers Festival itself) was striking in the lack of discussion of themselves as artists concerned primarily with formal issues or even freedom of expression. The indigenous media makers in the alliance, who came form all over the world, were all engaged in asserting the relationship of their work to broader arenas of social action. Such positions complicate structures of distribution and public culture in which the (media) artist's position is valued as being outside or critical of society, as in Adorno's view of art as an "intrinsic movement against society," a social realm set apart from the means-end rationality of daily bourgeois existence (Adorno 1970:336, quoted in Burger 1984:10).

Recent shows of indigenous film/video that have been organized by dominant cultural institutions situate them as new forms of aesthetic/political production yet continue to look for aesthetic innovation in the text itself, rather than in the relations of production and reception that shape the evaluation and mediation of the text in unexpected ways. Mainstream showcases, for example, continue to focus on "individual makers" in places associated with "auteurship" in the arts, such as programs of The Museum of Modern Art (1990, 1993). The New Museum (1990), or the Walter Reade Theater at Lincoln Center (1992), all sites of exhibition of indigenous media in New York City. In such venues, indigenous work is in tension with Western discourses that valorize the individual as a political or artistic agent in opposition to a broader polity. Although this has been changing as the broader zeitgeist in the West embraces multicultural and identity-based politics as frames for the exhibition of various expressive media, the structures for showing work in most cases still put forward "the artist," repressing the embeddedness of individual artistic production in broader social and political processes. For the most part, indigenous producers reject this dominant model of the media text as the expression of an individuated self and continue to stress their work as on a continuum of social action authorizing Aboriginal cultural empowerment.

In conclusion, I want to emphasize that the social relations built out of indigenous media practices are helping to develop support and sensibilities for indigenous actions for self-determination. Self-representation in media is seen as a crucial part of this process. Indigenous media productions and the activities around them are rendering visible indigenous cultural and historical realities to themselves and the broader societies that have stereotyped or denied them. The translational social relations built out of these media practices are creating new arenas of cooperation, locally, nationally, and internationally. Like the indigenous producers themselves, I suggest a model that stresses not only the text but also the *activities* and social organization of media work as arenas of cultural production. Only by understanding indigenous media work as part of a broader mediascape of social relations can we appreciate them fully as complex cultural objects. In the imaginative, narrative, social, and political spaces opened up by film, video, and television lie possibilities for Aboriginal mediamakers and their communities to reenvision their current realities and possible futures, from the revival of local cultural practices, to the insertion of their histories into national imaginaries, to the creation of new transnational arenas that link indigenous makers around the globe in a common effort to make their concerns visible to the world.

NOTES

From Faye Ginsburg, "Embedded Aesthetics: Creating a Discursive Space for Indigenous Media," *Cultural Anthropology* 9, no. 3 (1994). Reprinted by permission of the American Anthropological Association from *Cultural Anthropology* 9, no. 3. Not for sale or further reproduction.

Acknowledgments. For editorial comments on this and earlier drafts, I thank Debbora Battaglia, Paul Brodwin, Susan Harding, Toby Miller, and Fred Myers. Fieldwork on which this work is based could not have been done without the help of Fred Myers in 1988 and Françoise Dussart in 1992, in the logistics and languages of Aboriginal research in the field and out; I am deeply grateful to both of them. In addition, I want to thank the following people in Australia who shared their time and insights with me: Philip Batty, Freda Glynn, Annette Hamilton, Francis Jupurrurla Kelly, Ned Lander, Marcia Langton, Mary Laughren, Michael Leigh, Judith and David MacDougall, Michael Niblett, Rachel Perkins, Frances Peters, Nick Peterson, Tim Rowse, David Sandy, Neil Turner, and Peter Toyne. For research support, I am grateful to the Research Challenge Fund of New York University (1988) and the John Simon Guggenheim Foundation (1991–92). Portions of this piece were drawn from two essays (Ginsburg 1993b and 1994b). The Annette Hamilton quote used as the epigraph is from Hamilton 1993:5.

1. For a fuller development of this position, see Ginsburg 1994a.

2. These contradictions, some have argued, are typical of liberal welfare states and their indigenous populations, a system that Jeremy Beckett calls welfare colonialism (1988).

3. For examples of debates on Aboriginality, see Beckett 1988, Thiele 1991, Lattas 1991, and others in a special issue of *The Australian Journal of Anthropology* entitled Reconsidering Aboriginality.

4. I follow Annette Hamilton's use of the term *national imaginary*. Drawing on ideas from Benedict Anderson, Edward Said, and Jacques Lacan, Hamilton uses the term to describe how contemporary nation-states use visual mass media to constitute *imagined communities*. She uses Lacan's idea of the imaginary as the mirror-phase in human development when the child sees its own reflection as an "other": "Imaginary relations at the social, collective level can thus be seen as ourselves looking at ourselves while we think we are seeing others" (Hamilton 1990:17). As examples, she cites the current popularity of Aboriginal art and popular music, as well as films such as *Crocodile Dundee*, in which the outback and Aboriginal knowledge play a critical role, as if Australian appropriation of Aboriginal culture can justify "the settler presence in the country, and indeed . . . the presence of Australia as part of a world cultural scene" (Hamilton 1990: 18). Given current world conditions, representations of the Australian nation must take account of what Hamilton calls an increasingly "internationalized image-environment," in which images of indigenous peoples now carry a heavy semiotic load (1990). Aboriginal media have become implicated in the circulation of commodified images of Aboriginality, including "hi-tech primitives" engaged in their own televisual production. For a fuller discussion of this position, see Ginsburg 1993a.

5. For a discussion of the origins and use of the term *indigenous media*, see Ginsburg 1993a.

6. While the opportunities of such positions are obvious, there is some concern on the part of Aboriginal filmmakers that they are expected to confine their work to conventional or romanticized representations of Aboriginality, what Haitian anthropologist Micael-Rolph Trouillot calls "the savage slot" (Trouillot 1991).

7. Urban-based filmmakers such as Tracey Moffatt may be more oriented toward formal issues, although they, too, often couch their interests in terms of their social possibilities as *interventions* into dominant conventions of representation regarding Aboriginal men and women in popular culture, as was the case with both *Night Cries* (1990) and *Nice Coloured Girls* (1987). In the case of makers such as Moffatt, this language may be less a product of Aboriginal categories and more a reworking of available discourses in the independent cinema movement, of which she is a part.

8. For an interesting discussion of similar issues in relation to Aboriginal writing, see Muecke 1992.

9. For a fuller discussion of of the development of Australian Aboriginal media in different locales, see Batty 1993, Ginsburg 1991 and 1993a, Michaels 1987a, Molnar 1989, and O'Regan 1993.

10. Langton notes:

> One network was even broadcasting a drama series featuring a European acting in place of the original Aboriginal Character, Bony, from the novels of Arthur Upfield. . . . A new and welcome twist . . . was the appointment of Stan Grant, an Aboriginal journalist, to the position of anchor on *Real Life* [a nightly current affairs program]. [1993:21]

11. In 1978, the government established a separate Special Broadcast Service (SBS) initially to serve immigrant minorities. By the mid-1980s, the SBS altered its policy to include the presentation of Aboriginal radio and television programs and to take as its mandate the correction of popular misconceptions about Aboriginal history and culture.

12. Michael Johnson and Rhoda Roberts were the hosts for 38 programs that aired Tuesday nights at 7:30.

13. While the state-controlled and funded Australian Broadcasting Corporation (ABC) had been training Aborigines since 1980, by 1987 only seven Aborigines were employed there. That same year, the prime minister established the Aboriginal Employment and Development Policy (AEDP), which requires all industries to have 2 percent Aboriginal employment by 1991 (Molnar 1989:36–38).

14. As of 1993, APU had six Aboriginal staff who produce *Blackout*, a weekly late-night program on Aboriginal affairs, as well as occasional documentaries and dramatic works. As such, it is a precedent-setting model for including indigenous people and their concerns in the imaginary of the nation-state and beyond.

REFERENCES

Adorno, Theodor W.
    1970 Asthetische Theorie. Gesammelte Schriften, 7. Frankfurt: Suhrkamp.
Anderson, Benedict
    1983 Imagined Communities. Verso: London.
Appadurai, Arjun
    1990 Disjuncture and Difference in the Global Cultural Economy. Public Culture 2(2):1–24.

Batty, Philip
   1993 Singing the Electric: Aboriginal Television in Australia. *In* Channels of Resistance. Tony Dowmunt, ed. Pp. 106–125. London: British Film Institute.
Beckett, Jeremy
   1988 The Past in the Present: The Present in the Past: Constructing a National Aboriginality. *In* Past and Present: The Construction of Aboriginality. Jeremy Beckett, ed. Pp. 191–217. Canberra: Aboriginal Studies Press.
Bürger, Peter
   1984 Theory of the Avant-Garde. Theory and History of Literature, 4. Minneapolis: University of Minnesota Press.
Dutchak, Philip
   1992 Black Screens. Cinema Papers (March–April) 87:48–52.
Ginsburg, Faye
   1991 Indigenous Media: Faustian Contract or Global Village? Cultural Anthropology 6(1): 92–112.
   1993a Aboriginal Media and the Aboriginal Imaginary. Public Culture 5(3):557–578.
   1993b Station Identification: The Aboriginal Programs Unit of the Australian Broadcasting Corporation. *In* Visual Anthropology Review 9(2):92–96.
   1994a Culture and Media: A (Mild) Polemic. Anthropology Today (April): 5–15.
   1994b Production Values: Indigenous Media and the Rhetoric of Self-Determination. *In* The Rhetoric of Self-Making. Deborah Battaglia, ed. University of California Press. Forthcoming.
Hamilton, Annette
   1990 Fear and Desire: Aborigines, Asians, and the National Imaginary. Australian Cultural History 9:14–35.
   1993 Foreword. *In* Well, I Heard It on the Radio and I Saw It on the Television. By Marcia Langton. Pp. 5–7. Sydney: Australia Film Commission.
Langton, Marcia
   1993 Well, I Heard It on the Radio and I Saw It on the Television. Sydney: Australian Film Commission.
Lattas, Andrew
   1991 Nationalism, Aesthetic Redemption, and Aboriginality. The Australian Journal of Anthropology 2(2):307–324.
Leigh, Michael
   1992 Fade to Black: An Introductory Essay. *In* Cultural Focus. Cultural Futures. (Film festival catalogue.) Pp. 1–3. Canberra: Department of Foreign Affairs and Trade.
Michaels, Eric
   1986 Hollywood Iconography: A Warlpiri Reading. Paper presented at the International Television Studies Conference, British Film Institute, London.
   1987a For a Cultural Future: Francis Jupurrurla Makes TV at Yuendumu, Melbourne: Art and Criticism Monograph Series.
   1987b Aboriginal Content: Who's Got It—Who Needs It? Art and Text 23–24:58–79.
   1988 Bad Aboriginal Art. Art and Text 28(March–May):59–73.
Michaels, Eric, and Francis Jupurrurla Kelly
   1984 The Social Organization of an Aboriginal Video Workplace. Australian Aboriginal Studies 1: 26–34.
Molnar, Helen
   1989 Aboriginal Broadcasting in Australia: Challenges and Promises. Paper presented at the International Communication Association Conference, March.

Muecke, Steven
  1992 Textual Spaces: Aboriginality and Cultural Studies, Kensington: New South Wales University Press.
Myers, Fred
  1994 Beyond the Intentional Fallacy: Art Criticism and the Ethnography of Aboriginal Acrylic Painting. Visual Anthropology Review 10(1):10–43.
Nicoll, Fiona
  1993 The Art of Reconciliation: Art, Aboriginality and the State, Meanjin 52(4):705–718.
O'Regan, Tom (with Philip Batty)
  1993 An Aboriginal Television Culture: Issues, Strategies, Politics. *In* Australian Television Culture. Pp. 169–192. St. Leonards, Australia: Allen and Unwin.
Peters, Frances
  1993 Breaking All the Rules. (Interview with Jacqueline Urla.) Visual Anthropology Review 9(2):98–106.
Stanner, W. E. II.
  1956 The Dreaming. *In* Australian Signpost. T. A. G. Hungerford, ed. Pp. 51–65. Melbourne: F. W. Cheshire.
Thiele, Steve
  1991 Taking a Sociological Approach to Europeanness (Whiteness) and Aboriginality (Blackness). The Australian Journal of Anthropology 2(2):179–201.
Trouillot, Michel-Rolph
  1991 Anthropology and the Savage Slot: The Poetics and Politics of Otherness. *In* Recapturing Anthropology. Richard Fox, ed. Pp. 17–44. Santa Fe: School of American Research Press.
Turner, Neil
  1990 Pitchat and Beyond. Artlink 10(1–2):43–45.
Turner, Terence
  1993 Anthropology and Multiculturalism: What Is Anthropology That Multiculuralists Should Be Mindful of It? Cultural Anthropology 8(4):411–429.

Chapter Eighteen

Local, Global, or National?
Popular Music on Indonesian Television

R. Anderson Sutton

In this chapter, I wish to consider how television contributes to the negotiation between local particulars and global cultural flows outside "the West."[1] To what extent can nationwide television broadcasts in Indonesia accommodate local elements in their broadcasts of performing arts, including music, and to what extent can they localize global popular forms? In this chapter I address these questions with reference to popular music broadcasts on Indonesian television. By "popular music" I mean music that is packaged, commercially promoted, and disseminated as a commodity through the mass media and intended primarily as entertainment. The closest term in Indonesian might be *musik komersial* (commercial music), as the loanword *pop*, even in its broadest usage, refers to only one (albeit major) category of popular music, distinguished by elements of musical style from other popular genres.[2]

In Indonesia, as elsewhere, television is expected to connect the viewer with an imagined modernity that, for Indonesians, is foreign-derived, but reinterpreted and refashioned to fit internal needs. Popular music is a major arena for participation in modernity as well, and its prominent place in the programming schedules of all six Indonesian television stations attests to its importance in Indonesian cultural discourse. While Indonesian television offers an array of informational shows (mostly locally produced) and entertainment shows (many produced overseas and subtitled or dubbed), popular music shows represent a substantial portion of the entertainment programming. Many Indonesians hold strong opinions about popular music on television, some decrying its supposed insidious effects on indigenous values and sensibilities, others welcoming it as a source of pleasure whose experience brings Indonesians into Appadurai's "global now" (1996: 2–3).

I consider three sites of popular musical activity on Indonesian television: MTV (music videos from both Indonesian and foreign performers employing predominantly Western idioms), *dangdut* (a national genre, with roots in Indian film music and regional music from Sumatra, only recently and minimally represented on MTV in Indonesia), and *Dua Warna* (Two Colors, a postmodern pastiche of mainstream Indonesian pop and experimental "ethnic" music drawing on assorted Indonesian regional idioms).[3] Each site involves dialogic relations with local and global forces, but in different ways. I will argue here for a view of televised music as both subject to and resistant to global homogenization—subject to it in the pervasive borrowing of aural and visual idioms from abroad, resistant in the incorporation of local performers and visual and aural styles. Countering the arguments warning of global homogenization, Arjun Appadurai writes,

> What these arguments fail to consider is that at least as rapidly as forces from various metropolises are brought into new societies they tend to become indigenized in one or another way; this is true of music and housing styles as much as it is true of science and terrorism, spectacles and constitutions, (Appadurai 1996: 32)

Going a step further, I contend that some instances of what is touted as "local" might best be interpreted as tokenistic—mere ethnic tinge, reinforcing the hegemonic cultural order in which global, Western-based forms dominate. My interest in the popular music on Indonesian television arose during a period of research in 1997-98, when I was studying the representation of what are generally referred to as "traditional" performing arts on this medium. While the newest private station, Indosiar, broadcasts various genres of Javanese and Sundanese "traditional" arts weekly to much of the nation, the other private stations seldom offer traditional arts from any region. It is not economically viable, given the ethnic diversity of their audience and their reliance on advertising revenues. Broadcasts of "traditional" arts on the branches of the national television station, TVRI, range from relatively frequent, for example, in Yogyakarta (Java) and Den Pasar (Bali), to rare, for example, in Makassar (formerly Ujung Pandang, South Sulawesi). Yet all stations, including TVRI, broadcast forms of popular music. We will return briefly to the issue of "traditional" arts on television near the end of this chapter.

Indonesian Television Stations and the Distribution of Popular Music Broadcasts

Each of Indonesia's six stations (five privately owned, one government-owned) has developed a distinctive profile, setting itself off in some way from the others, although none broadcast exclusively one type of programming. Television broadcasting in Indonesia began with the establishment of the national government station, TVRI (Televisi Republik Indonesia) in 1962 in Jakarta. Since then, TVRI has expanded both its reach and its ability to offer local programming through thirteen branch stations around the nation with broadcast and studio production capabilities and nine additional stations with mobile units. Much of the programming, however, has been produced and disseminated nationally, forging and strengthening national unity through shared cultural experience.

For over a quarter century the government prohibited any competition to TVRI, but in the 1980s media laws were relaxed and the era of private, commercial television stations began, with the establishment of RCTI (Rajawali Citra Televisi Indonesia) in 1987. This first private station set itself apart from TVRI by creating a sophisticated image, targeting upper- and upper-middle-class audiences, with flashy productions and a mix of local and foreign programs. A second private station, SCTV (Surya

Citra Televisi), was founded in 1990, first based in Surabaya, but shortly thereafter in Jakarta. SCTV aims at a middle-class audience, especially young adults, with its own mix of local and foreign programs. At first conceived as a more "educational" alternative to either of the first two private stations, TPI (Televisi Pendidikan Indonesia [Indonesian Educational Television]) began broadcasting from Jakarta in 1991. Despite the initial emphasis on education, TPI's offerings have been largely in entertainment, including Indonesian music and dramas, but unlike its competitors it has targeted lower- and lower-middle-class audiences of all ages.

Members of former President Suharto's family have controlling ownership interests in three private stations: Siti Hardiyanti Rukmana (Mbak Tutut) in TPI, and Bambang Trihatmojo and his wife, Halimah, through the Bimantara conglomerate, in RCTI and SCTV. The pattern of ownership—private corporations whose controlling interests are in the hands of the ruling family—contrasts with the patterns found in most Western countries. But despite the deep economic involvement of the Suharto family, broadcast content has not been as strictly controlled as one might suspect. During the political protests against Suharto in May 1998, these private stations, rather than TVRI, brought the protest message to their viewers through relatively uncensored coverage.

The first station to be established and owned by a business interest not controlled by one of President Suharto's children, ANteve (Cakrawala Andalas Televisi), began broadcasting in 1993, with a rather different identity than the other private stations. The name Andalas is a literary term for Sumatra and this new station was conceived as the first station whose main offices and studio would be located in Sumatra (Lampung, South Sumatra)—not only outside Jakarta, but off the main Indonesian island of Java. However, like its competitors, it chose to be located in Jakarta for business reasons. It has emphasized sporting events and popular music among its main offerings, and in 1995 developed a cooperative agreement with MTV Asia, cultivating a "trendy" image and aiming its broadcasts at middle- and upper-class urban youth. The fifth and youngest private station is Indosiar (Indosiar Visual Mandiri), founded in Jakarta in 1995 by the Chinese business tycoon Liem Sioe Liong (Sudono Salim). Indosiar broadcasts a range of talk shows, dramas, and regional arts—mostly popular and commercial Javanese theatrical arts and other local content shows. It targets a wide audience and has won a dedicated following among many of the majority Javanese and Sundanese, whose traditional arts are featured regularly. This station also occasionally broadcasts regional popular music (*pop daerah*).

Terrestrial broadcast is by far the dominant mode of signal distribution. In the mid-1970s Indonesia began to use satellite technology (Palapa) to disseminate the TVRI signal to relay stations on various of Indonesia's many islands. Now there is a small but growing economic elite that own satellite dishes, downlinking CNN, TV Cinque, MTV Asia, and several Star channels, among others. Cable service is available in some districts of Jakarta, and there are plans for expansion there and in large cities (such as Surabaya), but it is expensive and still rare.

Indonesian television broadcast time was cut substantially after the beginning of the financial crisis in late 1997. As of mid-2000 several stations were broadcasting at all times except from late evening (post-midnight) to early morning (predawn). One can almost always find, on at least one of these stations, one or more popular music shows. ANteve, in particular, devotes enormous blocks of time to pop music shows, some produced by the ANteve staff, many produced by MTV Southeast Asia (and formerly by MTV Asia), and all of which, regardless of the national identity of the performers, employ the styles and idioms of Western popular music—rock, country, R&B, and rap. TPI emphasizes the throbbing sounds of Indonesia's widely popular *dangdut* genre, which is also featured in several shows on Indosiar, but only beginning to be heard on the other private stations.[4] RCTI and others have produced and broadcast glitzy shows in which top-selling pop music stars perform in collaboration with performers of what is now being called *musik etnik* (ethnic music)—music using instruments, scales, or styles of traditional music, primarily but not exclusively Indonesian.

How pervasive are music shows on contemporary Indonesian television? If we include those shows that mix banter with music videos, we find that in a total of 677.6 hours of broadcast on Indonesia's six stations from August 5 to August 11, 1998 (a typical recent week), 85.6 hours (12.6 percent) were music shows. These figures do not include the additional hours devoted to "traditional" arts (mainly on TVRI and Indosiar), one- to two-hour specials devoted to popular music (aired occasionally on all stations), nor do they include Indian movies, which are almost always musicals. The distribution of popular music broadcasts is uneven. ANteve devotes twenty-eight hours, or 24.1 percent of its weekly schedule, to music shows; TPI is not far behind with twenty-three hours, 18 percent of its weekly schedule. The choice of programming is, of course, driven by market considerations, weighing viewer tastes against costs. The cost to television stations of the music shows they broadcast varies widely. Those produced by a station for its own exclusive broadcast can be quite expensive, but music video programs may represent additional sources of income for the station (beyond fees for commercial advertisements), as recording companies pay fees to have some videos aired.

Both Sides Now: MTV on Indonesian Television

By far the most pervasive form of musical presentation on Indonesian television is the single-song music video—represented worldwide on music shows broadcast on MTV. Music videos (or video "clips"—the Indonesian term, from English, is *klip video* or *klip* for short) are seen regularly on all Indonesian stations and are routinely used to fill time between shows, in lieu of commercials.[5] Single-song videos, with singers lip-synching the lyrics and appearing in various scenes, have been seen on Indonesian television for several decades.[6] The style and content of recent videos, however, bear the unmistakable mark of American music videos seen on MTV.

MTV has a major presence in Indonesia today. Beginning in 1991, satellite dish (*parabola*) owners in Indonesia were able to view shows produced by MTV when it was part of the Star TV platform, with headquarters in Hong Kong. MTV was attracted to Asia particularly "because it included several countries like India and Indonesia that were increasingly open to commercial media ventures" (Banks 1996:

99). In 1994 MTV broke away from Star TV and set up offices in Singapore, where on May 5, 1995, it was launched as MTV Networks Asia (personal communication, Shabnam Melwani, MTV Asia, 10 September 1998). For the first eight months, this office managed two twenty-four-hour satellite programming services: MTV Mandarin (for Taiwan, Hong Kong, and mainland China) and MTV Asia (primarily for India, Indonesia, Singapore, Thailand, and the Philippines). In January 1996, realizing that tastes in South Asia were rather different from those in Southeast or East Asia, MTV added a third twenty-four-hour satellite programming service, MTV India, with extensive offerings of Indian film and pop music artists. In January 1999 MTV Asia reorganized as MTV Southeast Asia (twenty-four-hour), with a separate five-hour satellite service for MTV Korea. MTV shows can now be seen in Indonesia on the twenty-four-hour MTV channel carried on the satellite Palapa-C2, and over the air on ANteve, which in 1995 worked out a cooperative, revenue-sharing agreement with MTV Asia to broadcast a bloc of MTV shows.

Many of the videos are American, European, or Australian, but the MTV shows themselves are conceived and produced in Southeast Asia—in Singapore and Indonesia. Indeed, the plurality of networks (MTV Southeast Asia, MTV India, etc.) is MTV's market-driven strategy to localize its global product. Video jockeys (VJs) speak on some shows entirely in English, on others in a mix of English and Indonesian, and on the newest shows almost entirely in Indonesian. The shows with English-language announcing are broadcast as such via satellite, but for ANteve broadcast these are taped, subtitled in Indonesian, and broadcast a week later. In 1998 and 1999 three Indonesian VJs (all fluent in English as well as Indonesian) lived and worked in Singapore; two others worked in Jakarta, announcing Indonesian MTV shows in Indonesian, with only occasional short phrases in English ("now listen up"; "or something like that, anyway"; "well, that's it"), as if to legitimize the show as part of MTV's global kingdom. The use of English for the satellite channel is intended to make the broadcasts accessible to viewers in areas outside Indonesia (all the countries covered by MTV Southeast Asia), and to give these shows a trendy, international feel, playing on documented preferences of Indonesia's urban middle- and upper-class youth.

The videos played on MTV shows may be all or mostly of Western groups, but they are selected for (and sometimes by) Asian audiences. *MTV Asia Hitlist*, for example, presents a countdown of the top twenty videos, based on sales figures and viewer polls in MTV Southeast Asia's targeted countries (Malaysia, Singapore, the Philippines, and Thailand, in addition to Indonesia). The list often consists entirely of Western artists; Asian artists rarely make the top twenty. Yet there are numerous shows that offer either a mix of Indonesian and foreign artists or exclusively Indonesian artists, including several shows seen only on ANteve. The foreign artists are almost entirely Western; very rarely are other Asian artists seen on MTV in Indonesia, except by satellite. And the trend, as MTV follows its recent and much heralded "Go Local" strategy, is for viewers in one Asian country to see fewer artists and shows from other Asian countries than they could during the first several years of MTV Networks Asia (1995–1997). Satellite reception constitutes an increasingly significant part of the market in much of Asia, allowing viewers in each target country to see shows announced by VJs and featuring music videos from other target countries. Indeed, MTV programming on satellite clearly contributes to the internationalization of *pop Indonesia*, broadcasting a number of the Indonesian shows that play at least some Indonesian videos.

Three regular shows present videos by Indonesian performers only: *MTV 100% Indonesia* (produced in Jakarta), *MTV Ampuh* (an acronym for *Ajang Musik Pribumi Sepuluh*—the top ten Indonesian hits of the week), and *Salam Dangdut* (featuring the Indonesian hybrid genre *dangdut*). All three of these shows are announced entirely in Indonesian, except for the occasional phrase in English. The opening segment of *MTV Ampuh* consists of a young "modern" Indonesian couple, dressed in hip, Western clothes, seemingly on the run from several characters from Balinese and Javanese theatrical traditions—monkey characters as in Javanese dance drama (*wayang orang*) and the terrifying Balinese witch, Rangda. The segment ends with one of the demon kings triumphantly holding up a tablet, which then transforms into the show's title: *Ampuh* (meaning "magically powerful," or "potent," in Indonesian and Javanese).[7] *MTV Ampuh* continues the Balinese reference by incorporating brief phrases of *gamelan* music during each countdown. Since the shows feature Indonesian VJs, who introduce and play music videos by Indonesian pop groups, this show certainly has "local" content, even though the casual, youth culture style is typically (and deliberately) MTV-style global.

A video that won the Viewers' Choice award for MTV Asia in 1998, "Kala Cinta Menggoda" (When Love Tempts), was performed by the Indonesian pop superstar Chrisye. Explicit in its references to local culture, the video portrays young, rich, urban Indonesians at a masquerade party, all of them wearing distinctly Javanese masks. In this case, the reference is not to Indonesian "national culture," but to one of Indonesia's many "local" or "regional" cultures (Javanese). In another of Chrisye's videos, "Untukku" (For You), Javanese shadow puppets and Javanese female court dancers appear prominently, though not in the context of traditional performance.

Thus, even on the MTV viewed in Indonesia—the most "global" of the three approaches to televised music considered in this chapter—local input is evident at a number of levels. At the most general, the tastes of Asian viewers determine content on some shows. And Indonesian input abounds, from the VJ banter in Indonesian to the inclusion of Indonesian videos, entire shows devoted to Indonesian groups playing Western-style pop with Indonesian words (*MTV Ampuh* and *MTV 100% Indonesia*), some music videos whose visual content explicitly references local culture, and, most recently, even an entire show devoted to what is now considered a distinctly Indonesian genre (*MTV Salam Dangdut*).

While local and global content is negotiated within Indonesian MTV, many artists who appear frequently in American and European MTV broadcasts are excluded from the shows seen by Indonesian viewers, especially those shown terrestrially on ANteve. As in the early days of MTV in the United States, African American artists appear relatively seldom; and those who do are mostly those who perform the softest varieties of soul, R&B, and, rarely, rap.[8] Western videos by heavy metal groups celebrating wildness and rebellion are also absent, due not only to government censorship, but to notions widely shared by decision makers across the Indonesian television industry concerning the tastes and tolerance of the Indonesian viewing public.

Also excluded are some major genres of Indonesian popular music. *Pop daerah*, popular songs in regional languages (Javanese, Minang, etc.), are not included on MTV shows, though TVRI and Indosiar broadcast entire shows devoted to the genre. The other glaring omission until March 1999, by carefully weighed decision, was the enormously popular but still déclassé genre known as *dangdut*. In an August 1998 interview Daniel Tumiwa, marketing head for MTV in Indonesia, said he was intrigued with the idea of MTV "experimenting" with *dangdut*. He thought it very unlikely that MTV would incorporate this genre, however, since the music had associations with unsophisticated, lower-class Indonesians and this might tarnish the network's image. Yet eight months later, MTV Southeast Asia launched *MTV Salam Dangdut*, a weekly half-hour show devoted to *dangdut*. When I asked Tumiwa in August 1999 about this rather bold change in direction, he said that MTV was making efforts to "go local" and this was one of them. Yet the VJ Jamie Aditya (James Adityawarman Graham, b. 1970) treated this music with humor and parodic disdain, dressing and talking in a mocking imitation of lower-class Indonesian youth. At the same time, the producers have chosen only the most sophisticated videos for MTV, rejecting many of the cheaply produced, fuzzy, romantic or hip-grinding videos seen on other channels (especially TPI). This has enabled MTV to seek entry into a wider market of Indonesian youth (who like *dangdut*, but not some forms of Western pop) and to proclaim a new level of commitment to "local culture" (rather than flooding Indonesia with what locals consider polluting Western popular culture), and yet maintain its image of sophistication through the ironic posturing of the VJ.

MTV has adopted marketing strategies that give *pop Indonesia* (defined as a category of Indonesian popular music that conforms most closely to international pop expectations in musical style and ethos) and even *dangdut* a greater international platform, while making Western popular music more accessible to Indonesians. Indonesian VJs in Singapore interact with Western performers who appear on their shows. Sarah Sechan interviewed the British threesome 911 as MTV Asia's artist(s) of the month in August 1998, showing them interacting in a personable, informal, but respectful way with a young Indonesian VJ.[9] And international stars, such as Australian Natalie Imbruglia, utter a few well-practiced words of Indonesian as they beseech their Indonesian audiences on promotional ads to "nongkrong bersama saya di MTV" (hang out with me on MTV).

Recent surveys indicate that MTV reaches some 16 million households in Indonesia, that MTV shows are watched by 80 percent of urban Indonesian youth at least once a week, 33 percent watching at least some MTV every day (personal interview, Daniel Tumiwa, Jakarta Office of MTV, 10 August 1998). MTV is not just global or globalizing, however—it is also national, promoting those Indonesian artists who exclude regional elements (language, musical instruments, scales, forms, etc.) from their music, but who in turn may incorporate more specific, local elements in the visual dimension of their videos. In the case of MTV Southeast Asia, local may mean national, or even transnational within the region. The network has developed a marketing approach that skillfully blends and juxtaposes elements of the global and the local. As the media specialist Arif Dirlik notes,

> The radical slogan of an earlier day, "Think globally, act locally," has been assimilated by transnational corporations with far greater success than in any radical strategy. The recognition of the local in marketing strategy, however, does not mean any serious recognition of the autonomy of the local, but is intended to recognize the features of the local so as to incorporate localities in the imperatives of the global. (Dirlik 1996: 34)

MTV Networks Asia would seem to be no exception, but in Indonesia, at least, the extent of local determination suggests a more complex (and perhaps less bleak) view than Dirlik provides.

Class Act: Dangdut *on Indonesian Television*

Dangdut is Indonesia's de facto national music, derived from a mix of indigenous North Sumatran features with influences from Indian films, Arabic popular musics, and Western rock. But because of its popularity with the lower echelons of Indonesian society, the erotic nature of its beat, lyrics, and videos, and its association with Islam, stations cultivating a "sophisticated" audience (ANteve and RCTI) have avoided *dangdut*. Until 1999, MTV Asia did as well. Championed by East Javanese governor Basofi Soedirman and by former secretary of state Moerdiono, who has publicly described *dangdut* as "very Indonesian" *(sangat Indonesia)* (Simatupang 1996: 109), this music carries a different ethos than most of the Western-style Indonesian *pop* shown on MTV and other stations. This makes it no less problematic as a "national music" than is "country music" in the United States (associated as it is with a less sophisticated rural, and now lower-and lower-middle-class urban, white subculture). Yet *dangdut*'s popularity, on television as well as in cassette sales, demonstrates the firm place this genre holds among the Indonesian populace. The genre may sound Indian or Arabic in some ways, but is, as Hatch and others point out, clearly not Western in its sound (despite its reliance on mostly Western instruments: electric guitars, bass, keyboards, and drum set, and Indian *tabla* or *dangdut* drum). *Dangdut* enjoys some popularity in neighboring Malaysia, where Indonesian *dangdut* recordings sung by Malaysian artists are sold (Theodore 1996). MTV Networks Asia's Web site (www.mtvasia.com) describes *dangdut* as an Indonesian/Malaysian form, stressing its international presence. It also has imitators in Japan (Sandii Suzuki) and the Philippines (Maribeth), but lacks the international appeal of Celtic, African, or mainstream Western popular musics. For most listeners, it is still an Indonesian music, likened by Moerdiono to the nation itself: "from the people, by the people, for the people" (*dari rakyat, oleh rakyat, untuk rakyat*; *rakyat* is often used to identify the common people as distinct from the elite) (Simatupang 1996: 110).

Dangdut videos tend to stress the erotic, with the artists' hips gyrating irresistibly to the beat. Many of the newcomers to this genre in the video era have been young, attractive female singers, whose videos easily find a male audience. Most of the

Iwan, with futuristic dancers, music video for "Yang Sedong-sedang Saja." Shot from *In Dangdut*, broadcast on TPI on January 5, 1998. Text across the bottom of the screen is the first line of the song (and also its title), which translates as "[someone] Who's Just Average."

popular male *dangdut* singers are older men such as A. Rafiq, Meggy Z., and Mansyur S., whose videos are less likely to satisfy the romantic fantasies of consumers than those of younger singers. Many videos show the singer dressed in garb inspired by Indian film stars, usually romantically engaged with a young member of the opposite sex, whether happily or tragically. *Dangdut* videos in the last few years have become increasingly sophisticated, with MTV-inspired narratives and dreamlike discontinuities, moving away from the basic hip-grinding shots of the artist on stage (or as if on stage) to romantic vignettes, set in sylvan parks, luxurious mansions, or futuristic landscapes.

Many *dangdut* videos, in fact, cater to the male gaze by featuring attractive women and erotic dance movements. A video by the *dangdut* singer Iwan called "Yang Sedang-sedang Saja" ([Someone] Who's Just Average), for instance, features the male singer exclaiming, "she is not beautiful, she is not ugly, she's just average." What matters is that she is devoted/faithful, and his love for her is deeper than the Indian Ocean. The video opens with shots of the planets, then zooms to a close-up of Saturn and its rings. Iwan then appears in various sets with six dancers. As their costumes change from Indonesian batik dresses to spacesuits, the background shifts from one of green ooze to what looks like an asteroid shower as the dancers and Iwan appear to be moving through the galaxy.

Despite the identification of *dangdut* as "very Indonesian," the visual content of this music video portrays dancers with futuristic spacesuit-inspired costumes, planets, asteroids, galaxies, and other space references. The only hints at local culture are the few brief cuts of dancers in Indonesian batik. Indeed, many *dangdut* videos seem, in varying ways, to provide the viewer with a fantasy that intentionally removes the viewer from his or her local reality, whether it be through the depiction of luxury living (in Jakarta or wherever) or, here, outer space.

Those involved with *dangdut* programming at Indosiar told me in August 1998 that they altered *dangdut*'s image in order to make it more appealing to a broader Indonesian audience. This was good for *dangdut*, they said, and good for Indosiar in its quest for a broad spectrum of Indonesia's viewers. Their weekly hour-long show *Dangdut Ria* (Happy *Dangdut*), produced in a studio with artists present rather than as a series of videos, has a different theme each week, in a conscious—and often humorous—attempt to break with the usual image. Among other recent themes, which have included a New Year's celebration and even *wayang orang* (with artists dressed as characters from the Mahabharata and Ramayana epics in the style of Javanese *wayang orang* dance theater), I saw an hour devoted to a Mexican theme (9 August 1998). In this episode male performers were decked out in sombreros and ponchos and female performers wore Mexican lace or peasant tops and long skirts, and they were all on a stage depicting an old Mexican village, under a banner that read "Perkampungan Mexidhut" (Mexican Dangd[h]ut Village/Barrio). The host arrived by horse, dressed as Zorro, and called the hostess "señorita." Interspersed between humorous announcing and a range of *dangdut* songs were a short educational segment on varieties of Mexican cacti and cooking tips on chicken *fajitas* by the owner of a Mexican restaurant in Jakarta. This seems to be not an attempt to internationalize the genre—making it appeal to a Latin American audience—but rather an attempt to erase entrenched associations held by Indonesians about *dangdut* through ethnic caricature. (What could be less Islamic than a Mexican village?) The humorous elements in this and other *Dangdut Ria* programs reinforce their appeal to a broad Indonesian audience, while keeping them from the pretentious realm of international-style *pop Indonesia*.

Dangdut is not trendy, does not give its viewers a finger on the pulse of the world, of the global now. It is neither "traditional" nor "regional"; but neither is it "modern" in the same way that the more Western forms of *pop* are. Its use of electronic instruments and its strong presence in the electronic mass media (broadcast and recording) give it sufficient trappings of modernity for many Indonesians. It ties them in with modern entertainment technology because it is so unambiguously theirs in ways that *pop Indonesia*, which constantly shifts in imitation of international trends, is not. *Dangdut* is modern and local (as opposed to global), thereby challenging the too-facile dichotomy between traditional/regional/non-Western on the one hand and modern/international/Western on the other. *Dangdut* is not yet global, despite its popularity in Malaysia and its few imitators elsewhere, and the willingness of MTV Southeast Asia to experiment with a whole program devoted to *dangdut*, albeit presented within an ironic, ambivalent frame. Its presentation on Indonesian television contributes to its strong identity as a national music—incorporating some

Noer Halimah, with *dangdut* instrumentalists, dressed in Mexican peasant outfits, performing "Tanda Cinta." Shot from *Dangdut Ria*, broadcast on Indosiar, August 9, 1998. Text across the bottom of the screen translates as "Mexican Dangd[h]ut Village/Barrio."

foreign elements, but at the same time maintaining, through its cultivation of an "Eastern" style, resistance to the oft-feared onslaught of globalization.

Indigenized Exoticism: Dua Warna *on Indonesian Television*

The third site I would like to consider as part of Indonesia's television broadcast of popular music comes from *Dua Warna* (Two Colors), a program produced on the elite private station RCTI. This show features top-name popular musicians who perform pop songs in a glitzy studio, not only with their usual electric guitars, electronic keyboards and drum sets, but also with an ensemble of various non-electronic, non-Western, mostly Indonesian instruments. These Indonesian instruments are played by members of Kua Etnika (short for *kualitas etnika*, literally "ethnic quality" but also interpreted as *qua etnika*—"as if ethnic"), a group directed by Djaduk Ferianto, a veritable "ethnic music sensation" of the mid- and late 1990s.[10] One of the sons of Bagong Kussudiardjo, the famous Javanese dancer, choreographer, teacher, and arts manager extraordinaire, Djaduk grew up in the Javanese court-city Yogyakarta, in close contact with the music and dance not only of Java, but of the many other Indonesian regional traditions represented in his father's schools (see

Sutton 1991: 218). His Kua Etnika consists of nine or ten young male musicians, all Indonesian, specifically, Javanese (two are from Bali, one from North Sumatra). They play a range of instruments, including *gamelan* instruments of Java, Bali, and Sunda, drums from Java, Bali, Sunda, South Sulawesi, Ghana, and the West, boat-lutes from North Sumatra, South Sulawesi, and Kalimantan, bamboo flutes from various parts of the archipelago and Japan, a seemingly limitless variety of bamboo idiophones, and electronic keyboards.

Several producers at RCTI (Dradjat Usdianto, Jay Soebiakto, and Duto Sulistiadi) concocted the idea of combining pop music with more traditional and regional sounds. However, this is hardly new in Indonesia. There has been synthesis between Javanese music and Western music as early as the mid-nineteenth century. Anyone with access to Indonesia's mass media since the 1970s should be aware of the music of Guruh Soekarnoputra, the son of Indonesia's first president (Soekarno), who composed and arranged rock music with very obvious Balinese musical elements. Yet the RCTI idea, which took the name *Dua Warna*, was conceived to avoid representing one single Indonesian ethnic group over others. Djaduk, although Javanese, was well-versed in a range of Indonesian instruments and musical styles. He experimented with new musical patterns instead of repackaging existing traditional styles. To work on the arrangements, RCTI also enlisted the commitment of an American-trained electronic musician-composer-arranger, Aminoto Kosin, who told me in an interview (8 August 1998) that he had no real interest in Indonesia's regional traditions as such, had not studied them, but found it interesting trying to come up with an effective synthesis. Raharja, one of the Javanese musicians in Kua Etnika for the first three shows, noted to me that Aminoto would typically give Djaduk the basic framework of a song—its rhythm, melody, and form—asking Djaduk and his musicians to work up an accompaniment that fit. He would then add the pop instrumental arrangement, seldom seeking very substantial changes in what Djaduk and his musicians came up with (Raharja, personal communication, 1 October 1998).

The results of the collaboration between these two arrangers have been seen on five ninety-minute shows produced and broadcast by RCTI during evening prime time—twice on Indonesian Independence day (August 17, 1996 and 1997), and most recently on January 2, 1998. It is clear that the *pop* predominates over the *etnik*, particularly in the aural dimension. Javanese and Balinese pitched metallophone instruments (*saron* and *gendèr*) are retuned from the indigenous intervallic structures of *sléndro* and *pélog* to conform with the Western scale used by the pop musicians; drumming and other percussion patterns are tailored to support, rather than alter, the established rhythms of the pop musicians. Musical forms are not those of indigenous songs or pieces of any Indonesian region, but those typical of international pop music. In short, the *etnik* musical elements must work around the pop, and nearly all compromises are made by Djaduk and his ensemble. Philip Yampolsky's observations on the less prestigious genres grouped under the rubric *pop daerah* (regional pop), which use nearly all the idioms of *pop Indonesia* and whose main distinction from *pop Indonesia* is the use of regional languages rather than Indonesian, aptly describes the music of *Dua Warna*:

it is clear that in these encounters between Pop Indonesia and regional musics, Pop "wins" musically. One or two or even several symbols of the regional music may be present, but they bring no coherent or compelling message from outside. They are wholly subordinated to Pop, decorating the edges or the backgrounds. (Yampolsky 1989: 15)

When the show aired there was remarkable imbalance in the sound mix. Frequent shots of Djaduk and his musicians hammering away on Javanese or Balinese metallophones or beating various Indonesian drums appeared, but their sounds were barely audible. Two of the producers involved (Yogi Hartarto, 7 January 1998; and Dradjat Usdianto, 11 August 1998) informed me that the sound technician had kept the playback levels low for Djaduk's musicians in the final mix for fear of obscuring the pop singers and their pop accompaniment. They felt that a more balanced mix would have disappointed viewers and led to lower ratings. Duto Sulistiadi, executive manager for special events on RCTI, even expressed concern that this show might mess up Indonesia's music industry ("akan mengganggu industri musik di negeri kita") (*Republika*, 2 January 1998: 19). Yet there was clear agreement that, at least for RCTI viewers, too much "ethnic" music in the mix would have been disastrous.

Another indication of the unfulfilled promise of a successful musical mix was evident in the visual style, which showed members of Kua Etnika responding to each other's playing, but being largely ignored by the pop musicians. Only during the instrumental numbers—Western pieces such as Dave Brubeck's "Blue Rondo à la Turk" (2 January 1998) and "Mission Impossible" (17 August 1997)—do musicians of both "colors" seem to interact at all. The studio set and camera work for most numbers have been essentially the same: three or four cameras, nearly always in motion, show the pop star, his or her group, as the main attraction, with Djaduk and his group featured more at the beginning and at the end. The *Dua Warna* performance on January 2, 1998, of "Sang Nayaga" (The Venerable [traditional] Musician) by the very popular group Gigi ("tooth") and its outlandish Mick Jaggerish lead singer, Armand Maulana, was as typical as any. The song tells of traditional musicians (*nayaga*), who are no longer much appreciated in contemporary Indonesia. Only their instruments (frame drums, in this case) keep them company; their lives are increasingly lonely. This was already widely known as a hit song from Gigi's fourth album, 2×2 (released in 1997).

The set at the RCTI studio has dry ice producing occasional smoke or mist, musicians arrayed on platforms, a small audience seated on the floor, grass (possibly artificial), and Papuan totem sculptures. This number begins with a long instrumental introduction, during which we see a close-up of Purwanto playing the Javanese *rebab* (two-string fiddle) and other Kua Etnika members playing *bonang* (gong-chime) and large hanging gongs, then three members playing *rebana* (frame drums). Amidst lots of dry-ice smoke, Armand Maulana stands by a microphone. After a short shot of Kua Etnika members playing Javanese *saron* (metal-keyed instruments), lights flash on Armand briefly and the camera shifts to Dewa Budjana, Gigi's virtuosic lead guitar player. As we see another cameraman in a quick pan of these musicians, Armand jumps (literally) to Gigi's bass player, Opet Alatas. Armand cavorts with Dewa and with the drummer, Budhy Haryono. The camera shifts back to Kua Etnika, showing *saron* players at a forty-five-degree angle, then back to a close-up of Armand, whose face contorts as he sings. We then see a low-angle shot through tall grass (possibly artificial) that forms part of the studio set and we see a bird's-eye view of the drummer, Budhy. The camera then pans across musicians seated at the *saron* instruments, playing *rebana*. Djaduk Ferianto grooves as he plays a double-headed drum, then the camera focuses on Dewa for his guitar break, alternating between his calm face and his fluid hands. Armand then appears, kneeling. From behind the Kua Etnika instruments we see Djaduk on drum, alternating with an overhead shot of Budhy on trap set. During a long instrumental coda, Djaduk is again the focus, playing several drums, followed by a Kua Etnika musician playing *tarompet* (West Javanese double-reed). As the piece ends, Armand alone takes a bow and the small audience claps.

The visual references to local culture are obvious to most Indonesian viewers: Javanese *gamelan* instruments (*saron, bonang, rebab*); Indonesian frame drums associated with Islamic music (*rebana*); various Indonesian drums; Kua Etnika dressed in modified traditional Javanese dress; Papuan sculpture. But the main focus of attention, the pop singers and groups such as Gigi, play Western rock instruments (guitar, bass, drums), augmented by two electronic keyboard players. The premise of the show is the mixture of Indonesian pop with indigenous musical elements. Yet the choices made in the visual editing, like those in the audio mix, emphasize the pop, devoting most attention to the pop star (here Armand), and focusing on Djaduk and his group mostly in the instrumental introduction and coda. The rationale is that viewers will be more fascinated to see Armand prance and contort à la Mick Jagger than to see Djaduk and his group playing their instruments, seated on the ground.

According to producers, the use of "ethnic music" at RCTI was a sincere gesture to stimulate musical creativity, which turned into a more clearly commercial venture than was first envisioned. In the current economic crisis, however, RCTI has cancelled production of *Dua Warna*, though in August 2000 it produced a similar mix, involving Djaduk and Kua Etnika with arrangers and keyboardists Aminoto Kosin and Erwin Gutawa, a string orchestra, and various pop stars. I point this out not to criticize the producers, but to stress the extent to which the norms of *pop* clearly rule in the context of a national mass media such as television. In the area of radio and cassettes, which can and do operate on smaller scales and in particular locales, regional traditions fare comparatively better.

Dua Warna has participated in the dialogue between global and local. Here we have music that is inspired by multiple levels of global impact, and yet draws on local elements to create a self-consciously "less Western" sound and image than *pop Indonesia*: (1) the persistent impact of Western popular music in many (though not all) of its stylistic manifestations, and (2) the aesthetic impact of recent commercial world music/world beat, which exploits identifiably exotic/"ethnic" musical sounds in combination with established popular musical sounds and idioms. This music hopes to be newly "Indonesian," hence, national (or local as distinct from global), and in terms of its mostly sophisticated audience it has succeeded. But analytically I suggest that it is much more in the spirit of Western taste for an exotic tinge—

which fuels the world music/world beat market—than is either the *pop Indonesia* presented on MTV or the *dangdut* presented in videos and televised stage shows. In fact, this show represents, in explicit musical terms, the ongoing struggle between global and local forms and demonstrates the triumph of the Western popular idiom over any and all local Indonesian traditions, contrary to its creators' claims. The *gamelan* instruments are tuned to Western scale, and lightly decorate the contours and chords of the popular songs presented. The drums and other non-pitched percussion instruments fall into line, musically speaking, to enhance the backbeat and predictable syncopations. The result is pop music with an "ethnic flavor" (*nuansa etnik*). The very fact that the term "ethnic" (*etnik*) is now widespread in the discourse about Indonesian regional musical traditions, including prominently the discourse about this television show, is indicative of the marginalized space accorded these various traditions among popular musicians and, most importantly here, television producers.

Conclusion

Indonesian television is not a one-way medium in the flow of global cultural forms. Certainly the private stations, particularly ANteve with its MTV shows, fill the airwaves with great quantities of foreign pop music, just as multinational recording companies keep a ready supply of foreign pop music on the shelves of cassette stores throughout the country. But unlike the cassette stores, where the commodity sits on the shelf until it is bought, the foreign commodities presented in the form of videos on MTV are talked about by Indonesian VJs, foreign stars are interviewed, and the music is made to seem as if it "belongs" in Indonesia. Furthermore, both MTV Southeast Asia and MTV Asia have incorporated a growing number of videos of Indonesian pop musicians, placing them in the same trendy context as the big-name foreign stars, and giving them unprecedented exposure throughout the region. To a surprising extent, these broadcasts attempt both to glamorize *pop Indonesia* as a viable genre on par with the music of world-famous pop stars, and to de-exoticize these world-famous pop stars by making them familiar.

Dangdut has enjoyed television coverage for many years, which has undoubtedly contributed to its enormous popularity and its status as a "national" music; but programming has also tended to segregate it from other forms of popular music, particularly Western and Western-inspired pop. A genre that has numerous international influences, but a circumscribed audience, still mostly Indonesian lower- and lower-middle-class, *dangdut* is a "local" music in a very different sense than Javanese *karawitan* (*gamelan* music) or Minangkabau *saluang* (bamboo flute)—Indonesia's regional musics. Yet, from an international perspective, whether global or Asian, it is very much a "local" music, one that resists the hegemonic forces of Western pop, even as it paradoxically employs some of the stylistic features of Western pop, particularly in instrumentation (cf. Taylor 1997: 85). That at least some of Indonesia's national television stations devote airtime to *dangdut* has certainly contributed to the ongoing vitality of this music despite its problematic class associations.

In contrast, *Dua Warna* is not a broad genre of music, but simply a musical experiment, packaged in glitzy production and given prime airtime on Indonesia's upper-crust station. Its negotiation of local, global, and national forces is especially complex and contradictory, for in its self-conscious quest to Indonesianize *pop Indonesia* by combining it with various regional musical elements, it exoticizes the indigenous and champions the Western. The producers may be right that their viewers are not yet ready to accept greater exposure to indigenous musical traditions, that their insatiable taste for Western-style pop would have them turn off anything that represented a more even blend. I cannot deny that some form of dialogue is taking place here, with local elements working their way into the musical fabric of *pop Indonesia*. Yet it strikes viewers as a confirmation of the supremacy in Indonesia now of Western-style pop, and the subservient, marginal/exotic position of indigenous regional traditions and experimental music made on traditional instruments. No matter how radical or original, music made on these instruments is still perceived as "traditional" because it does not conform in sound or image to what is perceived to be "modern."

Placing local elements amidst musical symbols of modernity simultaneously contextualizes the global, making it more possible for Indonesians to feel a part of modernity, and legitimizes "local" (regional/traditional) cultural expression as compatible with the modern. Localness—representations of elements of Indonesian or Javanese or Minangkabau identities—abounds on Indonesian television in the late 1990s. Yet these elements are increasingly separated from the larger core of local cultural practice; they become arbitrarily exploited "nuances"—not quite the free-floating simulacra seen by Baudrillard to characterize much of the postmodern, mediatized world, but certainly signifiers no longer bound exclusively to particular localized interpretations. I have not considered the instances—albeit relatively few—of "traditional arts" on Indonesian television. Certainly there, too, much is changed as they are presented on television, not least the whole context of audience apprehension. What I have tried to argue here is that globalization, which would seem to be so readily promoted by national television, particularly when it goes into partnership with a transnational corporation such as MTV, is both aided and resisted by Indonesia's music television broadcasts.

It is important to bear in mind that Indonesian government policy has long been wary of globalization. Indonesia under Soekarno banned Western rock and roll during the latter part of his presidency (throughout the early 1960s). During the thirty-two years of Suharto's presidency, although Western popular music and local imitations were no longer banned outright, state discourse, from the president to small village officials, constantly warned of the aesthetic and moral dangers of excessive exposure to Western popular culture at the expense of local expression. The various branches of the national television station incorporate regional shows, including music, as part of cultural policy. And all stations, private and public, are by law supposed to limit their broadcast of foreign material to 30 percent of their broadcast day, even though this is neither fully observed nor strictly enforced. But as we have seen, the question of identity in popular music broadcasts is complex, constantly negotiating between these facile opposites. Language, video images, musical instruments, and vocal style provide "Indonesian-ness" in television broadcasts of popular music—transforming the local and continually engaging the global, now accommodating, now challenging. This engagement, of course, is not limited to the realm of broadcast, but it is evident there in high resolution. If culture is contested, as many now argue, then television—music television—seems a very good way to watch—and hear—that contestation unfold, in Indonesia as much as anywhere else in the world.

NOTES

I would like to thank the many people who have contributed to this essay, providing everything from raw scheduling data and promotional materials to extended discussions of media history and musical aesthetics. Many in the television industry spoke with me, often at length, concerning a range of issues covered in this essay. In particular, I would like to mention George (Chossie) Kumontoy at TPI; Yayang, Rusman Latief, Eka Prathika, and Wishnutama at Indosiar; Niniek Sidawati and Bambang Winarso at TVRI Jakarta; Anggit Hernowo, Yogi Hartarto, Dradjat Usdianto, and Ietje Komar at RCTI; Adhi Massardi and especially Amalia Ahmad at ANteve. At MTV in Jakarta, thanks to Bianca Adinegoro, "Bim-bom," and especially Daniel Tumiwa and Muthia Farida. And at MTV Singapore, thanks to Shabnam Melwani, who responded to my many questions via email. I am particularly grateful to Daniel Tumiwa and Amalia Ahmad for staying in touch by email, answering questions large and small as they have arisen. In addition, I appreciate the extended conversations concerning popular music on television that I had with the following: the *Dua Warna* music arrangers Aminoto Kosin and Djaduk Ferianto; the Kua Etnika musician Raharja; the anthropologists Lono Simatupang, Budi Susanto, and Made Tony Supriyatno; and my doctoral students in ethnomusicology, the composer and music critic Franki Raden, and the "creative pop" singer and teacher Nyak Ina (Ubiet) Raseuki.

1. Television in Indonesia and many countries in Asia and Africa is far more centralized than it is in the United States. In contrast, other media, such as commercial audiocassettes, are often produced by small, locally based companies in these countries. See, for example, Manuel 1993 on India, and Sutton 1985 on Indonesia. And while a few music television shows in Indonesia provide opportunities for viewer requests (via fax, email, letter, or occasionally telephone), it remains predominantly a one-way flow of communication, from the broadcaster to the viewing audience.

2. Hatch posits three main categories, each with subcategories: "Almost all *pop* songs sound recognizably western in ways that almost all *kroncong* and *dangdut* songs do not" (1989: 590). (*Kroncong* is a broad category of music characterized by acoustical string accompaniment with particular rhythmic configurations involving interplay of off-beat patterns. It has Portuguese roots, but has been indigenized in various ways over the course of several centuries. *Dangdut* is a pulsating popular music, similar to Indian film music and some popular musics of the Middle East.) Yet the term *pop* is also used in a narrower sense, as a subcategory of mellow, "middle of the road" music, distinct from the harder-edged *rock* and the Indonesian versions of *country*—all three of these sounding "recognizably western." *Cf.* Yampolsky's statement that "it is possible to use 'Pop' as an umbrella term for Pop Indonesia, Rock, and Country" (1989: 2, n. 3) This assessment, though dating from the late 1980s, still holds as of 2000.

3. My interest in the topic of music television in Indonesia developed gradually over a

period of what is now nearly thirty years of engagement with music in Indonesia. Trained as an ethnomusicologist in the 1970s, I set off in 1973–74 to conduct field research on the *gamelan* ensemble music of Java. After numerous visits to Java through the early 1990s, I began research in South Sulawesi, a part of Indonesia culturally quite distinct from Java and one whose music and related performing arts vie for legitimacy among various competing forms (Javanese and Western). My research on music television began in earnest in 1997–98 as I interviewed television producers, programmers, performers, and viewers. From an initial interest in the representation of "traditional," regional music, dance, and theater on television, I turned to popular music, due largely to the enormous amount of airtime I found devoted to music videos and live popular music shows. At a friend's house in Jakarta, I dubbed countless hours of music television, and obtained some videos from archives at RCTI in Jakarta and TVRI in Ujung Pandang (now Makassar), South Sulawesi. I asked friends and strangers alike about their viewing and listening habits and tastes. My audience research is, therefore, not based on systematic surveys, but on an admittedly random selection of viewers. This part of the larger picture remains in need of further research. Indonesian researchers are, to my knowledge, doing very little audience research of any kind, and certainly not on music television viewing. Several studies by foreign scholars offer in-depth ethnographic work with audiences: Caldarola 1990, a careful ethnography based on fieldwork in Kalimantan (Indonesian Borneo) prior to the era of private television; Kitley 1992, an excellent overview of Indonesian television as of the early 1990s; and Kitley 2000, a fine book-length study of Indonesian television, but with little mention of music television.

4. From the early 1980s until the rise of *dangdut* on private stations a decade later, TVRI devoted significant portions of its music shows, such as *Aneka Ria Safari*, to *dangdut*. During the 1970s, when television reached mostly the upper and middle classes, TVRI chose its music accordingly. But with the sharp increase in television viewership, particularly among the lower and lower-middle classes in rural as well as urban areas, TVRI responded by incorporating *dangdut*, music it knew this new viewership to enjoy.

5. Advertisements are seen on all stations except TVRI. Government broadcast laws forbid advertising on the national television station, and require private stations to pay 10 percent of their advertising income to TVRI, an especially burdensome ruling in the midst of drastically reduced advertising revenues precipitated by the economic crisis that began in late 1997.

6. Jay Soebiakto, a producer of music television shows for RCTI (including *Dua Warna*) and an independent producer of music videos, made the first Indonesian video seen on MTV, with "Pergilah, Kasih" (Go, Love), a song by the Indonesian pop star Chrisye, in 1990.

7. The acronym Ampuh, curiously incorporating the word *pribumi*, a racial term distinguishing "indigenous," Malay peoples from "foreign," Chinese and others, did not seem to strike those I questioned about it, including representatives of MTV, as potentially incendiary, even given the heightened sense of tension between *pribumi* and non-*pribumi* since the onset of the economic crisis.

8. In the many hours of MTV I watched in Indonesia during three weeks in August 1998, I saw the following: Boyz II Men, 98 Degrees with Stevie Wonder ("True to Your Heart" from the Disney film *Mulan*), Will Smith ("Just the Two of Us"), Lighthouse Family ("Lost in Space"), Brandy and Monica ("The Boy Is Mine"), and Whitney Houston ("Greatest Love of All"). Otherwise I saw no African American performers.

9. Goodwin has noted that MTV VJs "offer a girl/boy-next-door point of identification for MTV viewers" and that this "identification point established by the VJs is, unsurprisingly, a conscious MTV strategy" (Goodwin 1993: 55), MTV sought VJs who would not usurp the fame and larger-than-life image of the celebrity musicians. MTV's Indonesian VJs seem as

relaxed, unpretentious, and just slightly unprofessional as (some) American VJs, but in spite of their on-air style (or perhaps because of it), all three Singapore-based Indonesian VJs have won celebrity recognition. Indonesian VJ Nadya Hutagalung won Best Light Entertainment Presenter award in the Asian television awards, held in Singapore in January 1998, and she was recognized as one of twenty-five "Asian Trend Makers" in *Asiaweek* (6 March 1998). She and fellow Indonesian VJ Sarah Sechan were among ten television personalities named by television tabloid *Bintang Indonesia* as "Bintang Yang Paling Berkilau" (Most brightly shining stars) on Indonesian television for 1997. The Indonesian VJ Jamie Aditya was named by the same tabloid as one of ten "Bintang Baru Yang Potensial" (Promising new stars), as well as being chosen from a field of forty-seven nominees as "The Hip, Hot and Happening Bachelor" for 1998 by *Cleo* magazine (promotional literature from MTV Asia, Jakarta office, August 1998).

10. The term *etnik* or *etnika* is being used with increasing frequency in the discourse on Indonesia's music as a catchall to refer to non-pop, non-Western music, especially the countless regional traditions of the Indonesian archipelago. It has the advantage of avoiding the dichotomy between "traditional" and "modern," although other similar dichotomies are still implied. The term seems to be primarily used in the context of the music industry, by those whose primary concerns are with global, national, or supra-ethnic markets. Other terms persist, however. The biweekly tabloid published for private radio stations around Indonesia, *Eksponen* (renamed *Gong: Media dan Seni* in mid-1999), now incorporates a four-page insert with the rubric *musik tradisi* (traditional music), but the articles often make use of the term *etnik* and *daerah* (region, regional).

REFERENCES

Alfian and Chu, Godwin C., eds. 1981. *Satellite Television in Indonesia*. Jakarta: LEKNAS/LIPI; Honolulu: East-West Center, Communication Institute.

Appadurai, Arjun. 1996. *Modernity at Large: Cultural Dimensions of Globalization*. Minneapolis: University of Minnesota Press.

Aufderheide, Pat. 1986. "Music Videos: The Look of the Sound." *Journal of Communication* 36 (1): 57–93.

Banks, Jack. 1996. *Monopoly Television: MTV's Quest to Control the Music*. Boulder: Westview.

Barker, Chris. 1997. *Global Television: An Introduction*. Oxford: Blackwell.

Berland, Jody. 1986. "Sound, Image and Social Space: Rock Video and Media Reconstruction." *Journal of Communication Inquiry* 10 (1): 34–47.

Brown, M., and John Fiske. 1987. "Romancing the Rock: Romance and Representation in Popular Music Videos." *ONETWOTHREEFOUR: A Rock 'n' Roll Quarterly* 5 (spring).

Burns, Gary, and Robert Thompson. 1987. "Music, Television, and Video: Historical and Aesthetic Considerations." *Popular Music and Society* 11 (3): 11–25.

Caldarola, Victor J. 1990. "Reception as Cultural Experience: Visual Mass Media and Reception Practices in Outer Indonesia." Ph.D. diss., University of Pennsylvania.

Chen, Kuan-Hsing. 1986. "MTV: The (Dis)appearance of Postmodern Semiosis, or The Cultural Politics of Resistance." *Journal of Communication Inquiry* 10 (1): 66–69.

Denisoff, R. Serge. 1988. *Inside MTV*. New Brunswick, NJ: Transaction Books.

Dirlik, Arif. 1996. "The Global in the Local." In *Global/Local: Cultural Production and the Transnational Imaginary*, ed. Rob Wilson and Wimal Dissanayake, 21–45. Durham: Duke University Press.

Fiske, John. 1986. "MTV: Post Structural Post Modern." *Journal of Communication Inquiry* 10 (1): 74–79.

———. 1987. *Television Culture*. London: Routledge.

Frederick, William H. 1982. "Rhoma Irama and the Dangdut Style: Aspects of Contemporary Indonesian Popular Culture." *Indonesia* 34 (October 1982): 103–30.

Frith, Simon. 1984. "Can You Dance to It? Rock on TV." *Collusion* 4.

———. 1996. *Performing Rites: On the Value of Popular Music*. Cambridge: Harvard University Press.

Frith, Simon, Andrew Goodwin, and Lawrence Grossberg, eds. 1993. *Sound and Vision: The Music Video Reader*. London: Routledge.

Gehr, R. 1983. "The MTV Aesthetic." *Film Comment* 19 (4): 37–40.

Goodwin, Andrew. 1992. *Dancing in the Distraction Factory: Music Television and Popular Culture*. Minneapolis: University of Minnesota Press.

———. 1993. "Fatal Distractions: MTV Meets Postmodern Theory." In *Sound and Vision: The Music Video Reader*, ed. Simon Frith, Andrew Goodwin, and Lawrence Grossberg, 45–66. London: Routledge.

Hangguman, Willy. "Dangdut dan Orkestra, Sebuah Adonan Budaya" [Dangdut and orchestra: A cultural face-off/contest]. *Suara Pembaruan Online* 17 February (http://www.suarapembaruan.com/News/1997/02/170297/Budaya/bdy03.html).

Hatch, Martin F. 1989. "Popular Music in Indonesia." In *World Music, Politics and Social Change*, ed. Simon Frith, 47–67. Manchester: Manchester University Press.

Hughes-Freeland, Felicia. 1995. "Making History? Cultural Documentation on Balinese Television." *Review of Indonesian and Malaysian Affairs* 29 (1–2) (winter–summer): 95–106.

Ishadi, S. K. 1999. *Dunia Penyairan: Prospek dan Tantangannya* [The world of broadcasting: Prospects and challenges]. Jakarta: Gramedia.

Kaplan, E. Ann. 1987. *Rocking around the Clock: Music Television, Postmodernism, and Consumer Culture*. London: Routledge.

Kinder, M. 1984. "Music Video and the Spectator: Television, Ideology and Dream." *Film Quarterly* 38 (1): 2–15.

Kitley, Philip. 1992. "*Tahun Bertambah, Zaman Bertambah*: Television and Its Audiences in Indonesia." *Review of Indonesian and Malaysian Affairs* 26 (winter): 71–109.

———. 2000. *Television, Nation, and Culture in Indonesia*. Athens: Ohio University Center for International Studies.

Lewis, Lisa A. 1990. *Gender Politics and MTV: Voicing the Difference*. Philadelphia: Temple University Press.

Lockard, Craig A. 1998. *Dance of Life: Popular Music and Politics in Southeast Asia*. Honolulu: University of Hawaii Press.

Longhurst, Brian. 1995. *Popular Music and Society*. Cambridge: Polity Press.

Manuel, Peter. 1993. *Cassette Culture: Popular Music and Technology in North India*. Chicago: University of Chicago Press.

McDaniel, Drew O. 1994. *Broadcasting in the Malay World: Radio, Television, and Video in Brunei, Indonesia, Malaysia, and Singapore*. Norwood, NJ: Ablex.

Mulyana, Deddy, and Idi Subandy Ibrahim, eds. 1997. *Bercinta dengan Televisi: Ilusi, Impresi, dan Imagi Sebuah Kotak Ajaib* [In love with television: Illusion, impression, and image of a magic box]. Bandung: PT Remaja Rosdakarya.

Nugroho, Garin. 1995. *Kekuasaan dan Hiburan* [Power and entertainment]. Yogyakarta: Bentang.

Pioquinto, Ceres. 1995. "Dangdut at Sekaten: Female Representations in Live Performance." *Review of Indonesian and Malaysian Affairs* 29 (1–2 (winter–summer): 59–89.

Pour, Julius. 2000. " 'Trans TV' Mengudara Mulai Juni 2001" ["Trans TV" will air beginning in June 2001]. *Kompas Online*, 3 November (http://www.kompas.com/kompas-cetak/0011/03/DIKBUD/tran09.htm).

Sapada Makkasau, Andi Siti Nurhani. 1997. *Nuansa Pelangi* [Rainbow nuance]. Ujung Pandang: n.p.

Setiadi, Purwanto (with Endang Widya). 1997. "Bisnis Rekaman Lokal di Zaman MTV" [Local recording business in the era of MTV]. *SWA Online*, October (http://www.swa.co.id/97/0010/NONRUBRI.010.html).

Shuker, Roy. 1994. *Understanding Popular Music*. London: Routledge.

Simatupang, Gabriel Roosmargo Lono Lastoro. 1996. "The Development of *Dangdut* and Its Meanings." M.A. thesis, Monash University.

Siregar, Ashadi. 1995. *Sketsa-sketsa Media Massa* [Mass media sketches]. Yogyakarta: Bentang.

Soemanto, Bakdi. 1997. "Pengembangan Potensi Kebudayaan Daerah melalui Televisi" [Developing the potential of regional culture through television]. In Bercinta dengan Televisi, ed. Deddy Mulyana and Idi Subandy Ibrahim, 321–27. Bandung: PT Remaja Rosdakarya.

Sumardjan, Selo. 1991. "The Social and Cultural Effects of Satellite Communication on Indonesian Society." *Media Asia* 18 (1): 15–19.

Suryadi AG, Linus. 1994. *Nafas Budaya Yogya* [Breath of Yogyanese culture]. Yogyakarta: Bentang.

Susanto, Astrid. 1978. "Mass Communication Systems in Indonesia." In *Political Power and Communications in Indonesia*, ed. Karl D. Jackson and Lucian W. Pye, 229–58. Berkeley: University of California Press.

Sutton, R. Anderson. 1985. "Commercial Cassette Recordings of Traditional Music in Java: Implications for Performers and Scholars." *World of Music* 27 (3): 23–45.

———. 1991. *Traditions of Gamelan Music in Java: Musical Pluralism and Regional Identity*. Cambridge: Cambridge University Press.

Suzuki, Sandii. Web site (http://web.kyoto-inet.or.jp/people/kaki-y/eng/sindex0.htm).

Taylor, Timothy D. 1997. *Global Pop: World Music, World Markets*. New York: Routledge.

Tetzlaff, D. 1986. "MTV and the Politics of Postmodern Pop." *Journal of Communcation Inquiry* 10 (1): 80–91.

Theodore, K. S. 1996. "Dangdut 'Made In' Japan dan Malaysia" [Dangdut made in Japan and Malaysia]. *Kompas Online*, 16 September (http://www.kompas.com/9609/16/HIBURAN/dang.htm).

Whitely, Sheila. 1997. "Seduced by the Sign: An Analysis of the Textual Links between Sound and Image in Pop Videos." In *Sexing the Groove: Popular Music and Gender*, ed. Sheila Whitely. London: Routledge.

Wilson, Rob, and Wimal Dissanayake, eds. 1996. *Global/Local: Cultural Production and the Transnational Imaginary*. Durham: Duke University Press.

Wolfe, Arnold S. 1983. "Rock on Cable: On MTV: Music Television, the First Music Video Channel." *Popular Music and Society* 9 (1): 41–50.

Yampolsky, Philip. 1989. "*Hati Yang Luka*, an Indonesian Hit." *Indonesia* 47 (April): 1–17.

Chapter Nineteen

Marriages Are Made on Television
Globalization and National Identity in India

Divya C. McMillin

The stage lights are intense. The host squints under the added glare of the handheld camera lights and mops his brow. He addresses the middle-aged female participant before him

> *Host:* If you really wanted something, how would you communicate this to your husband?
> *Participant:* I'd ask him directly.

The camera pans the audience as they erupt with laughter. The host repeats, a little incredulously,

> *Host:* You would ask him directly?
> *Participant:* Yes, I would ask him directly, with no hesitation. If he can afford to buy it for me, he will; if he cannot, he won't.

The audience laughs as the host adjusts his glasses and says, "Your husband is a very good man."

The show is *Adarsha Dampathigalu* (The Ideal Couple), an Indian version of the *Newlywed Game*. Telecast Monday evenings from 7:30 to 8:00 on the private, regional, Kannada language cable channel, Udaya TV, it is one of the most popular shows in Bangalore, India, receiving a fan mail volume of around two thousand letters every week. The audience's laughter and the host's incredulity set the parameters of the patriarchal discourse unraveling on the stage. The laughter and incredulity signify their awareness that the female participant is a border crosser-crossing not only the boundary between the private sphere of the Indian household and the public sphere of the televised stage, but also the boundary between the male-authored role of submissive wife and the assertive role of outspoken woman.

This chapter is a critical examination of the hybrid program *Adarsha Dampathigalu* as a representation of the marriage of global and local cultures on Indian television. Audience anxiety and enjoyment of the husband-wife interaction on stage can be read as a symptom of the uneasy pleasure with which the larger nation accommodates processes of globalization. Hybrid programming, in which indigenous shows have appropriated Western formats, is a highly popular form of Indian television. While several of these shows rarely last beyond their first-run season, several others, such as *Adarsha Dampathigalu* on Udaya TV and the *Kiran Joneja* talk show on Star TV, endure, defying criticisms from politicians and women's welfare organizations alike that they "attract maximum viewership without caring about the effect and impact on the citizens, especially youths, thereby spoiling the culture and ethos of the country."[1]

The ideological construction of culture and national identity as unified and monolithic entities has been critiqued extensively.[2] Yet strategies of private television networks in accommodating resistance from national ideologues and catering to popular tastes have received scant attention in scholarship on globalization and national identity. Through narrative analysis of *Adarsha Dampathigalu* and ethnographic research at Udaya TV and at the national (Doordarshan) and transnational (Star TV and Zee TV) television stations during specific research phases spanning 1996 to 2000, this chapter addresses the following questions. First, how does *Adarsha Dampathigalu* accommodate the global and local in its hybrid programming? Second, how do private regional networks like Udaya TV compete with the state-sponsored national network Doordarshan and private transnational satellite channels such as Star TV and Zee TV? Finally, what may we conclude about the cultural landscape of Indian television in the twenty-first century? Textual analysis combined with ethnographic fieldwork facilitates a critical discussion of the strategies used by indigenous television networks to accommodate processes of globalization.

The Television Environment in India

Adarsha Dampathigalu debuted on Udaya TV on June 6, 1994, just one year after the channel was launched by its parent network, the Tamil language Sun TV based in Chennai, Tamil Nadu. A brainchild of Udaya TV's vice-president of programming, the show was introduced as part of an aggressive strategy to increase the channel's visibility in Karnataka and to convey to its audience that this channel, in its focus on Kannada language entertainment, would provide a refreshing change from the pedagogical narratives of the national network, Doordarshan.

Udaya TV was just one among several private, regional, vernacular language channels to crop up in the nation in the early 1990s. The government's 1991 economic liberalization policy dismantled, in urban areas, the monopoly status of Doordarshan. It also paved the way for the entry of private satellite and cable channels, foreign and indigenous. Hong Kong–based Star TV extended its footprint to India in 1992. Realizing the potential of the Indian market in the liberalized environment, Rupert Murdoch purchased 64 percent of Star TV in 1993 and the remaining 36 percent in 1994. Politicians and private entrepreneurs in India were quick to recognize the commercial success of Star TV and its then Hindi channel, Zee TV (now owned by Mumbai industrialist Subash Chandra). By 1993, private regional channels emerged in almost every state of the nation, such as the politically backed Sun TV in Tamil Nadu, the Zee-owned Asianet in Kerala, and the Eenadu (ETV) network in Andhra Pradesh. Barred from uplinking to the government-owned satellites INSAT 1D, IN-

SAT 2A, and INSAT 2B, private channels sought foreign satellites such as Russia's Rimsat and Gorizont or Singapore's INTELSAT. Although several independent, private channels provided competition to network channels for urban audiences all over the nation, it was clear by 2000 that these had not proved viable and only those that were part of larger networks and had political or industrial backing had managed to stay afloat. Also, regional, vernacular language networks were slowly gaining ground over the foreign, English, and Hindi language channels.

Cashing in on the success of regional television with its cultural and language-specific programming, Rathikant Basu, former head of Doordarshan and then Star TV, launched the TARA network (Television Aimed at Regional Audiences) in mid-2000.[3] With cable connections at 30 million in 2000, the reach of private television networks was still small, at 3 percent,[4] as opposed to the national network's reach of around 87.2 percent of India's one billion inhabitants.[5] Yet this small percentage formed a prime group since it comprised urban middle-class residents with sufficient purchasing power to consume the global and local products advertised on these networks.

Government Response to Private Channels

The government, which was quick with accusations of cultural imperialism against the transborder flow of foreign programming in the 1970s, bemoaned the degeneration of Indian culture in the 1990s as it reemerged, debased and polluted, in Western program formats. The anxiety-rhetoric of the Indian government is riddled with paradoxes. First, in the 1970s and 1980s, accusations of cultural imperialism accompanied sanctions to receive inexpensive sitcoms like *I Love Lucy* and *Diff'rent Strokes* from the United States.[6] Second, although these accusations continued into the 1990s, programming on Star TV, which included such shows as *Baywatch* and *Santa Barbara*, criticized for not having anything to do with Indian culture,[7] was not curbed because the government wanted to keep to its profitable policy of liberalization.[8] Finally, despite the lament that foreign programming leads to the "vulgarization of [Indian] culture and the commercialization of every aspect of human life,"[9] Doordarshan included such shows as *Dallas, Dynasty,* and *Carry On Behind* in its own programming to keep up with the entertainment-oriented programming of the privately owned global and local channels.[10]

In 1995 Doordarshan launched metro channels to supplement its regional channels in every major city of the country.[11] It entered an alliance with CNN in return for a U.S. $1.5 million fee and a fifty-fifty sharing of the revenue. Viacom, Time Warner, BBC Prime, and ESPN quickly followed suit and signed either flat fee or revenue-sharing contracts with the Indian behemoth. Even Murdoch's sports-and-movie formula was sidelined by Doordarshan's more-sports-and-more-movies formula. By 2000, Doordarshan's platform looked remarkably similar to that of Star TV with its Entertainment Channel, Music Channel, Business and Current Affairs Channel, and Sports Channel. Its aggressive commercialization was spurred on after it achieved autonomy from government control in November 1997. Autonomy from government influence was a dubious proposition since members of the government-appointed Broadcast Authority, expected to advise on the function and content of Doordarshan, had close ties to the Indian government.

Legislation for the regulation of content on cable and satellite television imitated government rhetoric in that it criticized private television content but did not stipulate measures to regulate this profitable industry. For example, the Cable TV Networks (Regulation) Bill, introduced in Parliament in 1993, was passed as the Cable Television Networks (Regulation) Act in 1995, and condemned objectionable content yet did not prohibit it.[12] The Indian General Rules of Conduct for TV and Radio Advertising also urged advertisers not to offend morality, decency, and religious sentiment, but did not require them to do so.[13]

From this brief description of the Indian television context, three things are important to remember. First, private networks were in a constant process of inventing and reinventing programs to stay afloat in an aggressively competitive environment. Although these channels posed a threat to Doordarshan in urban areas, the national network still led the field in terms of overall numbers because of its terrestrial telecast and rural reach. Second, state-controlled and private channels primarily targeted urban audiences. Although viewer language played an important role in defining niche audiences for each channel, networks aimed at general regional audiences since most people in India are bilingual or even multilingual. Finally, legislation carried little power even in the early 2000s because they lacked mandates and methods to check violations.

Hybrid Programming: A Cost-Effective Strategy

Situated a nation bred on films, private channels recognized that an easy way to circumvent prohibitive in-house program production costs was to obtain film rights and fill programming hours with movies or film-song countdowns. Regional channels raced against each other to obtain rights to vernacular language films. By 2000, Udaya TV owned rights to over 1,600 Kannada films and ETV owned rights to over 500 Telugu films. Besides lengthy hours of regional films, film-based shows such as *Superhit Muqabala* (Doordarshan), *Philips Top Ten* (Zee TV), *Boogie Woogie* (Sony TV), and *Sa Re Ga Ma* (Zee TV) flooded the channels. VJs for these shows were carefully chosen and were usually young, talented, and from urban backgrounds. For example, the moderators of Zee TV's *Sa Re Ga Ma, Close-up Antakshari,* and Sun TV's *Pattu Padava* (film music-based game shows) were trained singers themselves,[14] and most of the VJs on Channel [V] were born or brought up in England or the United States.[15] The producers of these shows were particular that anchors straddled both Indian and Western cultures and exuded an international character. Freedom, concern for the environment, and respect for women were carelessly tossed around between film videos and free-floating skits. Producers knew that "an all-English veejay [brought] abysmal ratings while an all-vernacular veejay [was] not hip enough for a country that generally worship [ped] English—Hinglish, Gujlish, Tamlish, Anythinglish [their Hindi, Gujarati, Punjabi, and Tamil hybrids]."[16]

Western program formats provided fodder for inexpensive Indian programming, resulting in such programs as *Surf Wheel of Fortune* (based on ABC's *Wheel of Fortune*; Surf is a brand of detergent) on Zee TV and *Movers and Shekhars* (based on NBC's *Jay Leno*) on Sony TV. *Kaun Banega Crorepathi* (based on ABC's *Who Wants to Be a Millionaire?*) on Star Plus led the field in ratings even eight months after its debut in December 1999.[17]

Although most of the programs were short-lived, some, such as *Adarsha Dampathigalu*, have proved viable and their viability is crucial to our understanding of how the local appropriates the global and packages this hybridity in a way that is nonthreatening to existing definitions of national identity. I invoke the term "hybridity," as mentioned earlier, to refer to television programming that incorporates foreign (primarily North American) formats within local themes and cultural contexts. The product may so completely appropriate the global that it seems for the most part an indigenous invention, such as *Adarsha Dampathigalu*, or may barely touch the local so that apart from language and characters, it seems a global clone, as in *Kaun Banega Crorepathi* or *Surf Wheel of Fortune*.

Economic liberalization in India allowed collaborations between the national network and foreign ones (such as the Doordarshan-CNN alliance or the Doordarshan-BBC alliance) and caused foreign ones to branch into local language networks (such as Star TV's Zee TV Hindi channel of the mid-1990s and its current EL TV Hindi channel). Such collaborations allowed these networks to capitalize on profitable hybrid programming intra-and internationally. Private regional networks further occupy the margins within India, and find themselves in a liminal space, continuously confronting state control, yet speaking to the present needs of the non– Hindi- or English-speaking audiences, hungry for innovative entertainment in their own languages and cultural contexts.

Private networks then push for a regional identity, yet package it within hybrid shows to deflect criticisms of regionalism and yet keep programs lucrative. Programs therefore are carefully crafted to represent the region through location, dress, accent, and language; and affirm the global through program format, theme, and use of English between vernacular sentences. The degree of interplay between global and local is contingent on audience conservatism, as we shall see in the case of *Adarsha Dampathigalu*. This program, although one of the most popular on Udaya TV, a channel that itself leads the Karnataka market,[18] is shrouded in controversy because it deals with marital relations—a taboo subject in conservative Hindu society. The show then becomes an ideological battleground for the collision between the global and the local, between patriarchy and female assertion, and between the domestic private sphere and the televised public sphere. By providing a stage for the unraveling of the male-authored mysteries of marriage, this show provides a space for female empowerment and thus challenges the restrictive myths of marriage and of female identity. This challenge strikes at the patriarchal heart of Hindu India and contests the very construction of national identity. To understand how *Adarsha Dampathigalu* becomes a symbol of the marriage of global and local and to comprehend the inauspiciousness of such a union, we need to understand the nature of Indian society and the restrictive myths surrounding the institution of Hindu marriage in India.

The Significance of Marriage in India in an Era of Globalization

Traditional Hindu society is based on a purity-pollution scale that places the Brahmin at the head of the cosmological body, and the sudra at the bottom.[19] Within these castes are further hierarchies of class and gender, with males dominating over females in each stratum.

> [The] marriage arrangement becomes the primary context for sorting out where a particular family, lineage, and kin group ranks in relation to others. Through marriage, a family's status may be maintained, strengthened, or weakened. Because a marriage affects the status of the entire family and its lineage, it is deemed too important a decision to leave to the persons actually getting married. Rather, the decision rests with the heads of extended family units. Consequently arranged marriages are the norm; marriages undertaken by the marrying parties themselves, so-called love marriages, are considered deviant, even dangerous.[20]

Marriage experiences also differ by caste, class within caste, religion, and region. Recognizing these complexities, Karve attempted a mapping of kinship and marriage by drawing together the overriding similarities among regions in India.[21] In major regions of the south (relevant to this analysis), Karve writes that families are patrilineal and patrilocal. A marriage between castes is seen as polluting to the higher caste. Such a union is considered *pratiloma*, and specifically refers to marriage between a woman from a higher caste and a man from a lower caste. Such a marriage goes against the hierarchical and patriarchal structure of society because the caste of the male is crucial in defining the status of the offspring in society.[22]

The inauspicious ability of a woman to breed across caste and class lines is a cause of hegemonic anxiety, translating into real religious and social strategies to control her freedom and confine her movement to the domestic sphere.[23] Vedic scriptures, Hindu mythology, and folklore award Hindu women great respect and power in their positions as virgins, mothers, and protectors. Hindu goddesses can take many forms: Mata (mother), Kali (destructor), Parvati (gentle consort), and even Durga (warrior). The rage of a woman is considered far more destructive than that of a man and hence, her power has to be restrained and directed toward procreation and protection. Her hair has to be braided or chignoned as a symbol of her restraint—unbraided hair is a sign of sexual freedom. Her jewelry denotes her marital status and her sari has to be carefully draped around her to conceal her womanly contours. This suppression of womanly powers defines a woman's role and function in society. She speaks when spoken to, and has to keep her eyes lowered in the presence of her husband, in-laws, and other men.[24]

Within the constraints of the post-Vedic discourse that define her roles and freedoms, a Hindu Indian woman is expected to make one great journey in her life: from *pihar* to *sasural*, from the home of her birth to the home of her marriage. She moves from her identity as daughter and sister to wife and daughter-in-law.[25] Marriage itself is considered a site where the bride's inauspiciousness is transferred from her family to the groom's family and she is accompanied by a *stridhaan* (dowry) to counter this inauspiciousness. During the marriage ceremony, the father or elder brother of the bride washes the feet of the bridegroom *(pao puja)* as a symbol of honor and respect of the groom and his family and as an acknowledgment of their superiority as wife-receivers.[26]

Hindu traditions and female restrictions continue in an era of globalization. Doordarshan's heavy pedagogical programs directed at rural audiences and women still cast the latter in traditional service-oriented roles whether in soaps, sitcoms, or documentaries.[27] However, competing frameworks of meaning in foreign and domestic programs where women occupy diverse roles and the increasing phenomenon of women working outside the home in India prompt private, regional television networks to formulate programs that acknowledge the changing roles of women.[28] The tensions surrounding the symbolic stage provided in *Adarsha Dampathigalu* for the exposition of husband-wife relationships reveal the institution of marriage as one constructed not through consensus, but through critical struggle. The public presence of the woman is a threat to the discourse of national identity as constructed by the Hindu conservatives in India. The show paves the way for female authorship, throwing her into the battleground to face the dominant groups (husbands on the stage and at home, and males at the heads of households, institutions, state, and nation) in a battle over the legitimacy of representation.

A space for the expression of female authorship comes with a heavy price. Private television networks such as Udaya TV cannot play with entrenched structures lightly —they necessarily face conflict from the keepers of this structure. How then, does *Adarsha Dampathigalu* accommodate such conflict to appease its viewers and censors and remain one of the most popular shows on Udaya TV even seven years after its debut in 1994? Textual analysis and ethnographic fieldwork at the station uncover some key strategies of this show.

Manipulating Global and Local

Adarsha Dampathigalu borrowed its premise from *The Newly Wed Game*, where married couples answered questions about each other and competed for grand prizes. The Indian version, however, had a twist: the couples were not newlyweds. They ranged in age from mid-twenties to mid-forties and had been married anywhere from two to fifteen years. The show lacked the spontaneity and boisterousness of the *Newlywed Game*. Participants did not whack each other with heart-shaped pillows, nor did they scream at each other for not guessing the right response. Far from it. The participants were tense and rarely smiled. The host often repeated his questions so the participants could understand him. He also had to instruct the participants how to perform on television and told them to "speak into the microphone," or to "face the audience while you talk." The "ideal" couple, chosen by the highest number of matched responses, could easily fool the audience into thinking they had lost judging by their closed, tight expressions. The crammed auditorium was about the only visual indicator that the show was a popular one.

Commenting on the lack of spontaneity on the show, the general manager of Udaya TV said Karnataka audiences were very conservative and spoofs on film stars or average participants, however lighthearted, were sharply criticized through scathing letters that flooded the station after any show that stepped out of the bounds of propriety. Viewer mail was still the primary source of audience information because the station lacked an audience research unit. *Adarsha Dampathigalu* had faced severe initial criticism because of its controversial topic. The host and vice-president of programming of the station, a veteran Kannada actor, said,

> The basic idea of *Adarsha Dampathigalu* is a lighthearted one [aimed] at trying to make the husband and wife understand each other . . . openness should be there. As a film director and actor I was really successful and popular. That might have been an added attraction of the program. Once I started contacting the people and talking to them, my knowledge of the problem [between husband and wife] also increased. But the openness of Indian people you cannot have and that's the problem.

The host's residual popularity from his days as a Kannada film hero no doubt added to the program's visibility and popularity, yet as a producer, he struggled to balance entertainment with pedagogy. Early episodes of *Adarsha Dampathigalu* rarely varied in format. Four couples, selected by a male leader of the city (invariably a government official) through lots drawn at the beginning of the show, would be seated across from each other, with husbands on one side and wives on the other. The game consisted of two rounds. In the first, each person would answer questions about his or her partner, while the partner was kept off-stage to be later asked the same questions. In the second round, each husband would read a love letter to his wife. The highest number of matched responses and the best love letter would determine the ideal couple. Between rounds, eight other couples would be called on stage through the same selection process. These were asked general knowledge questions.[29] The couple who answered all questions correctly in this round received a prize (a sari for the wife or shirt material for the husband). At the end of the show, an elderly gentleman from the audience would give away prizes to the winning and runner-up couples. The prizes consisted of gift hampers worth 1,000 rupees (U.S. $30) and 750 rupees (U.S. $25) respectively from local businesses.[30] All participants would receive a packet of detergent as a complimentary gift from a local business. The program would conclude with a brief dialogue between an elderly gentleman from the audience and the host, in which they justified the show and its purpose in discussing marital issues.

In the August 26, 1996, episode, chosen here for discussion as a representative of early versions of this show, *Adarsha Dampathigalu* employed certain narrative strategies that marked its difference from the *Newlywed Game*.[31] It differed in its existents (settings) and discourse. The entire show was recorded on the stage of a huge, packed auditorium. Handheld cameras accompanied by handheld lights panned the audience. It was obvious the auditorium was not air-conditioned as the audience members often fanned themselves and wiped their faces. The host too felt the heat and frequently mopped his brow. A banner advertising the main sponsor hung along the steps leading to the stage so that it entered the camera's eye view each time a participant was called on stage. The stage itself was quite bare except for a few potted plants. On either side of the stage, facing each other, were two rows of chairs. The chairs, made of aluminum and synthetic red leather, are commonly used for the bride and groom at wedding receptions. There was no background music or graphics, and the focus of the show was directed solely at the participants and their interaction with the host and the audience.

The host shared his narrator position with a government official, the director of the Karnataka History and Culture Department (identified as the second narrator hereafter), and with an elderly audience member (identified as the third narrator hereafter) at the beginning and end of the show respectively. The participants included twelve couples in all: four who competed for the main prizes, and eight who appeared in the intermediary general-knowledge round. The presence of the audience was frequently acknowledged by long shots of the packed auditorium.

The show itself was heavily edited, so that shots of participants walking down the aisle would suddenly cut to them answering questions on stage. A close-up of a participant responding to the host's questions would cut to his or her partner answering the same questions. This made for choppy, awkward sequences; participants appeared as if by magic on the stage without transition shots showing how they got there. Production quality was poor and amateurish and clearly differentiated the show from the somewhat slickly produced Kannada films that occupied the station's airtime from 10:00 P.M. onwards and on weekend afternoons.

The host identified himself with the real authors of the show—the producers and the network itself. He welcomed the audience to "This, *our* program, *our Adarsha Dampathigalu* on Udaya TV," and acted as a clear spokesperson for the network and architects of the show. The implied author of the program (what the viewer imagines the real author to be like) emerged in the host's narration. In welcoming the audience to "*our* program," he constructed an imagined community with not only the producers of the show but the audience itself, and placed the audience on the boundary —simultaneously negotiating between authorship and spectatorship. The host, network, and architects of the show, by allowing participants to write in their requests to be selected for the show and to compete with other participants, shared the writing of the narrative with the participants themselves. By sharing authorship, they provided the viewing public the illusion of empowerment and democracy by the systematic encouragement of participation and the seeming diminishment of the institutional voice. The host asked the participants such questions as "What do you think is most important in a marriage: compatibility, friendship, trust, or happiness?" and "Whom do you value the most, friends or relatives?"

At the end of each response, he would comment briefly on whether or not he thought the participant offered a wise response. Throughout, the host was able to maintain a certain distance from the participants, and this was further evident in his teasing comments. While these were made for the sake of humor, they often negated the validity of women's responses. We shall revisit this point later in this chapter. It is sufficient to say here that these teasing remarks placed the host in the role of arbitrator, deciding for the couples and the audience the legitimacy of each participant's comments.

The women, tight-faced and soft-spoken, were frequently asked to speak into the microphone so they could be heard clearly. Questions were far from personal and

Reprinted by permission of Udaya TV.

dealt with superficial matters such as taste in music and preferences among family members. The exchange between the third narrator and the host revealed a dialogue to legitimize the value of the show:

> *Third narrator:* (to audience) Does this make you angry? (to host) What is the primary goal of this program? What is the use of this program for viewing couples or people? Does this have any use for our society?
>
> *Host:* The purpose of this program is not to make fun of couples and their relationships, but to point to the importance of happiness in a marriage and of a couple's understanding of each others' likes and dislikes. They [the couples] should face and understand every issue together. Only then will the household be happy. From the letters and applications we have been receiving from participants who want to be on this show, we get the impression that we are achieving our goal. From the fact that I receive about 1,800 applications a week when I need only four couples for a show, I think we are a success.
>
> *Third narrator:* I can see that this show is accomplishing a lot of good—couples at home watching those on television can identify with similar situations and problems and learn from them, knowing that they are not alone. This is therefore a good show for all of us to learn from.

This bit of obviously "staged" dialogue was an effort at creating a public sphere. The third narrator was accompanied by his wife, who didn't say anything, but stood smiling by his side. By asking an elderly gentleman from the audience to pose these questions, the show identified its implied reader as not just the couples writing in to participate on the show, but the most conservative members of society from whom they may receive their strongest criticism. This indicated the authors' awareness that they were transgressing boundaries by shifting the private exchanges of a married couple to the public stage. In a follow-up interview, the host explained the need for the third narrator:

> There are critics who say this [show] is a mockery of husband and wife. So I didn't want a youngster to come on stage and comment on it. An elderly person who has watched the program, *who has seen the light*—I wanted him to comment on the program. So he came and said it is good, it is very good. . . . He is much more experienced in life. I know he was helping because of the letters we receive and the phone calls we get. (emphasis in original)

Viewer mail indicated that couples all over the state were using the show as a rubric for their own interactions. They learned about each other's idiosyncrasies so they would not fall short as did some of the participants on television. *Adarsha Dampathigalu* had moved from the televised stage into the home, reconfiguring husband-wife relationships and opening up dialogue between partners. It was interesting that by 2000, although the basic format of the show had not changed, *Adarsha Dampathigalu* had dropped the second and third narrators. No longer was their legitimizing function needed. The show had become one of the most sought-after, causing the vice-president of the network to often turn away advertisers or fall behind in his collection of payments. The most significant difference was the presence of a female cohost, who directed all her questions to the male participants (whom she addressed as "sir"), while the host directed his questions to the women and interspersed his cohost's questions with comments of his own to the men. A further difference between early and recent episodes was that the questions had grown more intimate. Participating couples were no longer asked general knowledge questions, but about their partner's personal habits—whether the partner was shy, talked too much, or was the more intelligent. The show had been shot in almost every district of Karnataka during its six years of telecast, and encouraged participation from even remote and rural areas of the state. Udaya TV had therefore turned from its focus on just urban, Kannadiga audiences to rural ones—a bold intrusion in an arena monopolized by Doordarshan.

The August 7, 2000, episode is discussed here as a representative of the more recent versions of the show. Although the game was still conducted on a stage inside a packed auditorium, the backdrop had changed from the jasmine flower string-lined black cloth of the early and mid-1990s to a diffused rainbow.[32] Also, the backdrop changed with almost every show depending on the current trend. For example, the *Titanic* lurched in the background for a February 14, 2000, show to signify undying love on Valentine's Day; and on the July 3, 2000, show, a medley of red, white, and

Reprinted by permission of Udaya TV.

blue colors was used, signifying American Independence Day. As with the episodes of the early and mid-1990s, a banner advertising the primary sponsor (in this case, Fair and Lovely Cream) occupied the center of the backdrop on the stage. The host had given up his Western sports coat and dark T-shirts of earlier episodes for a more traditional Indian kurta and pyjama—the native garb of North Indian men. While the host joked with participants and interrupted his cohost's questions and comments, the cohost limited her statements to the questions on her cue cards and improvised only when a participant needed further explanation.

The game itself consisted of three rounds. In the first, the partners' responses were matched, while the second round consisted of charades, in which husbands performed and wives guessed. In the third round, the couples guessed the price of gold jewelry and saris to win the same. Between the second and the third round, four couples were randomly drawn from the audience and competed in a game (in this episode, blowing balloons) for a grand prize of a gift hamper from a local business. Toward the end of the show, six randomly picked couples from the audience were asked to guess the price of various items: saris, shirts, ties, and jewelry, to win the same. As in earlier versions of *Adarsha Dampathigalu*, it was evident the show provided a lucrative avenue for small businesses such as sari dealers, jewelers, televi-

Reprinted by permission of Udaya TV.

sion stabilizer manufacturers, water heater makers, shirt and dhoti dealers, computer hardware dealers, and detergent and oil dealers (to name a few).[33] These businesses provided gift hampers for the prize winners, advertised their wares during intervals on the show, were all announced by the cohost as sponsors, and were listed in the acknowledgments at the end of the show.

Although the show seemed freer in its discussion of husband-wife interactions, the host served as a powerful moderator, curtailing this freedom in ingenuous ways, as is obvious in the following exchange:

> *Host:* (to male participant) Whom does your mother-in-law like more? Her younger daughter-in-law (indicating the man's wife) or her older daughter-in law?
>
> *Participant:* The question doesn't arise because we had a love marriage and are not allowed in my parents' house. (Audience laughter)
>
> *Host:* Who is the shy one of the two?
>
> *Participant:* (affirming his wife's earlier response) I am.
>
> *Host:* (with disbelief, facing the audience) You have just told us you had a love marriage—*how* can you be shy to go ahead with such a marriage? (emphases in original)
>
> *Participant:* No—you don't understand. When I got married, I was a different man. In

the nine years since we got married, I have become shy. (Audience roars with laughter)

Host: (laughing and moving to the front of the stage) Here he teaches us all a lesson: love marriage changes a man—it turns him from a bold person into a shy one.

By identifying the fatal flaw in a love marriage (in this case, the transformation of male qualities of boldness and defiance into female qualities of shyness and reticence), the host was able to deftly manipulate the potential threat of a stable love marriage into an affirmation that the arranged marriage was the one that endured. His teasing remarks function as a reminder that love marriage was a female-authored aberration, dangerous enough to reduce manhood. It warned all other men and women of its inauspicious powers. As indicated earlier in this chapter, the host's teasing remarks often negated the responses of female participants. Discrepancies between responses from husband and wife were usually blamed on the wife so that she emerged responsible for the inaccuracy. For example, when a wife responded that her husband was the more talkative of the two in response to a question on who talked more in the house, the host shook his head in disbelief while the audience broke into laughter. The husband's response in a later round claiming that it was his wife who talked more resulted in a quick response from the host:

> I knew it, I *knew* it. Listen you people (turning to the audience)—when a wife says her husband talks more, it means he is quiet at home, but talks more in public. That's because he needs to vent all that he has heard at home. (To the wife as audience continues to laugh) I *know* what goes on. But that's all right.

The host's relentless pursuit of the ideological "truth" imposed serious limitations on women's responses on this show. He regulated participants' comments by exhibiting disbelief at responses that defied the norm and endorsed responses that conformed to it. For example, he exclaimed at one point, "there's *no way* your husband can be the more lazy of the two—he just doesn't look it," and in another instance, he put his arm around a husband and said, "You have a good wife—she stepped onto the stage with her right foot first, she has brought harmony in your relations with your parents when things were not so good, and she has borne you a child—you are a very lucky man."

By questioning the husbands on whether or not they were aware of their wives' nonverbal expressions of unhappiness or disappointment, the show opened up a public space for husband-wife communication and legitimized this communication as crucial to a healthy marriage. Yet the host's judgmental statements needed further explanation. When asked about the need for his overt moralizing about the behavior of the husband and wife on stage, he said,

> There are people who want to talk very openly and they [asked] me, "Whatever we answer, are you going to [air] it?" I said, "that's for sure, I am not here to edit." [They said], "We want to talk about our sex life." I said, "I'm sorry, I don't—if you want to talk, you can, but the Indian mentality—think of your relatives and your friends. This is a very private matter between husband and wife." And they said, "Probably our grandmother is watching . . . we'd better not." So the openness, the people want [to talk], but . . . I'm still afraid, I am afraid to come open.

This narration of the participants' openness and the host's caution is interesting because he stated earlier that it was the audience in general that was very conservative. In the above narration, he was able to identify himself as one of those conservatives, afraid to telecast marital sexuality and defy traditional Hindu norms. These norms dictated that sexual relations between husband and wife were to be kept in the private sphere and, according to Vedic text, open to regulation by the husband's mother lest these relations alienate her son from his family. This narration brings us to an understanding of why the show has endured for six years on Udaya TV.

Although appropriating the global, the show had maintained the supremacy of the local and the host had proved himself time and again to be the keeper of the local, ensuring that the wives were not too outspoken and did not step out of the bounds of their "ideal" roles. The host performed a powerful role in addressing the hegemonic anxieties concerning the defiling or *pratilomic* marriage of global with local. His comments throughout the show, advising participants and audiences on codes of marital behavior, served the pedagogical function of a male head of the Indian household. Female assertion on the show was severely limited. Each show invariably ended with a brief comment to the audience such as the following, which wrapped up the August 26, 1996, show: "Did this show make you happy? If this show made you happy, we are happy, and the goal of this show is accomplished." With this, viewers and participants were left with a consensual picture of egalitarian marital harmony, a hegemonic strategy to gloss over critical differences that defined the lived experiences of the women. The local, therefore, appropriated the global for purposes of entertainment and consumption, but established its dominance in dictating how the global was to be organized and consumed within society. Udaya TV's overt strategies to uphold the local lead us to a discussion of how private satellite television networks negotiated through competition from the national and private transnational networks. These strategies solidify into the foundation of the Indian televisual landscape in the twenty-first century.

Strategies of Negotiation: The Indian Televisual Landscape in the Twenty-first Century

In 2000 the power of multinational corporations to connect subjects of the nation to global economic centers disregarding the national television hierarchy revived, with a vengeance, accusations of cultural imperialism from India's Hindu nationalist Bharatiya Janata Party (BJP) government. The BJP threatened to revoke the autonomous status of Doordarshan and reinstate government control over the floundering network. Private satellite television networks posed a threat because their broadcasts bypassed the national network and could be received by any household with a dish or cable connection. While British colonialism could be contained in the external material sphere,[34] private satellite television entered the inner spiritual sphere of the Indian home. Its narratives of individualism, freedom, and universalism could no longer be neatly set aside to be negotiated with in the external material sphere. As it crossed the private-public boundary, television as a conduit for global and local narratives, each propagating its own ideology, became the focus of hegemonic anxiety because it offered counternarratives to the dominant ideologies of Hindu supremacy mobilized by the BJP.

Despite government criticisms, private television companies knew that government sanctions on program content and network structure were far from an immediate threat. The task at hand was to consolidate their positions in regional arenas. Private regional channels recognized they could no longer operate independently in the face of competition for urban audiences from transnational networks such as Star TV and Zee TV. The only options were to diversify, acquire, or fold. Early in 2000, Udaya TV diversified into its film channel, Ushe TV, and its twenty-four-hour news channel, Udaya News. In June 2000 Zee Telefilms (ZTL) and Star TV battled to acquire the lucrative Rs. 300 crore (U.S. $68 million) Kerala based Malayalam network, Asianet, and its Kannada, Telugu, and Tamil regional channels.[35] By September that year, ZTL won, owning 51 percent of the company's stock. The most notable example, however, was the Mumbai-based UTV network's acquisition of the Telugu language Vijaya TV in April 2000. The chairman and the CEO of the network both stated that acquisition of regional channels was a crucial marketing strategy because there was room for at least three channels in each language per urban market. The network also obtained coproduction rights to a series of Fox Kids cartoons through its News Corp affiliation, the latter owning 12 percent of UTV's stock.[36]

With increasing competition among regional channels, especially now that most had network backing to support sophisticated in-house productions, local film industries received an unexpected boost. Theaters all over India experienced a slump in the mid-1990s, when regional channels stepped up their menus of classic and contemporary vernacular language films. By the late 1990s and 2000, regional channels were hungry for more talent not just in acting, but in production as well. Underutilized film studios were refurbished and several film actors, directors, and camera persons crossed over to television. The celebrity of the actors in turn promoted program visibility. At the same time, film studios increased their production of films because they had found an additional market in television audiences and regional channels bid against each other for first-run rights.[37]

Personnel at private regional and transnational channels were derisive of Doordarshan in general and noted that the sprawling and inefficient structure of the national network hindered its competitiveness. Doordarshan did own rights to films exponentially higher in number than any other network, yet internal corruption kept it from growing as rapidly in revenue as it could. Although its autonomy in 1997 did result in a greater proportion of entertainment programming, a culture of complacency still characterized the network and producers were not aggressive enough to counter competition from private networks. The network still dominates the field in terms of overall reach, but lags in urban viewership.[38]

The television industry in India is growing rapidly and will continue to grow for several years before it stabilizes. In the absence of strict government measures to check regulation violations, private networks and cable operators have found ways to organize themselves and stay afloat. Mergers and acquisitions have become the order of the day. Government criticism of foreign programs and of "immoral" local ones are no longer threatening to the viability of hybrid programs. Yet regional channels provide their own censors through hosts and audience response.

The success of *Adarsha Dampathigalu* points to an interesting correspondence between production and consumption of television. Without strict imposition of programming norms from the government, Udaya TV's producers and audiences negotiated between themselves the version of the show that could be transmitted to audiences at large. Conservative audiences communicated their opinions through letters and phone calls to the station. The host and producers of the show responded to that conservatism and were careful to keep the show within the bounds of Hindu propriety. The writing of the show between audience and network is indicative of a powerful and growing phenomenon in Indian regional television. As more and more regional networks emerge, each targeting niche audiences, there will likely be an intensification of channel loyalty and regional identification. In the context of politically backed networks such as Udaya TV's parent network, Sun TV, for example, these networks will provide a sympathetic space for regional politics. As television reconfigures husband-wife relationships, no matter how gradually, it is only a matter of time before it reconfigures the relation between region and nation.

NOTES

1. "Delhi High Court Issues Show-Cause Notice to TV Networks," *Economic Times*, August 1997, 4.

2. See, for example, David Morley and Kevin Robins, *Spaces of Identity: Global Media, Electronic Landscapes and Cultural Boundaries* (New York: Routledge, 1995); Purnima Mankekar, *Screening Culture, Viewing Politics: An Ethnography of Television, Womanhood, and Nation in Postcolonial India* (Durham: Duke University Press, 1999); John Tomlinson, *Cultural Imperialism* (Baltimore: John Hopkins University Press, 1991), 1–67.

3. Namrata Joshi, "A Babel in the Skies," *Outlook*, June 2000, 56–59.

4. "The Wiring of India," *Economist*, May 2000, 63–64.

5. "Doordarshan 2000: At a Glance," available from www.ddindia.net/bk1/content/html (23 June 2000).

6. Geetika Pathania, "Ambivalence in a STAR-ry Eyed Land: Doordarshan and the Satellite TV Challenge," *South Asia Graduate Research Journal* 1, no. 1 (1994).

7. J. Tusa, "International Satellite Television: Good Neighbor or Global Intruder?" *European Business Journal* 7, no. 4 (1995): 45–52.

8. Peter Shields and Sundeep Muppidi, "Integration, the Indian State and STAR TV: Policy and Theory Issues" (paper presented to the annual meeting of the International Communication Association, Chicago, 1996).

9. Tusa, "International Satellite Television."

10. Robin D. Crabtree and Sheena Malhotra, "The Genesis and Evolution of Commercial Television in India: A Case Study" (paper presented to the annual meeting of the International Communication Association, Chicago, 1996).

11. J. Banerjee, "Why Doordarshan's Getting Seedy," *Deccan Herald*, 12 January 1997, 1.

12. Government of India, *The Cable Television Networks (Regulation) Act: 1995 (With Rules, 1994)* (Allahabad: Law Publishers (India) Private Limited, 1995).

13. Pathania, "Ambivalence in a STAR-ry Eyed Land."

14. Suresh Nair, "The Host with the Most," *Times of India*, 29 June 1997, 6; J. Pinto, "Mad about the Game," *Times of India*, 7 August 1997, 1.

15. K. Manral, "India, Here She Comes," *Times of India*, 16 February 1997, 3.

16. Sudeep Chakravarthi, "Over the Top," *India Today*, 28 February 1995, 172–75.

17. Shankar V. Aiyar, and Anupama Chopra, "Great Gamble," *India Today*, 17 July 2000, 48–54.

18. "IMRB Connect," *Newsletter of Indian Market Research Bureau* 3, no. 1 (2000): 5.

19. For further discussion of the Indian caste system and marriage, see I. Karve, "The Kinship Map of India," in *Family, Kinship and Marriage in India*, ed. Patricia Uberoi (Delhi: Oxford University Press, 1993), 50–73. Also see Louis Dumont, *Homo Hierarchicus: The Caste System and Its Implications* (London: Weidenfeld and Nicolson, 1970).

20. L. Harlan and P. B. Courtright, "Introduction: On Hindu Marriage and Its Margins," in *From the Margins of Hindu Marriage*, ed. L. Harlan and P. B. Courtright (New York: Oxford University Press, 1995), 5.

21. Karve, "The Kinship Map of India."

22. Harlan and Courtright, "Introduction: On Hindu Marriage and Its Margins."

23. See G. N. Ramu, *Women, Work and Marriage in Urban India: A Study of Dual and Single-Earner Couples* (New Delhi: Sage, 1989).

24. Harlan and Courtright, "Introduction: On Hindu Marriage and Its Margins."

25. For further discussion of the complex identity of Indian women, see G. G. Raheja, "Crying When She's Born, and Crying When She Goes Away: Marriage and the Idiom of the Gift in Pahansu Song Performance," in Harlan and Courtright, *From the Margins of Hindu Marriage*, 19–59.

26. Louis Dumont, "North India in Relation to South India," in Uberoi, *Family, Kinship and Marriage in India*, 91–111.

27. See P. Krishnan and A. Dighe, *Affirmation and Denial: Construction of Femininity on Indian Television* (New Delhi: Sage, 1990), for an extensive analysis of programs of various genres on Doordarshan.

28. Mankekar, *Screening Culture, Viewing Politics*.

29. Examples of these questions were:

Who is the prime minister of India?
Who is the captain of the Indian cricket team?
Who was the winner of the 1996 Dada Phalke Award?

30. During this phase of the show the exchange value was one U.S. dollar to thirty-three rupees.

31. For a discussion of narrative theory, see D. Silverman, *Interpreting Qualitative Data* (London: Sage, 1995), 72–79; P. Alasuutari, *Researching Culture: Qualitative Methods and Cultural Studies* (London: Sage, 1995), 70–84; S. Kozloff, "Narrative Theory and Television," in *Channels of Discourse, Reassembled*, ed. Robert C. Allen (Chapel Hill: University of North Carolina Press, 1992), 67–100.

32. Jasmine is a fragrant flower in South India and is commonly worn by South Indian women. Jasmine garlands and strings are an integral part of many South Indian celebrations, especially weddings.

33. A dhoti is a lower cotton garment worn by South Indian men.

34. Partha Chatterjee, *The Nation and Its Fragments* (Princeton: Princeton University Press, 1993).

35. "Courtship for Channel Begins," *Deccan Herald*, 31 July 2000, Economy and Business, 3.

36. N. Vidyasagar, "UTV Riding High on Content," *Times of India*, 20 April 2000, Business Times, 1.

37. Srikanth Srinivasa, "Lights, Camera, Back in Action," *Deccan Herald*, 14 July 2000, Spectrum, 1.

38. For a critique of the political economy of television in India, see Divya McMillin, "Localizing the Global: Television and Hybrid Programming in India," *International Journal of Cultural Studies* 4, no. 1 (2001): 44–68.

Part V

Channelsurfing
Imagining Transnationalism

Culture and Communication

Toward an Ethnographic Critique of Media Consumption in the Transnational Media System

Ien Ang

The Power of the Popular: Beyond Ideology and Hegemony

The ethnographic thrust in audience studies has functioned as a way of relativizing the gloomy tendency of an older perspective within cultural studies, namely ideological criticism. A distinctive assumption of cultural studies is that the social production and reproduction of sense and meaning involved in the cultural process is not only a matter of signification, but also a matter of power.[1] The intimate connection of signifying practices and the exercise of power is a focal interest of cultural studies. As Grossberg (1983: 46) notes, "Once we recognize that all of culture refracts reality as well as reproducing it as meaningful, then we are committed as well to examining the interests implicated in particular refractions." Consequently, ideology was logically placed in the foreground of cultural studies to the point that the cultural and the ideological tended to be collapsed into one another; cultural processes are by definition also ideological in that the way the world is made to appear in a society tends to coincide with the interests of the dominant or powerful classes and groups in that society. The Gramscian concept of hegemony is mostly used to indicate the cultural leadership of the dominant classes in the production of generalized meanings, of "spontaneous" consent to the prevailing arrangement of social relations—a process, however, that is never finished because hegemony can never be complete. Since the communications media are assumed to play a pivotal role in the continuous struggle over hegemony, cultural studies became preoccupied with the question of how the media helped to produce consensus and manufacture consent (Hall, 1982). This set of assumptions has enabled us to understand the precise textual and institutional mechanisms by which the media function ideologically; how, that is, in processes of institutionalized cultural production particular meanings are encoded into the structure of texts, "preferred meanings" which tend to support existing economic, political and social power relations.

As a form of cultural critique, this kind of ideological analysis (only a simplified description is given here) is ultimately propelled by a will to demystify, denounce and condemn; it is a deconstructive practice which presupposes that the researcher/

critic can take up the marginal position of critical outsider. However, this perspective was soon sided by a countercurrent, which emphasized not top-bottom power, but bottom-top resistance, itself a form of (informal, subordinate) power. The well known work on youth subcultures (e.g. Hall and Jefferson, 1976; Willis, 1977; Hebdige, 1979), but also the emergence of ethnographic approaches to media audiences are part of the same trend. It is a populist reaction which stressed the vitality and energy with which those who are excluded from legitimate, institutional power create a meaningful and liveable world for themselves, using the very stuff offered to them by the dominant culture as raw material and appropriating it in ways that suit their own interests. Hall's (1980) encoding/decoding model opened up the space to examine the way in which the media's preferred meanings could be "negotiated" or even occasionally subverted in recalcitrant audience readings. John Fiske, the most exuberant ambassador of this position, has pushed it to an extreme in several provocative publications by virtually declaring the audience's independence in the cultural struggle over meaning and pleasure (e.g. Fiske, 1987a, 1987b). In this version of cultural studies the researcher/critic is no longer the critical outsider committed to condemn the oppressive world of mass culture, but a conscious fan, whose political engagement consists in "encouraging cultural democracy at work" (Fiske, 1987a: 286), by giving voice to and celebrating audience recalcitrance:

As Morris (1988:23) has remarked, what we have here is a "humane and optimistic discourse, trying to derive its values from materials and conditions already available to people." What, however, does it amount to as cultural critique? There is a romanticizing and romanticist tendency in much work that emphasizes (symbolic) resistance in audience reception, which, according to Morris, can all too easily lead to an apologetic *"yes, but . . ."* discourse that downplays the realities of oppression in favour of the representation of a rosy world "where there's always a way to redemption." Similar criticisms have been voiced by other critical theorists (e.g. Modleski, 1986; Schudson, 1987; Gripsrud, 1989).

But this kind of "selling out" is not the inevitable outcome of ethnographic work on media audiences. In this respect, it is unfortunate that the politics of reception analysis has all too often been one-sidedly cast within the terms of a liberal defence of popular culture, just as uses and gratifications research could implicitly or explicitly, in theoretical and political terms, serve as a decontextualized defence of the media status quo by pointing to their "functions" for the active audience (cf. Elliott, 1974). Similarly, research into how audiences create meanings out of items of popular culture has often been used as an empirical refutation of the elitist argument that mass culture stupefies, numbs the mind, reinforces passivity and so on. There is something truly democratic about this discourse, and I would be the last to want to question the importance of attacking the damaging impact of the high/low culture divide, which still pervasively informs—and limits—diverse cultural and educational policies, for example. However, revalidating the popular alone—by stressing the obvious empirical fact that audiences are active meaning producers and imaginative pleasure seekers—can become a banal form of cultural critique if the popular itself is not seen in a thoroughly social and political context. In other words, audiences may be active in myriad ways in using and interpreting media, but it would be utterly out of perspective to cheerfully equate "active" with "powerful", in the sense of "taking control" at an enduring, structural or institutional level. It is a perfectly reasonable starting point to consider people's active negotiations with media texts and technologies as empowering in the context of their everyday lives (which, of course, is *the* context of media reception), but we must not lose sight of the *marginality* of this power. As De Certeau (1984: xvii) has remarked about the clandestine tactics by which ordinary women and men try to "make do" in their everyday practices of consumption:

> this cultural activity of the non-producers of culture, an activity that is unsigned, unreadable, and unsymbolized, remains *the only one possible* for all those who nevertheless buy and pay for the showy products through which a productivist economy articulates itself. (Emphasis added)

To be sure, one of the important contributions made by ethnographic studies of reception is exactly the "signing", "reading" and "symbolizing"—the documenting, the putting into tangible discourse—of the fragmented, invisible, marginal tactics by which media audiences symbolically appropriate a world not of their own making. This is no doubt what Fiske meant by encouraging cultural democracy, and he is right. However, if audience ethnography wants to elaborate its critical function, it cannot avoid confronting more fully what sociologists have dubbed the micro/macro problematic: the fact that there are structural limits to the possibilities of cultural democracy *à la* Fiske, that its expression takes place within specific parameters and concrete conditions of existence. In short, we need to return to the problematic of hegemony.

If the euphoria over the vitality of popular culture and its audiences has tended to make the question of hegemony rather unfashionable in some cultural studies circles, it is because the popular came to be seen as an autonomous, positive entity in itself, a repository of bold independence, strength and creativity, a happy space in which people can arguably stay outside of, and resist, the hegemonic field of force. In fact, however, the relationship between the hegemonic and the popular should not be conceived of in terms of mutual exteriority; the hegemonic can be found within the very texture of the popular. As Colombian communication theorist Martin-Barbero (1988: 448) has noted, "we need to recognize that the hegemonic does not dominate us from without but rather penetrates us, and therefore it is not just against it but from within it that we are waging war". Therefore, he is wary of a "political identification of the popular with an intrinsic, spontaneous resistance with which the subordinate oppose the hegemonic." Instead, what should be emphasized is "the thick texture of hegemony/subalternity, the interlacing of resistance and submission, and opposition and complicity" (Martin-Barbero, 1988: 462). The resulting forms of cultural resistance are not just ways to find redemption, but also a matter of capitulation; invested in them is not just pleasure, but also pain, anger, frustration—or sheer despair.

In fact, Martin-Barbero's Latin-American perspective, informed as it is by the harsh and ugly realities which are a product of the subcontinent's unequal economic development, profound political instability and day-to-day social disorder, especially in the explosive urban areas, not only can help to undermine the Euro- and Americo-centrism of much cultural studies, but also, more positively, can (re)sensitize us to the messy and deeply political contradictions which constitute and shape popular practices. In Latin America, the popular is often nostalgically equated with the indigenous, and this in turn with the primitive and the backward—the disappearing "authentic popular" untouched by, and outside of the realm of modernity. From this perspective; the unruly, crime-ridden, poverty-stricken culture of the urban popular, concentrated in the *favelas*, the *barrios* and other slums, diffuses its subversions from there right into the hearts of the modern city centres, and could only be conceived of as contamination of indigenous purity, as an irreconcilable loss of authenticity. Against this vision Martín-Barbero (1988: 460) proposes to reconceptualize the indigenous as at once "dominated and yet as the possessors of a positive existence, capable of development". In this way, we can begin to see the urban popular not as inauthentic degeneration but as the truly contemporary site where powerless groups seek to take control of their own conditions of existence within the limits imposed by the pressures of modernity.

In the west, where everyday life is relatively comfortable even for the least privileged, the struggle for popular survival and self-affirmation seems to have lost its urgency. However, it is not true that, as Martín-Barbero (1988: 464) would have it, "in the United States and Europe . . . to talk of the popular is to refer solely to massness or to the folklore museum". In the developed world, too, the popular remains invested with intense conflict: this is the case even in such a seemingly innocent terrain as cultural consumption and media reception. To be sure, Martín-Barbero's assumption that popular culture is a subordinate culture that stands in a contradictory relation to dominant culture, is hardly unique and is well represented in British cultural studies too, particularly as a result of its Gramscian legacy (e.g. Bennett et al., 1986). However, this general theoretical assumption has not sufficiently succeeded in informing concrete analyses of media audiences. Instead, our understanding of media reception—one of the most prominent practices where the popular takes shape in today's "consumer societies"—is still governed by the unhelpful dichotomies of passive/active, manipulative/liberating, and so on. What a critical ethnography of media audiences needs to ferret out, then, is the unrecognized, unconscious and contradictory effectivity of the hegemonic within the popular, the relations of power that are inscribed within the texture of reception practices. The following section sketches out one of the trajectories along which we can begin to stake out this terrain.

The Hegemonic Specified: The Transnational Media System

To begin with, it is important to develop a concrete sense of the hegemonic forces that rule the world today. In too much cultural studies writing understanding of hegemony remains at an abstract theoretical level, evoked rather than analysed, by alluding to basic concepts such as "class", "gender" and "race". We need to go beyond these paradigmatic conceptualizations of hegemony and develop a more specific, concrete, contextual, in short, a more ethnographic sense of the hegemonic (Marcus, 1986).

A good point to begin with, although briefly, is the rather disturbing changes that the world media system—arguably an important locus of hegemonic forces—is undergoing at present. As we move towards the end of the century the communications industries, as part of the ever expanding capitalist system, have been in a process of profound economic and institutional restructure and transformation, which can be characterized by accelerated transnationalization and globalization. We can see this in the emergence of truly global, decentred corporations in which diverse media products (film and television, press and publishing, music and video) are being combined and integrated into overarching communications empires such as those of Bertelsmann, Murdoch, Berlusconi and Time-Warner. This process is accompanied by an increased pressure towards the creation of translational markets and transnational distribution systems (made possible by new communication technologies such as satellite and cable), transgressing established boundaries and subverting existing territories—a process which, of course, has profound political and cultural consequences (Robins, 1989; Morley and Robins, 1990). The currency of such notions as "the information revolution" and "postmodernity" are indicative of the perceived pervasiveness of the changes, and in our everyday lives we bear direct witness to these changes, through the turbulent transformation of our media environment, in both technological (cable, satellite, video) and institutional (new TV channels, dismantling of public service monopoly) terms.

These historical developments form, in very specific ways, the structural and global configurations of hegemony within which contemporary practices of media reception and consumption evolve. As we have seen, ethnographies of media audiences emphasize, and lend to celebrate, the capability of audience groups to construct their own meanings and thus their own local cultures and identities, even in the face of their virtually complete dependence on the image flows distributed by the transnational culture Industries. However, this optimistic celebration of the local can easily be countered by a more pessimistic scenario, pictured by Manuel Castells, who foresees "the coexistence both of the monopoly of messages by the big networks and of the increasingly narrow codes of local microcultures around their parochial cable TV's" (quoted in Robins, 1989: 151). In other words, would not the vitality and creativity of audiences in creating their own cultures merely amount to paltry manifestations of, in Castells' words, "cultural tribalism" within an electronic global village?

It would be ludicrous, I would argue, to try to find a definitive and unambiguous, general theoretical answer to this question—as the theory of cultural imperialism has attempted to do—precisely because there is no way to know in advance which strategies and tactics different peoples in the world will invent to negotiate with the intrusions of global forces in their lives. For the moment, then, we can only hope for provisional answers—answers informed by ethnographic sensitivity to how structural changes become integrated in specific cultural forms and practices, under specific historical circumstances. Only such a particularistic approach will allow us to avoid premature closures in our understanding and keep us alert to contextual specificities and contradictions.

However, an ethnographic perspective suitable for and sensitive to the peculiarities of our contemporary cultural condition needs to move beyond the restrictive scope delimited by the boundaries of the local, and to develop an awareness of the pertinent asymmetries between production/distribution and consumption, the general and the particular, the global and the local. In other words, ethnography's critical edge does not only have to reside in discovering and validating diversity and difference in an increasingly homogeneous world, as has been suggested by several authors (e.g. Van Maanen, 1988), it can work more ambitiously towards an unravelling of the intricate intersections of the diverse and the homogeneous (e.g. Lull, 1989). Furthermore, the ethnographic perspective can help to detail and specify the abstracting telescopic view invoked by structural analysis of the transnational global system:

> The ethnographic task lies ahead of reshaping our dominant macro-frameworks for the understanding of historical political economy, such as capitalism, so that they can represent the actual diversity and complexity of local situations for which they try to account in general terms. (Marcus and Fischer, 1986: 88)

In short, one means of examining the way in which the hegemonic and the popular interpenetrate one another is to trace the global in the local and the local in the global. . . .

Where the Global and the Local Meet: Nationality and the Struggle for Cultural Identities

One central issue, in which recognition of the intertwining of global and local developments has particularly strong theoretical and political consequences, is the issue of cultural identity. In the struggles that are fought out around this issue in many parts of the world today, the structural changes brought about by the trans-nationalization of media flows are often assessed and officially defined in terms of a threat to the autonomy and integrity of "national identity." However, such a definition of the problem seems a very limited and limiting one, because it tends to subordinate other, more specific and differential sources for the construction of cultural identity (e.g. those based upon class, locality, gender, generation, ethnicity, religion, politics, etc.) to the hegemonic and seemingly natural one of *nationality*. The defence and preservation of national identity as a privileged foundation for cultural identity is far from a general, self-evidently legitimate political option. After all, nations are themselves artificial, historically constituted politico-cultural units; they are not the natural destiny of pre-given cultures, rather their existence is based upon the construction of a standardized "national culture" that is a prerequisite to the functioning of a modern industrial state (Gellner, 1983). The desire to keep national identity and national culture wholesome and pristine is not only becoming increasingly unrealistic, but is also, at a more theoretical level, damagingly oblivious to the contradictions that are condensed in the very concept of national identity. Defining national identity in static, essentialist terms—by forging, in a manner of speaking, authoritative checklists of Britishness, Dutchness, Frenchness, and so on—

ignores the fact that what counts as part of a national identity is often a site of intense struggle between a plurality of cultural groupings and interests inside a nation, and that therefore national identity is, just like the popular identities in Latin America and elsewhere, fundamentally a dynamic, conflictive, unstable and impure phenomenon.

However, contrary to the subterranean tactics by which informal popular identities are created, the categories of national identity and national culture are invested with formal, discursive legitimacy and are at present still dominantly used as a central foundation for official cultural and media policies. It is this constellation that has been thrown into question by the electronic intrusions of the transnational media system, which does not care about national boundaries, only about boundaries of territory, of transmission and of markets. It is not just a question of "cultural imperialism", that older term that suggests the unambiguous domination of one dependent culture by a clearly demarcated other. The homogenizing tendencies brought about by the transnational era may be better characterized by the term "cultural synchronization" (Hamelink, 1983), and it poses quite a different problem as to the politics of cultural identity. The Mexican theorist, Garcia Canclini, has formulated the problem as follows:

> To struggle to make oneself independent of a colonial power in a head-on combat with a geographically defined power is very different from struggling for one's own identity inside a transnational system which is diffuse, complexity interrelated and interpenetrated. (Quoted in Martin-Barbero, 1988: 452)

In other words, in the increasingly integrated world system there is no such thing as an independent cultural identity; every identity must define and position itself in relation to the cultural frames affirmed by the world system. Ignoring this, which is the case when national identity is treated as a sacrosanct given; not only can lead us to undesirable unintended consequences, but is itself an act of symbolic power, both by defining an abstracted, unified identity for diverse social and cultural groups within a nation, and by fixing, in a rigid fashion, relationships between national "imagined communities" (Anderson, 1983).

Two more Third World examples can illuminate how a politics of national identity, or one that is propelled in its name, always implies a rearrangement of relations of cultural power, both locally and globally. The examples also point to the kind of concrete situations that ethnographies of reception could take up while holding together both local specificity and global pressures.

In its attempt to foster Malaysian identity, the Malaysian government ruled in 1989 that television commercials were no longer allowed to feature "pan-Asian" models (and still less Caucasian models or advertisements "suggesting Western superiority"). Instead, actors should represent Malaysia's main ethnic groups: Malays, Chinese and Indians: Ironically, however, the government had in the early 1980s taken precisely the opposite tack, directing advertising agencies to stop using racially identifiable models, reasoning that using mixed-race actors would be more adequate to promote Malaysian identity (Goldstein, 1989). What we see here is not only that national identity is a matter of selective construction, including some and excluding other elements from it (defining itself as much in terms of what it is not as in what it is), but also the very uncertainty and instability of what that identity is and should be. The inconsistency exemplified in this case glaringly elucidates the precariousness of a cultural politics that depends on the concept of national identity for its rhetoric and assumptions.

The second example describes a more popular case of cultural nationalism. In the Philippines, English, brought by the American colonizers at the turn of the century, has been the official language for nearly thirty years after the nation's independence in 1946. English was the language that served linguistically to unify a country inhabited by peoples who speak more than seventy regional languages and dialects. After the downfall of President Marcos in 1986, however, the country has seen the spectacular and spontaneous (i.e. unplanned) emergence of one of the native languages, Tagalog, as a popular national language. Tagalog, not English, was the language of street rallies and demonstrations and it became an emblem of national self-esteem. Now, most popular TV shows and comic books are in Tagalog, TV newscasts in Tagalog are drawing far larger audiences than those in English, and there is even a "serious" newspaper in Tagalog, breaking the previous English-language monopoly in this market. Politicians can no longer rely upon delivering their speeches in English only. (President Aquino's command of the indigenous language is said to have improved tremendously) (Branegan, 1989). If this turn of events would stir some optimism in the hearts of principled nationalists, it also has more contradictory consequences: it may lead, for example, to new, linguistically-based inequalities and social divisions. It is not unlikely that the use and command of English will gradually decline among the less privileged, while the upper and middle classes will continue to speak both languages. After all, on a global scale English is the language that gives access to economic success and social mobility.

These two examples reinforce Schlesinger's (1987: 234) claim that it is important for communication researchers

> not to start with communication and its supposed effects on national identity and culture, but rather to begin by posing the problem of national identity itself, to ask how it might be analyzed and what importance communication practices might have in its constitution.

Furthermore, we can see how the cultural constitution of national identity, as articulated in both official policies and informal popular practices, is a precarious project that can never be isolated from the global, transnational relations in which it takes shape. At a more general level, these cases give us a hint at the multiple contradictions that are at play in any local response to global forces.

There is also an opposite tack to take. While the transnational communications system tends to disrupt existing forms of national identification, it also offers opportunities of new forms of bonding and solidarity, new ways of forging cultural communities. The use of video by groups of migrants all over the world (e.g. Indians, Chinese and Turks) is a telling case. The circulation and consumption of ethnically specific information and entertainment on video serves to construct and maintain cross-national "electronic communities" of geographically dispersed people who would otherwise lose their ties with tradition and its active perpetuation (Gillespie, 1989). Thus, while official, national(ist) policies against further dissemination of the transnational media system seem to be less possible and more ineffectual than ever, social groups inside and between nations seem to have found informal ways to construct their own collective identities within the boundaries of the system that limits and binds us all.

The above cases have not been highlighted out of cross-cultural romanticism, but because things happening in distant places and among other peoples—often reified as an amorphous Third World—may offer us lessons that are relevant to our own situations. For example European national identities have recently been thoroughly put under pressure by the growing importance of an integrated European media policy, as for example in the EEC's directive for a *Television without Frontiers*. Culturally, this policy, which is an attempt to regulate the otherwise uncontrolled expansion of the transnational media system across Europe, is legitimized by pointing to the need to defend and promote some notional, supra-national "European identity," in which the spectre of separate national identities in Europe will presumably be represented. However, this sweeping pan-Europeanism, which is increasingly becoming a hegemonic force at the level of official politics, contains many contradictions. For one thing, it is clear that there is no agreement about what such a European identity should look like. Thus, the smaller nations (such as the Netherlands, Denmark and Greece) are suspicious about the dominance of the larger nations (France, Germany and Italy), while there is also a clash of visions and interests between nations who define themselves as part of a "Nordic" European culture and those that represent the "Latin" culture. Of course, this is not to say that the separate national identities themselves should be seen as harmonious givens to which we could resort as a safe haven (after all, the nations themselves are repositories of conflicting cultural identifications); rather, it is to suggest that the politics of European identity is a matter of cultural power and resistance, not simply a question of cherishing some "heritage," as official policy discourse would have it.

Troubling in this respect is the way in which such a "heritage" is artificially forged by the formulation of what is included in and excluded from the configuration of "Europeanness". This implies symbolic strategies that are sustained by constructing the image of a unified European culture that needs to be protected from the supposed threat of external, alien cultural influences. In his book *Orientalism*, Edward Said (1978) has already shown how the idea of "European" has benefited from the colonial period onwards from its claimed superiority to the culture of the "Orient". This "heritage" of latent and manifest racism still has troubling effects on ethnic relations in most European countries.

More recently, Europeanists have shown obsessive concern about the supposed threat of cultural "Americanization" as a consequence of the transnationalization of the media system. This blatantly ignores the fact, however, that American cultural symbols have become an integral part of the way in which millions of Europeans construct their cultural identities. Thus, official policies based upon a totalizing antagonism of "Europe" against "America" are necessarily out of touch with everyday life in contemporary Europe. If American popular culture seems so attractive to so many in the world, how do people incorporate it into their activities, fantasies, values and so on? What multifarious and contradictory meanings are attached to images of the "American way of life" in what specific circumstances? Surely, those meanings cannot be the same in different parts and among different groups and peoples living in Europe or, for that matter, in Latin America or South East Asia, but we know almost nothing about such differences. Against this background, pan-Europeanist discourse should not simply be seen as a counter-hegemonic response to the very real American hegemony in the field of cultural production and distribution, but as itself a hegemnic strategy that tends to marginalize the more elusive popular responses of ordinary Europeans. More specifically, I suggest that the official definition of "Americanization" as an unambiguous threat should be relativized by looking at the contradictory losses *and* opportunities allowed by it. As Marcus and Fischer (1986: 136) suggest:

> the apparent increasing global integration suggests not the elimination of cultural diversity, but rather opportunities for counterposing diverse alternatives that nonetheless share a common world, so that each can be understood better in the other's light.

What I have tried to conjure up, then, is the broad range of creative but contradictory practices which peoples in different parts of the world are inventing today in their everyday dealings with the changing media environment that surrounds them. The often hazardous and unpredictable nature of these practices makes them difficult to examine with too formalized methods: it is an ethnographic approach that can best capture and respect them in their concrete multi-facetedness. Here then lies the critical potential of an ethnography of audiences that evinces global and historical consciousness as well as attention to local detail. In the words of Marcus and Fischer (1986: 116), "since there are always multiple sides and multiple expressions of possibilities active in any situation, some accommodating, others resistant to dominant cultural trends or interpretations, ethnography as cultural criticism locates alternatives by unearthing these multiple possibilities as they exist in reality".

Its emphasis on what *is* rather than on what could be makes ethnography a form of cultural critique that is devoid of utopianism. But then we live in particularly non-utopian (or post-utopian) times—which is, of course, precisely one of the central features of the "postmodern condition" (cf. Lyotard, 1984; Ross, 1988; Rorty, 1989). The *de facto* dissemination of the transnational media system is an irreversible process that cannot be structurally transcended, only negotiated in concrete cultural contexts. In such a situation, a critical perspective that combines a radical empiricism[2] with open-ended theorizing[3] may be one of the best stances we can take up in order to stay alert to the deeply conflictive nature of contemporary cultural relations. It is a form of cultural critique which is articulated by "pained and disgruntled subjects, who are also joyous and inventive practitioners" (Morris, 1988: 26)

NOTES

From Ien Ang, "Cultural and Communication: Toward an Ethnographic Critique of Media Consumption in the Transnational Media System," *European Journal of Communication,* 5, nos. 2–3, (1990). Reprinted by permission of Sage Publications Ltd.

1. It is the place of power, conflict and struggle in the process of culture that characterizes the central difference between American cultural studies, of which Carey is a representative, and British cultural studies. The humanist idealism of the American perspective is countered by the grimmer and more cynical European perspective, with its eye never diverted from the social costs of any form of order and consensus.

2. Radical empiricism should emphatically be distinguished from vulgar empiricism. While vulgar empiricism has a built-in tendency towards conservatism because it takes "reality-as-it-is" for granted, radical empiricism questions that taken-for-grantedness precisely because it fully engages itself with the messiness of the world we live in. See Higgins (1986: 120).

3. According to Hall, such open-ended theorizing is necessary in order to keep cultural studies sensitive to historical process. "It is theorizing in the postmodern context, if you like, in the sense that it does not believe in the finality of a finished theoretical paradigm" Grossberg, 1986. 60).

REFERENCES

Anderson, Benedict (1983) *Imagined Communities.* London: Verso.

Ang. Ien (1985) *Watching Dallas.* London: Methuen.

Ang. Ien (1989) "Wanted: Audiences. On the Politics of Empirical Audience Studies", in E. Seiter, H. Borchers, G. Kreutzner and E. Warth (eds). *Remote Control: Television, Audiences and Cultural Power.* London and New York: Routledge.

Bennett, Tony, Colin Mercer and Janet Woollacot (eds.) (1986) *Popular Culture and Social Relations.* Milton Keynes: Open University Press.

Blumler, Jay G., Michael Gurevitch and Elihu Katz (1985) "Reaching Out: A Future for Gratifications Research", pp. 255–73 In K.E. Rosengren, L: Wenner and P. Palmgreen (eds), *Media Gratifications Research: Current Perspectives.* Beverly Hills: Sage.

Branegan, Jay (1989) "Bubbling Up from Below". *Time,* 21 August.

Certeau, Michel de (1984) *The Practice of Everyday Life,* (translated by Steven Rendall). Berkeley: University of California Press.

Elliott, Philip (1974) "Uses and Gratifications Research: A Critique and a Sociological Alternative", pp. 249–68 in J.G. Blumler and E. Katz (eds), *The Uses of Mass Communication.* Beverly Hills and London: Sage.

Fiske, John (1987a) "British Cultural Studies and Television", pp. 254–89 in R.C. Allen (ed.). *Channels of Discourse.* Chapel Hill and London: University of North Carolina Press.

Fiske, John (1987b) *Television Culture.* London and New York: Methuen.

Geertz, Clifford (1983) *Local Knowledge.* New York: Basic Books.

Gellner, Ernest (1983) *Nations and Nationalism.* Oxford: Basil Blackwell.

Gillespie, Marie (1989) "Technology and Tradition: Audiovisual Culture Among South Asian Families in West London". *Cultural Studies,* 3(2): 226–39.

Goldstein, Carl (1989) "The Selling of Asia", *Far Eastern Economic Review,* 29 June: 60–1.

Gripsrud, Justein (1989) " 'High Culture' Revisited", *Cultural Studies,* 3(2): 194–207.

Grossberg, Lawrence (1983) "Cultural Studies Revisited and Revised", pp. 39–70 in M.S. Mander (ed.), *Communications in Transition.* New York: Praeger.

Grossberg, Lawrence (ed.) (1986) "On Postmodernism and Articulation. An Interview with Stuart Hall", *Journal of Communication Inquiry*, 10(2): 45–60.

Grossberg, Lawrence (1988) *It's A Sin. Essays on Postmodernism, Politics and Culture*. Sydney: Power Publications.

Hall, Stuart (1980) "Encoding/Decoding", pp. 128–38 in S. Hall, D. Hobson, A. Lowe and P. Willis (eds). *Culture, Media, Language*. London: Hutchinson.

Hall, Stuart (1982) "The Rediscovery of "Ideology": Return of the Repressed in Media Studies", pp. 56–90 in M. Gurevitch, T. Bennett and J. Woollacott (eds), *Culture, Society, and the Media*. London and New York: Methuen.

Hall, Stuart, Dorothy Hobson, Andrew Lowe and Paul Willis (eds) (1980) *Culture, Media, Language*. London: Hutchinson.

Hall, Stuart and Tony Jefferson (eds) (1976) *Resistance Through Rituals*. London: Hutchinson.

Hamelink, Cees (1983) *Cultural Autonomy in Global Communications*. New York: Longman.

Hardt, Hanno (1989) "The Return of the 'Critical' and the Challenge of Radical Dissent: Critical Theory, Cultural Studies, and American Mass Communication Research", pp. 558–600 in J. Anderson (ed.), *Communication Yearbook 12*. Newbury Park: Sage.

Hebdige, Dick (1979) *Subculture: The Meaning of Style*. London: Methuen.

Higgins, John (1986) "Raymond Williams and the Problem of Ideology", pp. 112–22 in J. Arac (ed.), *Postmodernism and Politics*. Minneapolis: University of Minnesota Press.

Lull, James (ed.) (1989) *World Families Watch Television*. Newbury Park: Sage.

Lyotard, Jean-François (1984) *The Postmodern Condition* (translated by Geoff Bennington and Brian Massumi) Minneapolis: University of Minnesota Press.

Marcus, George E. (1986) "Contemporary Problems of Ethnography in the Modern World System", pp. 165–93 in J. Clifford and G.E. Marcus (eds), *Writing Culture*, Berkeley: University of California Press.

Marcus, George E. and Michael M.J. Fischer (1986) *Anthropology as Cultural Critique*. Chicago and London: The University of Chicago Press.

Martin-Barbero, Jesus (1988) "Communication from Culture: The Crisis of the National and the Emergence of the Popular", *Media, Culture & Society*, 10(4): 447–65.

Modleski, Tania (1986) "Introduction", pp. ix–xix in T. Modleski (ed.), *Studies in Entertainment*. Bloomington and Indianapolis: Indiana University Press.

Morley, David (1980) *The "Nationwide" Audience*. London: BFI.

Morley, David (1986) *Family Television: Cultural Power and Domestic Leisure*. London: Comedia.

Morley, David and Kevin Robins (1990) "Spaces of Identity", *Screen*, 30(1).

Morris, Meaghan (1988) "Banality in Cultural Studies", *Block* (14): 15–25.

Pratt, Mary Louise (1986) "Interpretive Strategies/Strategic Interpretations: On Anglo-American Reader-Response Criticism", pp. 26–54 in J. Arac (ed.). *Postmodernism and Politics*. Minneapolis: University of Minnesota Press.

Radway, Janice (1984) *Reading the Romance*. Chapel Hill: University of North Carolina Press.

Radway, Janice (1988) "Reception Study: Ethnograpy and the Problems of Dispersed Audiences and Nomadic Subjects", *Cultural Studies*, 2(3): 359–76.

Real, Michael (1989) *Super Media: A Cultural Studies Approach*. Newbury Park: Sage.

Robins, Kevin (1989) "Reimagined Communities? European Image Spaces, Beyond Fordism", *Cultural Studies*, 3(2): 145–65.

Rorty, Richard (1989) *Contingency, Irony and Solidarity*. Cambridge: Cambridge University Press.

Rosengren, Karl Erik (1988) *The Study of Media Culture: Ideas, Actions, and Artefact*. Lund

Research papers in the Sociology of Communication, Report No 10. Lund: University of Lund.

Ross, Andrew (ed.) (1988) *Universal Abandon? The Politics of Postmodernism*. Minneapolis: University of Minnesota Press.

Said, Edward (1978) *Orientalism*. New York: Pantheon Books.

Schlesinger, Philip (1987) "On National Idenity: Some Conceptions and Misconceptions Criticized", *Social Science Information*, 26(2): 219–64.

Schrøder, Kim (1987) "Convergence of Antagonistic Traditions? The Case of Audience Research". *European Journal of Communication*, 12(1): 7–32.

Schudson, Michael (1987) "The New Validation of Popular Culture: Sense and Sentimentality in Academia", *Critical Studies in Mass Communication*, 4(1): 51–68.

Siij, Alessandro (1988), *East of Dallas. The European Challenge to American Television*. London: BFI.

Van Maanen, John (1988) *Tales of the Field*. Chicago and London: The University of Chicago Press.

Willis, Paul (1977) *Learning to Labour*. London: Saxon House.

Chapter Twenty-one

Narrowcasting in Diaspora
Iranian Television in Los Angeles

Hamid Naficy

Producers and Production

Parviz Kardan, producer and host of Shah-re Farang, *had been a well-known actor and entertainer in Iran before his emigration first to England then to the United States. I interviewed him on a warm mid-morning in his shoe shop. He was the owner of and at the time the sole salesman in the store, located in a nondescript mall near the Los Angeles airport. The mall itself was eerily empty of customers, as was the shop, lined with rows of nondescript shoes. During my two-hour interview only one customer came, and he left empty-handed. Kardan spoke of the plays he had staged in London and bemoaned the crass commercialization of exile television. His weekly show did not generate sufficient income, forcing him to make ends meet by running the shoe shop. Television, his love, had to be his sideline.*

My interview with Hamid Shabkhiz, producer and host of Iran, *was set for late at night after the airing of his nightly show. It was a warm California night cooled by a gentle breeze. We met at his TV studio, which was also his house, a large ranch-style home in the San Fernando valley with a swimming pool in the back. He greeted me at the door and took me through his control room out into the backyard where I met his wife and his advertising agent. The lights from the rippling pool cast a variegated blue shade everywhere. The atmosphere was congenial and informal. Fruit and soft drinks were offered and I interviewed Shabkhiz while his wife in the control room compiled a weekly version of* Iran *for syndication to other U.S. cities (or as Shabkhiz would call them, provinces, shahrestanha). We were often interrupted by frantic phone calls, taken at poolside or in the studio. While Shabkhiz was on the phone, I interviewed Daryush Mirahmadi, the ad man. High-pitched voices from the editing machines shuttling forward and backward further punctuated our conversations. One or two customers, bringing artwork for their ads, came and went. Television was being made poolside: Our conversation, the editing of the syndicated show, and the business dealings continued well into the night.*

Homa Ebsan, producer and host of Didar, *lived in an upscale security condo in Orange County—in one of those large gated communities (read "stealth communities") that have sprung up everywhere in southern California. Her living room, where her show was usually taped, was a typical ethnic room, neat, decorated with all kinds of memorabilia from the homeland, from far-away family members, and from a professional life in radio and television before emigration. She had just been forced to take her show off the air and she was bitter about that, the sexism of the TV producers, and the loss of a forum for exposing the fast-assimilating Iranian children to the "authentic" culture of the homeland. Our conversation went on over a working lunch in her kitchen.*

Although many television shows are produced in studios, making television programs in exile is often a home-bound activity, like their viewing. Television production is part of the private lives of the producers. As a result, exile television inscribes more fully than does mainstream television the lives of its makers.

Minority Television

To maximize the size of its audience mainstream television has traditionally emphasized commonalities. Recent developments, however, have encouraged specialization and audience segmentation, making the industry particularly responsive to ethnic, transnational, and exilic differences. These developments include consolidation of cable television and its provision of lease-access to clients, including ethnic and exile communities, and government regulation of the industry, such as requirements to provide public access and minority ownership of stations. To this set of industrial and regulatory measures must be added the availability of inexpensive but sophisticated technologies, which tend to "democratize" television production and reception. Finally, the global news and information networks, program packaging consortia such as SCOLA, and videos imported from former homelands have created a very complex and intensified transnational traffic that feeds the nonmainstream form of television under study here.

These and other factors have enabled commercially driven television in the United States to surpass cinema as a vehicle of both the expression and the formation of minority identities. In Southern California, channel 18 (KSCI-TV), an independent station that dubs itself the "international channel," provides round-the-clock programming in some 16 languages produced by various diasporas in the United States or imported from their home countries.[1] There are also a number of local cable companies that air locally produced minority programs on a lease-access or public access basis. While there are many stations that target a specific ethnic or national group, KSCI-TV, by airing programs in so many languages, provides the most diverse ethnic and linguistic menu of any station in Los Angeles (and for that matter in the country).

In the following analysis, the menu of "minority television" is divided into three categories: ethnic, transnational, and exilic TV. Although these categories are flexible, permeable, at times simultaneous, and can merge under certain circumstances, there are distinguishing features that set them apart.

Ethnic Television refers to television programs primarily produced in the host country by long-established indigenous minorities. Black Entertainment Television (BET) is the primary example of this category, much of whose programming originates and centers on life and times in the United States. The homeland for these programs is ultimately located here and now, not over there and then. If its programming inscribes struggles, they are usually intracultural (within the United States), not intercultural. A good portion of the Spanish-language networks' programs also fall within this category.

Transnational Television is fed primarily by products imported from the homeland or those produced by American and multinational media concerns. Korean, Japanese, and Chinese programs fit this category. These programs locate their homeland outside the United States and they push to the background the drama of acculturation and resistance.

In some cases, reliance on imports gives a foreign government friendly to the U.S. administration direct access to program time, raising legal and political issues about unwarranted use of American airwaves for propaganda purposes (Holley 1986). The Korean-language broadcasts, for example, are produced by Korean Broadcasting Service in South Korea, a government-controlled body, and they are imported and distributed for broadcast in the United States by the government-owned Korean Television Enterprises. Station time is also subsidized by the government. As a result of such outside assistance, Korean producers of both radio and television programs have been able to block-book much of the prime-time hours of multiethnic stations in Los Angeles, pushing out other ethnic competitors. Spanish-language national networks in the United States (Univision, Telemundo, and Galavision) can be considered to be primarily transnational and only partly ethnic in that they are by and large produced by American or foreign multinational corporations and much of their programming is imported from Mexico, Venezuela, and Brazil.[2]

Exilic Television is by definition produced by exiles living in the host country as a response to and in parallel with their own transitional and provisional status. Television programs produced by Iranians, Arabs, and Armenians fall within this classification. Such programs are often produced by small-time individual producers, not by media conglomerates of the home or host societies. They tend to encode and foreground collective and individual struggles for authenticity and identity, deterritorialization and reterritorialization. Although they are relative newcomers, Iranians have been perhaps the most active users of television among all the minorities in this country. In fact, with the exception of Hispanic programming, Persian-language television tops all other locally produced transnational and exilic programming in the Los Angeles area. With the exception of *Aftab*, all Iranian programs aired in the area are produced outside Iran by entrepreneurs who oppose the Islamic government there.

Even though ethnic television, particularly BET and Jewish Television Network, is primarily focused on the culture, concerns, and personalities of a segment of the population in the United States, it can potentially reach mainstream audiences because it is spoken in English. As such, it is a form of "broadcasting." Transnational and exilic television, on the other hand, are examples of "narrowcasting" or "lowcasting" because they are aired in foreign languages.

In the process of developing infrastructure and experimenting with programming, a new exile genre of television has evolved, whose analysis will shed light on television's role as a facilitator of syncretic acculturation. On the one hand, exilic television creates a symbolic communitas in exile, and helps to consolidate collective solidarity based on descent; on the other hand, it procures cultural capital for the host society by reproducing its consumerist ideology, thereby obtaining the consent of its audiences to dominant values.

Iranian Exilic Television in Los Angeles

The first Iranian TV program aired in exile was a thirty-minute program called *Haftegi-ye Pars* (Pars weekly), only one episode of which was aired in 1978 by channel 52 (KVEA-TV). The first regularly scheduled program was *Iranian*, which began in March 1981 as a thirty-minute weekly show, and later expanded to one hour. This program is also the longest continuous Persian-language Iranian program abroad, lasting to the present in the same time slot. Since these initial efforts, a total of 62 regularly scheduled programs have been aired, with the current number standing at 26 shows, totaling over 17 hours of airtime per week. All of them are produced in Los Angeles.[3]

Although there has been a steady annual increase in the number of new shows, there has been considerable fluctuation in the fate of exile TV programs. Of the 62 regularly scheduled shows some 36 have disappeared. Every few months a television program dies to be replaced by one or more new shows—sometimes made by the same producers. This televisual ebb and flow is an index of the fluidity of life in exile—it parallels the ups and downs experienced by the other components of exilic popular culture. The fluidity is also related to the instability of funding sources and reliance on market forces. This fluidity hides a stable core of TV programs (*Iranian, Jam-e Jam, Jonbesh-e Iran, Sima-ye Ashna*), which are the oldest and perhaps the most watched shows, lasting for a decade or more. There are also a number of shows that have been on the air for more than four years (*Iran, Midnight Show, Jong-e Bamdadi, Pars,* and *Sobh-e Ruz-e Jom'eh*).

If exile TV was only regressive and nostalgic, as most Iranian intellectuals claim, one would expect its use to lessen with prolongation of exile and gradual acculturation. That the number of new TV programs has steadily increased and several programs have prospered indicates that exile TV is also an instrument of incorporation and acculturation, not just exilic identification. For a variety of sociopolitical reasons a great many Iranians seem finally to have accepted the physical fact of exile and reconciled themselves to a long period, perhaps a lifetime, of stay in the United States, prompting a gradual shift toward the host and away from the home country.[4]

Exilic television has been instrumental in both ushering in this shift and reflecting it. This is evident in that the authoritarian, univocal discourse of Iran and the past, the notion of the audience as an undifferentiated group of exiles, the rigid magazine format of programs, and the limited distribution system—which were so characteristic of the early period of communitas—have all begun to give way to certain structural features that organize the symbolic, ideological, and social milieu of exile in such a way as to encourage incorporation into the dominant universe of American consumer capitalism and its postmodern mode of cultural production. The chief direction that this new structuration has taken is toward rationalization of the production and distribution infrastructure and commodification of audiences, TV products, discourses, and fetishes of home and host cultures.

Production, Transmission, and Distribution Structures

Production

A number of TV producers have compared their output in exile to the output of the gigantic National Iranian Radio and Television (NIRT) during the heyday of its operation before the revolution, when it reportedly employed over 10,000 people. These producers (Manuchehr Bibian and Nader Rafi'i among them) contend that despite its size, NIRT did not produce a majority of its own programming. This is partially true—in 1974, for example, 40 percent of televised programs on NIRT consisted of foreign imports (Naficy 1981:358). In addition to producing the remaining 60 percent, however, NIRT created many hours of very expensive programs—serials, documentaries, and feature films—and it was engaged in a vast multidimensional effort to encourage and showcase Iranian performing arts nationwide. NIRT's programs, therefore, cannot be compared hour for hour with the simple and inexpensive magazine-format shows made in exile.

Although the producers' claim is largely self-serving, it is illuminating from a structural point of view. NIRT, like the TV broadcasters in many Third World and (until recently) Eastern and even Western European countries, was a centralized state-sponsored entity with a monopoly of national production and transmission. As a result, market forces were not a major criterion for programming; national developmental policies were.[5] Thus television producers learned to operate in an environment that was largely cushioned from budgetary constraints, direct market forces, and public tastes. Their programs tended to reflect the policies of the central government and the personal tastes of their makers.[6]

In exile, however, the situation has reversed entirely. Television production and transmission are not centralized; they are decentralized, indeed atomized, with 37 different producers creating 62 regularly scheduled programs in nearly a dozen years. Because exile programs are commercially driven, moreover, the producers are forced to be responsive to market forces, public tastes, and advertising dollars, as a result of which there is keen competition among them for advertising and suitable airtime. Despite this fragmented and conflictual relationship at the level of producers, there is a common technical, artistic, and commercial infrastructure undergirding the Iranian exile television industry, giving it a certain cohesiveness. This consists of production and advertising personnel—advertising agents, calligraphers, graphic artists, photographers, camerapersons, tape editors, writers, and musicians—who work simultaneously on a freelance basis with a number of producers. What keeps these professionals together is not their employment by a centralized state agency such as NIRT but their economic relationship in the civil society as freelance talents and clients. Thus the economic and political relationships between above-the-line personnel (the program makers) and those below the line (technicians and craftspeople) is markedly different in exile. Indeed, it is the gradual replacement of hierarchical relationships by economic relationships that is responsible for rationalizing and professionalizing exilic television, and for its functioning as a facilitator of assimilation.

Of course, economic activity seeks coalition, and it polarizes around wealth-producing nuclei, which in the case of exile TV has meant those producers who own their own production and editing facilities or who engage in brokerage of time—people whom producer Homa Ehsan calls "televisual godfathers."[7] These so-called godfathers not only produce their own programs but also assist others by providing them with facilities and services. Indeed, these are among the few producers who earn their living solely from their televisual activities.

Local and National Transmission

To accommodate the increasing population and the diversity of programs, and to position the audiences to receive advertisers' messages, a wide-ranging, advertising-driven schedule has emerged, supported by a proliferating Iranian business community. This schedule has grown from an exclusively weekend time slot containing a single thirty-minute program in 1981 to one that distributes 26 programs across all days and nights of a week in 1992, from early morning hours to past midnight. With the exception of *Assyrian American Civic TV, Bet Naharin, Diyar, Iran, Melli, Mozhdeh, Negah, and Shahr-e Farang*, which are currently cablecast, and *Aftab*, which is aired by KRCA-TV, all other programs are broadcast by KSCI-TV.

It must be noted here that the reach of broadcasting stations and cable companies that air minority programs is not equal. A broadcasting station such as KSCI-TV, for example, has a larger area of coverage, reaching many more viewers than local cable companies. According to the station, KSCI-TV reaches over five million TV households in the Los Angeles and San Diego areas and is carried by more cable companies in Southern California than any other independent commercial UHF station. Because of high demand and increasing cost of transmission on broadcast TV, however, many minority producers are forced to cablecast their programs. To reach a wider audience in a number of communities, these producers are forced to lease time on multiple cable channels, a logistically burdensome and expensive process.

By now Iranian television programmers can target their audiences and deliver them to advertisers more frequently at more propitious prime-time hours than before. Saturdays and Sundays are not considered prime time for mainstream American television, but are considered so for ethnic, transnational, and exilic television because of the supposed extended-family structure of the immigrants and exiles, and their habit of collective viewing on those days.[8] This is reflected in KSCI-TV's rate card, which charges the highest amount for time on weekend nights, weeknights, and weekend days, respectively.

The broadcast schedule of exilic television is very fluid. KSCI's printed schedule in *TV Guide* is not very reliable. Century Cable's own lease-access channel in West

Los Angeles, KCLA, does not publish a printed schedule because of its fluidity. Iranian programs have suffered from excessive changes in the schedule, often caused by the stations themselves, which seek to maximize their revenues by leasing time to the highest bidder. For example, in 1987 *Iran* was aired by KSCI-TV daily in the early evenings, then it was moved to twice a week in prime time, then to Sunday evenings, and finally canceled altogether. (Korean broadcasters, as previously noted, were able to block-book KSCI-TV's prime-time hours.) *Iran* was the first regularly scheduled show to be forced to move to cable and establish a beachhead there. Such a changing schedule interferes with audience loyalty and creates much anxiety among producers, emphasizing their exilic, not ethnic, status. As independent producers, most Iranian programmers must rely solely on advertising dollars from businesses to survive, although there are rumors that a few of them receive regular funding from factions opposing the Islamic Republic. Most of them must hold other jobs to make ends meet.

With the exception of early-morning news and magazine programs *(Sima-ye Ashna, Jong-e Bamdadi, Cheshmandaz)* and late night talk and phone-in shows *(Emshab ba Parviz, Harf va Goft,* and *Sokhani ba Ravanshenas),* which are usually transmitted or taped live, all other programs are taped and edited, then transmitted. All live programs are transmitted from KSCI-TV's studios in Los Angeles. Taped programs must be submitted hours before transmission to the TV stations or cable companies. Since Los Angeles is such a vast geographic area, it cannot be reached by any single cable company; as a result, those wishing to reach simultaneously the entire area via cable must make multiple copies of their programs for transmission by multiple cable channels.

In the early 1990s, the parent company of KSCI-TV created the International Channel Network, the nation's first and only twenty-four-hour, seven-day-a-week multilingual network, offering programs by satellite in sixteen different languages. The network is fed by two sources: programs imported from home countries, which constitute the bulk of the materials (100 percent of Korean and 70 percent of Japanese programming), and those produced in the United States. The network figures show that it reaches some thirteen million ethnic households nationwide, and the network touts the affluence of this audience, particularly the Asians, by stating that it "delivers a loyal, upscale audience with a concentration of households headed by a professional or independent businessperson."[9] It urges both cable operators and advertisers nationwide to use the network to penetrate the traditionally hermetic non–English-speaking markets, which are increasing rapidly and "which have higher levels of disposable income than the U.S. population as a whole."

Among the many languages broadcast nationally by the International Channel Network are Iranian programs, including morning programs *(Sima-ye Azadi, Jong-e Bamdadi, Cheshmandaz),* late-night programs *(Emshab ba Parviz, Sokhani ba Ravan-shenas, Harf va Goft),* and *Aftab.* Together, these add up to nearly 10 hours of Persian material per week, more programming than is done in Arabic, Russian, Hebrew, Italian, Armenian, German, and Hungarian. With the exception of *Aftab,* much of whose content is imported from Iran, all other Iranian programs are produced in Los Angeles and are transmitted live via satellite in their Los Angeles time slot. This means that morning programs aired at 7:30 A.M. and late-evening programs shown at 12:00 midnight in Los Angeles are seen on the East Coast at inconvenient time slots of 10:30 A.M. and 3 A.M., respectively.

The network has pushed its Asian audiences more than any of its other constituencies. As a result it has obtained national advertising for Asian programs from multinational companies such as AT&T, United Airlines, Bank of America, Mazda, Proctor & Gamble, Home Savings, Toyota, Japan Airlines, McDonald's, and Columbia Pictures. Iranian programs have so far received irregular advertising support from national American or Iranian businesses.

Syndication

Iranian producers from the start created a syndication network which involved distributing tapes of their programs for rebroadcast by local stations in cities with large Iranian populations across the United States, Europe, and the Middle East. A few producers claim that after traveling a circuitous route their programs reach inside Iran. Manuchehr Bibian of *Jam-e Jam TV*, for example, stated in an interview with me that copies of his program find their way into Iran by way of Persian Gulf countries without his involvement, sometimes with the commercials and other offensive materials removed. Likewise, Ali Limonadi contended that tapes of his *Iranian* program are smuggled from Europe into Iran by truck drivers who remove the tape from its cassette casing during transit. Once in Iran, the cassettes are reassembled and duplicated. According to Limonadi, some parts of his program, such as the satirical skits critical of the Islamic government, are removed in Iran before duplication and distribution.

In terms of contents, syndicated programs differ to some extent from those originally aired in Los Angeles. In the case of *Jam-e Jam*, *Iranian*, and *Iran*, for example, the Los Angeles–based commercials and news are removed and replaced with either other program matters or blank spaces to be filled in by local producers and advertisers elsewhere. The newscasts present special problems for tape syndicators because news is so ephemeral. The usual solution is to create weekly roundups of recent news. Another difference between Los Angeles and syndicated programs is in their varying broadcast schedules. *Iran*, which is aired daily in Los Angeles, is broadcast on a weekly basis in other cities. This necessitates assembling a special weekly program for syndication.

Political Economy of Exilic Television

Time Brokerage Network

At the same time that exile television producers have expanded their national reach through satellite transmission and tape syndication, they have worked to deepen their penetration within the local Los Angeles market. A type of brokerage network has developed by which a time broker contracts for more than one broadcast slot from the television station airing Iranian programs. Now, the broker can place in that slot a program that he or she has produced, lease that time to someone else for a profit, or lease the time to another programmer but reserve the right to insert a few minutes of ads into that program. This is a very good way of generating additional income and is one factor that complicates the accounting of the producers' income. Of the four time-leasing brokers in 1989 (Naficy 1990: 211–12) only two have remained. Over the years, Parviz Qarib Afshar, certainly a televisual godfather, has been able to put together a strong time-leasing brokerage operation, renting airtime from KSCI-TV and leasing it for profit to the shows *Cheshmandaz, Emshab ba Parviz, Harf va Goft, Jonbesh-e Iran, Jong-e Bamdadi, Sima-ye Ashna,* and *Sokhani ba Ravanshenas.*

In general, because of the relative smallness of the capital involved and low audience figures, syndication and network organizations are extremely rudimentary and financially unstable. By opening themselves to the host society's mode of competitive consumer capitalism, Iranian producers and brokers have also made themselves vulnerable to the vagaries of the marketplace, which means rapid fluctuation in their own fortunes as well as in the schedules of their broadcasts. In 1988 *Omid,* managed by veteran broadcaster Iraj Gorgin, attempted to become a multimedia organization by producing a daily radio program (*Omid*), a quarterly magazine (*Fasinameh-ye Omid*), and a daily morning and daily evening TV show (*Jong-e Bamdadi* and *Omid*). The daily cost, however, of producing and airing the evening show ($1,500) continually exceeded its advertising revenue ($1,000), and it folded within a few months.[10]

Despite such inherent instability, over the years a solid unchanging core of programmers has flourished, chiefly by astute programming, obtaining national advertising, and combining leasing of production facilities and airtime with syndication and networking. Potentially this can enhance their earnings sufficiently to place them someday in a position to deliver large, heterogeneous ethnic audiences in a number of locations nationwide to what could become national Iranian-American advertisers. Qarib Afshar's time-leasing brokerage and the satellite transmission of all his programs have already brought him within range of that vision.

Television's Exilic Economy

Most programs are run on a commercial basis, and clusters of advertisements frequently interrupt the flow of television texts. In fact, the amount of time devoted to commercials on Iranian TV increased so dramatically that by mid-1987 it reached an all-time peak of over 40 minutes per hour of programming. After much criticism from viewers, KSCI-TV and the program makers agreed on a limit of 20 minutes per hour of commercials, which seems to be holding with periodic violation.[11] Some programs contain many more minutes of indirect advertisements for products, however, especially in the field of entertainment.

The financial dimensions of the ad-driven schedule's political economy, supported by proliferating Iranian businesses, are also far-reaching, turning Iranian television into not only an exilic but also an ethnic economy. In fact, a number of producers, among them Manuchehr Bibian of *Jam-e Jam*, Nader Rafi'i of *Midnight Show*, and Hamid Shabkhiz of *Iran*, in their interviews with me credited Iranian television for making the community in Los Angeles become socially visible and economically viable. Bibian, for example, claimed that "wherever we started a new television program, Iranians increased in number." Although there is no definitive evidence in support of such a direct cause-and-effect relationship, exile television programs, Iranian businesses, and Iranian emigres have all proliferated in Southern California over the years. It is their generally high level of income, education, self-employment, and professional skill that allows Iranians as audiences, providers of advertisements, producers of programs, and consumers of products and services to have turned exile television into an economic and symbolic engine which will ultimately transform them from exiles into ethnics, and which injects millions of dollars annually into the U.S. and Iranian economies.

Businesses place commercial announcements for their products within television programs and pay between $3 and $6 for each second of the commercial,[12] depending on frequency of broadcasts, perceived popularity of the program, number of times and ad is repeated in one show, length of the period during which the ad is aired, and personal connection between advertiser and programmer. On average, a thirty-second commercial can cost between $90 and $180. If half-hour programs are assumed to contain a minimum of 10 minutes of advertisements and hour-long programs a minimum of 20 minutes, then producers of half-hour and one-hour shows earn for each show $2,700 and $5,400, respectively. My calculations show that the existing roster of 26 programs earns over six million dollars per annum from advertising. Of course, from this figure the cost of production and transmission must be subtracted.

There are other sources of income for producers that are not included in this calculation, such as financial contributions from political factions opposing the Islamic government and income earned from *syndication* of programs, because these figures are impossible to substantiate.[13] A few producers who own their own studios generate additional income by renting their facilities to other producers.[14] Based on these considerations, it can be safely said that the overall annual gross income of Iranian producers far exceeds six million dollars.

Iranian producers in four consecutive years, between 1989 (Naficy 1990:194–98) and 1992, spent over 1.2 million dollars annually to rent airtime from KSCI-TV and various cable companies to transmit their programs. Although these figures are not definitive because station rates vary, especially those of cable companies, and because stations may charge programmers rates slightly different from their standard schedule, they are close estimates. The cost of transmission for all Iranian programs since the beginning of exile TV will have to be in the tens of millions, but the cumulative figure is difficult to estimate because of the frequency with which programs have appeared, changed channels, or disappeared.

The figures for the cost of producing the programs are even harder to compute because producers use a variety of production houses with varying and personalized fee structures. The cost of production is high and the flow of ads, at least at first, was too slow for producers to make money, and a number of them lost money and went out of business.[15] Clearly, financial backing other than advertising revenues seemed to have been necessary for a program to survive long enough to become self-supporting. Indeed, this might have been a key reason, during the politically heated postrevolutionary period, that a few producers sought funding from exiled political factions—which were in need of legitimation through media exposure. Even though such politically motivated funding and such commercially motivated politicization have declined over the years, they have been significant features of the political economy of Iranian exile television. What sets Iranian programs apart from Korean, Japanese, and Chinese programs is the source of financing as well as programming. While Iranians rely almost completely on exile sources for programs and financial help, their Asian counterparts depend chiefly on programming and assistance from their home countries or their multinational corporations. As a result, Iranian programs are financially less stable, more prone to manipulation by exile groups, more responsive to market forces in exile and more reflective of the conditions of exile.

Station Politics

In the last decade, broadcast stations such as KSCI-TV, KDOC-TV, KRCA-TV, and a number of cable companies have carried Iranian programming. The possibility of using more than one station to air programs theoretically must increase the ability of producers to engage both in counter-programming and in reducing the cost of airtime by playing one station against the other. However, Iranian programmers have so far refrained from programming against one another. They have elected to access different channels, however, in order to get around the stations' attempts at censorship. A case in point is the *Sima-ye Azadi* program produced by the Mojahedin guerrilla organization. The program was taken off the air by KSCI-TV in 1986 but soon it found a new home in KDOC-TV, where it continued to broadcast until mid-1989. It returned to Los Angeles airwaves a few years later by broadcasting on KSCI-TV again.[16]

It is worth spending some time on examining these shifts by *Sima-ye Azadi* because they tell much about the ways that broadcast diversity can be obtained or curtailed in the United States, especially with regard to exile politics, which may not match U.S. foreign policy; the kind of cat-and-mouse game that political exile organizations play in gaining access to U.S. public opinion; and the relationship between broadcasting stations and exile producers.[17] *Sima-ye Azadi* was first aired in 1986 on KSCI-TV but it was taken off because, according to the station, the producer had failed to fulfill contractual obligations. These obligations appear to have been formulated by the station in cooperation with the U.S. State Department. In a 1986 letter, the State Department informed KSCI-TV that the Mojahedin was a "terrorist" organization and that all the following organizations "represented" it: Council of Resistance, Muslim Iranian Student Society, Iran Relief, and People's Mojahedin Organization of Iran. With this in mind, the station signed a contract (dated 1/9/1986) with Star Productions, producer of *Sima-ye Azadi*, in which the company promised it would

not air either in program content or commercial announcement, the activities or philosophy of the following groups:
a. National Council of Resistance
b. Moslem Iranian Student Society
c. Iran Relief
d. People's Mojahedin Organization of Iran
e. Any group related to the organizations listed above.
This includes, but is not limited to, on-air fund raising, invitations to rallies, demonstrations or meetings, editorial statements, etc.

The State Department apparently monitored the programs because two months later in a letter it informed the station that a few of the aired programs had contained interviews with three Mojahedin members who were tortured by the Islamic Republic. It continued:

> During the interview, there is frequent praise of the PMOI [Mojahedin] leader, Rajavi. No explanations were given as to the nature of PMOI, its role in bringing Khomeini to power, its ideology, or its extensive use of violence. Although the tapes contain no specific appeals for support for the PMOI, nevertheless, they appear fully within the PMOI's current propaganda line which goes roughly as follows: "the Iranian government is bad, the PMOI is against the Iranian government, the Iranian government represses the PMOI, therefore, the PMOI and its leader Rajavi are good and worthy of support."

The letter clearly posited that Star Productions' claim of no political affiliation and its promise to refrain from political proselytization were untrue. Because of this and the generally volatile politics of Iranians at the time, KSCI-TV hired an Iranian monitor to review for contents and amount of commercials all Iranian programs the station was airing. The monitor filed reports detailing contents of programs, including one for *Sima-ye Azadi*. Following the State Department's finding and the monitor's report, KSCI gave the organization four weeks' notice after which the program would be canceled on account of the "sensitive material thus far included." Less than four weeks later, KSCI-TV "reaffirmed" its decision to cancel the contract since the management did not "feel it is in the best interest of the station to continue airing" the program. Although Star Productions agreed to follow the policy standards outlined in the station's manual, and further promised "not to promote or encourage, or make representations political in nature so as to jeopardize licensing," the station stood fast and let the contract expire. In all fairness it must be noted that in fact the program continually proselytized in support of the Mojahedin ideology and the organization's political and military tactics against the Islamic government in Iran. Whether it was pressure from the State Department, the Mojahedin's violation of their contract, or the station's fear of losing its license at renewal time, the result was that the only anti-Khomeini program that was not also royalist was denied access.

After a period of hiatus *Sima-ye Azadi* resumed operation by moving over to channel 56 (KDOC-TV), where it continued its regular transmission until mid-1989. Although the program's contents had not changed, before each broadcast an announcement appeared stating that the producer was not a supporter of the Khomeini government in Iran. One inference that can be drawn is this: the Mojahedin had succeeded in dissociating itself from anti-American terrorism, which the State Department had worried about, while it continued to advocate anti-Khomeini terrorism, which the State Department was apparently not worried about. With this shift in the definition of "terrorism," *Sima-ye Azadi* was able to continue to air its programs until some time in 1989, when the organization relocated its headquarters from Paris to Iraq and suspended its propaganda activities in the United States to concentrate on military operations against the Islamic Republic.[18] In late 1991, the Mojahedin resumed its propaganda operations in the United States, including airing *Sima-ye Azadi* on its original channel, KSCI-TV. It is possible that the U.S. government's continued anti-Iranian foreign policy and the Mojahedin's relocation reassured KSCI-TV that leasing time to *Sima-ye Azadi* would no longer jeopardize its license.

The antiterrorism mindset in America in the late 1970s, of course, was consolidated by the taking of 52 Americans hostage in the American embassy in Tehran in 1979 and holding them for 444 days. The atmosphere in this country was poisoned for Iranian exiles and television producers. Limonadi, producer of *Iranian*, stated in an interview with me that in 1979, before the hostages were taken, he had signed a contract with KSCI-TV to air his program. With the taking of the hostages, however, the station became fearful of a backlash from American citizens for having given access to Iranians (citizens of a "terrorist" country) and it postponed the fulfillment of the contract until the hostages were released.

The State Department's labeling of a country (Iran), a group (Mojahedin), and a government (Islamic Republic) as "terrorist" acts somewhat like the Motion Pictures Association of America's labeling of films. It encourages compliance through self-censorship. The label warns the broadcasters about sensitive issues whose exposure may endanger the stations' license renewal.[19] In the same way that license renewal produces compliance and deference by television stations, the lease-access contract, containing a 28-day cancellation clause, recruits consent from exile producers. Access to multiple broadcast channels helps the producers, who are at the mercy of the stations that lease time to them, to manipulate the stations or attempt to get around one particular station's attempts at censorship.

Intermedia Rivalry

Although during the liminal period of Iranian exile television served to create exilic cohesiveness and national solidarity, it also nurtured a certain amount of political discord within the transplanted community. The chief reasons were economic and political competition and personal rivalries among various media producers, particularly those between publishers of periodicals and producers of television programs. Because of the Federal Communications Commission's regulative power, exile television programs are more circumspect than the periodicals in attacking each other, or in taking on the periodicals. Economic competition, however, appears to be the most significant reason for antagonism. According to a KSCI-TV official, the periodicals-television rivalry "comes down to economics," with both publishers and producers wanting larger shares of expanding advertising dollars.[20] One reason for the duration and nastiness of the rivalry may lie in the perceived effectiveness and desirability of television advertising over that in periodicals.

What complicates this economic rivalry is the fractious politics of exile groups working against the Islamic Republic. With the exception of the Mojahedin, none of the other opposition groups—which range from various shades of monarchism to Marxism—produce their own official television programs. Instead, they are said to clandestinely fund programs and periodicals in one or more of these ways: direct financial contribution to the owners; reimbursing TV producers for their travel expenses; paying producers and publishers for carrying "news" interviews with political figures,[21] and favoring a particular producer or publisher by placing advertisements with them. In its most insidious form, clandestine political sponsorship undermines the journalistic credibility of exile television because it not only politicizes but also commercializes their newscasts as well as the rest of their discourse. But this form of sponsorship serves the interests of exiled politicians: by appearing on television, they gain prestige and are recognized as leaders, thereby increasing their chances of obtaining funds from foreign governments opposing the Islamic Republic (such as Iraq, Saudi Arabia, or the United States). On the one hand, operating from behind the scenes confers on them power and the mystique of anonymity and removes them as targets of direct attack and criticism. On the other hand, audience perception of under-the-table machinations increases the sense of such politicians' power—although dislike of it is also present.

The manipulation of the news and interview processes through commodification, however, is not limited to politicians. Entertainers promoting their new albums and upcoming concerts and lawyers informing audiences about immigration laws often pay for the privilege of being interviewed on television. As a result of these financial and political practices, the line separating the program (text) and advertising (supertext) becomes blurred. Such textual ambiguity may be appreciated from a hermeneutic standpoint but it does tend to reinforce the negative public image of television producers as political or commercial hacks.

Another significant source feeding the intermedia discord is interpenetration of the private and public interests of producers. There is a duality in most people between self-interest and public interest.[22] The producers have resolved this duality by resorting to cleverness and deception—which is no different from the tactics used by non-Iranian producers. What makes the difference is that the producers attempt to raise funds by invoking sensitive and emotional issues: combatting the Islamic regime in Iran, nationalism, exilism, and serving the cause of displaced refugees and war children. As a result of these practices, television producers are accused of supporting the Islamic government under the guise of patriotism, receiving financial support from political factions in exile opposing the Islamic government while claiming otherwise, presenting views of one or another of the exile political factions while contending to be objective, and promoting personal gain while asserting service to the exile community.[23] There is always suspicion concerning corrupt practices[24] such as organizing allegedly fraudulent public service fund-raising events such as telethons.[25] The personal conduct of some producers reinforces the somewhat negative perception of them among many Iranians.[26]

One pathological symptom of the conflation of personal economic interest with public social interest is the manner in which exile TV producers, charged with allegations of the sort noted above, have used public airwaves to settle private scores, defend themselves, and launch direct countercharges against their detractors. These public contestations over personal integrity, sometimes fanned by periodicals, have had negative effects.

The regular program format has sometimes been disrupted to allow for the airing of charges and countercharges. When in April 1988 *Arya* TV charged that Homa Ehsan, producer of *Didar* (the first woman producer to air her program), had allegedly taken for her own personal use the money she had collected for Iranian immigrants, Ehsan abandoned her regular program format to deny the charge and defend herself.[27] Up to that point, *Didar* had been concerned with the familial self, and allowed expression of emotions more than did other television programs. It was focused on lifestyle, poetry, domestic issues, interviews with women, child-rearing practices, and children's performances. The set of Didar was domestic, resembling a comfortable Iranian guest room, suitable for rituals of hospitality (the show was taped in Ehsan's own living room). To defend herself, however, Ehsan felt obliged to shift from the private to a public, political orientation. Interviews with women and children and the display of children's performances gave way to Ehsan's own direct address to the camera, and her vernacular language also changed to more formal public utterances. The program lost much of its distinctiveness and soon ceased operation altogether, due to a drastic reduction in commercial sponsorship (particularly by physicians). With the demise of *Didar*, the women's voice was removed from the scene for some time.

The second negative effect of mixing personal benefit with public interest is the lessening of public trust in TV programs as organs of legitimate commercial enterprise and, in particular, of public good.[28] For a community whose psychology is so focused on sincerity, and which perceives cohesiveness to be more essential for its survival than differences, distrust may be very destructive. Farzan Delju, host of *Jonbesh-e Iran* (11/27/1988), warned in an emotional commentary that the "city of the angels" has become the "city of chameleons," in which Iranians often change colors. Whatever the ethical practices of *Jonbesh-e Iran*, this commentary was a call for upholding Iranian core values of sincerity and inner purity.

While anti–Islamic Republic politics, televisual fetishization of Iran, and disavowal of exile allowed television programs to create an exilic economy and, for some time, a symbolic collective unity, the commercialization of their political relations transformed them into intensely divisive, exploited, and exploitative political and commercial institutions. This is a clear indication that exilic ambivalence is structural. A few producers are themselves aware of this ambivalence. Rafi'i and Shabkhiz, of *Midnight Show* and *Iran*, noted in their interviews with me that exile TV programs created economic cohesiveness by linking consumers with ethnic businesses but they failed to produce political unity. Iraj Gorgin, producer of a series of cultural programs, emphasized this point in his interview:

> The role that Iranian television programs have played is perhaps a negative one, because they have created political polarization, not cohesion. This is because they are politically partisan and are always engaged in public feuds over personal interests. All these affect viewers negatively.

Such a tight imbrication of money and politics was more prevalent in the overheated liminal period following the arrival of the Iranians in America, when political factions were hoping to return triumphantly to Iran in the very near future. As the Islamic regime consolidated itself, however, and exile turned from a temporary sojourn into a long-term, perhaps permanent stay, financial and political divisiveness eased.

It surfaced again in 1992 with the advent of *Aftab*, a two-hour program that appears to be linked with governmental cultural institutions in Iran. The program positions itself as nonpolitical, but unlike all other exilic shows, the bulk of its contents (serials, plays, feature films, and cartoons) is imported from the state-run broadcasting networks and film organizations in Iran. Because of the higher quality of these materials, the program's emphasis on culture instead of politics, and its national transmission across the United States via KSCI-TV's International Channel Network, *Aftab* quickly attracted audiences and criticism. Royalist broadcasters and periodicals in Los Angeles vehemently criticized the program, accusing it of being an "agent" of the Islamic government. But when *Aftab* sought to attract advertisers, their begrudging tolerance turned into outright belligerence. Calls for boycotting the program and those who advertise on it were sounded, but to no avail, as businesses from Los Angeles to New York to Houston placed advertisements with it. Media frenzy against the "infiltration" into exile of a voice from inside Iran was so shrill that a respected Iranian communications expert, Kambiz Mahmudi, who himself opposes the Islamic government, was moved to criticize the exile media, challenging them to compete with the pro-Islamic program in the marketplace, leaving the ultimate judgment to audiences (1992:10). A number of TV producers, too, expressed support for *Aftab*, as for them the program (whose title translates as "sunshine") represented a ray of light in the claustrophobic discourse of exile television.

The response to *Aftab* indicates that at least a portion of Iranian audiences, businesses, producers, and critics have learned to separate personal politics from economic interests. It also shows how they can use their economic prowess and control of what they watch to pressure exilic media into a degree of compliance with their interests and wishes. At a more fundamental and personal level, this newfound tolerance for opposition viewpoints is a sign of democratization and assimilation. It is also an index of the gradual professionalization of exilic media and its critics, who are willing to follow codes and routines of journalism to gain ascendancy in the "civil society" of the host country instead of relying solely on promotion of personal and political connections, as was customary in the "traditional society" and "state society" of the homeland.

Political Demography of Exilic Television

Program Producers

Until 1992, all Iranian television programs opposed the Islamic Republic in Iran. In addition, they were all secular and predominantly royalist. These political tendencies turned most of the programs into partisan channels for antigovernment propaganda. As late as April 1992, representatives of the Iranian Mass Media Society of California took part in an anti-Islamic Republic political convention held in Los Angeles not as journalists *reporting* on the convention but as politicians organizing and participating in it. [29] Several reasons stand out for such partisan politics and attitudes. The first is that TV programs reflect the anti–Islamic Republic views of the exile community in Southern California. Many, but by no means at all, of the producers, segment producers, program hosts, musicians, pop stars, and political figures who appear on these programs openly admit to being against the Islamic Republic and in support of reinstatement of some form of constitutional monarchy in Iran under Reza Pahlavi, Mohammad Reza Shah's eldest son. Many producers envision an exclusively political mission for exilic media; in the words of Manuchehr Bibian of *Jam-e Jam* TV, this mission is to "wage a campaign against the current government in Iran and to offer the public political information" (Moslehi 1984:115). Iranian producers appear not to follow journalistic values in the West of "objectivity" and "fairness," which tend to conceal the politics of information and news. The high level of secularism among Iranians in exile, particularly the Muslims, also tends to separate exiles from the Islamic Republic. The separation of church and state has become a chief political demand for the exiles, who have tasted the bitter fruits of theocracy personally.

Another related reason for the politics of exile television might be that many program makers belong to minorities persecuted in Iran. Of the 46 different TV producers [studied here], 28 are Muslim, 12 Christian (6 Armenian, 5 Assyrian, 1 Protestant), 2 Jewish, and 4 Baha'i. Given that over 95 percent of the population in Iran is Muslim, the disproportionate representation of Iranian minorities among producers becomes clear. These minorities are also represented among technical personnel, ad agencies, and performers. The reluctance among American mainline media to accept programming supporting the current government in Iran is also a factor.[30]

Highly politicized exile programming partly results from the producers' general lack of formal training in journalism or television production. Of all the producers, [studied], less than four could be called journalists, trained to see the world through news values such as "objectivity" and "fairness." The irony of exilic television is that the news magazine format, which is the most prevalent, demands the application of these values that are in such short supply, rendering programs highly unreliable as sources of news. Although most producers had what we might call "show business" or media-related backgrounds before emigration, only seven of them had professional training in radio or television production and two in film directing. The liminal condition of exile also produces emotionalism and extremism of all kinds. In the case of exilic television, extremism expresses itself chiefly in conservative partisan politics.

The end result of the producers' fierce opposition to the Islamic Republic was an unfortunate and politically dangerous conflation early on of anti-Khomeinism with anti-Islam or anti-Shi'ism, leading many programmers to replay the same mistake made during the Shah's reign, that is, ignoring or dismissing Shi'i religion as a significant and legitimate fact of Iranian political life. The fetishistic iconography of program logos may be cited as an index of this monovocal politics. In the first ten years of exilic television, almost all program logos referred in one way or another to the Iranian map, flag, colors of the flag, secular and pre-Islamic monuments in Iran, and Iranian cityscapes and landscapes to the point of fetishizing them. During this period, however, none of the logos contained a visual that referred to the Islamic aspects of Iranian art, culture, and architecture. Any sign of Islam was effaced from representations of Iran.

In addition, the same partisan and extremist news values that caused them to misrepresent the politics of Iran pushed some exile producers to misrepresent the politics of Iranians in exile as well, thus rendering their audience the manipulated objects and themselves the manipulating subjects of exiled political factions. For example, when in May 1992 a brother of the late Shah of Iran was arrested by the Los Angeles police on the charge of dealing narcotics, royalist media refused to report the news and pressured others to comply with the ban. In the same month, *Jonbesh-e Iran* accused *Iran* and *Sima-ye Ashna* of being "errand boys" for the Iranian government apparently because they had inserted in their newscasts footage from Iran available by satellite to all broadcasters.[31] These partisan Los Angeles media seem to fear the penetration of any information into their discourse that does not match their royalist and anti-Islamist ideology.

The virulent anti–Islamic Republic and pro-monarchy discourses have gradually lessened, and there are a few producers who do take a more or less independent stance, regardless of the criticism they receive. A few television programs (for example, *Emshab ba Parviz* and *Cheshmandaz*) reported the news of Pahlavi's arrest despite warnings not to do so.[32] Independent-minded producers will inevitably come under criticism from all sides, from those in Iran and those in exile, from the political left to the right. Despite setbacks and detours, this move toward diversification, professionalization, and democratization is part of the creeping assimilation within the Iranian community, and it will steadily gain momentum.

Audience Demography

None of the rating services, such as Nielsen and Arbitron, compile regular statistics on viewing habits and preferences of so-called ethnic viewers, with the exception of Hispanic audiences. As a result, there is much uncertainty about the size, demographic profile, and preferences of audiences of transnational and exilic television. One source that provides a clue is the research conducted by individual stations airing these programs. According to the latest figures released by KSCI-TV, in 1987 the Iranian viewing audience in Los Angles was approximately 70,000 weekly households and 240,000 weekly viewers.[33] Iranian producers themselves claim much larger audience figures, based on inflated estimates of Iranians abroad (Naficy 1990: 171). The producer of *Jonbesh-e Iran* claims that more than two million Iranians worldwide watch his program (Ketab Corp. 1989:362) while the producer of *Sima-ye Ashna* stated in an interview with me (3/2/1990) that his program is seen by half a million Iranians from San Diego to San Francisco. Many also claim wide circulation abroad. The producers of *Jam-e Jam* and *Iranian* contend that copies of their shows are seen in Canada, Western Europe, Persian Gulf countries, and Iran itself.[34] The viewership worldwide is even harder to substantiate.

In the absence of an independent, reliable, and systematic rating service, both Iranian television producers and the stations that broadcast the programs must rely for audience reaction on letters and telephone calls from audiences, critical letters and columns appearing in exile periodicals, and personal contacts (especially in social gatherings and at parties). A few producers employ additional feedback methods, such as contests that encourage viewers to call in hope of winning a prize.[35] Advertisers, too, rely on similar methods, as well as on their own sales volume, to determine the effectiveness of ads.

The notion of viewers as groups of spectators (differentiated by age, gender, ethnicity, religion, and class) who can be addressed separately evolved gradually. Throughout most of its life, exilic television construed its audience as a homogeneous group of people uprooted from home and without roots here. It was seen to be not only homogeneous but also familial, as befits the Iranian self-perception and the condition of exile, both of which engender a desire for reunion and collective social constructions. A majority of producers in their interviews with me indicated that their target audience is foremost the entire "family." From the contents of their programs it becomes clear that the concept of the family encompasses not only the biological, nuclear, and extended family but also the social, national family of all Iranians in exile—both of which tend to suppress the individuality and differences of their members.

However, the survey of Iranians in Los Angeles County conducted in 1987–88 by UCLA sociologists Sabagh, Light, Bozorgmehr, and Der-Martirosian problematizes this notion by demonstrating the heterogeneity of Iranian exiles, and their varied reactions to programs based on class, education, age, and ethnoreligious affiliation. The survey included in-person interviews with 671 Iranian heads of households of four ethnoreligious groups (195 Armenians, 87 Baha'is, 188 Jews, 201 Muslims). Among other issues, they were asked about the types of videos and television programs they watch. The results show that the entire biological or national "family" may have been the producers' target, but each member of it was not addressed or reached equally.[36] . . .

Among factors that create differentiation within the exile "family" is internal ethnicity. Of those surveyed, Armenians generally watch television more than any other ethnoreligious group, whether it is American, Iranian, or Armenian TV. This viewing pattern, however, is not neutral. It seems to express on the one hand the high ethnic affiliation of Armenians and on the other hand their strong desire to assimilate into the dominant host society. Corroborating the ethnic affiliation theses, [my data show] that nearly 64 percent of Armenian-Iranians surveyed watch Armenian programs produced by non-Iranian Armenians (all Armenian-Iranians produce Persian-language shows that generally ignore Armenian nationalism, ethnicity, or issues). Supporting their assimilationist tendency, the same [data show] that more than any other subgroup Armenians watch American TV (nearly 80 percent). This tendency toward the host culture is also substantiated by [my data, which show] that 80 percent of Armenians watch English-language videos and only 3 percent watch Persian-language videos. But ethnically, Armenians do not have only a dual identity (Armenian and American); rather, as indicated by the high percentage of them (48.7) who watch Persian-language TV, their identity is a hybrid of three interethnic identities: Armenian, American, and Iranian.

Based on their television and video viewing patterns, Jewish Iranians seem to identify with Iranian ethnicity more than do Armenians, and they appear to favor assimilation into the host culture less than do Armenians. More Jews watch Iranian exilic TV and Persian-language videos, chiefly imported from Iran, than any other internal ethnic group.

Muslim respondents said they watched Iranian television less than any other group, perhaps pointing to their dissatisfaction with underrepresentation of Islamic values or the overly partisan anti-Islamist politics of the programs. Muslim Iranians may, however, be more acculturated than the other three subgroups, thus not in need of assistance from exilic television in that process.

It has already been noted that compared with native-born Americans or other high-status immigrants, statistically, Iranians in Southern California have an unusually high level of income, education, self-employment, and professional skills—all of which are indexes of their higher class status and necessary components of a viable exilic economy that can support television programs. In the UCLA survey of Iranian viewership, the data from education and income are taken as indexes of class. The higher the class aspiration, the more attractive assimilation appears. That education is associated with assimilation is clearly indicated by the figures showing that those with higher levels of education watch less Persian-language and more English-language videos. Corroborating the general trend in the United States, [my data] also show that the lower the level of education and income among Iranians, the higher is the amount of TV watching. Clearly, education is not only a source of class difference among the exiles but also an agent of their assimilation into the host society.

Income figures show that the lower the income of all Iranian ethnic groups, the more they watch videos and television, thus confirming the link established in the larger American society between lower income and higher TV watching. Low-income Baha'is, Jews, and Muslims watch more Persian-language television, while those with higher incomes watch more English language television, thereby affirming the link between higher income and the turn toward the dominant host culture. The pattern of viewership of Armenians of all income levels—more U.S. television, followed by Armenian and Persian-language television—seems to corroborate their gravitation toward both Armenian ethnicity and American assimilation.

Taken together, the data on education and income suggest that the higher the class status of the exiles, the more they aspire toward the dominant culture, although when income reaches a certain high level, as among some rich Jewish Iranians, assimilation to the host society becomes less important.

The viewership data was obtained from heads of households only, about 90 percent of whom were male, thus removing from consideration children, young people, and to a large extent women.[37] Data show that middle-aged and older Armenians (41–60 years) watch more Persian-language videos, followed by Armenian, American, and Persian-language TV, in that order. Elderly Armenians (60 years plus) watch more Persian, American, and Armenian TV, respectively. These figures confirm the expectation that the older generation's attachment to Iran and to Armenian culture is stronger than that of the younger groups. They also indicate that the older generation lacks knowledge of the English language and must rely more heavily on native languages. The trend for the younger generation (25–40 years) is similar in that it prefers Armenian, American, and Persian programs, in that order.

The older the Baha'is and the Jews, the more they tend to watch Persian-language videos and Persian-language broadcast television. Younger Baha'is and Jews watch more English-language TV followed by Persian-language TV. Among the Muslims, the older group (41–60 years) watches more American television followed by Persian television, while the younger group (25–40 years) watches more Persian-language videos than any other subgroup. The reason for the unexpectedly heavy use of Persian-language television by the younger Muslims may be sought in differences in income and other differences among Iranian internal ethnics. Generally, younger Muslims may be said to be economically poorer than their Armenian, Baha'i, and Jewish counterparts, and unlike them, they lack the kind of ethnoreligious networks and economic institutions that these minorities had formed in Iran and brought with them into exile. As a result, the younger Muslims more than other subgroups may be using Persian-language videos as a marker of their exilism and ethnicity.

From the analysis of the UCLA survey, it becomes clear that the target audience for exilic television—the Iranian exile "family"—is neither biologically nor demographically homogeneous, and its use of ethnic, exilic, and mainstream television varies depending on ethnicity, education, income, and age. An additional factor of diversity among Iranian exiles, which television producers have ignored, is language. With the exception of Assyrian programs and *You and the World of Medicine*, all other programs have been in Persian. Since Iranian minorities generally know Persian, this attempt at monolingualism has served to reinforce an Iranian solidarity in exile based on language. Such a solidarity, however, tends to exclude an important and growing population—that is, young people who have spent all or most of their lives in the United States and who do not know Persian or who prefer English.[38] Interest in Persian-language videos and TV programs increases with age. This information leads us to conclude that if teenagers had been surveyed they would have shown even less interest in these programs than the 25-year-olds who were surveyed.

The ethnic, religious, class, and generational diversity of Iranians flies in the face of the assumption of homogeneity of audiences that seems to have driven much of exilic television during most of its existence. The widespread dissatisfaction voiced by Iranians in conversations, on radio, and in periodicals about television must partly be attributed to the failure of program producers to take into account the diversity of their target audiences. Just because they all share the fact of displacement, a national language, and, to a large extent, opposition to the Islamic Republic does not mean that they have no differences. But until the late 1980s exile producers exploited the commonalities of their audiences and suppressed their differences for their own economic gain, and to enlist political solidarity favoring monarchist nationalism. As such they have acted more to consolidate Iranian ethnicity than to promote assimilation.

Since the late 1980s, however, a series of factors have contributed to modifying the homogenized notion of the audience as a unified biological or national family: proliferation of producers and programs; emergence of women producers; availability of multiple transmission channels, particularly cable television; specialization through targeting of microaudiences based on gender, age, education, profession, religion, and language; termination of the Iraq-Iran war; reduction in the bellicose mutual rhetoric of Iranian and American governments; and the reduction of the culture of politics and ascendancy of a politics of culture among the exiles.

All the women producers began (and ended) their shows in the late 1980s *(Didar, Ma, Sima va Nava-ye Iran)*. Live phone-in shows, transmitted nationally via satellite, began during this period *(Emshab ba Parviz, Harf va Goft, Sokhani ba Ravanshenas)*. Exile-produced serials increased in number and quality. A few shows, such as *Tapesh* and *Diyar*, attempted to target young audiences by programming music videos. The program *You and the World of Medicine* became the first regularly scheduled Iranian program in the English language. The political discourse of exilic television also widened, with the introduction in this period of the anti-government guerrilla show *(Sima-ye Azadi)*, the Assembly of God religious program *(Mozhdeh)*, and the somewhat pro-Islamic cultural program *(Aftab)*. Clearly this diversity of programming targets hitherto unaddressed constituencies, or creates constituencies where there were none. Such transformations show that one of the keys to the survival of Iranian exilic television will be its ability to keep up with its audiences and act as a means for both assimilation and exilic identification.

Over the past decade, Iranian exilic television has developed certain structures for production, transmission, syndication, time-brokering, cross-fertilization, advertising, and audience segmentation that have helped to create an ethnic economy and an Iranian national and exilic identity. At the same time, by rationalizing the industry and introducing market forces into production, transmission, and consumption, these structures have helped exilic television to facilitate the assimilation of its audiences.

NOTES

From Hamid Naficy, "Structure and Political Economy of Exile Television," In *The Making of Exile Cultures: Iranian Television in Los Angeles* (Minneapolis: University of Minnesota Press, 1993). Reprinted by permission of University of Minnesota Press.

1. The breakdown of these programs by languages on KSCI-TV is as follows (hours/week,

week of May 17, 1992): Arabic 3.0, Armenian 5.0, Cambodian 1.5, Mandarin 9.5, French 2.5, Tagalog/English 5.0, Deutsche .50, Hungarian .50, Hindi/English 1.0, Persian 15.5, Italian .50, Japanese 14.5, Hebrew 1.0, Korean 22.5, Russian 1.0, and Vietnamese 5.0. [SOURCE: compiled by the author from KSCI-TV data.] On the concept of "diaspora television," see Naficy 1993.

2. For example, 50 percent of the programs carried by Univision Television Network—the leader in Spanish-language programming in the United States, which reaches some 60 percent of Spanish-speaking audience—is produced in the United States, with the balance imported chiefly from Mexico and Venezuela (Puig 1992:D1). These programs, which are often modeled after proven U.S. or Latin American shows, neither adequately address problems of acculturation nor issues of diversity and specificity of various Latin American, Central American, and Chicano populations living in the United States. Instead, they appear, on the one hand, to reinforce the assimilation and Americanization of Latino populations (Valle 1988) and, on the other hand, the "cubanization" of Spanish-language programming.

3. In addition to these regularly scheduled programs, KSCI-TV has aired occasional specials produced by Iranian emigres. Some, such as *Iranian Jewish Senior Center Program* (aired in February 1986) or *Iranian Refugee Teletbon* (aired in March 1988), promoted the welfare of the Iranian community in exile. Others celebrated various national or religious occasions, such as Iranian New Year, Passover, Christmas, and Winter Solstice.

4. This is borne out by Bozorgmehr and Sabagh's study, which shows that since 1980 the "major mode of legal status attainment among Iranians" has been to "enter as nonimmigrants and subsequently change their status to immigrants." As a result, the number of Iranians who have become naturalized citizens increased at least twofold between 1984 and 1986 (1988:11). Ironically, naturalization, instead of suppressing nationalism, may be enhancing it—perhaps temporarily.

5. On the state of television broadcasting in postrevolutionary Iran, which is structurally similar to NIRT, see Sreberny-Mohammadi and Mohammadi 1991.

6. For an analysis of the use of broadcasting in a number of Third World countries, including Iran, see Katz and Wedell 1977.

7. These so-called godfathers of production are Ali Limonadi (Studio Cinegraphics, producer of *Iranian*), Manuchehr Bibian (Jam-e Jam Productions, producer of *Jam-e Jam*), Hamid Shabkhiz (producer of *Iran*), and Parviz Qarib Afshar (who uses the KSCI-TV facilities and produces *Sima-ye Ashna* and *Emshab ba Parviz*).

8. Author's interview with Rosemary Fincher, KSCI-TV station manager, 2/16/1988.

9. The description, profile, and program offerings of the International Channel Network are based on materials supplied to me in May 1992 by the network.

10. Interview with Iraj Gorgin, producer of the *Omid* programs, 4/23/1988, Los Angeles.

11. For examples of such criticism in exile periodicals, see *Iran News* (8/7/1987, p. 23), which claimed that hour-long television programs contained between 48 and 52 minutes of ads; *Payam-e Iran* (27 Esfand, 1367/1988, p. 6), which contended that hour-long TV programs contained 40 minutes of ads; *Rayegan* (1/22/1988, p. 35), which wrote that the hour-long *Jam-e Jam* program contained 45 minutes of ads. For additional criticism, see "Barresi-ye Televizionha-ye Yekshanbeh," *Rayegan* (5/13/1988, p. 22). Farhang Farrahi, "Chera Goruhi Javanan-e Porshur-e Vatanparast E'tesab-e Ghaza Konand Amma Yek Televizion Bekhahad az an Natayej-e Khosusi Khod ra Begirad?," *Rayegan* (4/8/1988, p. 5. "4 So'al az 4 Televizion," *Kabobnameb* (Ordibehesht 1361/1982):8. "Goft va Shonudi ba Tagi Mokhtar," *Par 27* (Farvardin 1367/1988):20–23.

12. The exact figures for advertising rates are unwritten, fluctuate over time and with individuals, and are held as proprietary information by competing producers, so they cannot

be independently verified. I have chosen to stay with the figures cited the most by the majority of producers (between $3 and $6 per second).

13. In interviews with me in 1989, Bibian of *Jam-e Jam* gave $4,500 as his monthly gross and Rafi'i of *Midnight Show* stated that his monthly net income was $3,500.

14. Limonadi of *Iranian*, who owns his own studio, stated in an interview with me that he makes approximately $3,500 per month from renting his facilities to other producers.

15. For example, Gorgin was in debt when his program, *Omid*, went off the air; Ehsan of *Didar* lost some $40,000 before closing down; and Bibian of *Jam-e Jam* lost over $100,000 in the first two years of his program. These figures are based on my interviews with the producers.

16. "Mojahedin" is the abbreviated name for *Sazman-e Mojabedin-e Khaiq-e Iran* (Organization of Fighters for Iranian People), a guerrilla organization that engaged in armed struggle against the Shah in the 1970s and, after a period of cooperation with the nascent Islamic government, turned to armed struggle against it in 1981. The headquarters of the organization at present is in Iraq, from where a number of incursions against the Iranian forces have been made. The organization produces and airs a regularly scheduled TV show in Iraq, *Sima-ye Moqavement*, which is beamed to Western Iran. This is in addition to *Sima-ye Azadi*, which it airs in the United States. For more on the organization, see Abrahamian 1989.

17. For more details of this case, see Naficy 1990:177–81.

18. This physical move by the organization fit the U.S. foreign policy at the time. This policy heavily favored Iraq against Iran and it must have finally established the Mojahedin's opposition to the Islamic government in Iran.

19. In contradistinction to the anti-Khomeini Iranian exiles, the anti-Castro Cuban exiles have received much direct help from the U.S. government because the politics of the latter either coincide or are dictated by the U.S. government. Radio Marti has been beaming anti-Castro programming from the U.S. mainland for quite some time and in 1990 the U.S. government began TV Marti with the same purpose.

20. Author's interview with Caren Garces, then community relations chief, 2/16/1988.

21. In my interviews with various television producers and ad agencies, I was told that leaders of monarchist political factions, such as Shapur Bakhtiar, Ali Amini, Ahmad Madani, and Reza Pahlavi, have regularly paid for their own "news" interviews inserted in Iranian TV newscasts.

22. For Iranians this duality of private *(andarun)* versus public *(birun)* resonates strongly with two other dyads: intimacy *(samimiat)* versus cleverness *(zarangi)* and interior *(baten)* versus exterior *(zaber)*.

23. Critics point to the excessive and single-minded commercialization of programs. See the "exilic economy" section for examples of such criticism.

24. For example, Manuchehr Buzarjomehri, the producer of *Melli* in the early 1980s, was arrested and apparently convicted on charges of possession and sale of narcotics.

25. A few telethon organizers, who also produce television programs, have been accused of having diverted to their own personal ends the funds they have collected under the guise of social service. In April 1989, Jamshid Kaveh, producer of *Arya*, ran a series of investigative reports in which he charged that Feraidun Farrokhzad, host of a telethon aired on November 20, 1988, and designed to help Iranian children captured by Iraq, had allegedly diverted to his own personal uses the $28,500 raised by the telethon. On the debate caused by the telethon and by *Arya*'s reports, see *Iran News* (11/25/1988, p. 29); *Rayegan* (4/28/1989, pp. 32–33); and *Javanan* (11/3/1989, pp. 36–37). Such charges and countercharges of misrepresentation and malfeasance are complicated and hard to sort out.

26. For example, KSCI-TV terminated *Parsian* on the grounds of the personal attacks of its producer (Parviz Sayyad) on an organizer of an Iranian beauty pageant (Faranak Qahhari). Likewise, *Iran* was canceled apparently because of its violation of U.S. election laws.

27. In denying the charges to me in an interview (Los Angeles, 5/1/1989), Ehsan counter-charged that attacks by Jamshid Kaveh, producer of *Arya*, were part of an organized effort by Shapour Bakhtiar's political faction to discredit her, thinking that she was supported by Ashraf Pahlavi's political faction. Although the Bakhtiar and Pahlavi factions are both monarchist, they differ in some respects and generally have been antagonistic to each other.

28. The periodical *Iran News* called distrust a "canker" that has invaded the exile community (11/25/1988, p. 29). Likewise, while lauding *Arya* TV's investigative efforts, *Khan-daniba* bemoaned the possibility that such reporting could frighten away philanthropists (Bahman 1367/1988, p. 6).

29. For a critique of this action, see "Sokhani az Nasher," *Asr-e Emruz* (4/13/1992, p. 2).

30. For a recent study on how U.S. news media more often than not followed the cues of foreign policy makers rather than using independent judgment in their reporting on Iran under the Shah, see Dorman and Farhang 1987.

31. See "Vahshat-e Saltanattalaban az Pakhsh-e Barnamehha-ye Sima-ye Jomhuri-ye Es-lami-e Iran dar Los Angjeles," *Kayhan Hava'i* (5/20/1992, p. 2).

32. Author's interviews with Parviz Qarib Afshar and Iraj Gorgin, producers of the two respective programs, Los Angeles, May 1992.

33. According to KSCI-TV's figures, the Iranian audience in 1987 ranked fourth in terms of number of households, after Filipinos, Japanese, and Koreans. These figures, however, seem to be based more on statistical probability of the population than on an actual survey of audiences.

34. Author's interviews with Manuchehr Bibian and Ali Limonadi, producers respectively, of *Jam-e Jam* and *Iranian*.

35. The producer of *Didar*, Homa Ehsan, gave a prize for the best name for her Persian cat and Hamid Shabkhiz of *Iran* gave a prize to the caller who named the largest Iranian city. If the contests seem insignificant, the viewers' responses are valuable for feedback-starved producers, especially if one takes seriously Shabkhiz's claim, in an interview with me, that on average he would receive between 100 and 125 calls after each show containing a contest. In an interview (5/10/1992), Parviz Qarib Afshar of *Sima-ye Ashna*, which is aired nationally via satellite, stated that he received 1,400 calls nationwide when he gave out a 900 telephone number.

36. The material in this section . . . is based on data from the study of Iranians in Los Angeles conducted by Georges Sabagh, Ivan Light, Mehdi Bozorgmehr, and Claudia Der-Martirosian. All interpretations here are mine.

37. Although 29 percent of the Armenian heads of household surveyed were female, control for gender showed no difference. Hence gender was eliminated from consideration.

38. This is true particularly of Armenian and Assyrian subgroups.

BIBLIOGRAPHY

Abrahamian, Ervand. 1989. *The Iranian Mojahedin.* New Haven: Yale University Press.
Bozorgmehr, Mehdi. 1992. *Internal Ethnicity: Armenian, Bahai, Jewish, and Muslim Iranians in Los Angeles.* Ph.D. dissertation, sociology, UCLA.
Bozorgmehr, Mehdi, and Georges Sabagh. 1988. "High Status Immigrants: A Statistical Study of Iranians in the United States," *Iranian Studies* 21:3–4. 5–35.

Bozorgmehr, Mehdi, and Georges Sabagh. 1991. "Iranian Exiles and Immigrants in Los Angeles," in *Iranian Refugees and Exiles Since Khomeini*. Asghar Fathi, ed. Costa Mesa, Calif.: Mazda Publishers. 121–44.

Bozorgmehr, Mehdi, Georges Sabagh, and Claudia Der-Martirosian. 1991. *Religio-Ethnic Diversity Among Iranians in Los Angeles*. Los Angeles: UCLA Center for Near Eastern Studies Working Paper No. 6.

Dorman, William A., and Mansur Farhang. 1987. *The U.S. Press and Iran: Foreign Policy and the Journalism of Deference*. Berkeley: University of California Press.

Holley, David. 1986. "South Korean Ownership of TV Firm Admitted," *Los Angeles Times* (2/ 11). Part II, 1.

Katz, Elihu, and George Wedell. 1977. *Broadcasting and the Third World: Promise and Performance*. Cambridge, Mass.: Harvard University Press.

Ketab Corp. 1989, 1991, 1992. *The Iranian Directory Yellow pages*. Los Angeles: Ketab Corp.

Light, Ivan H. 1988. "Los Angeles," in *The Metropolis Era: Mega-Cities*. Volume 2. Matteri Dogan and John Kasarda, eds. Beverly Hills: Sage Publications. 56–96.

Mahmudi, Kambiz. 1992. "Chera az Hozur-e Rasanehha-ye Hamegani-ye Vabasteh beh Rezhim-e Tehran Vahshat Darid?" *Payam-e Asbena* (Farvardin 1371/March 1992), 9–10.

Moslehi, Shahnaz. 1984. *Iranian-e Borunmarzi va Nemuneb-ye Los Anjelesi-ye an*. Encino, Calif.: Ketab Corp.

Naficy, Hamid. 1981. "Cinema as a Political Instrument," in *Modern Iran: The Dialectics of Continuity and Change*. Michael Bonine and Nikki Keddie, eds. Albany, N.Y.: SUNY Press. 341–59.

———. 1990. *Exile Discourse and Television: A Study of Syncretic Cultures: Iranian Television in Los Angeles*. Ph.D. dissertation in theater arts, UCLA.

———. 1993. "Diaspora Television: Middle Eastern Television in Los Angeles," *Afterimage* 20: 7, 9–11.

Puig, Claudia. 1992. "Univision President Bolts to Rival Telemundo," *Los Angeles Times* (5/ 27). D1,2.

Sabagh, Georges, and Mehdi Bozorgmehr. 1987. "Are the Characteristics of Exiles Different from Immigrants? The Case of Iranians in Los Angeles," *Sociology and Social Research* 71:2 (January 2). 77–84.

———. 1991. "Secular Immigrants: Religiosity and Ethnicity Among Iranian Immigrants in Los Angeles," manuscript. 1–36.

Sabagh, Georges, and Claudia Der-Martirosian. 1989. "Diversity Among Iranian Immigrants in Los Angeles," unpublished manuscript.

Sabagh, Georges, Ivan Light, and Mehdi Bozorgmehr. 1985. *Emergent Ethnicity: Iranian Immigrant Communities*. Proposal and Addendum to Proposal for National Science Foundation. Los Angeles:Department of Sociology, UCLA.

Sreberny-Mohammadi, Annabelle, and Ali Mohammadi. 1991. "Hegemony and Resistance: Media Politics in the Islamic Republic of Iran," *Quarterly Review of Film and Video* 12:4, 33–60.

Valle, Victor. 1988. "Latino TV Re-Creates U.S. Images," *Los Angeles Times* (8/18). Fl.

Chapter Twenty-two

Postnational Television?
Goodness Gracious Me *and the Britasian Diaspora*

Moya Luckett

BBC's Asian[1] sketch comedy, *Goodness Gracious Me*, started life on Radio Four in July 1996, a station "where white, middle-class listeners are in healthy supply."[2] In January 1998 it successfully transferred to BBC 2, a TV station catering to a similar demographic. Despite its lowly place in the schedule (it was shown at 11:15 P.M. on a minority channel), it attracted immediate critical acclaim and a very respectable audience of 2.83 million, escalating to 3.84 million for its second series when it was moved to a 9:30 P.M. slot.[3] In 1998 *Goodness Gracious Me (GGM)* won Best New British Television Comedy at the British Comedy Awards and was nominated the following year for Best Light Entertainment (Program or Series) at the British Academy Awards.[4] It stars four thirty-something Asians (Meera Syal, Sanjeev Bhaskar, Nina Wadia, and Kulvinder Ghir), who write many of its sketches. It is produced by Anil Gupta, previously Satyajit Ray's production manager on *Ganashatru* (1989, India) and script editor for ITV's satirical puppet show *Spitting Image*.[5] The show's acclaim, popularity, and genre are remarkable for an Anglo-Asian program focusing on life and customs in the Britasian diaspora. As the *Guardian*'s Phil Daoust notes,

> A few years ago, you could have shouted the words "Asian comedy" till you were blue in the face and no one would have had any idea what you were on about. Not only were there no high-profile Anglo-Asian comics; no one, black or white, seemed to think this was a gap that should be filled."[6]

Despite the much heralded Anglo-Indian film, pop music, and theater renaissance of the 1990s, seen in the emergence of acclaimed playwrights like Ayub Khan-Din and best-selling bands like Cornershop (whose very name plays with and against dominant Anglo-Indian stereotypes), Asians have remained in the margins of the nation's broadcast television. Remarkably, *GGM* is the only terrestrial network television show written by and starring Asians to receive a regular slot in the BBC's Britcom schedule. Nonetheless, the show's form, content, and popularity point to a significant change in the organization of terrestrial broadcast British television. It represents a move away from predominantly racially conceived programming for "minorities," with its concomitant focus on racial specificity, to genres designed to concentrate more specifically on diaspora and its experiences. This shift from what

A still from the title sequence for *Goodness Gracious Me*.

we might term "modernist" to "postmodernist" television inevitably follows a market-driven model and a population demanding entertainment and accessibility. By design, such diasporic shows would be largely accessible to white viewers precisely because their hybridity also involves mainstream white British life.

The concept of the Britasian renaissance refers to the youthful first-, second-, and third-generation British-born Asians who, during the 1990s, broke white Britain's dominant—and dominantly conservative—preconceptions about Anglo-Asian culture. Trendsetters and innovators in the high-fashion, high-visibility worlds of media, design, music, comedy, and new technologies, the new Asian entrepreneurs include the likes of Tahir Mohsan, "the 28-year-old boss of Time Computer systems . . . worth £27m and . . . one of the 500 richest people in the country."[7] Britasian celebrities include the *GGM* team, its former cast member and acclaimed musician Nitin Sawhney, who records for the Anglo-Asian Outcaste label (there is also an Outcaste club), and Asian bands like Cornershop and the 1999 Mercury Music Awards nominees, Talvin Singh and Black Star Liner.[8] Cool Asian style is showcased in a new magazine, *Second Generation*. It has also been officially sanctioned in Tony Blair's appointment of Waheed Ali, the young head of the television production company Planet 24, to Panel 2000, a group of young style leaders "chosen to help give Britain a 'cool' image abroad."[9] Perhaps unsurprisingly, *GGM* arrived in the midst of these transformations, although the cast's earlier accomplishments—such as Sanjeev Bhaskar's work with Nitin Sawhney as the Secret Asians stand-up duo and Syal's script for *Bhaji on the Beach* (Gurinder Chadha, 1994, U.K.)—arguably helped establish the foundations for the current Asian renaissance. As the *Guardian* reports,

> "The show came out at a time when the British Asian vibe was very current," says Syal. "It's trendy to be Asian at the moment. It was always trendy to be black, but never Asian. We used to be all tank-tops, side partings, too many kids and maybe a bit of mysticism. That was our slot." Others disagree: "Some Asians might want this to be the case," says Tariq Modood, professor in sociology at Bristol University. "But I am not convinced. I think people still think cool Asians are the exception to the rule. I think we are at a stage where people realize Asians are not all geeks, not where they think all Asians are cool."[10]

The "coolness" of Asian culture is a matter of debate, especially in an environment that has seen an increase in hate crimes, such as the 1999 Brick Lane bombings in the heart of one of London's leading Asian districts. Nonetheless, the increased visibility has produced new markets for Asian culture—some designed specifically for the diaspora, others for crossover audiences. In August 1999, for instance, the Bollywood producer and entrepreneur Sharad Patel announced he was building Sun City, a £210 million Asian leisure complex in Neasden, North West London, near the largest Hindu temple outside India "exclusively for Asians."[11] The *Observer* predicted that this "will be hailed by some as spectacular evidence that the Asian community is the most vibrant cultural and commercial force in Britain today—and condemned by others as a depressing symbol of its failure to integrate."[12] Sun City's planned facilities include a nightclub oriented toward new Anglo-Asian pop and dance music, a satellite television studio broadcasting Asian Sky TV, an eighteen-screen cinema showing Bollywood films, and a three thousand-seat arena designed to host "weddings of all religions"—presumably only those religions conventionally found in the Indian subcontinent.[13] Dr. Zubaida Haque of the Commission on the Future of Multi-Ethnic Britain endorsed the project, seeing Sun City as "a testament to the growing confidence of second- and third-generation people who now regard themselves as having multiple identities. They can be Bangladeshi, British, Asian and Bengali simultaneously."[14] Challenging the mainstream media, Haque argued that "it was no surprise Asians wanted their own cultural center when their tastes had largely been ignored by the mainstream." Seventy-three percent of Asian households, he noted, now subscribe to Zee TV, a satellite digital channel dedicated to Asian people. "The terrestrial television stations are failing us. In television, theater and museums, there is little sense that Asians play a strong role and have made great achievements here. If they continue to fail us, they will lose out on subscribers and advertising revenue."[15]

Terrestrial television is the term now used to describe Britain's network television: BBC 1, BBC 2, ITV, Channel 4, and Channel 5. Available without subscription (other than the cost of the compulsory £97.50 television license), these networks can be picked up with an antenna. Satellite television dominates the British pay television market (most homes have never been wired for cable). Satellite television debuted in 1989 with rival companies, Sky (Murdoch/News International) and British Satellite Broadcasting (BSB), which soon merged to form the dominant satellite provider,

British Sky Broadcasting (BSkyB). As with cable in the United States, there is a basic service with core channels; additional stations are available for a higher monthly subscription, an option that includes foreign channels and stations tailored for British and European diasporas. Zee TV, which shows Indian films, television, and programming catering to the Indo-Pakistani diaspora, is part of the expanded basic lineup, but it is available only on certain satellites, or ones fitted with an Astra 1D channel expander as it transmits at the very low end of the satellite spectrum, suggesting both the promise of ready availability and marginalization. Despite the rapid increase in satellite subscriptions throughout the 1990s, the vast majority of British homes still receive only terrestrial television, whose networks still dominate in terms of both ratings and visibility. Consequently, even a slot on BBC 2 or Channel 4 will often hold greater value than one on most cable networks. BBC 1 and ITV receive the largest ratings; BBC 2 and Channel 4 often fall behind the larger and more general interest cable and satellite networks, like Rupert Murdoch's Sky TV, by virtue of their emphasis on minority programming. Like many of the cable networks, Sky 1 is essentially filled with American programming (often from its sister channel, Fox) with a smattering of reruns. Other British satellite and cable offerings, like U.K. Gold, specialize in British reruns, producing a national cult television canon that often overshadows the first-run broadcast shows. Digital programming is the latest addition to the British television landscape, debuting on October 1, 1998, with Sky Digital, which was soon joined by rival OnDigital.[16] Besides the improved picture quality and increased channel access offered by these subscription companies, digital also promises a reworking and expansion of the nation's network television.

Indeed, as Haque's comments indicate, broadcast terrestrial television has been more reluctant than other media to accommodate British Asian culture, which has flourished perhaps most in dance music and the club scene (both of which are significantly oriented toward younger, more local audiences rather than national or transnational populations). Even on the stage, Ayub Khan-Din's *East Is East* "was the Royal Court's biggest hit for seven years and was widely held to mark the advent of Asian theater in the heart of London's West End."[17] Now an award-winning hit film, *East Is East* (Damien O'Donnell, 1999, U.K.) received a ten-minute standing ovation at Cannes and a Miramax international distribution contract.[18]

Karen Alexander laments the paucity of black (including Asian) British cinema in the 1990s. Still, her list of fourteen "black-themed,-penned,-directed and theatrically released [British] films in the '90s" greatly exceeds the number of terrestrial entertainment-oriented television shows that might be similarly categorized.[19] Of course, Alexander has a broader racial focus, although her definition of black British cinema is quite narrow and specific. Nonetheless, she cites four specifically Asian films, contrasting with the sole televisual instance of *GGM*. Like pop music, the stage, and the club scene, cinema does not have the same mass-market, national impulse as broadcast television. Anglo-Asian theatrical and musical successes demonstrate how aspects of this diasporic voice resist national address, addressing more specific audiences (like young clubbers or liberal theatergoers) in the service of preserving some "authenticity." Here, perhaps, lies one answer to a problem Alexander raises: "it seems ironic that the complexities of black British culture can be encapsulated in a love song or a dance track but fail to find articulation in one of the most modern of art forms, cinema [and, more markedly, television]."[20] It is less surprising that satellite and cable channels, such as Zee TV or Asianet, address this market as they are simultaneously both specialized and global, not national, in their scope. Of course for the Anglo-Indian diaspora, this is also a potential problem as the specificity of this incarnation of Asian culture is, of course, elided.

GGM fills this gap with its strong *Brit*asian sensibility. Remarkably, a few of the sketches actually center on specificities of the Anglo-Asian diasporic experience, such as the skit about Bharat Homes (a play on the mass-produced middle-income Barratt Homes that cluster the nation's housing estates). Bharat Homes come with all the details the Anglo-Indian could want—old suitcases above the closet, plastic covering on carpets and soft-furnishings, two nested sets of coffee tables, a plentiful supply of Tupperware, and concreted-over backyards. For any viewer outside this diasporic community, these observations alone would not be amusing as they play on inside cultural knowledge, so delivery and a louder laugh track are used to cue the spectator into the joke. But these sketches are rare; much of the show's comedy is more accessible, being based on parody, reversals (Indian/British, diaspora/India, diaspora/Britain, tradition/modernity, old/young) and genre appropriation, borrowing from Bollywood, British, and Hollywood films, television shows, commercials, music videos, and theater. For the first time on British television, Asians control the humor, casting our attention to the bizarre details of Indian, British, and Anglo-Indian cultures and foregrounding mutual cultural appropriations. "The reversal jokes were Anglo-Saxon–friendly jokes," says Gupta. "Jokes we knew white people would understand. They were entry-level sketches. We thought, 'If you like that, then once you're in, we'll do these other ones.' "[21]

GGM's focus is predominantly the Indian diaspora in contemporary Britain, with a special interest in the new Anglo-Asian youth culture articulated through creations like the Bhangramuffins, two young, happy, uninformed, and undereducated Asian hiphop-style men who speak with broad London accents, wear low-riding baggy jeans, caps, and trainers, and rap and repeat their catchphrase, "Kiss my chuddies." The show's primary representation of India owes more to the imperial era and the moment of partition than the present. Even sketches about contemporary Indian life, such as one featuring Indian University exchange students in England, frame their observations in *Passage to India*–style colonial rhetoric, presenting the United Kingdom itself in terms of colonial memory. As this reversal suggests, "India" here is constructed more in terms of memories, but memory here draws on two diverse traditions-the colonial empire and postcolonial migrations. Jokes point to the unreliability of memory, especially in the secondhand, cinematic, or novelistic incarnations that dominate contemporary British life, and show how these representations are more a primary cultural influence on life in Britain today than representative of a nation in its own right. This diasporic focus further suggests how, for the Anglo-Indian community, India might be as unrepresentable as it was for the Anglo colonists, becoming instead an absent present that touches and shapes contemporary life and customs.

GGM has received extensive newspaper coverage, including a lead column in the

Times, for opening up the sensitive area of diasporic life and culture in the most difficult and yet accessible way through humor.[22] The show has become structurally important, not just as a model for future programming, but also as a benchmark for studying the multicultural nature of Britain's television audience. Around 80 percent of the *GGM* audience is white, which for some implies that the show is failing to meet Asian needs. A closer look at the figures reveals that this is not the case. As the *Guardian* notes,

> Programs directed towards non-white people generally draw a high percentage of white viewers. *Black Britain* [a news and current affairs show aimed at the black population] despite having the word black in its title, attracts an audience that's 92 per cent white; the viewers for *Desmonds*, a Channel 4 sitcom set in a barber shop, were 88 per cent white. This is more a function of arithmetic than any racial conundrum. There are only 1.26 million Indians, Pakistanis and Bangladeshis in the country. Even if every one of them watched the program during the second series, there would be another 2.58 million to account for. *Goodness Gracious Me*'s . . . most staggering achievement has been its high penetration among Asian viewers—a group of people the BBC had previously failed to reach in any great number—more than half of whom watched the second series. "The Asian community feel they have something that belongs to them. Something they can identify with and call their own," says Ghir.[23]

These statistics also raise another question: how white is white? At its limits, this question was recently explored in Channel 4's documentary *Britain's Slave Trade*. Commenting on the show, a leading black television producer and media commentator, Trevor Phillips, noted that its researchers discovered "many 'white' [Britons] who can claim a slave ancestor. Most are pleased, but. . . . If nothing else we'll cause the Office for National Statistics some serious difficulties in ethnic monitoring: at what point in its history does a family with a black ancestor stop being mixed-race and become white?"[24]

Are the white viewers of *Black Britain* or *GGM* watching out of a sense of liberal duty, curiosity, or because in some way, they no longer identify solely as "white"? Furthermore, if the latter is the case, what might this suggest about contemporary national identity and the desirability of the nonwhite, multicultural other? In 1999 the Broadcasting Standards Commission published its report on television's representation of multicultural Britain, *Include Me In*. This document showcased *GGM* but, yet again, noted that it was an exception: "Many [nonwhite] respondents welcomed the program, although they found it difficult to name other examples."[25] Tellingly, the BBC as a public service broadcaster does not rely on advertising revenues. Nonetheless, ratings *do* guide its programming as the public demands popular shows in exchange for its license fee, foregrounding the consumerist pressures that have replaced the station's Reithian ethos. Significantly, *GGM* is still on the minority BBC 2. Despite its popularity, the show has not been moved to the more popular and populist BBC 1, as was the case with the 1999 British Comedy Award winner, *The Royle Family* (a sitcom about a northern, white working-class family).

British television has only relatively recently made an effort to cater to the black community, producing largely documentary and magazine-style programs that often address the nation's ethnic minorities en masse.[26] Most of the early efforts were specifically designed to address concerns that emerged into national consciousness after the racially inflected urban riots of the early 1980s, particularly the Brixton riots. Channel 4's near simultaneous debut in November 1982 opened up further ground for ethnic/racial programming with its remit to telecast material of minority interest.[27] The modernist strategy of rioting—a tactic oriented toward revolutionary change—received a peculiarly postmodern response. The nation's broadcasters formed programming divisions to deal with race and representation. The journalist Michael Collins notes that "the BBC's Afro-Caribbean department actually came into being as a result of the coverage of the Brixton riots in the early Eighties, when the network acknowledged that there was a particular voice among British viewers that wasn't getting aired."[28]

Even after this realization, it is arguable whether minority voices really were heard, or moreover, listened to. Audience fragmentation and the concomitant construction of "special-interest" broadcasting instead led to earnest, short-lived, low-budget, and often late-night programming without mainstream appeal, like *Eastern Eye* (aimed at Asian viewers) and *Bandung File* (which featured Bengali subtitles for non–English-speaking viewers). Most successful was *Black on Black*, which ran from 1982 to 1985. Hosted by a diverse group of presenters, including serious black journalists like the producer Trevor Phillips and the former pop singer Pauline Black, the show offered a combination of documentary-style reports, light entertainment and music for and from the Asian and Afro-Caribbean communities.[29]

Hardly surprisingly, these programs failed to meet audience needs, as Andrew Higson observed:

> The most critical audience [for Channel 4 in its first year] is that of ethnic minorities, especially Afro-Caribbeans and Asians, who are unable to perceive any focus to its ethnic programming policy, and call for more peak-time scheduling of programs with positive representations of their communities, in the realm of popular genres as much as so-called factual programming.[30]

Despite their earnest attempts to understand the specificity of their audience, programming decisions like Channel 4's early policy of each week alternating bimonthly shows aimed at Asians and Afro-Caribbeans suggested the interchangeability of minorities in the schedulers' eyes. The insistence on shows dealing with serious issues also smacked of a white liberalism that failed to understand documentary's limited appeal (especially for working-class audiences) and overlooked its potentially offensive ethnographic connotations.

Attempts to integrate Asians and Afro-Caribbeans into mainstream fictional television and the emergence of all-minority casts followed, but again, their success was limited. The combination of ratings-oriented television, its invariable ghettoization of anything non-mainstream, and the political pressures that produce television-by-committee made sensitive *and* entertaining programming almost impossible. In an attempt to move out of this impasse, Channel 4 fused all its ethnic and racial departments into one "multicultural department" in 1999 in order to "jettison the 'minority' tag that previously marginalized this breed of programs."[31] Meanwhile, the BBC maintained its "Asian" and "Afro-Caribbean" departments, and while some of its programming (like the 1999 documentary series. *Sikhs*) corresponds with the ethnographic tradition of minority television, it also produced *GGM*.

The departmental changes in television networks set up a crude binary between the commercial terrestrial channels (Carlton and Channel 4) and the BBC. While Channel 4 moved toward culturally specific minority programming (hence revealing an understanding that *diaspora*, not race, is dominant), the BBC's public service broadcasting ostensibly adheres to the more modernist, biological model of race. Digital and satellite networks, of course, take more risks as they have subscription revenue to play with and draw audiences and programming from around the world, leading to a greater variety of albeit ghettoized programming. If *Sikhs* and *Eastern Eye* fall more into the former category, then *GGM* definitely corresponds to the latter, and, in this regard, follows *The Lenny Henry Show*. Aired on BBC 1 (1984–85, 1987–88, 1995), the show featured Henry as a variety of characters representing Afro-Caribbean diasporic experiences. Henry has called for affirmative action and has his own production company, using his popularity to introduce the British public to multicultural experiences.[32] Nonetheless, he remains an exception. His show is not in the BBC's Afro-Caribbean department; like *GGM*, it is included within the Comedy and Entertainment division.[33] At one level, then, this suggests that famous black faces (like Henry's) cannot be ghettoized in the low-budget domains of racially oriented programming. Henry and the *GGM* cast's movement away from race per se and toward diasporic *culture* within the higher budgets of light entertainment possibly suggests another solution for (black) audiences' desires for culturally specific entertainment. These shows simultaneously address white audiences who recognize and identify with multicultural changes within the United Kingdom while offering other more culturally specific privileged levels of address to "minority" audiences—effectively killing two birds with one stone. One example of this privileged address occurs when characters speak Punjabi in *GGM*, even though this only interpolates a fraction of the Anglo-Asian audience. The executive producer, Jon Plowman, explains, "It's like watching *Frasier* or *Friends* when there's a joke you don't get but is clearly supposed to be funny . . . You think, 'Oh, that must be about being American' . . . it doesn't ruin the whole show for you."[34]

His analogy is important because it acknowledges that difference is not articulated here—or intended to be received—in terms of biological markers of race, but, rather, in terms of *culture*. *GGM* further develops this idea of culture, not race, in its playful attitude toward the "home land," which, whether it is India or Britain, exists predominantly as a cultural rather than racial/ethnic/physical space. Indeed, throughout its sketches, cultural confusion suggests the mobility of home, the very difficulty of defining and fixing space. This takes different incarnations, varying from the "more English than English" Kapurs, repeated characters who insist their name is pronounced "Cooper," and their friends the Rabindernaths/Robinsons, who fervently deny their Indian heritage, to another favorite, Mr. "Everything Comes From India," who insists on recovering Britain's linguistic, cultural, and material appropriations. Reclaiming William Shakespeare, all of Western literature, contemporary hair care products, and even mock Tudor mansions as "all Indian," he proclaims, "Do you think all we had in India was partition?" All these characters in *GGM* foreground how diasporic borrowings and reclamations move in both directions, extending also to the British desire for "authentically" Indian culture (today and back in the Raj), even when they have no idea what it might be.

In quintessentially postmodern fashion, the show offhandedly acknowledges that even in India the authentically Indian is lost, partly, perhaps, as a result of Western appropriations, but also, perhaps, as a result of continual national reimagining through media. This can be seen in a sketch where an Indian peasant couple play with Nintendo Game Boys as Rosie, a white-clad, colonial, aristocratic woman straight out of a heritage film, enters their hut without knocking or seeking permission. With an exaggerated sense of awe she proclaims her delight at their "authentic Indian memorabilia" before announcing that she is a folk art buyer for a chain store. Reversing the practice of imperial plundering of non-European heritage, the couple manage to sell her all their Western mass-produced junk, including a broken three-legged Formica table and a dirty Power Rangers quilt, by pretending that these are all historic artifacts, representations of a "genuine," "native" way of life. Rather than a neocolonial critique, this sketch (like many others) contests notions of native passivity, cultural purity, and Western supremacy-the "natives" have clearly sold junk to naive Westerners many times before. This colonial inversion serves to foreground the history of Anglo-Indian hybridity and the legacy of both nations' complex mutual cultural interaction. It also demonstrates how the desires for an "authentic" Indian culture are equally rooted in white fantasies, thereby rewriting the colonial experience as another, less progressive imperial diaspora.

Arguably, the deliberate lack of verisimilitude and realism in the sketch above—in terms of both its noncredible narrative logic and the artifice of the set—owes as much to a postmodern, postcolonial, postnational sensibility as to the conventions of multiple-camera sketch comedy, with its limited budgets and bright, high-key three-point lighting. The attraction of sketch comedy here might be its very nonrealist aesthetic-its use of clearly fake sets and the repeated appearance of the same principals in distinctly different roles, yet always recognizable as themselves. Like all sketch comedy, *GGM* does not hide ideology under the invisible realist metalanguage used by sitcoms and dramas, but instead foregrounds ideological conflict and divergent views of reality as part of its structuring principle. In this respect, it is worth noting that all "radical" British television shows-from *That Was the Week That Was* (BBC, 1962–64), to *Monty Python* (BBC, 1969–74) to *The Fast Show* (BBC, 1994–)—all fall within this genre, suggesting an association between political/cultural/national critique and nonrealist television. A similar argument can be made for American television. Of course, *GGM*'s difference here lies in its specific postmodern, postcolonial assault on realist television and its own contradictory stance on national and postnational identity.

This picture is further complicated by the show's frequent appropriations of Hindi cinema, also marked by its nonrealist aesthetic and genre appropriation and recombination. This is *not* to say Indian cinema is itself postmodern, but to reassert the prominence of Indian aesthetics within the show, a move that further highlights the ambiguity between "national" and "postnational" forms. The show's cast and writers knowingly play with this sense of the importance and pleasure of the nonrealist, as can be seen in Bhaskar's knowing parody of the Bhangramuffins' love for Indian cinema:

> We hear a lot of Westerners dissing these movies saying that they is not realistic, but we say: KISS MY CHUDDIES! They is not supposed to be realistic. The question shouldn't be: "Why aren't those films more like the real world?" but: "Why ain't the real world more like these films?" Why can't we do triple back somersaults when fighting 20 thugs, while only being armed with a spoon? Why can't we burst into song when we is on the bus? Let's face it, what world would you rather live in, innit? I blame Western society, man . . . Bollywood makes more movies than anywhere else, like in the galaxy man. So next time you go dissing my posse, just remember-my film industry is bigger than your film industry . . . innit![35]

But not all nonrealist forms are made equal, and certainly their political valences vary, even within a nation/culture. *Goodness Gracious Me*'s incorporations of Hindi cinema—its dances, brightly colored clothes, elaborate musical numbers, sudden shifts in genre, and appropriation of other national forms (like the "curry western")—sometimes seem to evacuate any meaning or cultural value. For example, operating in an MTV world of "just images," the rap/bhangra video parody for the Bhangramuffins' "Kiss My Chuddies" features sari-dressed dancers, while Bhaskar and Syal's westernized comic songs focus on the difficulties of love and arranged marriage. On first glance, such parodies may fit into a clichéd variety tradition as seen on countless 1970s television shows both in Britain and the United States. Yet they underscore a careful inversion of the Bollywood tradition of displacing desire and sexuality onto music. These banal songs feature frequent use of explicit language, which the bland variety show–style mise-en-scène and musical arrangement might cause viewers to overlook. For example, one country-esque song about the folly of love marriage contains lines like, "She was a greedy pig in bed. . . . It's like shagging a porcupine."

Cinematic appropriations include mini-film parodies and pastiche cinema advertisements like the one for Mountbatten's English Restaurant in Bombay, "just around the corner from this cinema," which together play with the position of the viewer-here watching television at home, now offered the role of spectator in an Indian movie theater. The show also plays to memories of British film audiences here. The "aged" and faded sixteen-millimeter film recalls the days when Indian restaurants advertised in movie theaters, when curry and, by extension, Indian food were still exotic.

Allusions to Hindi cinema suggest the importance of "national" culture in a postnational world, especially for diasporic populations, suggesting that hybridity does not necessarily imply dissolution. *GGM*'s filmic allusions and appropriations demonstrate the importance of Indian cinema as a vector of both national and postnational identity for groups as diverse as pop culture–obsessed youth, to those who refuse assimilation, to those liberal Anglo audiences who ally themselves with multicultural appropriation.

Cinema has been the dominant national mass medium in India, a nation where television was slow to catch on. Although television broadcasts started in the 1950s, many Indians received their first televisions in the 1970s and the medium has not

A still from "Jodhpur Station, 1947,"

disseminated as fast as elsewhere, possibly because of the nation's size and linguistic diversity, and possibly because of cinema's hegemony and its privileged national address. While it is hardly surprising that many of *GGM*'s India-set sketches are themselves filmic appropriations, these, in turn, foreground the interdependence of cinema/nation and the vexed status of the national within Indian culture. Furthermore, this dependence on already circulating images of nation, especially in nonrealist forms, further suggests that many in the diasporic audience know India only through Bollywood. Several popular sketches acknowledge cinema's central position in Anglo-Asian cultures, particularly in the repeated characters like Chunky LaFunga, a Bollywood star with over four thousand movies on his resumé, and Smitta Smitten, "showbiz kitten," a manic, delusional would-be gossip columnist who has no contact with Indian, British or Hollywood stars, but instead finds herself in men's public restrooms or outside Blockbuster rather than at the big premieres or celebrity parties.

One of the show's most elaborate cinematic sketches is a parody of *Brief Encounter* (David Lean, 1946) titled "Jodhpur Station, 1947." Shot in black and white with its low-key lighting romantically filtered through clouds of steam, the skit stars Bhaskar and Syal as two star-crossed lovers about to part forever to the strains of Rachmaninov's Second Piano Concerto. With their sensible tweeds, overcoats, Oxford shoes, and their very proper and precise articulation of a 1946 form of the King's English (an accent that has died out), they would almost fit perfectly into Lean's highly English film, save for their physiognomy and the color of their skin. They stand out from the crowd of shouting Indians-all of them dressed in "traditional" white flowing gowns and pants-while their final melodramatic moments together are interrupted by a series of peddlers and beggars. With the chivalrous help of her lover, the woman finally boards the train, which, in stereotypically comic-Indian fashion, is so full that her reserved seat is on the roof. Superficially, the sketch is funny because of its ridiculous incongruities-the couple's unexplained and unself-conscious Englishness, the blind beggar walking and waving a stick as he claims he has no limbs, and the seemingly unmotivated collision of India (as a "real" place) and British cinema (here a fiction and series of images). But this sketch offers a complex mediation on Anglo-Indian history and the diaspora. Set in 1947, not the 1946 of Lean's film but the year of independence and partition, the train and the lovers' separation become over-whelmingly symbolic of a nation being remade into new independent fragments, the final disruptive gesture of colonial power. At one level, the pun between their parting and the nation's partition is somewhat facile, but it also highlights the kinds of movement and family breakups that colonization inevitably produces, and with it, the formation of diaspora. Similarly, the train and the breakup of the couple enact the dissolution of family that is at the heart of both Western melodrama and Bollywood cinema. The reference to *Brief Encounter* further reminds us of the disruptive effects the conventions of polite Western society produce at home, keeping lovers apart, demanding a stiff upper lip, the renunciation of pleasure and emotional repression in the service of the national, imperial state. Individuals are thus subsumed within the national imagination, both at the heart of empire and under colonial domination. In this way, the sketch draws a correspondence between both nations, their shared heritage, and the sufferings of their average citizens. The correspondence is italicized here through the mundane pleasures and rituals both share: tea, railways, and a mutual love of cinema, a medium that, as this skit makes clear, explicitly shapes each culture's knowledge of the other.

The repeated reinscription of the postmodern as postnational is one of *GGM*'s characteristic and self-conscious structures. In one sketch, the Bhangramuffins muse about Eurostar, the train linking England to France, and its implications for "traditional English culture." As they travel to Europe by train, they fear that "the traditional British ways of life [will be] changed forever by the Euro changes . . . no more sticking pakoras up at Diwali parties." The humor clearly rises from the techno-bhangra boys' lack of awareness of their own role in the production of a postnational state. Their status as Anglo/Indian/Western hybrids reveals the confusion about the exact nature of the boundary between British and Indian culture. As this boundary becomes increasingly difficult for Anglo and Britasians alike to discern, it also under-scores their inability to understand India's distinct religious, ethnic, and secular traditions. Cultural confusion and ignorance of Indian tradition form the basis of Bhaskar's reviews of the holiday shows in the 1999 Christmas *Time Out* (London) television supplement, written in his Bhangramuffin voice: " 'Christmas is like the British Diwali, innit!' That's how one of our uncles explained it years ago, and it is still da best definition dat we ever heard. Unfortunately he didn't know nuffink about Diwali, so we got a bit stuck after dat."[36]

GGM's pastiches of Hollywood film and American television shows further underline how this postnational awareness by necessity extends beyond Indian and British shores. "The Six Million Rupee Man" sketch starts with a voice-over proclaiming, "we have the power, we have the capability . . . but we don't have the ideal exchange rate." It is precisely the exchange factor that limits how well Sanjeev Austin can be rebuilt as well as his adventures (here he is sent to buy sugar). This parody foregrounds the quintessential postmodern mix: the sketch is an Anglo-Asian pastiche of an American show, drawing on the writers' experience of watching this show in Britain as young Asians. Its purposefully weak narrative—linked to a weak economy-also highlights how much American television's transnational force relates to U.S. economic and cultural hegemony. Furthermore, this imaginary comic juxtaposition of Indian/American television programs points out the neocolonial economic consequences of Western hegemony as impoverished nations can only produce singularly weak narratives.

Throughout *GGM*'s sketches, then, a specific image of India emerges, one that dominates the Britasian imagination of the subcontinent. While the show mentions partition, it elides contemporary national boundaries between India, Pakistan, and Bangladesh to reconstitute the nation in its utopian wholeness. Despite privileging Punjabi over India's other languages, its narrative incorporates all religions and cultures, showing how in the diaspora, shared cultural similarities and histories might sit more comfortably together, although back "home," in what are now discrete nations, shared cultures are often at conflict with each other and violently riven by various nationalist movements. Sketches reveal how Asian cultural diversity exists in the diaspora with idealistic, minimal conflict. "East Meets Pest" features a Buddhist exterminator visiting a secular Westernized woman, and another skit is about a Muslim immigrant family whose only son converts to Judaism. Consoling his parents, he points out the similarities of both faiths, such as their shared food prohibitions, customs, and language: "You say "Salaam," I say 'Shalom,' . . . Jews and Muslims are both circumcised. . . . Have you ever noticed the uncanny resemblance between a rabbi and a Muslim cleric? The long beard, the glasses, the robes? Never picking up the check?" The son's westernized status is made all the more ludicrous in this London-set sketch as he now speaks with a New York accent (clearly aping Woody Allen) and wears an orange wig and glasses like George Costanza's father, Frank, in *Seinfeld* (NBC, 1990–98). The ridiculous stress on the complementary nature of violently conflicting religions here produces humor but also rearticulates the diasporic imagination's emphasis on multicultural unity rather than division, especially as it brings together Judaism's high Western profile and its more "Eastern" origins in proximity to Islam. But this parody of utopian multicultural rhetoric for once has a clearly defined target-we cannot even imagine a circumstance where these people would get along.

This utopian image of diasporic Indian unity lends itself very well to defining a market, especially as it draws upon a larger demographic that makes it more profitable to serve Asian (or, by extension, all diasporic) needs. This very image of India without partition and with harmonious interaction between its religious and cultural groups is also articulated in Patel's Sun City (even as it is at the center of the troubled national articulations in Hindi films) and is seen in his insistence that the center would be both secular *and* open to all religions. This image of a unified but independent India reconstructs for the diaspora a national image of lost possibility, countering news of increasingly antagonistic religious or ethnic nationalism, the rise of fundamentalism, and increased Indo-Pakistani border conflicts. In this light, Patel's harmonious rhetoric seems naively optimistic and market-driven when he asserts, "You can go to various parts of India and all the races and religions mix. In Indian restaurants you get food from more than one region. So why not at Sun City? There's not going to be any religion here. It's going to be a celebration."[37] His restaurant/ religion/region analogy also reinscribes the diaspora as simultaneously a *market* and a *commodity*, offering many choices without enforcing cultural boundaries and prohibitions. These sentiments are not universal; some in the diaspora police cultural boundaries. As the *Guardian* notes, despite wide acclaim from the nation's racial leaders, *GGM* has attracted fierce criticism from some in the Asian community. When it referred to the holy fire at a wedding ceremony as a "fondue," the Broadcasting Standards Commission upheld "in part" the complaints of twelve viewers who argued that the "religious symbol of the Hindu faith was unacceptably mocked." "It gives the English the opportunity to laugh at us without thinking about it," says Suman Bhuchar, an independent producer and freelance writer.[38] Interestingly, this controversy and much of the show's acclaim highlight its plays with language and the ways these are used to both evoke, unify, and debunk cultural identities. Puns like "Sanjeev Austin" abound, and, in classic knowing poststructural fashion, foreground the boundaries and ellipses between cultures and meaning as they are playfully juxtaposed and transgressed. These word games draw attention to otherwise unseen linguistic similarities (as with Kapur/Cooper, Dinesh/Dennis), while they showcase the writers' talents. Wordplay also hints at the increasingly polyglot nature of the British Isles; cultural commentators foreground the sheer number of languages spoken in England every day. Trevor Phillips notes that "London speaks 200-plus languages, and has 45 large ethnic communities," but this linguistic diversity pales in comparison with India's 1,600 languages.[39] This is, however, in keeping with India's status as a former colony, for, as Walter D. Mignolo points out, colonized countries speak the most languages and consequently have a high rate of illiteracy, as well as having greater numbers of polyglots and more fusion between languages. This multiplicity of tongues reveals colonization's impossible project, as the dominant Western language of the colonizer adds to the mix rather than replacing all minor languages.[40] Some languages have, of course, been destroyed, but the preservation of others demonstrates regional resistance to nationalization or imperialism, in addition to suggesting a preference for oral rather than written communication. The greater number of polyglots in India than in Britain also suggests a different relation to language, one that is more playful and inflects the spoken English of the diaspora. As Mignolo notes, the English spoken by colonized people does not carry with it the national history and ideology of the colonized person but rather is remade to carry a very different set of more personalized and localized memories and connotations.[41] Speaking multiple languages produces not just a facility with language, allowing the speaker to rework it for their own ends, but also divorces the language from its absolute associations with both concrete and abstract/ideological worlds while underscoring its non-national impulse. In this respect, Indian English is akin to pidgin, where, as Robert J. C. Young notes, "the vocabulary of one language [is] superimposed on the grammar of another-suggesting a different model from that of a straightforward power relation of dominance of colonizer over colonized." [42] For Young, pidgin represents a fertile hybrid, a language designed to express the interface between two cultures.

"Pidgin"-type languages are used in *GGM* and represent a consistent part of the humor (and even critique) of some characters, a strategy most highly developed in sketches dealing with the Kapur/Cooper family. Desperate to be considered a white, English upper-middle-class family, the Kapurs-like their friends the Rabindernaths/Robinsons-repress their Punjabi origins. They send their children to public schools, favor English culture, and adopt English names (Dinesh Kapur calls himself Dennis, his wife Ranchajeet, prefers Charlotte, Surjeet Rabindernath calls himself St. John Robinson, and his wife, Dina, goes by Vanessa). However, they cannot master standard English speech, and sometimes slip into Punjabi at moments of shock or fear (as when bricks are thrown through their window painted with the terrifying cliché "Paki go home"). Like pidgin speakers, they have mastered the vocabulary but not its syntax, and, similarly, they do not understand the history, memories, ideology, and multiple meanings built into the language. While they recognize its national impulse, they are excluded from this community as they only see each word in its denotative meaning, as a single, isolated unit, an understanding that parallels their own isolation. Their language is rigid and unplayful, largely because they try to control and bind it into their own national desires. Examples of their speech include, "Please do pursue me through into the parlor" and "Shall we evacuate to your lavatorial conwenieces?" The Kapurs' son, Sebastian, who has returned to his original name, Subash, was born in Britain, speaks fluent standard middle-class English as well as Punjabi, and is completely familiar with both sets of cultural traditions, but insists he is not English and wears hybrid Punjabi/Western dress.

Whereas the Kapurs' Indian-inflected English exposes their masquerade, the show's other hybrid forms reveal more liberating linguistic possibilities that exist within diaspora, highlighting how polyglot speakers might remake the English language through their deliberate deviations that carve out other cultural spaces. These vary from the trendsetting Bhangramuffins' reinvention of Anglo-Indian youth slang, now much aped in the general population, to the representations of older traditional Indian mothers who have deliberately not assimilated, even though they have spent most of their lives in the United Kingdom, who pepper their speech with Punjabi as a mark of resistance.

The careful use of language has been one of the show's most lauded characteristics. The *Guardian* observed, "The strength of Syal's writing is in the details, most notably her ability to capture the rhythms of Indian speech, so brilliantly parodied in *Goodness Gracious Me*."[43] The show's reception highlights Syal as author and controlling voice: "Meera Syal, author of the prize-winning *Anita and Me* and co-writer of the sketch show *Goodness Gracious Me*, has an agenda. She is interested in women suspended between two cultures: Indian tradition and liberal British society."[44] Without knowledge of the role of women within Indian media, the British (and, more recently, American) press has singled out Syal as the radical center of the show and as a singular departure for Indian women with her Western-style feminism.[45] Syal's incorporation within celebrity culture suggests that she offers an acceptable critique of Indian patriarchy but at the same time masks other diasporic or Indian contributions—such as the proactive work of Anglo-Indian feminist groups like the Southall Women's Collective or images of strong, independent women within Indian cinema—to a more global feminism.

The show's cast and writers explicitly state that women's rights represent the one area they will not compromise. As the *Guardian* notes, the show's critique of Indian national identity and customs is at its most acerbic when it interrogates the national-feminine:

> The one big exception to [its] resolutely upbeat, inclusive approach concerns the oppression of women, which the writers (Richard Pinto, Sharat Sardana, Sanjeev Kohli and the multitalented Meera Syal) clearly view as particularly severe among Asians. In one particularly telling sketch a doctor (Bhaskar) treats a woman (Wadia) for a "lack of Indian culture," then smacks her in the jaw to check the cure has worked. She just giggles—as she is supposed to.[46]

But the progressiveness of such a sketch is open to question, not least from the standpoint that it is equating violence against women with the East, erasing its presence in the West, and not forming some kind of coalition or association across cultures here, as the show characteristically does elsewhere. Furthermore, the stereotype of the typical Indian woman not only plays into a Western ignorance of Indo-Pakistani cultures, and the many different images and levels of feminine oppression that they uphold, but also forwards Western hegemony as the only solution for the diasporic woman, a hegemony that itself tends to marginalize femininity. Interestingly, this has occurred despite women holding the highest levels of political office in both India and Pakistan, although figures like Indira Gandhi (prime minister of India, 1966–77, 1980–84) and Benazir Bhutto (prime minister of Pakistan, 1988–90, 1993–96, and the first woman to head an Islamic state) can be reclaimed as Western-educated products of an international elite (therefore nationless) and/or rejected as corrupt.

The image of women as national icon and figure of some revolutionary power is also central to Indian cinema, seen perhaps most explicitly in Mehoob Khan's allegorical independence epic, *Mother India*. As Ashish Rajadhyaksha notes, Nargis's films with Mehoob Khan used the femme fatale and other feminine stereotypes to "combat the orientalization of India" and therein to articulate an independent national identity.[47] While Nargis's self-sacrificing mother represents the fertile origins of a new India, a more radical and explicitly postcolonial independent cinema, exemplified in such films as *Spices* (Ketan Mehta, 1987, India), interrogates the maternal metaphor while still positioning the nation as feminine. In doing so, they represent both revolutionary power and community building through women's ability to band together against male oppression, despite their different class and social status. In stark contrast, *GGM*'s feminine/feminist postcolonial voice presents the traditional Indian woman as a figure of gentle fun, at the margins of social and political life. This is most often caricatured through the figure of the aging mother, whose pride in her son's accomplishments takes the form of boasting and exaggeration, aimed at putting other women down and exerting her own power through male achievements. Unlike Nargis's hybrid of young, glamorous bride and revered mother, *GGM*'s Indian mothers (especially the repeated duo of the "Fiercely Competitive Mothers") are resolutely middle-aged or elderly. Dressed in matronly fashion (in either Western or Indian attire), they usually inhabit interiors (kitchens, back or passenger seats of cars, supermarkets, restaurants) and are most often seated, in a passive position. Their identities are wrapped up in their families, generally tied to husbands and sons, often to the point where they have lost touch with reality.

The strength and complexity of some of Hindi cinema's women, like Nargis, is negated in *GGM* in favor of representations of the "double oppression" of traditional Asian women who are marginalized as racial others within the diaspora and subordinated by Indian patriarchal traditions. As seen in the acclaimed "lack of Indian culture" skit, Indian gender relations are represented as violent, with "proper" Indian femininity marked as the ability to receive male violence with a smile. This also works against Britain's own tradition of Anglo-Indian radical feminism, as found in such groups as the Asian Women's Co-op (founded in 1986), the Asian Women's Advice and Activities Center (founded in 1992), and the Asian Women's Action Group (founded in 1989), to name just three London-based groups alone. Here, the show sidesteps one of the structuring and most complex aporias of postcolonial thought: the question of exactly *how* to maintain an Asian identity and benefit from Western feminism without evacuating the strengths found within traditional and contemporary Indian women's roles. Given woman's centrality to images of the nation in Indian popular culture, femininity becomes central to any understanding of the images of nation produced by the diaspora to support its own cultural identity. At the same time, they are also central to more recent postcolonial critiques of imperialism, partition, and the imposed reworkings of nationalism forced on India throughout its history.

GGM's representation of powerful female figures as predominantly educated, upper-middle-class professionals serves to white out the struggles involved in producing such a persona. Furthermore, it effects an erasure of the process by which a supportive marriage of Western feminism and Anglo-Indian culture might be produced. In this respect the text reenacts the problem it so often circumvents through elisions, puns, humor, and substitutions: the woman's "lack of Indian culture," the solution for which is either subjugation to native male oppression or the wholesale adoption of Western feminism. Ironically here the text's very "radicalism" on this ground reconstructs a traditional binary grid that fails to grapple with one of the central problems of Asian identity.

Feminist discourses have also been used to repackage *GGM* as yet another show that deals with British television's well-served audience of women. Ironically, this erases some of its potential cultural specificity. As the *Guardian* notes, "Along with children, youth, and single *men*, Britain's ethnic minorities are one of the groups recognized by the BBC as being most underserved."[48] Similarly, Trevor Phillips observes that women of color are better represented at executive levels than black men. He notes, "The one bright spot that I can see is the emergence of a posse of senior black and Asian program-makers just below executive level, most of them women."⁴⁹ This preponderance of women might have occurred because feminism—or at least feminine independence-more easily addresses concerns (and stereotypes) held by white audiences. Seemingly, the elevation of feminism over multiculturalism and diasporic concerns is a structural feature of British television, even among programs aimed at covering that lack. While the diversity of *GGM*'s female images foregrounds the obvious quotidian differences within the Anglo-Indian community—Islamic and Hindu mothers and grandmothers, thirty-something Britasian career women, twenty-something students, emotional but well-behaved teenage girls—these stereotypes tend to bypass the unstable and vexed identity of the Anglo-Indian hybrid. Ironically, and for extra comic effect, the show is as likely to show this figure as a white woman, married to an Asian man who affects a crazed parody of the passive but seductively dancing ingenue from Hindi films, another repeated and often despised character within the show.

Of course, this construction also comments on the possibly exotic appeal of Indian culture for whites (including, of course, the show's audience and the BBC's desire to reinvent itself as a multicultural broadcasting giant). This is linked to the colonial tradition, which highlights the gulf to be bridged by the hybrid as an unimaginable task. In the (Western) modernist imagination, this is still perhaps most famously associated with E. M. Forster's *A Passage to India* (1924) and disseminated across to the populist middlebrow in its televisual adaptation and through Merchant-Ivory's heritage/empire films. This aporia still exists in the self-proclaimed discourses of the (liberal) intelligentsia in multicultural Britain, as voiced, for instance, in Andrew Smith's report of his visit to India with former *GGM* cast member Nitin Sawhney: "In this huge nation, with seven major religions, 15 ethnic groups and 1,600 languages, there is little point in trying to control things. So everything is left to chance. You could see this as a kind of celebration of life. The problem is that it's easily exploited."⁵⁰ While Smith exhibits a more postmodern plurality, self-consciousness, and economic awareness, his perspective nonetheless represents the limits of the white Western subject: an inability to deal with such difference, particularly when it is overladen with similarity. Strangely, Sawhney's perspective is largely absent, save for moments where he can identify with either nation, but the article cannot deal with the possibility of simultaneous multiple identifications.

But clearly, the hybrid is not a problem for the popular imagination, as *GGM* and forms like techno-bhangra music clearly demonstrate. As this suggests, solutions to these modernist anxieties lie outside intellectual high culture and its middlebrow descendents. The desire to paint Britain as multicultural and postcolonial is, after all, rooted as much in the market/consumer culture and public relations as it is in *GGM*'s larger efforts to rework the nation as new, different, and exciting. Britain's multiple identities, fragmentation, and hybridity are fetishized, avowedly shared by all races. Ironically, as Robert J. C. Young suggests, this multiplicity might herald a new (national) stability:

Today's self-proclaimed mobile and multiple identities may be a marker not of contemporary social fluidity and dispossession but of a new stability, self-assurance and quietism. Fixity of identity is only sought in situations of instability and disruption, of conflict and change. Despite these differences, the fundamental model has not altered: fixity implies disparateness; multiplicity must be set against at least a notional singularity to have any meaning.[51]

Young notes that this historical fear of the unstable articulates another deeper anxiety about the heterogeneity of English identity, itself largely an Anglo-Celtic-Italian-Saxon-Viking-Norman-French hybrid, whose fears returned in its contact with the other.[52] As the hybrid has been re-understood as fertile, as social Darwinism has been exposed as culturally and scientifically unsound, as migration and travel have revealed the infinite differences and seductive similarities of all cultures, and as popular psychology and psychoanalysis have revealed the fragmented, multiple nature of all identity, instability becomes neither radical nor dangerous. If, as Wahneema Lubiano insists, "postmodernism [is] a sign of [the dominant group's] . . . lack of control," then a lack of control has become desirable, and thus marketable.[53]

Lubiano cites Jonathan Arac, who notes that a postmodern world is not "a world in which one can or should be too easily at home."[54] While these sentiments are generally placed in terms of loss, the critical reception accorded GGM reveals how desirable this position really is. Exported to "Sweden, the Netherlands, New Zealand, Australia and parts of South-East Asia," GGM's interrogation of Anglo-Asia enables all cultural groups to see themselves as in transit. It enables white British to see their culture as embedded in that long-ago encounter with India, a conflict that is no longer overwhelming or incomprehensible or undesirable on a North European island where curry has become the national dish. To be credible, then, television for the diaspora must highlight how both cultures are multicultural, fragmented, multiple, hybrid—all, of course, strategies that are completely compatible with the market and therefore economically somewhat conservative.

In terms of the market, GGM's open textuality and its absence of any central, ideological voice aid the show both in constructing Anglo-Asian identity and communities as complex, multifaceted, and diverse and in attracting the economically all-important white audience as well as the culturally important Britasian demographic. Multiculturalism is recast as an important market strategy, evoking Fredric Jameson's assertion that postmodernism is the dominant paradigm in contemporary society, embedded as much in consumerism and popular culture as in any elite discourse.[55]

I want to close with an image from GGM that captures this sensibility. One of the show's most popular repeated characters is an older woman used to lambaste the image of the nonconsuming Asian. Throughout the show, her behavior is ridiculed as inappropriate as she insists, for example, that she will not pay for spaghetti in an Italian restaurant as she can make it at home out of little strips of roti. Her ignorance and refusal to participate in the market reveal her dismissal of cultural difference, which the show associates with consumer society. Consumption and culture are allied as ways of preserving "authentic" tradition and sharing them with others. Ultimately, perhaps, GGM and the broadcasting strategies that led to its appearance on the schedule suggest that racial and cultural conflict, with their attendant riots and racially motivated violence (like the bricks thrown through the Rabindernath's window), can be made obsolete through the marketing of Asian and other minority cultures to ethnically, racially, and nationally diverse audiences. In this respect, postmodernism and postcolonialism rework difference into a market strategy rather than points of contention. Whether or not this is any solution is, of course, open to question, but as this tactic has become increasingly commonplace, it invites a greater interrogation of multiculturalism and the politics of pleasure, particularly the pleasures of the diaspora.

NOTES

1. I am using "Asian" here in the British context to refer to peoples from the Indian subcontinent rather than the accepted American use.

2. "Mirth of a Nation," *Guardian*, February 20, 1999.

3. Ibid.

4. Michael Collins, "Ghetto Busters," *Observer*, March 28, 1999.

5. "Mirth of a Nation."

6. Phil Daoust, "They Ain't Half Hot, Man," *Guardian*, March 8, 1999.

7. Nick Mathiason and Sonia Damle, "£200m Fun Palace to Celebrate Asian Culture," *Observer*, August 8, 1999.

8. Ibid.; "Mirth of a Nation."

9. "Britannia's 'Committee for Cool," *BBC News Online* (http://news.bbc.co.uk), April 1, 1998.

10. "Mirth of a Nation."

11. Mathiason and Damle, "£200m Fun Palace to Celebrate Asian Culture."

12. Ibid.

13. Ibid.

14. Ibid.

15. Ibid.

16. Available at http://www.users.zetnet.co.uk/csimon/tv_e.htm#Digital.

17. Maya Jaggi, "If You Want It Done Properly," *Guardian*, July 14, 1999.

18. Ibid.

19. Karen Alexander, "Black British Cinema in the 90s: Going Going Gone," in Robert Murphy, ed., *British Cinema of the 90s* (London: BFI Publishing, 2000), 112.

20. Ibid., 113.

21. "Mirth of a Nation."

22. Ibid.

23. Ibid.

24. Trevor Phillips, "For Those of You Watching in Black and White . . ." *Guardian*, September 20, 1999, G2 Media Section, 4.

25. Janine Gibson, "TV 'Failing to Reflect Multicultural Society,' " *Guardian*, December 8, 1999.

26. In Britain, the word "black" is used to describe the coalition between Asian and Afro-Caribbeans and is not a pejorative term.

27. Sylvia Harvey quotes the 1980 Broadcasting Act describing the new channel's service mandate, "to ensure that the programs contain a suitable proportion of matter calculated to

appeal to tastes and interests not generally catered for by ITV," "Deregulation, Innovation and Channel Four," *Screen* 30, nos. 1–2 (winter–spring 1989): 64.

28. Collins, "Ghetto Busters."

29. Harvey, "Deregulation, Innovation and Channel Four," 73.

30. Andrew Higson, "A Wee Trendy Channel," *Screen* 30, nos. 1–2 (winter–spring 1989): 88.

31. Collins, "Ghetto Busters."

32. Ibid.

33. "Mirth of a Nation."

34. Ibid.

35. Sanjeev Bhaskar, "Hooray for Bollywood!" *Observer*, November 21, 1999.

36. Sanjeev Bhaskar, "We Wish You a Mufffin Christmas," *Time Out*, December 22, 1999–January 5, 2000, section 2, p. 3.

37. Mathiason and Damle, "£200m Fun Palace to Celebrate Asian Culture."

38. "Mirth of a Nation."

39. Phillips, "For Those of You Watching in Black and White," 5.

40. Walter D. Mignolo, "Globalization, Civilization, Processes, and the Relocation of Languages and Cultures," in Fredric Jameson and Masao Miyoshi, eds., *The Cultures of Globalization* (Durham: Duke University Press, 1998), 38–41.

41. Ibid.

42. Robert J. C. Young, *Colonial Desire: Hybridity in Theory, Culture and Race* (London: Routledge, 1995), 5.

43. Carrie O'Grady, review of Meera Syal, *Life Isn't All Ha Ha Hee Hee*, *Guardian*, October 13, 1999.

44. Ibid.

45. As the BBC America Web site notes, "Meera Syal . . . was recently described by the *New York Times* as "a multicultural phenomenon." Available at http://www.bbcamerica.com/articles/goodness_gracious_me_goodness_gracious_me_s.html.

46. Daoust, "They Ain't Half Hot, Man."

47. Ashish Rajadhyaksha, "Nargis," in Geoffrey Nowell-Smith, ed., *Oxford History of World Cinema* (Oxford: Oxford University Press, 1996), 404.

48. "Mirth of a Nation."

49. Phillips, "For Those of You Watching in Black and White."

50. Andrew Smith, "The Outsider," *Observer*, September 19, 1999.

51. Young, *Colonial Desire*, 4.

52. Ibid., 3.

53. Wahneema Lubiano, "Shuckin' Off the African-American Native Other: What's 'Po-Mo' Got to Do with It?" in Anne McClintock, Aamir Mufti, and Ella Shohat, eds., *Dangerous Liaisons: Gender, Nation, and Postcolonial Perspectives* (Minneapolis: University of Minnesota Press, 1997), 206.

54. Ibid., 207.

55. Appiah, "Is the 'Post' in 'Postcolonial' the 'Post' in 'Postmodernism'?" In McClintock, Mufti, and Shohat, *Dangerous Liaisons*, 425.

Chapter Twenty-three

African American Television in an Age of Globalization

Timothy Havens

> The 'hood is only a section in a much larger city, state,
> country, and world. To exist in the coming century, it
> will be necessary to coexist with the world, and not
> simply to exist in the 'hood.
> —Todd Boyd, *Am I Black Enough for You?*

The increasing globalization of the television industry has opened a new arena of concern for scholars committed to racial justice. Stuart Hall notes that, in the predominantly white television industries of Western Europe, "black street styles and black bodies have become the universal signifiers of modernity and 'difference,'" resulting in portrayals of "Blackness" that do not significantly challenge the racial status quo (1995: 21). Karen Ross suggests that the economics of global television distribution and the ability of physical comedy to transcend linguistic borders create the "potential for negative stereotypes to circulate internationally," relegating "less popular and more challenging oppositional work to the margins" (1996: 172, 175). In support of Ross's claims, Kristal Brent Zook (1999) chronicled how the Fox Network canceled several innovative African American programs in 1994 as part of a strategy to increase its presence as a program distributor in Western Europe.

This chapter addresses how television representations of African Americans are shaped by the international television market. I begin by discussing the kinds of African American television programming that exist today and how current business practices in the global marketplace enable the distribution priorities of major U.S. producers and acquisition preferences of general entertainment European channels to restrict the diversity of African American televisual representations.

Globalization, however, is not *inherently* hostile to diverse Black television portrayals. The programming practices and preferences of buyers from niche channels and those of buyers from beyond Western Europe might enable a greater diversity of portrayals and greater involvement of African Americans and other minority television producers. Satellite distribution offers the possibility of creating a type of narrowcasting that may create a space for minorities worldwide to explore representational practices that counter mainstream portrayals without needing to appeal to national majority audiences. Though the basis for such cultural exchanges may seem questionable at first glance, historical, political, and aesthetic similarities among minority cultures worldwide make such exchanges possible—and they already occur in literature, popular music, and underground cinema.

Race and Television

For centuries, intellectuals and artists—particularly those of color—have believed in a link between the representations of Blacks in popular culture and wider social attitudes toward race. Since the 1950s, media effects researchers have investigated how "negative" portrayals enhance feelings of superiority among white viewers and inferiority among African Americans. Critical media researchers, meanwhile, sought to transcend the dichotomy of "positive" and "negative" media influences, instead envisioning television as a site of social discourse where claims about racial identity and difference are continuously made, challenged, and refashioned. In spite of their differences, both groups agree that the field of African American portrayals has historically been too restrictive and must be expanded.

Herman Gray has developed a useful typology for analyzing the degree to which African American television programs conform to conventional televisual modes. He distinguishes among three main types of African American television: assimilationist, pluralist, and multicultural. Assimilationist programs "are distinguished by the complete elimination or, at best, marginalization of social and cultural differences in the interest of shared and universal similarity" (1995: 85). Such shows include *Julia*, *Diff'rent Strokes*, and *Designing Women*, wherein African American and white characters exhibit few, if any, differences while narratives seldom address experiences relevant to African Americans. Essentially, these shows promote a vision of racial harmony that leaves the dominant racial order unchanged.

Pluralist shows like *Family Matters* and *The Jeffersons* accommodate expressions of cultural difference more explicitly than assimilationist shows through their creation of an African American world separate from the white American world. However, the characters we see and the lives they live differ only slightly from those of most white sitcoms. Although cultural differences exist, "the social and historical contexts in which these acknowledged differences are expressed, sustained, and meaningful are absent" (Gray 1995: 87). That is, the experiences of and struggles against oppression, which form the basis of African American cultural differences, never surface in these series. These shows also represent African American identity as homogeneous rather than diverse, conflicted, and contested.

Finally, multicultural shows like *Roc* and *A Different World* offer glimpses into the lives and experiences of African Americans from a decidedly African American viewpoint. These shows foreground African American cultural differences as well as the roots of those differences while expressing diversity through their recurrent characters. Multicultural shows provide "complex, even contradictory, perspectives and representation of black life in America" (1995: 90). A key question is thus whether and how the expansion of the U.S. television industry into international markets has affected the industry's reliance on any one of these typologies. In other words, does international distribution favor assimilationist, pluralist, or multicultural programming?

Global Television Distribution

Although international distribution has existed since the 1950s, not until the 1990s did these outlets become more than an ancillary business. U.S. distributors' revenues from film and television exports jumped fivefold between 1985 and 1992, with roughly 45 percent of these revenues from sales of television programs. Two main factors help explain this situation. First, the majors can sell shows with high production values cheaply on the international market because they get most of their revenues from domestic sales. As table 23.1 illustrates, in virtually every market—including the Western European markets—it is cheaper to purchase U.S. programming than to produce domestic shows.

The worldwide spread of new television channels is a second factor in the growth of international sales. The late 1980s and 1990s witnessed a surge in privately owned television channels, broadcast hours, and competition for U.S. programming as a

TABLE 23.1
Purchased Programming Cost Ratio

Country	Channel	1996
Austria	ORF	1.34
Belgium (N)	BRTN	2.34
Belgium (S)	RTBF	1.76
Denmark	DR	5.26
	TV2	4.04
Finland	YLE	4.28
	MTV	1.21
France	France 2	2.01
	France 3	3.17
Germany	ARD	5.62
	ZDF	3.56
Greece	ERT	2.23
Ireland	RTE	6.86
Italy	RAI	4.34
Netherlands	NOS	2.92
Norway	NRK	7.35
	TV2	1.79
Portugal	RTP	1.94
Spain	RTVE	1.94
Sweden	SVT	3.98
Switzerland	SSR	1.52
UK	BBC	2.97
	ITV	3.56
	Channel 4	2.52

The number reported is a multiplier representing how many times cheaper it is to buy imported U.S. programming versus self-producing programming. Parity = 1.0.
SOURCE: "European TV Programme Budgets" 1997.

TABLE 23.2
Top Eight Markets for U.S.
Television Rights Sales, 1996

Country	Sales in Millions of U.S. Dollars
Germany	$750
UK	$470
France	$315
Japan	$230
Italy	$230
Spain	$230
Australia	$200
Canada	$190

SOURCE: *Video Age International*, 16 June 1997.

result of worldwide deregulation, which affected the bottom lines of all the major distributors. In Western Europe, where channel growth has been most dramatic, the number of cable and satellite channels increased nearly twenty-fold between 1984 and 1996. Most of these upstart channels use programming acquired from U.S. distributors in order to build viewership and fill out their schedules.

Industry insiders agree that European buyers are more fickle today than they were five years ago, but Western Europe remains the primary destination for U.S. exports for economic and cultural reasons (see table 23.2). The countries of Western Europe have a greater concentration of wealth and higher GDPs than any other region in the world. They have the technological and economic capacity to support several channels that pay high prices for U.S. programming, and they offer a desirable market for advertisers. In 1998 U.S. distributors' revenues from international television outlets totaled almost $4 billion; Western European countries accounted for more than 60 percent of these revenues (Puopolo 1999). Moreover, the United States—Hollywood in particular—shares ties with Western Europe that translate into cultural similarities not shared with other regions of the world. One similarity is a common racial identity and history, which influences the kinds of programs traded.

Despite the importance of international sales revenues for U.S. distributors and the ubiquity of imported American programming throughout Europe, neither distributors nor buyers conduct regular audience research about U.S. imports. Some major distributors collect ratings data for the most popular shows in large markets, but the performance of most shows is never tracked because international markets are not distributors' primary targets (Duran 1999; Mulder 1999). From the buyers' perspective, imported shows typically do not attract the kinds of audiences that domestically produced programming does, so little economic incentive exists for conducting audience research. Also, many current and former public stations in Europe, which are often the main general entertainment channels in a market, remain biased against audience research because it smacks of commercialism. Some general entertainment channels conduct focus group research before buying imported shows; however, such research usually consists of an initial screening for a small number of viewers, with no follow-up research once a show has been purchased.

Instead of relying on audience research to make programming decisions, executives typically glean knowledge from one another about what kinds of programming "travel" internationally. The culture of international television is rife with speculation about why shows succeed or fail, which has become accepted wisdom among executives and is shared through trade magazines and discussions at television markets. These executives comprise a small, elite club: in 1997 a scant 154 acquisitions executives and deputies accounted for about 70 percent of international television sales for U.S. distributors (Puopolo 1999).

European Buyers and African American Programming

In the following sections, I refer to interviews I conducted with thirty-three international television executives regarding their impressions of the international marketability of African American situation comedies. Eleven of the executives work for international distribution wings of U.S. television producers; twenty are responsible for purchasing television from the international market; and two work for the National Association of Television Professionals and Executives (NATPE), which sponsors one of the largest international television festivals each year.

I discuss African American sitcoms because buyers and sellers treat them differently than dramas or television movies that feature African Americans. For international television executives, genre is the primary (though not the *only*) criterion in determining the marketability of shows. I focus on prevalent attitudes about African American sitcoms among buyers from general entertainment European channels and U.S. distributors who target such buyers.

African American sitcoms suffer from generally negative attitudes toward sitcoms among the main international players. Most people in the industry believe that comedy crosses national borders less easily than other genres. "First and foremost, what you need to know is that situation comedies are more difficult to sell internationally than action dramas," declared Mark Kaner, president of Twentieth Century Fox International Television. Likewise, Michael Puopolo, manager of international research for Warner Brothers International Television, said, "Sitcoms in general are not the most successful product. . . . A lot of it has to do with culture: better than any other culture, American culture transfers well to the rest of the world. However, American sitcoms don't translate as well" (Puopolo 1999).

If sitcoms in general sell poorly, African American sitcoms are thought to sell especially poorly. Buyers from general entertainment European channels agreed that African American sitcoms generally have less appeal for them than white American sitcoms. Puopolo asserted, "African American sitcoms in general do not do very well in the international marketplace." Jeff Ford of Channel 5 Broadcasting in the United Kingdom said that "Black comedies . . . seem not to travel as well broadly in prime time. What seems to happen is they are very popular with younger viewers. . . . But it's not going to appeal to the majority of the TV audience in the U.K." (1999). Torsten Dewi of the German channel Prosieben explained that African American sitcoms "[don't] translate very well to the German market for the simple fact that, I'm afraid to say, we don't have that many Blacks in Germany. It's just a question of demographics. We don't have an audience for that, so we have to build a strictly white audience" (1999).

Several points must be made about the presumed lack of international appeal associated with African American sitcoms by these executives. First, this belief is based primarily on the preferences of buyers from general entertainment European channels. Buyers from outside Europe and from niche channels tend to view African American sitcoms quite differently. European general entertainment channels, however, have the greatest influence on production decisions at the networks and the Hollywood majors because of their economic importance.

Second, buyers from general entertainment European channels tend to prefer pluralist shows that focus on nuclear families and nonracial themes. Frank Mulder of the Dutch public television consortium NOS explained that successful international shows address "all these things that happen in your own household" (1999). Dewi suggested that imported domestic sitcoms work best with German viewers because "family problems are the same all over the world" (1999). Yet no consistent themes appear to exist among the African American sitcoms sold internationally (table 23.3). Though this list is far from exhaustive, not least because information about which shows have been sold in which markets is proprietary information, a variety of series have sold well in a variety of markets, from the farcical follies of *Amos 'n' Andy* and *Damon* to workplace sitcoms like *The Show* and *Sparks* to shows that feature adult relationships like *Living Single* and *Martin*.

Notions about what constitutes universal family experiences are not objective, value-neutral facts about the world. The universal family themes buyers described refer to a particular set of domestic arrangements and problems associated with middle-class family life in predominantly white, developed capitalist nations, which conveniently fits the primary target demographics of U.S. networks and European general entertainment channels. Only African American sitcoms that limit their extratextual references to these concerns are considered "universal," even though shows with different references might have equal resonance for international viewers. Thus, dominant assumptions about the "universality" of family themes restrict the kinds of African American sitcoms that are sold internationally. The attitudes of some buyers from general entertainment Asian channels also help perpetuate the apparent universality of white U.S. and European programming. For instance, Sandra Buenaventura of Singapore Broadcasting Corporation has been paraphrased as saying that U.S. sitcoms "are increasingly focusing on Hispanics [*sic*] and other minority races with very little international appeal" ("Singapore's Majority Shopper" 1992).

The racial assumptions within these purportedly "universal family experiences" became clear when executives discussed the international appeal of *The Cosby Show*. Virtually every executive I interviewed claimed that *The Cosby Show* was a prime example of an African American show with "universal" appeal—and most referred to the show as "white." If *The Cosby Show* tells a "universal" tale of family, and *The*

TABLE 23.3

Internationally Traded African American Sitcoms

Title	Production Dates	Territories Sold into
Amos 'n' Andy	1951–53	Australia, Bermuda, U.K. [sold to but not aired in Kenya and Nigeria]
The Jeffersons	1975–85	Mexico, South Africa, Middle East
The Cosby Show	1984–92	approx. 70 territories, including U.K., France, Germany, Ireland, Spain, Italy, Turkey, Africa, South Africa, Mexico, Chile, Honduras, Pakistan, Australia, Denmark, Norway, Sweden, Netherlands, Belgium, Taiwan, Latin America, Israel, Lebanon, Kuwait, U.A.E.
A Different World	1987–93	South Africa, Germany, Spain, Australia
Family Matters	1989–98	Spain, Germany, Belgium, Middle East, Netherlands, Scandinavia
Fresh Prince of Bel-Air	1990–96	70 territories, including Indonesia, South Africa, Middle East, Spain, Germany, U.K., Netherlands, Scandinavia, Mexico, Chile, Colombia, Venezuela, France, Italy
True Colors	1990–92	Germany
Roc	1991–94	Middle East
Martin	1992–97	South Africa, Middle East
Hangin' with Mr. Cooper	1992–97	U.K., Middle East
Living Single	1993–98	Germany, South Africa, Middle East
Sister, Sister	1994–present	Latin America, Romania, Western Europe
Parent 'Hood	1995–present	Belgium, Western Europe
Wayans Bros.	1995–present	Belgium, Western Europe
Moesha	1996–present	France, Germany, Scandinavia, Netherlands, U.K., Spain, Latin America, Italy, Middle East
Cosby	1996–present	Scandinavia, Netherlands, Turkey, U.K., U.A.E., Australia, New Zealand, Africa, Middle East, Southeast Asia, Latin America, Belgium, Kuwait
Jamie Foxx	1996–present	Belgium, Western Europe
Sinbad	1996	Middle East
Sparks	1996–98	Germany, Scandinavia
Minor Adjustments	1996	Middle East
Between Brothers	1996–present	Kuwait
Smart Guy	1997–present	Western Europe
The Hughleys	1998–present	Mexico
Damon	1998	Romania, Belgium, Netherlands, Southeast Asia

Cosby Show is referred to as "white," it follows that the archetypal family these executives imagine is white. While I am not suggesting that Western television executives are part of a worldwide plot to spread white supremacy, this presumption colors the way they understand both the process of international cultural transfer and the appeal of minority programming like African American sitcoms. Though *The Cosby Show* was built on middle-class values such as economic mobility and individuality, it also attempted "to explore the interiors of black lives from the angle of African Americans" through its narratives, characters, and mise-en-scène, and ample evidence exists that these efforts appealed to nonwhite international viewers at least as much as the "universal" family themes (Gray 1995: 89; Havens 2000).

Multicultural African American sitcoms sometimes achieve international circulation by being packaged with Hollywood blockbusters. "Packaging" requires buyers to purchase a specified number of television shows, such as four sitcoms, in order to get the rights to a popular movie that the distributor also owns. *The Fresh Prince of Bel-Air*, for instance, was packaged with Will Smith's blockbuster *Independence Day*, placing the full muscle of a Hollywood major behind a series that reflected some measure of multiculturalism. In fact, the cross-promotion of Smith through the television series, first as an international pop star and later as an international film star, required the sitcom to integrate some degree of African American cultural integrity in order to maintain a consistent star persona for him.

African American cultural expressions in music and film encounter less resistance from international distribution executives, who believe that Black music appeals to the rebellious nature of teenagers everywhere, while movies create a visceral viewing experience that encourages fascination with the spectacular and the exotic. Television viewing, however, is conceived of as a family experience that encourages familiarity—at least among executives who target a general viewership. So the presence of a superstar like Smith can propel a multicultural African American sitcom into international distribution markets. However, the televisual cross-promotion of African American superstars does not guarantee the inclusion of cultural differences. Although Jamie Foxx, star of *The Jamie Foxx Show*, will appear in several Warner Brothers films in the near future, and Warner is actively promoting his sitcom internationally as a result, the series falls squarely within the definition of pluralist programming outlined by Gray.

Niche Channels and Non-European Buyers

Because niche channels focus on programming for a specific audience demographic, they have different purchasing criteria when it comes to African American sitcoms. For example, shows like *Moesha* that focus on teenage problems like dating and peer pressure offer more narrative diversity than typical domestic sitcoms, and include among their recurring characters a group of peers in addition to the nuclear family. Indeed, Zook (1999) argues that *The Fresh Prince of Bel-Air* contains a good deal of in-group humor, intraracial dialogue, and other textual traits that mark the show as minimally multicultural. And in recent seasons, episodes of *Moesha* have explored issues of single motherhood, gangs, and on-line dating (Braxton 1999).

Children- and teen-oriented niche channels seek out these kinds of series, as do general entertainment channels that devote specific dayparts to youth audiences. Eric Schnedecker, a former executive with Disney Channel España, explained that "[In] Spain, the *[Fresh] Prince of Bel-Air* was working like crazy. That's why at Disney Channel we bought *Moesha*. We bought *Moesha* because we knew that black comedies are [a] great success and so we thought *Moesha* . . . would work also very well" (1999). Obviously, this preference for youth-oriented African American situation comedy steeped in African American cultural references is quite different from the attitudes expressed by buyers from general entertainment channels. However, even

A Disney Channel España print advertisement for *Moesha*. Reprinted by permission of Disney Channel España, Buena Vista International, and Paramount.

these channels have similar preferences for African American youth sitcoms when they devote a portion of their daytime schedule to teenage viewers. According to Ford, from British-based Channel 5,

> [on] Channel 4 and BBC2 to some extent, they schedule things like *Fresh Prince* in [youth-oriented] slots . . . I think because they're a little more hip and the culture of music is obviously a very important part of those comedies . . . therefore it does touch with youth far more than possibly white sitcoms. (1999)

These comments demonstrate at least some variety in terms of buying preferences for African American sitcoms among international television executives in Western Europe. But buyers from general entertainment channels outside Europe demonstrate a greater range of preferences. This wider range, however, fails to find its way into either industry trade journals or commonsense assumptions of distributors from the Hollywood majors, whose opinions reflect mainstream European preferences and ultimately influence domestic U.S. television production.

Buyers from general entertainment channels in Latin America and the Middle East suggested that class differences and social struggles, which they associate with African American sitcoms, appeal to their viewers. "Black comedies will do better in Mexico or in Latin America [than white sitcoms] because the element of the underdog is there," insisted Ignacio Durán of Mexico's TV Azteca, "[a]nd this will probably cause an identification with the audience" (1999). In the same vein, Bassam Hajjawi of the Jordan-based International Distribution Agency said,

> [Most] of the Black situation comedies are about middle-class or lower-middle-class people. For many people in the Middle East, they associate and sympathize with that kind of life because they feel it's the kind of life they lead, too, and if they see these [white] situation comedies always with the high-brow politicians or the millionaires, they don't sympathize as much. (1999)

Several non-European buyers with whom I spoke also believed that some African American sitcoms included distinct forms of comedy and relations between characters that appeal to their primary audiences. TV Azteca's Durán suggested that comedic devices such as satire and bragging resonate with Latin American audiences. Khalid Abdilaziz Al-Mugaiceeb of Kuwait Television Channel 2 mirrored Durán's beliefs, contending that African Americans and Arabs share common cultures and senses of humor: "Black comedy, especially the women, the way they act, it's like Arabic women. The shaking heads and such, some of it's Arab. . . . Most of what we accept from all the comedy is Black. . . . [Culturally], it's more similar" (1999).

African American sitcoms also appeal to buyers from some African countries because of a history of cultural trade and similar political objectives. For instance, Cawe Mahlati, CEO of South Africa's Bophuthatswana Television (Bop-TV), explained why her channel purchases African American television programming:

> Because we are a Black station, the preference for acquisitions are television programs where African Americans appeared or acted. For a number of reasons: the one being that African Americans have got a very, very great influence in South African Black urban culture. . . . It makes sense . . . to show programming that contains images that people in South Africa can relate to. Secondly, as well, Bop Television has shown most of the movies that depict the African American experience in the U.S. There's a lot of resonance in South Africa for that kind of programming. (1999)

Mahlati mentioned the history of the civil rights and Black Power movements as well as contemporary hip-hop culture, slang, and humor as cultural similarities between Black South Africans and African Americans. As a quasi–English-speaking market, South Africa's channels provide fertile ground for distributors of African

American television programming. In 1998 the top ten programs were dominated by U.S. imports. Programs with Black characters do extremely well, especially dramatic shows with multiracial casts such as *Generations* and *New York Undercover*.

The purchasing preferences of niche channels and non-European general entertainment channels are distinct from mainstream European channels when it comes to African American programming. While these markets create some openings for multicultural African American sitcoms, however, they also impose limitations. Because sitcoms generally attract a younger demographic, niche channels prefer shows about teenaged and young adult life that allude to mainstream African American hip-hop. Meanwhile, though non-European channels may appreciate elements of multicultural African American sitcoms, most buyers are local elites whose preferences reflect dominant national worldviews and tastes, not those of local minorities. These buyers tend to pass on African American programming that contain more subversive expressions of cultural difference and minority politics.

An International Market for Minority Programming?

The current lack of international minority channels makes it impossible to judge their potential success, much less their likely buying preferences. But examining the structure of minority discourses, global popular music, and minority film and television culture reveals a distinct possibility that minority-targeted niche channels might not only prosper, but also provide a necessary distribution route for video and filmmakers whose work falls outside the mainstream. Comparing African American programming, which has been heavily studied, and exilic Iranian programming, which Hamid Naficy (1993, 1999) has documented extensively, reveals that these minority television cultures—which differ so markedly in history, size, and political leanings—have several common attributes, suggesting that a basis for minority television exchanges does, in fact, exist.

The idea that "cultural specificities" alienate viewers from other cultures is a compelling one; this assumption suggests that minorities from different parts of the globe have little basis for communication, including television exchanges. However, this assumption seems rooted in Western colonial ideologies that sought to divide non-Westerners in order to conquer them. As the literary scholars Abdul Jan-Mohamed and David Lloyd claim, "Western humanists find it inconceivable that Native-Americans, Africans, and others who have been brutalized by Euro-American imperialism and marginalized by its hegemony can have anything relevant to say to each other" (1990: 4). This shared experience of cultural, political, economic, and material exploitation, they argue, creates the conditions for homologous cultural practices that challenge the destructive individualism of Western culture.

Unfortunately, the current structure of ethnic and minority channels precludes us from being able to study minority cultural exchanges in the same way that literary scholars can. Ethnically oriented niche channels generally have either been owned by national governments and targeted at expatriate viewers or have suppressed internal difference to attract a single ethnic audience. For instance, governments in Turkey and China program satellite channels with nationalistic fare in order to target home-sick viewers abroad. Black Entertainment Television's (BET) domestic and interna-tional programming strategies target Black audiences around the globe. And exile Iranian television in Los Angeles smoothed over ethnic and religious differences among Iranian viewers in an effort to project a unified sense of Iranian identity (Naficy 1993). On the other hand, international gender-oriented niche channels such as the Latin American women's channel GEMS have become common, offering distribution outlets for unconventional portrayals of feminine desire (Curtin 1999). These channels point to the potential to articulate international audiences together along multiple axes of difference.

In popular music, ethnicity has become both a profitable commodity and a terrain of creative dialogue among and between minority peoples. Paul Gilroy (1993) argues that Black popular music has for centuries carried alternative political, aesthetic, and philosophical worldviews to cultures throughout the "Black Atlantic" region. An example of "antimodernist" expression, where assumptions about the superiority of white European music and cultural progress are undermined, Black popular music has recently found audiences beyond Black people, providing a model and a resource for minority musical expressions everywhere. Timothy D. Taylor argues that "the circulation of commodified musics and identities is pervasive and multidirectional," not simply a case of other minority musicians borrowing from Black music (1997: 76). And Sanjay Sharma has shown how British Asian popular music borrows from multiple ethnic traditions—including traditional Indian, Afro-Caribbean, and Afri-can American music—to create a space where "new meanings and practices are formed that open up the possibility of different ways of knowing and nodes of identification" (1996: 55).

Through the circulation of these popular musics, "[global] media and telecom-munications . . . have provided for a greater interconnectedness and interdependency for minority groups" (Kaur and Kalra 1996: 223). It is not that global capitalism has paved the way for understanding among minority cultures. Quite the opposite: the current moment "provides more ways of resistance, *and dominance*, than ever before" because of the pervasiveness of cultural exchanges ushered in by capitalism (Taylor 1997: 94, emphasis added). In popular minority music, musicians combine local, regional, and global aesthetic practices, "always attempting to get outside and beyond more traditionally bounded identities" (Taylor 1997: 126). Thus the global circulation of different music does not displace local cultures; rather, global pop music provides another resource alongside more traditional local musical styles, out of which con-temporary musicians may fashion new experiences of identity and new political projects.

Of course, music might facilitate cross-cultural circulation more easily than tele-vision programming because music uses sounds and beats rather than language. While the translation requirements associated with internationally traded television do complicate cultural trade, many series have overcome language barriers. Mexican and Brazilian *telenovelas*, for instance, have achieved notable success in virtually every region of the world. Meanwhile, the largely visual signifiers of African American youth culture have become a global lingua franca through visual media like advertising, film, and television, suggesting that some properties of the televisual text facilitate international circulation (Gray 1995: 148). In minority television cultures, these properties include parody, collectivism, and realism.

Self-parody is perhaps one of the most obvious and most controversial elements of African American sitcoms. While cognitive media researchers stress the ill effects of such portrayals, often deemed "negative," critical scholars have argued for the need to analyze the cultural politics of parodic portrayals rather than dismissing them. Watkins, for example, believes that parody is central to African American humor traditions and often carries stinging critiques of mainstream American culture, noting that "[t]he humor of nearly all minorities reveals a tendency toward self-deprecation"—which suggests a basis for cross-cultural minority comedy (1994: 30).

Naficy finds a similar self-parody in popular Iranian dramas of the eighteenth century, where contact between Iranians and the West gave rise to Iranian characters who excessively copied Western folkways. "[In] the surplus and satire of their imitation," he writes, these characters "criticized the Western way of life" (1993: 183). While such comedic characters were not transplanted to exile in Los Angeles, "tough-guy" serials that feature characters with an excess of parodic traits continue to be popular. Just as Naficy argues that one of the primary pleasures associated with "tough-guy" serials is the recognition of group-specific cultural allusions, Zook claims that "the most radical moments to be found in black TV . . . lay lodged in the inner folds of innuendo, comic asides, and in-group referencing" (1995). The attempt to keep cultural integrity alive in a hostile environment explains the continuing use of parody, as its subtlety can escape the surveillance of the dominant group because outsiders cannot decipher the codes.

A second characteristic common to both African American and exilic Iranian television programming is an attempt to "foreground collective and individual struggles for authenticity and identity" (Naficy 1993: 63). In exilic Iranian television, the creation of an exile community serves the economic ends of commercial television producers and advertisers while allowing exiled individuals to feel connected to a community. Televisual representations of an idealized, ancient homeland, free of the political division that led to exile, fulfill this requirement. Likewise, for African American viewers, "[frequent] references to Malcolm X in *The Fresh Prince of Bel-Air*, *Martin*, and *Roc* . . . in the form of posters, photographs, and T-shirts, invoked romanticized spaces of mythical unity" (Zook 1999: 8). In Iranian exile television, communal feeling is represented and nourished through the repetition of "the old 'authentic' self" associated with communal memories, while components such as advertising "confirm a new emerging 'consumer' self." This aesthetic strategy resonates with the cultural practices of the Black diaspora, where the dialectic between tradition and improvisation creates an aesthetic that Gilroy (1993) calls "the changing same."

Because African Americans have been relegated to comedic genres and caricatures throughout U.S. history, African American television producers often display a drive to inject shows with realist drama. According to Zook (1999: 80), producers of shows as diverse as *Frank's Place*, *South Central*, *The Fresh Prince of Bel-Air*, and *Roc* shared such a commitment. In one of the most daring attempts, an episode of *Roc* that centered around teenage gun violence included a full fifteen minutes without laughs. The preference for realist drama is prevalent throughout minority cinema practices as well. Ella Shohat and Robert Stam explain that "oppressed groups have used 'progressive realism' to unmask and combat hegemonic representations, countering the objectifying discourses of patriarchy and colonialism with a vision of themselves and their reality 'from within' " (1995: 180). Although realist drama may at times be problematic, often parading as "the truth" and masking its own construction, minority access to the genre nevertheless works to counteract traditional Western portrayals and expand the diversity of minority characters.

The cultural basis for minority television exchanges runs deep. Marie Gillespie (1995), for example, notes the appeal of Western ads that stress multiracial friendship among second-generation Punjabi youth in London. Soap opera researchers (e.g., Ang 1985) have demonstrated the cross-cultural appeal of feminine structures of feeling and "gossip culture" associated with the genre. My own research among young Kuwaiti viewers of *The Fresh Prince of Bel-Air* (Havens 2001) suggests that shared histories of Western oppression and stereotyping at the hands of Western media explain some of that show's appeal. More research into the common grounds of visual cultural expression among the world's minorities is in order if we hope to increase the viability of minority television exchanges in the future.

Possibilities for the Future of Black Media

The economics of international television distribution and the buying preferences of European general entertainment channels have encouraged African American television programming that can best be described as pluralist, depicting only minor cultural differences between whites and African Americans. Global television does not, however, require the death of more complex African American television portrayals. Comments from buyers in Latin America, the Middle East, Africa, and Western European satellite channels suggest an openness to different kinds of African American sitcoms. Programming that targets these markets could adopt textual strategies other than those designed for mainstream European channels—strategies that might include collectivism, satire, realism, and utopian multiculturalism.

One danger that globalization poses for minority cultures "is that cultural, ethnic, and racial differences will be continually commodified and offered up as new dishes to enhance the white palate—that the Other will be eaten, consumed, and forgotten" (hooks 1992: 39). But global satellite television may offer a space for the consumption and enjoyment of otherness with different intentions and consequences, where oppressed minorities could create and exchange television programming that bears the marks of subaltern experience, history, and cultural survival techniques. The politics of appropriation is often quite different when oppressed minorities practice it.

A loose network of minority satellite channels in different nations and regions of the world could not only provide new outlets for minority television, video, and film producers, but might also allow program sharing among channels to reduce production costs and perhaps even provide crucial additional revenues for minority producers. Cable access and other forms of "lowcasting" already provide important distribution outlets for minority creators seeking to sustain national, ethnic, and exilic identities (Naficy 1999). These channels and their constituents might also profit from "imported" minority programming.

Though television executives have begun to recognize the profitability of transnational channels targeting gender and/or ethnic groups, common misperceptions about the insularity of minority culture and the singularity of identity, rooted in discourses of whiteness, preclude them from imagining global minority programming. With such attitudes dominating the industry, minority producers and distribution channels may remain off the radar screens of the major international television players and out of their sphere of influence for some time.

Many activists and intellectuals might object that linking African American television programming with global minority programming would further balkanize white Americans and African Americans, ghettoize African American programming into "minority" channels, and abandon the struggle to confront and change racism in American television. But I do not intend to suggest an end to these important efforts to intervene in the politics of mainstream network television. Efforts to facilitate the creation of global minority programming must be appended to traditional media activism. Such an effort may result in a kind of feedback loop between minority and mainstream television channels, where some of the more popular minority shows might find their way into wider domestic and international distribution. In this way, the globalization of the media industries might multiply, rather than restrict, the variety of outlets for unique minority television.

REFERENCES

Al-Mugaiceeb, Khalid Abdilaziz. Director General, Kuwait Television Channel Two. Personal interview. 13 October 1999.

Ang, Ien. *Watching Dallas: Soap Opera and the Melodramatic Imagination.* Trans. Della Couling. New York: Methuen, 1985.

Boyd, Todd. *Am I Black Enough for You? Popular Culture from the 'Hood and Beyond.* Bloomington: Indiana University Press, 1997.

Braxton, Greg. "Hot Topics Thicken Plot for *Moesha.*" *Los Angeles Times,* 6 December 1999, F1.

Curtin, Michael. "On Edge: Culture Industries in the Neo-Network Era." In *Making and Selling Culture,* ed. Richard Ohmann. Hanover, NH: Wesleyan University Press, 1997.

———. "Satellite TV and Feminine Desire." *Journal of Communication* 44, no. 2 (1999): 55–70.

Dewi, Torsten. Commissioning Producer, International Co-Productions, Prosieben (Germany). Personal interview. 11 May 1999.

Durán, Ignacio. Vice President, International Affairs, TV Azteca. Personal interview. 15 April 1999.

"European TV Programme Budgets." *Screen Digest,* March 1997, 57–64.

Ford, Jeff. Controller of Acquisitions, Channel 5 Broadcasting (U.K.). Personal interview. 7 July 1999.

Gillespie, Marie. *Television, Ethnicity, and Cultural Change.* London: Routledge, 1995.

Gilroy, Paul. *The Black Atlantic: Modernity and Double-Consciousness*. Cambridge: Harvard University Press, 1993.

Gray, Herman. *Watching Race: Television and the Struggle for "Blackness."* Minneapolis: University of Minnesota Press, 1995.

Hajjawi, Bassam. President and CEO, International Distribution Agency (Jordan). Personal interview. 28 June 1999.

Hall, Stuart. Introduction to *Remote Control: Dilemmas of Black Intervention in British Film and TV*, ed. June Givanni. London: British Film Institute, 1995.

Havens, Timothy. "The Biggest Show in the World: Race and the Global Popularity of *The Cosby Show*." *Media, Culture, Society* 22, no. 4 (fall 2000): 371–91.

———. "Subtitling Rap: Appropriating *The Fresh Prince of Bel-Air* for Youthful Identity Formation in Kuwait." *Gazette: The International Journal for Communication Studies*. 63, no. 1 (2001): 57–72.

hooks, bell. *Black Looks: Race and Representation*. Boston: South End Press, 1992.

JanMohammed, Abdul R., and David Lloyd. "Toward a Theory of Minority Discourse: What Is to Be Done?" In *The Nature and Context of Minority Discourse*, ed. Abdul R. JanMohammed and David Lloyd. Oxford: Oxford University Press, 1990.

Kaur, Raminder, and Virinder S. Kalra. "New Paths for South Asian Identity and Musical Creativity." In *Dis-Orienting Rhythms: The Politics of the New Asian Dance Music*, ed. Sanjay Sharma, John Hutnyk, and Ashwani Sharma. London: Zed Books, 1996.

Mahlati, Cawe. CEO, Bophuthatswana Broadcasting Corporation. Personal interview. 3 May 1999.

Mulder, Frank. Director of Programme Acquisitions and Sales, Nederlandse Omroep Stichting. Personal interview. 16 April 1999.

Naficy, Hamid. "Between Rocks and Hard Places: The Interstitial Mode of Production in Exilic Cinema." In *Home, Exile, Homeland: Film, Media, and the Politics of Place*, ed. Hamid Naficy. London: Routledge, 1999.

———. *The Making of Exile Cultures: Iranian Television in Los Angeles*. Minneapolis: University of Minnesota Press, 1993.

Puopolo, Michael. Manager of International Research, Warner Brothers International Television. Personal interview. 11 May 1999.

Ross, Karen. *Black and White Media*. Cambridge: Polity Press, 1996.

Schnedecker, Eric. Program Director, Universal Studios Network. Personal interview. 3 May 1999.

Sharma, Sanjay. "Asian Noise or 'Noisy Asians'?" In *Dis-Orienting Rhythms: The Politics of the New Asian Dance Music*, ed. Sanjay Sharma, John Hutnyk, and Ashwani Sharma, 32–57. London: Zed Books, 1996.

Shohat, Ella, and Robert Stam. *Unthinking Eurocentrism: Multiculturalism and the Media*. London: Routledge, 1995.

"Singapore's Majority Shopper." *TV World*, September 1992, 18.

Taylor, Timothy D. *Global Pop: World Music, World Markets*. London: Routledge, 1997.

Watkins, Mel. *On the Real Side: Laughing, Lying, and Signifying, the Underground Tradition of African-American Humor That Transformed American Culture, from Slavery to Richard Pryor*. New York: Simon and Schuster, 1994.

Zook, Kristal Brent. *Color by Fox: The Fox Network and the Revolution in Black Television*. New York: Oxford University Press, 1999.

———. "Warner Bruthas." *Village Voice*, 17 January 1995, 36.

Chapter Twenty-four

Teletubbies

Infant Cyborg Desire and the Fear of Global Visual Culture

Nicholas Mirzoeff

Web search results for "Teletubbies" (about 5,431 matches)

"He warned us about the Teletubbies": www.ufomind.com/misc/
1999/jan/d06-001.shtml

"Infoculture: Tinky Winky isn't gay, says Teletubbies production
company": www.infoculture.cbc.ca/archives/filmtv 02101999_
tellytubbies.html

"See the Teletubbies Brutally Slaughtered": http://www.execution-
chamber.co.uk/tubbyindex.html

Four infant cyborgs live in a metallic berm. Their world has the preternatural calm of computer environments, where colors are bright and consistent, shadows sharp and well defined, and rain or wind is a welcome event. Their domestic needs are catered to by machines, one for food and one for hygiene. Time is measured by the rising and setting of an infant cyborg sun that smiles and laughs. The daily routine is marked out by loudspeakers that resemble old-fashioned telephone handsets. At regular intervals, windmills generate television signals that are received by the cyborgs' antennae and relayed to the others on a screen. Other entertainment is provided digitally. Welcome to the world of *Teletubbies*, now perhaps the most popular children's television show in the world. Tinky Winky, Dipsy, Laa-Laa, and Po are the avatars of a digital generation of infants who are already the television audience of the new century. The adults are not happy. The television critics are uncertain. The cyborgs are in raptures.

Parents

On April 6, 1998, PBS stations in the United States began showing episodes of *Teletubbies*, a British television show for very young children. The Tubbies quickly found a substantial audience, but few adults seemed very happy about it. In the chat rooms, in the playgrounds, in the aisles of Toys "R" Us, the parental word on *Teletubbies* was consistently that it was a "weird" show. The Tubbies themselves were especially weird. They are creatures resembling in outline a toddler wearing a romper

A still from *The Teletubbies*

suit and diaper, complete with rubberized feet, while their faces are those of especially calm dolls, with large, gently blinking eyes. Each one has its own distinctive color: Tinky Winky is purple, Laa-Laa yellow, Dipsy green, and Po red. Their activities include dancing, riding a scooter, playing with a ball, and jumping in puddles. None of these things are, of course, what is found odd. The dissonance is that the Tubbies are cyborgs whose goal is the production of a new childhood and, by extension, adulthood.

With a little rewriting, "weird" becomes "wired." The Teletubbies were explicitly envisaged by Anne Wood, who created the series for Ragdoll Productions, as providing a way for children to negotiate the digital planet: "We started with the idea that babies are growing up in a technological world, so we wanted to make a world that was safe and also in some way technological."[1] Wood rather understated the case, for by incorporating a television screen and antenna into the body of the Teletubbies, she has created a hybrid of machine and organism, that is to say, a cyborg. Unlike standard children's literature, which creates a world of animals and magic, or television environments like *Sesame Street* that are safely patrolled by adults, *Teletubbies* creates a technological world in which the infants are comfortably in charge of their cyberenvironment. The Tubbies live by themselves for themselves and are patently happy doing so. In an episode called "The Flying Toast," the Teletubbies set about making food for themselves using the Tubby Toaster. The Toaster begins to malfunction and produces a vast quantity of toast that is then cleaned up by the Noo-Noo, a form of intelligent vacuum cleaner. At no point in this story do the Tubbies become frightened or look for adult help. Far from going crazy, as William Carlos Williams would have it, the machines and cyborgs are getting on perfectly well. These infants are not awaiting the desire of the other. They have their own desire and it is both utopian and, in a certain sense, productive—even if only of Tubby Toast. In "Go to Sleep, Teletubbies," each Tubby gets up from their nap to play with their favorite thing. Rather than a parent restoring order, it is the other Tubbies who come and find the wandering cyborg.

Entertainment in Teletubbyland is electronic and digital. Each episode features a moment when the windmills spin and one of the Teletubbies "receives" a broadcast of "real" television pictures, showing children at play. The Tubbies thrust their stomachs forward in the hope of being the energized receiver but show no jealousy to the selected one. The desire to be a television seemingly produces no sense of lack. Within Teletubbyland, diversions are digital. The Tubbies sit down and watch as digitally generated carousels descend from the sky, as ships float on a virtual sea, or as cyberanimals parade past two by two. The feeling of displacement experienced by many analog-trained adults as they encounter the digitally friendly younger generation is given concrete existence by *Teletubbies*. Infants seem to immediately identify with the Teletubbies, as if they recognize that the Tubbies' world is more like their own than the outdated technologies of *Thomas the Tank Engine*, forever fighting off the diesel engines, or Dr. Seuss's fascination with housework.

At stake in the disruption caused by *Teletubbies* is what Anne Higonnet has called the "crisis of ideal childhood." This Romantic notion of childhood may be said to have begun with the declaration of Jean-Jacques Rousseau in *Emile* (1762) that "childhood is unknown."[2] Childhood was constructed as an age of innocence, suitable for play and exploration of the emerging self that had to be protected from the demands and desires of adulthood. Perhaps the clearest marker of these changes in the United States can be seen in the 1899 decision to create a special legal category for children that protected them from the full force of the law. These protections are now routinely set aside by the courts so that children may be tried "as adults" in precisely those violent and exceptional cases where it was formerly believed that children could not possibly understand the consequences of their actions. In December 1999, an eleven-year-old boy was convicted of first-degree murder as an adult in Michigan, even as the Department of Justice announced a 30 percent drop in juvenile violent crime.[3] As Higonnet concludes, "The image of childhood created in the eighteenth century has run its course and is now being replaced by another way of picturing childhood."[4] At the same time, there is a current of violence against pedophiles, those most actively perceived to have brought about the end of childhood innocence. Following the murder of the British eight-year-old girl Sarah Payne in July 2000, there was a nationwide surge of anti-pedophile violence, initiated by the "Name and Shame" campaign of the tabloid *News of the World*. In the southwest town of Portsmouth, residents of the Paulsgrove housing estate believed that no fewer than twenty pedophiles were living locally, driving four families into hiding. The list of alleged offenders was compiled in part on the Internet, according to Katrina Kassel, leader of the campaign. The local vicar, Father Gary Waddington, described the events as "social cleansing," drawing an explicit parallel with "ethnic cleansing" in the former Yugoslavia.[5] Forgotten or displaced in all this violence is the consistent evidence that over three-quarters of all offenses against school-age children in Britain are committed by their parents or relatives.[6]

Concurrent with the doctrine of childhood innocence was its other, the perverse and desiring child. Figures as diverse as Lewis Carroll and Sigmund Freud took the child to be a "knowing" and desiring subject. This aspect of children came to be regarded as abnormal and its extirpation was the subject of considerable social energy. Whereas in the nineteenth century, anxieties about child sexuality mostly concerned masturbation, they have now come to be expressed in wider terms of sexuality and sexual orientation. It was in a column named "Parents Alert," published in Jerry Falwell's *National Liberty Journal Online* in February 1999, that the religious Right notified the world that Tinky Winky was a "gay role model." The comment was part of a three-pronged attack on *Teletubbies*, *South Park*, and Disney. Falwell believes that Disney acts like characters from the film *Fight Club* (1999) and edits in single, obscene frames to its apparently wholesome entertainments, creating "subliminal messages" in "obviously planned offensives." By contrast to this rather wild allegation, the attack on Tinky Winky used what one can only call a semiotic approach: "The character, whose voice is obviously that of a boy, has been found carrying a red purse in many episodes and has become a favorite character among gay groups worldwide. . . . He is purple—the gay pride color; and his antenna is shaped like a triangle—the gay pride symbol."[7] Although the argument soon veered into the usual paranoia, asserting that further evidence came from the fact that a photograph of Tinky Winky appeared next to one of Ellen DeGeneres in the *Washington Post*, it was nonetheless accurate in stating that he was a gay icon. The PBS journal *Current* had even posted a remark to this effect in its online version a year previously.[8]

Falwell's attack made international news, despite its being posted to a section of his obscure Web site. Nonetheless, it seemed that he had touched a nerve. While the charge itself was ridiculed, there lurked an anxiety that the children of the global era are going to be different. Queer activists like Michael Musto responded by asserting that Tinky Winky was indeed queer and that it was a good thing for children to understand the full range of gender and sexual identities. While Musto correctly pointed out that purple is not a gay pride color, the patent red handbag seemed to both sides to be indubitably queer. Politically, these two could not be more different and there is no question that Musto's position is—to say the least—preferable. It is nonetheless noticeable that both are engaged in what Umberto Eco once called "guerrilla semiotics," the attempt to create alternative meanings from mainstream texts. In the age of intense media self-consciousness, where a soft drink can use the advertising slogan "Image Is Nothing," this strategy itself has become mainstream. During the 1998 impeachment hearings, the U.S. Senate preoccupied itself with a question as to whether President Clinton had sent a message to Monica Lewinsky by wearing a certain tie. One is reminded here of Michel Foucault's decrying the "poor technicians of desire—psychoanalysts and semiologists of every sign and symptom—who would subjugate the multiplicity of desire to the twofold law of structure and lack."[9] What is in the end most striking here is the consistent attribution of an active queer sexuality to characters that are intended to represent infants who are at best on the fringes of forming gender and sexual identity.[10] Children are now seen as mysterious and threatening just as much as they are perceived as innocent and in need of protection.

The crisis of childhood is itself a crisis of the middle-class family, whose entire raison d'être is the raising of children. The symptom of that crisis is widely perceived to be the thoroughgoing commodification of all aspects of childhood and family life. While families from the 1950s on welcomed the introduction of disposable diapers and packaged baby food, the perfect modern parents use a diaper service for environmental reasons and produce their own baby food from organic vegetables, using their Cuisinart. Of course for most parents, this approach is not a financially realistic option. Many have displaced these anxieties onto the television set as an icon of the crisis of childhood that has been part of public debate for nearly two decades. In this view, television is in general a bad thing for children and their access to it should be limited or even denied. Here social class is indexed in inverse relationship to the amount of television watched: the higher the viewing hours of children, the lower the social class.[11] In this last instance, children remain special for those who can afford it. While most parents allow their children to watch television, they guiltily respond to the moral panic surrounding children and television by attempting to control their viewing in terms of both content and duration.

For many media critics, *Teletubbies* crossed the final demarcation of the special world of childhood by explicitly marketing its product for children aged one to three. Anne Wood recalls that "We became aware that there were still children, younger children, who could get a lot more from television, and we hadn't quite reached far enough down to them." As a former English teacher, Wood envisaged Tellytubbyland as "a cross between the land where television comes from and a nursery rhyme land."[12] The producers of the show felt that they were simply catering to an already existing market and providing a better product. Kenn Viselman, who moved from Ragdoll to the Itsy Bitsy Entertainment Company, which handles *Teletubbies* in the United States and Canada, sees the issue in simple terms: "There's some discussion about whether kids should be watching TV at that age. But since parents are using TV as a babysitter, they might as well have good product."[13] The very success of *Teletubbies* proves that both the infant viewers and the adults turning on the televisions agreed in practice with the Itsy Bitsy point of view. On the other hand, implied in Viselman's comment is a critique of parents themselves, an implication others were not slow to develop. For whether childhood is equipped with wooden toys and handmade clothes or computer games and television programs, it is now unmistakably a commodity.

There is no doubting the success of the show. It has been sold around the world in quite remarkable fashion that was nonetheless implied by its very terms of existence. For when Ragdoll Productions licensed *Teletubbies* to the British Broadcasting Corporation (BBC), it retained the crucial North American rights for its subsidiary, the Itsy Bitsy Entertainment Company. The technically independent company BBC Worldwide, which markets all BBC products, had to sell the show to as many markets as possible to recoup the initial investment of 8.5 million pounds. *Teletubbies* is estimated to have earned tens of millions of pounds through such deals. The program marks a high point of the new British television system, which now involves many small independent companies creating product for the five terrestrial channels that still dominate the national market. These programs are then sold on to the global television market, where the real profits can be found, just as Hollywood cinema relies on the global market to offset any domestic losses. Anne Wood was named Veuve Clicquot Businessperson of the Year in 1999 as an index of the show's success. When France's Canal-Plus broadcast the show in October 1998, it completed a clean sweep of all European nations by the Tubbies. They are shown in South Africa, China, Mexico, Singapore, New Zealand, Australia, Israel, Japan, Bosnia, Estonia, Morocco, Korea, Malaysia, Hong Kong, and Thailand. *Teletubbies* can even be seen on in-flight entertainment systems and on hotel cable channels. The places in which the Teletubbies can be seen delineate one form of the global mediascape. This mediascape is not entirely self-identical. While even its British program makers saw *Teletubbies* as entertainment, the show has won educational awards in Japan, where the use of television in preschool is routine.[14] Despite such texture, the global culture of *Teletubbies* is more similar to itself than it is to the various locales in which it is screened. Even where some of the "real" television sequences are locally produced, as in the United States, the majority of *Teletubbies*, set in Teletubbyland, consists of the same sequences worldwide. The intriguing question is whether such global homogeneity is now producing a global experience of childhood in those relatively affluent households where television is available.

Critics

Television commentators in the mass media lined up to take shots at *Teletubbies* because it makes the commodification of global childhood visible. Even the online journal *Salon*, which one might expect to be more sympathetic to these digital creatures, recoiled from "the loathsome rat-baby visages of the four Tubbies." This distaste reflects the disparity between the baby-like appearance of the Tubbies and their advanced abilities as cyborgs to operate machines, fly kites, or feed themselves. The critic Joyce Millman backed up her dislike for the "inane mix of goo-goo talk and hallucinatory imagery" by asserting that "The British media hates the show. Parents hate the show. Child development experts hate the show."[15] The last assertion was certainly correct. *Teletubbies* has led pediatricians in the United States to move from a position of generalized hostility to television to a new medicalization of electronic media consumption in young children. The initial disquiet about *Teletubbies* was caused by their speech. Children's television programming usually tries to be as educational as possible, defining education as instruction in reading, writing, and arithmetic. *Teletubbies* not only refuses these conventions, it even has its characters speak like toddlers rather than little adults. Although there is a calm adult narrator, the Tubbies themselves prattle in baby talk, screaming "eh-oh" as a greeting, with repeated breaks for "Big Hug." Patricia Edgar, an Australian researcher into children's programs, denounced *Teletubbies* at the 1998 world summit on television for children as "regressive for any child who has gone beyond the babbling phase."[16] Her position found support from Dorothy Singer, who heads Yale University's Family TV Research and Consultation Center. Singer is against offering television to very young children at all and insists that "children need to be exposed to good language."[17] In seeming response to these worries, the American PBS version of *Teletubbies* dubs the narrator's voice into American-accented English, an oddity for the normally Anglophile channel. Perhaps the thought of toddlers babbling with an English accent was just too much to bear. The rather unlikely scenario that a child watching *Teletubbies* might forget how to speak articulates a wider fear that the hypervisuality of global culture is leading to a decline in literacy.[18] While the right wing in the United States argues for English-only education and the abolition of Ebonics, their counterparts elsewhere insist, for example, on the primacy of French music on French radio. These cultural politics can have drastic consequences.

Since the 1927 regulation of radio in the United States, broadcasters have been obligated to provide programming for children (among other requirements) in return for their use of a frequency. There has been a direct equivalency between the attempt such programs make to be educational and those children's programs regarded as being of high quality. *Sesame Street* is the classic example of a show that educates its viewers, and indeed it was perhaps responsible for preventing the 1994 Congress from abolishing all federal support for public television (although it was accused in the 1970s of promoting communism and other radical ideas).[19] *Teletubbies* is doubly scandalous in this context because it makes very little overt effort to educate its viewers, although the Tubbies are prone to counting slowly from one to four. But in a global economy, as President Clinton never tired of reminding his audiences, success "means giving every American the best education in the world."[20] In the minds of many parents and teachers, there is no time to be lost. If *Teletubbies* is not educating children, they must then be falling behind. At the same time that it fails to make children global producers, *Teletubbies* is seen as being responsible for turning innocent children into consumers. Ada Haug of the Norwegian station NRK asserted at the world summit that "this is the most marketing-oriented children's product I have ever seen."[21] The American critic Joyce Millman fumes that "*Teletubbies is* indoctrination, it *is* mind-control, it *is* a transparent attempt to institute brand-recognition and consumer craving in the youngest, most innocent viewers."[22]

Infantile Capitalism

Like all children's television, *Teletubbies* is not just a television program. You can now buy everything from Tubbies figurines to crockery and infant walkers. A single based on the theme tune called "Say Eh-Oh" reached number one in the British charts. A licensing deal with Hasbro, one of the largest global toy companies, generated some $80 million in sales and helped push Hasbro stock to a record price in April 1999 of $32.37 a share, four dollars higher than its arch-rival Mattel (it has since fallen considerably, to around $10 in August 2000). Hasbro is the subject of much trade union scrutiny, as many of its toys are made in China, where the code of practice adopted by the International Council of Toy Industries in May 1996 cannot be enforced or monitored.[23] Chinese workers are commonly paid in the region of twenty-five cents an hour in toy factories, according to the International Toy Campaign.[24] Even as its profits have risen, Hasbro has laid off workers in the United States since June 1997.[25] Hasbro Canada laid off all but fifteen of its once two hundred-strong workforce in Longueuil, Quebec, in pursuit of its corporate slogan, "One World, One Hasbro."[26] In 1999 Hasbro dramatically overestimated the market for *Star Wars* toys, causing it to lay off over 20 percent of its workforce, eliminating some 2,200 jobs. Positions were lost in Tijuana, Mexico, and Ashford, England, and the company relocated outstanding work to China.[27] Here what we still call First World and Third World countries both lost out to the global lowest denominator of the Chinese labor market. In such global capitalist enterprise, intellectual property rights and the carceral-industrial state can collide as well as converge. One striking case in September 1999 saw Spanish police arrest fifteen men who had set up a fake Teletubbies doll manufacturing business. One million items worth 650 million pesetas ($4.8 million) were seized, taking fifty officers fourteen hours to transport away. The fakers had managed to set up a deal with Brieve prison in Avila, where female inmates were paid $1.25 for sewing the dolls. Although this is a prison wage in the "West," it would be a desirable salary in Hasbro's legitimate factories in China. It seems that it is now possible for "Western" economies to compete with Asian labor practices only by sustaining a substantial prison population, giving the traditional phrase "the industrial reserve army" new meaning. Yet this "competitive" enterprise had to be suppressed in the name of intellectual property rights that digital activists are beginning to argue can no longer be defended.

In the era of "capturing eyeballs" as a form of generating profit, children's eyes are the most prized of all. Consider that J. K. Rowling's Harry Potter books occupied the first three places of the *New York Times* fiction best-seller list in 1999 before the astonishing success of the fourth installment in July 2000 caused the creation of a new list just for children's books. Video games marketed almost exclusively to boys aged six to eighteen grossed more revenue in 1998 than Hollywood films in the United States. *Pokémon* is a global phenomenon as a game and as a movie, precisely because adults cannot understand it. And when *Toy Story 2* does $80 million of business in its first weekend, beating the old cyborg Arnold Schwarzenegger by 250 percent, the new cyborgs are already in charge. Any hostility to the capitalization of childhood has in its own turn been commodified in the production of wooden, "traditional" toys that even come "distressed" to give the aura of long, loving play. Such toys are of course far more expensive than new plastic toys. Parents can thus purchase an ideal childhood that they themselves may not have experienced and offer it to their own children in place of the corrupting force of television. All the children within the commodity market are nonetheless learning the power of goods, even as the number of children growing up in poverty in the United States is higher in 2000 at 18.7 percent (13 million children) than it was in 1979 (16.2 percent).[28]

In Times Square, New York City, a giant Disney theater staging *The Lion King* looks out at what is about to become a flagship Toys "R" Us, with the nearby video game arcades marking the next stage in childhood capitalization. These spatial relations at the media center of global capital are symbolic in all senses of the term. There is no limit to commodification—if there ever was—and the child has become a privileged locus for the generation of hyperprofit—the new generation of profit that results from the successful catching of mass attention.[29] In all this global enterprise, the truly daunting challenge for parents in developed nations is how to provide their children with a rewarding childhood that does not come at the expense of workers around the world.

Medicalizing Media

American child development specialists have ignored such concerns, while creating a specific agenda of prohibitions and exhortations regarding television. In the official news magazine of the American Academy of Pediatrics, Jane M. Healy worried about the impact of "new shows targeted to children as young as one year" barely a month after the United States' debut of *Teletubbies*.[30] While those in medical science are often impatient with the critiques of medical practice emanating from scholars in science, gender, or media studies, essays of this kind seek to create a new hybrid of neuroscience and media criticism. As the global media begin to move beyond the control of the nation-state, this effort to rediscipline television as a medicalized object is of more than local importance. Healy argues that media exposure will damage the formation of the brain itself at this young age: "repeated exposure to any stimulus in a child's environment may forcibly impact mental and emotional growth, either by setting up particular circuitry ('habits of mind') or by depriving the brain of other experiences."[31] Readers will have noted that the condemnation of electronic media is nonetheless made in language ("circuitry") that metaphorizes the brain itself as an electronic medium. Nonetheless, Healy finds youthful television watching to be a major factor in the "negative outcomes" observed in contemporary schools, ranging from attention deficit disorder to "faltering academic abilities." While the former may be a clinical diagnosis (albeit a highly contested one), the latter is clearly a value judgment. By spending time watching television, young people are deprived of "close interaction with loving caregivers; engrossing hands-on play opportunities; and age appropriate academic stimulation." This remark implies that the prevalence of families with two working parents causes such failures and, observes Healy, they are "of course . . . partially responsible."[32]

Television is also a causal factor of educational problems because of its visual focus. A correlation is claimed between higher levels of television watching and lower academic scores: "This may be because television substitutes for reading practice, partially because the compellingly visual nature of the stimulus blocks development of left-hemisphere language circuitry."[33] Two assumptions are made here. First, Healy presents the brain's "circuitry" as dedicated hardware, as if it were a lighting circuit or refrigerator system, capable of only one activity. However, a far more prevalent metaphor sees the brain as a computer, capable of infinite numbers of calculations.[34] Even other neuroscientists have used very different models, such as Patrick Wall's conclusion in his analysis of pain that a "hard-wired, line-dedicated, specialized pain system did not exist. Rather, there is a subtle multiplexed reactive system that informs us simultaneously about events in the tissues and in the thinking parts of the brain."[35] This model seems far more productive if we are seeking to understand the complex relations of print and visual image than a competition for dedicated circuits. Second, the visual is assumed to be opposed to reading. In a widely publicized report, Sharon Begley claimed that "only 'live' language, not television" can teach a child language skills.[36] But it was as obvious to Dr. Seuss (who told children that "reading with your eyes shut is very hard to do") as to Jacques Derrida that reading is itself a visual practice.[37] It is only if we assume that the brain can use certain synapses only to look at television or to read, but not both, that a medicalized distinction between reading and watching television can be sustained.

In other words, a series of poorly grounded cultural and linguistic theories are being used to support a clinical diagnosis that television impedes childhood development in the earliest years of life. For every study that can be cited to support this theory, another can be found to refute it. For example, observations by media critics of people's viewing habits suggest that watching television is usually one of a range of activities being performed. A study of *Sesame Street* found that children on average look at and away from the television 150 times in an hour, presumably to engage in the accredited activities listed above.[38] In fact, the Children's Television Workshop, which produces *Sesame Street*, incorporates an awareness of these "distractors" into its extensive testing procedures.[39] It might seem that these figures provide support for the idea that television distracts attention, yet an Australian study showed that children who watch more television read significantly more books and significantly fewer comics than children who watch no television.[40] However, it is not my intent to get drawn into the game of "proving" what the effects of television are, for whatever they are, they are surely subject to so many variables of class, geography, gender, ethnicity, and so on in the new global audience as to be beyond effective generalization. The medical censors seek to control global media by creating a biological model for the effects of television that would presumably remain constant.

Healy does not in fact suggest a wholly medical solution to the problem, but rather advises pediatricians to "take a media history or ask about the amount of screen time as part of routine examinations."[41] In August 1999 the American Academy of Pediatrics went still further to suggest as a matter of policy that parents should avoid letting two-year-olds see television at all in order to promote "healthy brain growth and the development of appropriate social, emotional and cognitive skills."[42] At the same time the AAP adopted the notion of media questionnaires in pediatric examinations and the creation of a national media education policy. This education should seek to inform the media educated person that "all media messages are constructed; media messages shape our understanding of the world; individuals interpret media messages uniquely; and mass media has powerful economic interpretations."[43] If television is a virus that can contaminate the brain, then education is the innoculation that prevents that virus from crashing the system. In his 1992 novel *Snow Crash*, the science fiction writer Neal Stephenson imagined a computer virus so powerful that it could cause the cognitive functions of the brain to "crash" or malfunction. Now it is official medical policy that television is that virus.

The media education devised as a remedy shares some of the features of courses already taught in cultural and media studies programs. Should this be welcomed or worried about? It is the case that *Teletubbies*, the unnamed instigator of the change of medical policy, also poses a challenge to established methods of media analysis. Much of this work has concentrated on audience responses, either on the quantitative model derived from sociology or the qualitative model popular in cultural studies. In this case, neither method can yet be employed. A quantitative analysis of the *Teletubbies* audience is all but impossible as standard audience figures, like Nielsen in the United States and BARB in the United Kingdom, only track viewers aged four and over. Given that the controversy centers on the youngest, preverbal viewers, a qualitative research study would be equally impossible. Here Deleuze's caution as to the "indignity of speaking for others" needs to be remembered. If we cannot say for certain what *Teletubbies* means to infants, we can nonetheless investigate what it means as a text produced by adults for infants' consumption and thereby examine the limit between the adult and the child.[44]

Cyborgs

The Tubbies are cyborgs. Much has been written about the cyborg phenomenon in contemporary science fiction films and novels, stemming from Donna Haraway's famous "Manifesto for Cyborgs" (1985). Yet the posthuman body that Haraway announces is in effect simply a new apprehension of what it is to be human, for, as Judith Halberstam and Ira Livingston remind us, "You're not human until you're posthuman. You were never human."[45] In this context, what they mean is that there never was a time in which the human was totally distinct from the machine—or when the adult was neatly separated from the child.

The Tubbies recall not so much the destructive android of recent science fiction imagining, as the early modern fascination with the automaton. Mark Sussmann has described how "automata of the late 18th and early 19th centuries could play music, imitate human and animal movements, answer a limited set of questions, and otherwise dazzle audiences with clockwork *tableaux vivants* depicting pastoral scenes populated by articulated animals, angels, cupids and views inside miniature prosce- nium theatres."[46] *Teletubbies* is of course a pastoral scene populated by articulated cyborgs that incorporate little proscenium theaters into their bodies as televisions. Perhaps the most striking parallel between the Tubbies and the early modern history of automata comes with the career of Charles Babbage (c. 1791–1871), now famed as the inventor of the first computing devices, known as the Difference Engine and the later Analytic Engine. In his autobiography Babbage recalled a trip with his mother, when he was around eight, to see the Mechanical Museum. This spectacle of mo- dernity was the creature of John Joseph Merlin, a master designer of automata and other mechanical devices. Merlin took Babbage to see his pride and joy: two female figures made of silver, about twelve inches high. The second of these figurines was a dancer, who captivated Babbage: "an admirable danseuse, with a bird on the forefin- ger of her right hand, which wagged its tail, flapped its wings and opened its beak

...The lady attitudinized in a most fascinating manner. Her eyes were full of imagination and irresistible."[47] This childhood fascination first led Babbage to the distinctly marginal world of the theater. He contemplated becoming a theater designer, pondering the manufacture of colored stage lighting and even composing a ballet called *Alethes and Iris*, in which sixty women dressed in white would perform bathed in his colored lights and in front of a diorama. More famously, he then designed and built the automatic Difference Engine, a calculating machine that is now accepted as the ancestor of today's computers. In 1834 he exhibited it along with the very silver dancer he had seen as a child, which he had been able to purchase as an adult. Simon Schaffer points out that such dancers were made in part to serve as desirable commodities to exchange for goods in China, creating a "neat connection between passion, exoticism, mechanism and money."[48] If the notion of a mechanism can be extended to the Teletubbies, then it seems that Babbage's circuit is flowing again.

What should we make of these parallels with earlier experience? Once we might have been content to note the formal syllogism and pronounce upon the postmodern effects of reiteration and appropriation. Now cyberdiscourse would want to rewrite the example as part of a reformulated modernist narrative of technological progress. Neither solution seems quite satisfying. On the one hand, the precedents of the automata serve as a useful caution against the relentless proclamation of the unprecedented nature of digital culture. On the other, it is clear that the consumption of the mass medium of television is not the same as the secret cabinets of modern displays. Sheer force of numbers matters. An optimistic reading might say that if Babbage's encounter with the dancer produced the Difference Engine, who knows what technological marvels the Tubbies generation will create? In this reading, the cyberculture heralded by new technology is on the verge of creating what William J. Mitchell has called "e-topia."[49] Against that, the dystopic interpretations of child psychology and high culture both predict disaster on individual and societal levels, as school scores continue to fall and America bowls alone. In his study of popular entertainment, Richard Dyer identified a utopian element to such critically disdained formats as musicals, pantomime, and cabaret at the level of what he called the "nonrepresentational sign," that is to say, "colour, texture, movement, rhythm, melody, camerawork."[50] Teletubbyland is by definition a utopia in the literal sense, and the elements that Dyer identifies are exactly those that make *Teletubbies* a distinctive program. In short, *Teletubbies* represents an infants' utopia. It exists in a space of global media culture that is not real in the concrete sense but is precisely a virtual reality.

Perhaps the most striking aspect of *Teletubbies* is that its popularity with children has helped the show overcome all the opposition outlined above. Anecdotal accounts from Africa, Europe, and the United States all remark on how quickly the infant identifies with the program. It is not simply that the children fall in love with television via the Tubbies, because inevitably they will have seen television before seeing the Tubbies. Nor is it the seductiveness of what Raymond Williams famously named the "flow" of modern television. The producers of *Teletubbies* go to considerable lengths to prevent advertising from being shown during the show. In January 1999, Itsy Bitsy Entertainment took legal action against Mexico's TV Azteca in order to force the network to cancel its show *Telechobis*, an imitation version of the Tubbies. Negotiations with Azteca to show the original version broke down over the question of advertising, which the network wanted to show in the middle of the program. Lawyers for Itsy Bitsy declared, "That's something we don't permit, it confuses children as to what's Teletubbies and what's not, and it ruins the program."[51] It is certainly true that the program has very clear and extended opening and closing sequences that do not vary, which children quickly learn to identify as marking the limits of Teletubbyland. On the other hand, within the United States there is no such injunction against a repeated spot for Kellogg's Corn Flakes being used at the outset of each PBS broadcast, creating an identification of that product with Teletubbies.

What makes *Teletubbies* particularly appealing is that it acknowledges the spectatorship of infants as infants. This is perhaps the first moment in which the infant perceives the culture hailing it as a member of that culture. Or to put it in Louis Althusser's terms, *Teletubbies* interpellates infants as subjects. This is done quite literally with an extended sequence in which each Tubby greets and says goodbye to the viewer at either end of every episode. Each show is also figured as taking place over a "day" marked by the rising and setting of a sun with a baby's face. The sun also appears between segments, often laughing with pleasure. Infants can interpret the greetings of the Teletubbies and the laughter of the sun as being addressed to them because of the visual format of the program. The camera angles are low, mimicking the viewpoint of the child. The Teletubbies share the shape of the infant who wears diapers and a romper suit. The characters often look directly into the camera and wave or say something. It is noticeable that the youngest Tubbies watchers identify mostly with Po, the smallest Tubby, whom they clearly see as being like themselves.

There is, of course, a theoretical objection to this analysis. For the infant is surely pre-Oedipal, not yet able to identify itself as a subject. This model of subjectivity depends on Lacan's rereading of Freud and his famous mirror stage as a "formative function" of the ego or "I." Lacan sees the infant aged six to eighteen months as having a "primordial" sense of self, "still sunk in his motor incapacity and nursling dependence . . . before it is objectified in the dialectic of objectification with the other."[52] In this frame of reference, then, *Teletubbies* is nothing more than primary narcissism. But most (Western) children are now walking and eating solid food by eighteen months and may have been doing so for six to eight months. When Lacan wrote his paper, it was far more common for both cultural and economic reasons for women to nurse their children to the age of two or even later. By the same token, children were not encouraged to crawl and walk with the same enthusiasm as is common in contemporary Western culture. So it may be that the mirror stage now takes place much earlier than Lacan thought or that there are different mirror stages in different technocultures. Perhaps the mirror stage was specific to modern European culture and has now been superseded by something else. Crucially, the defining threshold for the beginning of childhood in so much critical writing on the gaze and gendered identity no longer appears secure but is rather at best variable and perhaps even extinct.

Cyborgs do not have a mirror stage. They become "self-aware." What makes *Teletubbies* disturbing is the sense that childhood and global capitalism are fusing to create a new cyborg hybrid of consumer, spectator, machine, and individual. The limit between adulthood and childhood has been drawn in terms of prohibitions, whether sexual or legal.[53] The cyborg child appears to adults to be eluding its limits, disrupting the sense of what it is to be adult. Adults therefore read the Tubbies as sexualized objects or as a symptom requiring medical attention in order to reinstate a limit that has now been passed. As Judith Butler cogently argues, "The subject is itself constituted through the embodiment of certain norms that establish in advance and with considerable social force what will and will not be a subject."[54] These norms are changing. While norms no doubt normally change, the current transition is visible as cyborgs on screen.

Despite considerable efforts by the BBC to prevent it, students and young adults in Britain have adopted *Teletubbies* as an icon of nonconformity.[55] This appropriation is part of a global youth fashion for the infantile that has seen the dummy or sucker become a hip-hop and rave accessory in London, New York, and Tokyo. This style is usually interpreted as a mix of regression and denial, part of the infantilization of the television audience. But infant cyborgs are not limited by biological age, unlike their ancestors, the replicants in *Bladerunner* that all died young. The utopian world of the Teletubbies may seem to self-defined adults to be little more than a front for the generation of profit. But in *Teletubbies* there is no visible authority figure, let alone money. In the Teletubbies' utopia, goods appear magically without the intercession of labor, imbued with a life of their own like Babbage's dancer. This is commodity fetishism with a twist—cyborg consumerism. The infant cyborgs do not respect the notion that commodities are owned by someone and hence are the key to profit. Napster—a computer program that allows users to exchange digitized music files—is already threatening to divest the music industry of its status as a generator of hyperprofit. The film industry is uneasily aware that its product may be next. Why are the cyborgs dancing? Say Eh-Oh.

NOTES

1. Anne Wood, "Making Teletubbies—Its Child's Play," www.bbc.co.uk/education/teletubbies/information/press relense

2. Anne Higonnet, *Pictures of Innocence: The History and Crisis of Ideal Childhood* (New York: Thames and Hudson, 1998), 26.

3. Proponents of stricter sentencing would no doubt claim that their policies are responsible for this decline. However, the pattern of falling juvenile violent crime is nationwide, whereas sentencing policy still varies widely.

4. Higonnet, *Pictures of Innocence*, 193.

5. Quoted in Keith Perry, "Families Flee Estate Hate Campaign," *Guardian*, 10 August 2000.

6. David Buckingham, *After the Death of Childhood: Growing Up in the Age of Electronic Media* (Cambridge: Polity Press, 2000), 66.

7. "Parents Alert," *NLJ*, 1999, www.liberty.edu/chancellor/nlj/feb99/politics2.htm,

8. "Eh-Oh!" *Current Online*, 1998, www.current.org/ch/ch803t.html

9. Gilles Deleuze and Felix Guattari, *Anti-Oedipus: Capitalism and Schizophrenia*, preface by Michel Foucault (Minneapolis: University of Minnesota Press, 1983), xiii.

10. One recalls Louis Althusser's analysis of the "implacable" ideological configuration of the family in his classic essay "Ideology and Ideological State Apparatuses," in *Essays on Ideology* (London: Verso, 1984), 50.

11. Ellen Seiter, "Power Rangers at Pre-School: Negotiating Media in Child Care Settings," in Marsha Kinder, ed., *Kids' Media Culture* (Durham: Duke University Press, 1999), 239–62.

12. Anne Wood, "Making Teletubbies."

13. Ibid.

14. Geoff Lealand, "Where Do Snails Watch Television? Preschool Television and New Zealand Children," in Sue Howard, ed., *Wired Up: Young People and Electronic Media* (London: UCL Press, 1998), 3.

15. Joyce Millman, "Tubbythumping," www.salon.com/media/1998/04/03media.html

16. Millman, "Tubbythumping."

17. "Eh-Oh!"

18. Nicholas Mirzoeff, *An Introduction to Visual Culture* (London: Routledge, 1999), 9–11; and Buckingham, *After the Death of Childhood*, 21–40.

19. Heather Hendershot, *Saturday Morning Censors: Television Regulation before the V-Chip* (Durham: Duke University Press, 1998), 153–55.

20. President William J. Clinton, "Remarks by the President to the AFL-CIO Biennial Convention," 24 September 1997, http://www2.whitehouse.gov/WH?New/html/199770924-5807.html

21. Cited in Millman, "Tubbythumping."

22. Ibid.

23. Robert Taylor, "Trade Unions and Transnational Industrial Relations," International Institute for Labour Studies, 1998, www.ilo.org/public/english/130inst/research/network/taylor.htm

24. International Toy Campaign, http://www.web.net/msn/3toy.htm.

25. Frank Pyke, "Local Development Initiatives and the Management of Change in Europe," Employment and Training Dept., International Labour Office, Geneva, 1999, www.ilo.org/public/english/60empfor/publ/etp31.htm.

26. Sarah Cox, "The Secret Life of Toys," *Georgia Straight* 5–12 November 1998, www.web.net/msn/3toy1.htm.

27. Milt Freudenheim, "Hasbro to Cut 20% of Its Jobs and Take $97 Million Charge," *New York Times*, 8 December 1999, C1, C6.

28. *New York Times*, 11 August 2000, A10.

29. See Jonathan C. Beller, "Cinema, Capital of the Twentieth Century," *Postmodern Culture* 4, no. 3 (May 1994), online at http://jefferson.village.virginia.edu/pmc/.

30. Jane M. Healy, "Understanding TV's Effects on the Developing Brain," 1998, www.aap.org/advocacy/chm98nws.htm.

31. Ibid.

32. Ibid.

33. Ibid.

34. Popular accounts of science are obsessed with such analyses of the brain, as neurosci-

ence seems now to represent the best contemporary avenue toward the explanation of consciousness.

35. Patrick Wall, *Pain: The Science of Suffering* (London: Weidenfeld, 1999).

36. Quoted by Marsha Kinder in her introduction to *Kids Media Culture*, 18.

37. Jacques Derrida, *Of Grammatology* (Baltimore: Johns Hopkins University Press, 1976).

38. Barrie Gunter and Jill McAleer, *Children and Television*, 2d ed., (London: Routledge, 1997), 31.

39. Hendershot, *Saturday Morning Censors*, 162–66.

40. Gunter and McAleer, *Children and Television*, 169.

41. Healy, "Understanding TV's Effects on the Developing Brain."

42. Ibid.

43. Ibid.

44. See Hendershot, *Saturday Morning Censors*, 6–11.

45. Judith Halberstam and Ira Livingston, *Posthuman Bodies* (Bloomington: Indiana University Press, 1995), 8.

46. Mark Sussmann, "Performing the Intelligent Machine: Deception and Enchantment in the Life of the Automaton Chess Player," *Drama Review* 43, no. 3 (fall 1999): 88.

47. Simon Schaffer, "Babbage's Dancer," 1998, http://ma.hrc.wmin.ac.uk.

48. Ibid., 4.

49. Ibid.

50. Richard Dyer, *Only Entertainment* (London: Routledge, 1992), 18.

51. Ibid.

52. Jacques Lacan, "The Mirror Stage as Formative of the Function of the I," in *Ecrits* (1949; London: Tavistock, 1977), 2.

53. Buckingham, *After the Death of Childhood*, 13–16.

54. Judith Butler, "Agencies of Style for a Liminal Subject," in Paul Gilroy, Lawrence Grossberg, and Angela McRobbie, eds., *Without Guarantees: In Honour of Stuart Hall* (London: Verso, 2000), 33.

55. Buckingham, *After the Death of Childhood*, 100.

Contributors

Ien Ang is a professor of cultural studies at the University of Western Sydney in Australia. Her research and teaching focus on the study of media audiences, postcolonial studies, theories of identity, ethnicity, diaspora, and multiculturalism, globalization and postmodernity, and contemporary Asia and the changing new world (dis) order. She is the author of *Watching Dallas; Desperately Seeking the Audience; Living Room Wars: Rethinking Audiences for a Postmodern World*; and *On Not Speaking Chinese: Living between Asia and the West.*

Arjun Appadurai is Samuel N. Harper Distinguished Service Professor of Anthropology and of South Asian Languages and Civilizations, and director of the Globalization Project at the University of Chicago. He is the author of *The Social Life of Things: Commodities in Cultural Perspective* and *Modernity at Large: Cultural Dimensions of Globalization*, and he is the co–founding editor of *Public Culture.*

Jose B. Capino is a doctoral student at the Department of Radio/TV/Film at Northwestern University. He has published essays on postcoloniality, documentary cinema, and the avant-garde. He maintains a filmmaking and playwriting career in the Philippines, where he recently translated Bizet's *Carmen* for the national theater company.

Michael Curtin is an associate professor of media and cultural studies in the Department of Communication Arts at the University of Wisconsin–Madison. He is the author of *Redeeming the Wasteland: Television Documentary and Cold War Politics* and coeditor of new BFI series on international screen industries. Over the past four years Curtin has been researching media industries in East Asia for a forthcoming book entitled *Playing to the World's Biggest Audience: The Globalization of Chinese Film and TV.*

Jo Ellen Fair is a professor in the School of Journalism and Mass Communication and director of the Global Studies Program at the University of Wisconsin–Madison. She is the author of many articles on race and ethnicity in the U.S. media's reporting on Africa, has given workshops in Namibia and Zambia, and has been involved in curriculum development of a media studies program at the University of Namibia.

John Fiske is an internationally renowned television and cultural studies scholar who has taught at universities in Europe, the United States, and Australia. He is the author of several books, including *Reading the Popular; Television Culture;*

Power Plays Power Works; and *Media Matters: Everyday Culture and Political Change.*

Faye Ginsburg is the David B. Kriser Professor of Anthropology at New York University and is the founding director of the Graduate Program in Culture and Media and the Center for Media, Culture, and History. Her research focuses on cultural activism and movements for social transformation. She is the author of *Contested Lives: The Abortion Debate in an American Community* and coeditor of *Conceiving the New World Order*. She is completing a book entitled *Mediating Culture: Indigenous Identity in an Age of Electronic Reproduction.*

Ramaswami Harindranath received his Ph.D. from the University of Leicester in 1996, and is at present a senior lecturer in cultural studies in the Open University, U.K. He has taught in universities in India and Malaysia, and published essays and articles on diverse topics such as audience research, new social movements, and the Internet and national identity. He coedited *Approaches to Audiences*, and is currently working on a book on cultural imperialism as well as a co-authored book on the controversy surrounding the film *Crash.*

Timothy Havens is an assistant professor of mediated communication at Old Dominion University. His work has been published in *Media, Culture, and Society* and the *International Journal for Communication Studies.* He is currently investigating how globalization has changed television programming practices around the world, with a particular emphasis on Central and Eastern European channels.

Edward S. Herman is an emeritus professor of finance in the Wharton School at the University of Pennsylvania, and is the author of numerous books, including *Manufacturing Consent* (with Noam Chomsky), *Triumph of the Market*, and *The Global Media* with Robert McChesney).

Michele Hilmes is a professor of media and cultural studies in the Department of Communication Arts at the University of Wisconsin-Madison. She has published three books on broadcasting history: *Hollywood in the Age of Television: From Radio to Cable*; *Radio Voices: American Broadcasting 1922–1952*; and, most recently *Only Connect: A Cultural History of Broadcasting in the United States.*

Olaf Hoerschelmann is an assistant professor in the Department of Radio, Television and Film at the University of North Texas. His publications focus on the history of U.S. broadcasting and on European media cultures, especially the relation between terrorism and cultural identities. He is currently completing his first book, *Rules of the Game: Quiz Shows, Audience Participation, and the Production of Knowledge*, a study of the history of quiz shows in American radio and television. The article included in this anthology is part of a second major research project entitled *RAF Memories: Terrorism, Media and Public Memory in Postwar Germany.*

Shanti Kumar is an assistant professor of media and cultural studies in the Department of Communication Arts at the University of Wisconsin–Madison. He is currently working on a book on satellite television in India. He has professional experience in multimedia, television, newspaper, and advertising industries in India.

Moya Luckett is an assistant professor of film studies in the English Department at the University of Pittsburgh. She has just completed a book on spectatorship, urbanization, and American cinema, 1907–1917, and is currently writing a manuscript on single femininity in American popular film and television from 1960 to the present. She has published articles in several anthologies and in *Screen*, the *Velvet Light Trap*, and *Aura*. With Hilary Radner, she coedited *Swinging Single: Representing Sexuality in the 1960s*.

Robert McChesney is a renowned media critic and a professor of communications at the University of Illinois at Urbana-Champaign. He is the author of several books, including *Telecommunications, Mass Media and Democracy; Rich Media Poor Democracy*; and *The Global Media* (with Edward S. Herman).

Divya C. McMillin is an assistant professor of media studies in the Interdisciplinary Arts and Sciences Program at the University of Washington–Tacoma. Her work has been published in such journals as the *International Journal of Cultural Studies*, *Continuum: Journal of Media and Cultural Studies*, the *Indian Journal of Gender Studies* and the *International Communication Bulletin*.

Nicholas Mirzoeff is a professor of art history and comparative studies at SUNY Stony Brook. He is the author of *Bodyscape: Art, Modernity, and the Ideal Figure* and *An Introduction to Visual Culture*, and has edited *Visual Culture Reader; Diaspora and Visual Culture: Representing Africans and Jews*; and *Visual Culture Reader 2.0*.

David Morley is a professor of communications at Goldsmith's University in London. His current research explores communications technologies, media markets, and cultural identities from the perspective of cultural geography, in relation to questions of globalization and cultural imperialism. He is the author of *Family Television; Television Audiences and Cultural Studies; Spaces of Identity: Global Media, Electronic Landscapes and Cultural Boundaries* (with Kevin Robins): and *Home Territories: Media, Mobility and Identity*.

Hamid Naficy is a professor of film and media studies at Rice University. He is the author of *The making of Exile Cultures: Iranian Television in Los Angeles* and *An Accented Cinema: Exicilic and Diasporic Filmmaking*. He has also edited *Otherness and Media* (with Teshome Gabriel) and *Home, Exile, Homeland: Film, Media and the Politics of Place*.

Lisa Parks is an assistant professor in the Film Studies Department at the University of California–Santa Barbara. She is finishing a book called *Cultures in Orbit: Satellite Technologies and Televisuality*, and has published essays in the journals *Television and New Media, Screen, Social Identities*, and *Convergence*. She has also produced activist videos for Paper Tiger TV and serves on the advisory board of CULT-STUD L.

James Schwoch is an associate professor at Northwestern University, where he holds appointments in the Center for International and Comparative Studies and the Department of Communication Studies. His research has been supported by, among others, the Center for Strategic and International Studies, the National Science Foundation, the Ford Foundation, the Fulbright Commission, and the National Endowment for the Humanities.

R. Anderson Sutton, a professor of music at the University of Wisconsin–Madison, received his Ph.D. in musicology from the University of Michigan. He is the author of three books and numerous articles on music in Indonesia, where he has conducted fieldwork on numerous occasions since 1973. At UW-Madison he is currently director of the research circle on Media, Performance, and Identity, and he has served twice as director of the Center for Southeast Asian Studies. His current research interests focus on music television in Asia.

Serra Tinic is an assistant professor of mass communication and media studies in the Department of Sociology at the University of Alberta. She publishes on popular culture, cultural studies, and consumer culture. Her research interests include issues of collective identity in a global media environment. She is currently working on a book project, *Imagining Canada in Hollywood North: Culture, Identity and the Globalization of the Vancouver Television Industry*.

John Tomlinson is a professor of cultural sociology and director of the Center for Research in International Communication and Culture at the Nottingham Trent University. He is the author of *Cultural Imperialism* and *Globalization and Culture*, and his current research explores the significance of speed in modern culture.

Mimi White is a professor and chair of the Department of Radio TV Film at Northwestern University. Her research and teaching areas include film, television, and media theory; feminist theory and film/television/popular culture; mass culture studies; and issues in media historiography. She is the author of *Tele-Advising: Therapeutic Discourse in American Television* and *Media Knowledge: Popular Culture, Pedagogy, and Critical Citizenship*, with James Schwoch and Susan Reilly.

Index

A. Rafiq, 328
A&E (Arts and Entertainment Network), 177
ABC (American Broadcasting Company), 28, 76
Aboriginal Invention of Television, The, 7
Aboriginal video and television, 7
Adarsha Dampathigalu, 341–342, 345, 347–355
Adda, Serge, 198
Adorno, Theodor, 315
AFP, 283
Africa, role of France in developing television broadcasting, 199–200
African American television: and the appeal of multiracial relationships in minority communities, 436; and Asian markets, 428; assimilationist programming, 424; commonalties with exile television and minority television cultures, 433–437; commonalties with foreign markets, 432; and community identity, 435; and European markets, 427–430; global distribution, 427–437; and globalization, 423–437; links between representation and social attitudes, 424; multicultural programming, 424–425; multicultural programming and "packaging," 429–430; niche marketing, 430–433; non-European markets, 430–433; pluralist programming, 424; and realist drama, 436; representation of class struggle as marketable, 432; self-parody as feature, 435; and the "universal," 428–429. *See also* Exile television
African Americans, as Other, 436; international appeal of Black music, 430; narrowcasting as a possible space for diversity, 423–424; television representations and restriction of diversity, 423–437. *See also* "Blackness," as signifier of modernity and difference
Aftab, 378, 391
Agence de Coopération Culturelle et Technique (ACCT), 203
Agence France-Presse, 27. *See also* Havas
Agency Alliance Treaty, 283
Ahmad, Aijaz, 165–166
Alexander, Karen, 405
Ali, Waheed, 403
Alienation, 48
All India Radio, 29
Allen, Robert C., 142
Allen, Woody, 414
Allende, Salvadore, 119
Althusser, Louis, 141, 451
Am I Black Enough for You?, 423
American Academy of Pediatrics, 447, 448
American Civil War, 235
American mass culture, 105

American Radio Relay League, 58
Americanization, 8, 40, 232; fear of, through transnational media, 371–372; the grammar of international television, 176; threat to British radio, 56. *See also* Globalization
Amnesty International, 255, 280
Amos 'n' Andy, 62, 428, 429
Anderson, Benedict, 161, 234
Ang, Ien, 7, 122–124, 128
Animals of the World, 195
Anita and Me, 416
AP (Associated Press), 22, 27, 283
Appadurai, Arjun, 87, 143–144, 304, 320–321
Appiah, K. A., 164
Aquino, Benigno, Jr., 263, 265
Aquino, Corazon, 262, 265, 266, 370
Aquino, Kris, 265
Arac, Jonathan, 420
Arnheim, Rolf, 298
Arnheim, Rudolf, 104
Art, high, versus industrialized, 277
Asian Sky TV, 404
Asian Women's Action Group, 418
Asian Women's Advice and Activities Center, 418
Asian Women's Co-op, 418
Assyrian American Civic TV, 381
AT&T, 58, 383
Attallah, Paul, 172
Attention deficit disorder, 447
Audience: active audience theory, 5, 129, 156, 158–159, 287, 364; research, 122–126, 287–289, 363; correlation between class and viewership, 395; the "creative," problems with the concept of, 288; creativity, 288; cultural proximity, 181–182; ethnographic approach, 372; feminization, 105; global audience/global market, 170; and irony, 123; marginality and limits of agency, 365; "nationwide," negotiation with the text, 124; as potentially resistant, 159; as public versus as consumers, 181; reception studies, 288; social process of viewing, 124; and "reading," 288. *See also* Cultural studies; Fiske, John; Hall, Stuart
Augusto, Pinochet, 33
Austen, Jane, 285
Australia, 7; Aboriginal civil rights movement, 312; Aboriginal media and ceremony, 307–309; Aboriginal presence on public television, 310–314; media of Aboriginal Australians, 303–316; role of Aboriginal media in formation of national identity, 305, 306; social construction of Aboriginal identity, 304–305
Aylesworth, Merlyn, 61, 63

Baader, Andreas, 216, 218–220
Babbage, Charles, 449–450, 452
Babitsky, Andrei, 237
Bad Aboriginal Art, 7
Badiday, Inday, 263–264, 267–270, 273
Baker, Martin, 119
Bakhtin, Mikhail, 137
Baldwin, Stanley, 59
Band Wagon, 66
Bandung File, 408
Bank of America, 383
Barber, Benjamin, 136, 228, 231
Barker, Chris, 138, 150
Barthes, Roland, 149
Basaey, Shamil, 232
Basu, Rathikant, 343
Bataille, Georges, 236
Bate, Fred, 61, 63
Baton Broadcasting Corporation, 182–183
Batty, David, 310
Batty, Philip, 308
Baudrillard, Jean, 48, 127–128, 218, 335
Baywatch, 150, 239n, 343
BBC (British Broadcasting Company/Corporation),
    24–25, 60, 62, 64, 75, 150, 402, 443, 452; formation,
    29, 55, 56, 57, 60; BBC Prime, 343; BBC Radio,
    146; BBC World Service, 27, 90; BBC Worldwide,
    443
BBC1, 404
BBC2, 402, 404
Beatles, the, 81
Bedevil, 304
Begley, Sharon, 448
Benjamin, Walter, 49, 94
Bennett, Tony, 140, 142, 366
Beresford, David, 296
Berger, John, 119, 286
Berlin Wall, fall of (1989), 226
Berlusconi, 367
Bertelsmann, 36, 367
Between Brothers, 429
Bhabha, Homi, 142, 162, 211–212, 223, 297
Bhaji on the Beach, 404
Bhaskar, Sanjeev, 402, 403, 413
Bhuchar, Suman, 415
Bhutto, Benazir, 417
Bibian, Manuchehr, 383, 385, 392
Bild-Zeitung, 214
Bill of Rights, 248
Birmingham school, 141
Black Britain, 407
Black Entertainment Television (BET), 377–378, 434
Black on Black, 408
Black, Pauline, 408
Black Skin, White Masks, 162
Black Star Liner, 403
"Blackness," as signifier of modernity and difference,
    423
Blackout, 311
Bladerunner, 452
Blair, Tony, 403
Blood Brothers, 311
Bold and the Beautiful, The, 150
Bollywood, 404, 412
Bourdieu, Pierre, 49, 288
Boyd, Todd, 423

Boyd-Barrett, J. O., 121–122, 126
Boys of St. Vincent's, The, 178
Bradley, Tom, 281
Braudel, Fernand, 299n
Brazil, 46
Brecht, Bertolt, 308
Breloer, Heinrich, 217, 219
Brennan, Timothy, 218–219
Brick Lane bombings, 404
Brief Encounter, 412–413
Britain: Afro-Caribbean community, 407–409; British
    Asian culture, 405; Commission on the Future of
    Multi-Ethnic Britain, 404; construction of ethnic
    Asian identity in England, 298; digital television,
    405; interpretation of documentaries, 160–161; na-
    tional identity and mobile identities, 419–420;
    race and television programming, 407–409; radio,
    54; radio broadcasting system, 24; satellite televi-
    sion, 404–405; television system, 404–405
Britain's Slave Trade, 407
Britasian, pop music, 434
Britasian Renaissance, 403–404
British royal wedding (1981), 296
British Satellite Broadcasting (BSB), 404
British Sky Broadcasting (BSkyB), 405
Brixton riots, 408
Broadcast over Britain, 64
Broadcasting: and national identity, 53–70; in the
    United States, 61; shortwave, 24–25
Broadcasting Standards Commission, 415
Brodmann, Roman, 213
Brown, F. J., 57, 58
Browne, Nick, 96
Brubeck, Dave, 332
Buback, Siegfried, 214
Budyonnovsk incident, 232
Buenaventura, Sandra, 428
Bundestag, 218
Burke, Martin, 175
Burrows, A. R., 64
Buruma, Ian, 212
Bush, George Herbert Walker, 284
Butler, Judith, 452

Caldwell, John, 75
Caldwell, Ron, 81
Camporesi, Valeria, 33, 66
Canada, 169; Canadian cultural identity, 172–184; Ca-
    nadian national audience, 170, 180–184; coproduc-
    tions with France, 172; coproductions with the
    U.S., 172; differences between Canadian and U.S.
    television programming, 178; Friends of Canadian
    Broadcasting, 182; national identity, 178; radio
    broadcasting system, 24; television and film pro-
    duction, 170, 170–184. *See also* CBC (Canadian
    Broadcasting Company)
Canadian Association of Broadcasters (CAB), 182–
    183
Canadian Radio-Telecommunications Commission
    (CRTC), 182, 183
Canal France Internationale (CFI), 200
Canal Horizons, 197–204
Canal Plus, 198, 444
Canclini, Garcia, 369
Candles in the Dark, 229–231
Capital Cities/ABC, 36

Capitalism: as cultural imperialism, 118; disorganized, 41. *See also* Cultural imperialism; Marxism and Neomarxism

Carey, James, 141–142, 291

Carroll, Lewis, 441

Carry On Behind, 343

Castells, Manuel, 367

Caughie, John, 100–101, 103, 106–107

CBC (Canadian Broadcasting Company), 175, 178, 181; "Keep the Promise" campaign, 182; unity train, 182; CBC Newsworld, 183

CBS (Columbia Broadcasting System), 28, 36, 177, 179, 278, 284; CBS News, 280; CBS Records, 37; origins in radio, 24–25; relationship with BBC, 61

Central Australian Aboriginal Media Association (CAAMA), 304, 311

Centre for Contemporary Cultural Studies, 141

Chakrabarty, Dipesh, 142

Chan, Wing-Tsit, 144

Chandra, Subash, 342

Channel 4, 104, 407

Channel 5, 404, 427, 431

Channels of Discourse, 142

Channels of Discourse Reassembled, 142

Channels of Resistance: Global Television and Local Empowerment, 8, 137

Chechnya, 226–239; national identity and the Budyonnovsk incident, 232; national identity and the role of religion, 231, 233; use of the internet in national identity formation, 237

Chee-hwa, Tung, 253

Chernomyrdin, Viktor, 232–233

Childhood, and television consumption, 447–449; Romantic image, 441–442; television viewing hours, 442

Children's Television Workshop, 448

Chile, 119–122

China, 46; corruption, 247; at the East-West Conference, 144; popularity of television, 252. *See also* Hong Kong

Chrisye, 325

Chuming, Martin Lee, 247

Cissé, Abdou Rahman, 196

Civil Rights Movement, 432

Clarke, Arthur C., 77, 79

Clash of Civilizations, 136

Class, 59; and radio, 67

Clifford, J., 288

Clinton, Bill, 235, 441, 445

Clogg, Richard, 235

Close-up Antakshari, 344

CNN (Cable News Network), 36, 83, 90, 150, 200, 322, 343

"CNN Defense Concept," 230–232, 233

Coca Cola, 121, 299

Coe, Paul, 312

Cold War, 4, 78, 103, 144, 213, 226–228, 236

College Literature, 148

Collins, Michael, 408

Columbia Pictures, 27, 37, 383

Columbia Workshop, 60

Columbo, 195

Columbus, Christopher, 285

Commercialization, 6

Commission on Population Control and the American Future, 89

Commission on the Future of Multi-Ethnic Britain, 404

Communications Act of 1934, 55

COMSAT (Communications Satellite Corporation), 78

Coniston Story, 309

Consoling Passions, 8

Constanduros, Mabel, 66

Convergence, 135

Cook, David, 127–128, 129, 131

Copycat Television, 146

Corner, John, 219

Cornershop, 402, 403

Corporate consolidation, 36

Corwin, Norman, 60

Cosby, 429

Cosby Show, The, 428–429

Council of Resistance, 386

Crawford Committee, 55

Cross-cultural communication, 277

Cross-demographic communication, 139–140; positionality, 146–148

Cultural imperialism, 4, 5, 113–114, 155; and American consumer-capitalist values, 120–121; capitalist values, 155, 159; as complicated by the transnational era, 369; as the critique of global capitalism, 157; as the critique of modernity, 157; as the "culture bomb," 155; defining the cultural, 113–115; the imperialist text, 119–122, 126; imperializing knowledge, 279; media effects, 113; as media imperialism, 157; and national identity, 157, 161; question of audience role, 121–122. *See also* Americanization; Audience; Media imperialism

Cultural Revolution, 250

Cultural studies: American, 141–142; audience reception studies, 288; Australian, 141–142; British, 104, 141–142, 366; ideological criticism versus audience studies, 363; and the postcolonial, 141–142; problems with definition, 141; theories of resistance, 364; as "traveling theory," 140–141; use value, 140

"Cultural Studies in/and New Worlds," 140

Cunningham, Stuart, 173

Cyborgs, 449; cyborg genealogy, 449–452; and the posthuman, 449

D'Acci, Julie, 8

Dallas, 7, 122–126, 159, 163, 181, 239n, 343; audience in Israel and the U.S., 159–160; ideology of mass culture, 122; Senegalese imitation, 203

Damon, 428, 439

Dangdut, 320, 326; and hybridity, 327–330

Daoust, Phil, 402

de Certeau, Michel, 365

de Gaulle, Charles, 296

Declaration of Independence, 248

Decolonising the Mind, 155

DeGeneres, Ellen, 441

DeGolyer, Michael, 247

Degrassi High, 184n

Deleuze, Gilles, 449

Delta Force, 222

Democracy, as master term, 44

Deniyev, Adam, 237–238

"Dependency theory," 115, 116; versus modernization theory, 116

Der Spiegel, 214–215
Derrida, Jacques, 141, 148, 150, 448
Descartes, Rene, 145
Designing Women, 424
Desmonds, 407
Deterritorialization, 44–45, 50
Dewi, Torsten, 428
Diaspora, 376; Black experience, 435; Britasian/Indo-
    Pakistani, 402–421; Britasian youth culture, 406;
    as location for pleasure, 420–421; as market and
    commodity, 415; as a postmodernist understand-
    ing of race and culture, 409
Didar, 376, 390
Different World, A, 424, 429
Diff'rent Strokes, 343, 424
Diop, Adrienne, 201
Diop, Boubacar Boris, 198
Diouf, Abdou, 19, 190, 198–199
DirecTV, 88
Dirlik, Arif, 327
Disney, 37, 119–122, 441, 446; comics in the Third
    World, 119–122; Disney Channel España, 430
Docudrama, 219
Documentary, 177, 213
Domestic, the: and formation of national identity,
    295–296; heritage politics, 50; as political space,
    294–297; the private as public, 295–296; role of
    television, 288–290; semantics of the everyday,
    291. *See also* Gender; Women
Dominance and Subordination, 164–165
Donald Duck, 119
Doordarshan, 342–344
Dorfman, Ariel, 8, 119–122, 126
Dowmunt, Tony, 8
Dr. Seuss, 441, 448
Dua Warna, 320, 330–334
Dudayev, Dzhokhar, 230, 235
Durán, Ignacio, 432
Dyer, Richard, 450
Dynasty, 101, 343

Early Bird, 74, 76
East India Company, 285
East is East, 405
Eastern Eye, 408, 409
East-West Center (Center for Cultural and Techno-
    logical Interchange between East and West), 144–
    145
East-West discourse, problems with comparative
    studies, 145–146
Ebonics, 445
Ebsan, Homa, 376
Eckersley, Peter, 64, 65
Eco, Umberto, 441
Economist, 232
Edgar, Patricia, 444
Egypt, radio, 54
Ehrlich, Paul, 79
Ehsan, Homa, 381, 390
Ellis, John, on flow, 95
Elsaesser, Thomas, 83, 212
Embedded aesthetics, defined, 306
Emile, 441
Encoding/decoding, 124, 364
Enculturation, 49
End of History, The, 136
English Family Robinson, The, 66

Enlightenment, subject, 248; universalism, 48; world-
    view, 43
Ensslin, Gudrun, 216, 218–220
Entertainment Tonight, 269
ESPN (Entertainment and Sports Network), 36, 343
Estonia, 233
Estrada, Joseph, 267
Ethnography, and tourism, 99
Ethnoscapes, 41
European Broadcasting Union, 76
European Economic Community (EEC), formation
    of integrated European identity, 371
Everyman's Theater, 60
Exile television, 107; clandestine political sponsorship,
    389; commercial television and advertisement, 384–
    386; demographic breakdown of audience, 393–
    397; demographic breakdown of Iranian exiles in
    Los Angeles, 392–393; emergence of female pro-
    ducers, 397; and the formation of minority iden-
    tities, 377–397; history of Iranian exilic television
    in Los Angeles, 379–380; as in instrument of in-
    corporation and acculturation, 379; Iranian, 107;
    Iranian communities in Los Angeles, 376–397; lo-
    cal and national transmission, 381; production,
    380–381; rivalry, 388–391; station politics, 386–388;
    syndication, 383; and terrorism, 386–388; time
    brokerage, 383–384; tolerance for opposing view-
    points, 391; women's programming, 390
Exoticism, indigenized exoticism, 330–334

Falwell, Jerry, 441
Family Channel, 229
Family Matters, 424, 429
Family Television, 288, 289
Family TV Research and Consultation Center, 445
Fann Océan, 203
Fanon, Frantz, 162, 278
FCC (Federal Communications Commission), 388;
    "Blue Book," 67
Fecan, Ivan, 179
Fecetti, German, 74
Fejes, Fred, 114, 115, 118, 121, 125, 126
Feminism, *Goodness Gracious Me,* and the conflict
    between Western feminism and Indian feminist
    traditions, 417–419. See also *Goodness Gracious Me*
    (GGM); Women
Feminist Television Criticism, 6
Feminist theory, 149; and cultural studies, 142; and
    the "other," 278
Ferguson, Marjorie, 135, 293
Ferianto, Djaduk, 330–333
Fetishism: commodity, 47; consumer, 47, 48; produc-
    tion, 47–48
Feuer, Jane, on flow, 95, 96, 288
Fight Club, 441
Film: and development of global media, 23, 27; Hong
    Kong, 47
Filmline International, 175
Filmstiftung Nordrhein-Westfalen, 217
Financescapes, 41, 42–43
Finland, radio, 54
Finn, Adam, 175
Firing Line, 262
First Australians, The, 311
First in Line, 311
First Nations Film and Video Makers World Alliance
    (FNFVWA), 314

Fischer, Michael M. J., 372

Fiske, John, 95, 97, 102, 106, 142, 158, 163, 288, 364. *See also* Cultural studies; Heterogenization

Flaubert, Gustave, 130–131

Flow, 3, 94, 450; under debate, 95–98; defined, 94; "discovery," 94, 99, 100; as ethnography, 100–101; historical perspectives, 104–108; and segmentation, 96; as "traveling theory," 99. *See also* Cultural studies

Follow the Sun, 65

"Forecast of Television, A," 104

Ford, Henry, 286

Ford, Jeff, 427, 431

Foreign Direct Investment (FDI), 22

Forster, E. M., 419.

Foucault, Michel, 141, 142, 286, 296, 441

Fox Network, 423

Foxx, Jamie, 430

Fragmentation, 287, 290. *See also* India

Frasier, 409

France. radio broadcasting system, 24; relationship with Senegal, 189–206; role in broadcasting in Africa, 199

Francophonie Summit (1989), 199–200

Francophonie Summit (1993), 203

Frankfurt School, 117. *See also* Cultural studies

Frank's Place, 435

Fresh Prince of Bel-Air, 429, 430, 431, 435

Freud, Sigmund, 441, 451

Friedman, Thomas, 136

Friends, 409

Fukuyama, Francis, 136

Galavision, 378

Ganashatru, 402

Gandhi, Indira, 417

Garofalo, G., 156–157

Gates, Daryl, 280–281

Gaumont Television, 175

Gaze, the, 98

GEMS, 434

Gender: and age, politics of, 295; gendered violence, 50; *Goodness Gracious Me* and presentation of Indian gender roles, 417–418; and radio, 67; relations, and television, 288–289; roles, policing of in Indian game shows, 341, 345, 347–355. *See also* Domestic, the; Women

Generations, 433

German Autumn of 1977: abduction of Hanns-Martin Schleyer, 214, 218–220, 222; assassination of Jürgen Ponto, 214–215; hijacking of Lufthansa airplane, 214, 216; Stammheim deaths, 216, 218–220

Germany: critique of post-war national identity through cinema, 212–213; early radio broadcasting system, 24; national identity and RAF as West German internal other, 214–224; 1967 visit of the Persian Shah, 213–214; preference in television programs, 173; radio, 54; representation and national identity formation, 211–224; repression of Nazi past in national identity, 223–224; student movement of the German Left, 214; symbols of national identity, 212

Ghir, Kulvinder, 402, 407

Giddens, Anthony, 163, 246

Gielgud, Val, 67

Gillespie, Marie, 298, 436

Gilroy, Paul, 434, 435

Gitlin, Todd, 219

"Glance theory," 97

Global capitalism, 155

Global corporate capital, ideology, 32–35

Global culture, 150. *See also* Heterogeneity; Homogenization

Global media: mediascapes, 304; origins, 21–23

Global Media: The New Missionaries of Corporate Capitalism, 6

Global mobility, and flow, 108

"Global Now," 74–75, 320; "time zoning," 87. *See also* "Global presence"

"Global presence," 75–76, 79–82, 84; mobility, 128; scheduled/canned liveness, 85–87

Global Television, 150

Global Television: An Introduction, 137

Global television, defined, 3

Global television studies: and cultural studies, 140–144; defined, 6–12; definition as a discipline, 136–140; as an incommensurate phenomena, 138, 139, 147; as intellectually distinct problems, 138, 139, 147; as interdisciplinary, 138, 139, 147; problems with definition, 141 147; teaching undergraduate students, 148–151

Global Village, 4, 5, 79, 84, 367

Globalization, 287, 367; civilizational heterogeneity and material homogenization, 228; decentered/polycentric corporations, 299; rhetoric, 135–137

"Glocalization," defined, 13; MTV Asia and the global local, 324

Golding, Peter, 117, 156, 157

"Going Public," 248

Good, the Bad, and the Ugly, The, 250–251, 254

Goodness Gracious Me (*GGM*), 402–421; appropriation of Hindi cinema, 410–411; Britasian humour, 406; conflict between feminism and multiculturalism, 417–419; criticism of Indian gender roles, 417–418; as desired Other, 419; feminism, 417–419; and Indian history as memory, 413; and language, 415–416; mobile identity, 419–420; as nonrealist television, 410; and permeability of racial identity, 407; as postmodernist television, 410–416; representation of India, 406, 411–413, 414; share of television audience, 406–407. *See also* Britain; Feminism

Graves, Cecil, 65

Gray, Herman, 424, 430

Green, Felix, 61

Grossberg, Lawrence, 140, 142, 143, 363

Guardian, 296, 402, 404, 407, 415

Guattari, Felix, 143

Guha, Ranjit, 142, 164

Gulf War, representations of U.S. involvement, 278–280, 282

Gunsmoke, 195

Gupta, Anil, 402

Habermas, Jurgen, 248

Hagerty, James C., 76

Halberstam, Judith, 449

Hall, Stuart, 70, 128–130, 141–142, 143, 290, 298, 363, 364, 423; managerial role of media, 130. *See also* Cultural studies

Hamilton, Annette, 303

Hangin' with Mr. Cooper, 429

Haque, Dr. Zubaida, 404

Haraway, Donna, 449
Hard, William, 62
Harris, Phil, 156, 157
Harry Potter, 446
Hartley, John, 135, 138–140, 146, 148, 288
Hasbro, 445–446
Hatch, Martin, 327
Haug, Ada, 445
Haut Conseil de la Radio Télévision (HCRT), 197
Havas, 22, 27, 283
Healy, Jane M., 447, 448
Hebdige, Dick, 364
"Hegelian didacticism," 148
Hegemony, 363, 365; translational media system as hegemonic power, 366–368
Herman, Edward, 6
Heterogenization, 40
Highlander, 175–176
Higonnet, Anne, 441
Higson, Andrew, 408
Hirsch, Paul M., on flow, 95, 96
Hitler, Adolf, 215, 215, 216
Hoggart, Richard, 138–140, 141–142
Hollywood, 23, 47
Home Territories, 7
Homogenization, 40, 287, 290, 321, 368; as Americanization, 169; instruments, 48; versus cultural fragmentation, 174
Homosexuals: Imelda Marcos as icon, 272; in Philippine talk shows, 262–266, 270–273; popularity of gay slang in the Philippines, 270–272; and Teletubbies, 441
Honda, 299
Hong Kong, 243–258; cultural distinction from mainland Chinese, 249–253; film industry, 47; local identity and the battle against corruption, 243–258; local identity as formed through television, 243–244; reaction to Tiananmen Square massacre, 252–253; representational shift around reintegration with China, 253–256; resistance to Chinese propaganda, 257; return to China, 243; Special Administrative Region, 245; the "rule of law" and public trust, 246–249; *See also* National identity
Hong Kong Transition Project, 247
Hoover, Herbert, 57
Hope, Bob, 76
Hoskins, Colin, 175
How People Use Television, 181
How to Read Donald Duck: Imperialist Ideology in the Disney Comic, 8, 119–122
Hughleys, The, 429
Huntington, Samuel, 136
Hussein, Saddam, 282
Hybridity, 156, 157, 158–163; and Britasian cultural identity, 411; hybrid television programming in India, 341, 344–345

I Love Lucy, 343
Identity, invention of tradition, 49
Ideology, 363
Ideoscapes, 41, 42, 43
Imagined communities, 234, 305, 369; definition, 234; mass media and political efficacy, 226–239; national identity and mass culture, 234. *See also* National identity
Imagined worlds, 42

Imbruglia, Natalie, 326
Imparja TV, 88
Impeachment hearings, 441
Include Me In, 407
Independence Day, 430
Independent Commission against Corruption, 244–246
India, 46, 79, 341–357, 417; competition among television channels, 356; at the East-West Conference, 144; game show and policing of national identity, 342, 351; history of television, 342–344; implications of cable and satellite broadcasting, 165; interpretation of documentaries, 160–161; national response to foreign programming, 343–344; radio, 54; role of English language, 344; satellite television, 343; TARA (Television Aimed at Regional Audiences), 343; traditional structures of Hindu marriage, 346
India Cabarel, 45
Indigenization, 40
Indigenous people: importance of community in Australian Aboriginal media, 309; indigenous media, 303–316; media and community responsibility, 313; media production in traditional communities, 305, 307–310; social construction of Australian Aboriginal identity, 304–305; use of media as social action, 306; use of national television, 305, 310–314; use of transnational networks, 305, 314–316
Indonesia, 320–336; ban on Western rock, 335; *dangdut* as national musical form, 326, 327–330; *dangdut* on television, 327–330; history of television, 321–322; pop Indonesia, 326; prevalence of television music shows, 320, 323; role of MTV, 323–327; use of satellite technology, 322
Indosiar, 321
INTELSAT (International Telecommunication Satellite Consortium), 78
International coproductions, 169; coventures, 171; history, 172; international joint ventures, 171; official coproduction agreements, 171; twinning packages, 171
International Council of Toy Industries, 446
International Monetary Fund (IMF), 26
International Toy Campaign, 446
Internet, 237
Interstate Commerce Commission, 58
Intimate Enemy, The, 142
Iran, 376, 392
Iran, 376, 379, 381, 382, 383, 385
Iranian Mass Media Society of California, 392
Iraq, 278, 282
Isaac, Godfrey, 57
Israel, reception of Dallas, 123–126
Italy, radio, 54
It's a Man's World, 146
It's That Man Again, 66
Itsy Bitsy Entertainment, 443, 451
ITU (International Telecommunications Union), 30
ITV, 402, 404
Iwan, 328

Jacka, Elizabeth, 173
Jam-e Jam, 379, 383, 385, 392
Jameson, Fredric, 51n, 127, 286, 420
Jamie Foxx Show, 429, 430

Jan-Mohamed, Abdul, 433
Japan: early television, 55; at the East-West Conference, 144; flow of ideas, 44
Jay Leno, 345
Jefferson, Tony, 364
Jeffersons, The, 424, 429.
Jewish Television Network, 378
Jihad vs. McWorld, 136, 228, 231
Johnson, Lyndon, 80
Joyrich, Lynne, 105
Julia, 424

Kaner, Mark, 427
Kardan, Parviz, 376
Kassel, Katrina, 441
Katz, Elihu, 7, 123–126, 156, 159–161, 163, 164, 296–297
Kaufer, David, 149
Kelly, Francis Jupurrurla, 308–309
KGB/FSB (Federal Security Service), 238
Khan, Chaka, 271
Khan, Mehonb, 417
Khan-Din, Ayub, 402, 405
King, Rodney, 280
Klinge, Matti, 230
Kohli, Sanjeev, 417
Korean Broadcasting Service, 378
Kosin, Aminoto, 331–332
Kosygin, Aleksei, 80
Kroker, Arthur, 127–128, 129, 131
KSCI-TV (the "international channel"), 377, 386–389; scheduling methodology, 381–383
Kua Etnkia, 330–333
Kunzle, David, 120
Kursk, 226
Kussudiardjo, Bagong, 330
Kuwait Television Channel 2, 432

Lacan, Jacques, 142, 162, 451–452
LaGrandeur, Kevin, 149
Langton, Marcia, 303, 305
LAPD (Los Angeles Police Department), 280–281
Larson, Gerald James, 145
Lash, Scott, 41
"Late Capitalism," 286
Latour, Bruno, 234
Le Soleil, 193, 197
Lean, David, 413
Lebed, Alexander, 234
Leckie, Keith Ross, 178
Lee, Benjamin, 248
Lenny Henry Show, The, 409
Levine, Michael, 173
Lewinsky, Monica, 441
Lexus and the Olive Tree, 136
Liar, Liar, 178–179
Liberal self, 143
Liebes, Tamar, 7, 123–126, 156, 159–161, 163, 164
Limonadi, Ali, 383, 388
Lincoln, Abraham, 235
Lion King, The, 446
Listener's Bureau, 67
Little Criminals, 178–179
Living Single, 428, 429
Livingston, Ira, 449
Lloyd, David, 433
Local, the, 48, 106, 174; as plural, 106

Localization, 287
Lodziak, C., 126–127
Lohengrin, 81
London Times, 407
Long Live the Election, 255
Lowe, Chad, 229
Lubiano, Wahneema, 420
Lufthansa, 211
Lull, James, 294, 368
Lyotard, Jean-François, 127, 372

Ma, Eric Kit-wai, 249–251
MacBride Report, 5, 31
MacDonald, Dwight, 105
MacMillan, Michael, 175
Madame Bovary, 130–131
Made in Hong Kong, 253
Magna Carta, 248
Mahlati, Cawe, 432
Mahmudi, Kambiz, 391
Malaysia, national identity as manipulated through media, 369–370
Malcolm X, 435
Mandela, Nelson, 296
"Manifesto for Cyborgs," 449
Mannix, 195
Mansyur S., 328
Manyu Wana, 310, 311
Maps: Eurocentric representation of the world, 282; as representations of power, 281–285. *See also* Representation
Marconi, 57
Marcos, Ferdinand, 33, 263, 370
Marcos, Imelda, 272
Marcus, George, 288, 372
Marshall Plan, 26
Martin, 428, 429, 435
Martin-Barbero, Jesus, 365–366
Marxism and Neo-Marxism, 5, 47, 116, 118, 142, 269; and cultural studies, 141
Maskhadov, Aslan, 235
Mass culture, as radio "chaos," 63–66
Matsushita, 36, 37
Mattel, 445
Mattelart, Armand, 8, 117, 119–122, 126, 293
Mattelart, Michelle, 122
Maulana, Armand, 332
MCA, 36
McBride, Mary Margaret, 68
McChesney, Robert, 6, 60
McFadyen, Stuart, 175
McLuhan, Marshall, 4, 5, 79, 84, 228
MCM, 200
Meaning of Exile Cultures, The, 107
Media consumption, role of ethnographic studies, 287–299
Media globalization, consolidation, 169
Media imperialism, 113–132, 115–116, 150; as cultural imperialism, 114–115; problem of assessing media effects, 116–117; problems with oversimplification of the concept, 189–190; television programming in Africa, 189–206. *See also* Cultural imperialism
Mediascapes, 41
Mediation of culture, 113
"Medium is the Message," 4
Meinhoff, Ulrike, 221

Men Behaving Badly, 146
Mercator, 282
Merchant-Ivory, 419
Mercury Theatre of Air, 60
Merlin, John Joseph, 449
Metz, Christian, 95
Mexico, 46
MGA, 27
MGM (Metro-Goldwyn-Mayer), 27
Michaels, Eric, 7, 306, 308–309
Midnight Show, 379, 385
Mignolo, Walter D., 415
Milano, Alyssa, 229
Millman, Joyce, 444, 445
Minor Adjustments, 429
Mir, 226
Miramax, 405
Mitchell, William J., 450
Mitchell-Thompson, Sir William, 64
Mitrani, Michael, 176
Mobility, 135
Modernity, 76; and representation, 131; as foreign derived, 320
Modood, Tariq, 404
Moerdiono, 327
Moesha, 429–431
Moffat, Tracey, 304
Mohsan, Tahir, 403
Mojahedin, 386–388, 399n
Moliére, 285
Monroe Doctrine, 25
Monty Python, 271, 410
Moran, Albert, 146
Morley, David, 7
Morris, Meaghan, 288, 364
Mother India, 417
Motion Pictures Association of America, 388
Movers and Shekhars, 345
Movie of the Week, 177
Mrs. Dale's Diary, 66
MTV (Music Television), 36, 150, 320, 411; prevalence in Indonesia, 326
MTV Asia, 322; absence of African American musical artists, 325; history in Asia and breakdown into regional MTV networks, 323–324; Salam *Dangdut*, 326
Mukerji, Chandra, 142
Mulder, Frank, 428
Murdoch, Rupert, 37, 139, 150, 156, 342, 343, 367, 405
Murdock, Graham, 117, 287
Music, in Indonesia, 320–336
Music video, 323, 327–330
Musto, Michael, 441
Myers, Fred, 310

Naficy, Hamid, 107, 433, 434, 435
Nair, Mira, 45
NAM (Movement of the Non-Aligned Nations), 30
Nandy, Ashis, 136, 142
Napster, 452
Narrowcasting, 376; audience specialization and segmentation, 377
Nation and Narration, 211–212
National Association of Broadcasters (NAB), 56, 60, 61

National Association of Television Professionals and Executives, 427
National identity, 106, 169, 341; Canadian, 178; formation, 53; formation within the transnational media system, 368–372; the "liberal state's dilemma," 216; Malaysian, 369–370; production of cultural identities through media, 297; use of the image of family, 222; use of the Oriental other, 222; West Germany, 211–224. *See also* Australia; Canada; Chechnya; Domestic, the; Germany; Hong Kong; India; Indonesia; Philippines; Russia; Senegal
National Liberty Journal Online, 441
National Sovereignty and International Communication, 115
Nation-state, role in global economy, 45–46
NATO (North Atlantic Treaty Organization), 26
NBC (National Broadcasting Company), 28, 36, 60, 64, 345; NBC Radio, 146; origins in radio, 24–25; relationship with BBC, 61
N'Diaye, Fara, 199
NDR (Norddeutscher Rundfunk), 217
Nelson, Cary, 148–149
Neoliberalism, 32, 35, 156, 165
Netherlands, radio broadcasting system, 24; reception of *Dallas*, 123–124
New German Cinema, 212–213
New Patterns in Global Television, 137
New Society, 119
New York Times, 446
New York Undercover, 433
Newcomb, Horace, 95, 96, 142
Newlywed Game, 341
News, 283–284
News agencies, Big Four, 22, 27. *See also* Associated Press; Havas; Reuters; United Press; Wolff
News Corporation, 37
News of the World, 441
Newspapers, 21–22
Nicoll, Fiona, 304–305
Nielsen Ratings, 181, 393, 449
Nigeria, 79
Nintendo Game Boy, 410
Nordenstreng, K., 115
Nothing but the Truth, 263
NRK, 445
NTV, 238
NWICO (New World Information and Communication Order), debate, 5, 29–32

Oboler, Arch, 60
Observer, 404
Olympics (1972), 193
Olympics, Tokyo (1964), 74
OnDigital, 405
One Man's Family, 66
Orientalism, 8, 142, 371
Ostankino Television Tower Fire, 226
Other, the: danger of being consumed, 436; desirability of the other, 407; enjoyment of otherness, 436; othering as a representational strategy, 278; RAF as West German internal other, 214; television as other, 102; terrorist as Other, 221–223; use of the Oriental other in national identity formation, 222
Our World, 74–90; lack of Second and Third World nations, 78, 88–90; origin, 76; representation of childbirth, 80

Outcaste, 403
Outer Space Treaty, 77, 78

Pac Rim initiative, 314
Paget, Derek, 219
Pahlavi, Reza, 392
Pakistan, 79, 417
Paldan. L., 165
Panel 200, 403
Panikkar, Raimundo, 146, 147
Paramount, 27
Parent 'Hood, 429
Passage to India, A, 406, 419
Passover, 297
Patel, Sharad, 404, 414
Pateman, T., 296
Paye, Moussa, 200, 204
Payne, Sarah, 441
PBS (Public Broadcasting Station), 76, 178, 439, 445
Perkins, Charles, 312
Perkins, Rachel, 311
Peters, Arno, 284
Peters, Frances, 311–314
Philippine Daily Inquirer, 272
Philippines, 262–273; Aquino assassination, 266; EDSA revolution, 266, 267; language and national identity, 370; role of celebrity in national identity formation, 267, 273; talk shows as representation of social reality, 266–267
Phillips, Trevor, 407, 408, 415, 418
Philosophy East-West, 145
Pinochet, Augusto, 119
Pinto, Richard, 417
Planet TV, defined, 10
Planet 24, 403
PLO (Palestinian Liberation Organization), 214
Plowman, Jon, 409
Pokémon, 446
Poland, 48
Police State Visit, The (Der Polizeistaatsbesuch), 213
Political economy approach, 5–6
Pollock, Jackson, 278
Poltergeist: The Legacy, 175–176
Ponto, Jürgen, 214
Pop music, 320, 336n
Popular culture, 365; fear of, 54; role of consumers, 288. *See also* Audience; Cultural studies
Population Bomb, The, 78, 79
Population Dilemma, The, 78
Population, explosion, 78
Population Explosion, The, 78
Postcolonial studies, 139; and cultural studies, 141–142
Postcolonial theory, 156, 162
Postmodernism, 127, 269, 372; characteristics of postmodern television, 410; as dominant group's lack of control, 420; and hyperreality, 127; and mobile identities, 419–421; postmodern geography, 286–287; as postnationalism, 413; in television, 403
Proctor & Gamble, 383
Project Link, 42
Prosieben, 428
Provincializing Europe, 142
Public/private split, 293
Pui-ying, Lily Yam Kwan, 245
Puopolo, Michael, 427
Putin, Vladimir, 235

Qarib Afshar, Parviz, 384

Race, 59; ethnicity and popular music, 434; possibility of alliance between minority groups, 434; and radio, 62; representations of race on television, 423–437; and television programming in Britain, 407–409. *See also* African American television
Racism, 371; hate crimes against Britasians, 404
Radio: "American chaos," 57–60, 63–66; broadcasting, 23–25; commercial, 29, 58–59; conflict between British and American systems, 61–63; history as global media, 23–24, 26–27; as public service, 66–69; scheduling, 66; state control, 53–54; women's radio programs, 67–69
Radio Four, 402
Radio France Internationale (RFI), 200
Radio Free Europe, 27
Radio Liberty, 27, 237
Radio Times, 64–65
Ragdoll Productions, 440, 443
Rajadhyaksha, Ashish, 417
Ramos, Fidel, 269
Raspe, Jan-Carl, 216, 218–220
Reagan, Ronald, 32
Red Army Faction (RAF), 211–224
Red Cross, 238
Reith, John, 58, 59, 61, 63
Repatriation of difference, 48
Representation: culture of power as a culture of representation, 277–285; as formative of experience, 129–132; ideological role of television, 290; maps as symbols of control, 281–285; news as imperializing force, 283–284; realism, 281; and scientific rationalism, 281. *See also* Ideology; Maps; News
Restless Years, The, 146
Rethinking Popular Culture, 142
Reuters, 22, 27, 283
Rhodesia, radio, 54
Richie, Lionel, 264
Ring Combination, 22
Roach, Colleen, 158, 164
Robertson, Pat, 229
Robins, Kevin, 7, 286–287
Roc, 424, 494, 435–436
Rockefeller Foundation, 89
Rockefeller, Nelson, 25
Romeo and Juliet, 81
Rorty, Richard, 141, 372
Rosenthal, Alan, 219
Ross, Andrew, 372
Ross, Karen, 423
Rousseau, Jean-Jacques, 441
Rowling, J. K., 446
Royal Canadian Air Farce, The, 182–183
Royle Family, The, 407
Russia: "Black August," 226; national identity formation after the Cold War, 231–232

Saerchinger, Carl, 61
Said, Edward, 8, 141–142, 162, 163, 164, 278, 371
Salazar, Oskee, 271
Salon, 444
Samarajiwa, Rohan, 117
Sandy, David, 312
Santa Barbara, 343

Sardana, Sharat, 417

Satellite technology, 74–90, 117, 150, 156, 227; and elimination of place, 293; emergence, 29–30; global hierarchy, 79; Outer Space Treaties, 77; Soviet perspective, 77; as technology of control, 282–283; visibility, 82–83

Satyajit Ray, 402

Saudi Arabia, 284

Sawhney, Nitin, 403, 419

Schaffer, Simon, 450

Schell, Maximilian, 229

Schiller, Herbert, 115–119, 121, 126, 159, 166

Schlesinger, Paul, 216–218, 221–222, 297

Schlesinger, Philip, 370

Schleyer, Hanns-Martin, 211–224

Schmidt, Helmut, 223–224

Schnedecker, Eric, 430

Schramm, Wilbur, 77

Schudson, Michael, 142

Schwarzenegger, Arnold, 446

Sconce, Jeff, 75

Sechan, Sarah, 326

Second Generation, 403

Secret Asians, 403

See True, 263–265, 267, 269, 271

Seinfeld, 414

Senegal, 189–206; *Fann Océan* and national identity, 203; formation of national identity through sénégalisation of television, 195–196; history of television broadcasting, 191–196; impact of international television on national values, 203–204; introduction of international radio broadcasting, 200; introduction of satellite subscription service, 196–204; *la mission civilsatrice*, 190; number of television receivers, 191; Office de Radiodiffusion-Télévision Sénégalaise (ORTS), 194; place within the francophone community, 189–206; Radiodiffusion-Télévision Sénégalaise (RTS), 196–197; Leopold Sedar Senghor, 192–195; television programming, 195

Senghor, Leopold Sedar, 190

Sesame Street, 440, 445, 448

Seven Sisters Dreaming: Tjukurpa Kungkarangkalpa Tjara, 307–308

Shabkhiz, Hamid, 376, 385

Shah, Mohammad Reza, 392

Shah-re Farang, 376, 381

Shakespeare, William, 285

Sharma, Sanjay, 434

Shohat, Ella, 436

Show, The, 428

Showbiz Lingo, 270–272

Siepmann, Charles, 67

Sikhs, 409.

Silent Explosion, The, 78

Silla, Mactar, 200

Silverstone, R., 290, 294

Sima-ye Ashna, 379, 386–388

Simpson, O. J., 203

Simpsons, The, 102

Sinbad, 429

Sinclair, John, 173, 176

Singapore Broadcasting Corporation, 428

Singer, Aubrey, 76

Singer, Dorothy, 445

Sister, Sister, 429

Situation comedies (sitcoms), 427

Six-Day War, 78

Six-Million Dollar Man, 414

Sky TV, 404

SkyDigital, 405

Smart Guy, 429

Smith, Andrew, 419

Smith, Anthony, 138

Smith, Will, 430

Smulyan, Susan, 55

Snow Crash, 448

Soap opera, 122–126, 130, 294

Social Darwinism, 420

Social knowledge, 128–129

Société Financire de Radiodifusion (SOFIRAD), 198

Soedirman, Basofi, 327

Soekarnoputra, Guruh, 331

Sony Corporation, 37

South Africa, 48; radio, 54

South Central, 435

South Park, 441

Soviet Union: breakdown of power, 230, 233; radio broadcasting system, 24

Space and place, 284; despatialization, 175; history of space as history of power, 286–287; "nowhere land" and "somewhere, USA," 176–180, 24; placelessness, 293; postmodern geography, 292–294; in postmodernity, 174–176; relationship between community and geography, 298; technological transformation, 291–292. *See also* Global mobility, and flow; Postmodernism

Spaces of Identity, 7

Spacks, Patricia Meyer, 266

Sparks, 428, 429

Speaking to Each Other, 139

Spices, 417

Spigel, Lynn, 95

Spitting Image, 402

Spivak, Guyatri, 137, 142

Springer Press, 214

Sprite, 441

Stam, Robert, 436

Standpoint knowledge, 106

Star Plus, 345

Star Productions, 386–388

Star Talk, 270, 271

Star Wars, 446

Starowicz, Mark, 175

StarTV, 88, 90, 322, 323, 342, 343

Stephenson, Neal, 448

Stern, 217

Street Legal, 181

Stuttgart-Stammheim, 216

Subaltern, 137; and cultural studies, 141–142; interlacing of resistance and submission, 365

Sud Quotidien, 197

Suharto, 33; control of television networks in Indonesia, 322

Sumatra, 320

Sun City, 404, 414

Surf Wheel of Fortune, 345

Sussman, Mark, 449

Syal, Meera, 402, 403, 416–417

Sykes Committee, 57–58

Sykes, Roberta, 312

Syncom, 74, 76

Taiwan, 255
Talk shows: Philippine movie, 262–273; Philippine public affairs, 263; role of gossip, 266
Talvin Singh, 403
Tanner, Elaine, 81
Tass, 27
Taylor, Timothy D., 434
Technological determinism, 4
Technology, 9
Technoscapes, 41, 41–42
Telegraph, 291
Telemundo, 378
Telenovelas, 434. *See also* Soap operas
Teletubbies, 439–452; as avatars of twenty-first century audience, 439; as cyborgs, 439, 449–452; as tools to negotiate the digital planet, 440; Tinky Winky as "gay role model," 441
Teletubbies, 439–452; and child development specialists, 447–449; as crisis of childhood, 440–444; crisis of middle class family, 442; criticism, 444–445; and flow, 450–451; global syndication, 444; as icon of nonconformity, 452; lack of applicable media analysis, 449; and the mirror stage, 451–452; merchandising and labour law, 445–446; as new image of childhood, 440; parental response, 439; as utopian, 450; and youth capitalism, 445–447. *See also* Childhood
Television: commercial, 55; domestic context, 288–290; emergence, 28–29; ethnic, definition of, 377–378; exilic, definition of, 378; global distribution of American programming, 424–427; hybrid programming, 341, 344–345; lack of audience research, 426; and mobility, 104; number of receivers worldwide, 191, 226; programs as travelers, 103; transnational, definition of, 378. *See also* Exile television
Television studies: American, 8; British, 7–8. *See also* Audience; Cultural studies
Television: A Critical View, 142
Television: An International History, 137
Television, Globalization and Cultural Identities, 137
Television: Technology and Cultural Form, 4, 95
Television: The Critical View, 6
Television Without Frontiers, 371
"Televisuality," 74–90; defined, 75
Telstar, 74, 76
Tent Embassy, 312
Terrorism, representation: in German docudrama and American film, 221–223; on West German television, 211–224
Thailand, sex tours, 45
That Was the Week That Was, 410
Thatcher, Margaret, 32
Thiong'o, Ngugi Wa, 155, 164
Third World: and Disney comics, 119–122; effect of transnational media, 117–118; and media imperialism, 115–116; role in *Our World*, 77, 81, 82, 88–90
This Hour Has 22 Minutes, 182–183
Thomas the Tank Engine, 441
Thomson-CSF, 193
Tiananmen Square, 248, 252–253. *See also* Hong Kong
Time, 37
Time Computer, 403
Time Out, 413
Time-Warner, 37, 169, 343, 367
Tintin, 200
Titanic, 351

Todesspiel, 211–224; as intersection of fiction and documentary, 219; promotion of broadcast, 217. *See also* Germany
Tomlinson, John, 5, 155, 156–157, 161, 165, 167
Toscanini, Arturo, 60.
Touré, Babacar, 200, 204
Town Meeting of the World, The, 74, 76
Toy Story 2, 446
Toys "R" Us, 439, 446
Tracey, Michael, 118, 126
"Trajectories: Toward an Internationalist Cultural Studies," 141
"Transnational Media and National Development," 115
Transnational elite, 155–156; as "cultural translators," 163–165; 161–163, 166
Transnational/Multinational Corporations, 22, 36–37, 116, 150, 277–278, 299; creation of markets and distribution, 367–368; and media imperialism, 114
Transparency International, 247
Travis, Major Joseph, 62
Trilogy Entertainment Group, 175
True Colors, 429
True Lies, 222
Tumiwa, Daniel, 326
Turner Broadcasting, 37
Turner, Graeme, 141–142
Turner, Nell, 307
TV Azteca, 432, 451
TV Cinque, 322
TV Guide, 381
TVB, 250, 255; relation with TVBS in Taiwan, 255–256
TV5 Afrique, 200–203
TVRI (Televisi Republik Indonesia), 321
Twentieth Century Fox, 27
Twentieth Century Fox International Television, 427

Udaya TV, 341
UN Conference on Trade and Development (UNCTAD), 32
UN Development Program, 192
Understanding Media, 4
UNESCO (United Nations Educational, Scientific, and Cultural Organization), 5, 26, 77, 192; flow studies, 103; Mass Media Declaration, 1978, 31
United Artists, 27
United States: national identity and scientific rationalism, 280; radio, 54; radio broadcasting system, 24. *See also* African Americans
Universal, 27
Universalization, 147; looking for the universal in the particular, 174–176; reduction to a bipolar world, 228–229
Univision, 378
UPI (United Press International), 22, 27, 283
Urry, John, 41
U.S. Radio Conferences, 57
Uses of Literacy, The, 138
Uses of Television, The, 6, 140
Uzbekistan, 237

Valery, Paul, 94
van der Keere, Pieter, 282–283
Viacom, 343
Video, as means of forming community, 370–371
Video games, 446

Vietnam War, 213
Virgin Mary, 266
Virilio, Paul, 233
Viselman, Kenn, 443
Voice of America, 25, 26–27

Waddington, Father Gary, 441
Wade, Abdoulaye, 199
Wadia, Nina, 402
Wall, Patrick, 447
Waller, Gary, 149
Wallerstein, Immanuel, 5, 115, 234
Warner Brothers, 27, 430
Warner Brothers International Television, 427
Washington Post, 441
Watching Dallas, 122–126
Waters, Malcolm, 174
Watkins, Mel, 435
Wayans Bros., 429
Wedding of Prince Andrew and Fergie, 101
Wegener, Ulrich, 223
Welles, Orson, 60
Westinghouse, 58
What's My Line?, 146
Wheel of Fortune, 345
Where the Spirit Lives, 178
White, Mimi, 3
Who Wants to be a Millionaire?, 345
Wide Wide World, 92n
Williams, Lord Francis, 77
Williams, Raymond, 3, 4, 7, 94, 95–97, 101, 102, 104, 141–142, 450; "discovery" of flow, 99

Williams, William Carlos, 440–441
Willis, Paul, 364
Winfrey, Oprah, 269
Wischnewski, Hans-Jürgen, 217
Wolff, 22, 28, 283
Women: characterized as television viewers, 105; gender roles in Hindu marriage, 346; lack of radio programming, 67–69; responses devalued in Indian game show, 354; women's radio programs, 60. *See also* Feminism; Gender
Wood, Anne, 440, 443, 444
"Work of Art in the Age of Mechanical Reproduction, The," 49, 94
World Bank, 26, 42
World Summit on Television for Children, 1998, 444–445
World Vision, 28
Worldwide Wrestling Federation, 200

Xiaoping, Deng, 256

Yeltsin, Boris, 232, 235
You and the World of Medicine, 396
Young, Robert J. C., 416, 419–420
Yun-Fat, Chow, 251

Zdanovich, Aleksander, 238
Zee TV, 342, 404, 405
Zeffirelli, Franco, 81
Zemin, Jiang, 256
Zimmerman, Friedrich, 223
Zook, Kristal Brent, 423, 430, 435